D0801529

FINANCIAL TIMES

Handbook of Management

FINANCIAL TIMES
Prentice Hall

Pearson
Education

FINANCIAL TIMES

Handbook of Management

SECOND EDITION

Edited by
Stuart Crainer and Des Dearlove

An imprint of Pearson Education

London · New York · San Francisco · Toronto · Sydney
Tokyo · Singapore · Hong Kong · Cape Town · Madrid
Paris · Milan · Munich · Amsterdam

PEARSON EDUCATION LIMITED

Head Office:
Edinburgh Gate
Harlow CM20 2JE
Tel: +44 (0)1279 623623
Fax: +44 (0)1279 431059

London Office:
128 Long Acre
London WC2E 9AN
Tel: +44 (0)20 7447 2000
Fax: +44 (0)20 7240 5771
Website: www.business-minds.com

First published in Great Britain in 1995

This edition published 2001

ISBN 0 273 64350 9

British Library Cataloguing in Publication Data
A CIP catalogue record for this book can be obtained from the British Library

10 9 8 7 6 5 4 3 2 1

Typeset by Pantek Arts Ltd, Maidstone, Kent
Printed and bound in Great Britain by Biddles Ltd, Guildford & King's Lynn

The Publishers' policy is to use paper manufactured from sustainable forests.

For Ro & Sara

CONTENTS

Introduction

For the manager in the front line there are no easy answers. The marketing man in Gdansk, Poland; the advertising executive in Savannah, Georgia; the CEO in the management suite in Tokyo – all labour under the same conditions. In management 2 + 2 does not necessarily equal 4.

This is an important realization. Recent years have seen the sometimes painful, but nevertheless welcome, dispersal of the cloud of illusion hanging over the development of management as a profession. From being fixated on solutions and elusive quick fixes, management has come of age. There is now growing appreciation that its allure and very substance are attributable to its uncertainty and a lack of readymade universal solutions.

After being contained as a rational and analytical art, management has broken its ties. Rationalism has given way to dynamism – solutions have been replaced by questions.

The *Financial Times Handbook of Management* is written in this new spirit. If you still believe in neat answers, look elsewhere.

The *Handbook* offers no immediate solutions to the problems confronting individual managers in unique situations. Instead, it raises issues, poses questions, and examines emergent management thinking and best practice from an array of angles. Its intention is to prompt further thinking and reading. The aim of the *Handbook* is to act as a starting point, leading into complex subjects, such as the changing nature of organizations.

The *Handbook* is an ignition point. It brings together a cornucopia of ideas, practices, and thinking. Not all of it may be immediately relevant to a particular manager's work today, but a career in management is likely to draw on virtually every subject covered here.

Management is perplexing and challenging, more complex than ever before and, for millions of managers throughout the world, a continual source of learning, stress, excitement, disappointment, and achievement. The *Financial Times Handbook of Management* hopes to capture the state of this indispensable, inspiring, and invigorating art.

STUART CRAINER AND DES DEARLOVE

Acknowledgements

The chief acknowledgement for any book of this nature must be to those who have generously chosen to contribute their insights and wisdom. Contributors to the *Handbook* have been gathered from throughout the world. We thank them all for their belief in the project and intellectual generosity.

The driving force behind this second edition of the *Handbook* was Richard Stagg, editor-in-chief of business books at Financial Times Prentice Hall. Richard is a true catalyst for the ideas changing the business world. The original idea for the *Handbook* belonged to Mark Allin.

Many of the usual suspects have provided ideas, insights, inspiration, and liquid refreshment at important junctures. Kjell Nordström and Jonas Ridderstråle reminded us what being funky actually means. Gerry Griffin explained all. Stephen Coomber provided research. Georgina Peters, our colleague at Suntop Media, helped with ideas and editorial support. We are especially grateful to George Bickerstaffe and Sally Lansdell who made a major contribution to the editing process.

PART ONE

The State of the Art

– CHAPTER 1 –

The rise of management

'Management means, in the last analysis, the substitution of thought for brawn and muscle, of knowledge for folklore and superstition, and of co-operation for force.' PETER DRUCKER

'If you ask managers what they do, they will most likely tell you that they plan, organize, co-ordinate and control. Then watch what they do. Don't be surprised if you can't relate what you see to those four words.' HENRY MINTZBERG

'To manage is to forecast and plan, to organize, to command, to co-ordinate and to control.'

HENRI FAYOL

'The function which distinguishes the manager above all others is his educational one. The one contribution he is uniquely expected to make is to give others vision and ability to perform. It is vision and more responsibility that, in the last analysis, define the manager.' PETER DRUCKER

Current reality

STUART CRAINER AND DES DEARLOVE

Management has always existed, but the way it is practised has changed fundamentally. While being by no means clear, the new first principles embrace learning and values, as well as the idea of corporate mortality.

SO long as there has been civilization, management has been practised. As Peter Drucker points out in his masterly celebration of the art, *Management: Tasks, Responsibilities, Practices*,[1] management is an ancient discipline that has been conducted and considered throughout history. The builders of the great monuments of the past, from the pyramids to the Great Wall of China, were involved in undertakings that demanded management if they were to succeed. The military leaders whose names litter history were similarly concerned with managing the people and the resources at their disposal to achieve clear objectives. Great religious leaders were also managers. (Indeed, a recent business book was entitled *The Leadership Wisdom of Jesus*.)

Although management has always been a fundamental activity, the recognition and study of management as a discipline and profession constitute a thoroughly modern phenomenon. While huge professional and educational edifices were built around the legal and medical professions, management remained largely unacknowledged. Only in the twentieth century did management come of age, gaining both respectability and credence.

Even now, the study of management is still in a fledgling state. While business schools like to give the impression of age-old permanence and wisdom, their lineage is relatively short. Indeed, by the standards of universities – especially in Europe – business schools scarcely register on the chronometer. (Oxford University is hundreds of years old; its business school is only now getting off the ground.)

Invented in the United States, the origins of the business school as we know it can be traced to the Wharton School at the University of Pennsylvania which was founded in 1881. The Wharton approach to business was numerical. Its bedrock was finance, and it was the management of money that was drummed into students from the earliest days. Other schools soon followed. These institutions grew out of a desire to train and educate future generations in management techniques and practices, an aspiration often supported by generous donations from industrialists.

Towards the end of the nineteenth century this desire led to the creation of a number of specialized departments and schools attached to leading US universities. For the first time commercial practices, and the philosophies that underpinned them, were elevated to the same sort of level as other academic disciplines. They have been unlikely and often uncomfortable bedfellows ever since.

The origins of the MBA, the best known business school qualification, date back to this period. Founded in 1900, the Tuck School at Dartmouth College claims to have had the first graduate programme in management. Although not technically an MBA, Tuck offered the first graduate degree in 1900. Originally it was a 'three, two' programme, with three years' study at undergraduate level at Dartmouth followed by two years at Tuck.

Postgraduate entry courses followed. Harvard Business School claims to have been the first business school to require a university degree for entry to its management programme. Founded in 1908, the school awarded its first Masters degree in the discipline in 1910.

The idea of business education quickly took off. Management education has been one of the great success stories of the last century. Over 100,000 MBA graduates now emerge blinking into the sunlight every year. Yet, for all the MBAs in the boardroom, management remains as open to constant redefinition as ever. The universal science is an irritatingly ill-defined one. It eludes simple codification. 'Managing is like holding a dove in your hand. Squeeze too tight, you kill it. Open your hand too much, you let it go,' baseball coach and player Tommy Lasorda once reflected.

Even now, there is little consensus as to what makes a manager, who is a manager, or what management involves. The more people you ask, the more confused you are liable to become. Travelling from country to country you quickly uncover differences in attitude and perception. In France, managers are usually referred to as *cadres*, a term founded on social class and education rather than managerial expertise or corporate standing. In Germany, engineers rather than managers run businesses. 'In the UK managers are very proud to be managers; in Sweden they are apologetic; and in Germany, managers see themselves as highly qualified specialists,' says leading management thinker Henry Mintzberg.[2] German managers emphasize their technical knowledge and competence. They believe that this, rather than an elevated position in the corporate hierarchy, invests them with authority. In contrast, UK managers emphasize their executive rather than their technical skills. In an age of global business and internationalization, such fundamental differences in outlook and practice provide enormous challenges for the organizations of the future and those who manage them.

In the past, a preoccupation with status and hierarchy enabled managers to explain away some of the inconsistencies. Grand-sounding titles hid a multitude of confusion. Unable to provide a concise answer when asked what they do, managers preferred to explain who they were in the organizational hierarchy. With hierarchies stripped away in many organizations, managers are now forced to confront the exact nature of their role and the new first principles of management.

Learning first and last

According to Peter Senge of the Massachusetts Institute of Technology:

'It is no longer sufficient to have one person learning for the organization, a Ford or a Sloan or a Watson. It's just not possible any longer to "figure it out" from the top, and have everybody else following the orders of the "grand strategist". The organizations that will truly excel in the future will be the organizations that discover how to tap people's commitment and capacity to learn at all levels in an organization'.[3]

Management is uniquely placed as a profession: it is driven by ideas. The emerging professional and practical agenda is not so much set by practitioners as by business schools, consulting firms, and an array of gurus. But these sources are not universally liked or even trusted. That there is scepticism about a great many of today's managerial ideas cannot be doubted. Managerial thinking is tainted with ever greater hype and hyperbole. And some of its ideas can be seen as driven by the media as much as by the research interests of academics or the needs of business.

Depending on your perspective, this situation can be attributed to the substantial financial rewards available for those who sweep the globe with the next bright idea, or as a sign of ever-increasing desperation among managers to find ways to make sense of the business world. Alternatively, and more positively, you can regard the merry-go-round of ideas as an indication of just how vital effective management is to the economies and people of the world.

Although there is clearly cynicism on the part of executives who receive a deluge of material on how best to run their businesses, if you read through the stream of management books you can detect some degree of consensus. No book is now complete without a fresh interpretation of ABB's remarkable performance under Percy Barnevik; GE's Jack Welch is feted and analyzed; Dell is examined and heads are shaken; Toyota's production methods are looked at in wonderment. At least when IBM was the premier corporate model you knew where you stood. Now we have ABB, whose structure works exceptionally well even though few seem to understand it – even if they work for the corporation; GE, which appears to have been reinvented through the drive and imagination of a single individual (and one who has, against all the prevailing wisdom, spent decades with a single employer); Dell, which cuts out the intermediaries while other e-businesses insert them; and Toyota, which manages to remain elusive, always one step ahead.

Managers yearn for clear, unequivocal messages, but that is no longer what they receive. They are saturated with reports and books on creating the global organization, at the same time as they are still asking what that means. When it comes to the huge international corporations detailed in case study after case study, our knowledge is extensive but highly fragmented.

There is a feeling that these companies possess something, but no one can quite encapsulate the entire message. There is no one great management book – though Peter Drucker has come pretty close to providing it. What one commentator pompously labelled 'the over-arching meta-narrative' is usually notable by its absence. Management continues to defy the theorists who would like to guide it into a corner and nail it down. It continues to escape. It carries on slipping through our fingers.

As a consequence, managers are on a continual quest for new ideas, new interpretations, and new corporate cures. Inevitably, they consume a fair number of placebos along the way. Yet, it is this quest for knowledge that marks management apart as a discipline. Fifty-year-old lawyers can afford to sit back and contemplate their bedrock of knowledge knowing that updating it will be an occasional chore; managers have no such luxury. If 50-year-old managers look back and contemplate their knowledge, they will quickly find they are out of a job. Management demands change and continuing development. There is no hiding place. Updating knowledge is an ever-present necessity.

Management, therefore, has become increasingly committed to the entire concept of learning. Albert Vicere and Robert Fulmer, two business professors from Penn State, have calculated that businesses worldwide spend more than $100 billion on training their employees every year. Dauntingly, they also estimate that over half of this is wasted, as much is carried out with no objective. The global executive education market has been calculated to be worth in excess of $12 billion. Business schools are believed to account for approximately a quarter of the total – about $3 billion.

If you add on all the many millions spent on management and business education at degree level, the figures become even more impressive – in 1995–96, 227,102 bachelor degrees in business were awarded in the US.

The profusion of training and development is driven by a realization that companies must become 'learning organizations' if they are to survive and prosper.

Harvard Business School's Chris Argyris, in a 1991 *Harvard Business Review* article, noted:

> *'Any company that aspires to succeed in the tougher business environment of the 1990s must first resolve a basic dilemma: success in the marketplace increasingly depends on learning, yet most people don't know how to learn. What's more, those members of the organization that many assume to be the best at learning are, in fact, not very good at it.'*[4]

The trouble, in practice, is that the learning organization is often regarded as an instant solution, yet another fad to be implemented. Earnest attempts to turn it into reality have often floundered. Even so, Peter Senge argues that the interest in the concept of the learning organization is proof that institutions and people are ready for major change:

> *'Our traditional ways of managing and governing are breaking down. The demise of General Motors and IBM has one thing in common with the crisis in America's schools and "gridlock" in Washington – a wake-up call that the world we live in presents unprecedented challenges for which our institutions are ill prepared.'*[5]

Values maketh the manager

The quest for ideas and the rise of learning as an important ingredient of organizational life are only part of the changing face of management. Another aspect is the growing importance of values in both management thinking and practice. The issue of personal and corporate values is clearly related to that of motivation and loyalty.

If you believed everything you read in the business press, the business world would be entirely populated by jargon-speaking free agents, flitting from project to project, from one interesting assignment to the next. According to the fashionable pundits, corporate loyalty is dead. Today's employees are loyal to no one but themselves.

Perhaps, for some, working life really is like that. Meanwhile, back in reality, many millions of people continue to work in much the same way, for much the same hours, as they have done for decades.

The champions of free agency would suggest that remaining with the same organization for 10, 15, maybe 20 years is mutually unsatisfactory. The employee becomes jaded, comfortable and complacent – hardly good news for any organization. The bright and ambitious new arrival is surely preferable to the cynical long-term resident with an eye on retirement and a gift for corporate manoeuvring.

The flip side of this is that an organization populated by people whose loyalty is at best fleeting and, at worst, elsewhere, is hardly likely to take the world by storm. Indeed, it is more likely to be riven with political intrigue, uncertainty, and insecurity. Short-term employees have eyes only for the short term; free agents are set on their individual freedom and success rather than team goals. 'Mercenaries tend to move on and not become marines. Can you build a company with a mercenary force?' asks Sumantra Ghoshal of London Business School, co-author of *The Individualized Corporation.*

Luckily perhaps, the talk of an army of mercenaries appears overblown. Research by Incomes Data Services found that in 1993, 36 percent of men had been with the same employer for 10 years or more. This was at the peak of downsizing mania. Interestingly, and surprisingly given the hysterical talk of the emerging promiscuous workforce, the equivalent figure for 1968 was only 37.7 percent.

More research from Business Strategies forecast that 79.2 percent of all employees would be in full-time permanent jobs in 2005 – compared with 83.9 percent in 1986. The revolution has been postponed.

For better or worse, people stick around. Even after downsizing, the flurry of demographic time bombs, and talk of Generation X, working life retains a strong element of security. It may be unfashionable to spend 30 years working for a single employer, but many people do. Some undoubtedly do so because they have limited opportunities elsewhere, limited ambition, or limited abilities. These are facts of life generally ignored by the free-agent propagandists.

But many actively choose to stay. They find their work and working environment stimulating, rewarding, or enjoyable. Indeed, some of the corporate titans of our age are devoted company loyalists. Perhaps the best known is GE's Jack Welch. Feted far and wide as the very model of the modern CEO, Welch joined the company in 1960. No one suggests that his loyalty has been misplaced.

With nearly 40 years of service, people like Jack Welch may appear to some as a throwback to a more naïve, even simplistic age. It was never meant to be like that. In the 1970s pundits envisaged the leisure age; in the 1980s they talked of flexible working, a world of teleworkers. Well, the technology now exists and teleworking remains a decidedly minority pursuit.

> *'The failure of teleworking to really catch on despite the availability of the technology, demonstrates that some sort of a physical relationship is important to people at work. People want to feel part of a team and of something much bigger. They want to be connected.'*

This is according to Gerry Griffin, director of global PR firm Burson-Marsteller and author of *The Power Game*.[6]

Corporate loyalty is engendered by the fact that conventional working life still holds a remarkable attraction. Its immediacy makes business sense. In business, being there remains of crucial importance. The psychological dynamics mean that conversations in corridors or over coffee actually move the business forward. Managers make an impact, make a difference, and get results by talking to people, walking around, and listening to others. They need to be there and for their people to be there. The reality is that people are loyal to the environment where they spend every day, and to their colleagues.

While the traditional attractions of office life remain, it is true that companies no longer have an aura of permanence. They change with accelerating regularity. The profusion of joint ventures, mergers, and acquisitions means that people's roles now change more regularly. In the past, people might have filled two or three roles in 15 years with a company. Now, they are likely to change positions every three years or so. This, perhaps perversely, can actually encourage them to stay. If you want a fast-moving, stimulating, constantly changing environment, why move when it is happening all around you and you're a player in making it work? If you stay with a company for 10 years or more, change will inevitably happen. You either develop your own skills and move forward with the organization, or you leave.

This is not to say that the corporate man of the 1950s and 1960s is alive and well. Blind loyalty is undoubtedly dead – and corporate man is now as likely to be corporate woman. Today's employees are more questioning and demanding. They are loyal, but confident enough to air their concerns, grievances, and aspirations. If they were customers, we would call them sophisticated. (It is perhaps significant that we tend not to.) People are now more likely to question the action behind the corporate rhetoric. As a result, the HR and internal communications functions are much more important. Indeed, internal communications has emerged as an industry in its own right, reflecting the need for companies to create communication channels to their own people.

Central to the demanding nature of today's employees is the notion of values. In the past and put simply, loyalty was bought. Job security, gradual progression up the hierarchy, and a decent salary were offered by the employer. In return, the employee offered unwavering loyalty and a hard day's work. Now, values determine loyalty. 'Every organization needs values, but a lean organization needs them even more,' GE's Jack Welch says. 'When you strip away the support systems of staffs and layers, people have to change their habits and expectations, or else the stress will just overwhelm them.'

A report produced by consultants Blessing/White, *Heart and Soul*, studied the impact of corporate and individual values on business. It observed:

> *'Values have two critical roles: a company that articulates its values enables potential recruits to apply a degree of self-selection. Values also*

provide a framework to match individual career goals with the organization's objectives.

The challenge for organizations is that values are more complex than mere money. Values cannot be simplistically condensed into a mission statement or neatly printed on an embossed card. In the past there was a belief in one set of values. Now, in more sophisticated companies, there is an awareness that the uniqueness of the firm comes from multiple values and cultures. Previously, people's needs were interpreted as being homogenous. Now, there are flexible benefits and working arrangements and recognition that people are motivated by different things. Money and power don't work for everyone.

With values becoming an increasingly important aspect of loyalty and motivation, it is little wonder that companies are paying them more attention. Indeed, in the modern world, companies are crucial in identifying and developing the values that shape society. In the past, value systems were created by the church and the state. Corporations are the great institutions of our current age and, in a secular world, they create the belief systems, the values into which people may – or may not – buy. The choice is ours.

'Companies increasingly resemble tribes,' says Jonas Ridderstråle of the Stockholm School of Economics.

'Companies have to find people who share their values. Recruiting is now about finding people with the right attitude, then training them in appropriate and useful skills – rather than the reverse. We can no longer believe in the idea of bringing in smart people and brainwashing them at training camps into believing what is right.'[7]

Clearly, for the better executives there is a choice. They work for companies that are in accord with their own value systems. If they don't want to work for a polluter, they will not. After all, people want to hold their heads up when they are with their peers. They don't want an embarrassed silence when they announce who they work for.

If a company gives real meaning to people's work, as well as the freedom and resources to pursue their ideas, then it's a good place to be. Values are the new route to developing loyalty among employees. Loyalty is not dead, it simply must be earned and, increasingly, earned in different ways.

Corporate mortality

Implicit in all this is the notion that companies and individuals who fail to learn or identify appealing values will cease to exist. In the disposable society, companies and executives are more disposable than ever before.

This has led to a variety of lines of enquiry. First, there are those who argue that corporate mortality is a healthy thing. Over 10 years, Andrew Campbell of the UK's Ashridge Strategic Management Centre and his co-researchers have exhaustively examined the role of corporate parents. (Cynthia Montgomery and David Collins at Harvard Business School and C.K. Prahalad and Yves Doz of France's INSEAD have also pursued this line of research.) 'Parent companies are competing with each other for the right to parent businesses,' says Campbell.

> *'They need to offer parenting advantage for their existence to be justified. And parenting advantage can only come from doing things differently from other parents. Corporate parents, therefore, must offer unique and specialist skills and knowledge.'*

The trouble is that the rise of the professional general manager encourages corporate parents, and corporate managers, to be alike rather than different. 'The manager is a hero in the Western world, but an impostor,' says Campbell.

> *'The concept of management has proved a huge distraction. The management side of running a company is trivial compared to the importance of being commercial or entrepreneurial, or having a particular specialist skill. Any organization needs to have people with the skills relevant to its business rather than concentrating on turning the marketing director into a rounded general manager.'*[8]

Indeed, Campbell goes on to suggest that we have become preoccupied with creating immortal organizations rather than those work in the present. 'Why do we want organizations to thrive for ever?' he asks.

> *'On average organizations survive for less time than the working life of an individual. They become dysfunctional and, at that point, they should be killed off. What is encouraging is that, first through management buy-outs and now through demergers, we are becoming more adept at bringing an end to corporate lives which have run their course and creating new organizations in their place.'*

The second line of enquiry is to examine what leads to corporate longevity. The most notable works in this field are Arie de Geus' *The Living Company* and James Collins and Jerry Porras' *Built to Last.*

Central to these books is the idea that the corporation is an important institution that needs to live for capitalist society to thrive. The trouble is that though companies may be legal entities, they are disturbingly mortal. 'The natural average lifespan of a corporation should be as long as two or three centuries,' writes de Geus, noting a few prospering relics such as the Sumitomo Group and the Scandinavian company Stora.[9] But, the reality is that companies do not head off into the Florida sunset to play bingo. They usually die young.

De Geus quotes a Dutch survey of corporate life expectancy in Japan and Europe that arrived at 12.5 years as the average life expectancy of all firms. 'The average life expectancy of a multinational corporation – *Fortune* 500 or its equivalent – is between 40 and 50 years,' says de Geus, noting that one-third of 1970's *Fortune* 500 had disappeared by 1983. He attributes such endemic failure to the focus of managers on profits and the bottom line rather than the human community making up their organization.

In an attempt to get to the bottom of this mystery, de Geus and a number of his colleagues at the Shell oil company carried out some research to identify the characteristics of corporate longevity. As you would expect, the onus is on keeping excitement to a minimum. The average human centenarian advocates a life of abstinence, caution and moderation, and so it is with companies. The Royal Dutch/Shell team identified four key characteristics. The long-lived were 'sensitive to their environment'; 'cohesive, with a strong sense of identity'; 'tolerant'; and 'conservative in financing'. (These conclusions are echoed in Jerry Porras and James Collins' equally thought provoking, *Built to Last*, which almost serves as a companion volume to de Geus' book.)

Key to de Geus' entire argument is that there is more to companies – and to longevity – than mere money making. 'The dichotomy between profits and longevity is false,' he says. His logic is impeccably straightforward. Capital is no longer king; the skills, capabilities and knowledge of people are. The corollary from this is that 'a successful company is one that can learn effectively'. Learning is tomorrow's capital. In de Geus' eyes, learning means being prepared to accept continuous change.

Here, de Geus provides the new deal: contemporary corporate man or woman must understand that the corporation will, and must, change, and it can only change if its community of people change also. Individuals must change, and the way they change is through learning. As a result, de Geus believes that senior executives must dedicate a great deal of time nurturing their people. He recalls spending around a quarter of his time on the development and placement of people. Jack Welch claims to spend half of his time on such issues.

According to de Geus, all corporate activities are grounded in two hypotheses: 'The company is a living being; and the decisions for action made by this living being result from a learning process.' With its faith in learning, *The Living Company* represents a careful and powerful riposte to the corporate nihilism which dominated during the early 1990s.

From certainty to chaos

If the sanctity of corporate life is now open to debate, it is just another sign that while management thinking once provided a healthy diet of answers, it now produces confusion and yet more questions. The debate about outsourcing, for example, is expanding from the simple cost benefits to contemplation of its repercussions for the nature of the company – boundaryless and more abstract than ever before, it is difficult to determine where, why, and how the actual organization begins and ends.

Increasingly, attention is focusing on the nature of the questions rather than the pithiness of the answers. Indeed, many would argue that there are no longer any answers. Here, managers find themselves in the uncomfortable and discomfiting world of chaos and complexity theory. There is much talk of fractals and cognitive dissonance; uncertainty and ambiguity are the new realities. Organizational metaphors have metamorphosed. The organization was once talked of in mechanical terms. Now it is variously described through natural and scientific metaphors as an amoebae or a random pattern.

Is such theory mere metaphorical colour or is it practically useful? Reaching a definitive conclusion on this is impossible – although, theorists suggest, that is just the sort of thing that managers will have to become used to. 'Complexity theory is intriguing. Going beyond the metaphor is the trouble,' observes Richard Pascale.[10]

Others insist that complexity is not simply a metaphor. Ralph Stacey, author of *Complexity and Creativity*, comments:

> *'Complexity is an effective metaphor and practically useful. Everything's a metaphor. It's not possible to make sense of anything apart from through a paradigm. It is a different way of making sense of human systems and so it is more important than another recipe or technique. Some people are quite hostile because acceptance of complexity undermines their way of thinking. To others it is a release.'*[11]

Systems thinking, the concept that all the activities in an organization are interlinked, fits comfortably with other popular notions of global networks and transnational organizations. It all seems to fit in some way, it's just that we don't have a master plan to reassemble it in the right way.

Where this leaves aspiring or practising managers is a matter of lively conjecture. They are, according to different commentators, either fearful of the uncertainty now surrounding them or upbeat, set on making themselves indispensable in the managerial marketplace. In reality, there is no stereotypical situation or attitude. Instead, there are a bewildering array of options, tools, techniques, new and old ideas. Either/or questions have become either/and. The freewheeling pragmatism offered by some offers all the answers and yet none at all. There is a thin line between order and chaos and this line is likely to become ever more blurred and indistinct in the years to come.

REFERENCES

1. Drucker, Peter, *Management: Tasks, Responsibilities, Practices*, Heinemann, London, 1974.
2. Author interview.
3. Senge, Peter, *The Fifth Discipline*, Doubleday, New York, 1990.
4. Argyris, Chris, 'Teaching smart people how to learn', *Harvard Business Review*, May–June 1991.
5. Senge, Peter, 'A growing wave of interest and openness', Applewood internet site, 1997.
6. Griffin, Gerry, *The Power Game*, Capstone, Oxford, 1999.
7. Interview with Stuart Crainer.
8. Ibid.
9. de Geus, Arie, *The Living Company*, Harvard Business School Press, Boston, 1997.
10. Author interview.
11. Ibid.

RESOURCES

BOOKS

Collins, James & Porras, Jerry, *Built to Last*, Random House, 1998.

Crainer, Stuart, *The Management Century*, Jossey-Bass, San Francisco, 1999.

Dearlove, Des & Coomber, Stephen, *Heart & Soul*, Blessing/White, 1998.

Drucker, Peter, *Management: Tasks, Responsibilities, Practices*, Heinemann, London, 1974.

de Geus, Arie, *The Living Company*, Harvard Business School Press, Boston, 1997.

Senge, Peter, *The Fifth Discipline*, Doubleday, New York, 1990.

WEB

www.themanagementcentury.com

ESSENTIALS

THE RISE OF MANAGEMENT

DRUCKER, PETER

FAR sighted and always opinionated, Peter Drucker was born in Austria in 1909 where his father, Adolph, was the chief economist in the Austrian civil service. Drucker worked as a journalist in London, before moving to America in 1937. His first book, *Concept of the Corporation* (1946), was a groundbreaking examination of the intricate internal working of General Motors. His books have emerged regularly ever since and now total 29. Along the way he has coined phrases and championed concepts, many of which have become accepted facts of managerial life.

The coping stones of Drucker's work are two equally huge and brilliant books: *The Practice of Management* (1954) and *Management: Tasks, Responsibilities, Practices* (1973). Both are encyclopedic in their scope and fulsome in their historical perspectives. More than any other volumes, they encapsulate the essence of management thinking and practice.

Drucker's book production has been supplemented by a somewhat low-key career as an academic and sometime consultant. He was Professor of Philosophy and Politics at Bennington College from 1942 until 1949 and then became a Professor of Management at New York University in 1950 – 'The first person anywhere in the world to have such a title and to teach such a subject,' he proudly recalls. Since 1971, Drucker has been a Professor at Claremont Graduate School in California. He also lectures in oriental art, has an abiding passion for Jane Austen, and has written two novels (less successful than his management books).

Drucker's greatest achievement lies in identifying management as a timeless, human discipline. It was used to build the Great Wall of China, to erect the Pyramids, to cross the oceans for the first time, to run armies. 'Management is tasks. Management is discipline. But management is also people,' he wrote.

> *'Every achievement of management is the achievement of a manager. Every failure is the failure of a manager. People manage, rather than* forces *or* facts. *The vision, dedication and integrity of managers determine whether there is management or mismanagement.'*

Drucker's first attempt at creating the managerial bible was *The Practice of Management*; he largely succeeded. The book is a masterly exposition of the first principles of management. In one of the most quoted and memorable paragraphs in management literature,

Drucker gets to the heart of the meaning of business life:

> *'There is only one valid definition of business purpose: to create a customer. Markets are not created by God, nature or economic forces, but by businessmen. The want they satisfy may have been felt by the customer before he was offered the means of satisfying it. It may indeed, like the want of food in a famine, have dominated the customer's life and filled all his waking moments. But it was a theoretical want before; only when the action of businessmen makes it an effective demand is there a customer, a market.'*

Drucker also provided an evocatively simple insight into the nature and *raison d'être* of organizations:

> *'Organization is not an end in itself, but a means to an end of business performance and business results. Organization structure is an indispensable means, and the wrong structure will seriously impair business performance and may even destroy it...The first question in discussing organization structure must be: What is our business and what should it be? Organization structure must be designed so as to make possible the attainment of the objectives of the business for five, ten, fifteen years hence.'*

With its examinations of GM, Ford, and others, Drucker's audience and world view in *The Practice of Management* is resolutely that of the large corporation.

In *The Practice of Management* and the equally enormous *Management: Tasks, Responsibilities and Practices* in 1973, Drucker established five basics of the managerial role: to set objectives; to organize; motivate and communicate; to measure; and to develop people. 'The function which distinguishes the manager above all others is his educational one,' he wrote. 'The one contribution he is uniquely expected to make is to give others vision and ability to perform. It is vision and moral responsibility that, in the last analysis, define the manager.'

Drucker identified 'seven new tasks' for the manager of the future. Given that these were laid down over 40 years ago, their prescience is astounding. Drucker wrote that tomorrow's managers must:

1. Manage by objectives.
2. Take more risks and for a longer period ahead.
3. Be able to make strategic decisions.
4. Be able to built an integrated team, each member of which is capable of managing and of measuring his own performance and results in relation to the common objectives.
5. Be able to communicate information fast and clearly.
6. Traditionally a manager has been expected to know one or more functions. This will no longer be enough. The manager of the future must be able to see the business as a whole and to integrate his function with it.
7. Traditionally a manager has been expected to know a few products or

one industry. This, too, will no longer be enough.

Recent years have seen Drucker maintain his remarkable work rate. In particular, his energies have been focused on non-profit organizations. His ability to return to first principles and question the fundamentals remains undimmed. At the millennium, Drucker remains worth listening to.

FAYOL, HENRI

EUROPE has produced precious few original management thinkers. It is surprising, therefore, that the achievements and insights of the Frenchman Henri Fayol (1841–1925) are granted so little recognition.

Fayol was educated in Lyon, France and at the National School of Mines in St Etienne. He spent his entire working career with the French mining company Commentry-Fourchamboult-Décazeville, and was its managing director between 1888 and 1918.

Fayol was important for two reasons. First, he placed management at centre stage. Frederick Taylor's Scientific Management emasculated the working man, but still treated managers as stopwatch-holding supervisors. Fayol emerged from a similar background in heavy industry. His conclusions, however, were that management was critical and universal. 'Management plays a very important part in the government of undertakings; of all undertakings, large or small, industrial, commercial, political, religious or any other,' he wrote. It was not until 1954, and Drucker's *The Practice of Management*, that anyone else made such a bold pronouncement in management's favour.

Fayol's second contribution was to ponder the question of how best a company could be organized. In doing so, he took a far broader perspective than anyone else had previously done. He concluded: 'All activities to which industrial undertakings give rise can be divided into the following six groups.' The six functions he identified were technical activities; commercial activities; financial activities; security activities; accounting activities; and managerial activities.

Such functional separations have dominated the way companies have been managed throughout the twentieth century. It may be fashionable to talk of an end to functional mindsets and of free-flowing organizations, but Fayol's functional model largely holds.

In many respects, Henri Fayol was the first *management* thinker. While others concentrated on the worker and the mechanics of performance, he focused on the role of management and the essential skills required of managers.

TAYLOR, FREDERICK W.

FREDERICK TAYLOR (1856–1917) had a profound effect on the

working world of the twentieth century and was a man of amazing versatility and brilliance. The inventor of what was known as Scientific Management, Taylor remains the patron saint of mass production, the champion of measurement and control.

The son of an affluent family in Philadelphia, Taylor was an engineer and a prolific inventor. At the core of his view of the business world was his theory of how working life could be made more productive and efficient. This was painfully simple. Taylor was the first and purest believer in command and control. In his 1911 book, *The Principles of Scientific Management*, Taylor laid out his route to improved performance.

Taylor's 'science' (which he described as 'seventy-five percent science and twenty-five percent common sense') came from the minute examination of individual workers' tasks. Having identified every single movement and action involved in performing a task, Taylor believed he could determine the optimum time required to complete it. Armed with this information, a manager could decide whether a worker was doing the job well.

The origins of Scientific Management lay in Taylor's observations of his fellow workers at the Midvale Steel Company. He noticed that they engaged in what was then called 'soldiering'. Instead of working as hard and as fast as they could, they deliberately slowed down. They had no incentive to go faster or to be more productive. It was in their interest, Taylor said, to keep 'their employers ignorant of how fast work can be done'.

Taylor regarded the humble employee as a robotic automaton. Motivation came in the form of piece work. Employees had to be told the optimum way to do a job and then they had to do it. 'Each employee should receive every day clear-cut, definite instructions as to just what he is to do and how he is to do it, and these instructions should be exactly carried out, whether they are right or wrong,' Taylor advised.

Taylorism was one of the first serious attempts to create a science of management. It elevated the role of managers and negated the role of workers. Armed with their scientifically gathered information, managers dictated terms. The decisions of foremen – based on experience and intuition – were no longer considered to be important.

The man most associated with the application of Scientific Management was Henry Ford, who used it as a basis for his model for mass production. But Taylor's thinking had a profound impact throughout the world. While his theories are now largely disregarded, his fingerprints can be seen on much of the management literature produced in the twentieth century.

– CHAPTER 2 –

The changing nature of organizations

'It was once the case that unless you were caught with your hand in the till, or publicly slandered your boss, you could count on a job for life in many large companies. Loyalty was valued more than capability, and there was always a musty corner where mediocrity could hide. Entitlement produced a reasonably malleable workforce, and dependency enforced a begrudging kind of loyalty. That was then, this is now.' GARY HAMEL

'It is clearly necessary to invent organizational structures appropriate to the multicultural age.'
VACLAV HAVEL

'Organizations are, in the last analysis, interactions among people.' RICHARD PASCALE

'The company is an economic vehicle invented by society. It has no rights to survive. But value systems and philosophies survive. People take it with them.' EDGAR H. SCHEIN

Creating the modern organization

GEORGINA PETERS

Modern organizations can trace their origins to the Incas in Peru, via Prussia and other unlikely byways. Georgina Peters describes how new forms of organization have continued to evolve and change.

ORGANIZATION has been one of the perennial bugbears of human civilization, and some attempts at it have been more successful than others. For example, at their peak the Incas controlled six million people spread over a huge area covering parts of modern Peru, Ecuador, Chile, Bolivia and Argentina. They spoke many different languages and dialects. Managing them and their lands was somewhat more problematic than contemplating how to manage a distant subsidiary.

The Incas had the advantage that force was one possibility. But, interestingly, their more peaceful means of persuasion were preludes to later organizational behaviour. The Incas decided on a highly standardized system of administration. This was based on units of ten and was the forerunner of the modern decimal system. To make sense of their land they divided it into four quarters, *suyus*, which met at the capital, Cuzco.

The Incas also invested heavily in infrastructure. Their road system eventually covered over 23,000 km, which meant that the army could move quickly to sort out trouble and that goods could move equally speedily, even though the Incas had no vehicles with wheels. The road system was combined with a highly complex logistical network. This was made up of way stations, imperial centres, forts, ceremonial centres, and other meeting and gathering points. Runners were specially trained to pass on messages. The system worked, but briefly: the Inca empire only functioned for 100 years.

Modern corporations dream of such longevity. Nevertheless, management pioneers were initially unwilling to contemplate organization as a serious issue. Henry Ford may have initiated mass production, but his view of how to organize his industrial giant was one-dimensional – if it existed at all. Ford chose to wrestle with the mechanical intricacies of production, cost control, and the product, while issues of the organization itself were ridden over roughshod. Scientific management pioneer Frederick Taylor was similarly myopic, considering that perfect tasks led to perfect processes that largely provided the structure necessary for a company to thrive.

With Taylor and Ford unhelpfully mute on the subject of the nature of organization, it took a German sociologist, Max Weber, to consider the organizational implications of their theories and practice. Weber looked around and noted the industrial trends, the factories with their supervisors and middle managers, the sheer scale of the new operations. Then, he envisaged the future of the organization itself. If these trends were to continue to develop, what would be the best way of organizing a business?

Weber's conclusions did not make for pleasant reading, especially for humanitarians. His vision of the future, encapsulated in *The Theory of Social and Economic Organization* (published four years after his death in 1924), suggested that it was inevitable that industrial growth would be depersonalizing.

While Karl Marx saw industrialization as trampling over the rights to the ownership of labour, Weber offered a more pragmatic view – the subjugation of individuals to organizations was reality, not a stepping stone to a proletarian utopia. People in large companies were required to put the cause of the organization before their own aspirations – and it didn't matter whether the corporation was building pyramids, fighting battles or making widgets.

'The capitalistic system has undeniably played a major role in the development of bureaucracy,' Weber wrote.[1]

According to Weber, the ultimate form of organization in the newly industrialized world was the bureaucratic system. This he envisaged as impersonal and entirely hierarchical: 'The organization of offices follows the principle of hierarchy; that is, each lower office is under the control and supervision of a higher one.' The organization operated as a machine. Each cog in the system – each bureaucrat – fulfilled a clearly defined role.

The machine's aim was to work efficiently: no more, no less. Efficient machines were productive and, therefore, profitable. 'The purely bureaucratic type of administrative organization,' wrote Weber, 'is, from a purely technical point of view, capable of attaining the highest degree of efficiency and is in this sense formally the most rational known means of carrying out imperative control over human beings. It is superior to any other form in precision, in stability, in the stringency of its discipline and in its reliability.'[2]

Weber did not advocate the bureaucratic system; he simply described it. As a sociologist, he was interested in scenarios rather than manifestos. The system was the extreme, the eventual outcome if the trends he observed continued. In many ways this bureaucratic world is similar to Orwell's *1984*: the nightmare scenario rather than a prediction.

Unfortunately, in some respects, the nightmare came to pass. Henry Ford was not alone. Corporations were routinely organized in ways similar to those imagined by Weber. The bureaucratic model built on unquestioning loyalty, subjugation, and stultifying hierarchies became the organizational role model.

It was no coincidence that it took a German to provide definitive insights into the bureaucratic model. The inspiration for Ford's control-led administrative system can be seen as the nineteenth century Prussian bureaucracy. Controlled by Heinrich von Stein, Gerhard von Scharnhorst, August von Gneisenau, and Helmuth von Moltke, the Prussian system would have delighted Ford. It was a triumph of control. There were detailed centralized materials requirements and logistical planning, bountiful rules, rigorously standardized operating procedures, a faith in functional administrative design, and tasks broken down into their simplest components.

Only very large organizations could take full advantage of the Prussian administrative system. Only they could afford to devote substantial amounts of resources to gathering and processing quantities of data for top management to use to co-ordinate activities and allocate resources. The logic was simple and conclusive: bigger organizations were better. Small may have been beautiful, but it wasn't productive or profitable. Corporate expansion was natural, limitless and good for business – and if proof were needed, you could have pointed to the success of Ford which was carrying the world before it in the 1920s.

The other German inspiration was a military one. During the First World War the German military bureaucracy under Ludendorff used sophisticated planning and control systems to mobilize the country's resources. This *Kriegwirtschaftsplan* was very similar to Ford's administrative system.

Another contemporary impressed by the Germanic approach was Lenin. *Gosplan,* the centralized planning system used in the Soviet Union to implement its long-term policies and strategic plans, simply adapted the *Kriegwirtschaftsplan*. Lenin later defined socialism as the best of all worlds: 'Soviets plus Prussian railway administration plus American industrial organization.'

Organizational thinking

While the nature of organization failed to spark interest in Taylor and Ford, many other contemporary theorists and practitioners were contemplating organizational issues. Organizational charts had been in use since the building of the railroads and the fledgling world of executive education had begun to explore organizational issues more systematically. In 1909 at Harvard Business School, Russell Robb gave a series of lectures on organizations. His approach merged military models with the new industrial reality. 'All organizations will differ somewhat from each other, because the objects, the results that are sought and the way these results must be attained, are different,' he said. 'There is no royal road, no formula that, once learned, may be applied in all cases with the assurance that the result will be perfect harmony, efficiency, and economy, and a sure path to the main purpose in view.'[3]

One of those who may have been in Robb's audience was Chester Barnard (1886–1961). Barnard had won a scholarship to Harvard to study economics. He dutifully and fruitfully attended Harvard from 1906 until 1909, but failed to receive a degree because he lacked a laboratory science. He joined the statistical department at AT&T and spent his entire working life with the company, eventually becoming president of New Jersey Bell in 1927. *Fortune* hailed Barnard as 'possibly [having] the most capacious intellect of any business executive in the United States'.

To Barnard, the chief executive was not a dictatorial figure geared to simple short-term achievements. Instead, part of his responsibility was to nurture the organization's values and goals. Barnard argued that values and goals need to be translated into action rather than meaningless motivational phraseology. He took what would today be called a holistic approach, arguing that 'in a community all acts of individuals and of organizations are directly or indirectly interconnected and interdependent'.

Barnard regarded the commercial organization simply as a means of allowing people to achieve what they could not achieve as individuals. He defined an organization as a 'system of consciously co-ordinated activities of forces of two or more persons'.

The rise of the modern organization

The genesis of the modern organization lies in the work of Alfred Pritchard Sloan, Jr. Sloan was precociously brilliant. He initially failed to get into the Massachusetts Institute of Technology because he was thought to be too young. When he was allowed in, to study electrical engineering, he was the youngest member of his class.

He began his working career as a draftsman in a small machine shop, the Hyatt Roller Bearing Company of Newark, New Jersey. Hyatt made Sloan. His influence, in spite of his age, was immediate. He pointed the company toward making antifriction bearings for automobiles and, in 1899 when still only 24, Sloan became the company's president. Hyatt was a beneficiary of the huge expansion in the automobile industry. Its bearings became the industry standard and it grew rapidly.

In 1916, Hyatt merged with the United Motors Corporation. A variety of other automobile industry suppliers also joined the company and Sloan became president. In 1918, United Motors was acquired by General Motors, and Sloan became vice-president in charge of accessories and a member of GM's Executive Committee, becoming president of the company in 1923.

Over five decades, Sloan reshaped General Motors and reinvented how it was managed.[4] He created a new cadre of highly professional, dispassionate, intelligent managers, who made decisions on the basis of the information available rather than always following their intuition. Decision making was the heart of management. Sloan was the first great professional manager. Peter Drucker wrote:

> *'As exemplified by Sloan, the executive is a professional first and foremost: objective, dispassionate, open-minded. His insistence on facts, on ample documentation, on considering all sides of a question, prevent his being opinionated, let alone bigoted.'*[5]

More damningly *Fortune* later observed: 'Alfred P. Sloan Jr was himself a man of limited interests who immersed himself totally in the construction of the company.'[6]

Sloan turned managerial decision making from a tumultuous, spontaneous art into an informed, commercially driven process. He took the amateurism (and some of the fun) out of business and replaced it with sober, respectable professionalism.

Sloan also created a new organizational form, which combined decentralized operations with co-ordinated centralized policy control. He organized the company into eight – five car divisions and three component divisions. In the jargon (invented 50 years later), these were strategic business units.

Ford had been able to achieve standardization and mass production by producing as narrow a product range as possible. Sloan wanted to produce a far greater range. Previously GM cars had competed for the same markets; to prevent that, Sloan gave each car division its own price and style categories. He also introduced annual model changes, creating a market for used cars. Each car division became an independent brand.

While Ford remained fixated on the Model T, GM moved progressively forward. The company's model changes were backed by extensive and carefully planned research, development, and testing. GM's expertise grew. The 1920s saw the introduction of Buick's four-wheel brakes, the Cadillac's shatter-resistant safety glass, chromium plating, automatic engine temperature control, hydraulic shock absorbers, automatic choking, adjustable front seats, and numerous advances in performance, dependability and manufacturing technology.

As GM thrived, its organization took firmer shape. Each of the company's units was made responsible for all its commercial operations. Each had its own engineering, production and sales departments, but was supervised by a central staff responsible for overall policy and finance. The operating units were semi-autonomous, charged with maintaining market share and sustaining profitability in their particular area. In a particularly innovative move, the components divisions not only sold products to other GM companies, but also to external companies.

Meanwhile the company's headquarters was kept to a manageable size. Its business was number crunching and it was able to carefully measure and keep up to date with the return-on-assets performance of each and every division.

Sloan's organizational model gave business units far more responsibility than they had ever before. The clarification of who was responsible for what was central to his approach. Once responsibilities were decided on, Sloan believed that it was inappropriate, as well as unnecessary, for top managers at the corporate level to know much about the details of division operations.

Sloan's multidivisional form meant that executives had more time to concentrate on strategic issues and operational decisions were made by people at the front line rather than at a distant headquarters. In effect, Sloan utilized the company's size without making it cumbersome. 'The multidivisional organization was perhaps the single most important administrative innovation that helped companies grow in size and diversity far beyond the limits of the functional organization it replaced,' say contemporary thinkers Sumantra Ghoshal and Christopher Bartlett.[7]

The multidivisional form created a trend among large organizations for decentralization. While in 1950 around 20 percent of *Fortune* 500 corporations were decentralized, this had increased to 80 percent by 1970. Among those taking the plunge was IBM. In 1956, chief executive Thomas Watson Jr announced his plans to decentralize the company into six autonomous divisions, each focusing on a product line. Later, in the 1980s, AT&T attempted to make the shift from being a production-based bureaucracy to a marketing organization.

One of the key supporters of this trend was Alfred Chandler. His classic book, *Strategy and Structure,* lauded Alfred Sloan's work at General Motors. Chandler argued that the chief advantage of the multidivisional organization was that:

> *'It clearly removed the executives responsible for the destiny of the entire enterprise from the more routine operational responsibilities and so gave them the time, information and even psychological commitment for long-term planning and appraisal.'*

Another who celebrated GM was Peter Drucker. His book *Concept of the Corporation* (1946) was a groundbreaking examination of the intricate internal workings of the company and revealed the auto giant to be a labyrinthine social system rather than an economic machine. In the UK the book was retitled *Big Business* as, Drucker later explained, 'both Concept and Corporation [were] then considered vulgar Americanisms'.

After being celebrated as a managerial hero by both Chandler and Drucker, the deficiencies of Sloan's model gradually became apparent. The decentralized structure revolved around a reporting and committee infrastructure that eventually became unwieldy. Stringent targets and narrow measures of success stultified initiative. By the end of the 1960s the delicate balance that Sloan had brilliantly maintained between centralization and decentralization had been lost – finance emerged as the dominant function – and GM became paralyzed by what had once made it great.

The multidivisional form, say Christopher Bartlett and Sumantra Ghoshal, was handicapped by having:

> *'no process through which institutionalized wisdoms can be challenged, existing knowledge bases can be overturned, and the sources of the data can be reconfigured. In the absence of this challenge, these companies gradually become immobilized by conventional wisdoms that have ossified as sacred cows, and become constrained by outmoded knowledge and expertise that are out of touch with their rapidly changing realities.'*

Re-engineering the organization

The organization of companies was given limited attention throughout the 1970s and 1980s. Managers tinkered at the edges. Then came the concept of re-engineering which was brought to the fore in the early 1990s by James Champy, co-founder of the consultancy company CSC Index, and Michael Hammer, an electrical engineer and former computer science professor at MIT. Its roots lay in the research carried out by MIT from 1984 to 1989 on 'Management in the 1990s.'

Champy and Hammer's book, *Re-engineering the Corporation*, was a bestseller that produced a plethora of re-engineering programmes at companies throughout the world, the creation of many consulting companies, and a deluge of books promoting alternative approaches. (Thanks to the popularity of re-engineering, CSC became one of the largest consultancy companies in the world.)

Champy and Hammer defined re-engineering as 'the fundamental rethinking and radical redesign of business processes to achieve dramatic improvements in critical measures of performance such as cost, quality, service and speed'. The basic idea was that organizations need to identify their key processes and make them as lean and efficient as possible. Peripheral processes (and, therefore, peripheral people) needed to be discarded. 'Don't automate; obliterate,' Hammer proclaimed.

The beauty of re-engineering was that it embraced many of the fashionable business ideas of recent years and nudged them forward into a tidy philosophy. There were strains of total quality management, just-in-time manufacturing, customer service, time-based competition and lean manufacturing. Big-name corporations jumped on the bandwagon and Champy and Hammer's book was endorsed, somewhat surprisingly, by no less a figure than Peter Drucker.

To Champy and Hammer, re-engineering was more than dealing with mere processes. They eschewed the phrase 'business process re-engineering', regarding it as too limiting. In their view the scope and scale of re-engineering went far beyond simply altering and refining processes. True re-engineering was all-embracing, a recipe for a corporate revolution.

To start the revolution, it was suggested that companies equip themselves with a blank piece of paper and map out their processes. This was undoubtedly a useful exercise. It encouraged companies to consider exactly what were their core activities and what processes were in place, and needed to be in place, to deliver them efficiently. It also encouraged companies to move beyond strict functional demarcations to more free-flowing corporate forms governed by key processes rather than fiefdoms.

Inevitably, the optimum processes involved more effective utilization of resources. Functional organizations (as opposed to process-based ones) tend to contain elements of self-serving protectionism. Different functions do not necessarily share knowledge or work to the same objectives as other functions. Clearly this is, at best, inefficient. As a result, some stages in processes were eliminated completely. Others were streamlined or made more effective through use of information technology. Having come up with a neatly engineered map of how their business should operate, companies could then attempt to translate the paper theory into concrete reality.

While the relative simplicity of the concept made it alluring, actually turning re-engineering into reality proved immensely more difficult than its proponents suggested. The revolution was largely a damp squib.

The first problem was that the blank piece of paper ignored the years, often decades, of cultural evolution that led to an organization doing something in a certain way. Such preconceptions and often justifiable habits were not easily discarded. Functional fiefdoms may be inefficient, but they are difficult to break down.

The second problem was that re-engineering appeared inhumane. As the name suggests, it owed more to visions of the corporation as a machine than a human, or humane, system. To re-engineering purists, people were objects who handle processes. Depersonalization was the route to efficiency.

Re-engineering became a synonym for redundancy and downsizing. For this the gurus and consultants could not be entirely blamed. Often, companies that claimed to be re-engineering – and there were plenty – were simply engaging in cost cutting under the convenient guise of the fashionable theory. Downsizing appeared more publicly palatable if it was presented as implementing a leading-edge concept.

The third obstacle was that corporations are not natural nor even willing revolutionaries. Instead of casting the re-engineering net widely, they tended to re-engineer the most readily accessible process and then leave it at that. As a result – and this was the subject of Champy's sequel, *Re-engineering Management* – re-engineering usually failed to impinge on management. Not surprisingly, managers were all too willing to impose the rigours of a process-based view of the business on others, but often reluctant to inflict it on themselves.

'Senior managers have been re-engineering business processes with a passion, tearing down corporate structures that no longer can support the organization. Yet the practice of management has largely escaped demolition. If their jobs and styles are left largely intact, managers will eventually undermine the very structure of their rebuilt enterprises,'

Champy noted in 1994 at the height of re-engineering's popularity. In response, he suggested that re-engineering management should tackle three key areas: managerial roles, managerial styles, and managerial systems. In retrospect, the mistake of re-engineering was not to tackle re-engineering management first.

A new breed of organization

Re-engineering did produce achievements in two areas. First, it encouraged managers to reconsider the thorny issue of how best to organize their companies. Second, Champy and Hammer advocated organizing along process rather than functional lines. This was significant in that it broke free of the rigidity inherent in functional organization. The trouble was that re-engineering replaced one form of organizational rigidity with another.

With rapid advances in technology, the 1990s were dominated by organizational issues. The book that set the agenda – despite being greatly maligned – was Tom Peters' *Liberation Management* (1992). It was, observed Karl Weick, written in 'hypertext'. 'Tomorrow's effective "organization" will be conjured up anew each day,' Peters announced.[8]

Peters eschewed traditional and functional notions of corporate structure. His exemplars of the new organization were notable for their apparent lack of structure. And herein lay his point. Companies such as CNN, ABB and The Body Shop thrived through having highly flexible structures able to change to meet the business needs of the moment. Free flowing, impossible to pin down, unchartable, simple yet complex, these were the paradoxical organizations of the future.

Key to the new corporate structures envisaged by Peters were networks with customers, with suppliers and, indeed, with anyone else who can help the business deliver. He wrote:

> *'Old ideas about size must be scuttled. "New big", which can be very big indeed, is "network big". That is, size measured by market power, say, is*

a function of the firm's extended family of fleeting and semi-permanent cohorts, not so much a matter of what it owns and directly controls.'

And networks must move quickly. The book's central refrain was fashion – 'We're all in Milan's *haute couture* business and Hollywood's movie business,' wrote Peters. 'This book is animated by a single word: fashion. Lifecycles of computers and microprocessors have shrunk from years to months.' The new model organization moved fast and did so continually, seeking out new areas to make it unique in its markets.

Clearly, this required quite different managerial skills than those traditionally needed by managers. Indeed, Peters said that the new organizational forms he depicted were 'troublesome to conceive – and a downright pain to manage'. The new skills are now familiar. Peters bade farewell to command and control, ushering in a new era characterized by 'curiosity, initiative, and the exercise of imagination'. It was, he argued, a step into the unknown for most organizations but also a return to first principles:

'For the last 100 years or so ... we've assumed that there is one place where expertise should reside: with "expert" staffs at division, group, sector, or corporate. And another, very different, place where the (mere) work gets done. The new organization regimen puts expertise back, close to the action – as it was in craft-oriented, pre-industrial revolution days ... We are not, then, ignoring "expertise" at all. We are simply shifting its locus, expanding its reach, giving it new respect – and acknowledging that everyone must be an expert in a fast-paced, fashionized world.'

Peters' view of the need for organizational change was followed by a welter of new organizational models: virtual organizations, network organizations, and the like. Among the most considered participants in this debate was the British thinker Charles Handy. Handy anticipated that certain forms of organization would become dominant. These were the type of organization most readily associated with service industries. First, and most famously, came what he called the 'shamrock organization' – 'a form of organization based around a core of essential executives and workers supported by outside contractors and part-time help'. Such organizations would resemble the way consultancy firms, advertising agencies, and professional partnerships are currently structured.

The second emergent structure identified by Handy was the federal one; not, he pointed out, another word for decentralization. He provided a blueprint for federal organizations in which the central function co-ordinates, influences, advises and suggests. It does not dictate terms or short-term decisions. The centre is, however, concerned with long-term strategy. It is 'at the middle of things and is not a polite word for the top or even for head office'.

The third type of organization Handy anticipated is what he called 'the Triple I' – Information, Intelligence, and Ideas. In such organizations the demands on personnel management are large. Handy explained:

> *'The wise organization already knows that their smart people are not to be easily defined as workers or as managers but as individuals, as specialist, as professional or executives, or as leader (the older terms of manager and worker are dropping out of use), and that they and it need also to be obsessed with the pursuit of learning if they are going to keep up with the pace of change.'*

The debate about organizational structures is continuing. In practice, however, the last ten years have seen the emergence of a distinctly new breed of corporation. The exemplars of this new generation are, among others, Asea Brown Boveri (ABB), Toyota, General Electric (GE) and Dell.

The matrix model

Asea Brown Boveri (ABB) is one of the most lauded and reported-on companies of our time. It is routinely decorated with corporate baubles as Europe's most admired company.

Headquartered in Zurich, Switzerland, ABB is the world's leading power engineering company employing over 213,000 people in 50 countries. A $31 billion company it is broken down into 35 business areas with 5,000 profit centres ('5,000 perceived companies,' says chief executive officer Göran Lindahl).

ABB came about from the merger of the Swedish company Asea, then led by the redoubtable Percy Barnevik, and the Swiss company Brown Boveri. It was the biggest cross-border merger since Royal Dutch Shell's oily coupling. Barnevik became the CEO of the resulting ABB and revolutionized its organization and performance until being succeeded by Lindahl in 1997.

The merger was announced on 10 August 1987. The corporate world was stunned by its suddenness. The *Wall Street Journal* said that it was a merger 'born of necessity, not of love'. This overlooked the uncanny fit between the two companies: it was truly a marriage made in corporate heaven. Brown Boveri was international, Asea was not. Asea excelled at management, Brown Boveri did not. Technology, markets, and cultures fitted together. Of course, whether this was luck or strategic insight is a matter of continuing discussion.

Then, quite simply, Barnevik made it work. 'The challenge set by Barnevik was to create – out of a group of 1,300 companies employing 210,000 people in 150 countries – a streamlined, entrepreneurial organization with as few management layers as possible,' write Kevin Barham and Claudia Heimer in their book examining the company, *ABB: The Dancing Giant*.[9] To enable this to happen, Barnevik introduced a complex matrix structure – what Lindahl has called 'decentralization under central conditions'. The company is run by an Executive Committee with the organization below divided by business areas, company and profit centres, and country organizations. The aim is to reap the advantages of being a large organization while also having the advantages of smallness.

Barnevik argues that the matrix system is simply a formal means of recording and understanding what happens informally in any large organization. The spider's web of the matrix is a fact of life.

Natural or not, the truth is that ABB's structure is complex, paradoxical, and ambiguous. As a corporate role model ABB is a complete non-starter. ('I do not believe that you can mechanically copy what another company has done,' advises Barnevik.) As a sophisticated means of managing this particular organization it has proved highly effective. What holds this 'globally connected' company together is deep-rooted local presence; global vision; cross-border understanding; global values and principles for managing creative tension; global connection at the top; and global ethics. In addition, it requires a CEO with the rare dynamism and intelligence of Barnevik. Imitators beware.

The management model

In December 1980, John Francis Welch Jr was announced as the new CEO and chairman of GE. At 45, Welch was the youngest chief the company had ever appointed. Indeed, he was only the eighth CEO of the company in 92 years.

When Jack Welch became top man GE's net income was $1.7 billion. By most measures, the company was growing at a healthy rate – by 9 percent in the previous year. Everything seemed rosy. More plain sailing was anticipated as the new chief got used to the job. After all, Welch was an insider. He was hardly likely to turn on the organization that had nurtured him so carefully. However, plain sailing was not on Welch's route map. Quiet, contented progress was not his plan: GE was shaken and then shaken again.

During the 1980s, Welch put his dynamic mark on GE and on corporate America. GE's businesses were overhauled. Some were cast out and hundreds of new businesses acquired. In 1984 *Fortune* called Welch the 'toughest boss in America'. The workforce bore the brunt of Welch's quest for competitiveness as GE virtually invented downsizing. Nearly 200,000 employees left the company and over $6 billion was saved.

Welch was known in the media as *Neutron Jack*. He was the man who swept away people while leaving the buildings intact. Not surprisingly, he wasn't the most popular man in GE or the wider corporate world. Within GE there were grave concerns about what was happening. But this was, Welch coolly reflected, part of the job. 'I didn't start with a morale problem. I created it!' he told Richard Pascale with typical forceful candor.

> *'The leader who tries to move a large organization counter to what his followers perceive to be necessary has a very difficult time. I had never had to do this before. I had always had the luxury of building a business and being the cheerleader. But it was clear that we had to reposition ourselves and put our chips on those businesses that could survive on a global scale.'*[10]

Perhaps Welch was too brutal, but there is no denying that by the end of the 1980s GE was a leaner and fitter organization. Any complacency that may have existed had been eradicated. In retrospect, Welch's greatest decision may have been to go in with all guns blazing. Dramatic though relatively short-lived change was preferable to incremental change.

Having proved that he could tear the company apart, Welch had to move on to Stage Two: rebuilding a company fit for the twenty-first century. Central to this was the concept of Work-out, launched in 1989. This came about, it is reputed, after a chance question was asked by Professor Kirby Warren of Columbia University. Warren asked Welch: 'Now that you have gotten so many people out of the organization, when are you going to get some of the work out?'[11] With typical gusto, Welch brought in 20 or so business school professors and consultants to help turn the emergent concept into reality. He called Work-out 'a relentless, endless company-wide search for a better way to do everything we do'.[12]

Work-out was a communication tool that offered employees a dramatic opportunity to change their working lives. As Janet Lowe explains in *Jack Welch Speaks:*

> *'The idea was to hold a three-day, informal town meeting with 40 to 100 employees from all ranks of GE. The boss kicked things off by reviewing the business and laying out the agenda, then he or she left. The employees broke into groups, and aided by a facilitator, attacked separate parts of the problem.*
>
> *'At the end, the boss returned to hear the proposed solutions. The boss had only three options: The idea could be accepted on the spot;*

rejected on the spot; or more information could be requested. If the boss asked for more information, he had to name a team and set a deadline for making a decision.'[13]

Welch the destroyer became Welch the empowerer. Work-out was part of a systematic opening up of GE. Walls between departments and functions came tumbling down. Middle management layers had been stripped away in the 1980s. With Work-out, Welch was enabling and encouraging GE people to talk to each other, work together, and share information and experience.

The next stage in Welch's revolution was the introduction of a wide-ranging quality programme. Entitled Six Sigma, this was launched at the end of 1995. 'Six Sigma has spread like wildfire across the company, and it is transforming everything we do,' the company reported two years on.[14]

Six Sigma spread the responsibility for quality. Instead of being a production issue, quality was recast as an issue for every single person in the company. 'We blew up the old quality organization, because they were off to the side. Now, it's the job of the leader, the job of the manager, the job of the employee – everyone's job is quality,' said Welch.[15]

The three stages of development – destruction; creation and quality – reshaped GE. It now operates in over 100 countries with 250 manufacturing plants in 26 countries. Its workforce totals 276,000, with 165,000 in the US. The company's 1997 revenues were $90.84 billion and net earnings $8.203 billion. The company's market value (according to the 1997 annual report) was the highest in the world: $300 billion. As a total entity, GE was ranked fifth in a *Fortune* 500. Nine of its businesses would be in *Fortune's* top 50 if ranked independently.

The broader lessons are equally significant. GE has succeeded because of a combination of professional management – driven by common sense rather than analysis – a strong culture (nurtured at its Crotonville training establishment), and vigorous, thoughtful leadership. It has refused to sit still.

The lean model

Toyota is the third biggest automobile maker in the world (behind GM and Ford). It sells five million vehicles a year (1.3 million in North America, 2 million in Japan and 0.5 million in Europe). Its 1998 sales were $88.5 billion with a net income of $3.5 billion.

Behind the Toyota story lurks the presence of W. Edwards Deming, the legendary American quality guru. While Western companies produced gas-guzzling cars with costly, large, and unhappy workforces in the 1970s, Toyota was forging ahead with implementation of Deming's ideas on total quality. By the time Western companies finally woke up and began to implement the quality gospel, Toyota had moved on.

Toyota progressed to what became labelled lean production, or the Toyota Production System. It was based on three simple principles. The first was just-in-time production. There is no point in producing cars, or anything else, in blind anticipation of someone buying them. Waste (*muda*) is bad. Production has to be closely tied to the market's requirements. Second, responsibility for quality rests with everyone and any quality defects need to be rectified as soon as they are identified. The third, more elusive, concept was the 'value stream'. Instead of seeing the company as a series of unrelated products and processes, it should be seen as a continuous and uniform whole, a stream including suppliers as well as customers.

Toyota's production philosophy and the carefully developed strength of its brand reached its high point in 1990 with the launch of the Lexus. This was initially greeted as a triumph for Japanese imitation. Media pundits laughed at the company's effrontery – 'If Toyota could have slapped a Mercedes star on the front of the Lexus, it would have fooled most of the people most of the time.'

But Toyota had moved the goalposts. It out-engineered Mercedes and BMW. The Lexus took seven years, $2 billion, 1,400 engineers, 2,300 technicians, 450 prototypes and generated 200 patents. Its standard fittings include a satellite navigation system and much more.

While the product stood up to scrutiny, where Lexus really stole a march on its rivals was through the ownership experience. Even when things went wrong, the service was good. An early problem led to a product recall. Lexus had dealers call up people personally and immediately. Instead of having a negative effect, this strengthened the channel: Lexus screwed things up like everyone else, but then they sorted the problem out in a friendly, human way. With the Lexus, Toyota demonstrated its capacity to stay ahead of the pack.

The new model

Michael Dell made history when he became the youngest CEO ever to run a *Fortune* 500 company. Along the way, he joined the ranks of the most revered entrepreneurs in America – as the man who took the direct sales model and elevated it to an art form.

The company Dell built is not the biggest in the world, nor are its products the most innovative. But Dell Corporation is that rarity: a corporate model, the benchmark for how companies can be organized and managed to reap the full potential of technology.

Dell's inspiration was to realize that PCs could be built to order and sold directly to customers. This had two clear advantages. First, it meant that Dell was not hostage to retailers intent on increasing their mark-ups at its expense. Dell cut out the middlemen. By doing so, he reduced the company's selling costs from a typical 12 percent of revenue to a mere 4 to 6 percent of revenue.

Second, the company did not need to carry large stocks. It actually carries around 11 days of inventory. 'The best indirect company has 38 days of inventory. The average channel has about 45 days of inventory. So if you put it together, you've got 80 days or so of inventory – a little less than eight times our inventory level,' says Dell.

In any language, high profit margins and low costs make business sense. In the fast-growing computer business they are nirvana. In its first eight years Dell Computer grew at a steady rate of 80 percent. It then slowed down to a positively snail-like 55 percent.

Emulators have come thick and fast. In an effort to keep ahead, Compaq introduced programs offering the ability to have PCs built-to-order. Crucially, these are still sold through intermediaries. The trouble for established companies like Compaq is that once the middlemen are in place it is very difficult to ease them out of the picture. Another Dell competitor, Gateway, opted for a half-way house approach – it introduced 'Country Stores' to provide potential customers with a physical site to learn about products in person, the equivalent of a car showroom and test drive.

Emulation is the purest form of desperation as well as flattery. Dell's insight was, after all, blissfully simple. 'There is a popular idea now that if you reduce your inventory and build to order, you'll be just like Dell. Well, that's one part of the puzzle, but there are other parts, too,' Dell has said. He explains the company's success as: 'A disciplined approach to understanding how we create value in the PC industry, selecting the right markets, staying focused on a clear business model and just executing.'

While the notion of selling direct is appealing, companies that do so are only as good as their ability to deliver. Dell's model creates a direct line to the customer that the company has proved highly adept at maximizing. Direct knowledge of the end consumer builds a satisfied customer base: increasing brand strength, lowering customer acquisition costs, and boosting customer loyalty. The result is 'mass customization', as opposed to the traditional method of broad market segmentation.

Dell has proved highly efficient in utilizing the full power of modern technology to create reliable logistic and distribution systems. It was among the pioneers of selling via the internet. 'The Internet for us is a dream come true,' says Dell. 'It's like zero-variable-cost transaction. The only thing better would be mental telepathy.' Dell's online sales alone exceed $3 million a day and, during Christmas 1997, it was selling $6 million worth of products every day online.

The beauty of the Dell model is that it can be applied to a range of industries where middlemen have creamed off profits. Its low overheads also mean that Michael Dell has no need to mortgage the business to expand. This year's model may be around for some time.

REFERENCES

1. Weber, Max, *The Theory of Social and Economic Organizations* (translated. A.M. Henderson and Talcott Parsons), New York, 1947.
2. Ibid.
3. Robb, Russel, *Lectures on Organization*, privately printed, 1910.
4. In 1937 Sloan became chairman of General Motors. He continued as chief executive until 1946. He resigned from the chairmanship in 1956, and became honorary chairman until his death in 1966.
5. Drucker, Peter, 'Alfred P Sloan's role', *Fortune*, July 1964.
6. Codtz, Dan, 'The face in the mirror at General Motors', *Fortune*, August 1966.
7. Ghoshal, Sumantra and Bartlett, Christopher, *Financial Times Handbook of Management*, FT/Pitman, London, 1995.
8. Peters, Tom, *Liberation Management*, Alfred Knopf, New York, 1992.
9. Barham, Kevin and Heimer, Claudia, *ABB: The Dancing Giant*, FT/Pitman, London, 1998.
10. Pascale, Richard, *Managing on the Edge*, Simon & Schuster, New York, 1990.
11. Vicere, Albert and Fulmer, Robert, *Leadership By Design*, Harvard Business School Press, Boston, 1988.
12. General Electric Annual General Meeting, 1990.
13. Lowe, Janet, *Jack Welch Speaks*, John Wiley, New York, 1998.
14. Byrne, John, 'How Jack Welch runs GE', *Business Week*, 8 June 1998.
15. Lowe, Janet, *Jack Welch Speaks*, John Wiley, New York, 1998.

RESOURCES

BOOKS

Barnard, Chester, *The Functions of the Executive*, Harvard University Press, 1968.

Barham, Kevin and Heimer, Claudia, *ABB: The Dancing Giant*, FT Pitman, 1998.

Peters, Tom, *Liberation Management*, Knopf, 1992.

Funky Inc.

KJELL NORDSTRÖM AND JONAS RIDDERSTRÅLE

Kjell Nordström and Jonas Ridderstråle argue that the time is right for an antidote to the traditional organization: welcome to Funky Inc.

LOVE them or hate them, companies remain the powerhouses of the capitalist system. Just think of a single fact: the 300 largest multinational companies control 25 percent of all productive assets on earth. A company such as Philip Morris has a larger annual turnover than New Zealand's GDP. Half of world trade is handled by multinational companies.[1] Forget the Romans or the British Empire. These global firms are the new empires roaming and running the world.

What is impressive about these empires is that they are built around an empty legal entity. Corporations are legal frameworks. They are shells. A company or a business firm basically consists of four different things: *capital*, dollars, nickels and dimes; *machinery* and *buildings*, the dirty and expensive hardware; *people*, the problematic software; and a basic *idea*, the most elusive element of all.

While we salute the massive power wielded by corporations we know that they will look and behave differently tomorrow. In a global, real-time, brain-based and messy world, the inflexible structures of the past do not stand a chance. Organizations come and go. They rise and fall. They change shape constantly. They leave the nations and regions in which they were born. They reorganize, realign, refocus. Nothing stays the same. But fear not, Funky Inc. is already here. Funky Inc. isn't like any other company. It is not a dull old conglomerate. It is not a rigid bureaucracy. It is an organization that actually thrives on the changing circumstances and unpredictability of our times. Its difference – and its perpetual search for difference – is visible both in terms of its looks and how it operates. Funky Inc. is:

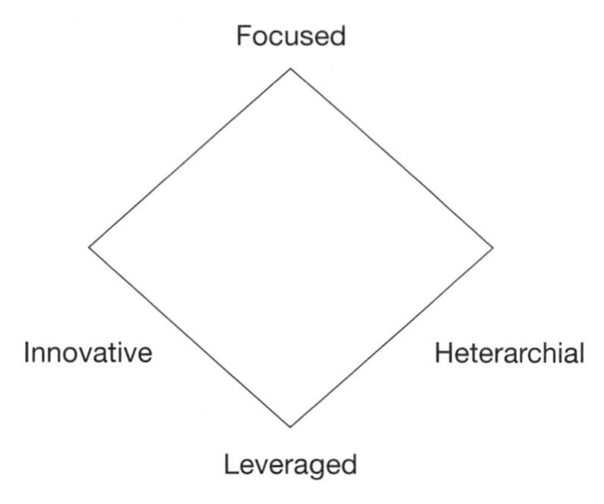

Funky Inc. is focused

Entering the age of abundance, we have to stop believing that organizations can master all things and situations. Stakeholders, inside and outside the firm, now have the power of choice. They all have access to international markets. None of them will accept middle of the road models. The excess economy is ruthless. For the demanding customer, only the best will do, and no one can excel at everything. Global competition in an oversupplied world with increasingly perfected markets kills average product offerings and performers.

There are also internal factors that prevent us from spreading our resources too thinly. No matter how much digitization, globalization and deregulation we may experience, we are still human beings with limited cognitive capacity. Our brains just don't have the bandwidth to handle excessive breadth. There is no way we can attend to everything with the same energy and emphasis.

Then there is the question of the internal climate of the organization. In non-focused firms, money is often reallocated from winners to losers, leaving people in the profitable businesses disappointed and demotivated. Likewise, there is a risk that the underperformers will doze off and rely on the others to save their necks yet again. Time is spent on political rather than productive matters. A sense of clarity and urgency is lacking.

In a society where money flows freely across borders, the shareholder will accept nothing else than continuous and fantastic value-creation. Increasingly perfected markets and total transparency prevent the pursuit of 'un-natural' synergies. The management team of any diversified organization is basically saying that it is better than the market at balancing risk and creating value. But, actors on the market can now evaluate each business separately. If they come to the conclusion that the sum of the parts is actually greater than the present whole, they will step in and dismantle the company. Why should some over-paid president manage my investments? If I want a diversified portfolio, I will put it together on my own or turn to an expert on such matters.

As an effect of increasing customer, employer and shareholder pressure, more and more hierarchies are being engulfed by markets. Perfected markets hate inefficiencies so inefficiencies disappear. Inept organizations are dismembered or they die. So, funky organizations do not aspire to be everything for everyone. Instead, they try to become something for someone. This focus has three elements.

Narrow focus

Funky Inc. is narrow, focused on one or just a handful of core businesses. The days of the large and diversified conglomerate are over. The antidote to mindless pursuit of synergies is to become intensely focused on those businesses where you clearly have a global competitive edge. Companies have to be turned from blunt instruments into sharpened precision tools.

Organizations are already honing themselves. How narrow a company is can be measured in terms of Standard Industry Codes (SICs), the number of different industries in which the firm is active. In the late 1970s, the average American firm scored a little more than four SIC, a few years back this measure was down to a little more than two.[2] Translation: the typical US company has lost some 50 percent of its body parts in less than 20 years.

Hollow focus

The second characteristic of focused Funky Inc. is that it is hollow. Focusing on only a few businesses just isn't enough. As strategy guru Gary Hamel sometimes puts it, you can take a fat man and cut off one of his legs, but that won't really make him any thinner. Every little process and activity in the firm must be exposed to the question: are we really world class? If not, outsource it. Buy it from someone else – someone who is better. Funky Inc. competes on the basis of its core competence and competents, the people who make competencies happen.

Once organizations really start trying to identify their core competencies, many of them realize that these are not always in the areas they thought they would be in. American Airlines, for example, realized that its real strengths were tied to SABRE, the booking system, rather than operating aeroplanes. In 1995, SABRE alone accounted for 44 percent of the company's pre-tax profits.[3] Sears discovered that its critical skills were in the fields of logistics and branding, rather than in running department stores. GE, IBM, and Xerox are all experts in the area of consulting. Their products have become nothing more than bi-products, a sideshow to the main action. Again, we can see the shift from atoms to bits. Atoms just aren't scarce enough so it is increasingly difficult to base competitiveness on access to them.

Focusing on your core competencies means sticking to what you excel at. Do it well. Do it fantastically well. Funky Inc. brings in other people to do the rest. Many successful firms no longer make what they sell. Timberland, for instance, is a shoeless shoe-company. Funky Inc. looks like the facades from an old Hollywood motion picture, nice on the outside, virtually empty on the inside save for one thing: brains.

You can call this new firm virtual, hollow, a spider's web, outsourced, a shamrock, or whatever you like. The important thing is that if we don't slim down, our chances of surviving and thriving in an excess economy are just that – slim. Call it hollow, but don't call it empty.

Targeted focus

The third and final element to Funky Inc.'s focus is that it is targeted. Funky Inc. targets tribes – core customers – and it doesn't matter what kind of tribe, where it's based or how large it is. What does matter is that they share a common vibe – values and attitudes.

Violent drug barons create tribes. Miguel Caballero is the Armani of the armoured apparel world. His company sells customized and fashionable bullet-proof vests. It has targeted a specific tribe. Its home base is Columbia where demand is great.[4]

Leg fetishists create tribes. A while back, we came across a magazine called *Legshow*. It is a global magazine for people obsessed with naked legs and feet. A small market, one would have thought. Surely, foot fetishists cannot form a huge percentage of society. The reality is that the publishers of *Legshow* make more money in relation to its turnover than you would ever imagine. Why? It dominates a certain tribe. *Legshow* has developed a profitable niche. It does not have a foothold in the market, but has a very large boot covering all of the market – globally.

The message is that if you focus your energy on creating and then exploiting an extremely narrow niche you can make a lot of money. The tribe may consist of one-legged, homosexual, dentists. It may be lawyers who race pigeons. But if you manage to capture these customers globally, you can make a lot of money. In an excess economy, we find riches in niches.

Funky Inc. is leveraged

The second crucial aspect of Funky Inc. is that it is leveraged. In recent years management and corporations have sought to solve the corporate puzzle through an obsession with minimization. Huge sprawling companies have sought to minimize bureaucracy, numbers of employees and to minimize time. Now, we need to maximize. Simply put, you cannot shrink to greatness. There is no way of creating new wealth by simply reducing costs and getting rid of people.

Once an organization has identified its basic businesses, the core capabilities and the target tribe, it needs to leverage its key resources. Funky Inc. needs to move on from corporate liposuction and anorexia to corporate bodybuilding – getting rid of the fat *and* letting the muscles grow.

In the machine age, leverage often meant real diversification – we needed different machines to make different products. But in a brain-based world, one and the same competence can be used to enter an array of industries, without being involved in the actual production of stuff as such. As noted earlier, the result is blur. The globally linked society forces firms to leverage competence in new ways and increased digitization enables and opens up the means by which this can happen. As with hollowing, leveraging is a three-stage process as shown in Figure 1.

Figure 1
Three stage leveraging process

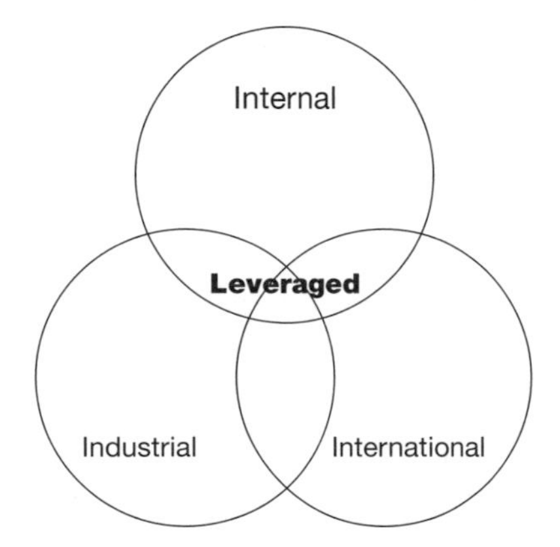

Internal leverage

The problem with most organizations is not that they know too little, but that they do not know what they know. Knowledge is dispersed without anyone having a clear picture of the total stock, how and where it flows, nor the location of specific capabilities.

To thrive, we must create a learning organization. This requires us to realize and acknowledge that we are not perfect. Unfortunately, this is often something which managers and companies are unwilling to contemplate. Building a learning organization is about increasing the rate of knowledge *transfer* and *transformation*. This starts with leveraging knowledge throughout the firm. We must move knowledge from individual levels to group and organizational levels. This sounds simple, but let us ask you three simple questions:

1. Are some of your colleagues better performers than the others?
2. Would you like the others to become as good?
3. What is being done about it?

Learning does not happen automatically, it must be managed. And the speed of a company will be determined not by the fastest and smartest people but by the slowest and least skilled. Enabling learning is one of the key tasks for any leader. Leaders must ensure the continuous transfer of knowledge across organizational boundaries. The individual parts must be able to reflect the whole. In effect, Funky Inc. must work in a similar way to the human brain.

Creating a learning organization is only part of the story. Customers do not pay companies – not even universities – for their learning abilities. They open their wallets for companies that can teach them something. So, in a real-time world we must decrease the time from insight to output.

Unless the capabilities can be put to good use they are virtually worthless. But creating such an organization is costly – IT investments, more travelling, co-location of key people and other measures do not come cheaply. The more important question, however, is whether you can afford not to invest in building a learning organization.

As a result, a critical task for any organization is to turn the core competents into core competencies. The funky firm transforms human capital into structural capital – just as the Scandinavian insurance company Skandia is trying to do.[5] They collect the knowledge of the gold-collar workers and excellent teams. By building systems containing this competence, the firm provides the others in the organization with an opportunity to learn and then use their new insights to help customers. Inevitably, this process calls for open communication and discussions throughout the entire company (and the external network). It may well be that the prime denominator of future competitive advantages will be related to which people are allowed to have what discussions about which topics with whom, when, and where.[6] The manager becomes a kind of talk-show host. Funky Inc. is built around forums, virtual and real, where people can meet, rather than boxes and arrows that isolate them in unbreakable silos.

But leveraging is not only a question of transferring skills across levels and transforming competents into competence, it also concerns transforming knowledge into forms which allow the organization to more effectively profit from it. Just as with many materials, any type of knowledge basically comes in three different forms: gas, fluid and solid. Gas is what we have in our minds. Fluid knowledge comes about when we discuss things with others. And solid knowledge is the stuff that is embodied in customer offerings, routines, systems, etc. In effect, a car, PC, a software program, an ice-cream or whatever is in reality nothing more and nothing less than frozen creativity. We get an idea (gas); start discussing it with others (fluid); and finally develop a customer offering (solid).

The more solid the knowledge, the more money one can make. As we begin to freeze creativity, we also create opportunities for greater economies of scale. Remember the CD-ROM? The first copy is incredibly expensive, but then costs drop dramatically. The problem with frozen creativity is that it is easy for our competitors to pick up a copy, take it to pieces and copy it. The icier it gets, the easier imitation becomes. No longer can we put our trust in patents. We must rely on our ability to develop processes that enable us to deep-freeze new pieces of knowledge faster than the others – decreasing the duration of the insight-output cycle. The alternative is to bundle our frozen knowledge with more fluid or gas-like stuff – to sell provices and serducts. Think about GE, Xerox, and IBM where the products are now little more than byproducts. But the real route to enhanced competitiveness is to combine and constantly bundle and re-bundle these different forms of knowledge – hyphenation.

How we create and leverage the knowledge of the firm are critically important questions. But increasing internal leverage does not mean creating a department for learning or knowledge management. Many companies in the West are now repeating the mistakes they made when realizing that Japanese firms constantly beat them on quality. The answer then, as it seems to be now when knowledge is concerned, was to set up a department to handle the task. Quality was made into a big thing for a selected few, and we ended up with a bunch of quality engineers or managers running around trying to fix all problems. Did it help? Not one bit. We must avoid making this mistake yet again. Instead, these responsibilities should be an integral part of everyone's job. Rather than knowledge management, the key to increasing internal leverage is knowledgeable management.

Industrial leverage

Leverage is not only internal. With a clear focus on their key capabilities, funky organizations also use their core competencies and competents to enter new industries. But they do so without trying to control all processes internally. The new logic means sticking to your competence, but utilizing these skills in more than one industry. Today, we see at least three different types of industrial leverage.

First, there is *attitude-based* leverage. Having understood the needs of, and targeted, a specific tribe, the organization may then use the fit in attitude to supply this tribe with more stuff. But it needs to convey the same vibe.

Second, many firms engage in *brand-based* leverage. Marlboro does it. Coca-Cola does it. Disney does it as a publishing, retailing, and theme park operating company. Consider Richard Branson's Virgin, which is involved in everything from airlines and railways, to clothing and cosmetics, from pensions to internet services. The organization slavishly applies the core values of the brand when deciding whether or not to enter a new industry.

Third, there are lots of cases of more purely *competence-based* leverage. Honda focuses on engines, but utilizes its knowledge to make cars, motorcycles, and so on. 3M is an expert on adhesives.

International leverage

No surprises, leverage needs also to be international. Funky Inc. is a global corporation. But global does not necessarily mean big. Midget multinationals – like *Legshow* – are already all around us.

While globalization is here, it is often not readily recognized in the organization of firms. Although most companies access global markets through exports, and many have their *assets* internationally dispersed in the form of foreign subsidiaries, few have managed to build global *administrative* structures and systems.

We also see clear differences across geography. To the typical US multinational, foreign usually equals marginal. But for many European multinationals, and particularly those from small countries such as Sweden, Finland, Holland, and Switzerland, foreign has always equalled 'most of it'. Early on, these companies had to come up with ways and solutions to tackle global challenges. The result is usually that the role of headquarters is not as pronounced. So if you want to learn more about managing across borders look to European firms such as Philips, Electrolux, Nokia, Heineken, Unilever, TetraPak and Nestlé, rather than Chrysler or Mitsubishi.

And then there is the fourth and most important stage of globalization – *attitudes*. No company we have ever come across is truly global in attitude. Home country standards are often applied relatively uniformly. Key persons usually come from the same country. Products are mostly developed at home with the requirements of the local market in mind. The typical multinational is still parochial and ethnocentric. Foreigners are often regarded as strange. Letting one of these managers loose in another culture is like inviting an elephant to dance in a china store.

Yet, only when we have become truly global in attitude can we reap all the other benefits of funkiness. To succeed, we need to move from conflict to reconciliation. We're not saying that it is easy to work in a global organization. Differences in culture and languages and large geographical distances provide demanding challenges. There will be disagreements and misunderstandings aplenty. Globalization may be seen by many as a necessary evil, but that does not make it less essential.

Funky Inc. is innovative

Funky Inc. is extremely innovative. In a real-time, globally linked surplus society it is just a matter of a few weeks, days or even hours before our friends from Bangalore, New York, Kuala Lumpur, Paris, Gdansk, Tokyo, Seoul, London or Santiago come here to copy our recipes. To remain unique, we must constantly sharpen our competitive edge.

By innovation we do not mean a dedicated department, a carefully fenced off group of boffins. We mean total innovation – a frame of mind that applies to everyone at the company, everything, everywhere, and that goes on non-stop. It turns the company into an idea and dream factory which competes on imagination, inspiration, ingenuity and initiative.

Innovation is not only a matter of technology – nuts and bolts. In fact, technology is often only a small part of it. Innovation concerns every little aspect of how an organization operates – administrative innovations, marketing innovations, financial innovations, design innovations, HRM innovations and service concept innovations. Going for total innovation, therefore, requires re-thinking every little aspect of how we operate. This means reinventing strategy, increasing speed and thriving on smartness. But above all, total innovation requires ignoring *and* listening to the customers, as well as promoting internal heterogeneity *and* homogeneity – moving from a world of focusing on either or to one of achieving both, simultaneously. We are not talking about striking a balance – Funky Inc. combines extremes rather than settling for average solutions.

Innovate through reinventing strategy

In a world where technology, institutions and values are in a state of turmoil, innovation is about rethinking what we are doing and about reinventing our industry. The US company Taco Bell, part of Pepsi Co., sells 'Tex-Mex' junk food. At one time, the company firmly believed that it was a player in the fast-food industry, and that the key to success was to increase market share, particularly in relation to other Tex-Mex restaurants. Reviewing the strategy, management realized that Taco Bell was really in the business of feeding people. The more challenging goal was to go for an increased share of stomach. In one second, the size of the market exploded from $70 billion to $550 billion. In five years, sales more than doubled. How? Well, if you are in the business of feeding people you had better go out looking for the customers, rather than just expecting them to find you. So, Taco Bell set up small, often portable restaurants at schools, hospitals, train stations, airports, libraries and other such places.

During the last few years, we have seen companies such as Dell, Amazon, Nike, and Starbucks, doing the same thing. They change the rules of the game. The uniqueness of these firms often rests with the soft and intangible aspects of their customer offerings rather than technology. Nike shifted its focus from being a shoe company to being a sports company. And then it shifted the focus from sports products as such to sporting performance and the superstars of sports. While most people don't talk about the characteristics of a particular basketball shoe or a golf putter, many are willing to dissect the performances of Michael Jordan or Tiger Woods from every angle.

Innovate through speed

Not only does a larger geographical market necessitate a sharper focus, it also decreases the time available to exploit our capabilities. In a real time society, getting faster to the future is obviously important. Funky Inc. operates in a world in which things are moving at a pace never before witnessed. Once we have a clear focus on our core competencies we need to act at the speed of light.

Traditionally, many European companies have been successful in what is usually referred to as mature industries. But, how can we then explain that a company like ABB generates half of its revenues from products introduced during the last three years? After you have erased the word synergy, please erase the word mature from your vocabulary and replace it with tired. We should no longer talk about mature industries or markets, but tired ones. Tired industries and markets are waiting for someone to do something revolutionary, radical, and interesting. If we are entering a real time economy, a remote control reality, people will zap to another company the instant they find that you are old, boring, and out of date.

Innovate through smartness

Working faster is of course not a question of trying harder – just try doing the wrong things twice as fast – it is a matter of working smarter. Even though the new economy comes without speed limits, creativity cannot be forced upon people. To be creative we need slack. We need resources and time. We need time to sit down and reflect. We need time alone. We need time to play around. We need time to experiment. We need time to have casual conversations with others. In Japan, people sometimes refer to 'nommunication', rather than communication. Nommu is Japanese for drinking – and for once we are not talking about Coke. The time spent together in a bar after office hours can be critical to the development of new ideas. A lot of venturing, mingling, socializing and relationship building in Silicon Valley is done in bars. So if thinking is working, put your feet back on the table, then leave the office and have a beer with your colleagues. Cut yourself some slack.

In a knowledge-based society, brains will always beat brawn. As it stands today, many organizations do not use knowledge – they abuse it. Something can be done and must be done. And no one can have a monopoly on creativity – not even a momentary one – not even Microsoft.

Ignoring and listening to customers

Contrary to popular belief, getting to know customer requirements is not very difficult. Let us tell you what all customers want. Any customer, in any industry, in any market wants stuff that is both cheaper and better, and they want it yesterday. The simple truth is that the typical customer will always ask for improvements within the present frame.

Radical innovation in a discontinuous world means forgetting about forecasting and listening to marketing studies. Of course, history is littered with people who ignored customers and paid the price. Still, listening to the wrong customers, or listening without thinking, can be real killers as well.

The reality is that we use and enjoy products that we wouldn't have wanted if they had been proposed to us at the very start of their development. We cannot expect the customer to think the unthinkable. That is our task. The responsibility for innovation always rests with the supplier. We must have the gifts and guts to imagine and work wonders. All this implies risk – total risk – and, at the end of the day, personal risk.

Does technology push really work? Just look at the US biotech company Amgen. It has been among the top-performers on the *Fortune* 500 in terms of profitability for the last 10 years. The business concept of Amgen is to take brilliant science and find a use for it. It may well be that if customers don't like your solutions they have the wrong problems. Unfortunately, in an age of abundance where the customers are in charge of the remote control, this is more problematic for you than for them.

If you are really innovative, you are also in a position to fire some of your customers. The typical company loses money on at least 50 percent of its customers. Trouble is, most companies do not have a clue about which these customers are. Clearly, the risks associated with voluntarily or involuntarily firing the wrong customers are immense. For Ford a 1 percent increase in customer loyalty is worth approximately $100 million per year in profits.[7] When an unhappy customer walks out the door how much money does your organization lose, if he or she decides never to come back? It could be $500, $5,000, perhaps even $50,000.

Paradoxically, Funky Inc. must also be extremely customized. We have to choose. Sometimes we must ignore the customer and do something radical and revolutionary, and in certain cases we must look upon the customer as a part of the firm and include them in value creation processes. In the age of the demanding customer, it is no longer enough to produce slides and slogans saying that the customer is king.

Customize, then do it some more. 3M's Post-it notes now come in 18 colours, 27 sizes, 56 shapes and 20 fragrances. All in all, more than half a million combinations are available. The modularized trucks of Scania allow you to build your personal truck – cafeteria style. Or why not build your own doll? Barbie now comes complete with 15,000 combinations. The management gurus were right. Mass customization is child's play. Change the outfit, the eyes, the colour, the hairdo, the clothes, the name – but don't even think about the legs. All for $40 (double the usual price).[8] To get the customized doll, you need to fill out a questionnaire. Anne Parducci, VP of Barbie's owner Mattel, claims that aim is to 'build a database of children's names, to develop a one-to-one relationship with these girls'.[9]

In a fragmenting world, niches are becoming ever smaller. Increasing individualization combined with changes in technologies and values mean that micro markets have overtaken mass markets. The next step is one-to-one manufacturing; one-to-one marketing; one-to-one everything; one customer–one solution. It is happening in industry after industry. We are entering a one-to-one society. Look at yourself in the mirror and staring back at you is the average size of a market segment in a surplus society. The new logic of the demanding customer is really simple. It is up to you to satisfy me, and I am not like you, you, or you.

Customization can occur in all aspects of the customer offering; customized products, customized prices, customized opening hours, customized promotion, etc. Total customization. Tele-operators and utility companies let us design our own profiles for pricing and paying bills. MTV targets programming and commercials for different regions in Europe.

The recent developments in production equipment open up many new opportunities. We can move from mass production to flexible production and now mass customization. With fewer tools we can produce more and better quality models.

Customization is also about your share of time. When and for how long are you prepared to do business with your clients? In an age of abundance, the customer decides when you can do business with him or her, not the opposite. In addition, in some situations certain customers are your best consultants (and, always, the cheapest). The modern manager has one great advantage. Customers and employees have never been as smart as they are right now. The sensible executive treats them as assets, not assholes. A natural solution is to move power close to those people directly involved with the customers on a daily basis. Those engaged in the moment of truth activities, as former Scandinavian Airline Systems president Jan Carlzon put it, must be given the means to master the situation.[10]

'Anything you can digitize, you can customize,' says Joseph Pine, author of *Mass Customization*.[11] 'Everything that can be digital will be,' claims New York-based digital change agent Razorfish.[12] So more or less everything is being customized.[13] Car rental company Hertz discovered that by doing *only* what each customer actually required, its Gold service was in fact less expensive to provide than its Standard service.

Combining heterogeneity and homogeneity

Making radical changes possible calls for a much more personalized company. Funky Inc. thrives on variation, difference, and diversity. Funky Inc. welcomes people who are prepared to challenge the *status quo*, and to break with existing norms and regulations. Funky Inc. refuses to take part in the look-alike game anymore.

Quite often people talk favourably about diversity, since it supposedly promotes a better atmosphere and equality. Though arguments alluding to the 'fun and fair' consequences of increased variation may seem nice and laudable, this is not the stuff that persuades the typical manager to change the mix of people at the company. Instead, let us give you three solid economic reasons why heterogeneity pays.

First, because $C=D^2$, where C stands for creativity and D for diversity.[14] Lack of diversity often results in groupthink and intellectual constipation. We all know what the others think, so what's the use in talking to them. From the point of view of innovation, opposites attract. Novelty is the result of constructive misfits and tension. Cacophony Inc. replaces calamity with creativity.

Second, more diversity generally decreases the average performance of a system but it also increases the standard deviation. The problem for Consistency Inc. is that in a world where the winner takes all, we do not compete on averages – we compete on exceptions. A firm with a lower average may well slaughter a rival with a higher average, if the latter organization lacks unique ideas that totally deviate from the norm.

Third, to ensure success, the complexity of our environment must be reflected in the composition of the firm. Most academics refer to this as the law of requisite variety. In practice, this means that when suppliers are from outside the home country of the organization this must be reflected in the make-up of the organization. If many of our customers are immigrants this, too, must be reflected. If we deal with really young or old people this must be reflected. If we increasingly do business with women this must be reflected.

Yet, most of us live and work in organizations built by and for 5 percent of the population – middle-aged white males. Many firms are so inbred that you somctimes expect the next person to walk through the door with an oversized head, red curly hair, and an extra eye in the middle of their forehead. Don't expect too much innovation at companies where 90 percent of the employees are the same gender, about the same age, have a similar educational background, dress the same way, and all play golf. Even if they go on annual strategy conferences to the Mediterranean or the Alps to be really creative, wild, and crazy, don't expect a great deal. A company with a board filled with white, male, 55-year-old Finns is unlikely to come up with an idea that is even slightly appealing to a young, coloured, female, lesbian, non-Scandinavian, Muslim. Are the men on the board going to recruit Muslim lesbians? Of course not.

What if you are continually turning down applications from people like Richard Branson? Or even worse, maybe these guys have stopped sending their CVs to you, because they know that you care about how people look, dress, the colour of their skin, and so on.

We are not suggesting that you should start recruiting all the cross-dressers in the world, but simply that you have to be prepared for the consequences of developing a brain-based firm. And, allowing people to be themselves and to look as they want appears a fundamental starting point.

The competitive reality is that organizations that are bogged down in issues of race, gender, age, sexual preferences, look and so on, will slip deeper down in the mire. They will encounter serious problems when competition moves softwhere. Intelligence is normally distributed. It is not the preserve of white, 45-year-old males.

Admittedly, an entire company of mavericks would be quite difficult to manage. We are not saying that you should move from hierarchy to anarchy. Instead, we are simply suggesting that sharing a number of things will be helpful. What can you share? The choice is endless. How about, shared ownership, rewards, identity, culture, language, knowledge and attitudes.

Funky Inc. is neither homogeneous nor heterogeneous it is *both*. Successful organization will evolve into organizational tribes – biographical organizational tribes.[15] And in a tribe people get the energy from one another. The Zulu's have a word for it: '*ubuntu*' (short for *unmunta ngumuntu nagabuntu*). This can be translated as: 'a person is a person because of other persons.' Or as Jung put it: 'I need we to be fully I.'

At McKinsey and several other consulting firms, all the employees have at least one thing in common. They are insecure overachievers.

This is a way of keeping people together and assuring some continuity in an otherwise discontinuous world. At Quad Graphics blood or marriage relates more than 50 percent of the 8,500 or so employees.[16] Once, someone even said that the Mafia gets more resignations than a company such as 3M with its extremely strong culture.[17] Have you thought of, identified and worked with, the lowest common denominator of your organization?

And just how do you get people to share your values? Short answer: find those who already do. Look at Hell's Angels or Greenpeace. We hire attitudes, says Herb Kelleher of Southwest Airlines.[18] The logic is that you can make positive people into good pilots, but turning great pilots with attitude problems into charming servers of customers is close to impossible. Funky Inc. recruits people with the right attitude, then it trains them in skill – not the reverse.[19] We can no longer bring in smart people and then brainwash them at training camps. Ideally, of course we try to attract people that are smart *and* share our values. But, if you are forced to choose, go for attitude. Lenin was right again. Find the revolutionaries. Do not try to change people.

The tribe is not necessarily restricted to the legal boundaries of the firm. Look at Harley-Davidson.[20] By inviting the consumer tribe it has targeted to join the organizational tribe, the firm has dramatically extended its community. It uses parties to initiate new members. Storytelling around the campfire keeps the messages moving throughout the tribe. Closing ceremonies and continuous reinforcement are also part of the deal. What Harley-Davidson and other Funky Incs have realized is that a tribe targeting another tribe does not merely have to produce value – the customers also want values.

Funky Inc. is heterarchical

Hierarchy builds on three key assumptions: your environment is *stable*, your processes are *predictable*, and your output is *given*. You know where you are, what you do, and what will happen – the same competitors, customers, suppliers, technologies and product offerings – year in and year out. As long as this holds true it is utterly stupid to organize in any other way. However, we seriously doubt that you would use any of those three words to describe your reality. And in a surplus society, an economy moving forward at turbo speed, and in companies heavily reliant on brain-power, traditional hierarchies will get constant nervous breakdowns.

Hierarchy holds other negative consequences. Jack Welch of GE expresses it bluntly when he argues that hierarchy is an organization with its face towards the CEO and its ass towards the customer. Is Welch right? Pleasing the boss sometimes seems more important than serving the consumer. Hierarchy is usually easier for us, but is it better for the customer?

Since hierarchy assumes that the sources underlying competitive advantage are given and eternal, the organizational challenge is to find a structure that will be an efficient exploiter of this specific combination of knowledge. So, we developed organizational structures that excelled in spitting out yet another standardized customer offering. But, in an age of abundance with total global competition, overcapacity in more and more industries, as well as increasingly powerful customers, we need to be different. We need innovation and renewal of our recipe. We need structures that support experimentation and the creation of novelty.

Funky Inc. applies organizational solutions capable of combining and re-combining knowledge across any type of border at the speed of light. And hierarchy simply is not for hyphenation and combination, it is for separation and division. So forget organizational pyramids with the CEO sitting atop. Who wants to work in pyramids, the greatest tombs ever created by man? Playgrounds must gradually replace the pyramids.

The funky model

The traditional hierarchical firm won't be a problem in the twenty-first century – it won't be around. The new organization will be heterarchical – containing many hierarchies of different kinds.

In reality, all firms have three overlapping hierarchical systems of positions, processes, and professions.[21] The positional structure is a contact book with addresses and numbers. The professional structure tells you something about the skills of people, and the process structure shows you what is actually going on. Everyone can be included in all of these categories, but in different places. The positional structures are manifested in our organizational charts. The process structures are represented by boundary-spanning activities and projects. The professional structures are a lot more messy and dependent on the skills of individuals placed all over the landscape of the firm, and increasingly also outside the legal boundaries of the company.

Historically, we have made the mistake of only recognizing the positional structure. Senior executives managed these structures, controlled all important processes and projects, and their professional knowledge was regarded as omnipotent. Many companies still make this mistake. The typical boss, no matter what type of organization or formal position in the hierarchy, is obsessed with knowing and controlling everything. The basic assumption has been that since people are stupid, they can only handle really simple jobs, so we had better have super-complex organizational structures.

Today, we need to transform complexity into simplicity. Jack Welch goes as far as to call bureaucracy the Dracula of organizational design. No matter how much we fight it, bureaucracy always comes back to haunt us. So we have to keep putting sticks through its heart.

In the face of an increasingly complex knowledge landscape we have got to strengthen the power of the professional and process structures. Firms need stronger project leaders as well as intellectual champions with sufficient organizational clout. But neither of these structures should dominate totally. If action drives the entire system the result is adhocracy and, if we let knowledge be the single organizing principle, the resulting structure is a meritocracy.

Total domination by one of the principles leads to bureau*crazy*, adho*crazy* and merito*crazy*, rather than anything else. All three aspects of the modern firm need to exist simultaneously – in our minds. And the latter point is critically important. The funky model is not a three-dimensional matrix. We will not solve problems by simply rearranging the boxes and arrows. It is a frame of mind, a philosophy. And we are not talking about a topless organization. The alternative to hierarchy is not *no-archy*. There is still a critical role for management to play. But they are no longer the only actors or stars.

The question must be whether we can see any companies successfully applying the funky model? Two of our colleagues recently studied the Danish hearing-aid company Oticon. With some $100 million in annual sales, about 1,000 employees and more than 90 percent of sales outside its home country, Oticon uses a 'spaghetti organization'. Just like in a boiling pot of spaghetti there is apparent disorder and chaos, but you can easily pull out a single strand of spaghetti and follow it from beginning to end. Every person in the firm belongs to a pool of resources. Any individual is tied to a project, a specialty profession, and to a people dimension. You are someone. You do something. You know something. Projects constitute the *modus operandi* at Oticon. At any given time there are some 90 projects. Specialty professions represent the functional organization where distinctive skills and expertise are developed. The people dimension refers to personal development. Rather than selecting people for fixed positions, Oticon tries to fit jobs to people. Successful? The firm will soon have been spaghetti managing for 10 years, and is one of the most profitable companies in its industry.

Seven features of the funky firm

So how will Funky Inc. work? Well, let us provide you with seven principles for organizing the firm. Some you will recognize, but the real trick is getting them all to work together in harmony.

Smaller

Throughout the twentieth century the predominant corporate myth was that big was good. From Henry Ford to Michael Eisner, Alfred P. Sloan to Jack Welch, size has been considered all-important. Bravado, of a peculiarly male kind, has dominated. The current fashion for bigger and bigger mergers is just the latest manifestation of this obsession. We may accept that quantity is not quality in virtually every other area of life, but in business organizations the two remain hopelessly intertwined and confused.

Now, those that are large are no longer in charge. In the mid-1970s, 20 percent of the US workforce were employed by *Fortune* 500 companies. Today, that figure is less than 10 percent.[22] Similarly, companies with less than 19 employees account for 50 percent of US exports – the *Fortune* 500 generates a mere 7 percent.[23]

Funky Inc. is small because, as pointed out by American commentator George Gilder: 'The smaller the space; the larger the room.'[24] We are creative in small teams. Maybe, the inhabitants of the Stone Age can teach us something. Back then, the average number of people in a tribe was some 40 individuals. On the African Savannah Plain 200,000 years ago, clans appeared to have had a maximum of around 150 members.[25] Nigel Nicholson of London Business School points to 'the persistent strength of small to midsize family businesses throughout history. These companies, typically having no more than 150 members, remain the predominant model the world over, accounting for approximately 60 percent of all employment'.

The optimum size of a company is a matter of perennial debate. Virgin chief, Richard Branson, argues that 50 to 60 people is enough. Bill Gates claims that around 200 is the maximum. Nathan Myhrwold, the R&D manager at Microsoft says that eight people is about enough. Although numbers vary, no one suggests that the 215,000 employees of a company like ABB is the optimum.

Of course, the mention of ABB is unfair. It has done more than virtually any other company to build smallness into bigness. This is done through building the company around a number of levels. First it has the dynamic working group consisting of some 2–5 individuals. Then it puts together 2–10 such groups into a dynamic business unit. How many such units can you have in a dynamic firm? Well, ABB claims to have approximately 5,000 such profit centres – the average unit having some 45 employees. Still, even Jack Welch admits that while GE is the fastest elephant at the dance – it is still an elephant. [26]

Flatter

The funky firm is flatter. Flatter so that the time from problem detection to solution implementation is reduced. Chrysler, for instance, increased its span of control from 20 people per boss in the late 1980s to some 50. In the future, the organization hopes to reach 100.[27] The need to flatten the firm is hardly big news to any of you, but this might be. There are two very different ways of making a company flatter. The first is to take a sledgehammer and hit the organization on the top while simultaneously raising the lower levels by means of training and education. The second way is to take your hand, reach into the centre of the organization and tear out the middle.

In the West we have had a preference for this second type of solution – getting rid of the middle. We all know how 'boring and conservative' middle managers are. Now, we believe there is an inherent danger to this. We may end up relying on 'seniles' managing 'juveniles'. Our experience is that often the best and most critical people sit in the middle. We only have to use them in the right way – as a value-adding link between the top and the bottom; translating vision into action and action into vision. Many Japanese companies no longer talk about bottom-up or top-down processes. Instead, they realize that real organizational action is dependent on processes better characterized as middle-up-down.

Temporary

Funky Inc. is temporary. By this we refer to working in projects and groups. Most of us know that teams are what Ed Lawler at the University of Southern California calls the Ferraris of organizational design. They are high performance, but also high maintenance and incredibly expensive.[28] Still, the changing circumstances of today's business world do not allow us to use one stable, unisex, one-size-fits-all structure. We have to be able to re-combine our key assets and turn the firm into a team-park. To succeed, we need to institute a culture which mixes aspects of caring, daring, and sharing.

One of the principal problems relates to the fact that people will have to become used to no longer having a job. At funky firms people have many jobs. Today, the woman in the room next to you is your boss – tomorrow you are hers. Our careers are becoming more like those of actors. In the morning you are playing Macbeth, and later that day you are the Terminator. Naturally, this will cause serious problems for those who find security in having a piece of paper saying 'job description' at the top. The new reality gives these people nightmares of Ingmar Bergman-ish proportions. One of the key tasks for leaders is to help people find themselves at ease with and enjoy this new situation.

Horizontal

Funky firms work horizontally, in processes. The vertical hierarchical logic builds upon the simple assumption that the smart ones are located at the top and the stupid ones at the bottom. Hierarchy divides people into those that think and those that merely do. In reality, however, we know that most opportunities and problems in a company occur horizontally – across functions, business areas, divisions, or countries. Moreover, there is little room for suppliers and customers in a vertical logic – they sit outside the firm.

As long as the preferred strategy was addition, through acquisitions, mergers, and diversification, the natural principle for structuring the firm was that of division. However, when the hallmark of a competitive strategy shifts to subtraction, through focusing and outsourcing, the preferred structural denominator should be multiplication – combining stuff from different parts of the network into new customer offerings. This is just simple management by metrics. If the main aim is to build an organization where the whole is greater than the sum of the parts, division is a highly inefficient method.

Circular

All really fast systems, such as our brain, use circular design. This principle is perhaps more difficult to grasp. It builds on the fact that we have a tremendous ability to self-organize once we get 360-degree feedback. Circularity is about organizational democracy. At your company who appoints the CEO? The board, of course. Well, in most organizations marked by knowledge intensity this is the task of the other members of the firm. The other professors mostly elect the dean at a university. The other partners appoint the head at McKinsey and most other consulting companies. This is also reflected in the shared ownership of the firm.

To check the circular qualities, we sometimes run a little experiment. We tell an audience that we want them to clap their hands in rhythm. It only takes three or four claps before they are all in rhythm. Still, people did not have a boss. In fact, if they had had one, they would probably never ever get in rhythm. In that situation people would soon have lost track of who is the boss. And just what is he or she doing? Just as in real life. However, as long as we get feedback from all around, we are amazingly good at spontaneous co-ordination – provided that we have a shared understanding of the words clap, hands and in rhythm.

The experiment may sound ludicrous, but exchange those words for global, product, and strategy. A shared language is critical for being able to manage without hierarchies. Otherwise we can have our meetings, make important decisions, and then realize that the other guys have abandoned the agreement claiming that it was a tactical rather than a strategic point, pertaining to the product concept, not the product itself.

Open

Unfortunately, simply changing internal structures won't suffice. Given that the firm is narrower and hollower, we also need to develop abilities to become increasingly networked. For Focused Inc. the future will mean more joint ventures, strategic alliances and partnerships. Not all assets can be kept internally. The network, rather than the single firm, is becoming the relevant unit of analysis and action. Co-operate with customers, suppliers, *and* competitors. Corporate adultery becomes OK, when you really need the skills and resources of a competitor. Business is not a zero sum game. This calls for a new type of logic.

It's our network/supply-chain against the others. The Seven-Up/RC bottling company brews arch competitors Lipton and Arizona ice-tea in the same tanks.[29] The Volvo S40 and Mitsubishi Charisma are both built in the same factory in Ghent, Holland. Two rivals under the same roof. But keep in mind the quality of your partners and the relationships is heavily contingent on your own attractiveness and willingness to give as well as take.

100101 measured

Control freaks of the world do not despair. Control will not disappear. It will only become more indirect. We do not foresee that the main use of IT for a lot of organizations will lie in increasing communication, co-ordination, customization, and external contacts. Instead, information systems will be used to increase control by measuring more things, new things, at multiple levels, and at a greater frequency than before. To a certain extent, this is a substitute for the loss of hierarchical control resulting from the introduction of new structures.

How many firms really measure not only their own but also their customers' market and mindshare? Are these guys the fastest growing in their industries? How many companies systematically organize knowledge about their competitors and suppliers? How many firms measure things such as: innovation, employee stuff, attractiveness, human exports, company demographics, environmental impact, and so on? How many companies measure their return on knowledge (ROK), return on decency (ROD) or return on people (ROP)? And just who is responsible for measuring all these new things?

We need appropriate goals. The sophisticated companies of today use stretch-goals, goals that challenge people to perform beyond what they thought was possible. At Toshiba the stretch-goal for a VCR was to make it with half of the parts, in half the time, at half the cost.[30] Stretch-goals are general. You do not tell the experts how to do it – you provide a challenging benchmark. Now, this is easier said than done. Not only are these goals hard to attain, it is also difficult to set them. It is difficult because we all have psychological limitations. Most of us know that the present way of doings things is not perfect, but we do believe that we are fairly close to the optimal solution. It is tricky to pose goals that almost seem ridiculous and unattainable.

To make real changes we have got to re-think our basic assumptions and break free from the logic of the past. We need what Konusuke Matsushita used to call: '*Torawarenai sunao-na kokoro*' – a mind that does not stick.

A recipe for success?

So you have focused, leveraged your competencies in all imaginable directions, created an innovative company that is anything but hierarchically organized. But are these changes adequate? Is this the recipe for future success? Short answer: NO! All the changes that we have proposed – all the traits of Funky Inc. – are merely necessary but not sufficient for securing future success. But they are necessary. Very necessary. The problem is that all companies are doing it. All organizations are refocusing, realigning, renewing, reorganizing, re-engineering, etc.

The word competition comes from Latin and literally means 'seeking together' or 'choosing to run in the same race'. But in an age of abundance the tracks are pretty crowded. The others are constantly stepping on your toes, pushing and elbowing you, trying to get to the customers first. So, and slightly paradoxically, the only (un)reasonable thing to do is *not* to compete. As soon as we start running alongside all the others, in our pursuit of marketshare, mindshare, or whatever-share, we risk ending up as one in the crowd – invisible to the customers. When we take part in the same race for top-talent as all the others it is hard for people to tell the difference.

The dirty little secret of market capitalism in all its many forms is that all successful companies have become so by killing the spirit of free enterprise. They have all succeeded in creating monopolies, at least for a short moment in time. Competitiveness comes about by not competing. Success arises from being different. And then being prepared to change again.

REFERENCES

1. *The Economist*, 27 March 1993.
2. Tapscott, Don, *Growing Up Digital*, McGraw-Hill, 1999.
3. Stewart, Thomas, *Intellectual Capital*, Nicholas Brealey, London, 1997.
4. *Business Week*, 3 November 1997.
5. Edvinsson, Leif and Malone, Michael, *Intellectual Capital*, 1997.
6. Michael Geoghegan of DuPont in Kao, John, *Jamming*, Harvard Business School Press, Boston, 1997.
7. Stewart, Thomas, *Intellectual Capital*, Nicholas Brealey, London, 1997.
8. *The Times*, 11 November 1998 and www.barbie.com.
9. *Fortune*, 28 September 1998.
10. Carlzon, Jan, *The Moment of Truth*, 1985.
11. *Fortune*, 28 September 1998.
12. www.Razorfish.com.
13. The example is borrowed from Don Tapscott.
14. John Kao, *Jamming*, Harvard Business School Press, Boston, 1996.
15. Our colleague Peter Hagström also talks about organizational tribes, though he gives the concept a slightly different meaning. Charles Handy uses the metaphor of organizations as membership communities.
16. *Fast Company*, August–September 1996.
17. *Fortune*, 16 January 1995.
18. *Fortune*, 2 May 1994.
19. This idea was proposed to us by our colleague Peter Hagström.
20. Wacker, Watts, *The 500 Year Delta*, Capstone, Oxford, 1997.
21. Hedlund, Hagström and Hedlund, Hedlund and Ridderstråle. Also see Nonaka and Takeuchi, 1995.
22. *Financial Times*, 1 March 1999.
23. John Naisbitt, in *Rethinking the Future*, Rowan Gibson (ed.), Nicholas Brealey Publishing, 1998.
24. *Fast Company*, September 1998.
25. Nicholson, Nigel, 'How hardwired is human behavior?', *Harvard Business Review*, July/August 1998.
26. *Fortune*, 11 January 1999.
27. *Financial Times*, 11 May 1994.
28. *Fortune*, 5 September 1994.
29. *Fortune*, 3 October 1994.
30. *Fortune*, 29 May 1995.

RESOURCES

BOOKS

Ridderstråle, Jonas, and Nordström, Kjell, *Funky Business*, FT.com, 2000.

WEB

www.funkybusiness.com

New World organization

EDDIE OBENG

Leaders of organizations are coming to recognize that the New World extends well beyond the publicized and high-profile activities of e-commerce companies and dot-coms to all their internal and external activities. They are beginning to realize that the speed of change, levels of complexity and the speed of information have irrevocably altered the business sphere – the group of enterprises influenced by or influencing the same entities. Eddie Obeng presents the new organization.

THE challenge is clear. Organizations need to possess speed, agility, be able to develop new capabilities, retain talent, manage global virtual teams, develop intelligent products, customize *en masse* and develop closer customer relationships than ever before.

And, so too is the solution. This lies in new business models, use of cyberspace especially the internet, local involvement of global leaders, new offerings delivered in new ways to new customers. The paradox is staying in control in a business environment which demands that you create new ways of operating which no one yet fully understands. The simplest way to understand the paradox is to contemplate which of these is the odd one out?

1. To run a formula one car using a steam engine.
2. To power a Boeing 737 with a water wheel.
3. To run a notebook computer using transistors.

4. To fuel a laser guided smart bomb with gunpowder.
5. To drive the screen of a palm pilot using valves.
6. To organize a new world global business model using a 100-year-old command and control hierarchical structure?

Did you guess right? Most people guess that number 6 is the odd one out. But why is it the odd one out? The reason is not that it is amusing, not because it is obviously the only one related to the topic being discussed here, not because it is the only one which spills on to two lines of text, but because it is the only one out of the six that we actually try to do.

The New World

Over the past decade, for many enterprises the pace of change in their business-sphere has easily outstripped the speed at which the organization can learn or respond to the change. As this happens business forecasts become more difficult to achieve or sustain, market capitalization valuations become less easily understood, the enterprise finds itself constantly under pressure to reorganize or merge – either to align resources to take advantage of recently identified opportunities or to avoid un-anticipated threats and issues. The enterprise finds itself investing substantially in technologies or activities in which it has little historical experience. Miles Flint, president of Sony Broadcast Europe, has reflected that in Sony its old world of analogue technology sold through a country-based channel needed to be replaced by a European digital solution based approach.[1]

The drivers of this transition are already well documented and understood – technology, aspirations/expectations, new economics – especially information economics, global reach. What is less well documented is the impact on old assumptions about the best way to run a successful enterprise.

Business model

In their simplest form Old World enterprises are usually based around a simple business model. The rely on few entities, there is a simple flow of money usually in exchange for goods – or services – or information). The focus is on the ability to provide superior offering at the expense of direct competing offers. The offers are based around a small range of technologies and are labelled as an industry. Diversified or divisional enterprises added a layer of financial control on top of this model to allow the management of the additional complexity through simpler financial measurements.

Success is based around doing 'more-of-the same' building on experience and exporting the offer to as many people as reachable. Because of scale advantages and reduced risk of repeated activity in a relatively stable market/industry the 'winning' company generally gains the largest share of market and highest customer loyalty, best supplier infrastructure and can generate superior profits as a result of this. The dominance created by the lead player/players, as well as the difficulty for customers to easily identify alternatives, offers leads to additional financial performance.

In contrast, New World enterprises tend to be based around complex or unusual models often involving knowledge rights or retention. There are complex flows of money. Often goods (or services – or information) are provided to one entity and paid for by a separate entity. The focus is on providing a faster and more comprehensive or value adding offering. Often direct competitors are identified as enterprises satisfying the same need. However, because of the increasingly multitudinous ways of satisfying each specific need it becomes more relevant to consider enterprises influencing or influenced by the same entities as being in the same 'business-sphere' rather than industry.

Success is based on a combination of providing new offerings in a different way, old offerings in a different way and new offerings in a traditional way. In general, success generally raises the bar and leads to a need to extend the business model. Innovative use of touchspace and cyberspace alter the cost of operations and the scale achievable. Active use of information economics – replication, network effects, bootstrapping – often leads to explosive exponential growth.

Capturing and sharing knowledge

In the Old World a year really was a short time. It was the basis of the budgeting cycle – a reasonable planning and implementation horizon. Why was it a short time? Because in an environment focused on doing more of the same, the few different or unanticipated issues which did occur were widely spread and did not cross-influence each other. As a result, knowledge acquired had a significant shelf life. The net result was that in an enterprise, the people with the longest experience of the industry were best placed to make strategic and tactical decisions. Knowledge was held at the top of the organization which was also where all the key controls on resourcing and finance were also held. By ensuring that the bulk of the people in the enterprise did what was demanded of them by the ones with the most knowledge, the security of an enterprise is best assured. As a result the management at the top closely determined the actions and focus of the rest of the organization. In order to deal with complexity, decisions and issues were aligned by function or segmented by department or division. Since the bulk of activity is repetitive and based on prior knowledge, little information is required to flow up or down the organization. In addition the volume of information flowing into the organization is low, often limited to structured market research, etc.

An important, but little recognized, fact is that information velocity, the maximum speed with which we can move units of data, increases faster than the rate of computing power. Many managers will be familiar with Moore's law which suggests a doubling of computing power every 18 months. Information goes faster – up by a factor of 10 every three years. Why is this important? It is important because there is a maximum speed at which a group of people can absorb information. Assuming a top management team of 25 in conversations the limit is about 1Mb/s.[2] This rate is fixed – true you can get more out of your 1Mb/s by concentrating on information – on answers rather than data – by making information graphical and colour based by using audible warnings, etc. but there is still a limit. Why is this a problem? – Well it wasn't. In the Old World this velocity was more than adequate. In the New World though, the issues starts at a local level where the simple speed around a local area network is two to three orders of magnitude faster – it is much faster to go across or around the organization than up it. The problem is amplified because the global/wide area networks operate at one to two orders of magnitude of the speed to management. Fast but lower than the local traffic. There are two frightening conclusions. First, the flow of information to the top management of a globally distributed organization will/has become a bottleneck to decisions and focus. Second, the flow of synergistic/knowledge management from one local operation through a formal process via top management to other local operations will not work.

Movement and realignment of resources

The third reason for the need to change is the increasingly debilitating effect of what I describe as the Petronius Paradox, named after a Roman centurion. At the pace of change suffered by organizations in the New World, it is difficult to sustain alignment of functional or divisional resources on the key priorities for very long. This leads to a constant reorganization cycle which is often exacerbated if there is rapid turnover of key executives. Furthermore, organizations that are unable to cope with the pace of the New World have two legitimate options: accelerate or die. But they often choose a third option – get really big and dominate the marketplace, then we won't need to go faster. This strategy drives the logic of consolidation affecting most business-spheres. Mergers and acquisitions have in the New World become part of business as usual. Every acquisition or merger – unless innovatively handled – simply leads on to additional pressure for realigning resources. In theory the process should be quick – instantaneous. In practice, because of the impact of reorganization on the status of individuals, their potential power positions and therefore relationships, their potential career opportunities, their role in the organization – and especially if they still have one after reorganization, far from being a quick logical process it is a slow emotional rollercoaster which takes months, if not years, to fade into the background noise of personal and organizational priorities.

Realignment of resources and people's roles and priorities in the New World should not be so intricately linked with power position and opportunity. But instead with the current challenge or opportunity and should allow individuals in the company to use their attitudes and capabilities to fulfill their potential.

Management/leadership balance

The final driver is the change in emphasis of the behaviours within the enterprise. Old World enterprises, with their focus on experience and procedure, could be effectively driven through standard management practices based on past activities. New or innovative challenges had, as always, to be led. The role of leadership was given to the senior managers – which it had to be, since with their powerful control levers they could actively prevent any change led from elsewhere in the enterprise. Leadership and management came from the top. In the New World the enterprise's agenda includes significant change, demanding a higher level of leadership. However, since most senior management teams are now bottlenecks suffering data or information overload, often relying on past and now obsolete experience, they may not be the best people to lead the change in many circumstances. So leadership shifts from the 'top' to 'who ever is in front' – and that might be anybody.

Not a matrix – a new dimension

The death knell of the old command and control hierarchy has sounded often before. As early as the last century, in the 1970s enterprises were experimenting with 'matrix organizations'. Success was limited because the duplication of the command and control structure which ensued allowed the creation of an intensely political and bureaucratic operating and working environment, and a mish-mash of confusing and confused accountabilities and responsibilities. Furthermore, the information requirements to sustain a matrix organization are tremendous and in the last century there were few tools capable of providing the information transparency required. The experiments usually ended as disappointments. (Even ABB, the much vaunted success story is dismantling its matrix.)

With the cyberspace and touchspace opportunities the New World gives us, it is possible to give ourselves another approach. However, any attempt to suggest a working organizational framework must satisfy certain conditions if it is to be practical and to be viewed with any sense of reality.

Conditions for a new organization for a New World:

- Enterprise objectives match – the organizational framework must recognize that enterprises exist usually to generate money. This is achieved through a range of entities in the business model.
- Allow personal aspiration, commitment, growth and development – without compromise.
- Ease of explanation – like the 'Old World garden fork' used to explain a hierarchy, the framework should be visually simple and easy to communicate to all from the new undergraduate recruit to the global chairman.
- Scalability – the framework should be capable of being interpreted at all levels of scale: individual, local team, global team, local enterprise, global enterprise, multi-global enterprise.
- Resilience flexibility and adaptability – must not be compromised.

- Comprehensiveness – the framework should be capable of fitting the majority of New World enterprises without additional modification.

Your last reorganization ever...

In order to break the Petronius Paradox it is essential to build an organizing framework which is designed, not around command and control, but instead around the key elements of an enterprise which remain constant in a changing business environment. The model must be complex enough to deal with the real issues involved, but not complicated. We base our model on what we refer to as dimensions of an organization.

• the productive dimension	Process
• the essential dimension	People – selection, recruitment, development, and roles
• the second dimension	Solutions & Offerings – Product, Service, Information
• the change dimension	Project and Change implementation
• the fourth dimension	Perspective & Strategy
• the group dimension	Virtual Teams, Networks
• the invisible dimension	Data, information, intuition & intelligence – knowledge for running the enterprise
• the multiple dimension	Growth, Acquisition & Divestment
• the sixth dimension	Programme Delivery for enterprise realignment
• the fourth dimension	Prospecting for Money, markets, sources of revenue, sources of value

- the tidying dimension — Policing and Auditing
- the focused dimension — Nodes for co-ordination & control
- the supportive dimension — Internal Professional Services
- the volume dimension — Core and emerging Capabilities
- the fifth dimension — Suppliers/Alliances & Partners
- the measured dimension — Performance, Financial & Non Financial

For a business enterprise with a goal of making money, the dimensions can be grouped around six purposes.

- Making money through processes and projects.
- Offering and solution development and relationship management.
- Providing leadership co-ordination and an appropriate working culture.
- High-quality internal application of professional services.
- Gaining access to appropriate suppliers/alliances and partnerships.
- Developing excellence in core current and future capabilities.

Taking these dimensions and purposes, we have developed a framework called the Organizational Pentagon or Organizational Grid. This differentiates between *accountability* – who the output is intended for – and *responsibility* – who has the authority to allow a response. Unlike the traditional organization, which represents as purpose, control and command, the pentagon centres on the purpose of the enterprise as a whole – making money. The final framework (see Figure 1) shows the teams and the areas they are accountable or responsible for.

The framework can be applied at an individual, team. enterprise, regional or global level without requiring additional explanation. There are five pre-requisites to the realistic and effective functioning of the pentagon.

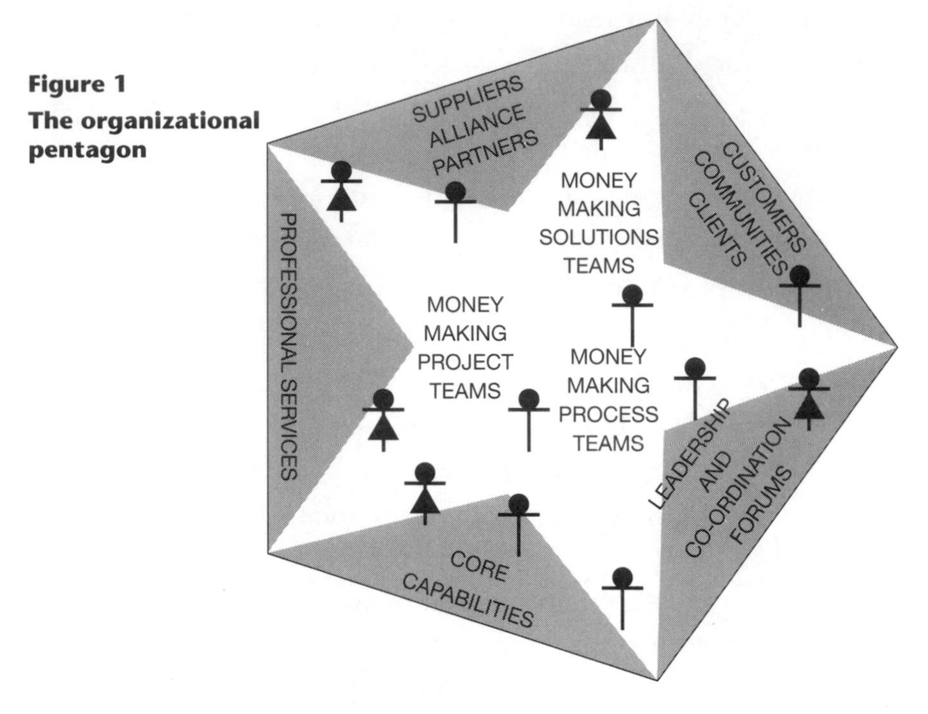

Figure 1
The organizational pentagon

Interdependence

Because of the potential for complexity in the model it is important to cross-link as many entities into systems as possible. Since there are always fewer systems than entities this not only simplifies running the organization but also reduces the need to police activities. In addition it makes it more difficult for non-moneymaking political activities to be added unwittingly to the agenda.

Separate accountability and responsibility. Focus accountability on the purpose

By ensuring that the accountabilities of every key role are clearly understood and set up, there is less opportunity for internal conflict. In addition, provided that the accountabilities are focused on moneymaking activities, the flow of money and resources to the delivery of the offerings or solutions is simply in the opposite direction to the flow of accountabilities.

Federalism: the best person to do it should do it – without duplication

This rule is best supported by the creation of transparent internal activities – the use of an intranet to ensure that there is not unwitting addition of complexity or duplication. Jacques Racloz, then Chief Executive of Novartis Pharmaceuticals, said, 'Federalism is essential to success. It allows alignment without confusion and internal fighting.'[3]

Virtuality: the effect is more important than the form

The active use of virtual structures, particularly virtual teams as a way of providing the agility and flexibility required become common.

Control must never outweigh leadership

Control is the hallmark of the Old World while leadership is a measure of the New.

REFERENCES

1. Leadership presentation Frontiers of Change Conference Impact, 1998.
2. Baughan, Kevin, *Nortel Networks,* 2000.
3. Kick off conference for the new Organizational Grid, Brighton, 1997.

RESOURCES

BOOKS

Obeng, Eddie, *New Rules for the New World,* Capstone, Oxford, 1997.

Davidow, William and Malone, Michael, *The Virtual Corporation*, HarperCollins, New York, 1996.

WEB

www.pentaclethevbs.com

Breaking out of organizational mindsets

DAVID BUTCHER

Every manager knows that organizations of today are very different to those of just a decade ago. The evidence is all around – not just in new economy businesses. Changes are evident in the debate which ebbs and flows in most companies around the question of how we should best organize our organization. David Butcher examines perceptions of organizations.

THERE are now so many possibilities for doing business in novel ways, so many potential arrangements that can be made with customers, suppliers and competitors. As if that were not enough, megatrends – such as the gathering vortex of global competition, the massive impact of information technology, and the rapidly changing landscape of multinational corporates – are shaking the foundations of organization. One way and another it must seem, from a management perspective, as though almost every fundamental principle of organizing has come under the microscope.

How strange it is, then, that in the world of management, certain ways of picturing organizations seem to persist. One might think that the continuous clarion call for managers to become enlightened architects of organizational form would lead to the creation of rich mental images of organizational life. But true examples of progressive management philosophies, based on rich and varied thinking about the nature of organizations, are not easy to find. There are the famous examples like Motorola, Virgin or ABB, but they get singled out precisely because they are unusual. Out in the organizational world at large there are undoubtedly unsung efforts to experiment with and revise the basic principles of organizing. But the old archetype of hierarchical authority structures still appears to loom large in practice, a curious phenomenon to say the least, given that the necessity for empowerment has been discussed in management circles for the past 25 years. Yet Chris Argyris, one of the founders of modern organization theory, has noted: 'Managers love empowerment in theory, but in practice the command-and-control model is what they trust and know best.'

This is evident, for example, in the many case studies of failed businesses, which have shown with stark clarity how first line, customer-focused managers see their products failing and the competition outstripping them, but wait for permission from the top to act. In the managerial mind's eye, organizations are essentially still pyramids of authority. They might be flat, inverted, or the multiple pyramids of matrix management, but that triangular form is ever present, an unmistakably dominant set piece.

This matters to the extent that any mental image of the social world may be advantageous or dysfunctional to us. Social psychologists have been able to show how these pictures influence behaviour in both obvious and subtle ways. The organizational pyramid illustrates this well. It represents the co-ordination and control necessary to create the economic efficiency that is supposed to govern managerial behaviour, and is based on a deep value about rationality which has underpinned Western society since the Industrial Revolution. Hierarchical control and co-ordination served management well for the greater part of the twentieth century because the fundamentals of the business world required it. Organizations were best managed as centrally planned command economies. But as that has given way to the need for great organizational flexibility and local variability, so the pyramid imagery has come to jar with the realities of managing a successful business. As Sumantra Ghoshal puts it:

> *'Companies are trying to implement their sophisticated, multidimensional third generation strategies, through their delayered, horizontal second generation organizations – but they are still trying to*

do that with first generation managers – managers whose personal sense of their roles and value added and whose personal skills and competencies have all been shaped by an earlier, outdated model.'

The profusion of metaphor

There is no question that other metaphors for organization are in use than that of the pyramid. Many, in fact. The organization theorist Gareth Morgan has captured the images that have been used historically, as well as some that are emerging as ways of picturing the complexity of the present day organizational world. Organizations, he has shown, are conceptualized through representations as diverse as machines, brains, psychic prisons, and instruments of domination. The machine metaphor leads us to work in terms of efficiency, logic, instrumentality and scientific principles, whereas if we think of an organization as a brain, then self determination and the sense of liberation that comes with accumulated knowledge may guide behaviour. The much-talked-of learning organization is, after all, an optimistic prospect. In contrast, the concept of a psychic prison creates a pessimistic image of deep dependence, a world where people become the victims of their own unconscious needs and anxieties. According to this perspective organizations are adult security blankets, their rules and regulations satisfying our need for certainty and order, as, for example, with bureaucracy, which defies logic from a customer point of view. But it is at least a relatively benign possibility, one that recognizes the inevitability of human frailties. On the other hand, if we think of an organization as a means of oppression, we are confronted with a rather darker picture of exploitation and abuse. This is more than repackaged Marxism to counter the evils of information age sweatshops. Household names like Nike and Disney have been publicly scrutinized for employee practices, and it is what lies behind the legislation to ensure equal opportunities in the workplace.

As Morgan points out, there are a host of possible images because organizations are many things at the same time. Often they are driven by ideas traceable to well established bodies of theory. Economists, for example, tend to have a deterministic picture of organizations. Within the behavioural theory of the firm, organizations have always been black boxes influenced by economic sub-systems. In the long term, the contribution of management to the survival of any one business is more or less irrelevant. Population ecologists use the living organism metaphor, but tend towards the same Darwinist view about the ability of an organization to control its own destiny. Like amoebae, businesses live and die at the mercy of global supertrends, which in today's world is why the life expectancy of FTSE 100 companies gets ever shorter. On the other hand, management theorists have often portrayed organizations as cultures, mini-societies defined by accepted practices and thinking patterns of which the natives are only partly aware. Supposedly these cultures can be engineered in pursuit of organizational effectiveness, although in practice that has proved exceedingly difficult to achieve, as now classic examples like IBM and Shell demonstrate.

Judging from their explanations for what goes on in everyday organizational life, managers tend to discover this wealth of imagery when it is pointed out, rather than through direct observation. Much of the time their experience appears to lead them directly towards highly selective pictures, which then dominate their understanding of the workings of organizations. It seems that more elaborate representations tend to come primarily through learning processes such as management education programmes or organizational change initiatives. Significantly, there is considerable doubt about whether these kinds of interventions have lasting impact on management thinking, at least as far as the latter are concerned.

Organization theorists are increasingly sceptical about the wisdom behind most attempts at orchestrated change programmes. This is hardly surprising when it is commonplace for organizational interventions such as business process re-engineering projects, or cross-business synergy building initiatives, to be scuppered by managerial indifference, cynicism and subversive resistance. Something is at work other than the clinical logic of change management, and it is to be found in the explanations of organizational life that seem entirely natural to street-wise managers. In fact there is probably no better way to reveal the organizational imagery used by management than through observing their reaction to top down imposed organizational change processes.

Above all, what they appear to notice is the impact of hierarchy together with the unofficial wielding of power in pursuit of vested interests. Pyramids and politics in other words. Perhaps some of the theory driven images are too inaccessible to articulate – people do not always know they are being exploited, for example, and if organizations are a means of satisfying unconscious drives, this particular understanding is, by definition, unavailable to explain one's own organizational surroundings. Other metaphors may be too abstract to connect with immediate experience, or be too deterministic for comfort. After all, embedded in the concept of hierarchy is the idea of co-ordination and control. To shatter the illusion could be deeply disturbing. But the impact of direct experience also has great significance in explaining the clear images of organization that managers are so often guided by. As mental pictures of organizational life, both hierarchical authority and the political clash of conflicting interests are undeniably real in their consequences.

Why does it matter if management relies on these particular ways of picturing organizations? There are three significant reasons. In the first place there is the much documented dysfunctional effect of hierarchical thinking in the context of the contemporary business environment. The reduction of hierarchical management has been a primary objective in the efforts of organizations to reinvent themselves in a horizontal configuration. Second, the political metaphor, whilst of great explanatory value to managers, often troubles them because it does not sit easily with the rationality of co-ordination and control. One of the important consequences of this is that it has yet to be properly developed as a constructive way of improving business performance. Lastly, it is becoming increasingly more difficult to think of organizations as separate from one another, the more business to business collaborative relationships become the norm. There are a host of variations on such themes as strategic alliances, joint ventures and customer–supplier intimacy, all designed to foster new levels of co-operation between firms working in the same field, rival companies, and supply chain interfaces. These arrangements are both contractual and constructed around mutual trust, and are sufficiently widespread for organization theorists to argue that the concept of the rational organization with distinct borders is under serious threat of extinction. In this scenario boundary management is everything. It is an inherently political activity of balancing separate identity with mutual dependency.

The arguments for de-emphasizing hierarchical control are now very well rehearsed. Hierarchical assignment of tasks worked well when central planning worked well, but those days are gone. Local autonomy and accountability are essential preconditions for creating true organizational agility. Within multinationals agility has meant dramatically scaling down the centre, and finding the right balance between corporate guidance and local independence. Yet this remains exceedingly difficult to achieve, and even the more successful examples are usually acknowledged to rely on the special contribution of a few larger than life leading figures. Not all corporates can have such leaders, and the centre often still looms large in the lives of far-flung local outlets and operational facilities. Business unit leaders get stranded in the middle, caught between playing to the rules of corporate control and realizing the ambition of building a vibrant local business. Companies within industries like pharmaceuticals or automobile production illustrate this well. Plant managers are sometimes accused by their staff of selling their souls to the devil who controls corporate careers, when what they are seeking to do is accommodate corporate efforts to maintain a global manufacturing strategy, without which survival is impossible. They can end up pleasing nobody, an outcome that is likely to be repeated so long as the imperative of deeply embedded hierarchy dominates organizational thinking.

More fundamentally still, hierarchy is in principle obsolete in the knowledge economy. Intellectual capital possessed by knowledge workers implies management based on fragile coalition rather than control. Most important of all, top management is dependent on knowledge possessed by the new, the young, the professionals, and those people at the margins in their organizations. Henry

Mintzberg likens the role of senior executive to that of orchestra conductor – there by common consent, but in a creative capacity, not a managerial one. Perhaps if you are Bill Gates, or Andy Grove of Intel, this seems the most natural thing in the world. How could organizations such as these thrive on a diet of hierarchical control?

Yet even in the most knowledge-driven businesses like universities, consultancies, or high technocracies, strategy is often still decided by the Executive, managers continue to answer to their seniors, and the golden rule still applies – do not sidestep the authority of the boss. Of course people inside these organizations are at times highly critical in private about the contribution of their bosses to the business. But mounting any real challenge is often perceived to be very difficult, at least if it is not also going to become career limiting. That said, there has to be a significant doubt as to whether businesses can afford to wait for managerial relationships to mature sufficiently to drive the organization with minimal hierarchy. Time may not be on their side.

The political metaphor

The political metaphor probably dominates management thinking in equal measure to that of the pyramid, but there the parallel ends. Understanding organizations as political systems contrasts hugely with the idea of hierarchy. Politics, more often than not, is a concept with negative connotations such as self interest, misuse of power or clandestine wheeling and dealing. One director of an international investment bank said that the 'P word', as he puts it, is not to be used in his presence. His colleagues have learned to respect his wishes on this. But he represents the sentiments of those managers who are inclined to see political activity is an illegitimate organizational aberration. The more extreme their reaction, the more they seek to exempt themselves and, as they would sometimes have it, take the moral high ground.

Of course this perspective only captures one component of the political metaphor. Managers who understand their organizations as natural arenas for competing interests see the potential for constructive politics. They would recognize major differences in the positions of two senior executives as inevitable, and more importantly, valuable, so long as the motives of both are worthy. When they build relationships to win support for their own agendas they tend to see themselves as working within the best traditions of politics.

One executive in the telecommunications giant Ericsson exemplifies this perspective. He regularly travels to conferences with the real purpose of ensuring several hours of conversation with influential colleagues on long haul flights. It is intrinsic to achieving his aims. Lobbying, pre-meetings, and alliances are simply part and parcel of the action rather than being the stuff of cloak and dagger subterfuge. But it is a mindset possible only once there is an acceptance that most significant decisions are legitimately made this way, a mental leap too far for some.

Much of the research on organizational politics has shown it to be an alternative rather than mainstream managerial frame of reference. There are few appraisal schemes that actively assess political skills, for example. In a recently published book, which comprehensively addresses the role of politics in organizational change, the authors, Dave Buchanan and Richard Badham, conclude that management development has largely ignored the issue of political competence. Most businesses, it seems, have still some way to go before they can claim to be working with a fully fledged model of managerial politics. In most there is not even an acceptable language to describe it. Phrases like 'internal market' or 'creative entrepreneurship' represent only the first steps in defining politics constructively. In consequence, the positive and negative faces of the political metaphor are simultaneously a potent influence and a source of untapped potential.

To those who understand it, the political frame of reference extends beyond the internal dynamics of organizations. The dominant mode of doing business is rapidly becoming that of supply chains, partnering, strategic alliances and networked coalitions of interested parties. The politics of common destiny and collaboration play as important a part in relationships between organizations as does adversarial competition. This is an environment in which industries, federal synergies of companies, and geographical clusterings often make more sensible starting points for analysis than the business prospects of individual organizations. Even the high volume retailers are coming increasingly to accept the dependency inherent in their industry. Where are the boundaries of a business whose survival depends on the fortunes of several other 'distinct' organizations? Simple answers are increasingly elusive. In many industries financial, physical, legal and knowledge separateness are increasingly being surrendered as a deliberate strategic choice.

The rational mindset

The rational control mindset, however, is one of unitary organization. It has a strong historical association with boundary maintenance. Identifying with the business you manage, the same one that pays you and can dispense with your services if it so chooses, represents an uncluttered world view. The pluralistic politics of mutual dependency do not. But sensitive and finely balanced politics are even more prone to negative interpretation than the more straightforward variety. To complicate matters, strategic business partners continue to use the rhetoric of competition to communicate leadership messages to their employees, resulting inevitably in confusion. This is particularly evident, for example, when joint venture capital projects begin to fail. The respective top management teams start to communicate less openly with each other, and advise their project managers to follow suit. Not surprisingly, industries in which firms compete primarily on cost, like construction, have even more difficulty in embracing the politics of collaboration. In consequence, neither of the dominant metaphors of pyramids and politics serve adequately the reality of organizational interdependency endemic in the contemporary business environment.

The significance of organizational mindsets lies in the impact they have on managerial behaviour. Once they cease to be useful, or worse, persistently reinforce mistaken thinking, it is time to dismantle them. When they are theoretical abstractions that can be hard enough, which is why it has taken some 20 years to recognize the basic limitations of both the learning organization and the culture metaphors. A mindset rooted in social values represents another order of difficulty altogether. It is an irony that the vice-like grip of the pyramid metaphor can best be broken by recognition of the unacceptable face of politics. It does beg the question of how much unrealized potential lies in organizational mindsets yet barely embraced by management.

RESOURCES

BOOKS

Peters, Tom, *Liberation Management*, Knopf, New York, 1992.
Simon, Herbert, *Administrative Behavior*, Macmillan, New York, 1947.

ESSENTIALS

THE CHANGING NATURE OF ORGANIZATIONS

ADHOCRACY

COINED by the leadership expert Warren Bennis in the 1960s, and popularized by futurist Alvin Toffler, adhocracy is basically the opposite of bureaucracy. An adhocracy is an organization that disregards the classical principles of management where everyone has a defined and permanent role, in favour of a more fluid organization where individuals are free to deploy their talents as required.

Essentially, the concept was an attempt to answer the question of how companies should create an appropriate organizational model for the future. It addresses the nature of managerial work and the strategy formulation process, as well as social issues. (From a historical perspective, the organizational form can be seen as an evolution from Simple Structure, to Machine Bureaucracy, to Divisionalized Form, to Adhocracy.)

The concept was explored by Alvin Toffler in his 1970 book *Future Shock*. An adhocracy is a non-bureaucratic networked organization. Toffler notes:

> *'This form is already common in organizations such as law firms, consulting companies and research universities. Such organizations and institutions must continually readjust to a changing array of projects, each requiring somewhat different combinations of skills and other resources. These organizations depend on many rapidly shifting project teams and much lateral communication among these relatively autonomous, entrepreneurial groups.'*

Toffler has gone on to assert that the social and cultural institutions that currently exist have become unwieldy and outdated. The problem, he claims, is a lack of flexibility. 'Why is it that all our institutions seem to be going through a simultaneous crisis?' he asks. 'The answer is that we have sets of institutions that were designed either for agrarian life ... as parliaments were, or ... the Industrial Age, but no longer meet the requirements of today.' What is needed, Toffler suggests, is a wholesale move to adhocracy.

The concept was further developed by strategy theorist Henry Mintzberg, for example in 'Strategy-making and the Adhocracy'. Mintzberg's adhocracy represents smaller-scale, fluid, often temporary structures. Typically, a group of line managers, staff, and operating experts come together in small product, customer, or project-focused teams. Informal behaviour and high job specialization are typical characteristics of these adhocracies. Teams have their terms of reference (decentralization) provided by more senior management and a team's scope for action and membership may run counter to the command structure of the rest of the organization.

Mintzberg distinguishes between two types of adhocracies. The *operating adhocracy* works on behalf of its clients (for example a creative advertising agency or consulting firm), while an *administrative adhocracy* serves itself (and offers a model for a wide range of companies).

Along with the benefits of a more fluid organizational form, Mintzberg observes, are some potential drawbacks. One problem, he notes, is that managers in an adhocracy may spend too little time on making strategy. They may be sucked into just responding to problems rather than proactive analysis and formulation of radical, corrective programmes. An effective adhocracy, he says, must balance the need for action in the short term with the need to take a longer-term view of changes occurring within its environment.

AGILITY

LIKE adhocracy, the concept of corporate agility is a response to the need for companies to be more adaptive to changing market conditions. It recognizes that speed of response to market opportunity and threats and flexibility are what distinguishes many successful companies from their lumbering rivals.

Sometimes linked with the emergence of virtual organizations, a number of writers and academics have written about agility. Tom Peters and Richard Pascale are among those who have propounded it in recent years. But if the movement has a principal architect, it is Roger N. Nagel, an expert on competitiveness.

Nagel focuses on agile manufacturing and agile competition, and co-authored the 1995 book *Agile Competitors and Virtual Organizations* with Steven L. Goldman and Kenneth Preiss. The book defined agility at the organizational and individual level:

> *'For a company, to be agile is to be capable of operating profitably in a competitive environment of continually, and unpredictably changing customer opportunities. For an individual, to be agile is to be capable of contributing to the bottom line of a company that is constantly reorganizing its human and technological resources in response to unpredictably changing customer opportunities.'*

Nagel, Goldman, and Preiss present agile competition as a system, with four strategic dimensions:

1. **Organizing to master change and uncertainty**: An agile company is organized in a way that allows it to thrive on change and uncertainty. (There is no single right structure or size, it can support multiple configurations.)
2. **Leveraging the impact of people and information**: In an agile

company, management nurtures an entrepreneurial company culture that leverages the impact of people and information. People are seen as an investment in future prosperity.

3. **Co-operating to enhance competitiveness**: Co-operation – internally and with other companies – is an agile competitor's operational strategy of first choice.
4. **Enriching the customer**: An agile company is one that is perceived by its customers as enriching them in a significant way, not only itself.

Agility allows companies to migrate from one business to another. In Nagel's view, agility is more than simply speed of action; the ability to adapt and make lateral moves is more important.

BARNARD, CHESTER

CHESTER BARNARD (1886–1961) was a rarity: a management theorist who was also a successful practitioner. Barnard won an economics scholarship to Harvard, but before finishing his degree he joined American Telephone and Telegraph to begin work as a statistician. He spent his entire working life with the company, eventually becoming President of New Jersey Bell in 1927.

Although he was the archetypal corporate man, Barnard's interests were varied, and he also found time to lecture on the subject of management. His best known book, *The Functions of the Executive*, collected together his lectures. The language is dated, the approach ornate but comprehensive. Much of what Barnard argued strikes a chord with contemporary management thinking. For example, he highlighted the need for communication so that every single person could be tied into the organization's objectives. He also advocated lines of communication that were short and direct.

To Barnard, the chief executive was not a dictatorial figure geared to simple short-term achievements. Instead, part of his responsibility was to nurture the values and goals of the organization. For all his contemporary-sounding ideas, Barnard was a man of his times – advocating corporate domination of the individual and regarding loyalty to the organization as paramount.

Even so, Barnard proposed a moral dimension to the world of work. 'The distinguishing mark of the executive responsibility is that it requires not merely conformance to a complex code of morals but also the creation of moral codes for others,' wrote Barnard. In arguing that there was a morality to management, Barnard played an important part in broadening the managerial role from one simply of measurement, control, and supervision, to one also concerned with more elusive, abstract notions, such as values.

CORE COMPETENCIES

INSTEAD of identifying what business they are in, the core competencies approach calls on companies to identify the distinctive and differentiating competencies that lie at their heart. Identifying core competencies allows an organization to nurture and build from its strengths rather than pursuing red herrings for which it does not possess appropriate skills. A clear understanding of core competencies can also help a company decide which areas of its business are non-core and better outsourced, and which are so vital to its competitive position that they must be maintained at all costs.

While there are clear drawbacks to religious adherence to the tenets of core competencies, the concept marks an important development. Once, differentiation was regarded as being solely concerned with products. Companies sought to develop their products to compete. Now, differentiation is increasingly identified with the skills, knowledge, and aspirations of the organization. Differentiation comes from the 'soft' areas of branding, organizational innovation, and service. As a result, differentiation is more human and harder to achieve than ever before.

Actually identifying a company's core competencies is fraught with difficulty. The champions of the concept of core competencies have been the American academics Gary Hamel and C.K. Prahalad, authors of *Competing for the Future*. They suggest that a core competence should provide potential access to a wide variety of markets; make a significant contribution to the perceived customer benefits of the end products; and be difficult for competitors to imitate. In practice, these are highly demanding tests. As a result, what tends to emerge is a wish list of what the company would like to be good at, a compendium of vague aspirations.

Part of the problem is that there is confusion between personal competencies and corporate competencies. The temptation for companies when they set out in pursuit of competencies is to start with the personal. These are relatively easy to establish. Companies can then synthesize the skills of their people into generic competencies that apply to the firm as a whole. This is not what Hamel and Prahalad intended. The end result of the bottom-up approach may be personally beneficial but, from a corporate viewpoint, is usually confusing. Instead, Hamel and Prahalad advocate that companies take a much broader view, seeking out links between activities and skill areas.

For those organizations able to determine a persuasive and useful list of their core competencies comes the next stage: developing strategies that are driven by those competencies. Herein lies what some consider the greatest danger of the neat theory. If a company seeks out markets, mergers and acquisitions in areas where its core competencies would be most advantageous, it may well be entering markets about which it knows nothing.

In effect, the concept of core competencies encourages companies to diversify. They need to go where their competencies would be put to the most effective and profitable use. Unfortunately, corporate history is littered with unhappy experiences of diversification.

Another weakness to the core competence argument is that a business's critical competencies and insights often reside among a small coterie of people, not necessarily senior managers. In a knowledge-intensive and information-intensive age, this is increasingly the case. If the people depart so, too, do the competencies.

GENEEN, HAROLD

A FORMIDABLE mythology has built up around the career and management style of Harold Geneen (1910–1997). Born in Bournemouth on England's genteel south coast, Geneen became the archetypal bullish American executive, a remorselessly driven workaholic who believed that analytical rigour could – and surely would – conquer all.

Harold Geneen qualified as an accountant after studying at night school. He then began climbing the executive career ladder working at American Can, Bell & Howell, Jones & Laughlin, and finally Raytheon, which was taken over by ITT. He joined the board of ITT in 1959 and set about turning the company into the world's greatest conglomerate.

Geneen's basic organizational strategy was that diversification was a source of strength. By 1970, ITT was composed of 400 separate companies operating in 70 countries. Keeping the growing array of companies in check was a complex series of financial checks and targets. Geneen managed them with intense vigour and a unique single-mindedness. As part of his formula, every month over 50 executives flew to Brussels to spend four days poring over the figures. 'I want no surprises,' he announced. He hoped to make people 'as predictable and controllable as the capital resources they must manage'. While others would have watched as the deck of cards fell to the ground, Geneen kept adding more cards, while managing to know the pressures and stresses that each was under.

Facts were the lifeblood of the expanding ITT – and executives sweated blood in their pursuit. According to Geneen:

> *'The highest art of professional management requires the literal ability to smell a* real fact *from all others – and, moreover, to have the temerity, intellectual curiosity, guts and/or plain impoliteness, if necessary, to be sure that what you do have is indeed what we will call an* unshakeable fact.'

By sheer force of personality, Geneen's approach worked. Between 1959 and 1977, ITT's sales went from $765 million to nearly $28 billion.

ITT rapidly disintegrated following Geneen's departure in 1979. His followers were unable to sustain his uniquely driven working style. The underside of ITT was exposed – it had worked with the CIA in Chile and been involved in offering bribes. The deck of cards tumbled to the floor.

HANDY, CHARLES

CHARLES HANDY (born 1932) is a bestselling writer and broadcaster. His work is accessible and popular. Because of this it is dismissed by some. Yet, Handy has brought major questions about the future of work and of society on to the corporate and personal agenda.

Irish born, Charles Handy worked for Shell until 1972 when he left to teach at London Business School. He spent time at MIT, where he came into contact with many of the leading lights in the human relations school of thinking, including Ed Schein.

Handy's early academic career was conventional. His first book, *Understanding Organizations* (1976), gives little hint of the wide-ranging, social and philosophical nature of his later work.

It was in 1989 with the publication of *The Age of Unreason* that Handy's thinking made a great leap forward. The age of unreason that he predicts is:

> *'A time when what we used to take for granted may no longer hold true, when the future, in so many areas, is there to be shaped, by us and for us; a time when the only prediction that will hold true is that no predictions will hold. A time, therefore, for bold imaginings in private life as well as public, for thinking the unlikely and doing the unreasonable.'*

In practice, Handy believes that certain forms of organization will become dominant. These are the types of organization most readily associated with service industries. First, and most famously, is what he calls 'the shamrock organization' – 'a form of organization based around a core of essential executives and workers supported by outside contractors and part-time help'. The consequence of such an organizational form is that organizations in the future are likely to resemble the way consultancy firms, advertising agencies, and professional partnerships are currently structured.

The second emergent structure identified by Handy is the federal one. It is not, he points out, another word for decentralization. He provides a blueprint for federal organizations in which the central function co-ordinates, influences, advises, and suggests. It does not dictate terms or short-term decisions. The centre is, however, concerned with long-term strategy. It is 'at the middle of things and is not a polite word for the top or even for head office'.

The third type of organization Handy anticipates is what he calls 'the Triple I'. The three 'Is' are Information, Intelligence, and Ideas. In such organizations, the demands on personnel management are large. Explains Handy:

> *'The wise organization already knows that their smart people are not to be easily defined as workers or as managers but as individuals, as specialist, as professional or executives, or as leader (the older terms of manager and worker are dropping out of use), and that they and it need also to be obsessed with the pursuit of learning if they are going to keep up with the pace of change.'*

As organizations change in the age of unreason so, Handy predicts, will other aspects of our lives. Less time will be spent at work – 50,000 hours in a lifetime rather than the present figure of around 100,000. Handy does not predict, as people did in the 1970s, an enlightened age of leisure. Instead, he challenges people to spend more time thinking about what they want to do. Time will not simply be divided between work and play – there could be 'portfolios' that spilt time between fee work (where you sell time), gift work (for neighbours or charities), study (keeping up to date with your work), home work and leisure.

Handy has reached his own conclusions. He says he has made his last speech to a large audience. He now sets a limit of 12 to his audiences, reflecting that 'enough is enough'. Handy has become a one-man case study of the new world of work on which he so successfully and humanely commentates. At a personal level, he appears to have the answers. Whether these can be translated into answers for others remains the question and the challenge.

MATRIX MODEL

AN organizational structure adopted by many multinational companies, the matrix model, is an attempt to deal with the complexities of managing large organizations across different national markets. It was developed by the electronics company Philips after the war, and represents a compromise between centralization and decentralization.

Under a simple matrix management system, a marketing manager in, say, Germany reports ultimately to a boss in that country, but also to the head of the marketing function back in the company's home country. The two reporting lines (more complicated matrix structures have multiple reporting lines) are the two sides to the matrix, which has a geographical and a functional axis.

As a theoretical model, the matrix is a neat solution to the complexity of large companies. However, in reality, power cannot be evenly balanced, and conflicts inevitably arise. When you add in additional complexity such as cross-functional reporting lines in project teams or start-up operations, managers can find themselves trying to please several different bosses at the same time.

Many multinationals continue to operate as matrix management structures simply because they haven't come up with a better model. In the beginning, organizations were neat, hierarchical, and linear, with simple chains of command. Worker A reported to manager B, who reported to senior manager C, who reported to board member D, who reported to the managing director or CEO. Corporate life was relatively simple, understandable and clear cut.

As companies became bigger, they began to organize themselves differently. In the 1920s, the American company DuPont championed federal decentralization. This gave the headquarters responsibility for core central functions such as finance and marketing. Business units were granted greater autonomy and responsibility for their own performance. This approach was championed by Alfred P. Sloan at General Motors, and later emulated by the likes of General Electric and Shell.

Federal decentralization brought professional rigour to management. However, its fundamental flaws were that one central function tended to emerge as the dominant one; it did little to share value, information, and knowledge between units; and it helped create an entire layer of headquarters-based middle managers whose value-adding role was increasingly difficult to determine.

The inevitable rebuff to decentralization is centralization, taking power back to the corporate centre. The trouble is that this involves a degree of dictatorship and commitment that few senior managers can carry through for any length of time.

Matrix management is a middle way. It is a hybrid of decentralization and centralization. A matrix organization is organized in such a way that each unit has at least two bosses. Instead of being based around a linear chain of command, the matrix is multidimensional – depending on how many dimensions are deemed to be useful or practically possible. An organization may include regional managers; functional managers; country or continental managers; and business sector managers.

Herein lies the problem. The mythical matrix boss is seven headed. Matrix management is complex, ambiguous, and confusing – little wonder that it has generally had a bad press. In *In Search of Excellence*, Tom Peters and Robert Waterman were dismissive of matrix organization as 'a logistical mess', arguing that 'it automatically dilutes priorities' and that structure should be kept as simple as possible. The hackneyed criticism is that a matrix organization is 'an organization in which nobody can make any decision on his or her own, but anybody on his own can stop a decision being made'.

While these criticisms are generally justified, the matrix organization may be, in fact, a more realistic delineation and description of responsibilities and hierarchies. Built around a network of responsibilities, it fosters broader perspectives. Managers don't view matters within the narrow perspectives of their unit, their function, or their fiefdom. Instead, they have to view them from a variety of perspectives – local, corporate, national, international, global, functional.

Matrix management can be made to work – some large European multinationals, perhaps most laudably Asea Brown Boveri (ABB), have done so. At its heart, however, lies an element of ambiguity and uncertainty with which managers remain uncomfortable. The trouble is that management theorists and researchers are virtually all agreed that ambiguity and uncertainty are the new facts of corporate life. Matrix management – in one form or another – may be the most appropriate means of making organizational sense of these disturbing realities.

SHAMROCK ORGANIZATION

IN recent years, the organizational structure most appropriate for the future has been widely discussed. British management thinker Charles Handy has been one of the most considered participants in this debate. He anticipated that certain models of organization would become dominant. These were the type of organization most readily associated with service industries.

First and most famously came Handy's Shamrock Organization.[1] This describes a type of organizational structure with three parts – or leaves – 'a form of organization based around a core of essential executives and workers supported by outside contractors and part-time help'. The consequence of such an organizational form is that organizations in the future are likely to resemble the way consultancy firms, advertising agencies, and professional partnerships are currently structured.

This model, or variations of it, is often used to explain the move to outsourcing non-core functions. In Handy's analogy, the first leaf of the shamrock represents the organization's core staff. These people are likely to be highly trained professionals who make up the senior management. The second leaf consists of the contractual fringe – either individuals or other organizations – and may include people who once worked for the organization but now provide it with services. These individuals operate within the broad framework set down by the core, but have a high level of discretionary decision-making power to complete projects or deliver contracts.

The third leaf includes the flexible labour force. More than simply hired hands, in Handy's model, these workers have to be sufficiently close to the organization to feel a sense of commitment ensuring that their work – although part-time or intermittent – is carried out to a high standard.

The second emergent structure identified by Handy was the *Federal Organization* – not, he pointed out, another word for decentralization. He provided a blueprint for federal organizations in which the central function co-ordinates, influences, advises, and suggests. It does not dictate terms or short-term decisions. The centre is, however, concerned with long-term strategy. It is 'at the middle of things and is not a polite word for the top or even for head office'.

The third type of organization Handy anticipated is what he called 'the Triple I' – Information, Intelligence, and Ideas. In such organizations the demands on personnel management are large. Handy explained:

> *'The wise organization already knows that their smart people are not to be easily defined as workers or as managers but as individuals, as specialist, as professional or executive, or as leader (the older terms of manager and worker are dropping out of use), and that they and it need also to be obsessed with the pursuit of learning if they are going to keep up with the pace of change.'*

More recently, Handy has suggested that successful organizations of the future will be what he calls 'membership communities'. His logic is that in order to hold people to an organization that can no longer promise them a job for life, companies have to offer some other form of continuity and sense of belonging. To do this, he suggests, they have to imbue their members with certain rights.

Handy is, in fact, advocating some notion of the federal organization, built on the principle of subsidiarity. This places a large degree of trust in core professionals and other knowledge workers. Under Handy's membership community model, the centre is kept small and its primary purpose is to be 'in charge of the future'. Only if the organization is severely threatened does decision-making power revert to the centre. This allows the company to react quickly in a crisis. The rest of the time, decision making is highly decentralized.

REFERENCE

1. Handy, Charles, *The Age of Unreason*, Century Business Books, London, 1989.

1

THE VIRTUAL ORGANIZATION

MUCH beloved of management theorists, the notion of the virtual organization has more than one interpretation. To some people, the virtual concept refers simply to the ability of companies to use IT to allow people in different locations, and even on different continents, to work together effectively. For others it goes further, describing an amorphous organization, made up of project teams that form to fulfil a specific purpose and disband at a moment's notice.

From the traditional images of machinery, the organization has become an elusive, ever-changing amoeba. Describing the organization of the future, American writers William

Davidow and Michael Malone say:

> *'To the outside observer, it will appear almost edgeless, with permeable and continuously changing interfaces among company, supplier and customers. From inside the firm, the view will be no less amorphous with traditional offices, departments and operating divisions constantly re-forming according to need.'*

The end result is the virtual organization.

The theory on which the concept is built is perfectly sensible. Technology enables companies to dismantle their cumbersome headquarters buildings, the costly bricks and mortar of the conventional business. Employees can work at home or occasionally in satellite offices when required. Linked by networks of computers, communicating by e-mail and modems, people become more productive if freed from the burdens of commuting and the regularity of office life. With no expensive tower blocks to support, organizations make massive cuts in operating costs. The virtual organization is life and profit enhancing.

The ability of employees to communicate and share information also means that the patterns of decision making are fundamentally altered, with no necessity for co-ordination from the centre. If we think of individual workers as dots on the organizational map, then one justification for traditional structures was to provide a framework to direct their efforts. But as soon as you can connect each dot – or computer terminal – to any other, the need for a formal structure disappears. If we go a step further and think of those dots as light bulbs connected with the power of communication, then, theoretically at least, a virtual organization can instantly light up any pattern or configuration of skills required, and can switch it off just as quickly.

The virtual organization is well understood and a logical extension of technology. But virtual organizations are, as yet, notable by their absence. There are organizations that appear virtual to customers, but are not truly virtual in reality. Internet banking seems more virtual than the bank down the road, but even e-banking companies have their conventional headquarters buildings. Companies may relocate to cheaper alternatives, but they are still choosing to invest in reassuring concrete. If the arguments for the virtual organization are so persuasive, why are so few decision makers persuaded?

First, virtual organizations are off-puttingly fashionable. They remain terminally associated with smart and creative companies. Ad agencies, design companies, and software houses are thought to be candidates for virtuality, not less esoteric manufacturers. This is a limit of perception rather than reality. A manufacturer in Dudley can benefit from organizing itself in a virtual way as much as one in Palo Alto.

The second stumbling block is that the virtual organization requires a quantum leap rather than steady evolution. Making it work requires more than short-term enthusiasm on the part of senior managers. It demands some understanding of the technical possibilities – as well as a harmonious and respectful relationship with corporate IT specialists.

This brings us to the third obstacle. The virtual organization uses IT as a primary corporate resource. The trouble is that many organizations continue to regard IT as a function, rather than a dynamic organizational tool.

This list could be supplemented by the crucial fact that people, and managers in particular, remain wedded to their offices. With its social rituals, human interest, and politics, office life retains a strong attraction.

Given the apparent difficulties in creating truly virtual organizations, the way forward may rest with compromise solutions – such as hot-desking or the use of virtual teams, groups that are accountable for the achievement of transient or short-term objectives. For most companies, true virtual working is still some way off.

WEBER, MAX

The German sociologist Max Weber (1864–1920) was the original champion of the bureaucratic model of organizations. In terms of management theorizing he has become something of a *bête noir*, the sociological twin of Frederick Taylor, the king of scientific rationality.

Weber observed emerging organizations in the fledgling industrial world. Weber argued that the most efficient form of organization resembled a machine. It was characterized by strict rules, controls, and hierarchies and driven by bureaucracy. This Weber termed the 'rational-legal model'.

At the opposite extreme was the 'charismatic' model where a single dominant figure ran the organization. Weber dismissed this as a long-term solution – once again, he was the first to discuss this phenomenon and examine its ramifications. No matter what Peters and Waterman say, history bears Weber out – an organization built around a single charismatic figure is unsustainable in the long term.

The final organizational form that Weber identified was the traditional model where things were done as they always have been – such as in family firms in which power is passed down from one generation to the next.

If it was pure efficiency you required, there was, said Weber, only one choice:

> *'Experience tends universally to show that the purely bureaucratic type of administrative organization – that is, the monocratic variety of bureaucracy – is, from a purely technical point of view, capable of attaining the highest degree of efficiency and is in this sense formally the most rational known means of carrying out imperative control over human beings.'*

In *The Theory of Social and Economic Organization*, he outlined the 'structure of authority' around seven points:

1. A continuous organization of official functions bound by rules.
2. A specified sphere of competence.
3. The organization of offices follows the principle of hierarchy.
4. The rules that regulate the conduct of an office may be technical rules or norms. In both cases, if their application is to be fully traditional, specialized training is necessary.
5. In the rational type it is a matter of principle that the members of the administrative staff should be completely separated from the ownership of the means of production or administration.
6. In the rational type case, there is also a complete absence of appropriation of his official position by the incumbent.
7. Administrative acts, decisions and rules are formulated and recorded in writing, even in cases where oral discussion is the rule or is even mandatory.

Modern commentators usually cannot resist the urge to scoff at Weber's insights. It was an undoubtedly narrow way of doing things and one that seems out of step with our times. Yet, in the early part of the twentieth century, it was a plausible and effective means of doing business. Like all great insights, it worked, for a while at least.

– CHAPTER 3 –

The changing nature of managerial work

'The mad rush to improve performance and to pursue excellence has multiplied the number of demands on executives and managers. These demands come from every part of business and personal life, and they increasingly seem incompatible and impossible.' ROSABETH MOSS KANTER

'The way we are doing things is not the best way. The micro-division of labour has fostered a basic distrust of human beings. People weren't allowed to put the whole puzzle together. Instead they were given small parts because companies feared what people would do if they knew and saw the whole puzzle. Human assets shouldn't be misused. Brains are becoming the core of organizations – other activities can be contracted out.' CHARLES HANDY

'There is joy in work. There is no happiness except in the realization that we have accomplished something.' HENRY FORD

'We do what we are and we are what we do.' ABRAHAM MASLOW

'Work expands so as to fill the time available for its completion. General recognition of this fact is shown in the proverbial phrase It is the busiest man who has time to spare.*'* C. NORTHCOTE PARKINSON

'The man who does not work for the love of work but only for money is not likely to make money nor find much fun in life.'

CHARLES M. SCHWAB

What managers do

DAVID W. BIRCHALL

Do we know what managers really do? David Birchall examines a number of studies and considers how the demands on managers and organizations are changing today.

THROUGHOUT the twentieth century researchers and observers were eager to know more about what managers actually do. There is an assumption that if we can establish what particularly successful managers do, we can then encourage and train others to emulate this behaviour and also be more effective as managers. Even now, in the twenty-first century, solutions to the managerial imponderables are difficult to find – despite decades of intensive research and observation.

In fact, the legacy of early management thinkers remains deeply embedded in many of our organizations and managerial practices. For all its high-technology and modernity, management today owes much to the work of people at the end of the nineteenth century. Their classical studies of management were based more on observation and reflection than research. Frederick Taylor (1856–1917) was one of the first to write about management, advocating what was then termed a 'scientific approach'.

Early management theory

Taylor's book *Principles of Scientific Management* was published in 1911.[1] Its contribution to management thinking and practice has to be put in the context of the industrial times in which he lived. Much of the labour entering the newly established factories was untrained and unused to any form of industrial work. Taylor advocated the subdivision of work into simple jobs. Management could then devote its energies to understanding how best to do the primary tasks: the scientific selection and training of the workers, motivating them to perform in accordance with management's principles, and planning and controlling the productive activity. Taylor's pioneering work focused on the level of supervisor and foreman rather than more senior levels of management.

Recognized as the 'father of work study', Taylor's principles have been widely adopted and, even now, are still applied in many organizations involved in mass production or mass processing of paper work.

Frenchman Henri Fayol (1841–1925) took another approach. In *Industrial and General Administration* (1916),[2] Fayol enunciated five elements (and 15 principles) of administrative management: planning, organizing, co-ordinating, commanding and controlling. These elements have been widely disseminated to generations of managers and formed the basis of later writings. In 1937 Luther Gulick modified the list to include staffing, reporting, and budgeting.[3] And in a 1931 study of the state, the Roman Catholic Church, the military, and industry, Mooney and Reiley advocated four main principles[4]:

1. The co-ordination principle, which directed attention to the unity of action towards a common purpose.
2. The scalar principle, which defined the hierarchical flow of authority and the definite assignment of duties to sub-units of an organization.
3. The functional principle, which stressed the need for specialization of duties.
4. The staff principle, which answered the need for advice and ideas by line executives.

As with Taylor, these ideas very much reflected the times in which the writers lived and worked. Dominant in their thinking was a strong expectation of respect for authority among the management classes, a lack of training and development for the workforce, the influence of a bureaucratic model of organization, and the relatively inward-looking nature of the managerial role.

Generally operating in a suppliers' market, organizations were not under great pressure to change other than to improve profitability for shareholders by carefully planned productivity improvement. Labour was in plentiful supply and there was little government intervention regulating the employment contract, allowing employers to hire and fire at will.

As a result, it would be easy for today's managers to dismiss these theories. Taylor in particular has been routinely castigated for many years. The world of paper-pushing bureaucracy and harsh manual labour is far removed from modern reality. But, although the context has changed, many of the ideas of scientific management remain in place. Taylorism lives on in highly functionalized organizations intent on relentless supervision rather than empowerment.

Since these writers, there has tended to be greater emphasis on the human aspects of the managerial role and on leading rather than commanding. For example, American political scientist Mary Parker Follett (1868–1933) believed that in a democratic society the primary task of management is to create a situation where people readily contribute of their own accord. She repeatedly emphasized the need for managers to learn from their own experience by systematically observing, recording, and relating to the overall situation. She saw the manager as responsible for integrating the contributions of specialisms such as marketing, production, cost accountancy, and industrial relations so that they contributed effectively for the benefit of all.

In 1953 Louis Allen was sponsored by the National Industrial Conference Board in the US to investigate what management methods were most effective, which new management techniques had proved most effective, and what companies should do to manage more effectively. This was the managerial equivalent of seeking the Holy Grail.

Allen continued the original research over a 15-year period and in his 1973 book *Professional Management* put forward four functions of management based on a belief that managers think and act rationally: planning, organizing, leading and controlling.[5] He broke these functions down into 19 management activities:

1. **Planning function:** forecasting, developing objectives, programming, scheduling, budgeting, developing procedures and developing policies.
2. **Organizing function:** developing organization structure, delegating, developing relationships.
3. **Leading function:** decision making, communicating, motivating, selecting and developing people.
4. **Controlling function:** developing performance standards, measuring, evaluating and correcting performance.

These and similar ideas about the nature of managerial work have been influential on later researchers, but more importantly on those actually managing organizations. However, these formulations of management work are not without their critics.

Generally, they are seen as focusing on a rational view of organization that tends to omit the human and political side. Also, in the main, they lack support from empirical studies. They attempt to produce a general theory of management work while disregarding the diversity of such work in different types of organization and in different functions, such as marketing, production, or finance. They are based on observations of a particular society that is greatly different from many of those in which we now live. Probably most importantly, they focus on what it was believed managers *should* do rather than what they *actually* do, and they fail to give any priority to the various roles or to relate them to superior performance.

Despite these limitations, the propositions may still have some validity in certain types of organization, though interpretation of meaning and translation into action is probably much different from that intended by the original authors.

Empirical studies

In recent years, studies have rigorously attempted to research what managers actually do by undertaking empirical work. Just as the early writings of management theorists have inherent weaknesses, so do these later studies. Nevertheless, several research approaches have merit.

Many studies have relied on questionnaires asking managers about their work and the emphasis placed on various activities. Others have requested that managers complete diaries detailing their activities or used direct observation with the researcher present throughout the manager's working day. These observation studies have employed a variety of approaches: activity sampling, critical incident, sequence of episodes, unstructured and structured observations.

The model, explicit or implicit, always limits questionnaire studies used by the investigator to underpin the design of the research study. So if the investigator were influenced by classical management theory, the survey questions would reflect this theory. Diaries, while useful in giving an impression of the work carried out, suffer from the unreliability of managers when recording activities and the difficulties of then classifying their records.

Observational studies are usually confined to a small sample that cannot claim to be representative of management generally. In the case of observation, it is not always possible to see what a manager is doing because so much activity is cerebral, and it is particularly difficult to interpret the purpose of much of the observed activity.

Many of these studies have contributed more to our understanding of the characteristics of managerial work than to the actual content of the manager's job. They have revealed that much management time is spent with other people. In 1964 an early study of this type reported that 20 percent of managers' time was spent with superiors, 33 percent with peers, and 50 percent with subordinates. Fifty percent of the activities were planning or programming, 20 percent were dealing with technical matters, and 10 percent with personnel administration.[6]

Probably the most influential and widely cited observational study is that of five chief executives in the US undertaken by Henry Mintzberg. In *The Nature of Managerial Work*, published in 1973, Mintzberg claimed the following.

1. There is a similarity in managerial work whether carried out by the company president, the health service administrator, or the general foreman. He categorized it into 10 basic roles and six sets of work characteristics.
2. While differences exist arising from functional or hierarchical level, the job can largely be described according to common roles and characteristics.
3. The managerial job is made up of regular and programmed duties as well as non-programmed activities.
4. The manager is both a generalist and a specialist.
5. The manager is reliant on information, particularly that which has been verbally received.
6. Work activities are characterized by brevity, variety, and fragmentation.
7. Management work is more an art than a science, reliant on intuitive and non-explicit processes.
8. Management work is increasingly complex.[7]

Mintzberg's model of managerial work identified three overall categories and specific roles within each.

1. **Interpersonal category**
   a. The figurehead role where the manager performs symbolic duties as head of the organization.
   b. The leader role where the manager establishes the work atmosphere and motivates subordinates to achieve organizational goals.
   c. The liaison role where the manager develops and maintains webs of contacts outside the organization.
2. **Informational category**
   a. The monitor role where the manager collects all types of information relevant and useful to the organization.

b. The disseminator role where the manager transmits information from the outside to members in the organization.
c. The spokesman role where the manager transmits information from inside the organization to outsiders.

3. **Decisional category**
   a. The entrepreneur role where the manager initiates controlled change in their organization to adapt to the changing environment.
   b. The disturbance handler role where the manager deals with unexpected changes.
   c. The resource allocator role where the manager makes decisions on the use of organizational resources.
   d. The negotiator role where the manager deals with other organizations and individuals.

While it proved highly influential, this research is also not without its critics. Later researchers have experienced difficulties in categorizing their observations according to the Mintzberg framework. A focus on individual activities is also criticized as likely to lead to failure to understand the big picture. Other descriptors are seen as equally valid: later in the 1970s researchers carried out a factor analysis of data collected against the Mintzberg framework and derived six factors:

1. Managing the organizational environment and its resources.
2. Organizing and co-ordinating.
3. Information handling.
4. Providing for growth and development.
5. Motivation and conflict handling.
6. Strategic problem solving.[8]

This research went on to study managerial effectiveness in two organizations. It reported that the managerial behaviour resulting in effectiveness varied between the two organizations, suggesting that the context in which managers are working will determine the work activities required for success.

While much of this early research has been influential in how managers view their role within the context of organization design, it is based on observation of organizations that were operating in an environment much removed from the situation now facing many businesses. Numerous studies were undertaken in the US at a time when it was the most powerful manufacturing nation. The threat of Japanese manufacture and service industry had not dawned on the average American. Customer focus, total quality management, just in time, distributed computing, empowerment, key organizational competencies, partnership sourcing, and continuous change and improvement were not yet articulated as concepts. Strategy formulation was still the exclusive domain of executive management and execution the province of middle management. Much of the research was based on observing the way managers function in their world, rather than looking at changes taking place and how they might affect the way management might be carried out in the future.

Management work in the modern organization

Over 700 managers – in a variety of organizations and at all levels of management – were surveyed at the Singapore Institute of Management at the beginning of the 1990s. From factor analysis, five 'mega-components' of management work were identified:

1. Goal setting and review.
2. Creating a conducive working environment.
3. Managing quality.
4. Relating to and managing the external environment.
5. Managing performance.[9]

The strongest contributing factor to the mega-components was 'managing organizational climate', which focused on encouraging and supporting employee involvement and contribution. The second most dominant was 'organizational work control', which combined with mega-component number five and dealt with the importance of policies and procedures in ensuring the smooth functioning of the work organization. The strategic aspects of the work are reflected in analysis of the external environment and goal setting and review.

Clearly, there are differences in management practices in Singapore compared to Western management. However, the expressions used to describe the components reflect the current management agenda, including quality and performance management, and the underlying factors bear a similarity to those identified by earlier researchers such as Mintzberg.

How do managers do what they do?

Clearly, understanding what managers do is important when trying to understand how organizations function and how one might go about training managers to achieve high performance levels. However, these various studies tell us little about the attributes needed for superior performance. More recent research has focused on the key competencies required for superior managerial job performance.

The roots of much of this work can be traced back to the extensive work done by Richard Boyatzis for the American Management Association.[10] This study, published in 1982, involved over 2,000 managers who held 41 different jobs in 12 different public and private organizations. The researchers set out to develop a generic model of managerial competencies applicable in different contexts and organization types.

Boyatzis defined job competency as an underlying characteristic of a person that results in effective and/or superior performance. The underlying characteristic may be a motive, trait, skill, aspect of one's self-image, or a social role, but it is manifest in an observable skill. The resulting model comprises 12 competencies in six clusters (see table 1).

Clearly, competence in itself does not result in high performance. The theory of motivation evinced by Porter and Lawler in their 1968 book *Managerial Attitudes and Performance*[11] suggests that perfor-

Table 1[12] *Boyatzis' managerial job performance key competencies*

Cluster	Competency	Threshold competency
Goal and action management	* *concern with impact* * *diagnostic use of concepts* * *efficiency orientation* * *proactivity*	
Leadership	* *conceptualization* * *self-confidence* * *use of oral presentations*	* logical thought
Human resource	* *managing group process* * use of socialized power	* accurate self-assessment * positive regard
Directing subordinates		* *developing others* * spontaneity * use of unilateral power
Focus on others	* *perceptual objectivity* * self-control (trait) * stamina and adaptability (trait)	
Specialized knowledge		* specialized knowledge

Note: Italics for the most relevant to executive levels of management; self-control is a competency for entry level jobs only.

mance will only result where the person has opportunities to perform and the motivation to do so in addition to the skills (or competencies) required by the job. In addition, if the goals for the task are not clear, the combination of motivation, opportunities, and competencies will still not result in high performance levels.

Rosemary Stewart in *Managers and their Jobs* found that managers with the same job requirements will use their time and energies differently.[13] Given each person's unique combination of competencies, knowledge and understanding, and aspirations, it is not surprising that managers operate differently in seeking to achieve the same organizational goals. Each will accommodate to the job, as well as modify the job to suit themselves.

The benefit of competence models is as much to assist managers in self-assessment and the identification of development needs as in recruitment and allocation of managers to organizational roles.

The research available gives some idea of the work carried out by managers as well as the personal competencies required for effective performance at senior levels. Yet it has become clear that there is no one best theory of management work and managerial competencies. Applied to any one organization, the models inevitably appear deficient. In attempting to develop a universal theory, the investigators have had to compromise and overlook industry or organization-specific requirements.

Additionally, much of the research is based on current practice and may well not reflect what managers will be doing, nor how they will be doing it, in the future.

The changing world of organizations and its impact on management

The last few years have probably seen changes in the organization and management of work as dramatic as at any period since the emergence of the large corporate entity. Depending on the background of the commentator, the explanations for radical change will differ. There is no doubt that factors such as global competition, the convergence of information and communications technology, and the emergence of the digital economy, recession in most Western economies in the 1990s, the emergence of customer power, and changing political philosophy have all contributed to the changes.

As a consequence, it is clear that much of the work undertaken by middle management no longer requires the considerable number of layers of management that has for so long been a feature of the large organization. In part this results from a recognition that front-line employees, with proper training and support, as well as the support of powerful IT systems, may be capable of dealing directly with the customer and responding on behalf of the organization to the specific needs of that customer.

If one accepts that there is much unrecognized talent at the point of contact with the customer and that empowerment is an appropriate strategy, then it follows that there is less need for immediate supervision. The employee dealing directly with the customer now takes the queries and decisions previously taken by the supervisor. So a task that used to take up a great deal of management time in hierarchical structures is now possible with minimal intervention.

The impact of modern technology on lower and middle managers can be compared to the effects of the introduction of automated production processes on shopfloor workers. In both cases, a large proportion of the workforce was no longer required.

Many organizations, when in the process of empowering their front-line staff, have reassessed the role of first-line management. Rather than the traditional supervisory role of allocating work, determining how it should be done, and ensuring progress, the first-line manager in many organizations has become a facilitator. The manager has more of a support role, assisting staff in meeting customer needs, training and developing staff, and counselling them.

Another change affecting management has come about because the complexity of the design of many products and services is increasing, pressures are growing to compress the time from concept to market, and in many industries the costs of developing new products are proving beyond the capability of any one organization. Companies that were previously in competition are having to combine resources in order to share the costs and risks of new product development. In many cases, duplication of effort in the various organizations has been eliminated, with resulting reductions in employee and management numbers.

Companies previously adopted a policy of vertical integration to control the production processes through to market, but many are now changing their approach to one of specialization in areas within their supply chains where the potential for added value is greatest. Each organization will then form new relationships with suppliers and customers in order to protect its position and develop a strategic advantage through its unique supply network or constellation.

Concentration on core activities has led organizations to divest those parts not seen as central to their strategy or have them undertaken by other companies. This reduction in size has resulted in a need for fewer managers, particularly in support functions. Then, as these support functions have themselves been reviewed and deemed no longer central to the strategy, they in turn have been outsourced.

Work previously undertaken in functional departments has become too complex and specialized for organizations to carry the numbers of technical specialists needed to deal with the business problems encountered. So there is a strong move towards the use of consultants, whether legal, marketing, or management. The use of external consultants may well be more cost effective than retaining in-house staff. In addition, it allows companies to choose the most appropriate skills available, with the prospect of appointing someone whose knowledge base is up to date through exposure to the way similar problems have been tackled in a variety of situations and organizations. This broad exposure can have additional benefits in making sure that the organization does not take an insular view. This again reduces the need for managers, particularly in functional departments.

Much of an organization's work is now carried out in projects. Some industries, such as construction, have for many years used subcontracting as the basis of project sourcing. Other sectors have been slower to adopt this approach but now it is widespread. Projects may be managed internally and sourced from a range of outside providers, or an outside contractor may be appointed to manage the total project on a turnkey basis. Again, this policy enables the organization to utilize the most suitable resources rather than retaining internal staff with less specialized expertise to do the work.

By concentrating on a focused core activity and keeping employment levels to a minimum, the organization is able to manage its lower number of direct employees more effectively. Given the greater dependence on this group of key personnel – sometimes called 'gold-collar' employees – they are likely to be well rewarded and well trained. If this is not the case, they are likely to see the alternative of being a contract employee as financially rather more attractive and no more risky than being directly employed.

Companies are seeking ways of maintaining commitment and contribution without any guarantee to employees of a job for life. With no long-term security, employee expectations of immediate rewards are higher than would have been the case in the large bureaucracy of the 1970s and 1980s with its 'job for life' policy and generous pension provisions.

There remains a shortage of first-class personnel in many professional areas, including management. Numerous managers who have left the umbrella and safety of the large corporate have found that their new lifestyle has not left them disadvantaged, financially or otherwise. Their example serves to unsettle the corporate man or woman who is committed to the organization but realizes that the company has dispensed with the services of a large number of their colleagues.

In addition, as business becomes more global, the economics of sourcing activities change. Certain types of work can easily be transferred to areas where labour costs are significantly lower or for political reasons. The economics of production may be distorted by tax breaks and other financial incentives. With companies increasingly thinking on a global scale, they also need their managers to have a range of new skills and aspirations. Some will not be able to adjust, and others will have to make way for managers from other national backgrounds in order to achieve the organization's desire to become truly international.

As organizations attempt to become more customer facing, they depend more and more on having excellent front-line staff who can offer high levels of customer service and provide information about changing customer needs and the impact of competition in the marketplace. Partly as a result of this change, the role of senior executives is also changing. They need to involve people at all levels to ensure that they remain in touch. They also have to win the commitment of staff to the organization's mission and strategy. More emphasis is being put on a manager's ability to gather views from a wide range of stakeholders and integrate them into a shared vision, mission, and strategy. There is also an emphasis on the strategic leadership role, translating strategy into action and developing strong core values. Just as the focus at lower levels of management has moved more to counselling, senior executives are having to pay much more attention to the development of their successors. It is also important for them to help create a learning culture and a learning organization.

Probably the greatest contributory factor to the reduction of management in organizations is the realization that managers are a highly expensive resource – the more senior, the greater the cost. Many organizations have recognized that they can have greater control over their costs if they employ consultants, as and when necessary, to carry out special assignments previously undertaken by in-house management, without the ongoing expensive overhead of the employee. In a fast-changing world, flexible employment contracts are attractive to employers for work that is non-standard and not a core activity.

We are seeing the realization of what Charles Handy calls the 'shamrock organization'.[14] This comprises a central core with a lean organization, supported by a network of suppliers for non-core activities and a network or peripheral staff brought in to carry out specialist and project-based activity.

New roles for a new era

Despite all these changes, the general principles of management espoused by the early thinkers still seem remarkably robust. However, three vital differences are apparent in how work is undertaken.

First, management is no longer the sole prerogative of an elite group called 'managers'. The functions of management are being much more widely shared within an enterprise.

Second, while goals and a clear sense of direction remain fundamental, who decides and agrees those goals and the strategies for their implementation are very different from those in earlier times.

Third, organizations still need leadership and direction, but the style of approach required is changing as organizations become much more open and responsive to customer needs.

Nevertheless, there is still a need for management and a role for managers. They are likely to fall into two broad categories:

1. Those managing within the smaller corporate structure or in organizations servicing the corporate. Some of the latter companies will have been created specifically for the

purpose, and in seeking to widen the base of their business they will probably be highly entrepreneurial.

2. Independent or networked managers providing specific services to both of the other groups.

Those managers wishing to stay within the larger corporate structure will have to be prepared for continual change, at both the organizational and personal level. In order to remain useful to the organization, they will have to adapt quickly to the business's changing needs. The more successful managers will be those who anticipate the direction of changes and prepare themselves for new roles and ways of working. Organizations will have to be prepared to invest more resources in the development of key managers, but those managers will also have to be more proactive in demanding and using opportunities for personal development.

Much of that development may well come through non-conventional methods such as distance learning, mentored on-the-job learning, secondments, and project assignments. Distance learning will become available 'on-tap' for many more managers, at a time and place to suit their personal needs. Consequently, more development will be delivered on a 'just-in-time' basis, when managers are confronted by a particular problem. Managers will also put emphasis on gaining qualifications to demonstrate their competence, and on ensuring their marketability outside the organization, so the qualifications deemed important will reflect capability rather than academic achievement.

Rewards will have to be commensurate with risks. Since increasing length of service makes alternative employment more difficult to obtain, companies may have to pay a premium to retain the people they want.

Managers will have to develop new frameworks to guide their actions in a rapidly changing business environment. For example, the emphasis on core activities and outsourcing requires managers to exercise rather different skills to those required in the effective management of direct employees. Managing contractors and contract staff in new-style partnership arrangements demands a non-adversarial framework or conceptual model. Getting the best out of these suppliers depends on more subtle approaches to relationship building and management, as well as high-level commercial skills. Managers will have to be capable of developing these new models, internalizing them, and adjusting their behaviour appropriately.

Many managers will find themselves managing people who spend much of their time outside the office. Employers will accept more flexible ways of working for managers and their staff and be concerned more with work outputs than the management of the input. Such work arrangements are based on trust, performance measurement, and individual appraisal. Managers will have to adjust their ways of both thinking and working in order to make these new arrangements work.

Those managers in the peripheral workforce will have to spend considerable time networking. This will no longer necessarily be playing the internal political games of a large organization to promote their own career, but to maintain a number of contacts to generate consultancy assignments. So they may well have to develop networking skills as well as competence in marketing and sales.

Delayering and the introduction of budgetary responsibility even for junior managers have resulted in considerable levels of responsibility at a relatively young age and with relatively limited prior experience. More far-sighted companies are investing considerable resources in training new entrants to cope with these new demands.

It is important for new entrants to get a breadth of experience at an early stage, probably by transferring laterally between functions or product divisions. By doing this they can prepare themselves for more senior levels or, alternatively, a career as a consultant. Traditionally, the latter has been used as a path to senior positions in organizations and it may well prove the ideal route for aspiring executives.

The nature of many consultancy assignments will be political. A consultant needs to be able to enter an organization and quickly assess the sources of power and influence and how they might affect the outcome of the assignment. The skills required may well be different to those that led to a reasonably successful career in a large organization.

Some consultants will spend part of their time as interim managers, standing in before replacements are found for those who leave, or to cover for illness. Others will specialize in turnarounds, spending relatively short periods in any one business.

The consultant may be called on to carry out specific investigative work, although many organizations are equally concerned about implementation. In such cases the assignment may include the development of a strategy for implementation and then a contribution to the process, for example through running training and development programmes. Again, the skills needed to design and deliver a development programme are outside the range of experience of most corporate managers.

It is obvious from this discussion that independent managers will have to devote a large amount of time to updating and self-development. This will be achieved partly through experience on assignments of different types and in varying contexts. It will also require a concerted effort to read widely in order to maintain understanding of broad business developments as well as in the specialist areas of expertise being offered to clients. Research skills will be important to keep adding value for clients. The choice of clients will also be important to the consultant, as the key to future success will be an impressive client list along with personal recommendations resulting from high-quality delivery.

The new generation of manager – the all-rounder

One thing is certain about the new style of managers – they will be much more competent in a broader range of activities. They will possess a broad understanding of business principles and a range of competencies, some of which will be at a high level.

There will be a particular requirement to understand how technology can be applied to move the business forward, as well as to have personal competence in the use of technology to aid managerial effectiveness. It will be less important for the manager to have computer literacy skills than competence in recognizing how IT can assist in the management process and then deploying it effectively.

So how will IT change the way managers work? We have already seen the widespread adoption of tools such as spreadsheets. However, in many ways the spreadsheet is fairly unsophisticated. Expert systems will be used increasingly in executive decision making, which will create problems for those who have difficulty understanding not only the opportunities that expert systems offer, but also their limitations.

Managers will make more use of international data sources in decision making. For the consultant with a particular expertise, electronic networks will enable services to be sold and provided globally. Networks such as the Internet also enable managers to keep in touch with the latest thinking in their area of expertise, something vital to the success of the independent consultant but also the corporate manager who wants to keep ahead of the demands of their job and build their reputation and career.

Probably the fastest growing application at present is groupware. Using electronic networks, this has been designed to enable teams of people to work more effectively – particularly where time and distance separate them. It can facilitate the operation of distributed teams and virtual organizations, whether for a specific project or for an ongoing business venture. The potential is considerable, although the barriers to making its application effective are equally significant.

Electronic communication is a new art form and managers currently have a clear preference for face-to-face meetings rather than remote communication. This is largely because they can pick up cues from body language and other non-verbal signals. They also use these opportunities to pick up other information peripheral to the meeting, but vital to their role and position in the company. Electronic meetings preclude much of this information.

Managers without this source of information often feel naked and politically exposed. The reality is that the technology is here to stay and managers will have to adjust. If they need other kinds of information they will have to find new ways of obtaining it. It may well be the case, however, that managers will have more time to concentrate on their main purpose – establishing goals and managing complex organizations to achieve them.

Possibly the greatest potential lies in releasing the organization's creative capabilities. The traditional bureaucracy did not welcome creativity. Ted Levitt, in a classic 1963 article in the *Harvard Business Review*, wrote:

> *'One of the collateral purposes of an organization is to be inhospitable to a great and constant flow of ideas and creativity... The organization exists to restrict and channel the range of individual actions and behavior into a predictable and knowable routine. Without organization there would be chaos and decay. Organization exists in order to create that amount and kind of inflexibility that is necessary to get the most pressingly intended job done efficiently and on time.'*[15]

1

Many companies are still working to this model. However, those that are moving towards being customer focused are endeavouring to harness the creativity of all stakeholders, including all employees as well as those in interfacing organizations such as customers and suppliers. Managers have a key role to play in this process by fostering an innovative climate and encouraging risk taking.

The companies that will be successful in the new decade are those that innovate in order to get ahead of their competitors. They will be innovating in a number of areas, including:

- Challenging existing business assumptions to identify the customers and products/services they most want to have as well as preferred delivery channels.
- Identifying and developing new methods of delivery, e.g. e-business.
- Product/service improvement.
- New products and services.
- Identifying, attracting, and looking after external and internal customers more effectively by building stronger customer relationships.
- Doing whatever they can to increase efficiency and/or reduce costs.

Research at Henley Management College in the UK has led to the formulation of eight working hypotheses that form the basis of critical success factors leading to the innovative organization[16]:

- Situational empowerment.
- Remuneration systems that reward trial and error.
- Clear understanding of customers' needs and external changes, well articulated within the organization.
- A mixture of training for innovation and change as well as specific skills, both 'hard' and 'soft'.
- Top executives' internal focus of control should be such that executives are convinced of their own ability to influence their situation.
- An innovation fund that at least matches competitors'.
- Explicit targets for innovation.
- High-quality managers.

Executive management has to create a vision of where it wants the organization to go and then agree an appropriate strategy for getting there. For many this will lead to a streamlining of the organization to increase its focus and long-term profitability. Middle management, in particular, will be a continuing target for change. Some organizations may well have already introduced the type of changes in the way management is undertaken that are identified above, but many have still to follow.

The primary stimulus will be corporations rather than governments or individuals themselves. These corporations will be responding to market pressures, reacting to global competition, and seeking ways of doing what they can best do, but doing it much better.

REFERENCES

1. Taylor, Frederick W., *Principles of Scientific Management*, Harper, New York, 1911.
2. Fayol, Henri, *Industrial and General Administration*, Pitman, London, 1916.
3. Gulick, Luther H. and Urwick, Lyndall F. (editors), 'Notes on the theory of organizations' in *Papers on the Science of Administration*, Columbia University Press, New York, 1937.
4. Mooney, J.D. and Reiley, A.C., *Onward industry: the principles of organisations and their significance to modern industry*, Harper, New York, 1931.
5. Allen, L.A., *Professional Management: new concepts and proven practices*, McGraw Hill, Maidenhead, 1973.
6. Kelly, J., 'The study of executive behaviour by activity sampling', *Human Relations*, 17, 1964.

7. Mintzberg, Henry, *The Nature of Managerial Work*, Prentice Hall, New Jersey, 1973.
8. Morse, J.J. and Wagner, F.R., 'Measuring the process of managerial effectiveness', *Academy of Management Journal*, 21, 1978.
9. Tan, J.H., *Management work in Singapore: developing a factor model*, Henley Management College/Brunel University, 1994.
10. Boyatzis, Richard E., *The Competent Manager: a model for effective performance*, John Wiley, New York, 1982.
11. Porter, L.W. and Lawler, E.E., *Managerial Attitudes and Performance*, Irwin Dorsey, Homewood, Illinois, 1968.
12. After Boyatzis, R.E., *The Competent Manager: a model for effective performance*, John Wiley, New York, 1982 (Table 12-1 'Summary of Competency Results').
13. Stewart, Rosemary, *Managers and their Jobs: a study of the similarities and the differences in the way managers spend their time*, Macmillan, London, 1967.
14. Handy, Charles, *The Age of Unreason*, Business Books, London, 1989.
15. Levitt, Ted, 'Creativity is not enough', *Harvard Business Review*, Vol 41, 1963.
16. Birchall, D.W., Swords, S., Brown, M. and Swords, D.F., *Growth and Innovation*, Henley Management College, 1993.

RESOURCES

BOOKS

Boyatzis, Richard E., *The Competent Manager: a model for effective performance*, John Wiley, New York, 1982.

Handy, Charles, *The Future of Work*, Blackwell, Oxford, 1984.

Mintzberg, Henry, *The Nature of Managerial Work*, Prentice Hall, New Jersey, 1973.

Schwartz, Peter, *The Art of the Long View*, Doubleday, New York, 1991.

WEB

www.henleymc.ac.uk

Work beyond 2010

RICHARD SCASE

Richard Scase highlights the changes that will increasingly affect the way businesses operate.

IN the past, companies functioned as internally integrated systems: creating structures, functions, and tasks as they grew that managed all of their activities 'in-house'. This enabled the directors to keep a tight control over these various activities and was most often undertaken by applying the principles of hierarchical line management. Managers gave orders and workers dutifully executed them. A culture of compliance predominated and the organization, with the aim of functioning like a well-oiled machine, operated by reference to precisely stipulated job descriptions.

The management of information is a good case in point. In the past this was a straightforward corporate activity. It was conducted by tiers of line managers whose responsibilities were to ensure that information was managed on a 'need to know' basis. The structuring of this information was hierarchical and reflected the needs of the organization rather than customer requirements. Structured on the basis of specialist departments – sales, marketing, accounts, and so on – companies were highly fragmented in their internal and external operational practices.

This meant that the management of information was highly focused and localized. It could rarely be integrated across the organization to develop customer-driven innovative products and services. It was also difficult for companies to focus on their core corporate competencies and leverage them for competitive success.

If there were any centralized corporate handling of data it was of a non-strategic kind – for example customer accounts, staff payrolls, and so on. This explains the old-fashioned popularity of computer mainframes. Different departments stored data on them that was used for their own specialist purposes; it was not a shared resource.

This paradigm is well known and large numbers of businesses still try to function in this way. However, it neglects organization's hidden inefficiencies. The growing recognition of these inefficiencies is bringing about a core rethink of how businesses should operate and, with this, a reappraisal of the role of management. The outcome is the emergence of new organizational forms that will have repercussions for the future nature of work and employee skills.

Intellectual capital and innovation

Traditional forms of organization are becoming redundant because the future business will not be a manufacturing enterprise. By the year 2010, only 10 percent of the labour force in the UK will be engaged in manufacturing.

The twenty-first century will witness the continuing growth of the information economy, with businesses trading on the basis of the various value-added services that they can provide. This means their key asset is intellectual capital and not, as in the past, machinery and the capacity to produce standardized products for either high-volume or niche markets (as is the case for large numbers of small and medium-sized enterprises).

Intellectual capital is the knowledge a company possesses to be innovative in continuously developing new products or services that are relevant for gaining competitive advantage in its targeted markets. In other words, in an information economy, IT is the basis for a company's core competencies. Everything else that may have been undertaken within traditional, highly integrated enterprises can now be outsourced, often on a global basis. The key challenge for businesses is to nurture creativity and innovation. It is the ability to do this that will differentiate successful, high-performing and competitive businesses from the rest.

How can creativity be nurtured so there is continuous innovation? Many lessons can be learned from the ways in which many small and medium-sized enterprises operate. Those that are high performing have a clear vision. The founding owners have a strong idea of where they want their businesses to go – and, importantly, so do their employees. There is an employer–employee partnership in which the vision is shared. The principle may be simple, but its implementation requires the presence of a range of organizational features:

- That there is open, honest, and fluid communication around all matters that are likely to affect the company's future.
- This, in turn, demands the existence of a culture of high trust between employers and employees.
- This in itself requires that employees are trained and given the capacity to develop their own talents for their own self-development as well as for the good of the enterprise. They must feel that they are stakeholders, participating in the rewards of the company as it grows. This can be in a variety of forms, ranging from equity stakes (as in many business partnerships) to profit sharing and career prospects.

It is within such organizational contexts that creativity is nurtured. These features account for the rapid growth of many small and medium-sized firms in such diverse industries as high technology, bioscience, professional services, advertising, and entertainment. Often the organizational attributes are structured around the 'charisma' or the personalities of the founder-owners. Although this can be an advantage, it is not an absolute necessity. What is vital for high performance is continuous innovation through leveraging the creativity of employees through the organizational processes mentioned above.

Product innovation through employee creativity requires the psychological contract between employer and employee to be redefined. There must be a shift from compliance to internalized commitment. Essentially, this means that employees are excited by their jobs – they eat, sleep, and drink their work. Their jobs are at the heart of their personal identities and inherent to their notions of self. Again, it is only through managing the business as a partnership between employers and employees that this can be achieved.

The physical workplace

If, in the past, the workplace was where work was done, in the information economy it is where ideas are exchanged and problems solved. This normally requires close working relationships among colleagues and the cultivation of positive team dynamics. It not only puts a premium on selecting employees who are technically competent, but also on recruiting people who are personally compatible with others in the business. The architecture and design of the workplace need to facilitate communication and teamwork.

Through the strategic use of information networks, companies can now operate as highly decentralized yet tightly integrated operating units spread across the globe. At the same time, and on a global basis, they can develop and pursue their business strategies through supply chain partnerships and strategic alliances.

This capability gives companies flexibility in their business practices. These are not steady-state organizations. On the contrary, they have mobility in both their internal and external operations. This continual change is driven by the need for continuous innovation. The outcome is the ever-transforming corporation that is forever redesigning its internal processes and its external trading linkages. If organizations of the past were characterized by stability, those of the future have the paradigm of constant change.

What is striking about businesses that compete on the basis of their intellectual capital is how they convey the physical impression that nothing much is being produced. This is because the workplace is designed to encourage face-to-face encounters among colleagues for problem solving and generating new ideas. A high proportion of floor space is designated as 'public areas', consisting of comfortable sofas arranged around vending machines. These areas are the nerve centres of creative businesses. Through discussion in these areas, colleagues develop ideas and then return to their 'private spheres' (and this is increasingly at home instead of at the workplace) to explore further the potential and feasibility. These thoughts will then be fed back to colleagues in the coffee area on a later occasion.

It will become taken for granted that staff should not have their own desks or exclusive use of office space. Hot-desking will be commonplace. People will spend less time working in offices. It may be necessary for them to attend corporate premises for meetings with colleagues but, increasingly, more time will be spent working on projects at home and away from the office with customers and business partners.

In the US roughly 24 percent of the labour force is mobile. In the UK the figure is 35 percent and growing. By 2010 it will reach over 60 percent – a staggering change in the patterns and culture of work. This will reduce the need for large corporate buildings, which will contribute to a sharp reduction in overhead costs – a hidden but substantial contribution that network systems can make to business profitability.

The process of innovation is not formally structured. It is not a specialist or compartmentalized activity, as is often the case in traditional manufacturing companies. Instead, it is located at the very heart of the business process. Employers cannot tell employees to be creative – intellectual capital does not operate in this way. What employers can do is provide the organizational and architectural contexts that facilitate employee creativity, and then reward employees so they have a stakeholder's interest in the outcomes of innovation. This often means more than simply material rewards. It can be part ownership of patents, as in bioscience, or the opportunity for professional recognition, as in the entertainment industry.

Location is also an important factor for leveraging creativity and fully utilizing the intellectual capital of a business. Why is it that the centre for the global entertainment industry continues to be in congested Los Angeles? Why do advertising agencies locate in parts of London and software companies in the UK's Thames Valley? It is because these geographic areas constitute clusters of tacit knowledge, of intellectual skills from which all firms benefit. Pools of talent become geographically concentrated and then shape the character of local infrastructures. Therefore the local labour markets from which these companies recruit consist of pools of appropriate intellectual capital. In many ways these are similar to the industrial districts of the early Industrial Revolution, where cultures became established that enhanced the capabilities of each of the separate businesses.

The limits of the virtual workplace

There are limits to the extent to which information technology can completely abolish the need for the workplace. A barrier to the adoption of the virtual organization, enabled by information technology, is the need for those with intellectual capital to interface in spontaneous and unstructured ways to leverage creativity to develop innovative products and services. In order for companies to be competitive in the information economy, they need to redesign their operational processes, management styles and cultures. This will require self-confident leadership in which openness and informality are encouraged. The design and architecture of their workplaces will need to embody these assumptions. Businesses will have to function as partnerships of all their aspects, from strategic decision making to the structuring of reward systems.

Without these mechanisms in place, intellectual capital – as the core asset of the information-based business – will simply walk out of the door. Unlike machinery in factories, people – especially those with creative knowledge – cannot be bolted to the floor.

RESOURCES

BOOK

Scase, Richard, *Britain in 2010*, Capstone, Oxford, 2000.

WEB

www.scase.org
www.forview.com

Making excellent decisions

SAM HILL

'Executives do many things in addition to making decisions. But only executives make decisions. The first managerial skill is, therefore, the making of effective decisions,' Peter Drucker has observed. Sam Hill presents a blueprint for excellent decision making.

STRATEGY is all about making the right decisions, or not making the wrong decisions, at the right time. Those companies that consistently make more right decisions more often succeed. Those that do not, fail.

Companies understand this of course, and devote considerable resources to making the best decisions possible. They employ the best trained MBAs and send their star managers to intensive six-week training programmes at the finest universities in Boston and Lausanne. They invest billions in sophisticated management information and decision support systems to provide the managers with the data they need to make good decisions. And they support them with armies of management consultants who bring the best and most current insights of academics and thought leaders.

Nonetheless, there remains a demonstrable difference in how well organizations make decisions. There are many reasons for this. One of the most important, though, is that in this era of chaotic competition and empowered organizations, excellence in decision making requires not just institutional excellence but individual excellence. There is no time to elevate every decision to corporate headquarters where pointy headed specialists will ponder it thoroughly. The executive or manager on the front line must be able to make good decisions in real time. They must be able to do so consistently. They must be able to do so both on major decisions and on what may appear to be minor ones, since there is no way of knowing when either a small decision or an accumulation of them will have strategic impacts.

Therefore, if we wish to create and implement successful strategies, we must invest in teaching those in the organizations both to understand strategic decisions and to make the right decisions themselves.

There are six rules of decision-making excellence.

Rule 1. Be timely

For every decision, there is an appropriate timeframe. False urgency is wasteful, since it often means decisions will need to be rethought as more data comes in. However, lateness is criminal, since it results in last minute crises or even worse, decision by default. As soon as any decision surfaces, identify the appropriate timeframe for resolution. Work to the deadline.

Recently one of my energy clients received a call from an internal task force negotiating a transfer price with another business unit. He listened quietly while they explained the complexities of forward price curves, risk premiums, buy backs, timing of payments, and so on. Finally, they paused for breath, and he asked, 'When do we need to make a decision?' Well, they replied, at the latest within 18 months' time. What had occurred is that a task force to set up the systems interface had created a master list of issues, each of which had then been assigned to various team members. Somehow a decision which required nothing more than monitoring had floated right up the priority list. But by refusing to make the call now, the business unit president had avoided creating a pricing agreement which would almost certainly have required a complete rethink in a year's time. In this case, delay was the right non-decision.

Every decision has its day. For some it is today, and for some it is tomorrow, and for some it is never. It is important not to wait too late and miss the decision window, but it is a similarly dangerous mistake to make the call too early, before all the available information is in.

Rule 2. Isolate

Most decisions are like the ball of yarn that belongs to a kitten, messy and scraggly, replete with tangles of facts and loose ends. Excellent decision makers first isolate the real decision from all this clutter. That is not to say all those other bits and pieces aren't important, but for most decisions there is a hierarchy, and that the key is to handle the most important, pivotal decision first.

Kraft makes a cheddar cheese in a small round can, invented to feed soldiers in the Second World War. It is manufactured in Australia and sold in countries where refrigeration is not always available, and is a mainstay of rural diets in many parts of the world. In 1988 a combination of currency movements and raw material prices made the price of Australian cheddar rise sharply in proportion to European cheese. The question facing management: should Kraft shift production of canned cheese from Australia to Germany or Portugal? There were many complications. Were the two factors which had created the cost differential temporary or permanent? Would the proposed changes to the EC coming in 1992 increase the differential or reverse it? Would shipping costs offset the gains? What would the loss of volume do to economics of the Australian operation? Could the taste profile be replicated with European cheese rather than Australian? If not, would consumers accept a different product? We filled three whiteboards with questions.

Surrounded on three sides by walls of unresolved issues, we first envisaged a six month study, complete with econometric models and primary consumer research. However, after some reflection we realized that the huge volumes of cheese required would demand a considerable expansion of European plant capacity. So the revised decision became, 'What volumes and margins would be required to justify buying a new plant or moving the existing equipment from Australia?' Thus the real decision was not whether to move the cheese production, but whether to build a new plant in Europe. We quickly discovered that building a new plant with that configuration of equipment would be prohibitively expensive. So we did not need to find out consumer reactions or any of the other issues involved.

Invest a bit of time up front defining the decision before making a major investment in prosecuting it.

Rule 3: Triangulate

There are three basic approaches to solving problems: intuition, experience and analysis. Each type has both strengths and weaknesses. Each is particularly appropriate to particular types of situations. The best decision makers are those who have learned to combine the three into a balanced 360-degree perspective. This is far harder than it looks, since most of us have a natural bias toward one type of decision making and tend to favour it, even when another might well provide a better answer.

The acceptance of intuition as an appropriate decision-making tool in business comes in and out of fashion. When a Richard Branson or Howard Schultz creates a huge business on little more than a gut feel, we are appropriately awed. When an Edgar Bronfman attempts the same, with less success, we are less forgiving. In fact intuition should play an important role in any decision maker's toolkit. The strengths of intuition as a decision-making approach are that it is fast and can provide answers that are brilliant, providing breakthroughs and leaps that can create or destroy companies. Its primary weakness is that it is a very individual tool. It's hard to explain and hard to document, and as a result hard to check for quality.

Experience is far more well accepted, but in fact should be treated far more sceptically than it often is. The advantage of experience is again that it is fast, and in that the costs of acquiring it occurred some time in the past, cheap. It is very compelling and is often the best way to sell decisions internally and externally. However, it too has drawbacks. One is particularly important. That is, experience relies on the performance of a complex mental retrieval function. What situation in our personal or group database most closely matches this one? What did we learn? And should we repeat the decision or reverse it based on that experience? There are never two exactly identical situations. However simple, each varies slightly in some obvious or not-so-obvious way than the one before. Since it will never be perfect, when is close enough good enough? An over reliance on experience can lead to absurd results, as when industry pioneer Ken Olsen of Digital Equipment scoffed at the idea that any home would ever need a computer, and decided not to devote resources to developing the PC.

Finally, there is analysis. Like intuition, analysis is controversial. Proponents love its rigour and repeatability. Detractors question its slowness. The advantages of analysis are that it is repeatable and predictable. Unlike either intuition or experience, it can be taught in a formal setting, a characteristic which allows rapid mass production of decision makers. The disadvantages are that it is slow, very costly and for a certain set of situations often produces an incorrect decision. There are many situations where analysis is inappropriate, but two stand out. First, analysis of people is a suspect process. People decisions are always best made using experience and intuition. Second, analysis does not cope well with situations where there is a major discontinuity. That is, analysis requires data, which is always historical. If there is a sudden shift which makes that historical data irrelevant, then analysis is helpless, adrift on an ocean of uncertainty with torn sails and a broken rudder. Analysis failed to accurately predict the size of the markets for mainframe computers, cellphones and the internet. In each case, a discontinuity made the historical data useless.

Nonetheless, on balance the positives of analysis outweigh the negatives. Thus in many industries we increasingly see the hyper-analytical companies rising to the top. This is especially true in data rich industries. Success stories include Providian and CapOne in financial services, D.E. Shaw in trading, and Target in retail. All consistently outperform their peers through skilful deployment of analytics in decisions.

Again, the best decision makers are those who best deploy all three modes. The Enron's and GE's have created business after business through their unique abilities to combine intuition with experience and analysis.

Rule 4: Write it down

Back in the 1970s, the epitome of old-style management was the legendary 'memo to file.' It was derided as an anachronism, a bureaucratic device to cover one's backside. Gradually the discipline faded away, and few companies have replaced it with a similar documentation. As a result, many of my clients have revisited the same decision three or four times due to management changes. Succinct and effective documentation is a key component of a complete decision-making process. Working through the decision on paper is useful at many points. Early on, it provides a way to capture all the various issues and organize them. Later, it provides a record of the decision and the logic behind it, so if assumptions or key variables change, it is not necessary to restart from scratch.

Rule 5: Make the call

The American general George Patton reputedly said, 'The best decision is the right one, second best is the wrong one, and worst is no decision.'

Rule 6: Be humble

A good decision is one that correctly uses all the available and relevant data in an appropriate timeframe. A consistent commitment to good decision making will over time result in more right ones. However, no approach will ensure that every decision is right. Most decisions are by their nature a close call, with tradeoffs and marginal economics. Seldom does a manager have all the information he or she needs to resolve these conflicts. Even more important, in most decisions there is considerable uncertainty, uncertainty that with frustrating regularity makes good decisions wrong and bad decisions right.

My most humbling experience happened several decades ago. One of my clients developed a newly patented chemical ingredient. Following an extensive period of testing and development, the chemical was finally ready for its US release. After agonizing discussions with the European head office, the US sales force agreed to a price that they felt was the maximum amount their customers would be willing to pay. When discussions finished, it was late in the day. The meeting with their largest customer was the next morning. The VP of Sales had committed to fax a quote to the customer's hotel room before the meeting. On his way out, he handed his secretary a hand written contract with the proposed price expressed in dollars per kilogram.

But this was an American secretary, and it was the early 1980s, and although the scrawled note appeared to say '$ per kg', that made no sense to her. She had to make a decision, to call the VP at home or to sort it out herself. She made an executive decision, and typed in a unit with which she was more familiar, '$ per lb'. The next morning the customer screamed and accused my client of extortion, but finally agreed to terms as stated. The secretary's typo instantly turned an industry also-ran into a major chemical company and created billions in shareholder value. But it was a bad decision nonetheless, a lucky one, but a bad one. The secretary could have called the executive at home, she could have consulted the dictionary, she could have asked a colleague. Instead, she used an unnecessarily limited set of data and introduced a huge level of risk into the discussion.

It is a bad practice to get overly confident in your decision-making ability, or overly self critical. A dash of humility seems about the right measure.

Decisions matter. While it is impossible to make every decision right, it is well within reach to making every decision good. Achieving this standard requires excellence at both the institutional and the individual levels.

RESOURCES

BOOKS

Baron, Jonathon, *Thinking and Deciding*, 2nd edition, Cambridge University Press, Cambridge, 1994.

Dearlove, Des, *Key Management Decisions*, FT Pitman, London, 1997.

Yater, J. Frank, *Judgement and Decision Making*, Prentice Hall, Englewood Cliffs, New Jersey, 1990.

ESSENTIALS

THE CHANGING NATURE OF MANAGERIAL WORK

Decision theory

AN entire academic discipline, decision science, is devoted to understanding management decision making. Much of it is built on the foundations set down by early business thinkers, who believed that under a given set of circumstances human behaviour was logical and therefore predictable. The fundamental belief of the likes of computer pioneer Charles Babbage and Scientific Management founder Frederick Taylor was that the decision process (and many other things) could be rationalized and systematized. Based on this premise, models emerged to explain the workings of commerce which, it was thought, could be extended to the way in which decisions were made.

In general, management literature defines two different types of decisions:

1. **Operational decisions** are concerned with the day-to-day running of the business. Typical operational decisions might involve setting production levels, or the decision to recruit additional employees.
2. **Strategic decisions** are those concerned with organizational policy and direction over a longer time period. So, a strategic decision might involve determining whether to enter a new market, acquire a competitor, or exit from an industry altogether.

Madan G. Singh, chair of information engineering at Manchester Institute of Science and Technology, prefers an alternative breakdown of decision levels, which recognizes some of the changes taking place within companies. He divides the decision makers in an organization into three levels:

- Day-to-day decisions.
- Tactical decisions.
- Strategic decisions.

Day-to-day decisions, he says, are those made by front-line staff. Collectively, they make thousands of decisions daily, most of them in a short timeframe and on the basis of concrete information: answering a customer's request for information about a product, for example. Their decisions usually have a narrow scope and influence a small range of activities.

Tactical and strategic decisions, on the other hand, are both longer-term decisions. The data needed to make them is much broader, extending outside the organization, and the information derived from that data is less precise, less current and subject to more error. Tactical decisions cover a few weeks to a few months, and include decisions such as the pricing of goods and services, and deciding advertising and marketing expenditures.

Strategic decisions are those with the longest time horizon – one to five years or longer. They generally concern expanding or contracting the business or entering new geographic or product markets.

To help managers cope with all these decisions, there are numerous models, frameworks, tools, techniques, and software programs. Decision-making models assume that the distilled mass of experience will enable people to make accurate decisions. They enable you to learn from other people's experiences. The danger is in concluding that the solution provided by a software package is *the* answer.

Decision theorizing suggests that effective decision making involves a number of logical stages. This is referred to as the 'rational model of decision making' or the 'synoptic model'. The latter involves a series of steps: identifying the problem; clarifying the problem; prioritizing goals; generating options; evaluating options (using appropriate analysis); comparing predicted outcomes of each option with the goals; and choosing the option that best matches the goals.

Such models rely on a number of assumptions about the way in which people will behave when confronted with a set of circumstances. These assumptions allow mathematicians to derive formulae based on probability theory. These decision-making tools include such elements as cost/benefit analysis, which aims to help managers evaluate different options.

Alluring though they are, the trouble with such theories is that reality is often more confused and messy than a neat model can allow for. Underpinning the mathematical approach are a number of flawed assumptions, such as that decision making is consistent; based on accurate information; free from emotion or prejudice; and rational. Another obvious drawback to any decision-making model is that identifying what you need to make a decision about is often more important than the actual decision itself. If a decision seeks to solve a problem, it may be the right decision but the wrong problem.

The reality is that managers make decisions based on a combination of intuition, experience, and analysis. Despite the growing body of evidence that many of the best business decisions are not strictly rational, the belief in 'decision theory' persists. This is a very Western view. Eastern cultures take a variety of different approaches.

The Japanese, for example, have traditionally relied on a consensus-building process – *ringi* – rather than a decision-making formula. Under this system, any changes in procedures and routines, tactics, and even strategies are originated by those who are directly concerned with those changes. The final decision is made at the top level after an elaborate examination of the proposal through successively higher levels in the management hierarchy. The acceptance or rejection of a decision is the result of consensus at every echelon.

In the West, the emphasis is on finding the right answer and moving on to implementation as speedily as possible. The Japanese, in contrast, tend to place the emphasis on defining the right question. They are especially good at managing a process by which they reach a consensus on the need to make a decision about a particular issue. Once that consensus has been reached, it is possible to move quickly because there is broad agreement that a decision is needed.

– CHAPTER 4 –

Managing globally

'There will be two kinds of CEOs who will exist in the next five years: those who think globally and those who are unemployed.' PETER DRUCKER

'International life will be seen increasingly as a competition not between rival ideologies – since most economically successful states will be organized along similar lines – but between different cultures.' FRANCIS FUKUYAMA

'Japanese people tend to be much better adjusted to the notion of work, any kind of work, as honourable.' AKIO MORITA

'Think globally, act locally, think tribally, act universally.' JOHN NAISBITT

Global strategy in the twenty-first century

GEORGE S. YIP

What does it mean for a company to be excellent at global strategy, asks George Yip. He considers different modes of globalization and outlines how to operate as a Global Network Maximizer.

IN the 1980s and the mid-1990s, many companies were still debating whether they should globalize. In the twenty-first century this debate has ended. Companies now assume that they should globalize unless they can find very good reasons not to.

The spread of the web provides one compelling reason. Any company that mounts a website has instant global reach and overseas customers follow very quickly, with corresponding demands for delivery and service. In my book *Total Global Strategy*, published in 1992, I set out a set of general globalization drivers that are pushing nearly all businesses to globalize, and a set of specific industry globalization drivers that affect different industries differently.[1] Both these sets of drivers are stronger now than then.

The world has seen great convergence in customer needs and tastes, the drastic reduction of many government barriers to free trade and investment, an acceleration of globalization enablers in communications, and a surge in globally applicable new technological products and services. All this does not mean that every industry has become entirely global. But today, nearly every industry has a significant global segment in which customers prefer products or services that are much more global than they are local. Around the global segment are still regional, national, or sub-national niches. The size of the global segment varies, from very large in the personal computer industry to relatively small in many parts of the food industry. But the global segment is increasing in size in nearly all cases.

Increasingly, global strategy is also converging with global excellence. Global strategy requires a company to manage effectively on an integrated basis, but the company needs to be excellent to be able to do that. Global strategy also means being able to deploy a company's best achievements in any country to the rest of the world. But what does it mean for a company to be excellent at global strategy?

Overall global strategy and organizational forms

In globalization, strategy and organization are inextricably intertwined. The organizational form facilitates some types of international strategy and not others. Individual companies typically evolve over time from one form to another as their international activities and strategies evolve. Today, multinational companies can take one of three main forms: internationalist, federalist, or global maximizer.[2]

The internationalist

Most companies start with what might be termed an 'internationalist' strategy and organization (Figure 1). In this posture, home market activities dominate and foreign activities are often opportunistic, without too much investment or adaptation. A simple test is whether the company could survive without its international activities.

Many American companies took this approach as they focused first on their enormous home market. Some, like Chrysler, never got beyond this stage. Many quite large and most *Mittelstand* (mid-sized) German companies are still in this mode. Most Japanese exporters started in this fashion and the cornerstone of their success in the 1970s and 1980s was the exploitation of their home market as a base for overseas expansion.

As the extent of international revenues increases most companies move on to other forms. For example, the US brewing giant Anheuser-Busch is now trying to break out of this mode as it increases its international activities. Companies that cannot grow organically beyond this stage typically have to acquire internationally or be acquired (or, as Wall Street bankers put it, to 'eat lunch or be lunch'). The latter has been the fate of Chrysler and Mazda in the automotive industry and in 2000 of Ben and Jerry's, the socially responsible US ice-cream maker, whose new owner, Unilever, will leverage its worldwide distribution capabilities to take Cherry Garcia and Peace Pops global.

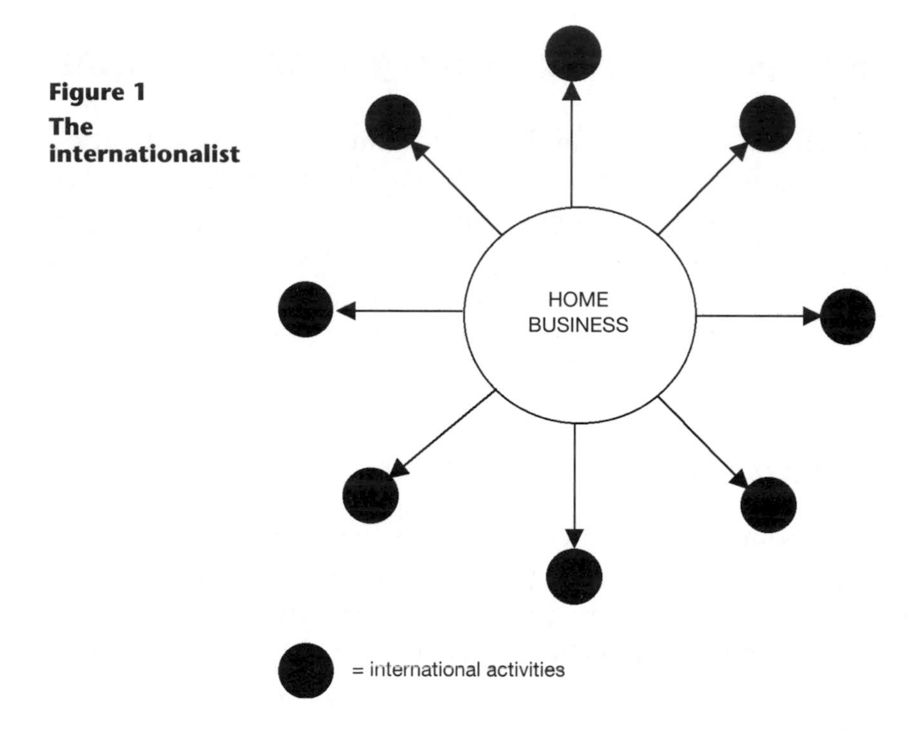

Figure 1
The internationalist

Some companies are stuck in this form, typically because they compete in regulated industries that allow only limited internationalization; because of being in sensitive industries such as defence, where home governments discourage the overseas relocation of critical activities; or in industries where the minimum efficient scale of operations, particularly production, is so great that concentration is best. Typical companies and industries are British Aerospace and Northrop Grumman in their defence-related businesses; British Telecom and other national telecom service operators; most airline companies; most utility operators; most law firms; and many media companies.

For internationally blocked industries, there are three main paths for globalization. First, they can make acquisitions of foreign participants in the same industry, if allowed. But there are severe restrictions in many industries on foreign ownership, including in airlines, defence, and media. Rupert Murdoch had to become a US citizen in order to be able to buy US radio and television companies.

Second, they can form international strategic alliances. British Airways continues to seek to build a transatlantic alliance that can operate as seamlessly as will be allowed by national regulators. Its global One World alliance (co-led with American Airlines), the Star Alliance (spearheaded by the United States' United Airlines) and the pan-European Qualiflyer alliance[3] all seek to achieve in alliance mode what their members are not allowed to do as national air carriers.

Third, companies in blocked industries can hire out their expertise to foreign partners or customers, or globalize in unrestricted activities. For example, Singapore Airlines has many training and support contracts with other carriers and also operates globally some specialized airline-related businesses, such as catering. Thames Water, one of the UK's largest utility companies, is using both acquisition and technology-transfer modes in its globalization efforts. In summary, internationalists face a hard challenge of achieving and maintaining global excellence when most of the world is blocked for many of their most critical activities.

The federalist

The classic multinational form has been that of the federalist (Figure 2). In this mode each international subsidiary operates most, if not all, of the value chain, and has considerable autonomy. The home market becomes just another country and the head office primarily a holding company.

This mode was particularly common among European multinationals from the 1950s to the 1980s. With relatively small home markets, such as Switzerland or the Netherlands, and in an earlier era of high transportation costs, poor communications and large differences in country tastes, companies like Nestlé, Unilever, and Philips created a far-flung chain of subsidiaries where the country manager was king. The success formula for these companies was the transfer of home country competencies (such as products, technology, or marketing know-how), a globally uniform management system and set of standards (extensive and common procedures), use of local managers leavened by expatriates, and significant independence in local business decisions. So the product had to meet Unilever's worldwide standards and had to be developed and marketed 'by the book', but it could be called by different names in different countries or be a different product even though under a globally common name such as 'Omo', perhaps the world's least consistent global brand.

The federalist model has great advantages where adaptation to the local environment, including customer tastes and government rules, is critical. With global convergence, most industries no longer favour this approach. So companies like Philips struggled in the 1980s to convert to a global mode, and Procter & Gamble reorganized in the late 1990s from a regionally based organization into just seven global strategic business units.

Some remaining industries still have mostly federalist companies and constitute the current frontier in global change. These include accounting and engineering consulting services. In all these industries knowledge of national environments is still critical. So most firms continue to operate as loose multilocals, although most are making efforts to achieve more global integration. Advertising agencies have moved somewhat faster, spurred by the advent of global advertising in the 1980s and by the pre-emptive claims of Britain's Saatchi and Saatchi to be the world's first advertising agency able to deliver global advertising.

The global maximizer

The third mode, the global maximizer, constitutes genuine global strategy. Japanese companies provided the most extreme applica-

Figure 2
The federalist

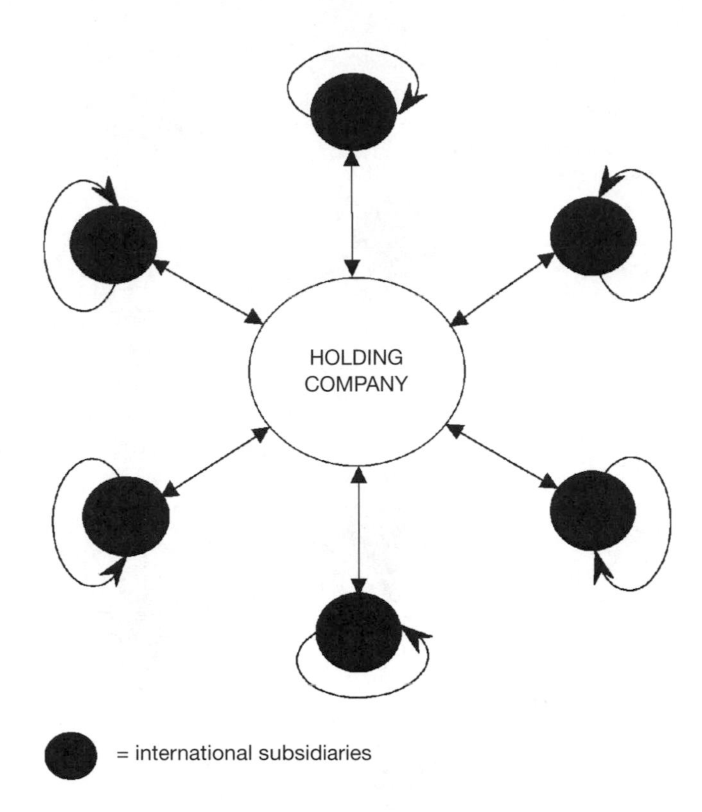

tion of the first version of this model: pure global strategy. In the 1970s and 1980s, firms such as Toyota and Matsushita swept world markets with globally standardized products made in a small number of factories, mostly based in Japan.

By the 1990s, a more complex form of the global maximizer had emerged, the global network maximizer (GNM) (Figure 3).[4] In this form, multinational companies break up the value chain and locate individual activities in as few locations as possible. No part of the organization, whether headquarters or subsidiary, is self-sufficient. Instead, all work together in a network. Perhaps the prime current example is ABB Asea Brown Boveri. Most leading American, European and Japanese companies are now converging on this model, albeit from different starting points.

The internet and the web have consolidated the dominance of the GNM as the key model for multinational companies for the foreseeable future. The GNM model seeks to reduce duplication of activities. As an electronic network, the web, through both intranets

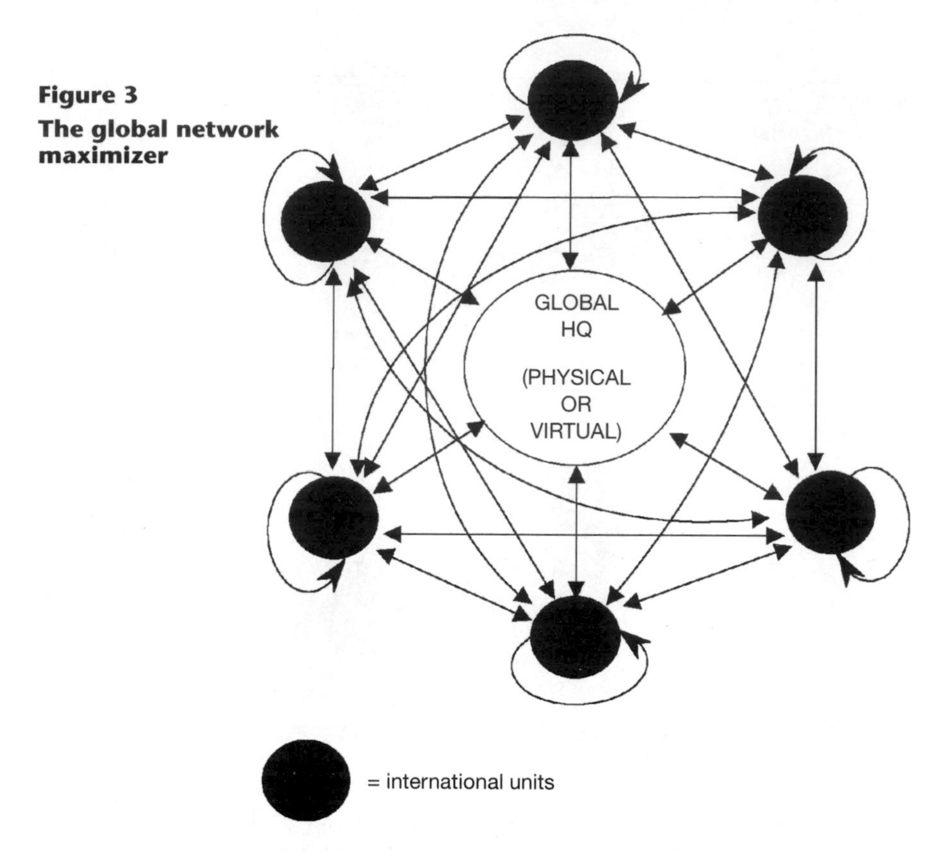

Figure 3
The global network maximizer

and extranets, offers the potential to complete this process of deduplication. This model is, therefore, also ideal for internet-based 'new economy' companies, many of which are 'born global'. The rest of this article focuses on how to operate the GNM model.

Globalization of individual activities[5]

I am often asked, 'What is the world's most global company or the most globally effective?' My answer is that different companies excel in globalization of different activities but none excels in all – not surprising given the complexity of global management of even a single activity. In addition, global excellence does not always mean the most global standardized solution. For each activity, global excellence means being able to develop and implement the most appropriate combination of global, regional and national solutions.

Global research and development

Global excellence in R&D means being able to access new knowledge and capabilities anywhere in the world and develop globally appealing products and services that can be produced on a globally competitive basis.

In terms of accessing knowledge, multinational companies have historically concentrated their R&D activities in their home countries, thereby greatly reducing their ability to access overseas knowledge and innovation. This mattered less when the creation of new knowledge was the near-monopoly of North America, Western Europe and Japan (Kenichi Ohmae's Triad economies),[6] also the home bases of most multinationals. However, the exponential rise in technology and knowledge creation has created a global diaspora of expertise. Global companies now need to access knowledge and development capabilities not just in Triad nations but in emerging economies such as China, India, and Russia.

Several routes exist: physically setting up R&D overseas but keeping these units plugged into the global network, by electronic means constantly and in-person sometimes; hiring scientists and technologists from overseas; or frequent visits to and other contacts with countries that are sources of innovation. For example, Canon conducts R&D activities in eight facilities in five countries, Motorola has 14 facilities in seven countries and Bristol-Myers Squibb has 12 facilities in six countries.[7] Microsoft has invested in an R&D centre in Cambridge, UK, in order to tap into the expertise of Cambridge University, Cambridge's Science Park, and the area's phenomenon of 'Silicon Fen'.

Global products and services

The output of global R&D should be global products and services, but these are seldom totally standardized worldwide. Instead, such products are designed with global markets in mind, and they have as large a common core as possible. Some industries and categories, such as ethical pharmaceuticals and express package delivery, allow the potential for a very large common core, while others, such as furniture and legal services, allow for less commonality. Most companies now actively seek to maximize this global core, even if, for marketing reasons, they do not talk about global products as such.

Honda's Accord passenger automobile illustrates the new kind of thinking in designing global products. Developing a new automobile platform costs over US$1 billion. But a major challenge is that US drivers prefer wider cars, and hence platforms, than do drivers in Europe and Asia. Thus many companies operate with at least two platforms or even completely different product lines between the US (and Canada) and the rest of the world. Honda's solution in the late 1990s was to develop the world's first adjustable-width automobile platform. Its development cost was about halfway between that for one platform and that for two. Such global products cannot be developed on a country-by-country basis but only on a globally integrated basis. In the service sector, American Express leads the world in offering a range of credit cards with a very high degree of global commonality. An American Express Gold Card provides the same core functionality whatever the home country of the card holder.

Global sourcing and production

Global sourcing and production have to reconcile several conflicting objectives: cost, productivity, quality, reliability, protection of expertise, and trade barriers. So there is a seldom a single sourcing and production configuration that can maximize all of these objectives, merely optimize them. Hourly labour costs now range from US$30 an hour in Germany to under 25 cents in Indonesia, or a ratio of more than 100:1. With such large differences, even companies in non-labour-intensive industries need to think seriously about where to locate activities. Furthermore, companies should not be put off by the low *average* productivity in low-cost economies. These figures include all the unmodernized, often state-owned companies. The whole point is to achieve higher levels of productivity by making investments and transferring technology and expertise. Motorola, the proselytiser of 'six-sigma' quality, excels at operating world-class manufacturing in developing countries.

As described, for the global network maximizer, the global solution typically means a network of sourcing and production nodes in different countries, specializing by product or sub-activity. For example, Nippon Denso, a Japanese producer of air conditioners and other automobile parts, operates an Asia-Pacific network in which starters, alternators, and wiper motors are made in Thailand, engine ECUs, alternating current amplifiers, and relay arms in Malaysia; compressors and spark plugs in Indonesia; meters in the Philippines; and evaporators and condensers in Australia.[8]

Global logistics

Global logistics embody the challenge for global companies to deliver their intermediate and final products anywhere in the world in a cost-effective and timely manner. The solution can seldom be one single distribution hub, but a network of hubs, exemplified by the systems of the global delivery companies, such as FedEx, DHL, and UPS. Another issue is whether to use a globally common distribution system or a differentiated one. Coca-Cola has achieved great success by replacing local distribution systems with its effective and efficient standardized distribution methods.[9]

Global marketing and selling

Global marketing and selling strive for the appropriate balance of global uniformity and local adaptation in all elements of the marketing mix, but with a probable bias in favour of uniformity, unless a good case can be made for local exceptions. This means casting aside the previous conventional wisdom that companies should globally standardize the marketing process but not the marketing content. Global excellence in marketing now means looking for uniformity. For example, Unilever recognized that it was hampered by marketing too many different brands around the world. In 1999 it began an initiative to reduce the number of brands from over 1,600 to about 400. And Diageo's United Distillers Vintners unit focuses on nine 'global power brands'.

Research on global marketing shows that different elements of the mix need to have different degrees of global uniformity, with brand names and packaging the most uniformity; pricing, advertising, and distribution moderate uniformity; and selling and promotion the least.[10] Germany's Beiersdorf, the marketer of the Nivea brand, provides an excellent example of global marketing that maintains tight and effective worldwide consistency.

However, companies can go too far. In the late 1990s British Airways made an attempt to reposition itself as a global rather than just a British airline by replacing the national flag on the tails of its planes with art designs from around the world. Domestic opposition mounted and the designs were dubbed 'global graffiti'. British Airways ended this experiment after just a few years.

Global customer service

Customers today require service anytime, anywhere. As the world's leading global retail bank, Citibank goes even further. Its global motto is that customers can do business with it 'anytime, anywhere, anyway'. Citibank invested hugely in the 1990s in both physical infrastructure, such as branches and ATMs, and computer and communication systems to make real its boast.

Hewlett-Packard is a global leader in computer-based customer support services for its customers. It maintains a globally standardized set of services that range from site design to systems integration to remote diagnostics. This global standardization includes seamless service at any hour of the day or night from anywhere in the world.[11] To do so, H-P maintains a global chain of 30 customer response centres, integrated into a global network.

Global capital and financial management

Global companies now seek to diversify their shareholder bases geographically by listing on multiple exchanges and doing other things to encourage foreign shareholders. Broadening the shareholder base increases demand for the company's shares and also provides exposure and insight into the needs of foreign capital markets. Recent transatlantically merged companies, such as Daimler-Chrysler and BP-Amoco, actively manage their multiple shareholder bases.

Today, the globally excellent company should keep track of the global mix of its shareholders. In general, excellent approaches to global capital and financial management include improving access to company information, reducing the real after-tax cost of capital, minimizing currency risk, and improving global treasury management.[12]

Global human resource management

In the internationalist model companies tend to rely on expatriates, while in the federalist or multilocal model they aim to have as many local managers as possible. Global excellence now requires a balance of global, regional, and national managers. A global network can be operated only if many members have had international experience and also have many interpersonal connections and shared experiences.

Furthermore, individuals can take different roles at different stages of their career or family lifecycle. Global companies need to invest in building a portfolio of the necessary capabilities, not just in technical or business terms, but in terms of language and cultural capabilities and types of international experience.

Japanese and Korean companies may find it difficult to incorporate foreign nationals into their management systems, but they also invest heavily in preparing their own nationals for foreign assignments. Samsung puts executives through a one-year programme before they are sent abroad, and also spends two months debriefing them on return at its Global Management Institute. AMP, a US producer of electrical connectors, began an extensive programme in 1992 to develop what it calls 'globe-able leaders'.[13] Statoil, the Norwegian oil company, finds that many of its international opportunities lie in Central Asia. Few Norwegians speak the languages of Kazakhstan or Uzbekistan! Perhaps it should fund students in Norwegian schools to learn those languages.

Global governance and leadership

Lastly, excellence in global governance and leadership means getting the best top executives and board members from anywhere in the world. Few of even the largest multinational companies have representation from all continents on their boards, even though non-executive directors provide an easy source of such expertise. Some companies, such as Portugal's innovative Sonae group, now have global advisory boards as a way to tap this global expertise without having to change their legal boards. And for top management, companies are beginning to follow the example of top football (soccer) teams, such as Real Madrid and Chelsea, by searching for the best talent worldwide.

The global challenge

Global strategy sets very tough challenges for companies. They need to be globally excellent in nearly every activity, and find the right balance of global, regional, and national solutions. This concept is best summed up in the philosophy at Beiersdorf: 'As global as possible, as local as necessary.'

The global company does not have to be everywhere, but it has the capability to go anywhere, deploy any assets, and access any resources, and it maximizes profits on a global basis. Now global companies also need to do it all very fast – at internet speed. And if they do not do all this, their competitors will. Globalization means there is no place to hide.

REFERENCES

1. These drivers were also summarized in Hans Wüthrich's contribution to the 1995 edition of *The Financial Times Handbook of Management*.
2. I thank José de la Torre of the Anderson School at UCLA for sharing with me these three models and their conceptualizations.
3. Qualiflyer includes Swissair, Austrian Airlines, Sabena, Air Portugal, Turkish Airlines, AOM, Crossair, Lauda-air, and Tyrolean.

4. See Bartlett, Christopher A. and Ghoshal, Sumantra, *Managing Across Borders: The Transnational Solution*, Boston, Harvard Business School Press, 1989; and Nohria, Nitin and Ghoshal, Sumantra (contributor), *The Differentiated Network: Organizing the Multinational Corporation for Value Creation*, San Francisco, The Jossey-Bass Business & Management Series, Jossey-Bass Publishers, 1997.
5. This section has benefited from my association with the Deloitte & Touche programme on 'Innovative Leaders in Globalization'.
6. Ohmae, Kenichi, *Triad Power: The Coming Shape of Global Competition*, Free Press, New York, 1985.
7. Kuemmerle, Walter, 'Building Effective R&D Capabilities Abroad', *Harvard Business Review*, March–April 1997.
8. See Kondo, Mari and Yip, George S., Chapter 16 'Regional Groupings–ASEAN, APFTA, APEC, Etc', in George S. Yip, *Asian Advantage*, Reading, MA, Addison-Wesley, 1998; and *Asian Advantage: Updated–After the Crisis*, Cambridge, MA, Perseus Books, 2000.
9. Ohmae, Kenichi, *The Evolving Global Economy: Making Sense of the New World Order*, Boston, MA, Harvard Business School Press, 1995.
10. Yip, George S., 'Patterns and Determinants of Global Marketing', *Journal of Marketing Management*, 13, pp. 153–164, 1997.
11. Lovelock, Christopher H. and Yip, George S., 'Developing Global Strategies for Service Businesses', *California Management Review*, Vol. 38, No. 2, Winter 1996, pp. 65–86.
12. *Innovative Leaders in Globalization – Program Discussion Document*, New York, Deloitte Touche and World Economic Forum, 1998. See also *Innovative Leaders in Globalization*, Deloitte Touche Tohatsu, New York, 1999.
13. Marquardt, M. and Reynolds, A., *The Global Learning Organisation: Gaining Competitive Advantage through Continuous Learning*, Homewood, Illinois, Irwin, 1994.

RESOURCES

BOOKS

Bartlett, Christopher A. and Ghoshal, Sumantra, *Managing Across Borders: The Transnational Solution*, Harvard Business School Press, Boston, 1989.

Marquardt, M. and Reynolds, A., *The Global Learning Organisation: Gaining Competitive Advantage through Continuous Learning*, Irwin, Homewood, Illinois, 1994.

Nohria, Nitin and Ghoshal, Sumantra (contributor), *The Differentiated Network: Organizing the Multinational Corporation for Value Creation*, Jossey Bass, San Francisco, 1997.

Ohmae, Kenichi, *Triad Power: The Coming Shape of Global Competition*, Free Press, New York, 1985.

Ohmae, Kenichi, *The Evolving Global Economy: Making Sense of the New World Order*, Harvard Business School Press, Boston, 1995.

Yip, George S., *Total Global Strategy: Managing for Worldwide Competitive Advantage*, Prentice Hall, Englewood Cliffs, NJ, 1992.

WEB

www.georgeyip.com

1

Global advantage

MARCUS ALEXANDER

Complex and multi-faceted, globalization defies simplification. Corporate practice, from Disney to *Playboy*, suggests that there is much more to globalization than homogenization. Marcus Alexander believes that when it comes to corporate strategy, the blend is the thing.

GLOBALIZATION, if it is a single thing at all, is a very complex thing. The term provides a collective label for a whole series of trends and changes related to the significance of geography in shaping organizations and the interactions between them. For example, many local markets are globalizing as their governments reduce import restrictions and tariffs or as other countries reopen trade relationships. This not only means that goods and services become available from other parts of the world, but that the nature of competition changes from local to global, in turn affecting the way local firms must operate in order to survive and thrive. My own experience of working in Saudi Arabia, South Africa, and China in the recent past has brought home to me the massive impact that this shift in global competition can have on culture and ways of working inside the organization, as well as on balance of payment figures or brands on the shelf.

A somewhat different type of globalization concerns the homogenizing of tastes across geographies. Food, once highly local in style, has become more global in many respects. This is not simply what has been called the culinary imperialism of America being rolled out across the world via Coca-Cola and McDonald's. The changing economics of transportation and increased experience of foreign travel have enabled consumers to break away from largely national determinants of taste and resegment across countries on more individual lines. It is not that everyone is moving to a single global standard, but that shared tastes transcend national borders. Some consumers are moving toward a traditional Italian diet whether they live in London, Toronto or Stockholm, while others eat increasing quantities of Chinese-style stir-fries whether in New York, Adelaide or Madrid. In this context, globalization simply means that geographic location is no longer the key determinant of behaviour.

Other forms of globalization can also be distinguished. More and more firms have a presence in multiple locations across the world rather than simply exporting from a home base. But, perhaps more importantly, as such firms seek to standardize approaches or gain purchasing economies, they increasingly demand co-ordinated, multi-country support from their suppliers. This requires the suppliers not only to be present in different parts of the world, but to manage the relationships between their local units in new ways.[1]

Even without a physical presence in more than one country, organizations, like individuals, are no longer isolated from economic events far away. The globalization of capital markets and increasing international trade flows mean that local economies are heavily, and rapidly, affected by what is going on thousands of miles away – just as individuals are instantaneously linked, via CNN or BBC World, to events whose impact was once muted by distance and time.

Parenting advantage

These different strands of globalization are, therefore, having a profound effect in many areas. In particular, they are creating opportunities and threats in the realm of corporate strategy.

Corporate, or group-level, strategy is different from business-level strategy. It addresses two basic questions concerning multibusiness companies: why does it make sense to have a particular combination of businesses within the same group; and how should the parent organization relate to its business units?

At Ashridge Strategic Management Centre we have long argued that the key to both questions is the development of what we label 'parenting advantage'.[2] That is to say, the fundamental logic for any multibusiness group should be that the businesses are worth more under the ownership and guidance of this particular parent than they would be either individually or under alternative ownership. The whole should not only be worth more than the sum of the parts, but should ideally be worth more than the potential value of the parts in other wholes.

Sadly, as many years of research have shown, corporate strategy in practice often fails these tests or even fails to address them at all.[3] Parents frequently buy businesses of which they are not even particularly suitable owners, let alone the best, for reasons of growth, balance, desired diversification, or simply fashion. Furthermore, many parents own businesses that they are inadvertently damaging through inappropriate capital allocation, bureaucratic delays, or unsuitable advice. However capable the parent is in some general respects, our research has shown that they will only be suitable owners of a particular business if their skills and culture fit with that business.

As a brief aside, two things are clear about mergers and acquisitions: that they are extremely popular; and that they frequently cause problems. Study after study has concluded that acquisitions, on average, are value destroying for the acquirer. Going back to 1987, Michael Porter demonstrated in a classic *Harvard Business Review* article that even among 33 leading US companies, more than half the acquisitions they made were subsequently divested or shut down, often in a period of five to 10 years.

Even surveys of CEOs, usually leading proponents of any acquisitions made, are surprisingly downbeat. A typical *Acquisitions Monthly* poll, for example, found CEOs claiming only 37 percent of their acquisitions to be 'very successful' or even 'somewhat successful'.

Academics argue about exact numbers, but most conclude that around two-thirds of acquisitions fall well below expected performance, many of them proving actively damaging even at a direct cost level without accounting for indirect costs such as wasted management time and tarnished reputations. The prize of success can indeed be great, but evidence clearly shows that success is rare.

For a business to gain significant value from membership of a group, three conditions must apply:

- There must be some opportunity for enhancing performance that the business managers would not be able to obtain by themselves (for example, sharing complex best practices across parallel units in different countries).
- The parent must have relevant skills in addressing these opportunities (for example, an ability to install systems, manage career development, or facilitate knowledge transfer that enables the business to benefit from best practices around the group).
- The parent must not cause damage in other respects due to a misfit with the business (for example by using an

Figure 1 Ashridge portfolio matrix

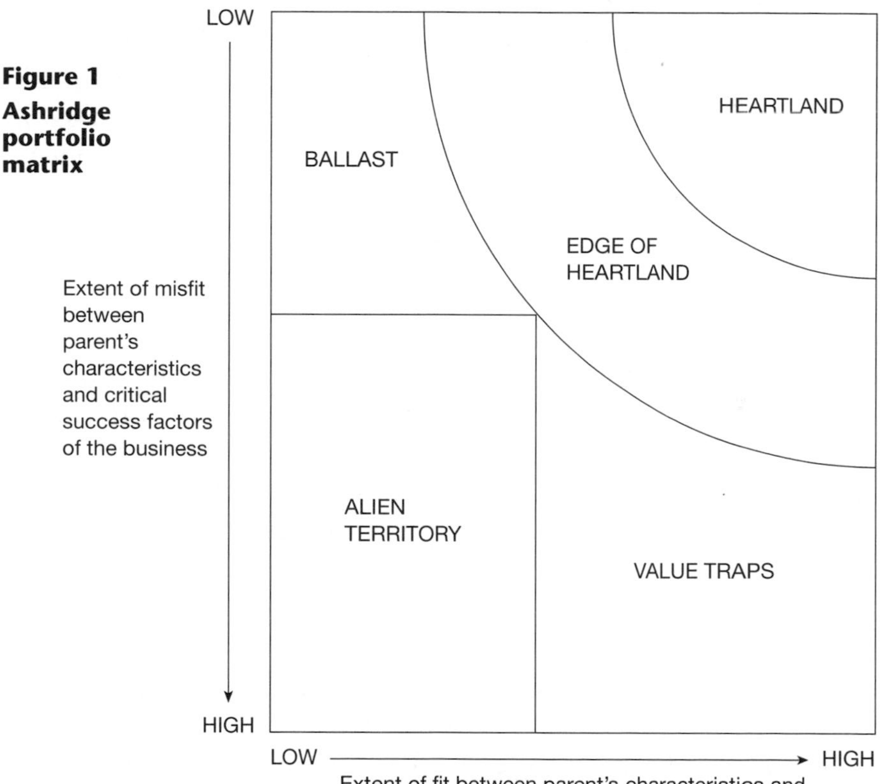

inappropriate budgeting process or applying group-wide policies that are harmful to some of the businesses, even if they are helpful to others).

The extent to which these conditions apply in practice is captured in the Ashridge portfolio matrix (see Figure 1). The horizontal axis relates to the first two conditions: is there a significant opportunity to enhance business value that this parent is able to get at? The vertical axis relates to the last condition: is misfit between the parent and the business likely to cause problems?

- Heartland businesses gain from group membership and suffer little damage.
- Alien territory businesses, in contrast, are likely to be damaged over time and to gain little advantage from being in the group, even if they start off profitable.
- Ballast businesses (which may quite often be described as core businesses by the parent) are safe from much parental damage but would be little or no worse off if they left the group, while being freed from an extra layer of management and complexity.
- Value traps do gain some benefit from the parent's actions, but they may also suffer significant damage due to other areas of misfit.[4]

Globalization affects all three of the conditions underlying this matrix. First, it creates opportunities that are often hard to exploit from within a single business unit. For example, cross-country co-ordination may be difficult for each local business to orchestrate on its own. A parent may be able to create overlay structures, as some advertising agencies do; set up an organizational matrix, as ABB did in the 1980s; or redefine the business unit scope, as TI did with its businesses in mechanical seals and small-diameter tube. All of these moves have given their individual business units an advantage over stand-alone rivals or others with less suitable parents.

Second, globalization is affecting the skills of parents themselves. The tighter links between different parts of the world make simple geographic division, where each regional head looks after their own area in isolation, less tenable.

This is leading to more physically virtual parent organizations – and constant travel or video conferencing for many senior executives. Tolerating cultural diversity is no longer enough. Parent managers are having to cope with it directly, rather than subdivide their tasks into more homogeneous geographic blocks. Information technology and expanding communication bandwidth require the parent to react to events across the globe more rapidly and with a more complex, integrated understanding than was once the case.

Finally, with regard to the third condition, globalization is opening up a whole series of potential pitfalls for parents. Areas of misfit between the parent and specific businesses that were previously unlikely to cause real damage may now become significant value destroyers. For example, dominant cultural maps that were acceptable in home markets or were once mediated through layers of local managers at what was regarded as a safe distance from head office may now cause havoc in a shrinking world.

The foregoing argument has mainly dealt with the problems and opportunities of parenting – owning a business – but it is worth pointing out that acquisition is not the only method of acquiring additional outside expertise or resources. Corporate alliances are an increasingly attractive alternative. There is good reason for this.

For example, spotting the trend to 'convergence' in the mid-1980s, AT&T hoped to combine core competencies in computing and communications. After failing to build adequate computer competency in-house, it identified NCR as an appropriate acquisition target and paid $7.5 billion to bring it on board in 1991. However, it seems to have had few clear mechanisms for integrating the two skill sets. As a result, early experiments were tentative and half-hearted and the ownership of NCR made little fundamental difference to AT&T's corporate capabilities.

The lesson to learn is that if the parent has no clear sense of how to combine the relevant resources, simply acquiring them is unlikely to help. In contrast, if it does have a very clear sense, it may not always need to acquire the complementary resources in order to achieve combination.

For example, Coca-Cola, McDonald's and Disney have a global alliance that creates significant value for all three parties. It combines McDonald's distribution strengths with Coca-Cola's brand marketing and image and Disney's strength in developing branded 'characters'. Combining these resources is not particularly complex, it merely involves planning promotions that jointly develop all three brands and physically moving products through McDonald's distribution system.

Although each partner's resources are therefore valuable to the others, there is no need for merger in order to gain the benefits; alliance is a much more appropriate vehicle. It should be pointed out, nevertheless, that alliances are not always plain sailing, nor are the rewards to the partners always equitably divided.

The meaning of globalization

In order to exploit the opportunities presented by globalization while avoiding the pitfalls, parents need to develop a sophisticated understanding of what globalization really means in the context of their particular businesses. A good framework for starting this investigation was put forward by Christopher Bartlett and Sumantra Ghoshal in their work on the transnational organization (see Figure 2).[5] Their research showed that different parents adopted different positionings with regard to seeking global integration across their businesses or encouraging local responsiveness to individual market needs. Global companies tend to have a single, integrated way of doing things, which is rolled out across the world. Multinationals, in contrast, have a collection of businesses that are heavily tailored to local needs.

Historically, the contrast could be seen in the oil industry, for example between Exxon's global approach and Shell's more multinational positioning. Both of these positionings can be highly successful, but in an increasing number of industries advantage is

Figure 2
The transnational organization

Source: Bartlett and Ghoshal, 1989

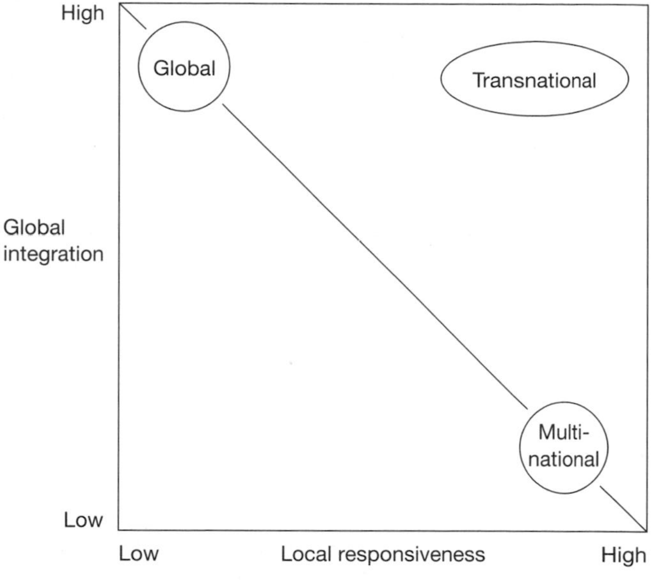

now being gained by combining both attributes rather than trading them off against each other. This is the role of the so-called transnational corporation. It gave rise to the famous maxim 'think global, act local' and the challenging contradictions espoused by Percy Barnevik at ABB.[6] In a more racy setting than power turbines, it has also inspired Christie Hefner, CEO of *Playboy*, to abandon her father's global American export mentality. Her, more successful, transnational model exploits globally the intellectual property of *Playboy*'s photo library, brand, and logo, while responding to local tastes through joint ventures in 14 non-American markets.

As noted, globalization is a complex concept, and each of the axes of this framework can be usefully disaggregated to clarify understanding. Global integration, for example, may apply to brand values, delivery standards, backroom services, knowledge management, purchasing clout, or a number of other aspects of the business. Nestlé has worked hard to ensure global integration of key brand values, for instance, but would happily accept different execution of those brand values, and often different recipes, tailored to local contexts. BASF has gained purchasing economies by integrating its global needs for certain chemical raw materials, but does not attempt to integrate all its purchases. Andersen Consulting has spent considerable resource in building its KX (Knowledge Exchange) system to aid global knowledge transfer, but tailors its detailed service offering to local needs.

A similar disaggregation of the horizontal axis brings out further richness of choice. Local responsiveness is sometimes simply equated with local language use. However, many dubbed advertisements reveal how much more than language is at issue. The offering itself may need to be significantly different: even the largely global McDonald's sells goatburgers in India and serves wine in Paris. Furthermore, pricing may need to vary in the light of local competitive conditions, even if the offering is essentially the same. Such conditions may differ as much between the centre of Saudi Arabia and the West Coast around Jeddah as between Los Angeles and Amsterdam. Customer focus may also need to be tailored, as accounting firms and banks have discovered in serving different European markets.

As a result, finding the right combination of global integration and local responsiveness is a key challenge for many parents in globalizing industries. Even highly successful companies, such as Disney, have found this a sizeable challenge. The original combination at Euro Disney (symbolically renamed Disneyland Paris after changing its approach) did not work at all well. While the staff, or 'cast' in Disney-speak, were multilingual and culturally diverse, and the rides had a French-speaking Mr Toad and dubbed Cinderella, pricing was entirely based on the American model. This was skewed toward eating, merchandise sales, and multi-day visits. European visitors, especially the French, tended to come only for one day, bring a packed lunch, and refrain from indulgent purchases of Mickey Mouse ears and Dumbo pencil cases. This almost bankrupted the operation until a French general manager was appointed and a considerable reblending of local and global elements took place.

At a broader level, Disney illustrates the very two-edged nature of globalization with regard to corporate strategy. Globalizing trends in the travel industry have made Florida an accessible destination for many European families. At this level, globalization has generated growth for Disney's Magic Kingdom at its home base. In contrast, the globalization of brands made new theme parks in Japan and Europe potentially attractive, leveraging Disney's animatronics expertise, crowd management skills, and use of famous characters. As the Euro Disney experience shows, globalization is not a simple process of homogenization. Worse still, it brings active problems to manage as well as opportunities. Failure to coordinate release dates, video sell-through prices, merchandise agreements, or product windowing leads to far bigger problems in a time-compressed, space-compressed world than was ever the case in a more discretely divisible and fragmented one.

Given the complexity of its relationship with corporate strategy, it may seem dangerous even to talk about globalization as a single concept. Certainly it is multifaceted and, rather like the concept of Europe, should not be used too simplistically. However, creating a clear focus on the shifting role of geography in shaping business activity is valid and timely. At some stage, globalization may even seem parochial to Martian corporate strategists!

REFERENCES

1. Janine Nahapiet, 'Managing relationships with global clients: value creation through cross-border networks', available as a working paper from Templeton College, Oxford. See also George Yip and C.J. Lovelock, 'Global strategies for service businesses', *California Management Review,* Vol. 38 (2) winter, 1996, pp. 64–86.
2. For a brief summary of Parenting Advantage theory, see Marcus Alexander, Andrew Campbell, and Michael Goold, 'Parenting advantage: the key to corporate-level strategy', *Prism,* Second Quarter 1995 (published by Arthur D. Little).
3. For a discussion of some of the major problems of corporate strategy in practice, see David Sadtler, Andrew Campbell and Richard Koch, *Break-Up!,* Capstone, Oxford, 1997.
4. For a fuller description of this matrix, see Andrew Campbell, Michael Goold and Marcus Alexander, 'Corporate strategy: the quest for parenting advantage', *Harvard Business Review,* March–April 1995, Reprint 95202.
5. Christopher Bartlett and Sumantra Ghoshal, *Managing Across Borders: the Transnational Solution,* Harvard Business School Press, Boston, 1989.
6. For the classic exposition of Barnevik's views on the transnational, see William Taylor, 'The logic of global business: an interview with ABB's Percy Barnevik', *Harvard Business Review,* March–April 1991, Reprint 91201.

RESOURCES

BOOKS

Goold, Michael, Campbell, Andrew and Alexander, Marcus, *Corporate Level Strategy; Creating Value in the Multibusiness Company*, John Wiley & Sons, New York, 1994.

Sadtler, David, Campbell, Andrew and Koch, Richard, *Break-Up!*, Capstone, Oxford, 1997.

WEB

www.ashridge.ac.uk

ESSENTIALS

MANAGING GLOBALLY

HOFSTEDE, GEERT

ACCORDING to *The Economist,* Geert Hofstede (born 1928) 'more or less invented [cultural diversity] as a management subject'. Few would deny that this is the case. The Dutch academic has exerted considerable influence over thinking on the human and cultural implications of globalization.

Hofstede trained as a mechanical engineer before becoming a psychologist. He spent time working in factories as a foreman and plant manager; was chief psychologist on the international staff of IBM; and joined IMEDE, the Swiss business school, in 1971. He is now Emeritus Professor of Organizational Anthropology and International Management University of Limburg in Maastricht.

In Hofstede's hands, culture becomes the crux of business. He defines it as 'the collective programming of the mind which distinguishes the members of one group or category of people from another'. Hofstede's conclusions are based on huge amounts of research. His seminal work on cross-cultural management, *Culture's Consequences,* involved over 100,000 surveys in over 60 countries. The sheer size of Hofstede's research base leads to perennial questions about how manageable and useful it can be.

Each society faces some similar problems, but solutions differ from one society to another. Hofstede identified five basic characteristics distinguishing national cultures. These dimensions are:

- **Power distance**: the extent to which the less powerful members of institutions and organizations expect and accept that power is unequally distributed.
- **Individualism**: in some societies the ties between individuals are loose, while in others there is greater collectivism and strong cohesive groups.
- **Masculinity**: how distinct are social gender roles?
- **Uncertainty avoidance**: the extent to which society members feel threatened by uncertain or unknown situations.
- **Long-term orientation**: the extent to which a society exhibits a pragmatic, future-oriented perspective.

MORITA, AKIO

AKIO MORITA (1921–1999) was the co-founder of Sony and the

best known of the new wave of Japanese businessmen who rose to prominence in the West in the 1980s.

Trained as a physicist and scientist, he founded a company with Masaru Ibuka (1908–1997) immediately after the end of the Second World War. In 1957, the company produced a pocket-sized radio and a year later renamed itself Sony (*sonus* is Latin for sound). In 1960, it produced the first transistor TV in the world.

And increasingly, the world was Sony's market. Its combination of smaller and smaller products at the leading edge of technology proved irresistible. In 1961, Sony Corporation of America was the first Japanese company to be listed on Wall Street and, in 1989, Sony bought Columbia Pictures, so that by 1991 it had more foreigners than Japanese on its 135,000 payroll.

Morita and Sony's story parallels the rebirth of Japan as an industrial power. When Sony was first attempting to make inroads into Western markets, Japanese products were sneered at as being of the lowest quality. Surmounting that obstacle was a substantial business achievement.

Morita and Sony's gift was to invent new markets. Describing what he called Sony's 'pioneer spirit', Morita said: 'Sony is a pioneer and never intends to follow others. Through progress, Sony wants to serve the whole world. It shall be always a seeker of the unknown.' While companies such as Matsushita were inspired followers, Sony set a cracking pace with product after product, innovation after innovation. It brought the world the handheld video camera, the first home video recorder, and the floppy disc. The blemishes on its record were the Betamax video format, which it failed to license, and colour television systems. Its most famous success was the brainchild of Morita, the Walkman. The evolution of this now ubiquitous product is the stuff of corporate legend.

OHMAE, KENICHI

BORN 1943, there is no doubting Kenichi Ohmae's credentials as a modern Renaissance man. He is a graduate of Waseda University, the Tokyo Institute of Technology, and has a PhD in nuclear engineering from Massachusetts Institute of Technology. He is also a talented flautist and sometime adviser to the former Japanese Prime Minster Nakasone. Ohmae joined McKinsey in 1972, becoming managing director of its Tokyo office. McKinsey Americanized him as 'Ken', but the ambitions of his thinking remained resolutely global.

Ohmae's work is important for two reasons. First, he revealed the truth behind Japanese strategy making to an expectant Western audience. Second, he has explored the ramifications of globalization more extensively than virtually any other thinker.

Ohmae's first contribution was to explode simplistic Western myths about Japanese management. Forget company songs and lifetime employment, there was more to Japanese management. Most notably, there was the Japanese art of strategic thinking. This, said Ohmae, is 'basically creative and intuitive and rational' – although none of these characteristics were evident in the usual Western stereotype of Japanese management.

Ohmae pointed out that unlike large US corporations, Japanese businesses tend not to have large strategic planning staffs. Instead, they often have a single, naturally talented strategist with 'an idiosyncratic mode of thinking in which company, customers, and competition merge in a dynamic interaction out of which a comprehensive set of objectives and plans for action eventually crystallizes'.

Ohmae also noted that the customer was at the heart of the Japanese approach to strategy and key to corporate values.

> *'In the construction of any business strategy, three main players must be taken into account: the corporation itself, the customer, and the competition. Each of these "strategic three Cs" is a living entity with its own interests and objectives. We shall call them, collectively, the "strategic triangle",' he said. 'Seen in the context of the strategic triangle, the job of the strategist is to achieve superior performance, relative to competition, in the key factors for success of the business. At the same time, the strategist must be sure that his strategy properly matches the strengths of the corporation with the needs of a clearly defined market. Positive matching of the needs and objectives of the two parties involved is required for a lasting good relationship; without it, the corporation's long-term viability may be at stake.'*

The central thrust of Ohmae's arguments was that strategy as epitomized by the Japanese approach is creative and non-linear. (Previously, the Japanese had been feted in the West for the brilliance of their rationality and the far-sighted remorselessness of their thinking.)

> *'Phenomena and events in the real world do not always fit a linear model. Hence the most reliable means of dissecting a situation into its constituent parts and reassembling them in the desired pattern is not a step-by-step methodology such as systems analysis. Rather, it is that ultimate non-linear thinking tool, the human brain. True strategic thinking thus contrasts sharply with the conventional mechanical systems approach based on linear thinking. But it also contrasts with the approach that stakes everything on intuition, reaching conclusions without any real breakdown or analysis.'*

Ohmae went on to suggest that an effective business strategy 'is one by which a company can gain significant ground on its competitors at an acceptable costs to itself'. This can be achieved in four ways: by focusing on the key factors for success (KFSs); by building on relative superiority; through pursuing aggressive initiatives; through utilizing strategic degrees of freedom. By this, Ohmae means that the company can focus on innovation in areas that are 'untouched by competitors'.

The second area that Ohmae has greatly influenced is globalization. In *Triad Power* (1985), he suggested that the route to global competitiveness is to establish a presence in each area of the Triad (United States; Japan and the Pacific; Europe). Also, companies must utilize the three Cs of commitment, creativity, and competitiveness.

To Ohmae, countries are mere governmental creations. In the 'interlinked economy' (also made up of the Triad), consumers are not driven to purchase through nationalistic sentiments, no matter what politicians suggest or say.

'The essence of business strategy is offering better value to customers than the competition, in the most cost-effective and sustainable way,' Ohmae writes.

> *'But today, thousands of competitors from every corner of the world are able to serve customers well. To develop effective strategy, we as leaders have to understand what's happening in the rest of the world, and reshape our organization to respond accordingly. No leader can hope to guide an enterprise into the future without understanding the commercial, political and social impact of the global economy.'*[1]

He suggests that corporate leaders should concentrate on building networks.

> *'We have to learn to share, sort and synthesise information, rather than simply direct the work of others. We have to rethink our basic approach to decision making, risk taking and organizational strategy. And we have to create meaning and uphold values in flatter, more disciplined enterprises,'*

Ohmae concludes. We will, it seems, have to forget the past in order to create the future.

REFERENCE

1. Ohmae, Kenichi, 'Strategy in a world without borders', *Leader to Leader*, Winter 1998.

TRANSNATIONAL CORPORATIONS

THE transnational corporation is a concept developed by Harvard Business School's Christopher Bartlett and London Business School's Sumantra Ghoshal. (Ghoshal joined London Business School in 1994 and was formerly Professor of Business Policy at INSEAD and a visiting professor at MIT's Sloan School.) At the heart of

Ghoshal and Bartlett's work during the late 1980s and early 1990s is the demise of the divisionalized corporation, as exemplified by Alfred Sloan's General Motors.

Their work on globalization and organizational forms came to prominence with the book *Managing Across Borders* (1989), which was one of the boldest and most accurate pronouncements of the arrival of a new era of worldwide competition and truly global organizations.

Bartlett and Ghoshal, unlike others, suggest that new, revitalizing organizational forms can – and are – emerging. Crucial to this is the recognition that multinational corporations from different regions of the world have their own management heritages, each with a distinctive source of competitive advantage.

The first multinational form identified by Bartlett and Ghoshal is the *multinational* or multidomestic firm. Its strength lies in a high degree of local responsiveness. It is a decentralized federation of local firms (such as Unilever or Philips), linked together by a web of personal controls (expatriates from the home country firm who occupy key positions abroad).

The second is the *global* firm, typified by US corporations such as Ford early in the twentieth century and Japanese enterprises such as Matsushita. Its strengths are scale efficiencies and cost advantages. Global-scale facilities, often centralized in the home country, produce standardized products, while overseas operations are considered as delivery pipelines to tap into global market opportunities. There is tight control of strategic decisions, resources, and information by the global hub.

The *international* firm is the third type. Its competitive strength is its ability to transfer knowledge and expertise to overseas environments that are less advanced. It is a co-ordinated federation of local firms, controlled by sophisticated management systems and corporate staffs. The attitude of the parent company tends to be parochial, fostered by the superior know-how at the centre.

Bartlett and Ghoshal argue that global competition is now forcing many of these firms to shift to a fourth model, which they call the *transnational*. This firm has to combine local responsiveness with global efficiency and the ability to transfer know-how – better, cheaper, and faster.

The transnational firm is a network of specialized or differentiated units, with attention paid to managing integrative linkages between local firms as well as with the centre. The subsidiary becomes a distinctive asset rather than simply an arm of the parent company. Manufacturing and technology development are located wherever it makes sense, but there is an explicit focus on leveraging local know-how in order to exploit worldwide opportunities.

Ghoshal and Bartlett conclude that, in the flux of global businesses, traditional solutions are no longer applicable. They point to the difficulties in managing growth through acquisitions and the dangerously high level of diversity in businesses that have acquired companies indiscriminately in the quest for growth. They have also declared obsolete the assumption of independence among different businesses, technologies, and geographic markets that is central to the design of most divisionalized corporations. Such independence, they say, actively works against the prime need: integration and the creation of 'a coherent system for value delivery'.

Today's reality, as described by Ghoshal, is harsh: 'You cannot manage third generation strategies through second generation organizations with first generation managers,' he says.[1] 'Third generation strategies are sophisticated and multidimensional. The real problem lies in managers themselves. Managers are driven by an earlier model. The real challenge is how to develop and maintain managers to operate in the new type of organization.'

While *Managing Across Borders* was concerned with bridging the gap between strategies and organizations, the sequel, *The Individualized Corporation* (1997), moved from the elegance of strategy to the messiness of humanity. In it, Bartlett and Ghoshal examine the factors that are likely to be crucial to the success of the organizational forms of the future.

One of the phenomena they examine is the illusion of success that surrounds some organizations. 'Satisfactory under-performance is a far greater problem than a crisis,' Ghoshal says, pointing to the example of Westinghouse, which is now one-seventh the size of GE in revenue terms. 'Over 20 years, three generations of top management have presided over the massive decline of a top US corporation,' he adds. 'Yet, 80 percent of the time the company was thought to be doing well.'

The explanation he gives for this delusion of grandeur is that few companies have an ability for self-renewal. 'You cannot renew a company without revitalizing its people.' And Ghoshal contends that revitalizing people is fundamentally about changing people. The trouble is that adults don't change their basic attitudes unless they encounter personal tragedy. Things that happen at work rarely make such an impact. If organizations are to revitalize people, they must change the context of what they create around people. 'Companies that succeed are driven by internal ambition. Stock price doesn't drive them. Ambition and values drive them. You have to create tension between reality and aspirations,' he says. 'We intellectualize a lot in management. But if you walk into a factory or a unit, within the first 15 minutes you get a smell of the place.'

As vague and elusive as 'smell' sounds, Ghoshal – no touchy-feely idealist – believes that it can be nurtured. 'Smell can be created and maintained – look at 3M. Ultimately the job of the manager is to get ordinary people to create extraordinary results.'

To do so requires a paradoxical combination of what Ghoshal labels 'stretch' and 'discipline'. These factors do not render obsolete attention to strategy, structure, and systems. Businesses can still be run by strict attention to this blessed corporate trinity. These are, in Ghoshal's eyes, the legacy of the corporate engineer, Alfred Sloan, and the meat and drink of business school programmes. They are necessary, but he adds a warning: 'Sloan created a new management doctrine. Sloan's doctrine has been wonderful but the problem is that it inevitably ends up creating downtown Calcutta in summer.'

REFERENCE

1. International Management Symposium, London Business School, 11 November 1997.

TROMPENAARS, FONS

DUTCH consultant and author Fons Trompenaars (born 1952) takes as his subject the universal one of cultural diversity: How do we think? How do we behave in certain situations? How does that affect the way we manage businesses? And what are the skills essential to managing globally?

'Basic to understanding other cultures is the awareness that culture is a series of rules and methods that a society has evolved to deal with the recurring problems it faces,' says Trompenaars.

> *'They have become so basic that, like breathing, we no longer think about how we approach or resolve them. Every country and every organization faces dilemmas in relationships with people; dilemmas in relationship to time; and dilemmas in relations between people and the natural environment. Culture is the way in which people resolve dilemmas emerging from universal problems.'*

Brought up by a Dutch father and a French mother, Trompenaars studied at top American business school Wharton. He spent three years with Shell, finishing up working on a culture change project. He then worked part time for the company before founding the Center for International Business Studies. He is now developing his research and ideas further through the Trompenaars-Hampden-Turner Group.

Trompenaars' book, *Riding the Waves of Culture*, was published in 1993. Now in his mid-forties, he has a troubled relationship with the American business world, which tends to regard his work as concerned with diversity, racial and sexual, rather than different cultures. Undeterred, Trompenaars remains dismissive of the American (or any other) managerial model – 'It is my belief that you can never understand other cultures. I started wondering if any of the American management techniques I was brainwashed with in eight years of the best business education money could buy would apply in the Netherlands, where I came from, or indeed in the rest of the world.' The answer he provides is simply that they do not.

To the ethereal world of culture, Trompenaars has brought enthusiastic vigour. His books are based around exhaustive and meticulous research. At the heart of this research is a relatively simple proposition: the only positive route forward for individuals, organizations, communities, and societies is through reconciliation. 'Our hypothesis is that those societies that can reconcile better are better at creating wealth. More successful companies are those which reconcile more effectively,' says Trompenaars. The rich don't get even; they get on with each other.

The wide range of fundamental differences in how different cultures perceive the world provides a daunting array of potential pitfalls. 'We need a certain amount of humility and a sense of humour to discover cultures other than our own; a readiness to enter a room in the dark and stumble over unfamiliar furniture until the pain in our shins reminds us of where things are,' says Trompenaars. Most managers, it seems, are more intent on protecting their shins than blundering through darkened rooms.

Homing in on the dramatic success of the East Asian 'tiger economies' is Trompenaars' latest book, *Mastering the Infinite Game* (written with long-term collaborator, Charles Hampden-Turner of Cambridge's Judge Institute of Management Studies). Not surprisingly, Trompenaars and Hampden-Turner identify fundamental differences in Western and Eastern values. The West believes in rule by laws (universalism), while the East believes in unique and exceptional circumstances (particularist); winning is opposed by negotiating consensus; success is good opposes the belief that the good should succeed.

The differences between West and East have been much debated and there is little to disagree about in Trompenaars and Hampden-Turner's list. But that is not their argument. Instead, this remains the same: reconciling different values is key to success – and it is something Eastern cultures have proved marvellously adept at achieving. While the East settles the difference, the West remains obsessed with splitting the difference. This is a cultural imponderable that is enough to make even Fons Trompenaars despair.

– CHAPTER 5 –

Managing responsibly

'For the merchant, even honesty is a financial speculation.' CHARLES BAUDELAIRE

'Just being honest is not enough. The essential ingredient is executive integrity.' PHILIP CROSBY

'Go ahead and be inconsistent. You're not a wind-up toy. If they are consistent in values, which they are, then we have nothing to worry about.' HERB KELLEHER

'The market is a mechanism for sorting the efficient from the inefficient, it is not a substitute for responsibility.' CHARLES HANDY

The new economy as a values shift

DONALD N. SULL AND JONATHAN WEST

The world is undergoing a revolution in values that will have far-reaching implications for business and society, claim Donald Sull and Jonathan West. The fundamental shift is from the bureaucratic to the entrepreneurial ideal, heavily influenced by the internet.

THE debate rages on as to whether we are shifting from the 'old economy' to a 'new economy'. Both sides agree, however, that the transition – real or imagined – is fundamentally technical and economic. A profound transformation *is* under way, but it is concerned with more than technology or economics. What we are witnessing is actually a revolution in values that will have far-reaching implications for business and society. The basic shift is from the bureaucratic to the entrepreneurial ideal.

A shift from bureaucratic to entrepreneurial values does not simply mean that large, bureaucratic organizations are being replaced by small entrepreneurial firms, although that is happening as well. More profoundly, we believe that the ideologies that underlie these two organizational forms are trading places. The ideal of bureaucracy is rapidly losing its claim as a source of economic progress, just as the entrepreneur is emerging as the hero in the ongoing drama of creative destruction. If this analysis is correct, established organizations steeped in bureaucratic values will suffer a decline in their legitimacy and status. This, in turn, will prevent them from attracting and retaining the talented employees they need to fuel future growth.

This shift in values has happened before. History provides several historical examples of comparable shifts including the replacement of Roman civic religion by Christianity, the fall of agrarian community values at the end of the twentieth century, and the collapse of Communism. 'History doesn't repeat itself,' as Mark Twain observed, 'but it rhymes.' By studying historical shifts in societal values, we can discern some underlying similarities in how the process unfolds. Although separated by time and geography, historical values shifts generally follow a similar three-stage process of gradual decay, a tipping point when new values abruptly replace the old, followed by the gelling of the new order.

Bureaucratic dry rot

The first stage in a values shift is a gradual weakening of the grip that a society's dominant values exert over its citizens. This erosion proceeds imperceptibly at first, as people continue to pay lip service in public to values they disregard in private. Roman citizens, for example, continued to worship the civic deities long after they had lost faith in the power of these gods. The dominant values lose their hold when they prove impotent in the face of external threats and fail to meet people's need for meaning. Rome's failure to defeat the Barbarians and the old gods' failure to inspire combined to undermine Rome's civic ideology.

This gradual erosion in social values resembles dry rot in wood, an insidious process in which bacteria eat away at the cellulose that provides wood with its hardness. The decay proceeds imperceptibly as the bacteria advances. In the advanced stages of dry rot, a wooden house can appear perfectly sound to the casual glance, but can collapse at any moment.

Bureaucratic values are now in the late stages of dry rot. Yet a century ago they provided a solid foundation for American economic growth. In his influential book *The Search for Order*, historian Robert H. Wiebe argues that the twin forces of industrialization and urbanization disrupted the established order of America's small farming communities. The bureaucratic ideal of rational processes and clear hierarchical structure provided a powerful antidote to the chaos resulting from the rise of complex organizations on a national scale. In business, the rise of professional management enshrined the bureaucratic ideal in the practices of America's most admired industrial enterprises. The progressive movement, led by Teddy Roosevelt, brought the same enthusiasm for rational management and bureaucratic order to public administration.

While bureaucracy entered the twentieth century as a conquering hero, it exited a spent force. Like the decline of Rome's civic gods, bureaucracy's decay can be traced to both impotence in response to environmental shocks and failure to inspire. Over the past few decades, the failure of large bureaucratic organizations to resist nimble upstarts has been played out in industry after industry, including not only 'new economy' industries, like computers and software, but also such 'old economy' heavyweights as steel, airlines, computers, retailing, and financial services.

The culmination of this trend may have been *Fortune*'s 1992 cover labelling General Motors, Sears and IBM as dinosaurs doomed to extinction. These conspicuous failures led business strategists to shift the focus of competitive advantage from the established incumbent protecting its turf with barriers to entry – think Xerox circa 1970 – to agile attackers like Canon. The wave of layoffs by large companies in the 1980s and 1990s brought this shift home to hundreds of thousands of employees who lost their jobs as large companies floundered.

As large companies surrendered market share, they also lost their hold on the hearts and minds of employees. Through most of the twentieth century, employees enjoyed the status and legitimacy that came from working with established companies, and wore the company pin as a badge of honour. As the well-oiled bureaucracies broke down in the face of new entrants, however, employees felt more acutely the constraints of being a cog in the machine. Employees who came of age in the 1960s felt their individual initiative stifled by the need for endless approvals. They also saw the results of their actions obscured by the company's large size, and politics replace individual performance as the basis for recognition and reward. By breaking the link between individual effort and reward, bureaucracies deprived employees of the opportunity to make a difference and stripped work of its meaning.

The dry rot in dominant values is accompanied by experimentation at the periphery; several sects blossomed amid Rome's decline, for example. The gradual erosion of bureaucracy also encouraged experimentation with alternative values and institutions that rectified the shortcomings of bureaucracies. Leveraged buyouts, for example, attempted to re-establish the link between individual initiative and results by combining ownership and management. Companies like The Body Shop and Ben & Jerry's attempted to restore meaning to work by recasting the corporation as an agent of social activism.

The entrepreneurial ideal provides the starkest contrast to bureaucracy. Many entrepreneurs explicitly define themselves in counterpoint to bureaucrats in big companies – they see themselves as free agents instead of suits. Individual initiative is often lost in a large company, while the link between individual effort and results is transparent in a smaller enterprise. Their very size insulates large bureaucracies from market forces, while product and capital markets quickly reward success and penalize failure in small companies. Exposed to the bracing forces of market competition, results replace politics as the basis for recognition and reward in small companies. While the reality may not match the ideal in every small company, entrepreneurial values present a distinct alternative to bureaucratic values.

The tipping point

The second stage in a values shift is the tipping point, in which a new value set abruptly replaces the old. The term 'tipping point' comes from epidemiology and refers to the moment at which a long-simmering infection overcomes its most serious growth barrier to become an epidemic. Tipping points are, by their very nature, non-linear, because the infection builds strength over time while its obstacles to growth may decline slowly. The reversal of fortune, however, comes abruptly, and with surprising force. A values tipping point can occur with the same abruptness and force as an epidemic; recall how fast Communism fell.

The explosive growth of the internet has triggered a tipping point in which bureaucratic values implode as the entrepreneurial ideal explodes. Many observers have confused the internet with the revolution, but we believe that it is simply a catalyst that attacked established bureaucracies at their weakest point – responding to discontinuities – while dramatically expanding the opportunities for aspiring entrepreneurs. Entrepreneurship of course preceded the current internet frenzy, and bureaucracy will survive it, just as craft work survived the second Industrial Revolution. The internet has, however, fundamentally shifted the balance of legitimacy between bureaucratic and entrepreneurial values.

Established companies acutely feel the symptoms of their fading legitimacy. Large enterprises find it difficult to recruit the best and brightest. The proportion of the Harvard Business School class of 1999 joining start-up companies was double that of the previous year. Says Antonio Borges, former dean of the French school INSEAD: 'Fifty years ago students dreamed of running General Motors; ten years ago they dreamed of working at Goldman Sachs; five years ago it was McKinsey. Now they dream about running their own company.' More than one-third of INSEAD MBAs end up running their own company five to 10 years after graduating, as do two-thirds of Harvard graduates.

Even leading corporations like Walt Disney and McKinsey find it difficult to stem the tide of talented employees leaving to join start-ups. Moreover, many of the employees left behind in large companies feel disheartened. One senior executive in a highly admired corporation recently confided that he removed his business card from his briefcase, so fellow passengers would not view him as a 'loser' because he worked for a large company.

Established companies are not the only institutions feeling the shock of their tipping point. Consider the business press. A host of new magazines, including *Business 2.0, The Industry Standard, Red Herring,* and *Upside,* have sprouted to celebrate the success of recent start-ups, while established journals like *Fortune* and *Business Week* have scrambled to dramatically increase their coverage of small companies. Business schools are also responding to a groundswell of student demand by increasing courses on entrepreneurship and e-commerce. In a particularly symbolic move, the Harvard Business School recently replaced its required course on general management with a class on entrepreneurship.

Institutionalizing the entrepreneurial ideal

The current internet bubble will burst and most of today's start-ups will fail, but the business world will never return to the *status quo ante*. When the smoke clears, we believe that the entrepreneurial values will stand triumphant over the fallen bureaucratic ideal. Existing institutions that recast themselves as entrepreneurial ventures, such as Enron, Cemex, Lucent and GE, will thrive in the new economy. Those companies that cling to their bureaucratic heritage will, like old soldiers, slowly fade away.

A few guidelines for survival in the new world follows:

Make the leap of faith

Our analysis has several implications for managers in traditional companies. The most important, by far, is how they frame the current revolution. While information technology and location in entrepreneurial hot-houses like Silicon Valley or Boston play a critical enabling role, the change is fundamentally about the shift from bureaucratic to entrepreneurial values. The internet has exposed a fault line between the 'old economy' of bureaucracy and a 'new economy' that glorifies the entrepreneurial ethic. This gap will quickly grow to an unbridgeable chasm. Leaders of traditional companies must, therefore, commit to the entrepreneurial values in their organization. The test of whether they succeed is clear: are they able to attract and retain the most desirable employees?

While making the leap of faith is difficult, it is possible, as the experience of GE, Enron, Nokia and Lucent demonstrates.

Go all the way

Committing fully to entrepreneurship will raise fundamental questions about every aspect of a traditional bureaucracy. How can we break up our enterprise into small businesses? How will we co-ordinate the units? How far will we go in providing incentives that match the market? How do we attract and retain people who aren't like us? How do we handle employees who want to leave? How do we spin off businesses? How do we kill projects that aren't panning out? Managers in most companies try to avoid answering or even contemplating these difficult questions, but the key tests of commitment to entrepreneurship will come in how managers answer them.

Don't wait

If our analysis is correct, the need to leap is critical. For many companies it may already be too late. Thus managers must resist the temptation to avoid the leap. Delay can leave your company stranded on the wrong side of the chasm separating the old from the new economy.

RESOURCES

BOOKS

Gibbon, Edward, *The Decline and Fall of the Roman Empire*, Penguin, London, 1952.
Handy, Charles, *Beyond Certainty*, Hutchinson, London, 1995.
Wiebe, Robert H., *The Search for Order: 1877–1920*, Hill and Wang, New York, 1967.

WEB

www.harvard.edu
www.people.hbs.edu/dsull/bio.html
www.people.hbs.edu/jwest/bio.html

Corporate governance

DEAN LEBARON AND ROMESH VAITILINGAM

As Dean LeBaron and Romesh Vaitilingam report, shareholders demand high returns on their equity investments, while executives of public companies typically want a peaceful life with good remuneration and minimal outside intervention. These conflicting interests and how to achieve some kind of alignment between them – to give corporate managers the incentives to act in the best interests of corporate owners – are the central questions of corporate governance. They have become increasingly important as instead of choosing 'exit' – simply selling their holdings in underperforming companies – investors are beginning to exercise their voice – telling management to change their ways.

IN the 1980s, the most powerful external pressure on executives for stock market performance was the threat from corporate raiders, poised to bid for companies with underperforming shares. Latterly, challenges have come more from institutional investors, the activist shareholders who demand long-term value creation from the companies whose shares they own. This activism has been most dramatic in the United States, and has been supported by regulation; for example, the SEC has mandated the reporting of value creation in the proxy statement.

In the UK too, the pressures have shifted from the threat of takeovers to shareholder activism, often around the subject of top managers' pay and its weak relationship to corporate performance. For example, guidelines on remuneration published by the investing institutions' professional bodies (the National Association of Pension Funds and the Association of British Insurers) demand a clearer link between performance and pay. In turn, many UK companies now explicitly target the creation of shareholder value.

Inside corporate governance

The 1970s and 1980s saw the growing dominance of institutional shareholders with an ability and propensity to trade away their unhappiness with the way their assets are employed. Meanwhile, Bob Monks was Assistant Secretary of Labor, the federal official responsible for supervising the public interests of pension funds – exactly the right place to observe the lack of interest of institutional investors in taking part in corporate decision making, effectively enfranchising managements whose stewardship of assets was questionable.

When Monks left public service, he applied this lesson to develop a profitable investment management style resuscitating slack companies. In early 1990 he launched Lens, a fund that takes active equity positions in companies whose management needs shaking up. He appealed to shareholders and directors to function as they were legally charged, to monitor and, as a late resort, remove hard-of-hearing managements who forget that they are employees, not owners. The investment record of Lens has been outstanding, surpassing the S&P 500 every year since 1990.

In 1991, Monks electrified the investing world by running a credible race for director of Sears Roebuck as a unique way of calling attention to that company's failed strategies. Sears changed, as did Eastman Kodak, Westinghouse, American Express, and several other companies in which Monks and Lens have asserted their rights as shareholders. It helps that as a candidate for an activist board seat, Monks is well qualified as a successful businessperson and public leader. He is not a single-issue advocate with nothing else to offer, but a fully skilled manager that any board would be privileged to have as a member.

Lens describes itself as an activist money manager, buying stock in a limited number of companies that meet two investment criteria: they must be underperforming in the light of strong underlying values, and susceptible to increased value through shareholder involvement. Once the fund has established its position, it approaches company management and directors, with the goal of enhancing value for its clients and other shareholders. Creating value requires specialized knowledge, hands-on involvement, and vigilance. It is the fund's activism, coupled with expertise in law, corporate governance, and business, that gives it a measure of control in its investments beyond that available to passive managers.

Physically and intellectually imposing, Bob Monks puts his stamp on any activity in which he engages. A successful investor for over 40 years – the founder of Institutional Shareholder Services, the world's premier proxy advisory firm, and former chairman of the Boston Company, a prominent institutional investor – Monks has an unrivalled understanding of how to lead shareholders in cost-effective initiatives to increase value.

After leading the charge to wake up US shareholders to their stake in corporate affairs, Monks has been taking the message to Europe and Asia in response to the increasing globalization of capital markets. Markets outside the United States are following his lead in examining rules for shareholder participation and giving new energy to their firms. The 1998 strategic alliance between Calpers (the California Public Employees Retirement Scheme) and Hermes (the UK pension fund for British Telecom and the Post Office) is a good example of such international shareholder activism, as is the role of Lens and Hermes in removing the chief executive of the UK's Mirror Group in early 1999.

Like growing numbers of people in the business and investment community, Monks has adopted the new tools of adaptive complexity and computer simulations to demonstrate his points about shareholder activism. His book, *The Emperor's Nightingale*, describes how corporations behave through the stages of their lifecycles, and shows that synergy really does exist – not as a single burst of energy but as a continuous, healthy adaptation to business conditions. He does not condemn corporate managers for their ironclad budgets, rigid forecasts, and attempts to control the uncontrollable. Rather, he provides informed support for the view that business must consist of smaller independent units, which pursue their own aims but collectively achieve what is beyond their individual capability.

Counterpoint

The corporate and investing worlds are typically constituted of interconnected networks of trustees, executives and managers. These create a wide variety of conflicts of interest that can make corporate governance less effective than it should be.

Bob Monks comments:

> *'The question of the ineffectiveness of institutional investors is most important, particularly as it relates to "conflict of interest". Even the best chief executive of a fiduciary organization is not going to be willing to be activist, or to be perceived as activist, because "my customers don't like it". Until the government enforces the fiduciary laws respecting conflicting interests, there has been an attitude of benign neglect in the Anglo-American world. Thus, we have the irony that among institutional investors, only those least qualified by education, training, and outlook are free to be activist.'*

The concept of corporate governance has its roots in the legal structure giving companies unique status with an allocation of powers among owners, managers, customers, and society. But do many advocates of shareholder activism go too far, pushing the interests of shareholders too strongly to the exclusion of other 'stakeholders'? After all, a firm is not just a bunch of shares, but a collection of relationships between its owners, managers, employees, customers, suppliers, and society as a whole. Thinking of the firm as a social institution rather than a capital market vehicle has important implications for corporate governance.

Bob Monks comments: 'I don't think of the firm so much as being "social" as being a question of "power": who has the power to create reality, whose standards will prevail?'

Stock option plans have become increasingly popular among UK and US corporations, as they are generally regarded as effective tools of corporate governance, rewarding executives for enriching their shareholders. But such corporate compensation plans are due for a major overhaul and reform. At present, they are a travesty, and may become a source of litigation and anger on the part of workers and shareholders. Not only has executive pay increased the gap between lower-level workers and senior executives, but these executives have given themselves attractive golden parachutes that pay off handsomely in the event they are let go for incompetence or any other reason.

Furthermore, executive pay is increasingly tied to stock incentives or stock options. On the surface this seems fine, except that if the stock price goes down, options are nearly always rewritten to the lower stock price. This is a compensation scheme under which the executive cannot lose. Compensation by this technique is not typically a deduction in income and does not reduce reported earnings per share, though it should, because it is a regular part of the compensation package. But in the United States, the Business Roundtable has bullied the accounting profession and the US Senate to the extent of creating an accounting practice that does not take the current cost of options into the profit and loss account.

Another concomitant of executive remuneration increasingly tied to stock prices is that companies and investors are accused of short-termism. There is a very simple solution if we want long-term ideas and focus on the part of our companies. Instead of having executives paid with bonuses or stock options related to current results, we could change the timeframe to three to five years' hence. In other words, a chief executive would be paid according to the results of the company three to five years from the time in which the bonus or option was set.

In the event of a sustained market decline, executive compensation could become a critical issue with potentially big payoffs for lawyers: when shareholders lose money in an absolute sense and then find that executive compensation has been high; when options have been ratcheted upwards to be more attractive and adjusted when the stock price goes down, so that it is always a winning strategy for the executive; and when executive compensation includes very large payments for severance. Executive compensation could be the touchstone for the next market decline.

Where next?

Corporate governance is all about the relationship between investors and the companies in which they invest. But what does 'investor relations' really mean? To the practitioner, it means a craft of communication striving to be a profession. To a shareholder receiving its output, it is a necessary way to understand markets and companies. To corporate officials, it is a convenience to fend off the time-consuming quest for information that is often a distraction from running a business. All these views are correct, but they are far from the full story of investor relations today.

An unprecedented 18-year bull market has multiplied all financial service tasks. Abby Joseph Cohen of Goldman Sachs notes that compensation for financial service workers has been the only area of wage inflation in the present business cycle. And many others note that financial assets are the only inflating assets in a deflationary economy. It is reasonable to look at the macro influence of a bull market creating the need for ever more competent and ever more highly paid investor relations people. But that is not the whole story either.

At its base, investor relations is about communication of fact. Usually, it is what is today called 'push' through releases, attractive venues, and targeted sources. Investor meetings and lunches have given way to conference calls and internet group e-mails in turn to global video conferences. Facts are still distilled by lawyers but, curiously, with the most important facts withheld during blackout periods when the most significant developments are taking place.

With computer databases and search capabilities, remarkable things can be done to turn masses of data into information. Most of the innovations have already taken place in the corporate world, especially in comparative retail sales. Now, they are finding their way into finance: for example, screening of the type used at www.fortuneinvestor.com can survey 16,000 securities on 600 variables; and charts of historical activity on almost anything are available at www.bigcharts.com and www.yardeni.com. Hundreds of tools like these are converting the 'push' from investor relations into a 'pull' by users in control of what they want, what they do with it, and the conclusions to be reached.

Investor persuasion is moving to the user through the empowerment of technology. The nub of judgement remains in an elusive corner of agency finance, behavioural sciences, and computation. But each single user has access to machinery to do the chores, which is low cost, readily available, global, and instantaneous. Like Microsoft endorsing the internet, which may ultimately be its downfall, so the alert investor relations person will provide these tools to make the user's job easier and better.

The next steps for investor relations are straightforward:

- Companies, funds, and countries that wish to inform their constituency should maintain and publish FAQs (frequently asked questions), a common practice in industry. All questions, with whatever favourable or unfavourable answer, can be made available on a bulletin board. It is the next step to the ultimate in transparency, when the answers are created automatically regardless of the questions asked.
- Companies should actively trade their own shares with open disclosure of transactions on an instantaneous basis. Companies would reveal their own interplay between business conditions, availability of capital, and their assessment of prospects by their actions.
- In the same vein, insiders would be encouraged to trade with no reservations on when, except that they would have to be identified as an insider.

Technology makes all these possible and investor relations would be advanced, providing the user with live, real, and significant, individually customized information individually customized. It is possible today. But no one has done it.

Bob Monks comments:

'I would add a fourth bullet point to the summary of the next steps for investor relations: as "institutional" ownership approaches the 50

percent level in the OECD world, the question arises repeatedly, quis custodiet ipsos custodes – *who is watching the watchers?*

'I believe that internet technology will allow trustees to communicate with pension beneficiaries, mutual fund operators with the beneficial owners, and union trustees with the membership. The mechanics of communication and consent will need to be worked out over the next 50 years. What is important is to require that there be some requirement on the trustees to take into account the fact that they are acting for others. Modern technology provides a relatively cheap and reliable means for doing this.'

RESOURCES

BOOKS

LeBaron, Dean and Vaitilingam, Romesh, *The Ultimate Investor*: the people and ideas that make modern investment, Capstone, Oxford, 1999.

LeBaron, Dean and Vaitilingam, Romesh (with Pitchford, Marilyn), *The Ultimate Book of Investment Quotations*, Capstone, Oxford, 1999.

Monks, Bob, *The Emperor's Nightingale: Restoring the Integrity of the Corporation*, Perseus Books, 1999.

Monks, Bob and Minow, Nell, *Watching the Watchers: Corporate Governance for the Twenty-First Century*, Blackwell Publishers, 1996.

Monks, Bob and Minow, Nell, *Corporate Governance*, Blackwell Publishers, 1994.

Monks, Bob and Minow, Nell, *Power and Accountability*, HarperBusiness, 1991.

WEB

www.deanlebaron.com – Dean LeBaron's website.

www.ragm.com and www.lens.com – Bob Monks' websites.

www.hitachi.com – an example of a corporate bulletin board.

www.fortuneinvestor.com; www.bigcharts.com; and www.yardeni.com – examples of websites with various historical data and investment management tools.

Corporate values

DES DEARLOVE AND STEPHEN COOMBER

A growing number of companies from the new and old economies have explicit values statements. Des Dearlove and Stephen Coomber consider the reasons for the rise of the values-based organization and assess the effectiveness of values statements as a management tool.

CORPORATE values are in vogue in the management world. Unlike the mealy-mouthed mission statements that many companies foisted on employees in the 1980s and 1990s, the power of values lies in capturing what is authentically believed within a company. New economy companies are embracing them as a way to preserve their distinctive cultures and inspire employees.

Amazon.com, for example, famously has its six core values: customer obsession; ownership; bias for action; frugality; a high hiring bar; and innovation. These it hopes provide the springboard for its vision as 'the world's most customer-centric company. The place where people come to find and discover anything they might want to buy on line'.

They may have the instincts of entrepreneurs but the paradox of the dot-coms is that many profess the aspirations of social revolutionaries. They wear their values on their sleeves. Companies like Amazon claim to offer a new sense of meaning and purpose to working life. They recognize that the new generation of workers want more than just a pay cheque at the end of the month. Since the early days, Amazon has had the stated aim of revolutionizing business. Its values are part of the appeal. 'It's like the Cultural Revolution meets Sam Walton. It's dotcommunism,' *Time* magazine observed recently.

One of the latest to proclaim the importance of values is David Pottruck the president and co-CEO of the brokerage firm Charles Schwab. Widely regarded as a leader in online share dealing services, Schwab has embraced the internet with remarkable zeal – and, more unusually for a traditional business, a great deal of success. In *Clicks and Mortar*, the book Pottruck co-wrote with Schwab colleague Terry Pearce, he outlines the importance of values in the 'passion-driven growth' of the firm. Recalling the decision to write down the Schwab values, he says:

> *'Until then, it hadn't dawned on us that the firm had gotten big enough that we needed to communicate the fundamentals of the culture explicitly. In a way it was like the drafting of the Declaration of Independence. It put in writing what we understood to be the truths of our company, truths that we had been operating with for a number of years, but that could now stand as a beacon to guide our actions not just as a company but as individuals within that company.'*

The entire management team worked on the project. Eventually five core values were agreed: fairness, empathy, teamwork, responsiveness, and constantly striving to be worthy of customers' trust. 'We set out to etch the vision and values we believed to be cultural DNA into the mind and heart of every Schwab employee,' Pottruck says.

Why are values coming to the fore now?

So why the sudden outbreak of values? Diane Newell is managing director for Europe at Blessing/White, a consultancy that specializes in helping companies communicate their values. Values, Newell says, are in tune with the new business environment, where passion and energy are seen as a source of competitive advantage.

> *'Because of the influence of new technology – not just the internet – we're all having to reinvent the rules of business. It's not unique to the dot-com world, but because they are passion-driven from the start, the issue of culture and values is more explicit for them at the moment. Dot-coms also have to deal with very rapid growth. That sort of growth precludes the use of rules and procedures.*

'Most are started by one or two people, so the values that drive the business are very personal to them. That's infectious for the people who join. But rapid growth means that you no longer share a coffee with everyone. They quickly realise that they can't instil the passion, the spirit and the values on a one-to-one basis anymore. At that point, it becomes really important to articulate their values and communicate them to their people.'

Values are also seen as a way to attract bright people to small growing businesses. Take de Baer Corporate Clothing, for example. A sort of designer label for companies, de Baer provides bespoke corporate clothing. Founded by chief executive Jacqueline de Baer, the company designs and manufactures natty staff uniforms which interpret the brands of the likes of Marriott Hotels, Boots Opticians and the Odeon Cinema in Leicester Square.

As befits its stylish products, de Baer sees itself as an international company with personality. It aims to create a culture that will attract young talent looking for an informal and fun environment to work in. The company's values include fun, integrity, openness and learning.

'For us it's been incredibly important,' says Jacqueline de Baer.

'If you start a company then the company takes on a lot of your personality. As it gets bigger it's very important to identify the personality of the company. It might still be 75 percent the personality of the founder but there may be other elements. Defining the values is very powerful. The values can guide you in all sorts of ways, especially in speeding up decision making. We are very clear on what we are trying to do.'

The company also uses values to guide recruitment decisions. Every new person to join at management level has a telephone interview to discuss their values before being asked to the first formal interview. At other levels within the organization, questions aimed at identifying values are incorporated into the first interview. 'It's more than just empowering decision making. I recruit against the values,' says Jacqueline de Baer.

Why take values seriously?

Values may be popular with up-and-coming companies, but they are not a new idea. The fact is that they have been a staple of successful organizations for decades. Well-managed companies have always found it useful to spell out what they stand for. The fact is that a set of core values underpins many of the most famous and long-lived companies.

General Electric, one of the outstanding old economy success stories of recent times, subscribes to a set of core values. Among them are 'setting stretch goals', and 'simplicity'. Other long-lived companies such as Disney, Sony and Merck also subscribe to an explicitly stated set of values, or guiding principles.

Indeed, it would be much easier to dismiss the whole idea of values if they weren't found in such prominent and successful organizations. Some of these companies go to remarkable lengths to preserve their values:

- Merrill Lynch has its five 'Principles' engraved on plaques lining the corridors of its world headquarters.
- Johnson & Johnson has its values written down in a book – the 'Credo' – which dates back to the founding fathers of the company.
- Cadbury Schweppes has set out the company's values in a document called the 'Character of the Company'.
- Hewlett-Packard has the H-P Way, which employees write out by hand and pin up next to the picture of their family.

These companies place their values above profit maximization. Yet research suggests that they outperform companies that put profits first, providing a better return to shareholders over time. The companies identified by James C. Collins and Jerry I. Porras in *Built to Last*, for example, had outperformed the general stock market by a factor of 12 since 1925. All were values-driven businesses.

To separate the impact of values from other aspects of company performance, however, is almost impossible. The best companies don't even try. Many of the CEOs we spoke to seemed unworried by their inability to measure the impact. 'You can feel it,' one CEO told us. CEOs are driven by bottom-line results, not vague concepts. Quantifying cause and effect goes with the job. So why do a growing number of CEOs seem prepared to accept the case for values on faith?

Towards a new psychological contract

Values seem to offer a handle on changes taking place to the relationship between individuals and organizations and the need to create a new framework for the future based on mutual self interest – what Charles Handy has described as 'proper selfishness'.

In recent years a number of developments – including the move to non-hierarchical corporate structures, increased mobility and the end of the jobs for life culture – have undermined the traditional organizational framework, and the relationship between employer and employee. The old psychological contract between employee and employer – whereby workers gave their loyalty and commitment in return for job security – has been swept away. In its place, companies must find new ways to establish a bond with employees.

There is a growing support for the idea that values have an important role to play in this. They can help build bridges between employees and company. In their book *The Leadership Challenge*, Barry Posner and Jim Kouzes assert, that shared values:

- Foster strong feelings of personal effectiveness.
- Promote high levels of company loyalty.
- Facilitate consensus about key organizational goals.
- Encourage ethical behaviour.
- Promote strong norms about working hard and caring.
- Reduce levels of job stress and tension.
- Foster pride in the company.
- Facilitate understanding about job expectations.
- Foster teamwork and *esprit de corps*.

Even national governments are taking the issue seriously: the Norwegian government has announced an initiative to distil the country's core values. We examined a number of claims made about values. In particular that they:

- Engender loyalty among employees. As the balance of power begins to shift in favour of the individual knowledge worker, a crucial issue is how to recruit, retain and engage the very best staff. Could values provide a basis for a new psychological contract to replace job security?
- Provide a framework to motivate employees and devolve responsibility for decision making. Many companies have tried unsuccessfully to introduce 'empowerment'. Could values help support an empowered workforce?
- Offer fixed points of reference in a rapidly changing world, providing a degree of stability and continuity during periods of upheaval or times of corporate crisis. Moreover, it was suggested by some that 'aspirational values' can support the actual process of change. Given that organizational change continues to figure prominently on many companies' agendas, and will do for the foreseeable future, what role can values play?

What are values?

First it is necessary to understand what values are. Where do they come from? How do the individual and the company benefit from understanding, articulating and living their values? These are key questions in beginning to understand the issue of values and their relevance in the workplace.

Different companies have different names for their core values. Values, beliefs, principles, 'essential and enduring tenets' – call them what you will – the point is not by what name they are known but what they are understood to mean. Some confusion results from imprecise use of these terms. One of the most authoritative definitions, in our view, is that of Collins and Porras. Core values, they say, are: 'The organization's essential and enduring tenets – a small set of guiding principles; not to be confused with specific cultural or operating practices; not to be compromised for financial gain or short term expediency.'

Organizational goals (specific targets that help to realize a vision) are not values; neither are mission or purpose (the fundamental reason for existence); nor should values be confused with vision (a picture of the intended future). All these have their place in a successful company. Values, however, it could be argued, are the precursor, the foundation on which the others are built.

Values, then, run deep. They are timeless guiding principles that drive the way the company operates – everything it does – at a level that transcends tactical or even strategic objectives. The key which unlocks the power of values is interpretation. This is the missing link between the theory and the effective practice. The issue we explore here is the practical difference they make to a company.

Many of those we spoke to – including a number of CEOs – pointed to clear business benefits, even though they were unable to quantify the effect. Evidence does exist, however, to support this assertion. A four-year study of between nine and 10 firms in each of 20 industries, carried out by Professor John Kotter of Harvard Business School, and his colleague John Heskett, found that firms with a strong culture based on a foundation of shared values, outperformed the other firms in the study by a huge margin:

- Their revenue grew more than four times faster.
- Their rate of job creation was seven times higher.
- Their stock price grew 12 times faster.
- Their profit performance was 750 percent higher.

Yet, until very recently values have been largely ignored in management literature. We believe that this is because they are considered the softest of 'soft' issues. The very idea that abstract notions such as honesty and respect for people might make a fundamental difference to the business is one that was out of step with traditional management disciplines. Values can be perceived by businesspeople and business commentators alike as abstract notions, muddying the corporate waters and obscuring the principal *raison d'être* – making a profit.

There is, too, a sense that companies should not involve themselves in such sensitive issues. Some people are concerned that values may cross the line between professional and private lives and may be used as a form of brain washing to exploit employees. Real as these concerns may be, they result from a misunderstanding. Values, as we describe them here, are primarily concerned with what happens in the workplace. We would never suggest that companies should attempt to dictate the spiritual life or beliefs of private citizens.

Where do values come from?

The identification of an organization's core values is a task not to be undertaken lightly. If values are to be effective, this cannot be a superficial exercise. They cannot be plucked from the air. The key is to capture what is 'authentically believed', not what other companies select as their values or what the outside world thinks should be the values. Charles Handy notes in *The Hungry Spirit*: 'It is inadequate to borrow beliefs. We have to work them out for ourselves'. If a company comes under pressure for whatever reason, its guiding principles will only help if they are 'true' for that company.

Usually few in number – typically between three and 10 – values are the essence of the company's identity, the corporate DNA. The values shout from the roof-tops 'this is what our company passionately believes in'.

Despite their current popularity, it is clear that values are no quick fix. Defining a set of principles is just the beginning. To benefit, an organization has to live and breathe its values; it is necessary to make the connection between what the employee and the organization are trying to achieve. That requires the translation of the organization's values into something individuals can put into practice during their everyday working lives.

Table 1 Values

Organization	Values
Disney	Imagination and dreams; no cynicism; the promulgation of wholesomeness American values.
Cadbury-Schweppes	Competitive ability; quality; clear objectives; simplicity; openness; responsibility to stakeholders.
Merrill Lynch	Client focus; respect for the individual; teamwork; responsible citizenship; integrity.
Merck	Corporate social responsibility; unequivocal excellence in all aspects of the company; science-based innovation; honesty and integrity; profit, but profit from work that benefits humanity.
Sony	Elevation of the Japanese national culture and status; being a pioneer – not following others, but doing the impossible; respect and encouragement of individual ability and creativity.
IKEA	Innovation; humbleness; simplicity; looking after the interest of the majority; will power.
Reuters	Accuracy; independence; accountability and openness; speed, innovation; customer focus.
US army	Loyalty; duty; respect; selfless-service; honour; integrity; personal courage.

Successful values-driven businesses do not try to achieve an exact match between organizational and individual values. 'Values clones' is not the aim; rather, it is to use values to establish common ground as a platform to support a more effective organizational culture.

We believe that companies can improve their performance, by:

- Distilling their core values (core values cannot be created but must be 'discovered'), and communicating them to employees.
- Strengthening the link between the values and aspirations of individuals and those of the organization, using mutual interest to engage the talents and commitment of workers.
- Using values as the cultural glue to 'connect' employees and support a social community based on shared goals.

1

Linking organizational and individual aspirations

To understand the impact of values, let us consider them first from the perspective of the organization, and then from the perspective of the individual. For the organization, values can support a number of goals – but only if staff can translate them into something meaningful to them as individuals. For example, companies can use values to support:

- Vision/strategy.
- Cultural continuity – 'organizational glue'.
- Empowerment.
- Community.
- Commitment.
- Corporate transformation.
- Crisis management.

From the individual's perspective, organizational values – if translated into action – offer a route to:

- Self-fulfillment.
- Identity.
- Decision-making guidelines and frame of reference.
- A sense of belonging.
- Career development in step with their aspirations.
- Continuity in the face of change.
- A moral compass to cope with any eventuality.

These two sets of benefits overlap. So, for example, the organizational goal of building strong culture fits with the individual's quest for identity; the need to create a sense of community fits with the individual's desire for a sense of belonging. As management commentator Charles Handy has observed: 'Work has always been a major strand in people's self-description, and therefore a major component in their identity.'

Companies therefore must seek to find a way of catering for the needs of the individual within the workplace. It is not about creating an exact match between organizational and individual values. Rather, it is about finding common ground, and translating organizational values into actionable behaviour that individuals can live in their everyday working lives.

Our own research suggests that the stronger the bridge between the organizational and individual values, the more direct the link with business performance. A common mistake, however, is to look at corporate values in isolation from individual values. The two must be linked. The business case resides in the ability to harness corporate and individual aspirations. The companies that use values most effectively invest the time and effort to help employees identify the common ground.

As noted earlier, it is difficult – if not impossible – to prove a direct link, but values-driven businesses appear to enjoy important advantages over other organizations in a number of areas, including:

- Staff recruitment, development and retention.
- Motivation, and achieving alignment between organizational and individual goals.
- Change management.
- Crisis management.

Recruitment and retention

Recruiting and retaining the best people has always been a vital issue for successful companies. The current talent shortages experienced by many companies suggest that it will be even more critical in future. As the competition for skills increases, values-driven businesses appear to have an edge.

'When it comes to attracting, keeping, and making teams out of talented people, money alone won't do it,' observes Xerox PARC's John Seely Brown. 'Talented people want to be part of something that they can believe in, something that confers meaning on their work and their lives.'

Values have two critical roles: a company that articulates its values enables potential recruits to apply a degree of self-selection. Values also provide a framework to match individual career goals with the organization's objectives.

Values represent the bedrock of an organization's culture. In his book *The Living Company* Arie de Geus talks about 'introception', the awareness of one's own position relative to others, within an organization – how 'the values of the company coexist with the values of individuals within the corporation – and every member is aware of this co-existence'.

> *'There is no ambiguity about who belongs and who does not...,' he says 'the company's members know who is prepared to live with the company's set of values. Whoever cannot live with those values, cannot or should not be a member....Members must share the set of institutional values at the core of the company persona.'*

With reduced job security, individuals are more discerning about which organizations they want to work for. Organizations with strong 'employer brands' are increasingly attractive. A company with a clear set of values offers employees a chance to work with the company for something they both believe in. Explicit reference to values such as 'respect for the individual' provides a signal about working conditions and the opportunities for training and development.

'Maximum contribution and maximum satisfaction is the goal,' says Steve Daniels, HR director at Ulster Bank, which has recently been through a major values initiative.

> *'In the new paradigm you can't base the relationship on false premises. We can't offer a job for life, but we can offer skills for life. The question that organizations have got to start having an answer for is: "What's in it for me?" How can we structure jobs and career structures around their values, while we're still making profits?'*

Values offer a foundation upon which loyalty and trust can be built. If employees identify with the values of a company they are more inclined to trust the organization – and to give their active commitment to its objectives. Frederick Reichfield has tried to calculate the 'loyalty effect' on performance. He estimates that disloyalty from stakeholders – employers, shareholders, staff and customers – can cut performance and productivity by 50 percent.

Engaging staff commitment

A highly motivated workforce, it is widely acknowledged, can make the difference between success and failure. Human capital, London Business School's Professor Sumantra Ghoshal has noted, is now the primary source of sustainable competitive advantage. Companies will have to find ways to mobilize the active commitment – rather than passive acceptance – of their people.

Charles Handy says: 'A match of corporate and individual souls releases those "E" factors (energy, enthusiasm, effort, excitement, excellence, etc.). Without that match, work and life are dull.' Dull will not be acceptable to workers in the future, in Handy's view. They are individuals and expect to be treated as such.

The match does not have to be exact. Indeed, our findings suggest that a precise fit between individual and organizational 'souls' – or even values – is neither feasible nor desirable. But an organization which links strategic and operational objectives to explicit values – and translates that link to the everyday work of employees – will enjoy greater commitment.

For example, a company that has a goal of improving delivery times, or customer service standards can appeal to a core value – such as 'excellent customer service'. If individual workers buy into the core value, they are more likely to play an active role in achieving that goal.

But there is another important aspect to this issue. Much of the last decade has been spent trying to create empowered workforces. There is ample evidence to indicate many empowerment initiatives have failed. A major factor, we suggest, is because management hierarchies have been removed for the sake of expediency without providing a meaningful framework for individual decision making. Values may fill this void. They offer a compass: always pointing true North.

'We had tried other things. We'd got as far as a mission statement, top-down, which we stuck on the wall. And even had made into laminated cards,' observes Steve Daniels, of Ulster Bank. 'But we had not engaged with the individual. The question we hadn't addressed is: what's in it for me? That's the critical question.'

Adds John Pocock, CEO of the UK IT consultancy Druid Consulting, 'If you've got people who are excited by the company values – and you weed out people who aren't – you get people who are highly motivated to work in the company style. That gives you business momentum.'

A decision-making framework

The companies we spoke to also confirmed that empowerment is a key benefit of introducing explicit values statements. A number of comments from interviewees support the notion that values can create a framework for discretionary decision making.

'Every day most individuals are faced with challenges and problems,' says Karrin Nicol, global HR director, sales and marketing, SGI (Silicon Graphics) which has recently introduced a major values programme.

> *'The values and expected behaviours we have articulated for each value can be a tremendous help in helping an individual sort through these issues. They can help guide decision making and I think can make the individual more independent in solving problems.*
>
> *'It is a way to get 10,000 employees around the world focused on the same values and behaviours. People outside the headquarters especially want to feel a connection to the main part of the company and I believe stating the values and constantly referring to them in everyday situations helps the organization make that connection.'*

Adds John Duncan, director of organizational development and training at the Texas-based oil exploration company Apache Corporation:

'In today's society, people are much more comfortable working for a company that has values. Those values help employees make decisions. They provide them with the context to make good decisions.'

'I know a lot of CEOs are reluctant to give up authority. But with values in place they are not giving up authority, they are ensuring that the appropriate authority is exercised throughout the company no matter how far away from the centre. With a values statement, the CEO can rest assured that other people will make the right decision, too.'

Values can also help in the boardroom. Notes John Pocock of Druid:

'The values give the framework. With the framework in place, we can drive the business forward without having to worry about the direction. It actually helps with the decision making. For example, we were wondering whether we should set up a company training centre. The answer is yes, because teamwork is one of our values.'

Managing change

As the globalization of markets and impact of new technology continue, there is one point on which all business people agree – the pace of change is accelerating. Change management is becoming a critical competence. Change places stress on an organization.

The challenge for organizations is making the successful transition from one structure to another, from one method of management to another, from one culture to another – without losing sight of what made the company successful in the first place. Change, however, often creates fear, resistance and other unconstructive behaviour.

The danger is that when the organization is placed under stress the values may be the first thing to go out of the window. As MIT's Peter Senge has noted: 'The more stress we put on our organizations the more their tendency will be to revert to their most primitive behaviours.'

Common issues for companies experiencing rapid change are:

- Lack of continuity – employees often feel disoriented, there is nothing solid to hang on to.

- Resistance driven by fear.
- Culture conflict. Companies that acquire or merge with others with a very different culture.
- Lack of clarity about what the organization is trying to achieve and what it means for them as individuals.

As a result, organizations undergoing change are in danger of losing the commitment of employees along the way. Values can support change management in two ways, by:

- Providing fixed points when all else appears to be changing.
- Creating organizational aspirations that employees are inspired to attain.

The work of late Milton Rokeach, a leading expert on human values, supports this view. He observed that values fall into two categories – 'means values' and 'ends values'. One interpretation of this is that 'ends values' are values that we aspire to, while means values are the standards by which we measure ourselves.

In the organizational context, ends values can be used as the catalyst to provoke change, and inspire new behaviours – what we want to be like. Means values, provide continuity and reassurance for employees. They invoke the best of the existing culture.

Organizational crisis

There is another special role for values. A clearly articulated set of values appears to offer a touchstone at difficult points in the life of an organization.

A number of examples indicate that values can act as a guide for companies in times of crisis, helping them preserve their identity and integrity *in extremis*. Some of these are well documented, although they have not always been viewed through the lens of values. An example of values under pressure is the Tylenol murders.

The Tylenol crisis started in the autumn of 1981 with the news that seven people had met mysterious deaths on Chicago's West Side. The deaths were soon linked to the analgesic Extra-Strength

Tylenol. It appeared that some Tylenol capsules had been laced with cyanide, 65 milligrams as it turned out, 10,000 times more than the amount needed to kill a human.

From the very start Johnson & Johnson put people's safety before profits. The company told consumers not to use the product, ceased production, pulled advertising and recalled all Tylenol capsules. Recalling the product meant removing more than 30 million bottles of Tylenol from the shelves; more than $100 million worth.

What made Johnson & Johnson decide on this course of action? The answer was revealed in an article published by the *New Jersey Bell Journal* and written by Lawrence G. Foster in 1983. Foster, Corporate Vice President of Johnson & Johnson at the time of the poisonings, explained how the senior management turned to the company's values, enshrined in a document called the *Credo*, to help guide them through the crisis.

'It was the *Credo* that prompted the decisions that enabled us to make the right early decisions that eventually led to the comeback phase,' observed David R. Clare, president of Johnson & Johnson at the time.

Written in the 1940s by Robert Wood Johnson, the company's long-standing leader, '*Our Credo*' set out the company's responsibilities to its stakeholders – to 'consumers and medical professionals using its products, employees, the communities where its people work and live, and its stockholders'.

Johnson believed that a company should have social responsibilities and that these should come before profit. If Johnson & Johnson stayed true to its *Credo* then the profits would follow. He was right. Despite the Tylenol murders incident Tylenol is still one of Johnson & Johnson's most successful products. Other companies might have dealt with the crisis differently.

What the organization does when faced with a crisis is the acid test of the values-driven business. On 22 February 1999, Levi-Strauss announced that it was to close 11 of its owned and operated factories, making 5,900 employees redundant, on top of 7,400 in 1998. CEO Robert Haas, is on record as saying: 'A company's values – what it stands for, what its people believe in – are crucial to its competitive success. Indeed values drive the business.' For a company which claims to be values-driven, these are clearly tough times. How do you square massive redundancies with being a values-driven company?

The fact is that any company which claims to be values-driven is open to criticism in such circumstances, and Levi's is no exception. A critical article in *Fortune* in April 1999, declared: 'Levi-Strauss is a failed utopian management experiment.' A measure of its commitment to values is how a company deals with a crisis.

Says Alan Christie, director of public affairs:

> *'When business circumstances compelled us to close facilities, a decision arrived at only after all alternatives had been explored, the severance packages we provided to our employees and their communities were recognized to be well above industry norms. These are behaviours consistent with our commitment to "responsible commercial success". Like all businesses, we must, on occasion, make tough decisions. Our values don't prevent us making those decisions, but they do help us to make them in the right way.'*

Management legacy

The notion of organizational legacy is one which we developed in the course of our research. As economic conditions change with the passage of time there is often pressure within companies to deviate from the values, drop them altogether, or take on new ones. The question that then has to be answered is can values change or be replaced, or are they sacrosanct?

Opinion varies on this point. 'Our basic principles have endured intact since our founders conceived them,' said John Young, former CEO of Hewlett-Packard in 1992. 'We distinguish between core values and practices; core values don't change, but the practices might. We've also remained clear that profit – as important as it is – is not why the Hewlett-Packard company exists; it exists for more fundamental reasons.'

Writing in *Fortune* magazine, Thomas A. Stewart draws a different conclusion: 'Over time self-interest distorts corporate values... To bring them back, top management must constantly reiterate, refresh, reinterpret and rename.'

'Many of our core values – integrity, openness, quality, having global brains – cannot change if we are to remain successful,' says GE spokesman Bruce Bunch. 'But our value of "seeing change as opportunity" leads me to suspect our values could change in other areas as times, technologies and opportunities change.'

Equally important is the issue of review. Should values be dropped once they have served their purpose or should they be valid for all time? If it is accepted that values are sacred, are they open to periodic reinterpretation?

In any long-lived company, we suggest, generations of CEOs will preside over the 'corporate values', inheriting them from their predecessor, passing them on to their successor. In *The Living Company* Arie de Geus, writes about the managers of long-lived companies: 'They succeeded through the generational flow of members and considered themselves stewards of the longstanding enterprise. Each management generation was only a link in a long chain.'

So it is with values. Stewardship is an idea that is increasingly relevant to business. How successive leaders deal with this 'corporate legacy', however, is rarely discussed. In a sense they act as custodians of the values conserving them on behalf and for benefit of the company. If the original sense of the values has been lost, if the values have evolved in the wrong direction it will be the top team's role to redefine and reinterpret the values so that they are relevant.

The issue of corporate legacy, we believe, is an area that is ripe for further research. How do senior managers view their relationship with the 'corporate values'? Do they recognize a responsibility as custodians of those values?

At one of our case study companies, Apache Corporation, the HR director made specific reference to the notion of legacy. Asked how a hard-bitten oil company got involved with values in the first place, John Duncan explained:

> *'It came from the chairman. He's 76 years old. He's starting to think about his legacy; what he hopes to leave behind for the company. He read* Built to Last *and it crystallised his thinking. He knows he won't be around for*

ever, but he views this company as one that should be built to last. The book was the catalyst. He decided that we needed to identify our core values. That is the best way to safeguard the company in the long-run.'

Cadbury-Schweppes can trace its history back to the 1800s when John Cadbury first started selling tea and coffee in Birmingham, England. In 1976 Sir Adrian Cadbury, then chairman, took steps to ensure that the Cadbury values would be permanently enshrined after the merger with the beverage company Schweppes. He also took the opportunity to restate the Cadbury values in a modern context.

The Cadbury values were printed in a document, *The Character of the Company*. They include a commitment to: competitive ability, quality, clear objectives, simplicity, openness and responsibility to stakeholders. As Kevin Hayes, managing director of Cadbury's Asia Pacific operation, observed: 'Values don't lose their power. They are handed down in an almost legendary way from one generation of managers to the next.'

Alignment/congruence

Alignment holds the key to the values-driven business. For values to have a significant impact there *must* be a degree of alignment between the values of the company and employees.

As GE's Bruce Bunch puts it: 'Companies must pay attention to the values employees have, just as employees need to be aware of their company's values. Over time, each can change, but if there is not a high degree of congruence in the end, neither party will be happy, and the relationship will not be successful.'

There are a number of dimensions to the alignment issue. At one level it is about how our working lives align with the other parts of our lives. But it is also to do with how employees behave at work. As Thomas A. Stewart observes: 'If you want [employees] to do as the company thinks best, then you must hope that they have an inner gyroscope, aligned with the corporate compass.'

It is not necessary for the workforce to buy into the entire set of values a company has espoused. This is an important point. In research conducted by Brian P. Hall (President of Values Technology) and the Maltese sociologist the Revd Canon Benjamin Tonna, 125 different values were found to be the basis for all human behaviour. Each individual's behaviour, however, was based on approximately 15 values.

The significance of this is that it will be extremely unlikely that the company and its employees will hold the same 15 or so values. Would an exact match between company and employees even be desirable?

Companies need diversity. If all the pieces of the corporate puzzle were the same it would make a very poor picture. Values-clones are not the aim.

A company that does not combine its own goals and vision with its employees is like a taxi that sets off without its passengers. It's a situation where no one wins. The taxi fails to carry out its business productively. The passengers fail to reach their destination. Values can help build a bridge between a company and make sure that both passengers and taxi arrive at a mutually satisfying destination.

Research by Barrie Posner and Warren Schmidt found that employees who had the greatest clarity about *both* personal and organizational values had the highest degree of commitment to the organization. Those individuals that were unclear about their own and the organization's values had low commitment and were the most alienated from their work (see Figure 1).

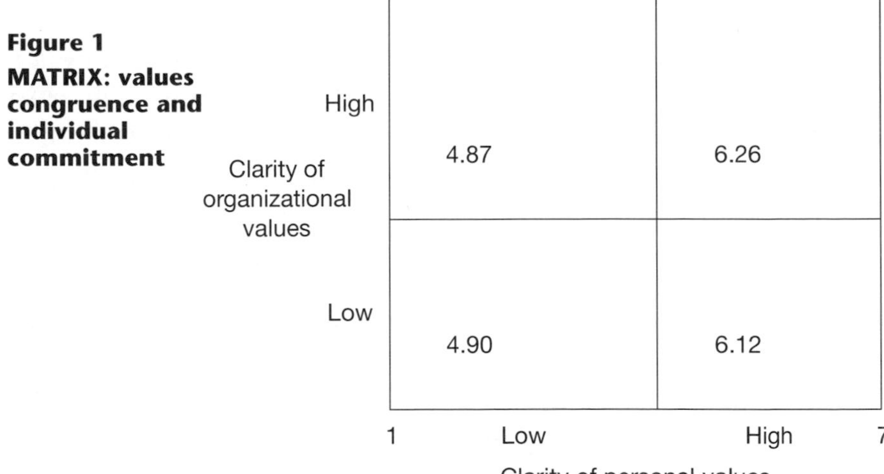

Figure 1
MATRIX: values congruence and individual commitment

The cells represent the degree of clarity about personal and organizational values. The numbers in the cells represent the extent of individuals' commitment to their organization on a scale of 1 to 7, with 1 being low and 7 being high.[1]

RoseAnn Stevenson, an HR manager at Boeing, analyzed values statements from 77 different companies. She found 19 commonly identified values. Although no one value appeared on all 77, the most commonly mentioned were: integrity; involvement; achievement; quality; creativity/innovation; respect; learning; fairness; and customer service.

Despite finding 19 common values, she observed little agreement on the meaning of these values. For the value of integrity, there were no fewer than 185 different interpretations. It is the interpretation – and most particularly the translation of values into individual actions or behaviours that is the critical element. Companies that miss out this stage will fail to get the benefits.

Living the values

It is not enough for senior management to simply pay lip service to the organization's values. To obtain the benefits they must live them every day.

Anyone can pluck some values out of the air, write them down and pin them on the wall – some companies have done just this. The hard bit is living those values and standing by them through thick and thin. This is why companies should be absolutely clear that the values they articulate are truly the ones they believe in.

Part of the problem is the 'credibility gap'. It is no use hanging the chosen cardinal values in the hallways of corporate HQ when the company acts in a way that shows it pays no attention to them. Thomas A. Stewart says: 'There's a technical term for values that look good on the wall but don't add value to the business. The term is "bullshit" and even an MBA can smell it.'

Jack Welch carries a laminated card in his pocket bearing the GE values. Failure to live to those values is grounds for dismissal. At one meeting Welch surprised his audience saying: 'Look around you: there are five fewer officers here than there were last year. One was fired for the numbers, four were fired for (lack of) values.'

So how do companies get the full benefit from their 'core values'? One thing that companies can do is ensure that they practise the values that they preach. This comes not just through stating what the corporate values are. Nor even does it necessarily follow from implementing systems that reinforce the values; although this may help. The real test is how a company reacts in situations when following the values conflicts with other, some would say essential, aspects of corporate life.

For Merck's 100th anniversary the company published a book entitled: *Values and Visions: a Merck Century*. As the following example shows, the company also provides one of the best examples of a company living its values. Mectizan was a drug designed to combat Onchocerciasis – known as 'river blindness'. River blindness is caused when a water borne parasitic worm enters the body and making its way through the body ends up in the eyes where it causes irreparable damage leading to blindness. This disease is particularly prevalent in third world countries afflicting over a million people.

Merck recognized that while this was potentially a large market, it was not a wealthy one, with the majority of end users unable to afford the product. However, the company pressed on with the drugs development, and production, hoping that government agencies, or other bodies, would step forward to buy the product. In the event none did. What did Merck do? It gave the drug away, free to all who needed it. It also helped distribute the product ensuring it reached those who needed it.

When asked why Merck did what they did, the CFO replied that not to have done so, could have demoralized scientists who worked for a company expressly in the business of 'preserving and improving human life'.

People like us

Some people see values as a soft issue. They are tempted to dismiss it along with discredited corporate gestures that includes mission statements, vision statements and the like. Poorly executed values are likely to be equally ineffective. However, those companies which have already committed to values and make them work do not regard them as window dressing – quite the reverse, in fact.

That does not mean that they can measure the effects; it simply means that they recognize the impact. As GE's Bruce Bunch explains:

> *'Our values are a roadmap to how we want to succeed. That seems quite practical and not at all soft or fuzzy. Many of them – setting stretch goals, and using speed for competitive advantage – have a clear and direct impact on our success in the marketplace. But being anti-bureaucracy and complexity, we have never attempted to measure how many cents per share each value contributes to the bottom line.'*

So much for those who have already made the leap of faith. But how can values help other companies succeed in the twenty-first century? With the dismantling of the old relationship framework of hierarchy and job security, organizations that do not provide a new basis for the relationship will find it increasingly difficult to secure the commitment of their employees. Values, potentially, offer a sustainable alternative.

Values-driven businesses would seem to have important advantages in a number of areas that will become increasingly important in the next few years. In particular, values can help support:

- Recruitment and retention.
- Motivation and empowerment.
- Identity.
- Alignment.

At the same time, values-driven businesses may be better able to manage:

- Organizational change.
- Crisis management.
- Corporate longevity.

The idea is not without its critics, however. Over the years, advocates of corporate values have encountered their fair share of cynicism. Some commentators and journalists dismiss the idea as yet another example of hollow management rhetoric – which, in some cases, it is. At the other extreme is a persistent lobby that lambastes companies for over stepping the line between work and the personal lives of employees. Corporate values, these critics say, are a form of corporate brainwashing.

'It is an important issue,' says Blessing/White's Diane Newell. 'There used to be a relationship between organizations and individuals where you did what you had to do and then went home to get on with your life. You left your private life at the door. Some people were very comfortable with that. It didn't demand that you were deeply committed to the company or cared about the business. The trouble is that if those companies are competing with companies where people do care, then they may lose out.

'The idea that we need to engage people's spirit, passion and energy is OK. But the idea that it has to be for life is potentially dangerous – that would be turning companies into cults. Commitment has to be voluntary. The company cannot demand employees sign up to it like a cult or religion. Undying loyalty cannot be part of the deal. It has to be an adult to adult relationship.'

It is no panacea, or quick fix. As Ulster Bank's Steve Daniels observes:

'Once you jump off the cliff with values, if you aren't really committed to them you can do more damage than good. You've got to stay with it through the good times and the bad times. You've got to be committed. Once you open the Pandora's box, you can't just expect to close it again.'

REFERENCE

1. Posner, B.Z. and Schmidt, W.H., 'Values Congruence and differences between the interplay of personal and organizational value system', *Journal of Business Ethics*, 12, 1993, 174.

RESOURCES

BOOK

Dearlove, Des and Coomber, Stephen, *Heart & Soul*, Blessing White, 1998.

ESSENTIALS

MANAGING RESPONSIBLY

CORE VALUES

DISTINCT from the concept of core competencies, core values are concerned with what an organization stands for. The term may be a relative newcomer to the business lexicon, but the notion of a set of values as an important aspect of corporate life is not.

Although not always described as 'values', many companies have long recognized the importance of possessing a set of guiding principles. The evolution of the concept can be traced through some of the most influential business books over the last 50 years. Indeed, the notion of values has had an enduring impact on the development of thought since ancient times.

'Values,' the Greek philosopher Aristotle observed, 'are qualities, human excellence, reflected through our habits, skills, and behaviours.' Honesty, integrity, wealth, fairness – these are all values to which we can relate on an individual, personal basis. In the twentieth century, values began to be explored in the context of business and corporations.

In his 1963 book *A Business and Its Beliefs,* Thomas Watson Jr, then CEO of IBM, observed: 'Consider any great organization – one that has lasted over the years – I think you will find it owes its resiliency not to its form of organization or administrative skills, but to the power of what we call beliefs and the appeal these beliefs have for its people.'

When Watson talks about beliefs, he is talking about fundamental principles or standards, about what is valuable or important to IBM, the organization. He is talking about values. Similarly, Tom Peters and Robert Waterman thought corporate values important enough to warrant an entire chapter in their 1982 book *In Search Of Excellence.* For them, the terms beliefs and values were interchangeable. Other writers touched on the subject with varying degrees of interest.

But the debate took a leap forward in 1994 with *Built to Last,* an influential book by James C. Collins and Jerry I. Porras. These two business academics from Stanford University set out to identify the qualities essential to building a great and enduring organization, what the authors called 'successful habits of visionary companies'. The companies they wrote about had outperformed the general stock market by a factor of 12 since 1925.

For Collins and Porras, 'corporate values' are of paramount importance when building a lasting company. These are, they say, 'the organization's essential and enduring tenets – a small set of guiding principles; not to be confused with specific cultural or operating practices; not to be compromised for financial gain or short term expediency'.

For Hewlett-Packard, for example, values include a strong sense of responsibility to the community. For Disney, they include 'creativity, dreams, and imagination' and the promulgation of 'wholesome American values'.

Organizational goals (specific targets that help to realize a vision) are not values; neither are mission or purpose (the fundamental reason for existence); nor should values be confused with vision (a picture of the intended future). All of these have their place in a successful company. However, it could be argued that values are the precursors, the foundation on which the others are built.

Corporate values, then, are the fundamental beliefs for which a company stands. They are the essence of a company's identity, a corporate DNA. Long lasting, possibly immutable, values are guiding principles by which a company can chart its course across the business seas. The rougher the seas, the more important it is to have values to navigate by.

PART TWO

Foundations of Management

– CHAPTER 1 –

Strategy

'Unless structure follows strategy, inefficiency results.' ALFRED CHANDLER

'We all know a strategy when we see one.'
GARY HAMEL

'The real challenge in crafting strategy lies in detecting the subtle discontinuities that may undermine a business in the future. And for that there is no technique, no programme, just a sharp mind in touch with the situation.' HENRY MINTZBERG

'The job of the strategist is to achieve superior performance, relative to competition, in the key factors for success of the business.' KENICHI OHMAE

'Strategic thinking rarely occurs spontaneously.'
MICHAEL PORTER

'Deploy forces to defend the strategic points; exercise vigilance in preparation, do not be indolent. Deeply investigate the true situation, secretly await their laxity. Wait until they leave their strongholds, then seize what they love.' SUN TZU

What is strategy and how do you know if you have one?

COSTAS MARKIDES

Strategy bewilders and confuses at every turn. This led *The Economist* to claim that: 'Nobody really knows what strategy is.' Costas Markides examines the chasm at the heart of our knowledge of strategy.

WHAT is strategy, *really*? Despite the obvious importance of a superior strategy to the success of an organization and despite decades of academic research on the subject, there is little agreement among academics as to what strategy really is. From notions of those strategy as positioning to those of strategy as visioning, several possible definitions are fighting for legitimacy. Lack of an acceptable definition has opened up the field to an invasion of sexy slogans and terms, all of which add to the confusion and state of unease.

Not that the confusion is restricted to academics. If asked, most executives would define strategy as 'how one could achieve their company's objectives'. Although this definition is technically correct, it is so general that it is practically meaningless. One can put almost everything under the 'how' umbrella to make this definition a motherhood.

Needless to say, this state of affairs is unfortunate. Perhaps nothing highlights this confusion better than the following: in November 1996, the most prominent strategy academic, Michael Porter of Harvard, published a *Harvard Business Review* article[1] grandly entitled: 'What is strategy?' This was followed only a few months later by another famous academic, Gary Hamel of London Business School, with an equally impressively titled article:[2] 'The search for strategy.' That after 40 years of academic research on the subject, two of the most prominent academics in the field felt the need to start searching for strategy goes to show how much confusion we have managed to create regarding such a crucial business decision.

Although part of the confusion is undoubtedly self-inflicted, a major portion of it stems from an honest lack of understanding as to the content of strategy. I would like to propose a view of strategy based on my research on companies that have strategically innovated in their industries. These are companies which not only developed strategies that are fundamentally different from the strategies of their competitors but that also turned out to be tremendously successful.

Based on my research on these successful strategists, I would like to propose that there are certain simple but fundamental principles underlying every successful strategy. When one goes beyond the visible differences among strategies and probes deeper into their roots, one cannot fail but notice that all successful strategies share the same underlying principles or building blocks. Thus the building blocks of the successful Microsoft strategy are the same as the building blocks of the strategy which propelled Sears to industry leadership a hundred years ago. My argument is that by understanding what these building blocks are, they can be used to develop a successful strategy.

The building blocks of strategy

Strategy must decide on a few parameters

In today's uncertain and ever-changing environment, strategy is all about making some very difficult decisions on a *few* parameters. It is absolutely essential that the firm decides on these parameters because they become the boundaries within which people are given the freedom and the autonomy to operate and try things out. They also define the company's strategic position in its industry. Without clear decisions on these parameters, the company will drift like a rudderless ship in the open seas.

What are these parameters? A company has to decide on three main issues:

- *who* will be its targeted customers and who will it *not* target?
- *what* products or services will it offer its chosen customers and what will it *not* offer them?
- how will it go about achieving all this – what activities will it perform and what activities will it not perform?

These are not easy decisions to make and each question has many possible answers, all of them *ex ante* possible and logical. As a result, these kinds of decisions will unavoidably be preceded with debates, disagreements, politicking and indecision. Yet a firm cannot be everything to everybody, so clear and explicit decisions must be made. These choices may turn out to be wrong but that is not an excuse for not deciding.

It is absolutely essential that the organization makes clear and explicit choices on these three dimensions because the choices made become the parameters within which people are allowed to operate with autonomy. Without these clear parameters, the end result can be chaos. Seen in another way, it would be foolish and dangerous to allow people to take initiatives without some clear parameters guiding their actions.

Not only must the company make clear choices on these parameters, it must also attempt to make choices which are different from the choices its competitors have made. A company will be successful if it chooses a *distinctive* strategic position (i.e. different from competitors). Sure, it may be impossible to come up with answers which are 100 percent different from the answers of our competitors, but the ambition should be to create as much differentiation as possible.

Given the importance of coming up with clear answers to these three issues, the questions are: Who comes up with possible answers to these questions? Who decides what to do out of the many possibilities? How long do the decisions remain unchanged?

Who comes up with ideas?

Given the right organizational context, strategic ideas (on who to target, what to sell and how to do it) can come from anybody, anywhere, anytime. They may emerge through trial and error, or because somebody has a 'gut feeling' or 'got lucky' and stumbled across a good idea. They may even emerge out of a formal strategic planning session. However dismissive we are of the modern corporation's formal planning process, the possibility still exists that some good ideas can come out of it. No matter how the ideas are conceived, it is unlikely that they will be perfect from the start. The firm must therefore be willing and ready to modify or change its strategic ideas as it receives feedback from the market. But the first task of strategy must be to generate as many strategic ideas as possible, from which we choose what to do and what not to do.

In general, there are numerous tactics at our disposal to enhance creativity at the idea-generation stage. Let me list a few of them:

- Encourage everybody in the organization to question the firm's implicit assumptions and beliefs (i.e. the firm's sacred cows) as to who our customers really are, what we are really offering to the customer and how we do these things. Also encourage a fundamental questioning of the firm's accepted answer to the question: 'What business are we really in?'
- To facilitate this questioning, create a positive crisis. If done correctly, this will galvanize the organization into active thinking. If done incorrectly, it will demoralize everybody and create confusion and disillusionment throughout the organization.
- Develop processes in the organization to collect and utilize ideas from everybody – employees, customers, distributors, etc. At Lan & Spar Bank in Denmark, every employee is asked to contribute ideas through a strategy workbook; at Schlumberger in France, they have an internal venturing unit; at Bank One in the United States, they have a specific customer centre where all customers are encouraged to phone and express their complaints; at my local supermarket, they have a customer suggestion box. Different

organizations have come up with different tactics but the idea is the same: allow everybody to contribute ideas and make it easy for them to communicate their ideas to the decision makers in the organization.

- Create variety in the thinking that takes place in a formal planning process. This can be achieved not only by using a diverse team of people, but also by utilizing as many thinking approaches as possible.
- Institutionalize a culture of innovation. The organization must create the organizational environment (i.e. culture/structure/incentives/people) which promotes and supports innovative behaviours.

This is not an exhaustive list of tactics that could be used to increase creativity in strategy making. I am sure that other tactics and processes exist or can be thought of. The principle though remains the same: at this stage of crafting an innovative strategy the goal must be to generate as many strategic ideas as possible. From this plethora of ideas, we then have the luxury of choosing.

Who decides?

Even though anybody in the organization can come up with new strategic ideas (and everybody *should* be encouraged to do so), it is the responsibility of top management to make the final choices. There have been many calls lately to make the process of strategy development 'democratic' and 'flexible' – to bring everybody in the organization into the process. The thinking here is that the odds of conceiving truly innovative ideas are increased if thousands of people rather than just five or ten senior managers put their minds to work. And this much is true. But the job of choosing the ideas that the firm will actually pursue must be left to top management. Otherwise, the result is chaos, confusion and ultimately a demotivated workforce.

Choosing is difficult. At the time of choosing nobody knows for sure whether a particular idea will work, or whether the choices made are really the most appropriate ones. One could reduce the uncertainty at this stage by either evaluating each idea in a rigorous way or experimenting with the idea in a limited way to see whether it works. However, it is crucial to understand that uncertainty can be reduced but cannot be eliminated altogether. No matter how much experimentation we carry out and no matter how much thinking goes into it, the time will come when the firm must decide one way or another. Choices have to be made and these choices may turn out to be wrong. However, lack of certainty is no excuse for indecision.

Not only must the firm choose what to do but it must also make it clear what it will not do. The worst strategic mistake possible is to choose something but also keep the firm's options open by doing other things as well. Imagine an organization where the CEO proclaims that: 'Our strategy is crystal clear: we will do ABC,' while at the same time the employees see the firm doing XYZ as well as ABC. In their eyes this means one of two things: either the firm does not really have a strategy or top management is totally confused. Either way, the organization is left demoralized and confidence in senior management is shattered. Organizations that say one thing and then do another have failed to make clear choices as to what they will do and not do with their strategy.

The difficult choices made by Canon in attacking Xerox highlight the importance of choosing an explicit strategy. At the time of the attack, Xerox had a lock on the copier market by following a well-defined Xerox's and successful strategy, the main elements of which were as follows. Having segmented the market by volume, Xerox decided to go after the corporate reproduction market by concentrating on copiers designed for high-speed, high-volume needs. This inevitably defined Xerox's customers as big corporations, which in turn determined its distribution method: the direct sales force. At the same time, Xerox decided to lease rather than sell its machines, a strategic choice that had worked well in the company's earlier battles with 3M.

Xerox's strategy proved to be so successful that several new competitors, among them IBM and Kodak, tried to enter this market by adopting the same or similar strategies. Canon, on the other hand, chose to play the game differently. Having determined in the early 1960s to diversify out of cameras and into copiers, Canon segmented the copier market by end-user and targeted small and medium-sized businesses while also producing PC copiers for the individual. Canon decided to sell its machines through a dealer network rather than lease them, and while Xerox emphasized the speed of its machines, Canon elected to concentrate on quality and price as its differentiating features. IBM and Kodak's assault on the copier market failed, but Canon's succeeded: within 20 years of attacking Xerox, Canon emerged as the market leader in volume terms.

There are many reasons behind the success of Canon. Notice, however, that just like Xerox did 20 years before it, Canon also created for itself a *distinctive strategic position* in the industry – a position that was different from that of Xerox. While Xerox targeted big corporations as its customers, Canon went after small companies and individuals; while Xerox emphasized the speed of its machines, Canon focused on quality and price; and while Xerox used a direct sales force to lease its machines, Canon used its dealer network to sell its copiers. Rather than try to beat Xerox at its own game, Canon triumphed by creating its own unique strategic position.

As in the case of Xerox, these were not the only choices available to Canon and undoubtedly serious debates and disagreements must have taken place within the company as to whether these were the right choices to pursue. Yet, choices were made and a clear strategy with sharp and well-defined boundaries was implemented. Canon was successful because, like Xerox, it chose a unique and well-defined strategic position in the industry – one with distinctive customers, products and activities.

Strategy must put all our choices together to create a reinforcing mosaic

Choosing what to do and what not to do is certainly an important element of strategy. However, strategy is much more than this. Strategy is all about combining these choices into a system that creates the requisite fit between what the environment needs and what the company does. It is the combining of the firm's choices into a well-balanced system that is important, not the individual choices.[3]

The importance of conceptualizing the company as a combination of activities cannot be overemphasized. In this perspective, a firm is a complex system of interrelated and interdependent activities, each affecting each other: decisions and actions in one part of the business affect other parts, directly or indirectly. This means that unless we take a holistic, big-picture approach in designing the activities of our company, our efforts will backfire. Even if each individual activity is optimally crafted, the whole may still suffer unless we take interdependencies into consideration. The numerous local optima almost always undermine the global optimum.

The problem is that human beings can never really comprehend all the complexity enbedded in companies. We therefore tend to focus on one or two aspects of the system and try to optimize these sub-systems independently. By doing so, we ignore the interdependencies in the system and are therefore making matters worse. Since it takes time for the effect of our actions to show up, we do not even see that we are the source of our problems. When the long-term effects of our short-sighted actions hit home, we blame other people and especially outside forces for our problems.

In designing the company's system of activities, managers must follow four principles:

1. the individual activities we choose to do must be the ones that are demanded by the market;
2. the activities we decide to perform must fit with each other;
3. activities must not only fit but must also be in balance with each other;
4. in designing these activities, it is important to keep in mind that the collection of these activities will form an interrelated system.

Not only should we pay particular attention to the inter-relationships in this system, but we should also be aware that the structure of this system will drive behaviour in it. What our people do in the firm is conditioned by this underlying structure. Therefore, if we want to change behaviour, we will have to change the structure of the system.

Strategy must achieve fit without losing flexibility

Creating the right fit between what the market needs and what the firm does can backfire if the environment changes and the firm does not respond accordingly. We are all familiar with the story of the frog: when a frog is put in a pot of boiling water, it jumps out; when, instead, the same frog is put in a pot of cold water and the water is slowly brought to a boil, the frog stays in the pot and boils to death. In the same manner, if a company does not react to the constant changes taking place in its environment, it will find itself boiled to death.

This implies that a company needs to create the requisite fit with its current environment while remaining flexible enough to respond to (or even create) changes in this environment. But what does it mean when we say that a firm must remain flexible? The way I use the term here, it means three things: a firm must first be able to identify early enough changes in its environment; it must then have the cultural readiness to embrace change and respond to it; and it must have the requisite skills and competencies to compete in whatever environment emerges after the change. Thus flexibility has a cultural element to it (i.e. being willing to change) as well as a competence element to it (i.e. being able to change).

Strategy needs to be supported by the appropriate organizational environment

Any strategy, however brilliant, needs to be implemented properly if it is to deliver the desired results. However, implementation does not take place in a vacuum. It takes place within an organizational environment which we, as managers, create. It is this organizational environment which produces the behaviour that we observe in companies. Therefore, to secure the desired strategic behaviour by employees, the firm must also create the appropriate environment – that is, the environment that promotes and supports its chosen strategy.

By environment, I mean four elements: the organization's culture; its incentives; its structure; and its people.[4] A company that wants to put into action a certain strategy must first ask the question: 'What kind of culture, incentives, structure and people do we need to put in place so as to support the successful implementation of our strategy? In other words, to create a superior strategy, a company must think beyond customers, products and activities. It must also decide what underlying environment to create and how exactly to create it so as to facilitate the implementation of its strategy.

However, deciding on what kind of culture, structure, incentives and people to have is not enough. The challenge for strategy is to develop these four elements of organizational environment and then put them together so that, on the one hand, they support and complement each other, while on the other hand, they collectively support and promote the chosen strategy. As was the case with the activities which I described above, this is the real challenge for strategy: not only to create the correct individual parts; but also to combine them to create a strong and reinforcing system.[5]

Achieving internal and external fits will only bring short-term success. Inevitably, fit will create contentment, overconfidence and inertia. Therefore, while a company aims to achieve fit, it must also create enough slack in the system so that, as the firm grows or as the external environment changes, the organizational environment can remain flexible and responsive.

Finally, if business conditions oblige a strategic change of direction, the internal context of the organization must change with it. This is extremely difficult. Not only do we need to change the individual pieces that make up the organizational environment, but we must also put the new pieces together to form an overall organizational environment that will again fit with the new strategy.

No strategy remains unique for ever

There is no question that success stems from the exploitation of a distinctive or unique strategic position. Unfortunately, no position will remain unique or attractive for ever. Not only do attractive positions get imitated by aggressive competitors, but also – and perhaps more importantly – new strategic positions keep emerging. A new strategic position is simply a new viable Who–What–How combination – perhaps a new customer segment (a new Who), or a new value proposition (a new What), or a new way of distributing or manufacturing the product (a new How). Over time, these new positions may grow to challenge the attractiveness of our own position.

You see this happening in industry after industry: once formidable companies that built their success on what seemed to be unassailable strategic positions find themselves humbled by relatively unknown companies who base their attacks on creating and exploiting new strategic positions in the industry.[6]

New strategic positions – that is, new Who–What–How combinations – emerge around us all the time. As industries change, new strategic positions emerge to challenge existing positions for supremacy. Changing industry conditions, changing customer needs or preferences, countermoves by competitors and a company's own evolving competencies give rise to new opportunities and the potential for new ways of playing the game. Unless a company continuously questions its accepted norms and behaviour, it will never discover what else has become available. It will miss these new combinations, and other, more agile players will jump in and exploit the gaps left behind.

This means that a company must never settle for what it has. While fighting it out in its current position, it must search continuously for new positions to colonize and new opportunities to take advantage of. Simple as this may sound, it contrasts sharply with the way most competitors compete in their industries: most take the established rules of the game as given and spend all their time trying to become better than each other in their existing positions – usually through cost or differentiation strategies. Little or no emphasis is placed on becoming different from competitors. This is evidenced from the fact that the majority of companies which strategically innovate by breaking the rules of the game tend to be small niche players or new market entrants. It is indeed rare to find a strategic innovator who is also an established industry big player – a fact that hints at the difficulties of risking the sure thing for something uncertain.[7]

There are many reasons why established companies find it hard to become strategic innovators. Compared to new entrants or niche players, leaders are weighed down by structural and cultural inertia, internal politics, complacency, fear of cannibalizing existing products, fear of destroying existing competencies, satisfaction with the status quo and a general lack of incentives to abandon a certain present for an uncertain future. In addition, since there are fewer industry leaders than potential new entrants, the chances that the innovator will emerge from the ranks of the leaders is unavoidably small.

Despite such obstacles, established companies cannot afford not to strategically innovate. As already pointed out, dramatic shifts in company fortunes take place only when companies dramatically change the rules of the game in their industries. Strategic innovation has the potential to take third-rate companies and elevate them to industry leadership status; and it can take established industry leaders and destroy them in a short period of time. Even if the established players do not want to strategically innovate (for fear of destroying their existing profitable positions), somebody else will. Established players might as well pre-empt that.

The culture that established players must develop is that *strategies are not cast in concrete.* A company needs to remain flexible and ready to adjust its strategy if the feedback from the market is not favourable. More importantly, a company needs to question continuously the way it operates in its current position and search for new positions to colonise.

Continuously questioning your accepted strategic position serves two vital purposes: first, it allows a company to identify early enough whether its current position in the business is losing its attractiveness to others (and so decide what to do about it),[8] and second, and more importantly, it gives the company the opportunity to explore proactively the emerging terrain and hopefully be the first to discover new strategic positions to take advantage of. This is no guarantee: questioning accepted answers will not automatically lead to new unexploited goldmines. But even a remote possibility of discovering something new will never come up if the questions are never asked.

REFERENCES

1. Porter, Michael, 1996, 'What is Strategy', *Harvard Business Review*, November–December, pp. 61–78.
2. Hamel, Gary, 1997, 'The Search for Strategy', London Business School working paper.
3. The idea that the firm is a complex system of interrelationships and that it should be viewed and managed as such is one of the founding principles of 'system dynamics' as developed by MIT's Jay W. Forrester. A powerful and managerial exposition of system dynamics and systems thinking principles can be found in: Senge, Peter, *The Fifth Discipline*, Doubleday, New York, 1990. See also: Meen, David E. and Keough, Mark, 1997, 'Creating the Learning Organization: An Interview with Peter Senge', in *The McKinsey Quarterly Anthologies: Business Dynamics*, 1997, pp. 79–93; and Meen and Keough, 1992, 'The CEO as Organization Designer: An Interview with Professor Jay W. Forrester', *The McKinsey Quarterly*, 2, 3–30.
4. What I call here 'environment' is what is widely known as the 7S framework developed by McKinsey & Company. The 7S are: style, strategy, structure, systems, skills, staff and superordinate goals.
5. This point is made forcefully and in much more detail in Nadler, David and Tushman, Michael, *Competing by Design: The Power of Organizational Architecture*, Oxford University Press, New York, 1997.
6. For additional details, see my article: Markides, Castas, 1997, 'Strategic Innovation', *Sloan Management Review*, 38(3), Spring, 9–23.
7. Markides, Castas, 1998, 'Strategic Innovation in Established Companies', *Sloan Management Review*, 39(3), Spring, 31–42.
8. If this happens, value will migrate from one strategic position to another; see the excellent study by Slywotzky, Adrian J., *Value Migration: How to Think Several Moves Ahead of the Competition*, HBS Press, Boston, 1996.

Strategy and control

JOHN KAY

John Kay considers the illusion of control on which the idea of strategic thinking was developed, and explores the potential contribution of a resource-based view.

IT is the early 1960s. Robert Macnamara, recruited from US car maker Ford to run the Department of Defense, is managing the first stages of the Vietnam War on computers in the Pentagon. John Kenneth Galbraith, detesting the world Macnamara represents, writes of the New Industrial State, in which giant mechanistic corporations run our lives.

The Soviet Union is ahead in the space race and while most of the West loathes the Russian empire, they do not dispute the claims made for its economic success. Every newly independent colonial territory looks forward to the realization of its development plan. British Prime Minister Harold Wilson talks of the white heat of the technological revolution; George Brown gives Britain its first, and only, national plan.

It is in this environment that the idea of business strategy is created. The early texts are by Igor Ansoff and Ken Andrews. Its principal journal is called *Long Range Planning*. It is founded on an illusion of rationality and the possibilities of control.

It is a world that will soon fall apart. Macnamara will be transferred to the World Bank, but history will note the failure of each of his careers – CEO, Secretary of State, international statesman. Half a million hippies will gather at Woodstock to celebrate the demise of the New Industrial State; and – although few people saw it then – the Soviet Union is on an unstoppable path from totalitarianism to disintegration.

Yet the delusion of control has continued to define the subject of business strategy. In the heady 1960s, no major firm was without its strategic plan. Few are without one today, although few devote the resources to it that they once did. The plans contain numbers, neither targets nor forecasts, which purport to describe the evolution of the company's affairs over the next five years.

But planning and strategy are no longer conflated. The delusion of control has changed its form if not its nature. What matters are vision and mission. Charismatic CEOs can transcend the boundaries of the firm. Their achievements, and those of the companies they inspired, could be restricted only by the limitations of their executive imagination.

However, companies are not restrained only by imagination. They are limited by their own capabilities, by technology, by competition, and by the demands of their customers. So visionary strategy has been succeeded by an era in which the cliché 'formulation is easy, it is implementation that's the problem' holds sway. If strategizing consists of having visions, it is obvious that formulation is easy and implementation the problem: all substantive issues of strategy have been redefined as issues of implementation.

As organizations stubbornly fail to conform to the visions of their senior executives, we should not be surprised that organizational transformation has become one of the most popular branches of consultancy.

Or perhaps the CEO's vision is of the external environment, rather than of the internal capabilities of the firm. The future belongs to those who see it first, or most clearly. Nevertheless, it is not just that forecasting is hard – although that difficulty should not be underestimated. Even if you do see the future correctly, its timing is hard to predict and its implications are uncertain.

US telecoms carrier AT&T understood that the convergence of telecommunications and computing would transform not only the company's own markets but much of business life. This was a perceptive vision, not widely shared. But the company failed to see – how could it have? – that the internet was the specific vehicle through which the vision would be realized, or that its merger with US business machines manufacturer NCR was an irrelevant and inappropriate response. While there are many examples – take General Motors or International Business Machines – of companies that suffered from failing to see the future even after it had arrived, there are almost no companies building sustainable competitive advantages from superior forecasting abilities.

Thoughtful strategy, then, is not about crystal balls, or grand designs and visions. The attempt to formulate these at the level of national economies is now seen to have been at best risible and at worst disastrous – as with Soviet economic planning, Mao's Cultural Revolution, or the improvement strategies of almost all developing countries. What has been true of states is true also in companies. No one has, or could hope to have, the knowledge necessary to construct these transformational plans. Nor – however totalitarian the structures they introduce, in governments or corporations – does anyone truly enjoy the power to implement them.

The subject of strategy

Business strategy is concerned with the match between the internal capabilities of the company and its external environment. Although there is much disagreement of substance among those who write about strategy, most agree that this is the issue.

The methods of strategy, and its central questions, follow from that definition. The methods require analysis of the characteristics of the company and the industries and markets in which it operates. The questions are twofold. What are the origins and characteristics of the successful fit between characteristics and environment: why do companies succeed? How can companies and their managers make that fit more effective: how will companies succeed?

I once thought that these core questions of strategy – the positive question of understanding the processes through which effective strategies had been arrived at, the normative question of what effective strategy should be – were quite separate. I now believe that they are barely worth distinguishing, and that the conventional emphasis on the vision is a product of the illusion of control.

Strategy is not planning, visioning, or forecasting – all remnants of the belief that one can control the future by superior insight and superior will. The modern subject of business strategy is a set of analytic techniques for understanding better, and so influencing, a company's position in its actual and potential marketplace.

Evolving modern theory

Strategy, as I have defined it, is a subject of application, rather than a discipline – rather as, say, geriatrics is to underlying disciplines of pharmacology or cell biology – and the obvious underpinning disciplines for strategy are economics and organizational sociology. Still, this is not how the subject developed in practice.

When the content of strategy was first set out 30 years ago, industrial economics was dominated by the structure–conduct–performance paradigm, which emphasized how market structure – the number of competitors and the degree of rivalry between them – was the principal influence on a company's behaviour. Market structure was determined partly by external conditions of supply and demand, and partly (unless antitrust agencies intervened) by the attempts of firms to influence the intensity of competition.

This was a view of markets aimed at public policy, not business policy. It was correctly seen as having little relevance to the basic issues of business strategy. The neglect of the internal characteristics of companies is obvious and explicit. While some of the strategic tools developed by consultants in the 1970s – such as the experience curve and the portfolio matrix – might advantageously have had an economic basis, in practice microeconomic theory was largely ignored.

Not until 1980, with the publication of Michael Porter's *Competitive Strategy*, did economists attempt to recapture the field of strategy. But this was ultimately to prove a false move. Porter's work – essentially a translation of the structure–conduct–performance paradigm into language more appropriate for a business audience – suffered from the limitations of the material on which it was based. His 'five forces' and value chain are usefully descriptive of industry structure, but shed no light on the central strategic issue: why different firms, facing the same environment, perform differently.

Much of the organizational sociology of the 1960s addressed strategic issues. Chandler's magisterial *Strategy and Structure*, or the empirical work of Tom Burns and G.M. Stalker, addressed directly the relationships between organizational form and the technological and market environment. But academic sociology was largely captured by people hostile to the very concept of capitalist organization. The subject drifted into abstraction, and further away from the day-to-day concerns of those in business.

More recent insights into the nature of organizations have come either from economics or from the accumulated practical wisdom of which Charles Handy and Henry Mintzberg are, in different ways, effective exponents. Porter's attention ultimately reverted to the public policy concerns of his former mentors in the Harvard economics department, as in *The Competitive Advantage of Nations*.

Strategy today – rents and capabilities

At about the same time as Porter first wrote about strategy, *The Strategic Management Journal*, today the leading journal in the field, was established. The currently dominant view of strategy – resource-based theory – has been principally set out in its pages. It also has an economic base, but has found its inspiration in different places and further back in history. It draws on the Ricardian approach to the determination of economic rent, and the view of the firm as a collection of capabilities described by Edith Penrose and George Richardson.

Economic rent is what firms earn over and above the cost of the capital employed in their business. The terminology is unfortunate. It is used because the central framework was set out by David Ricardo in the early part of the nineteenth century, when agriculture was the dominant form of economic activity. Economic rent has been variously called economic profit, super-normal profit and excess profit – terms that lack appeal for modern businesspeople. Most recently Stern Stewart, a consultancy, has had some success marketing the concept under the term 'economic value added'. The problem here is that value added – the value added that is taxed – means something different. Nor does my own attempt to call it 'added value' help. Perhaps economic rent is best. The title doesn't matter; the concept does.

The objective of a firm is to increase its economic rent, rather than its profit as such. A firm that increases its profits but not its economic rent – as through investments or acquisitions that yield less than the cost of capital – destroys value.

In a contestable market – one in which entry by new firms is relatively early and exit by failing firms is relatively quick – firms that are only just successful enough to survive will earn the industry cost of capital on the replacement cost of their assets. Economic rent is the measure of the competitive advantage that effective established firms enjoy, and competitive advantage is the only means by which companies in contestable markets can earn economic rents.

The opportunity for companies to sustain these competitive advantages is determined by their capabilities. A company's capabilities are of many kinds. For the purposes of strategy, the key distinction is between distinctive and reproducible capabilities.

Distinctive capabilities are those characteristics of a firm that cannot be replicated by competitors, or can only be replicated with great difficulty, even after these competitors realize the benefits they yield for the originating company. Distinctive capabilities can be of many kinds. Government licences, statutory monopolies, or effective patents and copyrights are particularly stark examples. But equally powerful idiosyncratic characteristics have been built by companies in competitive markets. These include strong brands, patterns of supplier or customer relationships, and skills, knowledge, and routines that are embedded in teams.

Reproducible capabilities can be bought or created by any firm with reasonable management skills, diligence, and financial resources. Most technical capabilities are of this kind. Marketing capabilities are sometimes distinctive, sometimes reproducible.

The importance of the distinction for strategy is this: only distinctive capabilities can be the basis of sustainable competitive advantage. Collections of reproducible capabilities can and will be established by others and therefore cannot generate rents in a competitive or contestable market.

Matching capabilities to markets

So the strategist must first look inward. The strategist must identify the distinctive capabilities of the organization and seek to surround these with a collection of reproducible capabilities, or complementary assets, that enable the firm to sell its distinctive capabilities in the market in which it operates.

While this is easier said than done, it defines a structure in which the processes of strategy formulation and its implementation are bound together. The resource-based view of strategy – emphasizing rent creation through distinctive capabilities – has found its most widely accepted popularization in the core competencies approach of C.K. Prahalad and Gary Hamel. But that application has been made problematic by the absence of sharp criteria for distinguishing core and other competencies, which allows the wishful thinking characteristic of vision-based and mission-based strategizing. Core competencies become pretty much what the senior management of the corporation wants them to be.

The perspective of economic rent – which forces the question 'why can't competitors do that?' into every discussion – cuts through much of this haziness. Characteristics such as size, strategic vision, market share, and market positioning – all commonly seen as sources of competitive advantage, but all ultimately reproducible by firms with competitive advantages of their own – can be seen clearly as the result, rather than the origin, of competitive advantage.

Strategic analysis then turns outward, to identify those markets in which the company's capabilities can yield competitive advantage. The emphasis here is again on distinctive capabilities, since only these can be a source of economic rent, but distinctive capabilities need to be supported by an appropriate set of complementary reproducible capabilities.

Markets have product geographic dimensions, and different capabilities each have their own implications for the boundaries of the appropriate market. Reputations and brands are typically effective in relation to a specific customer group, and may be valuable in selling other related products to that group. Innovation-based competitive advantages will typically have a narrower product focus, but may transcend national boundaries in ways that reputations cannot. Distinctive capabilities may dictate market position as well as market choice. Those based on supplier relationships may be most appropriately deployed at the top of the market, while the effectiveness of brands is defined by the customer group that identifies with the brand.

Since distinctive capabilities are at the heart of competitive advantage, every firm asks how it can create distinctive capabilities. Yet the question contains an inherent contradiction: if irreproducible characteristics could be created, they would cease to be irreproducible. What is truly irreproducible has three primary sources: market structure that limits entry; firm history that by its very nature requires extended time to replicate; tacitness in relationships – routines and behaviour of 'uncertain imitability' – that cannot be replicated because no one, not even the participants themselves, fully comprehends their nature.

So companies would do well to begin by looking at the distinctive capabilities they have rather than at those they would like to have. And established, successful companies will not usually enjoy that position if they do not enjoy some distinctive capability. Again, it is easy to overestimate the effect of conscious design in the development of firms and market structures.

The evolution of capabilities and environment

Strategy, with its emphasis on the fit between characteristics and environment, links naturally to an evolutionary perspective on organization. Processes that provide favourable feedback for characteristics that are well adapted to their environment – and these include both biological evolution and competitive market economies – produce organisms, or companies, that have capabilities matched to their requirements.

Recent understanding of evolutionary processes emphasizes how little intentionality is required to produce that result. Successful companies are not necessarily there because (except with hindsight) anyone had superior insight in organizational design or strategic fit. Rather, there were many different views of the firm capabilities a particular activity required; and it was the market, rather than the visionary executive, that chose the most effective match. Distinctive capabilities were established, rather than designed.

This view is supported by detached business history. Andrew Pettigrew's description of ICI shows an organization whose path was largely fixed – both for good and for bad – by its own past. The scope and opportunity for effective management strategic choice – both for good and for bad – were necessarily limited by the past. This is not to be pessimistic about the potential for strategic direction or the ability of executives to make important differences, but to reiterate the absurdity and irrelevance of using the blank sheet of paper approach to corporate strategy.

New paradigm

The resource-based view of strategy has a coherence and integrative role that places it well ahead of other mechanisms of strategic decision making. I have little doubt that for the foreseeable future, major contributions to ways of strategic thinking will either form part of that framework or represent development of it. To use the most overworked and abused term in the study of management, after 30 years or so, the subject of strategy is genuinely acquiring what can be described as a paradigm.

RESOURCES

BOOKS

Andrews, Kenneth, *The Concept of Corporate Strategy*, Irwin, Homewood, IL, 1965.

Ansoff, H. Igor, *Corporate Strategy*, McGraw Hill, New York, 1965.

Barney, J., 'Firm Resources and Sustained Competitive Advantage', *Journal of Management* 17, 1991.

Burns, Tom and Stalker, G.M., *The Management of Innovation*, Tavistock Publication, 1961.

Chandler, Alfred, *Strategy and Structure*, MIT Press, Cambridge, 1962.

Handy, Charles, *Understanding Organisations*, Penguin, London, 1976.

Kay, John, *The Business of Economics*, Oxford University Press, 1996.

Mintzberg, Henry, *The Structuring of Organizations*, Prentice Hall, Englewood Cliffs, 1979.

Montgomery, C.A., 'Of diamonds and rust', in Montgomery, C.A. (ed), *Resource based and evolutionary theories of the firm*, Kluwes, Boston, 1995.

Penrose, E., *The Theory of the Growth of the Firm*, Oxford University Press, 1959.

Pettigrew, Andrew, *The Awakening Giant*, Blackwell, Oxford, 1985.

Porter, Michael, *Competitive Strategy*, Free Press, NY, 1980.

Porter, Michael, *The Competitive Advantage of Nations*, Free Press, NY, 1990.

Scherer, F.M., *Industrial Market Structure and Economic Performance*, Houghton Mifflin, Boston, 1970.

Bases of competitive advantage

GEORGE S. YIP

There are many different bases of competitive advantage, as George Yip describes. He offers a hexagon of different categories: customer market, products and services, business system or value chain, assets and resources, partners, and scale and scope.

HOW many bases of competitive advantage does a company need? Many business academics and gurus have suggested that companies need to focus on just one basis of advantage. Michael Porter has famously argued that there are only three possible bases of competitive advantage: differentiation, cost, or focus, and that companies can choose only one.[1] Other bestselling authors have argued that market leaders pursue only one discipline.[2]

However, the reality seems otherwise. The most successful companies have multiple bases of competitive advantage. New companies may start out with just one basis of competitive advantage, but they rapidly add many others if they are to sustain their success. Dell Computer started out by offering low cost as its advantage. But then it added speedy delivery, accessible service, and eventually a broad and high-quality product range. Meanwhile, it has consistently invested in and reconfigured its business so that it continues to be able to provide high quality products and services at a lower cost than its premium segment rivals.

Successful companies also get into trouble if they lose one or more bases of competitive advantage. Over the decades, British Leyland

and its predecessor and successor companies gradually lost almost every basis of competitive advantage. The furore over the sale of Rover by BMW has probably fatally weakened the Rover brand as one of this company's last remaining bases of competitive advantage. Perhaps its last asset lies in the MG brand name, still highly evocative to sports car fans.

British Airways transformed itself from the mid-1980s to the mid-1990s, adding virtually every basis of competitive advantage. But today, the company faces a deteriorating cost position (partly from the long-term strength of the pound sterling and from pressure by younger carriers with lower cost structures).

It has also become very clear with the rush of internet company public offerings that dot-coms need multiple bases of competitive advantage. Amazon.com's success with customers depends on several bases: having the largest range of books; a very user-friendly system including its patented one-click ordering; initially its relationship with the United States' largest book wholesaler and its warehouse, since replaced with Amazon's own warehouses; and its expansion to other product categories. In contrast, one-legged dot-coms, such as lastminute.com (the British vendor of travel and entertainment bargains), raise serious doubts as to their sustainability unless they add bases of advantage other than their wide range of offers.

The hexagon of competitive advantage

While there are many different bases of competitive advantage, companies may find it useful to think about six categories of advantage: customer market, products and services, business system or value chain, assets and resources, partners, and scale and scope. Figure 1 depicts these categories around a hexagon, illustrating the idea that a company can start from any corner, but needs eventually to add strength at every point.

Customer market advantage

Being the first company to enter or create a new market, or the first to serve a group of customers, constitutes one of the most common

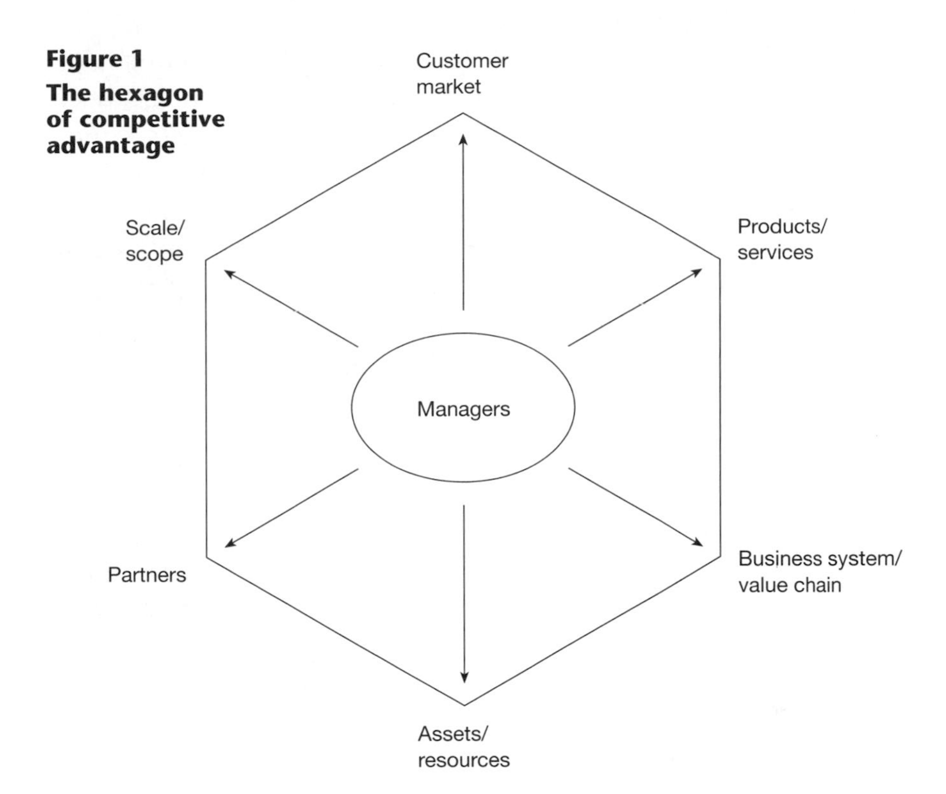

Figure 1
The hexagon of competitive advantage

early bases of competitive advantage. Initially, such a company has no competitors at all, which is the ultimate competitive advantage.

When Xerox created the market for plain paper photocopiers it was in a position of total dominance, protected by its patents and unique products. Market dominance is a better way of viewing Xerox's competitive advantage at this stage rather than, say, product superiority. There simply were not any competitive products. Many new dot-coms also have this as their first basis of advantage (which also makes clear that once competition comes in, dot-coms need other bases of advantage).

It is also important to note that some successful companies never achieve an advantage in terms of market or customer dominance, other than through other bases such as product superiority that lead to preference by customers in market segments. A quintessential example is Singapore Airlines, which, starting from one of the smallest countries (Singapore even today has a population of fewer than 3 million), has become one the world's leading airlines and consistently one of the most profitable and most highly rated among business travellers.

Lastly, owning a customer market can be a major basis of advantage even if the customers do not like the company. It has been estimated that in Britain the average bank account lasts longer than the average marriage. Do customers love their banks? No. But they stay with them out of inertia. In contrast, some companies have such a good relationship with their customer base that the latter will buy almost anything from them: in the case of Britain's Virgin group, everything from air and train travel to music to investments; and Britain's easyGroup is following the same path, expanding from air travel to internet cafés, car rental and banking.

Product and service advantage

Having a superior product or service is, of course, a very common basis of competitive advantage. Such superiority can range from minor items to very major ones.

Toyota's innovation of a coffee cup holder in its automobiles represents perhaps one of the smallest yet most successful product-based advantages. This product feature, costing less than .01 percent of the total value of the car, gained Toyota many sales in the US during the brief period before its competitors imitated it. At the other extreme, product superiority can be so great as to constitute a new category that in turn yields the additional basis of advantage of market dominance.

Product superiority can also be built up slowly over time. Both Singapore Airlines and Toyota, starting from initial positions of product inferiority, continually improved their product until they achieved superiority in many aspects of their offering. Only continuing product superiority has kept Apple Computer alive in its fight against the Microsoft standard, outnumbered more than 10 to one in its installed base. At the same time, companies may be successful with inferior products, most famously in the case of Microsoft's DOS operating system.

We also have to be careful to understand the underlying reality of an apparent product-based source of competitive advantage. Often, this advantage springs from other bases in the hexagon. For example, the bestselling book *The Discipline of Market Leaders*[3] cites as a primary reason for Hertz's success in the automobile rental market its product superiority, such as in its faster, more efficient express service (Gold Service in the United States). But why can Hertz offer a service superior to that of its competitors? Is it because Avis and National do not know how Hertz does it? No. There are no secrets in the car rental business. Nor is it because Avis and National do not have the desire to imitate Hertz. The real barrier to imitation lies in the sixth base of competitive advantage: scale. By virtue of being larger than its competitors, Hertz has more buses circling airports, larger facilities, more cars and more staff. It is these scale-based advantages that yield the advantage of product superiority and not the other way around. So Hertz is not number one because it offers superior service; it is able to offer superior service because it is number one.[4]

Business system/value chain advantage

The value-adding chain, also known as the business system, comprises all the activities that a business conducts. A typical sequence begins with research and development, runs through production, and finishes with selling, marketing, distribution, and after-sales services. The value chain can provide advantage if a company is superior in one or more elements of the chain. Many companies have built up superiority in particular elements over long periods: 3M's superior research and development capability, Procter & Gamble's marketing skills, Dell Computer's distribution system, Sony's innovative designs, Toyota's superiority in production operations, and companies such as American Express in customer service.

An alternative or additional source of value chain superiority is to co-ordinate the chain better than competitors. The just-in-time movement can be interpreted as an effort at better co-ordination of the value chain. The enthusiasm for business process re-engineering also qualifies as a way of obtaining competitive advantage through reconfiguration of the value chain. Southwest Airlines became the most profitable airline in the US partly through redesigning its value chain in order to speed up turnaround. This required the co-ordination of several elements of the business system: the passengers, the check-in process, the boarding process (boarding not by row numbers but by position in the row – window seats first, then centre seats, then aisle seats), and in terms of operations and turnaround service of inbound and outbound flights.

A number of Hong Kong hotel chains, such as the Peninsula and the Regent, are renowned for their impeccable service, the best in the world. But this service is merely the tip, experienced by guests, of an entire business system dedicated to supporting the point of customer interface.

One way of viewing the efforts at achieving value chain superiority is that they all have the same end objectives of delivering products and services better, faster, or cheaper.

System assets/resources

Assets – tangible ones, which can range from factories to patents, and intangible ones, such as brand names and reputation – provide another powerful basis for competitive advantage. Perhaps the most interesting aspect of asset-based competitive advantage is that these assets have often been generated in much earlier periods.

One of Coca-Cola's primary bases of competitive advantage is the fact that it has the best-known brand name in the world (confirmed in numerous surveys). Yet the power of this brand name has been built up over a period of 100 years through continual investment in advertising and other forms of promotion, as well as association with Coca-Cola's high-quality products.

Another key basis of Coca-Cola's advantage is its asset of both its physical distribution system, comprising many company-owned bottling plants and trucks, warehouse, and other distribution facilities, as well as its less tangible network of franchised bottlers. This asset has also taken decades to build up. So a very high proportion of Coca-Cola's current competitive advantage is based on assets built up by previous generations of managers.

Brands are a particularly tricky form of asset. For example, some analysts value Microsoft's brands at over $50 billion. But people do not buy Microsoft products because of the brand. Without the patents and installed base, Microsoft's brands are worth almost nothing.

Sometimes an asset-based advantage can come from a complementary asset rather than one that is directly in the company's value chain. Not least among Singapore Airlines' competitive advantages is the fact that its base, Singapore's Changi airport, is one of the world's finest and is owned by the Singaporean government, also a major shareholder in the airline.

For many natural resource companies, assets are often the sole basis of competitive advantage. This is the case for many state-owned energy companies, whose primary competitive advantage is the fact that they have assets in the ground – oil and gas reserves – that can be extracted at lower cost than those of rival countries. Generally, companies operating in the natural resource sector typically owe their competitive advantage to ownership or access to low-cost and/or high-quality sources of raw materials. As one executive from a major mining company put it: 'Ownership of the ore in the ground is our only source of competitive advantage.' Like any other basis of competitive advantage, assets and resources can be underutilized, perhaps more so. The dramatic improvement in Disney's fortunes from the late 1980s to the late 1990s, under Michael Eisner's stewardship, lay primarily in his ability to make much better use of the company's underexploited assets of film properties, brand names and characters.

Partner advantage

Having the right partners can also provide a very powerful basis of competitive advantage. Rover was in serious difficulties until it acquired Honda as a new joint venture partner in the 1980s. Honda was able to help Rover so much that the British company became a valuable property and was able to sell itself to BMW, much to Honda's chagrin (but perhaps subsequent relief, seeing that BMW turned out to be not such a successful partner).

Many companies have gone on to surpass their partners. Microsoft's true initial basis of competitive advantage was its partnership with

IBM, but its fortunes have certainly prospered much more than those of IBM. Numerous Asian manufacturers have begun as original equipment suppliers to American and European partners, only to overtake them later. The emphasis on strategic alliances illustrates the criticality of having the right partners. Indeed, US chemicals producer Dow Corning identifies its ability to create and manage alliances as one of its critical sources of competitive advantage.

Scale and scope advantage

Companies can also gain advantage from economies of scale or of scope. Economies of scale consist in the reduction in unit cost with increased production volume, while economies of scope come from sharing costs across multiple products or lines of business.

Market share usually drives these economies. Depending on the industry, economies of scale may flatten out at relatively small market shares. Such industries are fragmented ones in which no competitor can dominate the industry or gain a large share, such as many retailing sectors, apparel manufacturing and the like.

Economies of scale and scope, or even just sheer size, can yield many advantages, some of which may not be obvious to the companies themselves or their competitors. We have already mentioned the example of Hertz's express service. Other companies recognize that size is perhaps their main advantage. In early 2000, Barclays Bank began an advertising campaign in Britain to stress how 'big' the company is, linking bigness to customer benefits such as being able to provide free internet banking. By inference, Barclays was admitting that it could offer few other advantages.

Adding to bases of advantage

While it is important to be superior in some basis of advantage, the real power comes not from being good in one base, but from putting together multiple bases of advantage. The really successful companies are those that manage to build on their initial base of advantage, increasing the advantage in that base, while continually adding others.

Singapore Airlines provides an example of a company that started from one base of advantage and rapidly added others.

- Like many other companies from developing countries, its first source of competitive advantage was low labour costs, giving it an advantage in the business system. So, initially, Singapore Airlines was able to offer cheaper flights.
- Another source of advantage was its ability to attain very high levels of service, partly due to cultural factors and partly due to management attention. So it was rapidly able to add an advantage in the product/service corner of the hexagon.
- As mentioned earlier, the Singapore government, which owns Singapore Airlines, contributed significantly to building up a collateral asset, Changi airport, as an asset-based source of competitive advantage. The company has consciously used its fleet of planes as a source of competitive advantage, continually upgrading them, and proudly advertises that it has the world's youngest fleet of planes.
- It has also assiduously built up a network of partners through alliances. These alliances improve the feed of passengers and also encourage passengers from Asia to use Singapore Airlines in order to make easier connections in the United States and in Europe.
- Despite all this success, Singapore Airlines is still a relatively small airline, and does not enjoy many economies of scale and scope relative to its competitors.
- Lastly, as discussed earlier, Singapore Airlines has never enjoyed an advantage in terms of dominance of a market or customer base, given how small its home country is. While the city of Singapore is geographically convenient as a hub for flights between Europe, North America, Southeast Asia and Australasia, other nearby airports are similarly convenient – Kuala Lumpur, Jakarta, Bangkok. As these neighbours upgrade their airport facilities and the quality of service of their national carriers, Singapore Airlines will face increased competition.
- Singapore Airlines is also facing another source of competition. It has found that even Singaporeans are not

> particularly loyal to their national carrier, when faced with the lure of frequent flyer miles from major American carriers. So, it offers its own frequent flyer programme by participating in a pan-Asian consortium, Passages.

The hexagon can also be used to explain how companies lose their competitive advantage. PanAm used to be the most respected airline in the world. It began with market dominance, by being the first to offer international air service in 1928. Over 50 years it built up superior product and service, such that it became renowned for offering the world's best airline service. PanAm created an efficient business system that allowed its planes to fly around the world and to be serviced in remote locations. It also built up assets and resources, including fleets of planes, such as the Boeing Stratocruiser, the first double-decker aeroplane with its upstairs lounge for first-class passengers. Its brand name became so respected that it was able to put that name on a major office building in New York City and attract tenants. PanAm also achieved scale by becoming the world's largest international carrier. But it never did develop good alliances with partners, nor was it particularly good at playing competitive games. It was this lack that undermined its position when conditions changed.

Of course, the first basis of advantage that PanAm lost was its market dominance. Carriers from many other countries began to offer competing services. But PanAm's real problem came with deregulation of the US airline industry in 1978. Suddenly, domestic carriers, such as United Airlines and American Airlines, which had acted as feeders to PanAm's international flights, now sought to go international themselves. With their large domestic networks, these airlines were in a much better position than PanAm to feed passengers on to international flights. PanAm now really paid for its lack of partners, and it also had a piece of tragic bad luck. By virtue of its near-identification as America's national carrier, it was targeted by terrorist bombers, and the loss over Lockerbie, Scotland, sent PanAm's fortunes spiralling downwards at the worst possible moment in 1988.

But before this disaster, PanAm was already suffering the disadvantages of the first mover. Because of union contracts, the oldest airlines such as PanAm tended to have the most restrictive work conditions and the least motivated, long-serving employees.

Similarly, PanAm began to suffer from having aged equipment. So it was caught in a downward spiral of declining revenues and inability to upgrade its assets. By 1991, PanAm had lost almost every basis of advantage and went into bankruptcy, selling off its last assets: its routes, planes and brand name.

Role of managers in bases of advantage

What is the role of managers in bases of competitive advantage? They should not be deluded into thinking that they themselves are the advantage. Their job is to identify, build, and sustain advantage. Having good managers is not itself nearly sufficient for success. Just recall how until 1990 or so, everyone wanted to hire IBM's managers.

Peter Lynch, the spectacularly successful manager of Fidelity's Magellan Fund, once wrote: 'I like to buy a company that any fool can run, because eventually one will.' What he meant is that a company's bases of competitive advantage come first. Advantages take years to build up and years to run down. Managers need to remember that they are temporary custodians who have received a set of advantages. Their job is to sustain and add to those advantages.

REFERENCES

1. Porter, Michael E., *Competitive Strategy: Techniques for Analyzing Industries and Competitors*, Free Press, New York, 1980.
2. Treacy, Michael and Wiersema, Fred, *The Discipline of Market Leaders*, Addison-Wesley, Reading, Mass, 1995.
3. *Ibid.*
4. Hertz is now only the second largest car rental company in the United States, behind Enterprise rent-a-car, but it is still the largest for business and vacation rentals, as Enterprise focuses on accident replacement vehicles.

RESOURCES

BOOK

Yip, George, *Total Global Strategy*, Prentice Hall, Englewood Cliffs, NJ, 1992.

WEB

www.georgeyip.com

Strategic supremacy through disruption and dominance

RICHARD D'AVENI

Richard D'Aveni explains how companies can achieve strategic supremacy.

THE evolution of business strategy has sometimes been a search for a general theory that explains success and failure. Many managers try to adopt one viewpoint to guide their strategic thinking: five forces, core competencies, hypercompetition or whatever. Others have tried to use them all simultaneously. Some have become disillusioned with their chosen paradigm(s) because it doesn't seem to work. Others have argued that strategy is based only on creating stable industry structures but discovered that stability (while desirable) is impossible when outside disruptions caused by increasing globalization or knowledge intensity are uncontrollable.

Each of the major popular strategic paradigms is really a different way to create wealth and strategic supremacy. Disillusionment occurs because practitioners and theorists have not recognized these differences and when it is appropriate to use each model.

Moreover, because rivals and customers won't be content to maintain the current environment the battle for strategic supremacy is continuous. By understanding the pattern of turbulence in the current competitive environment, managers can develop better strategies that lead to and maintain strategic supremacy.

There are four different competitive environments: equilibrium, fluctuating equilibrium, punctuated equilibrium and disequilibrium. They each require different strategies for success. Each requires that the incumbent leader and the challenger or disrupter formulate a different strategy to maintain or shift the current playing field.

Equilibrium

The equilibrium environment is characterized by long periods of little or no turbulence. Incumbent leaders control an equilibrium environment by creating barriers to entry for potential competitors and restraining rivalry within the industry. A powerful company extracts monopoly profits from captive customers without fear of attracting invaders seeking to capture its abnormally high profits. It creates profits by exercising monopoly power over buyers and monopsony over suppliers only when barriers are high and rivals agree to mute their competitive activities. A company using these norms of behaviour, forms an industry structure that offers it a protected competitive space.

Challengers might focus on disruptions that tear down or leap over the existing barriers of the incumbent leader.

Fluctuating equilibrium

The fluctuating equilibrium environment is characterized by rapid turbulence based on frequent disruptions that enhance existing competencies. This environment allows industry leaders with core competencies to sustain their leadership by layering new competencies on top of old ones. This, in turn, forces everyone else to catch up and allows the leader to leverage its core competencies into new product markets while others are still catching up.

Challengers in this fluctuating environment try to destroy the underlying core competencies of the leader and shift the environment to punctuated equilibrium or disequilibrium. Ideally, the disruption should turn the incumbent's strengths into weaknesses by making its competencies obsolete or a burden.

Punctuated equilibrium

A punctuated equilibrium environment is characterized by brief dynamic periods based on discontinuous change or competence-destroying revolutions. These dynamic periods are followed by longer periods of convergence (where the market organizes around the new common standard established by the revolution) and greater stability. Punctuated equilibrium environments are prevalent in industries where radical technological changes are followed by an emergent dominant design. This dominant design or standard creates a period of stability until the next technological revolution and the cycle repeats itself.

Industry leaders in the environment form fairly stable structures during the periods of convergence but then shift those structures rapidly during the periods of reorientation. Therefore they cannot organize or strategize during a convergent period as if they were in a stable environment. Companies can sometimes balance between flexibility and stability by using alliances to enhance flexibility and less formal mechanisms such as product standards to create stability. These alliances and standards, however, can be shifted rapidly when a new opportunity or need for disruption arises.

In this environment the challenger defines the playing field with a contrarian strategy. When the incumbent seeks to create stability, the challenger is disruptive. When the incumbent seeks to lead the next revolution, the challenger launches a counter-revolution by sustaining and improving the old environment. In this way the incumbent faces increased costs and friction for its strategies and the challenger has an opportunity to seize the initiative.

The leader faces the challenge of knowing when and how to respond to the next revolution. It has the option of pre-empting the revolution by waiting until discontinuity occurs and guiding or even absorbing it by acquisition of its leading proponent. Or, if it has vast resources, it can dampen the disruption.

If the leader has more limited resources it will try a less expensive approach to make the revolution irrelevant. For example, it may hedge its bets by using joint ventures that give it the option to emulate the new business model or gain access to revolutionary technologies after their success is proven.

In general, incumbent leaders prefer to dampen potential revolutions or hedge their bets so they can sustain their position as long as possible before incurring the risk and expense of adopting every potential revolution.

Disequilibrium

Disequilibrium, perhaps the most challenging and hypercompetitive environment, is characterized by frequent, discontinuous disruptions. Many high-tech industries, newly deregulated markets and unlikely low-tech industries such as pet foods and auto retailing face frequent, competence-destroying changes.

Successful incumbents in this environment constantly create new competencies to replace obsolete ones, continually leaving and disrupting the market themselves before their rivals do. Leaders gain advantage because their slower-moving opponents spend even more energy catching up and reacting.

Challengers have to disrupt this environment frequently, efficiently and in matchless ways or shift the environment to be less disruptive.

There are no clear lines of demarcation between the four environments. An environment of punctuated equilibrium in which the disruptions become increasingly more frequent becomes a disequilibrium environment.

Classifying the exact line between environments is less important than understanding the different dynamics and successful strategies for achieving strategic supremacy in each. The firm's perspective determines the environment it is currently in. One firm in an industry might see competence-destroying turbulence while another may experience competence enhancement in which its core competence is still valuable.

The goal of incumbent leaders and challengers in each environment is to achieve strategic supremacy by controlling the degree and pattern of turbulence. Strategic supremacy means not only control over the environment but also the paradigm used for the creation of wealth.

Different rules or norms of competition create profits differently in each environment. In an equilibrium environment dominant firms can profit by shutting out rivals and using power over buyers and suppliers to extract monopoly profits. In environments of fluctuating equilibrium, dominant firms use core competencies to profit from customers seeking to use these unique competencies. In punctuated equilibrium dominant firms make profits from the first-mover advantage of a revolution that sets a new industry standard and then positioning themselves to react to the next revolution. The dominant firm in disequilibrium profits by constantly improving and creating value through innovation.

RESOURCES

BOOKS

D'Aveni, Richard, *Hypercompetition*, The Free Press, New York, 1994.

D'Aveni, Richard, *Competing in Highly Dynamic Environments*, The Free Press, New York, 1995.

High speed strategy in large companies

PAUL STREBEL

Paul Strebel summarizes the main components of the high-speed strategy process in high-tech companies and describes the challenges these present to large companies trying to install them, and how some large, fast-moving companies are meeting these challenges. Those that succeed have an advantage over smaller companies in rolling out a successful business model.

THE traditional strategy process in large companies is not up to the speed required in today's fast-moving environment. It is usually too slow, being based on annual planning cycles; backward looking, trying to explain what went wrong; and too static, reflecting the fit between existing industry conditions and company competencies. By contrast, high-tech companies in the new economy make and implement strategic decisions much more rapidly. Large companies, in general, because of their size, face several major challenges in trying to adopt these processes.

The high-speed strategy process in high-tech companies

Research on the strategy process in high-tech companies in California suggests two main process components in companies with high-speed strategy: rapid bottom-up experimentation on the front line, and strategic road mapping through creative conflict (the clash of alternative viewpoints) at the top.[1]

Rapid bottom-up experimentation involves exposing concepts to customers, discussing prototypes with suppliers, running simulations, trying new products out as soon as possible, and perfecting them in the marketplace. Rather than driving initiatives from the top down, based on forecasts and plans, fast-moving companies encourage and nurture initiatives on the front line, from the bottom up. They collect real-time data and make decisions about which initiatives to invest in, based, wherever possible, not on opinion but on facts.

At the top, high-speed companies are fast and willing to think 'out of the box'. Ideally, they consider numerous alternatives before making a decision. The alternatives emerge from the bottom-up initiatives, as well as from scenarios reflecting business and technology trends, consideration of competitors' moves, and the interaction of a diverse management team.

However, a creative clash of alternative viewpoints requires the management of conflict at the top. Conflicts can be resolved constructively when management has higher-level values and goals to guide decisions. Everyone has their say, the leadership decides, and the dissenters agree to support the decision in pursuit of the higher goal. If facts later prove the decision wrong, then it is quickly changed. In effect, rather than a strategic plan, these companies develop a strategic roadmap that provides alternative paths to the same higher-level goal.

Bottom-up experimentation and strategic road mapping are essentially interlinked processes of organizational learning about work in a rapidly changing environment. When discussing high-speed strategy with executives, I have found it useful to depict the activities involved in the form of the learning cycles shown in Figure 1.

Strategic road mapping, based on future intelligence, scenarios, competitor responses, and the clash of alternatives, is now part of the strategy process package offered by several well-known consulting companies. Rapid bottom-up experimentation is part of innovation management packages, as well as the options view of strategy: dealing with high uncertainty requires experimentation to develop a portfolio of strategic options that open doors to the futures that may unfold.

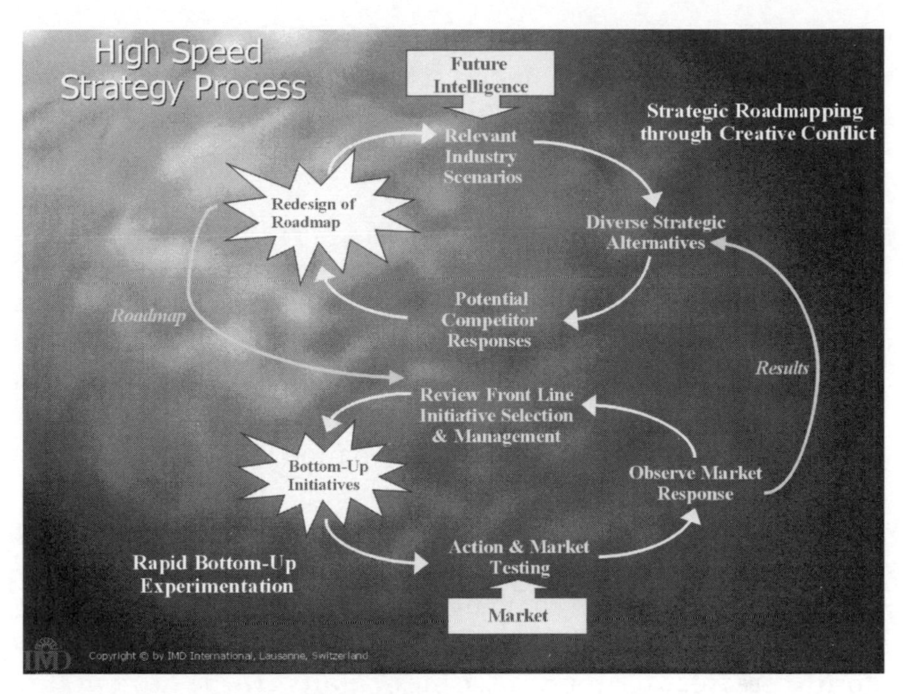

Figure 1 High speed strategy process

High-speed strategy is only possible, however, if its two process components are tightly linked together. Here, there is a big difference between large and small companies. In the latter, strategic road mapping and bottom-up experimentation are naturally intertwined in the daily life of the firm, with the same individuals often involved in both processes. In large companies this is not the case, and the implementation of high-speed strategy is much more difficult.

Challenges faced by larger companies

The first challenge for large companies is to energize the organization to produce bottom-up experimentation. It is well known that the mindset, politics, culture, and systems behind the past success that produces large companies are a heavy legacy that, unless radically modified, suffocate rule-breaking initiatives. The literature on innovation points to the importance of creating a culture that tolerates honest failure, the open exchange of business ideas, the rotation of talent through project teams, and multi-channel access to resources. Not only is this difficult to put in place, but it is often not enough to produce a rapid flow of initiatives in the face of a conservative mainstream culture.

The second challenge is the distance between the top and the front line in large companies. Getting feedback into strategic thinking at the top from front line experimentation and customers and suppliers is no easy matter, nor are the communication of the strategic roadmap to the front line and the shaping of incentives and support systems. All of this is complicated in global companies by language and differences in national culture. The time lag between a change in direction at the top and its full comprehension throughout the company makes it impossible to shift direction rapidly and frequently without disorienting people.

This is part of a third challenge: the difficulty of reorganizing rapidly to exploit new opportunities. Large companies are commonly organized around business units with bottom-line responsibility. The push for, and the rewards based on, business unit performance result in competing business 'silos' between which there is little co-operation. Reorganization usually involves shifting the focus of bottom-line responsibility to a dimension that cuts across the original organizational silos. The resistance in the old silos to managing along the new dimension, plus the communication difficulties already mentioned, make rapid reorganization in large companies very difficult.

A fourth challenge is to get focus amid the multiplicity of competing initiatives that emerge once the organization is energized. Large companies have a larger portfolio of businesses, plus the resources to support many more initiatives than smaller companies. In addition, there are more top managers, each with their own favourite projects. This often results in an overload of change and growth initiatives, causing confusion on the front line. On top of this, the politics that occur between senior managers from different businesses with different perspectives, delay critical choices and further aggravate the lack of focus.

How successful large and fast companies deal with these challenges

The practice in three successful large and fast companies, Cisco, Nokia and Enron, suggests an emerging pattern for dealing with these challenges.

Direct contact between the top and the front-line innovation champions to energize the organization

Top management in all three companies directly stimulates front-line innovation. They recognize that in a rapidly moving environment their company's future depends on the success of its innovation champions. And nothing stimulates the emergence of innovation champions more than attention, support, and recognition from the top.

John Chambers, CEO of Cisco is continually involved in the purchase of new start-ups with leading-edge technology and high-energy, innovative managers. Special attention goes to retaining the acquired managers, who are quickly integrated into Cisco's organization with new opportunities and freedom to take the initiative, plus direct access to the top. (Chambers has 70 vice-presidents reporting to him from around the world.) These entrepreneurial managers help Cisco maintain its flow of growth initiatives and front-line experiments; several of them are leading major parts of the company.

At Enron, the direct role of top management in stimulating the flow of bottom-up initiatives has been especially marked. Creating the new trading markets for gas, electricity, pulp and paper, surplus bandwidth on fibreoptic networks, and so on, was true pioneering in the sense that there were no start-ups to buy. In the case of the gas and electricity derivative markets, CEO Ken Lay and COO Jeff Skilling were the entrepreneurs. Front-line employees, with the personal involvement of Jeff Skilling, developed the markets for pulp and paper, surplus bandwidth, and weather derivatives. The way in which Skilling encouraged and supported David Cox, Thomas Gros, Lynda Clemmons and others, to develop these new markets is now part of oft-repeated business stories.

At Nokia, the lack of hierarchy means that top management is very closely involved with front-line initiatives, while the lack of pretentiousness and the informality of the Nokia culture make it easy for front-line managers to access the top management team. *Fortune* magazine calls Nokia 'perhaps the least hierarchical big company in the world ...'[2]

It's 'often profoundly unclear who's in charge'. Top managers like Matti Aluhuhta, president of Nokia Mobile Phones, periodically spend several days closeted with middle managers in seminars elaborating their change and innovation initiatives. And 'Nokia's cafeteria is where employees can often corner CEO, Jorma Ollila'. He also spends several months of the year in Silicon Valley to keep in touch with the latest Valley activity, especially with the new start-ups Nokia has recently bought.

Virtual network to shorten the distance between customers, suppliers, the front line and the top

The notion of a virtual organization has also been around for some time, but large company examples are rare. Our three are among the more successful large company exponents of this approach. All of them use virtual networks to bring the voices of the customers and suppliers deep inside the company.

Cisco is especially advanced. It practices what it preaches about using the web to speed up business: in net language, it 'eats lots of its own dog food'[3]. The company does 90 percent of its sales over its extranet, the internet connection with its customers, and answers more than 80 percent of customer service questions online. 'It has saved me over 1,000 engineers,' says Chambers, 'I put them into building new products.'[4] Upstream, over 30 component factories run by contract suppliers are tied into a virtual organization centred on its three assembly plants. The extranet integrates and radically shortens the response time of this supply chain, by facilitating the exchange of test, design and order information.

Internally, as well, Cisco makes extensive use of the web. The internet is the primary tool for recruiting talent and personnel management. Particularly impressive is the way Cisco uses the web to speed up the flow of financial information. Chief Financial Officer Larry Carter can analyze the financial contribution of every customer order and can consolidate and close Cisco's accounts within a day at any time.[5]

Apart from the now standard uses of an intranet for internal communication, virtual project team management, and the like, Enron's new business model is all about using derivatives and technology to create virtual marketplaces between itself and its partners. Thus, EnronOnline.com is an internet-based trading system for energy commodities and derivatives, the 'first web-based system enabling companies to buy and sell the full range of wholesale energy products online'. As a complement, it has also started EnronCredit.com to provide 'innovative credit risk management for the B2B world'. Enron pioneered this unit to take advantage of a big gap between what it and other utilities need to manage their corporate risk and what is available in the credit markets.

Located in a small country, Nokia has been forced to work with virtual teams from early on. In 1991, Pertti Kerhonen, a 29-year-old vice-president at the Camberley R&D facility in England, co-ordinated the development of a multi-standard phone with researchers, designers, marketers, and production people around the world, including outside suppliers, most of them located at a distance. Today, relying on a network of colleagues around the world to get things done is part of life for many at Nokia. The use of the virtual organization goes along with a highly hands-off management style. Most assignments of importance are given to a team. 'The objective is to always have decisions made by people who have the best knowledge,' says Matti Aluhuhta.[6] And it doesn't matter where they are.

Continual acquisition and reorganization to capture new strategic opportunities

Whereas small companies, by virtue of their size, are very flexible, large organizations have to work at flexibility to speed up the strategy execution process. At all three companies we've been discussing, reorganization and acquisition integration are part of ongoing corporate life.

From 1993 to early 2000, Cisco made 53 takeovers costing more than $23 billion. Normally, the mainstream culture of a large organization would snuff out the entrepreneurial spirit of acquired start-ups. As an antidote, Cisco has developed a well-honed process for integrating the start-ups into its organization. There is a special acquisitions group of 60 people that screens target firms for their compatibility with Cisco culture and prospects for a rapid financial return, and then manages the integration process. In 1999/2000, Cisco also started three major new alliances, with Motorola to provide business networking services, with Qwest communications to develop the US's largest internet-based network, and with GTE, Whirlpool, and Sun to develop a home appliance networking device.

Although Enron started its move into energy trading with home-grown initiatives, it has begun making acquisitions and alliances, like Cisco and Nokia, to maintain the pace of business innovation and growth. In 1998/1999, Enron began power trading in Australia and Argentina. It acquired control of a power utility in Brazil and continued to build its US portfolio of power plant interests. Enron acquired a UK water company and formed Azurix, a global water business. In addition, it reorganized its gas operations in China and India, and formed a joint venture with SK Group to distribute and market gas in South Korea.

At Nokia, the New Venture Organization (NVO) is the incubator for capturing new strategic options beyond the company's existing business portfolio. There are new initiatives, or equity participations in promising small companies, that do not fit into the mainstream organization. Most recently, these have been in the e-commerce and telephony technology areas. In addition, when there is a critical internal mass of new business, it is grouped into a new division. In 1999, Nokia combined its wireless and internet businesses into new units, Nokia Internet Communications to provide solutions to Internet Service Providers and Nokia Home Communications to serve the home. In the mainstream business itself, the exponential growth in mobile telephones also has been creating an ongoing organizational revolution. In 1999, Nokia signed major alliance contracts with several advanced telecom operators, Sprint, Telefonica Celular (Brazil), and Docomo (NTT Japan), as well as deals for its WAP software in HP and IBM servers.

Strategic confidence and cohesion at the top to provide focus and take appropriate big bets

In an uncertain, rapidly evolving environment, the multiple options created by an energized bottom-up organization can quickly degenerate into gridlock, if top management does not execute with cohesion and have the confidence to make the strategic choices necessary to provide focus and take advantage of major opportunities.

At Cisco, John Chambers provides cohesion and focus at the top: 'John listens ... But once Chambers decides to move, he expects "everybody to be in line".' And the big moves have been implemented with relentless focus: acquisitions to get away from Cisco's original dependence on internet routers to an offering incorporating the most complete range of networking products in the industry, with everything being driven by customer service. Stories abound on the importance of customer satisfaction and how Chambers checks on critical customer problems every night, no matter where he is.[7]

It was Ken Lay and Jeff Skilling, themselves, who directed the big shift at Enron from traditional utility to surplus capacity trader and market maker. They saw and took the opportunity presented by the drop in oil prices in the mid-1980s, the resulting crisis in the US gas pipeline industry as customers switched to oil, and the eventual deregulation of the industry, to begin trading surplus pipeline capacity. As mentioned above, they have provided the decisive guidance since then, in all the other major moves Enron has taken to focus on and develop new opportunities.

Although they have rotated positions, the same top team of five executives has been in place at Nokia since Ollila took over in 1992. This is the team that took Nokia from old-world conglomerate to focused telecom equipment company. Ollila himself got the CEO job in large part because he had turned around the then ailing mobile phone division. He was also at the centre of one of

Nokia's most important competitive moves, the decision to turn mobile phones into a branded product. One of his favourite quotes is from Confucius, 'The task of the leader is to have them think they did it themselves.' Despite the difficulty of telling who's in charge at Nokia, there is no doubt who is providing the focus.

The advantage of large companies in a fast-moving environment

Considering the challenges they face because of their size, one might ask whether large companies have any advantage over smaller ones in a fast-moving environment. The answer is that they can leverage competence and focus resources far more effectively than a network of small companies when rolling out a successful product and business model. Once they make the breakthrough, they can take it much further than a small company. All three of our examples built their success on the rollout of a successful business model: Cisco with its broad range of networking equipment, Enron with its surplus capacity derivatives, Nokia with its branded mobile phones.

However, riding the breakthrough wave requires a high-speed strategy capability. Competitors without this capability fall off the wave; there are many incremental innovations and adjustments needed to stay ahead. We have argued, based on the literature on high-tech companies and the practice at Cisco, Enron and Nokia, that the key components of a high-speed strategy capability in large companies are:

- Rapid bottom-up experimentation on the front line.
- Strategic road mapping through the creative conflict at the top.
- Direct contact between the top and the front-line innovation champions.
- Virtual networking to shorten the distance between customers, suppliers, the front line and the top.
- Continual acquisitions, alliances, and reorganization to capture new strategic opportunities.
- Strategic confidence and cohesion at the top to provide focus and take appropriate big bets.

This list can be reduced to the last four items, because if they are in place, the first two must be also. Acquisitions of start-ups, alliances, and innovation champions are the stuff of rapid bottom-up experimentation. Direct contact between the top and the front line, plus networking to bring the voices of customers and suppliers inside, make the clash of ideas at the top inevitable. Strategic confidence and cohesion are necessary to manage these and provide focus.

The outstanding question is whether this is enough to be able to catch another breakthrough wave. Some researchers have argued that large companies cannot make the revolutionary breakthroughs.[8] However, two of the companies we have been looking at did exactly that, Enron and Nokia. And both capitalized on existing experience and hardware to do it: Enron had power plant capacity to trade, and one of Nokia's divisions was part of the original Nordic cellular system. Making a breakthrough by combining the 'old' with the 'new' economy is clearly possible. In both cases, however, it was not existing, but new management that achieved it.

REFERENCES

1. Eisenhardt, K., 'Making Fast Strategic Decisions in High-Velocity Environments', *Academy of Management Journal*, Vol 32, No 3, 1989, pp. 543–575; Eisenhardt, K. and Tabrizi, B., 'Accelerating Adaptive Processes: Product Innovation in the Global Computer Industry', *Administrative Science Quarterly*, Vol. 40. 1995, pp. 84–110.
2. Fox, J., 'Nokia's Secret Code', *Fortune*, 1 May 2000, pp. 31–38.
3. 'Cisco Systems: The Dogfood Danger', *Economist*, 8 April 2000, pp. 72–74.
4. Byrne, J. A., 'The Corporation of the Future', *Business Week*, 31 August 1998.
5. 'Cisco Systems: The Dogfood Danger', *Economist*, 8 April 2000, pp. 72–74.
6. Fox, J., 'Nokia's Secret Code', *Fortune*, 1 May 2000, pp. 31–38.
7. Serwer, A., 'There's Something about Cisco', *Fortune*, 15 May 2000, pp. 38–52.
8. Utterback, J., *Mastering the Dynamics of Innovation*, Harvard Business School Press, Boston, 1994.

RESOURCES

BOOKS

Gilbert, X., 'Using Collective Learning to Focus Frontline Energy', *Focused Energy: Mastering Bottom-up Organization*, Strebel, P. (ed), Wiley, 2000.

Strebel, Paul, *Breakpoints: How Managers Exploit Radical Business Change*, Harvard Business School Press, Boston, 1992, Chapter 11.

Strebel, Paul (ed), *Focused Energy*, John Wiley, 1999.

Utterback, J., *Mastering the Dynamics of Innovation*, Harvard Business School Press, Boston, 1994.

Strategy in the knowledge economy

W. CHAN KIM AND RENÉE MAUBORGNE

W. Chan Kim and Renée Mauborgne on why strategy in the knowledge economy must be more than just beating the competition.

AT the heart of most strategic thinking is competition. Yet strategy driven by competition usually has three unintended effects:

- Imitative, not innovative, approaches to the market.
- Companies act reactively.
- A company's understanding of emerging mass markets and changing customer demands become hazy.

The reason is that when asked to build competitive advantage most managers look at what their competitors are doing and then seek to do it better. In other words, their strategic thinking regresses towards the competition. As a result, companies often achieve no more than an incremental improvement on what the competition is doing – imitation not innovation.

For the past 10 years we have looked at companies that have recorded ongoing and high levels of growth and profits compared to their competitors. The strategies they have followed are what we call 'value innovation'. This is fundamentally different from adding layers of competitive advantage or trying to outperform competitors. Value innovation focuses on offering quantum leaps in value for customers. The key is the simultaneous pursuit of radically superior value and lower costs.

Starbucks, Virgin Atlantic, Enron, Bloomberg, Home Depot, Wal-Mart and others are examples of companies that have succeeded by consistently focusing their innovative efforts on customer value and lower costs.

Value innovation places an equal emphasis on both value and innovation. Value with no innovation stresses improving the net benefit to the customer or value creation. Innovation with no value can be too technology driven. Value innovation grounds innovation in buyer value.

While innovation itself may be random, value innovation is not. It deliberately seeks quantum leaps in customer value.

There are five key ways in that value innovation differs from conventional strategic logic:

1. While many companies may allow industry conditions to dictate what is possible, probable and profitable, value innovators see their industries as inherently malleable and challenge the inevitability of industry conditions.
2. While the orthodox strategy may be to focus on outpacing the competition, value innovators aim to dominate the market by introducing a major advance in buyer value that makes the competition irrelevant.
3. Traditionally, companies focus on customer segmentation, customization and retention. But value innovators seek key value commonalties that will allow them to capture the mass market even if they have to lose some customers.
4. Most companies start by more fully exploiting their existing key assets and capabilities but while value innovators do the same they are not constrained by them. They are willing to tear down and rebuild if necessary.
5. Conventional companies concentrate on improving traditional industry products and services. Value innovators think in terms of a total customer solution, even if this means going outside traditional industry boundaries.

Thus value innovation differs from traditional strategy in both the height of its ambitions and the breadth of the way it defines customers. The focus on incremental improvements slips to the background and it identifies its target market not merely as its own or its competitors' customers. It also seeks to pull in buyers that have never patronized an industry. Companies may often look to their customers for inspiration, but the best ideas often come from listening to competitors' customers and people who are not even, as yet, in your market.

For example, in 1991 US golf club manufacturer Callaway Golf launched the 'Big Bertha' club. The product soon dominated the market, taking increased market share and, more importantly, growing the total market. The reason is that in a highly competitive market Callaway did not focus on the competition. Rivals had fiercely benchmarked each other, resulting in very similar clubs with over-sophisticated enhancements. Callaway looked at why in the 'country club' market, more people played tennis than golf. The answer was that small club heads made hitting a golf ball difficult. 'Big Bertha's' large club head made it easier and more fun, attracting both existing and new players.

Callaway Golf did not look at how it might beat other golf club manufacturers by offering an improved solution to the traditional goal – how to hit a golf ball further. Instead it looked at offering a solution to a customer problem – how to hit a golf ball more easily. By redefining the problem in this way Callaway grew the market by attracting customers who previously had not wished to play golf.

Value innovators seek to create new and superior value. A conventional focus on retaining and better satisfying existing customers promotes a fear of challenging the *status quo*. Value innovators monitor existing customers but also pursue non-customers.

The conventional strategic objective is to gain a competitive advantage by offering improvements against industry benchmarks. But this type of benchmarking is not what value innovation is all about. Value innovation changes industries. For example, Bloomberg's value innovation leapfrogged existing market leaders to redefine an industry. Reuters and Dow Jones' Telerate were providing online stock price date. Bloomberg offered smart terminals capable of data analysis that allowed traders and analysts to make decisions more quickly and accurately, allowing it to rapidly become the market leader and leave the others in the dust.

Note, though, that while value innovation is the essence of strategy in the knowledge economy, it is not enough on its own. Any strategy that attracts customers will be copied. Value innovators therefore also need to deploy the tactics that traditionally preserve the first mover's advantage, and often these will be incremental improvements to the original value innovation. In this respect, value innovation produces a punctuated equilibrium – major change followed by periods of refinement and consolidation.

When they find superior value, value innovators deploy capabilities that exist both within and outside their companies to exploit it. Value innovators frequently have a network of partners that provide complementary assets and capabilities.

For example, SMH, creator of the Swatch, had no expertise in the mass watch market, in plastics mounding or even in design. It did have an idea of superior value – the wristwatch as a fashion accessory – plus the insight to create, buy or borrow the expertise needed to produce it.

To make value innovation a reality companies have to go beyond conventional competence-based thinking that takes an inside-out approach and ask, what would we do if we were starting anew? That opens the creative scope and range of opportunities that companies consider.

Quantum leaps in value almost always involve major changes in behaviour and working practices. These will not be achieved without people willingly co-operating with the innovation process and making their skills and experience available to a company.

But the key to gaining this willing co-operation is the idea of 'fair process'.

Exercising 'fair process' – fairness in the process of making and executing decisions – is a powerful way to recognize people's intellectual and emotional worth. Fair process promotes trust and commitment whereas treatment perceived as unfair makes people hoard their ideas and drag their feet. Fair process involves three basis principles:

- **Engagement**: involving people in decisions that affect them by seeking their ideas and allowing them to challenge the ideas and assumptions of others.
- **Explanation**: everyone involved or affected should understand the reasons for decisions and why their ideas were accepted or rejected.
- **Establishing clear expectation**: people must know what the objectives are, how their performance will be judged and who is responsible for what.

Fair process and value innovation create a positively reinforcing cycle. Success in value innovation strategy that results from fair process strengthens the group and increases people's belief in the process, thus perpetuating the collaborative and creative models that are the basis of value innovation.

Most companies strive to deliver fair outcomes but do not distinguish this from fair process. Fair outcomes ensure that individuals receive the resources they need or material rewards in exchange for co-operation. But to induce knowledge creation and voluntary co-operation between individuals companies must go beyond fair outcomes to fair process.

Fair process it is about being even-handed, consistent and open to challenge.

Fair process is often not easy for managers. It forces them to be candid and to explain themselves. Just rewards are important, but people are also concerned with how they are treated. If people feel respected and think that decision-making processes are fair they will accept decisions even if they don't benefit from them. Fair process creates an objective, meritocratic culture based on a belief in the intellectual and emotional worth of all employees.

People possessing knowledge are the key resource of companies that follow value innovation strategies. But this resource is increasingly independent and mobile. To capture it, companies must meet expectations of both fair outcome and fair process.

RESOURCES

WEB

www.insead.fr

Coping with strategic risk

COLIN EDEN

Strategic management is risk management, claims Colin Eden. He outlines the key areas of strategic risk and advocates responses to risk that reduce the turbulence from which so many organizations see themselves as suffering.

ORGANIZATIONS are becoming progressively more involved in increasingly complex ventures. Globalization and the need for projects to involve many partners through strategic alliances and joint venture partnerships has provided many organizations with experiences of unexpected disasters of sometimes enormous magnitude. These experiences focus the mind, and it is immensely attractive to believe that there might be tools and methods for managing the complexity that is considered to be causing such disasters.

The types of risks facing large organizations are changing. Because strategic alliances and partnerships are increasingly common, working across time zones and cultural boundaries is adding even more complexity. The significance of currency fluctuations is now an everyday aspect of running major projects where suppliers and partners are sometimes embedded in unstable economies.

An inability to manage strategic risk has meant that many large organizations have gone out of business or been absorbed by their competitors. This might suggest that increased caution in decision making is required. On the contrary, more complexity and the associated risk demand more aggression in the assessment of risk, and more importantly in the management of the risk.

What are the key areas of strategic risk?

Political risks

Primary among these tend to be regulatory and planning risks, where progress on major projects or new products depends on expectations about, for example, approvals for new roads or safety regulations. Construction of the Eurotunnel was disrupted extensively by continual changes in safety requirements, particularly following the Zeebrugge and Kings Cross transport disasters.

In turn, political activity can depend on stable, or at least predictable, government. In many parts of the world, the shift away from communist central planning towards privatization has left some bidders used to working with experienced government floundering as they face government with little or no experience of dealing with the privatization process.

Customer risks

In addition to risks associated with government as the customer, the structure of decision making in customers can change violently. It is typical of an organization to take for granted, without thinking, that its customers will continue to make decisions in the same way they have always done. 'We've done so much work for them before, we know how they operate, and know how to work with them.' And yet, with increasing change in the structure and strategic orientation of business, these assumptions are becoming significant risks. Sometimes, for example, marketing people take control from engineers and start imposing totally different ways of managing contracts. An underestimation of the changing strategic context of customers can lead to a severe underestimation of major risks.

Partner and supplier risks

Some organizations determined that the best approach was to adopt a policy of transferring risk to suppliers and partners. This policy often proved to be wholly mistaken, as managers found that they had transferred risk to subcontractors and partners who had no capability to manage that risk. These risks came back to haunt the very organization that had thought they were rid of them – sometimes with dire consequences. Indeed, in some instances organizations have been forced to acquire a subcontractor in order to avoid their going bust. Joint risk assessment using expertly facilitated risk workshops and an involvement of in-house lawyers in a background role can avoid the worst outcomes of lose/lose mutual risk transfer.

Joint venture risks

Collaboration is notoriously difficult. Truly finding and explicitly recognizing joint goals that neither organization could achieve on their own – what are often called 'meta-goals' – is problematic, particularly when a joint venture involves two or more organizations who will otherwise be competing in similar markets. If these cannot be found and recognized then there is no likelihood of 'collaborative advantage' and so there is a greater probability of serious strategic risk unfurling as the project is delivered.

People risks

Assumptions about the availability of skilled staff at managerial and blue-collar levels are often mistaken. Managing global complexity is difficult and there are few people available who have significant experience in managing strategic complexity on that scale. The shift of skills from traditional enterprise to smaller-scale operations associated with, for example, dot-com organizations, is leaving larger organizations unusually exposed. The increasingly mobile and disloyal labour force, particularly of knowledge workers as well as more mobile manufacturing workers, is increasing the strategic risks associated with delivering complex projects. The behaviour of some competitors in terms of employment practices, and what would be illegal attitudes in some countries, can result in unexpected and non-traditional advantages.

Reputation risks

The public view of an organization's strategic behaviour has often had a devastating impact on future strategies. Shell's attitudes projected by the Press, and other surprisingly powerful stakeholders, during the Brent Spar and Nigerian episodes, for example, seriously affected Shell's reputation among some of its customers. The behaviour of Barclays Bank in relation to ATMs and rural branches certainly affected its reputation – though the full strategic consequences are yet to be clearly understood. It is, of course, possible that these strategic behaviours were well understood by decision makers, and that the outcomes and risks were assessed and chosen. What is not doubted is that there was an impact on reputation.

More obvious strategic risks are:

- Market risks.
- Operational risks.
- Financial risks.

Market risks

In this category, the most serious strategic risk follows from a misunderstanding of competitor behaviour and competencies through arrogance and unquestioning blindness. Here, management teams operate in ways that mean they cannot question their own self-confidence and market prowess. Sometimes over-confidence can be an important attribute that helps organizations get through difficult times. However, more often it leads to blinkered strategies that do not openly recognize the realities of market and competitor change. It is a condition known as 'groupthink'.

Operational risks

Obvious risks include an inability to deliver promised design and so concomitant manufacturing and warranty risks follow, with risk of subsequent shortening of the product lifecycle. Less obvious are the significant risks that derive from demands to deliver new products to a compressed or accelerated timescale. This may follow from competition launching earlier than expected. However, project acceleration against already aggressive timelines can easily cause so much disruption and consequential delay that delivery dates get worse rather than better.

Financial risks

The inaccurate assessment of the liquidity or credit capability of suppliers is sometimes devastating in its impact, resulting in forced acquisition. More evident are the risks associated with currency exchange, interest rates, recession, localized inflation, and so on. Although obvious, it is still surprising how many organizations do not undertake simple 'scenario' analyses as the basis for exploring risk management strategies.

Is strategy making redundant?

These circumstances have led some organizations to consider serious strategy making as almost redundant, on the grounds that the business world is now too turbulent.

A risk is only a risk if it potentially attacks strategic aspirations. Turbulence only matters when it matters. What matters is what affects, in a disastrous manner, the attainment of desired outcomes – the organization's aspirations. Therefore, one organization's turbulence is another's stability. The major purpose of strategy making is to manage turbulence by reducing it. Some organizations thrive on turbulence because they have strategically designed their organizations to manage that turbulence. For them, turbulence would be the lack of all the characteristics that for another organization would indicate turbulence. Turbulence is a subjective matter and is, crucially, related to the ability to manage and control – and that is what strategic thinking must do.

So why is this? It is because strategic management has been advertised as something akin to planning, to stability, to budgets and action programmes. It has not been presented as something that is highly contingent, in form and nature, to a specific organization.

Strategic management is risk management

As senior managers try to develop an understanding of the strategic issues facing the organization, they seek to anticipate the kind of strategic problems and disasters that might affect a successful strategic future.

The key strategic responses to strategic uncertainty – risk – are power, structural, and technical. These are the responses that reduce turbulence.

Typical power responses to strategic risk

The most common responses are to dominate or eliminate risk. It is most attractive to be paid for the risk by having the power to set your prices accordingly. In this case, power may derive from relationship management, for example historically trusting relationships between supplier and government. Alternatively, more power may be leveraged through product uniqueness or market dominance (including a monopoly position), although this is usually only a temporary power base.

It is the inappropriate, or unthinking, use of power that leads to the transfer of risk to other organizations that are unable to manage the risk. Effective power responses depend on sound stakeholder analysis and so effective stakeholder management strategies.

Structural responses to strategic risk

It is important to design at least parts of the organization so that it can recognize early on the direction in which uncertain situations will unfold, and so respond to change and uncertainty in an opportunistic, flexible and effective manner. Of course, design of organizational structures is not all; the ability to use a range of appropriate technical responses is also paramount.

Technical responses to strategic risk

Strategy-making techniques can be applied such as stakeholder analysis and management, scenario planning or alternative futures exploration, cross-impact analysis designed to capture the interactions between strategic risks, and the application of cause-mapping techniques that can recognize the 'systemicity' of strategic risk. Not only does the mapping capture the relationship between each of the risk triggers and the issues they may create, it also encourages questions about the strategic consequences of those issues. In addition, when the cause mapping is captured from the group senior managers, using a computer-supported group decision support system, then the supposed attack on the organization's aspirations can easily be outlined.

Most of these technical responses demand a change in attitude to the assessment of risk, from overly bureaucratized risk assessment undertaken at too low a level in the organization, to a 'workshop-based' method involving those with powerful tacit and subjective knowledge based on substantial experience and with the power to act on their deliberations. Senior staff must make explicit the sort of events that might trigger risks across all of the categories discussed above. In one sense, they are creating for themselves a 'risk register'. However, as with a traditional technical risk register, creating it as a list misses the key feature of strategic risk – that the risks interact with one another.

Whatever technical responses are developed must address the fact that strategic risks interact with each other. The pattern of interactions gives the clue to which 'bundles' of risk are most significant and also indicates which are most potent – in the sense of acting as drivers for the unfolding of dangerous scenarios.

RESOURCES

BOOKS

Bernstein, Peter, *Against the Gods: The remarkable story of risk*, John Wiley, New York, 1998.

Chapman, C. and Ward, S., *Project Risk: Management process, techniques and insights*, Wiley, 1997.

Eden, C., Williams, T., Ackermann, F. and Howick, S., 'On the Nature of Disruption and Delay', *Journal of the Operational Research Society*, 51, 1-00, 200.

Williams, T. M., Ackermann, F. and Eden, C., 'Project Risk: Systemicity cause mapping and a scenario approach', in Kahkones, K. and Artro, K.A. (eds), *Managing Risks in Projects*, E & FN spun, London, 1997, pp. 343–52.

The communication advantage

PAUL A. ARGENTI AND JANIS FOREMAN

Paul A. Argenti and Janis Foreman explain why following the teachings of Aristotle can help involve key organizational constituencies in helping formulate and implement strategy.

SINCE the 1970s numerous studies have identified how organizations develop their strategies and, in some instances, how they succeed or fail when moving from a formulated strategy to its implementation. Some of these studies also discuss the importance of communication to the process of implementing strategy, but none of them considers communication to be a central focus. Even studies of strategic implementation make communication a peripheral concern, focusing instead on issues such as organizational structures and processes, reward systems and resource allocation. Despite the importance of these issues, the lack of focus on communication leaves a significant gap in managers' understanding of how to move from formulating to implementing strategy.

So how can senior management use communication effectively to formulate a strategy and to ensure that strategy is implemented?

Unlikely as it may seem, let's turn to the ancient Greek philosopher Aristotle and his work *On Rhetoric* to see the theoretical basis for bridging the gap between strategy and communication. We can use Aristotle's constituency focused approach to persuasion as a departure point for building a communication framework that can be used by 'expressive organizations'. These organizations risk expressing their values in the marketplace to attract and form relationships with varied constituencies on which both their survival and success ultimately depend.

In Aristotle's day, the fourth century BC, the fundamental unit of organizational life was the city state, in his case Athens. But despite the historical and cultural gap between our own and Aristotle's time, *On Rhetoric* contains two important elements that inform our understanding of how expressive organizations can effectively design and communicate their vision statements and strategic plans.

The first of these is Aristotle's notion of 'deliberative rhetoric', or speeches made in political assemblies where debate occurs for or against a particular kind of future for an organization – in Aristotle's case the city state, and in ours the expressive organization. The second element is his constituency focused approach to communication – that is, the centrality of the audience to persuasive discourse.

In today's expressive organization, deliberative rhetoric is most akin to the discourse of strategy formulation and implementation. For example, the whole idea behind Gary Hamel's notion of 'strategic revolution' is to postulate a future and move constituencies towards it. Under the leadership of CEO Arthur Martinez, Sears, Roebuck and Company put this idea into motion by developing a new vision statement in the mid-1990s – to be internalized by its constituencies – that was a hallmark of the company's huge transformation.

In *On Rhetoric* Aristotle used a constituency focused approach to consider the individual speaker persuading others to think or act according to the speaker's agenda. Aristotle grants a central role to the audience as judges – not merely spectators or recipients – of a particular argument. We have adapted this approach to look at the communication challenges that expressive organizations and their chief spokespeople face as they attempt to formulate and implement strategy.

Each element of the framework – the organization, its messages, its constituencies and its constituency responses – focuses attention on specific challenges for implementing strategy successfully.

The organization must determine its objectives for a particular communication with each constituency (what does the organization want each constituency to do?); evaluate the resources available to accomplish the task (what kind of money, human resources and time does the organization have available?); and determine the organization's overall reputation (how does each constituency receive the organization?).

A good way to see the benefits of a constituency focused approach to formulating and communicating strategy is to examine an organization that employs such an approach, such as Navistar.

Although CEO John Horne of Navistar – a heavy truck manufacturer headquartered in Chicago – did not formally design and use such an approach, his ideas about communication evolved to clearly illustrate his focus: persuading the company's multiple constituencies to help formulate and implement the organization's strategy.

When Horne took over as CEO in 1993 he recognized that the company had significant problems with its constituencies – employees, unions, senior management, the financial community and the media. The company was plagued with a history of union conflict, including a long strike in the 1970s. In turn, the general discontent of the workforce made investors lose confidence in the company's ability to prosper.

Believing that he had to bring his employees on board before raising the confidence of the financial community, Horne supported early initiatives to gather information from employees about their concerns. He used a three-pronged approach: extensive plant visits; an employee survey with follow-up; and direct involvement of union representatives in employee issues.

The dialogue established between senior management and plant employees became so successful in raising morale and in formulating strategy that plant visits became a formalized communication practice by the autumn of 1996. As a result, each month a member of the senior management group visits every plant. Meetings include the senior manager and 30 or 40 employees representing a cross-section of the plant. Senior management brings back what they learn at the plant and, in this way, the employees' voices are brought into top management's discussion of strategy. This continuing discussion has allowed the company to create its message collaboratively with this constituency, a role for communication that Aristotle envisaged long ago in his study of rhetoric.

Navistar's communication group extended this collaboration with employees by conducting extensive employee research to design an employee survey. Survey results, which were presented jointly by management and union leaders and published in newsletters, became the basis for action plans.

The CEO also initiated and maintains dialogue with another vital constituency, union representatives. Union members have been invited to join education and training committees and to recommend changes in this aspect of employee life.

Along with plant employees and union representatives, Horne also targeted senior management as a key internal constituency with which he wanted to improve communications. He instituted a 'leadership conference' in 1995, a three-day meeting for the top 550 managers in the firm. On the first day he learned that only 24 percent of the top executives knew that the company had a strategy. By the end of the conference, 98 percent knew. Leadership conferences continue to be a permanent component of the company's approach to communication.

When the company turned its attention to the external world, its first concern was understandably with its customers. Customer focus is, in fact, one of the core values it espouses. Since Horne became CEO, the company has taken actions to revitalize this core value – researching customers' overall experience and expectations of the brand, rethinking each target market group, holding press conferences and giving speeches at industry events to project Navistar as an industry leader. Among other things, the company has also worked to extend its brand image beyond that of 'reliability' and 'durability' – qualities that customers identified – to also include technological leadership and excellence for its extensive distribution network.

To address the scepticism of another external constituency, the financial community, about Navistar's ability to resolve its union problems, senior management developed a powerful, consistent story about how the company was going to solve its difficulties. They decided that, although management would take the blame for the problems, the company needed the employees to work collaboratively with them to help solve them.

As for the media – another key constituency – Horne persisted in opening up a dialogue with them even in the face of media stories that exacerbated the strife between unions and management and resulted in low morale in the plants. Despite initial lack of trust on both sides, the CEO's willingness to respond to questions and his ability to present a consistent story about the company's strategy gradually improved media relations.

As a result of Horne's constituency focused approach to communication he has been able to change the image of the company, raise employee morale, and improve its overall reputation and financial status.

Given these effects on an organization's image, morale, reputation and bottom line, public interest in rhetoric still pervades today. In the 4th century BC, Aristotle's work grew up alongside Athenian democracy and its need for public debate in the contested arenas of the law courts or public assemblies where issues of great consequence to the individual or the state were decided. Today, however, expressive organizations face other, but no less compelling, challenges: the need to influence and motivate key constituencies and to engage them in formulating as well as implementing strategy.

RESOURCES

BOOK

Aristotle, *Complete Works Volumes 1 and 2*, Barnes, Jonathon (ed.), Princeton University Press, 1984.

ANSOFF, IGOR

IGOR ANSOFF (born 1918) was one of the key figures in the formulation of a clear concept of strategic management. Ansoff was born in Vladivostok, the son of an American father and a Russian mother. In 1936, the Ansoff family moved to New York. Igor Ansoff trained as an engineer and mathematician. He worked for the RAND Corporation, and then the Lockheed Corporation where he was a vice-president.

In 1963 he left industry for academia, joining Carnegie-Mellon's Graduate School of Business Administration. He joined the San Diego-based US International University in 1983, where he is now Distinguished Professor of Strategic Management.

Ansoff's first – and most important – book was *Corporate Strategy*, in which he sought to make sense of the broader implications of what he had learned at Lockheed. He believed that there was 'a practical method for strategic decision making within a business firm' that could be made accessible to all.

Ansoff's work struck a chord. Until then, strategic planning had been a barely understood, *ad hoc* concept. It was practised, while the theory lay largely unexplored. The result was a rational model by which strategic and planning decisions could be made. The model concentrated on corporate expansion and diversification rather than strategic planning as a whole. From this emerged the Ansoff Model of Strategic Planning, an intricate and somewhat daunting sequence of decisions.

Central to this was the reassuringly simple concept of gap analysis: see where you are; identify where you wish to be; and identify tasks that will take you there. Ansoff can also lay claim to introducing the word 'synergy' into the management vocabulary. He explained it with uncharacteristic brevity as '2 + 2 = 5'. In addition, he examined 'corporate advantage' long before Michael Porter cornered the field 20 years later.

To the contemporary observer, Ansoff's work can appear excessively analytical and highly prescriptive. In an era where corporate change is increasingly recognized as a fact of life, thinkers argue that solutions are ever more elusive. Ansoff's model was better suited to a world of answers than one beset by turbulence and uncertainty.

BALANCED SCORECARD

THE Balanced Scorecard is a strategic management and measurement system that links strategic objectives to

comprehensive indicators. It recognizes that companies have a tendency to fixate on a few measurements that blinker their assessment of how the business is performing overall. The Balanced Scorecard focuses management attention on a range of key performance indicators to provide a balanced view.

The concept was originally put forward by David Norton, co-founder of the consulting company Renaissance Solutions, and Robert Kaplan, the Marvin Bower Professor of Leadership Development at Harvard Business School. It is explored in their book *The Balanced Scorecard: Translating strategy into action* (1996).

Kaplan and Norton compared running a company to flying a plane. The pilot who relies on a single dial is unlikely to be safe. Pilots must utilize all the information contained in their cockpit. 'The complexity of managing an organization today requires that managers be able to view performance in several areas simultaneously,' said Kaplan and Norton. 'Moreover, by forcing senior managers to consider all the important operational measures together, the Balanced Scorecard can let them see whether improvement in one area may be achieved at the expense of another.'

In many ways, it is simple common sense. Balance is clearly preferable to imbalance. Kaplan and Norton suggested that four elements need to be balanced:

- First is the customer perspective. Companies must ask how they are perceived by customers.
- The second element is 'internal perspective'. Companies must ask what it is at which they must excel.
- Third is the 'innovation and learning perspective'. Companies must ask whether they can continue to improve and create value.
- Finally, there is the financial perspective. Companies must ask how they look to shareholders.

According to Kaplan and Norton, by focusing energies, attention and measures on all four of these dimensions, companies become driven by their mission rather than by short-term financial performance. Crucial to achieving this is applying measures to company strategy. Instead of being beyond measurement, the Balanced Scorecard argues that strategy must be central to any process of measurement – 'A good Balanced Scorecard should tell the story of your strategy'.

BOSTON MATRIX

SO influential was the Boston Matrix that a whole generation of senior managers grew up with cows, dogs, stars and question marks as a way to classify their businesses. The Boston Matrix became an icon in an era of strategic planning.

Until the 1960s, models were the impenetrable domain of economists. The man largely credited for bringing business models into the mainstream was an Australian, Bruce Henderson (1915–1992), founder of the Boston Consulting Group (BCG).

Sometimes called the 'Dog star' matrix for obvious reasons (see Figure 1), the Boston Matrix epitomized a generic view of strategic decision making. It is, in fact, a simple two-by-two matrix (a format popular with management consultants ever since) that measures market growth and relative market share for all the businesses in the company's portfolio. Each business can be placed on the matrix and classified accordingly.

The hypothesis of the Boston Matrix is that companies with higher market share in faster-growing industries are more profitable. The further to the left a business is on the Boston Matrix, the

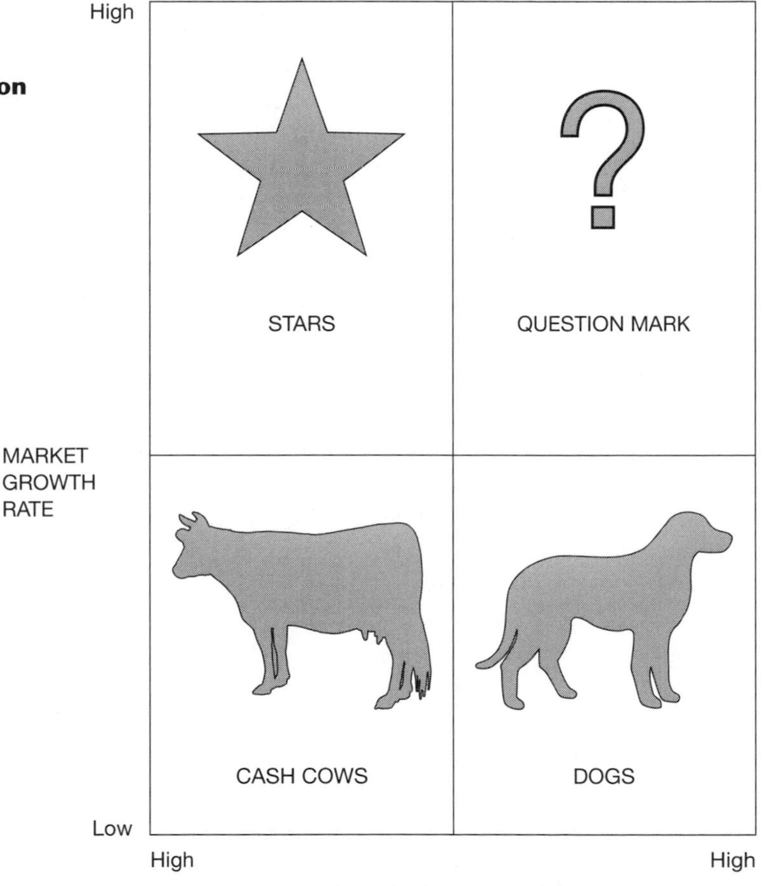

Figure 1 The Boston Matrix

stronger the company should be. (The matrix can be applied to individual products or entire businesses.)

Refinements have been added along the way. On its original matrix, BCG superimposed a theory of cash management that included a hierarchy of uses of cash, numbered from one to four in their order of priority. This identified the top priority as cash cows, characterized by high market share and low growth. Investment in cash cows is easily justified, as they are dull, safe, and highly profitable. Next in line are the stars (high growth; high market share), although their investment requirements are likely to be significant. More problematic is the third category, question marks (problem children, or wildcats in some versions) where there is high growth and low share. Any investment in them is risky. The final category is the aptly titled dogs, where low market share is allied to low growth. Dogs should not be approached.

The Boston Matrix proved a highly popular innovation. From a business point of view, it had the characteristics of any great model: it was accessible, simple and useful. However, it was also limiting. Measuring corporate performance against two parameters is straightforward, but potentially dangerous if these are the only two parameters against which performance is measured. A product of its time, the matrix offered a blinkered view of a world where growth and profitability were all that counted.

As a business tool, however, the Boston Matrix had a significant and long-term impact. Of equal significance was its influence on the management consulting industry. It spawned a host of imitators. Today, no consultant's report is complete without a matrix of some sort. More importantly, BCG could be said to have introduced the first off-the-shelf consulting product (although it wouldn't see it that way). Companies required the big idea. They wanted to see how they fared on the matrix and how it could shape their strategies. The consulting firm product was born.

Previously, consultants had gone in to client companies to solve specific business problems. The success of the Boston Matrix marked a change in approach. As well as problem solving, consultancy became concerned with passing on the latest ideas, the frameworks, models, and matrices that were in vogue. Problem solvers became pedlars of big ideas. This opened up huge new vistas for the management consultancy profession, which it has been assiduously – and profitably – chasing ever since.

CHANDLER, ALFRED

ALFRED CHANDLER (born 1918) is a Pulitzer Prize-winning business historian. After graduating from Harvard, he served in the US Navy before becoming, somewhat unusually,

a historian at MIT in 1950. He has been Straus Professor of Business History at Harvard since 1971.

Chandler's hugely detailed research into US companies between 1850 and 1920 has formed the cornerstone of much of his work. Chandler observed that organizational structures in companies such as DuPont, Sears Roebuck, General Motors, and Standard Oil were driven by the changing demands and pressures of the marketplace. He concluded that the market-driven proliferation of product lines led to a shift from a functional, monolithic organizational form to a more loosely coupled divisional structure.

Chandler was highly influential in the trend among large organizations for decentralization in the 1960s and 1970s. In his classic book, *Strategy and Structure*, he praised Alfred Sloan's decentralization of General Motors in the 1920s. He argued that the chief advantage of the multidivisional organization was that 'it clearly removed the executives responsible for the destiny of the entire enterprise from the more routine operational responsibilities and so gave them the time, information and even psychological commitment for long-term planning and appraisal'.

While the multidivisional form has largely fallen out of favour, another of Chandler's theories continues to raise the blood pressure of those who care about such things. He argued that strategy came before structure. Having developed the best possible strategy, companies could determine the most appropriate organizational structure to achieve it. In the early 1960s, this was speedily accepted as a fact of life.

More recently, Chandler's premise has been regularly questioned. In an ideal world, critics say, companies would hatch perfect strategies and then create neat structures and organizational maps. Reality, however, is a mess in which strategy and structure mix madly.

HAMEL, GARY

GARY HAMEL (born 1954) has established himself at the vanguard of contemporary thinking on strategy. Hard hitting, opinionated and rigorously rational, Hamel summarized the challenge of the 1990s, in a typically earthy phrase, as 'separating the shit from the shinola, the hype from the reality and the timeless from the transient'.

As well as being visiting professor of strategic and international management at London Business School, California-based Hamel is a consultant to major companies and chairman of Strategos, a worldwide strategic consulting company. His reputation has burgeoned as a result of a series of acclaimed articles in the *Harvard Business Review* as well as the popularity of the bestselling *Competing For the Future*, co-written with C.K. Prahalad, and *Leading the Revolution*. Along the way, Hamel has created a new vocabulary for strategy that includes strategic intent, strategic architecture, industry foresight (rather than vision) and core competencies.

The need for new perspectives on strategy is forcefully put by Hamel: 'We like to believe we can break strategy down to Five Forces or Seven Ss. But you can't. Strategy is extraordinarily emotional and demanding. It is not a ritual or a once-a-year exercise, though that is what it has become. We have set the bar too low.' As a result, managers are bogged down in the nitty-gritty of the present – spending less than 3 percent of their time looking to the future.[1]

Hamel's argument is that complacency and cynicism are endemic. 'Dilbert is the bestselling business book of all time. It is cynical about management. Never has there been so much cynicism.' It is only by challenging convention that change will happen. 'Taking risks, breaking the rules, and being a maverick have always been important, but today they are more crucial than ever. We live in a discontinuous world – one where digitization, deregulation and globalization are profoundly reshaping the industrial landscape,' he says.[2]

Hamel argues that there are three kinds of companies. First are 'the real makers', companies such as British Airways and Xerox. They are the aristocracy: well-managed, consistent high achievers. Second, says Hamel, are the takers, 'peasants who only keep what the Lord doesn't want'. This group typically has around 15 percent market share, such as Kodak in the copier business, or Avis.

Third are the breakers, industrial revolutionaries. These are companies that Hamel believes are creating the new wealth, and include the likes of Starbucks in the coffee business. 'Companies should be asking themselves, who is going to capture the new wealth in your industry?' he says.

When Hamel talks of change, he is not considering tinkering at the edges. 'The primary agenda is to be the architect of industry transformation not simply corporate transformation,' he says. Companies that view change as an internal matter are liable to be left behind. Instead, they need to look outside of their industry boundaries. Hamel calculates that if you want to see the future coming, 80 percent of the learning will take place outside company boundaries. This is not something companies are very good at.

Many will continue to ignore Hamel's call for a revolution. 'There is a lot of talk about creating shareholders' wealth. It is not a hard thing to do. Just find a 60-year-old CEO and set a 65-year-old retirement age and then guarantee a salary based on the share price growing.' The trouble is that it is here, at the stock-option-packed top of the organization, that change needs to begin. 'What we need is not visionaries but activists. We need antidotes to Dilbert,' Hamel proclaims.

REFERENCES

1. International Management Symposium, London Business School, 11 November 1997.
2. Hamel, Gary, 'Killer strategies that makes shareholders rich', *Fortune*, 23 June 1997.

HENDERSON, BRUCE

WHILE managers may rely on experience to predict how their business will respond to their actions, strategists and economists rely on their models, which are amalgams of many different experiences.

The man who brought business models into the mainstream was the Australian Bruce Henderson (1915–1992). Henderson was an engineer who worked as a strategic planner for General Electric. He then joined the management consultancy Arthur D. Little before leaving in 1963 to set up his own consultancy, the Boston Consulting Group (BCG).

BCG is regarded by some as the first pure strategy consultancy. It quickly became a great success. Within five years, BCG was in the top group of consulting firms – where it has largely remained. It has been called 'the most idea-driven major consultancy in the world'.

The first model discovered – or rediscovered in this case – by Henderson was something of an antique. In the 1920s, an obscure company called Curtiss Aircraft came up with the concept of the 'learning curve', which also became known as the 'experience curve'. This posited that unit costs declined as cumulative production increased because of the acquisition of experience. The idea had been applied solely to manufacturing. Henderson applied it to strategy rather than production and found that it still worked and provided a useful, practical tool.

The model for which Henderson and BCG are best known is the Growth/Share Matrix. This measures market growth and relative market share for all the businesses in a particular firm. The hypothesis of this particular framework is that companies with higher market share and growth are more profitable.

BCG then superimposed on the matrix a theory of cash management that included a hierarchy of uses of cash, numbered from 1 to 4 in their order of priority. Richard Koch comments in his *Financial Times Guide to Strategy:* 'Bruce weaved it all together in a coherent philosophy of business that highlighted more clearly than ever before the compelling importance of market leadership, a low cost position, selectivity in business, and looking at cash flows.'[1]

REFERENCES

1. Koch, Richard, *Financial Times Guide to Strategy*, FT/Pitman, London, 1995.

MINTZBERG, HENRY

HENRY MINTZBERG (born 1939) is one of the most interesting of

2

management thinkers. Eschewing the guru seminar-trail, he forges a unique intellectual path.

Mintzberg is a great debunker of received wisdom. He is cheerfully quotable – 'Great organizations, once created, don't need great leaders'; 'Delayering can be defined as the process by which people who barely know what's going on get rid of those who do.'

Mintzberg is Professor of Management at McGill University, Montreal and Professor of Organization at INSEAD in Fontainebleau, France. His first book, *The Nature of Managerial Work*, examined how managers worked. Not surprisingly, managers did not do what they liked to think they did.

Mintzberg found that instead of spending time contemplating the long term, managers were slaves to the moment, moving from task to task with every move dogged by another diversion, another call. The median time spent on any one issue was a mere nine minutes.

From his observations, Mintzberg identified the manager's 'work roles' as:

- **Interpersonal roles**
  Figurehead: representing the organization/unit to outsiders.
  Leader: motivating subordinates, unifying effort.
  Liaiser: maintaining lateral contacts.
- **Informational roles**
  Monitor: of information flows.
  Disseminator: of information to subordinates.
  Spokesman: transmission of information to outsiders.
- **Decisional roles**
  Entrepreneur: initiator and designer of change.
  Disturbance handler: handling non-routine events.
  Resource allocator: deciding who gets what and who will do what.
  Negotiator: negotiating.

Mintzberg's work on strategy has been highly influential. In particular, he has long been a critic of formulae and analysis-driven strategic planning. He defines planning as 'a formalized system for codifying, elaborating and operationalizing the strategies which companies already have'.

Mintzberg identifies three central pitfalls to today's strategy planning practices. First, the assumption that discontinuities can be predicted. Forecasting techniques are limited by the fact that they tend to assume that the future will resemble the past.

Second, that planners are detached from the reality of the organization. Planners have traditionally been obsessed with gathering hard data on their industry, markets, and competitors. Soft data – networks of contacts, talking with customers, suppliers and employees, using intuition and using the grapevine – have all but been ignored.

To gain real understanding of an organization's competitive situation soft data needs to be dynamically integrated into the planning process. Writes Mintzberg: 'While hard data may inform the intellect, it is largely soft data that generate wisdom. They may be difficult to "analyze", but they are indispensable for synthesis – the key to strategy making.'

The third and final flaw identified by Mintzberg is the assumption that strategy making can be formalized. The left side of the brain has dominated strategy formulation with its emphasis on logic and analysis. Alternatives which do not fit into the pre-determined structure are ignored. The right side of the brain needs to become part of the process with its emphasis on intuition and creativity. 'Planning by its very nature,' concludes Mintzberg, 'defines and preserves categories. Creativity, by its very nature, creates categories or rearranges established ones. This is why strategic planning can neither provide creativity, nor deal with it when it emerges by other means.'

By championing the role of creativity in strategy creation and in providing carefully researched rebuttals of formulaic approaches to management, Mintzberg has provided new insights into strategy. 'The real challenge in crafting strategy lies in detecting the subtle discontinuities that may undermine a business in the future,' he says. 'And for that there is no technique, no program, just a sharp mind in touch with the situation.'

PASCALE, RICHARD

RICHARD PASCALE (born 1938) first came to the attention of a large audience with the advent of the Seven S framework, one of the most renowned and debated management tools of the 1980s. The framework emerged from a series of meetings during June 1978 between Pascale, Anthony Athos, then of Harvard Business School, and the McKinsey consultants Tom Peters and Robert Waterman, who were already involved in the research that was to form the basis of *In Search of Excellence*. The Seven Ss (strategy, structure, skills, staff, shared values, systems, and style) are a kind of *aide memoire*, a useful memory jogger of what concerns organizations.

From Pascale's perspective, the Seven Ss presented a way into comparisons between US and Japanese management. Pascale and Athos concluded that the Japanese succeeded largely because of the attention they gave to the soft Ss: style, shared values, skills, and staff. In contrast, the West remained preoccupied with the hard Ss of strategy, structure, and systems. These conclusions formed the bedrock of *The Art of Japanese Management* (1981), one of the first business bestsellers.

Pascale was a member of the faculty at Stanford's Graduate School of Business for 20 years. He has since worked as an independent consultant and is the author of *Managing on the Edge* (1990).

In addition to the Seven S framework, Pascale's work is significant for a number of reasons. First, he was among the first researchers to provide original insights into Japanese approaches to business and management.

The second influential area was vision, which he and Athos championed. Today, corporate visions are a fact of life, although many fail to match the Japanese practice mapped out by Pascale and Athos in which visions are dynamic, vivifying *modus operandi* rather than pallid or generic statements of corporate intent.

The third element of Pascale's work is in the related areas of corporate mortality and corporate transformation. In the late 1980s and 1990s, Pascale drew attention to the fragile foundations on which our grand corporate assumptions are made. *Managing on the Edge* begins with the line 'Nothing fails like success'. 'Great strengths are inevitably the root of weakness,' Pascale argued, pausing only to point out that from the Fortune 500 of 1985, 143 had departed five years later.

To overcome inertia and survive in a turbulent climate requires a constant commitment to what Pascale labels 'corporate transformation'. Incorporating employees fully into the principal business challenges facing the company is the first 'intervention' required if companies are to thrive. The second is to lead the organization in a way that sharpens and maintains incorporation and 'constructive stress'. Finally, Pascale advocates instilling mental disciplines that will make people behave differently and then help them sustain their new behaviour. In the latter element, Pascale cites the work of the US army, in which a strong culture allows minds and behaviour to be changed through rigorous and carefully thought-through training.[1]

In his recent work, Pascale has coined the term 'agility' to describe the combination of skills and thinking required of the organizations of the future. Pascale and his co-researchers believe that there are 'four indicators that tell us a great deal about how an organization is likely to perform and adapt'. These are power (whether employees think they can have any influence on the course of events); identity (to what extent individuals identify with the organization as a whole, rather than with a narrow group); contention (whether conflict is brought out into the open and used as a learning tool); and learning (how the organization deals with new ideas).[2]

The trouble is that these four elements, under normal circumstances, tend to coagulate and the organization eventually stagnates. Pascale says that this can only be avoided if an organization pursues seven disciplines of agility – which range from the self-explanatory 'accountability in action' to the more elusive and painful 'course of relentless discomfort'.

Pascale's vision of the future is a troubling one. To survive, companies must continually move on, using the agility engendered by their individuals and culture to ask questions, discuss the undiscussible, and shake things up. Case studies of this in practice are few and far between.

REFERENCES

1. Pascale, Richard, Millemann, Mark and Giola, Linda, 'Changing the way we change', *Harvard Business Review*, November–December 1997.
2. Golzen, Godfrey, 'The next big idea', *Human Resources*, March–April, 1997.

PORTER, MICHAEL

IF Peter Drucker is the intellectual giant of management thinking and Tom Peters its most charismatic populist, Michael Porter (born 1947) is perhaps the thinker with the greatest influence.

Porter is precociously talented and intellectually persuasive. He could have pursued a career as a professional golfer, but chose instead to take a Harvard MBA. While completing his PhD at Harvard, Porter was influenced by the economist Richard Caves, who became his mentor. He joined the Harvard faculty at the age of 26, one of the youngest tenured professors in the school's history.

Porter has served as a counsellor on competitive strategy to many leading US and international companies and plays an active role in economic policy with the US Congress and business groups, as well as acting as an adviser to foreign governments. Porter has also exerted a huge local influence on the state of Massachusetts.

In his 1980 book *Competitive Strategy: Techniques for Analyzing Industries and Competitors*, Porter developed the model still regarded as essential reading for strategy makers and MBA students the world over. His timing was impeccable. Publication of his model coincided with a wholesale rethink of Western business principles. In the 1970s, corporate America had watched in horror as Japanese companies stole market share in industry after industry. Initially, US companies put Japanese competitiveness down to cheap labour, but by the end of the decade it was dawning on them that something more fundamental was occurring. Porter encouraged a complete re-evaluation of the nature of competitiveness and changed the way companies thought about strategy for ever.

Porter's genius has lain in producing brilliantly researched and cogent models of competitiveness at a corporate, industry wide, and national level. He took an industrial economics framework – the structure–conduct–performance paradigm (SCP) – and translated it into the context of business strategy. From this emerged his best-known model: the five forces framework.

In his 1980 book Porter wrote: 'in any industry, whether it is domestic or international or produces a product or a service, the rules of competition are embodied in five competitive forces'. These five competitive forces are:

2

- **The entry of new competitors**: new competitors necessitate some competitive response that will inevitably use some of your resources, thus reducing profits.
- **The threat of substitutes**: if there are viable alternatives to your product or service in the marketplace, the prices you can charge will be limited.
- **The bargaining power of buyers**: if customers have bargaining power they will use it. This will reduce profit margins and, as a result, affect profitability.
- **The bargaining power of suppliers**: given power over you, suppliers will increase their prices and adversely affect your profitability.
- **The rivalry among the existing competitors**: competition leads to the need to invest in marketing, R&D, or price reductions that will reduce your profits.

The five forces, he asserted, shape the competitive landscape. Initially, they were passively interpreted as valid statements of the facts of competitive life. But by laying them bare, Porter provided a framework for companies to understand and challenge the competitive markets in which they operate. For strategy makers, the five forces represented levers on which any strategy must act if it is to have an impact on a company's competitive position.

'The collective strength of these five competitive forces determines the ability of firms in an industry to earn, on average, rates of return on investment in excess of the cost of capital. The strength of the five forces varies from industry to industry, and can change as an industry evolves,' Porter observed.

A late addition to his book was the concept of generic strategies. Porter argued that there were three 'generic strategies', 'viable approaches to dealing with ... competitive forces'. Strategy, in Porter's eyes, was a matter of *how* to compete. The first of Porter's generic strategies was differentiation, competing on the basis of value added to customers (quality, service, differentiation) so that customers will pay a premium to cover higher costs. The second was cost-based leadership, offering products or services at the lowest cost. Quality and service are not unimportant, but cost reduction provides focus to the organization. Focus was the third generic strategy identified by Porter. Companies with a clear strategy outperform those whose strategy is unclear or those that attempt to achieve both differentiation and cost leadership.

'Sometimes the firm can successfully pursue more than one approach as its primary target, though this is rarely possible,' he said. 'Effectively implementing any of these generic strategies usually requires total commitment, and organizational arrangements are diluted if there's more than one primary target.'

If a company failed to focus on any of the three generic strategies, it was liable to encounter problems. 'The firm failing to develop its strategy in at least one of the three directions – a firm that is *stuck in the middle* – is in an extremely poor strategic situation,' Porter wrote.

> *'The firm lacks the market share, capital investment, and resolve to play the low-cost game, the industry-wide differentiation necessary to obviate the need for a low-cost position, or the focus to create differentiation or low cost in a more limited sphere. The firm stuck in the middle is almost guaranteed low profitability. It either loses the high-volume customers who demand low prices or must bid away its profits to get this business away from low-cost firms. Yet it also loses high-margin businesses – the cream – to the firms who are focused on high-margin targets or have achieved differentiation overall. The firm stuck in the middle also probably suffers from a blurred corporate culture and a conflicting set of organizational arrangements and motivation system.'*

When *Competitive Strategy* was published in 1980, Porter's generic strategies offered a rational and straightforward method for companies to extricate themselves from strategic confusion. The reassurance proved short lived. Less than a decade later, companies were having to compete on all fronts. They had to be differentiated, through improved service or speedier development, and be cost leaders, cheaper than their competitors.

Porter's 1990 book, *The Competitive Advantage of Nations*, must be ranked as one of the most ambitious books of our time. At its heart was a radical new perspective of the role and *raison d'être* of nations.

His research encompassed 10 countries: the UK, Denmark, Italy, Japan, Korea, Singapore, Sweden, Switzerland, the US and Germany (then West Germany). Porter has since extended his study to include, India, Canada, New Zealand, Portugal, and the US State of Massachusetts.

Porter sought to examine what makes a nation's firms and industries competitive in global markets and what propels a whole nation's economy to advance. 'Why are firms based in a particular nation able to create and sustain competitive advantage against the world's best competitors in a particular field? And why is one nation often the home for so many of an industry's world leaders?' he asked. 'Why is tiny Switzerland the home base for international leaders in pharmaceuticals, chocolate and trading? Why are leaders in heavy trucks and mining equipment based in Sweden?'

Porter identified a central paradox: companies have become globalized and more international in their scope and aspirations than ever before. This, on the surface at least, would appear to suggest that the nation has lost its role in the international success of its firms. 'Companies, at first glance, seem to have transcended countries. Yet what I have learned in this study contradicts this conclusion,' said Porter.

'While globalization of competition might appear to make the nation less important, instead it seems to make it more so. With fewer impediments to trade to shelter uncompetitive domestic firms and industries, the home nation takes on growing significance because it is the source of the skills and technology that underpin competitive advantage.'

SCENARIO PLANNING

SCENARIO planning involves testing business strategies against a series of alternative futures. The technique was invented in the 1940s by Herman Kahn, the famous futurist from the Rand Corporation and the Hudson Institute. The term scenario – meaning a detailed outline for the plot of a future film – was borrowed from Hollywood by Kahn's friend, screenwriter and novelist Leo Rosten.

Kahn was best known for his scenarios about nuclear war – and for his trademark phrase, 'thinking the unthinkable'. Other early pioneers of scenario thinking also tended to look at the macro level: the future of mankind, for example, or the economy of an entire region.

Although only now coming into wider use, scenario planning has been practised in one form or another in the business world since the early 1960s. It was first used by a far-sighted team of planners at the oil company Royal Dutch Shell. They began to build on Kahn's work, developing their own version of the scenario approach as a possible answer to two questions: 'How do we look up to 20 to 30 years ahead?' and 'How can we get people to discuss the "unthinkable" together?' Using the technique, they foresaw the energy crises of 1973 and 1979, the growth of energy conservation, the evolution of the global environmental movement, and even the break-up of the Soviet Union, years before these events happened.

What Shell realized, however, was that managers need these grand scenarios to be translated into something more recognizable. To have practical use in business, the story has to be focused on a particular audience or issue. Learning to focus scenarios on a specific business purpose was part of the company's contribution to the practice.

In the 1990s, a string of books – including *The Art of the Long View*, by futurist Peter Schwartz, *The Living Company*, written by former Shell manager Arie de Geus, and *The Age of Heretics* by Art Kleiner, who interviewed Shell managers – drew attention to scenario planning, placing it firmly on the management agenda. It is no coincidence, of course, that the technique came to the fore at a time when so many seemingly unassailable companies were wrong-footed by changes in their trading environments.

Although sometimes confused with disaster planning or contingency planning – which deals with how a company should respond when things go wrong – scenario planning is a way to identify both threats and opportunities that flow from decisions. According to Clem Sunter, head of scenario planning at Anglo American Corporation and another leading authority on the technique: 'Scenarios are to organizations what radar is to a pilot. They help us look for the first signs of changes that can profoundly affect how we work, and make us think about our responses.'

SEVEN S FRAMEWORK

The Seven S Framework is no more than a simple distillation of the key elements that make up an organization's personality. Developed around 1980 by two business school academics – Anthony Athos and Richard Pascale – and a group of consultants at McKinsey and Company – including Tom Peters and Robert Waterman – it provides a useful checklist for thinking about what makes a business tick. It advocates examination in seven basic areas, all beginning with S: strategy, structure, systems, style, skills, staff and shared values.

The Seven S model was neatly alliterative, accessible, understandable, and with its logo (later named 'the happy atom') highly marketable. Managers seemed to like it. This was a business theory to fit all occasions encapsulated on a single page.

Pascale and Athos introduced the Seven S model to a mass audience in *The Art of Japanese Management*, published in 1981. Peters and Waterman also featured the framework in *In Search of Excellence* a year later (despite the fact that Tom Peters initially thought the framework 'corny').

The attraction of the Seven Ss is that they are memorable and simple. The framework is a model of how organizations achieve success. Inevitably, a model that simplifies something as complex as organizational behaviour is open to abuse, misinterpretation, and criticism. The Seven S framework has suffered more than its fair share. (Contrast this with the generally positive response still reserved for Michael Porter's five forces model of competitiveness, which simplifies something equally complex but does so in a far more analytical and academic way.)

Today, when Japanese companies have fallen off their pedestal and the cult of 'excellence' started by Peters and Waterman seems to have finally run its course, it is easy to forget how influential the ideas behind them were. For the first time, the Seven S framework enabled meaningful comparisons between companies from completely different sectors, national cultures, and histories. As a way to cover the basics, it remains a useful concept.

No one ever ran a business with a framework. The Seven Ss are a helpful summation of the main issues bedeviling managerial life. But they are only practically beneficial as a memory jogger, a structure around which to build, or as a filter to determine key issues. They are not, never could be, and were never intended to be, set in stone.

Like the Boston matrix, the Seven S framework belongs to an era that is gone. The simple truths it uncovered are no longer considered worthy of our attention. But as a milestone in the evolution of management theory, it still has much to tell us.

STRATEGIC INFLECTION POINT

THE strategic inflection point is a term associated with Andy Grove, chairman of the microprocessor company Intel and one of the best-known figures in the computer industry. Strategic inflection points, he says, occur when a company's competitive position goes through a transition. It is the point at which the organization must alter the path it is on – adapting itself to the new situation – or it risks going into decline. It is concerned with how companies recognize and adapt to 'paradigm changes'.

'During a strategic inflection point, the way a business operates, the very structure and concept of the business, undergoes a change,' Grove writes. But the irony is that at that point itself nothing much happens.

'That subtle point is like the eye of a hurricane. There is no wind at the eye of the hurricane, but when it moves the wind hits you again.

'That is what happens in the middle of the transformation from one business model to another. The irony is that, even though these are the most cataclysmic changes that a business can undertake, more often than not those changes are missed.'

Grove was so enamoured of the term that 'Strategic Inflection Points' was the original title of his 1996 book, until the publishers rejected it in favour of the more memorable *Only the Paranoid Survive*.

In the real world, the need to spot paradigm changes is most acute for high-tech companies such as Intel. Indeed, it was IBM's original failure to spot the switch from mainframe to personal computers that allowed Intel and Microsoft to create their dominant market positions. Both companies have inculcated their cultures with the lesson.

Grove explicitly recognizes that the pace of change in the modern business world is such that entire markets and industries can change almost overnight. This places an increasing burden on strategy makers and involves the ability to discard current assumptions to shape the future of the industry – before someone else does. Grove calls this '10x change', and it can either undermine the business model or create tremendous new growth opportunities.

The trouble with traditional strategic planning approaches is that they tend to extrapolate the past to create a view of the future. As a result, they often preserve, rather than challenge, industry assumptions. Traditional planning processes tend to analyze external factors individually, therefore missing the power that is unleashed when trends converge. The concept of strategic inflection points recognizes this phenomenon and gives it a name.

SUN TZU

THE link between the military and business worlds has existed since time immemorial. Its starting point, as far as it is possible to discern, is Sun Tzu's *The Art of War*, written 2,500 years ago.

The authorship of *The Art of War* remains clouded in mystery. It may have been written by Sun Wu, a military general who was alive around 500 BC. His book is reputed to have led to a meeting between with King Ho-lü of Wu. Sun Wu, not having a flipchart available, argued his case for military discipline by decapitating two of the king's concubines. This proved his point admirably.

The book returned to grace business bookshelves in the 1980s. The attraction of the military analogy is that it is clear who your enemy is. When your enemy is evident, the world appears clearer whether you are a military general or a managing director. Sun-Tzu is an aggressive counterpoint to the confusion of mere theory. After all, among his advice was the following: 'Deploy forces to defend the strategic points; exercise vigilance in preparation, do not be indolent. Deeply investigate the true situation, secretly await their laxity. Wait until they leave their strongholds, then seize what they love.'

Managers lapped up such brazen brutality. Yet, *The Art of War* is more sophisticated than that. Why destroy when you can win by stealth and cunning? 'If you are near the enemy, make him believe you are far from him. If you are far from the enemy, make him believe you are near,' wrote the master. 'To subdue the enemy's forces without fighting is the summit of skill. The best approach is to attack the other side's strategy; next best is to attack his alliances; next best is to attack his soldiers; the worst is to attack cities.'

While the imagery of warfare continues to exert influence over managers, it appears to be on the wane. Contemporary business metaphors are as likely to emerge from biology and the environment as from the traditional sources of engineering and warfare.

– CHAPTER 2 –

Managing human resources

'We can never wholly separate the human from the mechanical side.' MARY PARKER FOLLETT

'How come when I want a pair of hands I get a human being as well.' HENRY FORD

'Your most precious possession is not your financial assets. Your most precious possession is the people you have working there, and what they carry around in their heads, and their ability to work together.' ROBERT REICH

'The person who figures out how to harness the collective genius of the people in his or her organization is going to blow the competition away.' WALTER WRISTON

Succession planning

WILLIAM BYHAM

A dramatic change is required in organizations' succession management policies, argues William Byham, if they are to nurture the executive talent they require to compete.

TRADITIONAL succession management/planning systems are failing, resulting in a dearth of ready-to-promote managers. In traditional succession management systems, senior managers spend an inordinate amount of time considering and naming potential replacements for themselves and their subordinate managers. Labels such as 'ready now' or 'ready in two years' are often applied.

These systems are often very expensive, forms driven, bureaucratic, and out of touch with organizational strategy. There is usually very little focus on skill development, most of the attention concentrating on job placement. Most importantly, the majority of traditional programmes are inaccurate – fewer than 30 percent of senior management positions are filled by these handpicked backups. If organizations are going to have the executive talent they require, a drastic change is needed.

There are five factors to consider.

Downsizing

Managements have suddenly become victims of their own success. Many of those who not long ago proclaimed how completely they had eliminated 'all those superfluous middle managers' now lament the shortage of leadership talent. As helpful as it may have been, episodes of re-engineering – or whatever label one wishes to apply – have wiped out not only the trainees but also the training ground itself. American Management Association research, for example, notes that while middle managers account for between 5 and 8 percent of American workers, they have accounted for as much as 25 percent of the US jobs eliminated in recent years. And middle managers represent 60 percent of outplacement firms' clients.

Lack of interest

Not surprisingly, many of the managers who lost their jobs, as well as many who escaped the corporate axe, have also lost their appetite and enthusiasm for corporate high command and leadership. In their eyes, the executive suite is a cold and indifferent place, to be avoided. What many aspiring executives now desire is not just career success but also personal happiness and a less stressful life. *Industry Week* magazine dubs it 'downshifting', and the results of both corporate and media surveys show a clear trend toward declining promotions and walking away from pressure-packed jobs, their financial rewards notwithstanding.

Appeal of entrepreneurship

Executives are willing to work hard and put in long hours – but on their own terms. The lure of running 'your own show' is attracting countless young leaders who once would have raced up the ladder of a blue-chip corporation. The dramatic and well-documented rise of small but high-potential companies testifies to this trend, as do the availability of venture capital, the rise of new industries, a resilient economy, and retired and semi-retired corporate executives who will lend their hands and heads to start-ups, often for minimal compensation.

Lack of succession planning

In many organizations succession planning is not even a consideration. The once-reliable 'farm club' comprised of 'assistant to' grooming positions is long gone. Amid cost cutting and job slashing, top management never considered future needs. Worse, the middle managers who have survived rarely have the breadth of experience that high-level positions demand.

Niche-oriented society

Our ability to define ever-more narrow market niches and demographic slices has been a boon for marketers, but it has also produced a troublesome side effect. Hiring and human resources managers alike are now inclined to typecast and pigeonhole managerial talent, to the point that those who have toiled in one business sector may not even be considered for a post in another. 'Once in chemicals, always in chemicals,' or so it appears.

This dwindling supply of talent is only part of the problem, however. A consequence of our increasingly competitive and fast-moving society is that leadership positions are more demanding than ever. In today's flattened and intensively competitive organizations, the competencies required for success at senior levels demand individuals who can:

- Shape and articulate vision and mission.
- Build business relationships and partnerships.
- Serve as effective change agents.
- Develop and articulate new business strategies and guide their execution.
- Grasp technology and seize marketing and entrepreneurial opportunities.
- Deal with people and issues throughout the world.

Of course, corporations are not impotent in this regard. As a preliminary step, an organization must determine the extent of its problem. It must define the executive roles and associated competencies it needs to reach its ultimate business objectives and conduct a census of who's available within the organization.

Nevertheless, old methods simply won't work – most companies don't have the tools needed to identify fairly and accurately both current shining stars and unsung individuals who have quietly turned in stellar performances in operations around the world. Indeed, companies that have used assessment centres and multiple-perspective instruments ('360°s') have often found more latent talent than they imagined they possessed.

What can organizations do?

Armed with this information, organizations have three options for building the leadership corps they need. Two are short term, the other takes a longer perspective. The odds are that a combination of the three will be required. Whatever options are selected, action needs to begin immediately, before the anticipated exodus of executives turns into a stampede.

Make it more attractive for key executives and managers to stay

The most expedient action is to keep current talent from retiring. As attractive as it may appear, retirement remains a difficult decision for most people. Not every executive is ready to hang up their skills. Indeed, many will want to continue working in some capacity, at least on a part-time basis. Letting them deliver invaluable assistance, advice and counsel to the enterprise they know best makes sense; it also pre-empts the risk of their helping competitors.

Hire talent from the outside – more effectively

At first blush, raiding other companies looks like a consummate quick fix. Fresh ideas typically arrive with new talent groomed elsewhere. But hiring outsiders is no panacea, as high-profile failures of senior executives have shown. Given the cost of executive search, the effect of organizational turmoil, and the ramp-up time required for new managers, such waste cannot be tolerated.

Assessing outside talent more thoroughly is an obvious way to improve recruiting results. Organizations that have upgraded their evaluation technology using modern assessment centres and other methodologies have shown dynamic improvement in 'hit rates'. Another quick fix is to recruit from a broader base than some organizations traditionally consider, such as women executives and overseas talent.

Overall, however, raiding other enterprises to ease the leadership dearth is a stopgap alternative at best. As more organizations face the challenge and try the same solutions, the costs of recruiting seasoned executives will rise dramatically.

Acceleration pools

A longer term and more effective approach to maximum development is the 'acceleration pool system'. This is a process by which an organization assures that its key positions will be filled with qualified candidates. It succeeds by establishing a pool of individuals who have been selected for their basic skills and then developed through training and job experiences to maximize their potential contributions to the organization at large – and not to a specific position.

This is a startling change from when corporations deluded themselves into thinking they could predict an individual's career path. The dismal record from that era warns against repeating it. The acceleration pool system differs from traditional succession planning in many ways, including:

- The system rests on the premise that while everyone is developed, only the company's best and brightest qualify for accelerated development. In the acceleration pool, they receive stretch assignments, special developmental experiences, and accelerated growth and educational opportunities. They also go through an updated and redesigned assessment centre (see page 322), staffed with outside professionals, and receive expert feedback and coaching.

- Acceleration pool candidates are prepared for assignments with measurement systems, coaching, and clear job and learning accountabilities. Traditional replacement planning assignments, by comparison, only delivered unplanned learning, had little structure, and the coaching they offered came mainly from the HR department. Taskforce and other special assignments are fully leveraged to speed learning in an acceleration pool.
- Movement in the acceleration pool is based on performance and achieved development. Candidates must make effective use of each development assignment and achieve stretch performance goals. They cannot just serve time. Job assignment decisions are made only relative to the next opportunity – they are not planned two or three positions out.
- The acceleration pool offers no presumption of upward movement or implicit guarantee of promotion – as was typically the case with succession planning and traditional talent pools.
- At regular intervals (every six or 12 months) individuals in the pool are reviewed relative to their career development needs at that moment, personal interests, and the company's management needs. One such review, for example, might conclude that a lateral move would be in everyone's best interests. Ongoing evaluation ensures that individuals will be stretched to the extent of their capabilities – all without the paperwork nightmares that once brought companies to their knees.
- Individuals can be in an acceleration pool for between one and 15 years, depending on when they enter, their performance, and the urgency of the organization's needs;

ASSESSMENT CENTRES

THE modern executive assessment centre is very different from those run by companies such as AT&T and Bell 40 years ago. Here is how one works.

- Approximately two weeks in advance, the executive receives information about the hypothetical organization in which they will be involved. This includes extensive background information on the organization, key employees, plans for the future and so on. They also often receive a videotape to help them visualize the outputs of the hypothetical organization and to acquaint them with some of the people with whom they will interact. Sometimes they are asked to study a proposed reorganization plan or other corporate issue and bring along their analysis.

- On arriving at the assessment centre, which is staffed by professional assessors, the executive is briefed further about what is currently happening at the hypothetical organization and then goes to a room fully equipped with all modern communication devices. There is access to the hypothetical organization's e-mail and voice mail systems. Faxes can be sent and received.

- The executive receives an outline of the day's (in some cases the session lasts one-and-a-half days) activities indicating when meetings are scheduled and what they are about. During times between these events, they have time to prepare and handle in-basket items, as well as items that come in via e-mail, voice mail, fax and so on. They can respond to these items in any way they choose.

- Executives do not deal with other assessees in the centre. In group situations, assessment professionals role-play the other executives. Similarly, when exercises require the executive to handle a personnel problem, an assessment professional assumes the role.

- Throughout the assessment process, the individual is treated as a respected adult and may spend as little or as much time preparing for individual or group meetings, writing reports, and so on as they deem appropriate.

also the door is always opened for late bloomers. A sophisticated performance – and competency-based selection system assists with decisions about entry and departure. By comparison, traditional talent pools for management trainees accepted members only at the bottom and dismissed them once they joined the ranks of middle management.

Underlying assumptions about businesses today further distinguish the acceleration pool:

- Business strategy, organizational structures and jobs themselves change frequently.
- Jobs are fluid, marked by continual changes in responsibilities and reporting arrangements.
- Individuals can move both horizontally and vertically.
- Development can include assignments outside the organization (with suppliers or customers, for example).
- Since it is impossible to plan future jobs with any accuracy, the focus shifts to the next assignment and development actions.

Traditional succession planning, by comparison, counted on such assumptions as consistent business strategies, stable organization structures, fixed jobs and vertical movement.

Not all members of senior management will come from the acceleration pool, of course. Most organizations still plan to get 15 to 20 percent from outside their ranks in order to infuse management with new ideas and perspectives.

In conclusion, corporations can neither hunt future talent as they once did, nor relegate action to the back burner as many have done in recent years. And if tending to leadership development means momentarily turning a blind eye to investors, so be it. In time, they will praise organizations that act for the long term.

Organizations that persist in maintaining the *status quo* court more than short-lived difficulties. They stand a good chance of seeing their organizations trampled and being forced to accept a final option – going out of business.

RESOURCES

BOOK

Byham, W.C., Smith, A. and Paese, M., *Grow Your Own Leaders*, DDI Press, Bridgeville, PA, 2000.

WEB

www.ddiworld.com

Empowerment

D. QUINN MILLS AND G. BRUCE FRIESEN

Increasingly popular, though perennially misunderstood or poorly applied, empowerment has become an all-embracing term, explain D. Quinn Mills and G. Bruce Friesen. It is nevertheless a simple concept, which cannot be practised half-heartedly, occasionally, or in isolated pockets of an organization if it is to work successfully.

EMPOWERMENT can be succinctly defined as the authority of subordinates to decide and act. It describes a management style. The term is often confused with delegation but, if strictly defined, empowerment goes much further in granting subordinates authority to decide and act. Indeed, within a context of broad limits defined by executives, empowered individuals may even become self-managing.

A careful definition of empowerment allows clear distinctions to be drawn from more traditional management styles. For example, a committee is not an empowered team – it studies and recommends; an empowered team takes action. Traditional employees execute instructions; empowered individuals act on their own initiative to achieve company goals.

Colloquially, the term empowerment is not so precisely used. Many people speak of 'empowerment' when they mean not freedom of action but merely the opportunity for consultation about decisions that superiors will make. In reality, this is employee participation. Others use empowerment as a synonym for autonomy; that is, authority without constraint. They regard empowerment as implying full independence of action for the employee. True empowerment is more than 'participation' but less than 'autonomy'.

Organizations typically use empowerment to improve employee productivity and customer satisfaction. The link between empowerment and productivity is straightforward: people freed to innovate in the workplace tend to find more efficient ways to perform their work. The link between empowerment and customer satisfaction is equally straightforward, but less well known. Empowerment permits many decisions about customer service to be made at the point of contact by those providing the service, for example. Less time is wasted seeking a supervisor with appropriate authorization to take action; as a result, customer requests are typically filled more quickly and satisfaction rises.

Empowerment as a management style is not a new idea. Burns and Stalker (1964) observed its use in laboratories where complex experiments were being performed by multidisciplinary scientific teams. Rather than rely on managers to co-ordinate team activity, the scientists collaborated to make their own work decisions; their managers handled administrative tasks.

In their book *Doing Deals* (1988), Eccles and Crane observed similar behaviour among investment bankers. Rather than relying on managing directors to co-ordinate work on specific deals, banking associates networked among themselves to get the work done; directors focused on client relations or administrative matters.

In *The Age of the Smart Machine* (1988) Harvard Business School's Shoshana Zuboff reported similar experiences from the factory floor. Her study of technology-intensive industry suggests that employees had considerable say in the management of these workplaces. Their routine work was performed by process-controlled machines; their managers worried about resource procurement and administrative issues.

The elements of empowerment

Effective empowerment requires executive commitment. Hybrid or partial solutions – mixing elements of empowerment with elements of traditional management – will not work. This cure is worse than the disease it treats, generating mixed signals that can trigger institutional paralysis. As outlined below, major elements of the enterprise – including its organizational structure; employee, manager, and executive roles; executive style; and even its basic reward and control systems – must be transformed to support empowerment.

Changing organization structure

Traditional management uses hierarchy as an organizing device to reduce administrative costs. It takes only a few managers to control thousands of subordinates using hierarchy; consider the typical army. However, hierarchy generates managerial efficiency at a price, that of inefficient communication.

Time is lost as field data percolates up and decisions down through layers of authority. If data skip layers going up, incomplete decisions result; if decisions skip layers going down, incoherent implementation results.

Modern management, in an environment that demands immediate responsiveness, needs faster internal communication than hierarchy can deliver. And so it turns to empowerment, embedded in a network organization structure to give it substance.

Three modifications of hierarchical structure are required to create network structure:

- **Decisions down – not up**: the benefit of perspective, which pushes decisions upwards from the point of action in a hierarchy, is traded for the benefit of responsiveness, which pulls decisions downwards to the point of action in a network.
- **Work generalized – not specialized**: hierarchy typically divides managers from employees and then divides employees by specialization. Network organizations tend to collapse these basic distinctions. To cope with broader job duties, employees augment their technical skills with problem-solving training so that they *can* make decisions too.

- **Communication horizontal and vertical – not just vertical:** hierarchy uses vertical communication channels. Ideas spread as managers transmit them; only managers are formally entrusted to speak on behalf of their groups in the company. Networks use point-to-point communication channels. Anyone, regardless of rank, may ask anyone else for information through electronic media such as instant messaging.

Table 1 details the differences between traditional hierarchy and empowered network structure.

Table 1 ***Features of organization***

	Traditional	Empowered
a. Decision making	Issues pass up to the closest manager with sufficient perspective to make the decision. *priority* = completeness	Issues pass down to the employee closest to the customer with sufficient data to make the decision. *priority* = timeliness
b. Employees	– Specialized. – Arrayed by function. – Perform narrow jobs. – Only receive orders.	– 'Generalized'. – Arrayed by team. – Perform broad jobs. – Make decisions too.
c. Management	– Holds all authority. – Arrayed in many levels (narrow span of control).	– Shares authority. – Arrayed in few levels (wide span of control).
d. Communications	Data shared only on a 'need to know' basis. Subordinates and peers communicate only through supervisors and managers. Vertical channels used to issue commands and control activities.	Data widely shared, few secrets allowed. Everyone talks to others regardless of level or position. Data flow from point to point; command and control are not tied to communication.

Changing management roles

What do managers do in an empowered organization? The short answer is plenty! The same turbulence that drives decision making down to the point of action makes new demands on management too, as seen in Table 2.

Table 2 ***Management roles***

	Traditional 'control'	**Empowered 'support'**
a. Executives	Make decisions. Review results. Control firm's responses.	Delegate decisions. Plan for the future. Develop vision.
b. Managers	Supervise people. Monitor activity. Make work assignments. Report to the top.	Support team building. Manage systems. Coach teams. Report to the top.

Time constraints and competitive pressures require managers to be sensitive and quick to respond to subtle changes. Missing a turn in a key trend can destroy a firm. Executives no longer have the luxury of time to review results, make operating decisions, and exercise control over activities; this is a *backward* orientation that may cause a company to crash.

Empowerment asks executives to shed daily decision making so that their attention can be directed *forward* to vision and planning. This is not always easy for them to do because they are held accountable for corporate performance and so face the temptation to assert control over activities. But knowing that the organization will be better able to meet performance goals if *all* of its people feel responsible for doing so is a strong incentive to change.

Empowerment also changes the role of the middle manager. An empowered organization places employees in broad, process-oriented teams rather than narrow functional jobs. These teams are driven by goals, not by orders; their performance is measured by results, not behaviour; and those managers with titular responsibility for them do not direct, rather they let employees use their own judgement to make decisions and drive communication. In shifting from traditional control to an empowered support orientation, managers are asked to facilitate work, maintain communication channels, and manage resources.

Facilitate work

Management's role as intermediary between executives, who set strategy, and employees, who carry it out, does not disappear under empowerment. Managers must continue to help translate strategy into team goals and relay team concerns back to the top. But the role does change to one of facilitation rather than intervention.

Traditional management asks managers to extract obedience, maintain conformity, and reprimand failure. Empowerment requires more supportive behaviour. Managers must learn to coach by example, counsel those who ask for help without judgement, and maintain tolerance for innovation.

Maintain communication channels

Managers assume considerable responsibility for enabling communication under empowerment. As communication channels are composed of people as well as technology, this responsibility becomes one of managing the quality of relationships so that communication proceeds smoothly.

There are two types of communication channel: intra-team and inter-team. Managers have limited dealings with intra-team communications; members interact directly. However, managers must be prepared to help new members blend into a team. People are not expected to assimilate naturally.

Managers have greater dealings with inter-team communication. While freedom to communicate extends broadly, natural limits will appear. If an employee does not know anyone in another team, for example, they must have a point of reference – someone who knows who and *how* to call.

Someone must also serve as the external contact point for a team. That person must have credibility *beyond* the team and influence *in* the team.

A manager with experience in the industry and the company is well positioned to be both a point of reference and a point of contact for the team. It is important, however, to remember that being a contact point does not mean becoming a gatekeeper; the role is one of *connection*, not *filter*.

Manage resources

Managers still select and hire employees, arrange training, help administer performance appraisal, and may also administer rewards. Although they do not supervise, they maintain a perspective on team functions and should be the first person in when a team encounters problems it cannot solve for itself.

While team members will have multiple skills, they may not have the experience needed to analyze more complex business situations. These situations will be picked up by the manager, who is in a position to tap outside expertise or solve the problem for the team.

Changing management 'style'

A study of executives conducted at the Harvard Business School found four basic elements of managerial style: the ability to administer (e.g. organize work); the ability to assert 'control' (e.g. hold people to procedures); the ability to demonstrate empathy (e.g. relate to others); and the ability to generate vision (e.g. to see (and plan for) the future).[1] Successful managers in traditional firms tend to score highly on administrative and control elements, which are key to traditional management, and less highly on empathy and vision, which are not.

An empowered company is ill served by a managerial style heavy on administration and control. Those managers whose self image requires them to dominate others will not be happy in an empowered environment, which requires empathy and vision to operate smoothly. Those managers whose style enables them to act as diplomats or coaches will thrive in the empowered environment.

Changing incentives

While empowerment and traditional management both rely on intrinsic and extrinsic rewards to elicit performance, each deploys a somewhat different mix of these rewards. These differences are summarized in Table 3.

Table 3 ***Rewards***

	Traditional	Empowered
a. Rewards are	Primarily extrinsic (money and benefits). Little intrinsic possible.	Lean to intrinsic (but extrinsic often equal to traditional).
b. Basis for pay	Job duties performed. People supervised.	Business results. Team output.
c. People receive	Fixed salary. Small bonuses. (Pay for behaviour)	Variable salary. Large bonuses. (Pay for performance)

Empowered firms tend to emphasize intrinsic rewards; empowerment was *designed* with autonomy, variety, and involvement in mind. Traditional firms can make only limited use of intrinsic rewards – employee involvement is not a hallmark of hierarchy – and must rely on less effective extrinsic incentives such as increased pay tied to promotions in rank.

The famous pay studies of Fredrick Herzberg, among others, have shown that increasing intrinsic motivators – such as autonomy – generates a *sustained* increase in performance, while increasing extrinsic motivators – such as pay – at best generates a *temporary* increase in work performance. However, managers using empowerment do not have it all their own way.

As the scope of hierarchy is reduced, people can no longer expect personal advances in rank; they can only gain pay when their teams do well. This can limit individual extrinsic incentives (and, as Herzberg also showed, limiting pay can reduce performance too). Further, empowered firms tend to rely more heavily on results than on specified behaviour, so 'pay for performance' becomes the norm. Good employees can be hurt by poor team performance, reducing their motivation.

Changing control systems

Empowerment also uses different control mechanisms than traditional management to guide the firm. Elements such as vision or goal setting and performance indicators like unit profitability or cost gain importance; the close supervision of specific behaviours found in traditional management becomes less important. Other differences in control systems are detailed in Table 4.

Table 4 ***Control systems***

	Traditional	Empowered
a. Vision setting	Limited activity.	Critical activity.
b. Goal setting	Top-down activity	Bottom-up process.
c. Performance appraisal	Supervisor/Manager only. Closely guarded process. One-on-one assessment. Relies on managerial judgement.	Customers have input. Team mates may share. May have team element. Uses 'results-based' performance data.
d. Choosing leaders	Boss/bosses appointed to lead work groups. Critical management activity.	Leadership rotates inside a work team. Personal control is much less important.

Empowerment uses a 'control' cycle that begins with vision, moves to mission statements and goals, and concludes with measurement. As teams achieve goals they are rewarded *and left alone*. Should a team fail to achieve its goal, management steps in, reviewing resources (skills, people) or redefining goals.

2

Vision

Vision provides the frame of reference within which mission statements are written and goals selected. If vision is ill formed, mission statements will be vague and goal achievement hard to measure. But how do you know when you have a good vision?

- It must be consistently and easily comprehended by *all* who hear it; length dilutes clarity.
- It must be articulated in as inclusive a fashion as possible. Involvement in the process counts nearly as much as the end product. If a few people write the vision, the process is not inclusive – even if the result is outstanding.
- It must be *action oriented* – not a forecast or a prediction.
- It must 'stretch' the firm – if a vision is too easy to realize it will not challenge those who hear it.

The National Aeronautics and Space Administration's (NASA) vision in the 1960s – 'to put a man on the moon' – is an example of a good vision. It is short, action oriented, created a similar image in the minds of everyone who heard it, and stretched the existing organization.

The raw material for vision flows from strategic industry analysis. The company uses such data to answer the questions in Table 5.

Table 5 ***Articulating a vision***

- Who are our customers?
- What do our customers want from us?
- Who are our competitors?
- How do they compete with us?
- Who are our suppliers?
- Why are our suppliers important to us?
- What are the principal drivers of cost in the firm?
- How does our 'business system' create value?

Good mission statements address *all* key corporate constituencies: the customers, employees, investors and community in which the firm operates. A mission statement should not be confused with goals: it provides a *context* for goals and tells teams how to shape their goals to suit the firm's purpose.

Goals

Goals must exhibit several characteristics to be effective:

- They must be *understandable,* otherwise those who are given them seek further input before acting. Since they cannot act on their own, it follows that they have not been empowered.
- They must *contain a time dimension* so that those being empowered will know when their progress will be measured. This helps them to accept empowerment and stop looking for direction.
- They must be *achievable.* Goals that are too ambitious will demotivate as people realize they cannot reach them. Goals that are too easy will demotivate as they insult those to whom they are assigned.
- They must be *carefully drawn,* broad enough to support independent action, but not so broad that confounding factors prevent their achievement. For example, monthly sales goals for a product requiring a two-month sales cycle are too narrow; measurement occurs before a single sale is closed. On the other hand, asking a team to keep the company stock price above target is too broad; share prices are influenced by factors beyond the control of any one team.
- A good goal is one that *can be aligned* with other goals across the organization to facilitate co-ordination among teams. If various team goals 'roll up' into collective company goals, then team activities should be complementary too.

Measurement

Measurement completes the loop of vision, goals, and measurement, which lets management exercise control without the close supervision of traditional management. There are four types of measurement: financial, market driven, operational, and organizational. Each has advantages and drawbacks.

Financial measures

Financial measures range from the simple (spending against budget) to the complex (profit, rate of return). Such measures are useful in an empowered environment because they are based on objective data that are typically already quantified by the team in its normal functioning, which makes them easier to track than if they had to be charted separately. But it is important to remember that financial measures may not be practical.

Even empowered teams may not be able to control all cost inputs and so reported profits may not be entirely under their control. Also, it makes no sense to track rates of return on assets for teams if assets among them are shared. Pushing financial measures on teams under such conditions will only cause inter-team rivalry to see who can saddle whom with 'joint' costs.

Market-driven measures

Market-driven measures include market share data, customer retention rates, or even customer satisfaction indicators. These measures may be derived from industry sources, third party surveys, or internal surveys.

Market measures are useful for an empowered team because they drive customer responsiveness, but they also have drawbacks. Although the data on which market measures are based may be easy to quantify, they are less objective than financial data. Further, measures like market share data will be more objective than customer satisfaction data, which relies not only on recall but also on application of fixed rating scales to a subjective experience. Finally, market measures may not be appropriate where a team has no real customer. Some firms assign an 'internal' customer to such teams, but this may not produce the same results as real customers.

Operational measures

Operational measures include productivity or quality indicators. Such measures are useful for an empowered team because they focus the team on efficient operation.

Although operating data may be the equivalent of financial data in its objectivity and ease of tracking, there are still caveats to its use. For example, a team located at a station in the middle of a production process may not be able fully to control either the timing or quality of its inputs. So appropriate allowances must be made if operational measures are to provide effective feedback.

Some teams may operate in businesses where data on efficiency is elusive, for example in the service sector. The fact that data is harder to obtain does not mean operational measurements should be abandoned; it does mean that this data needs to be weighted for a relative loss of objectivity.

Organizational measures

Organizational measures are the most subjective. They include such ideas as innovation, harmony, and co-operation observed in team settings. Data for such measures must be obtained by team surveys or external observation.

A great deal of work has been done to build survey instruments that can track organizational measures to determine how well the team is functioning. Critical incident techniques are also available to help observers filter data.

Practising empowerment

Traditional management uses managers as a focal point. It presumes that managers identify strongly with company objectives and so can be trusted to administer rewards and punishments on behalf of the company. Traditional management also presumes that most employees are unable to think for themselves (or the company) and so should be asked only to obey orders. Neither assumption is consistent with modern experience. Many firms have found their executives not acting in the corporate interest, while society heaps ridicule on order takers, regardless of their status as managers *or* employees.

Empowerment does not use managers as a focal point. It presumes that employees have brains and ambitions and so it asks them to internalize vision and goals so as to develop commitment, as managers do. When used properly, empowerment can transform motivation, allowing a company to motivate without close supervision.

Traditional management uses the asymmetric distribution of power found in hierarchy for purposes of co-ordination. Specialized workers have limited perspective; they *must* turn to managers to make decisions in ambiguous situations because only managers can see the context in which to act.

Empowerment deliberately reduces employee specialization and broadens employee perspective through building teams, writing broad job descriptions, providing administrative training, and allowing point-to-point communication so that managers need not be the only decision makers. But the psychology that puts managers in charge remains hard to break – for while broadening perspective can *encourage* initiative, getting employees to *take* initiative is another matter.

Empowerment continues to assign managers the roles of rewarding and punishing behaviour; of setting performance criteria and goals; and of hiring and firing. And so employees can still perceive that there is a risk in taking initiative. Practising empowerment also requires changes in employee psychology.

Fault tolerance

Managers may find employees setting self-imposed limits on their perception of empowerment unless steps are taken to introduce fault tolerance to the workplace. Fault tolerance changes the psychology of the workplace by explicitly setting conditions under which mistakes are not punished.

In setting fault tolerance, managers must carefully consider their still large powers of influence in the firm. If they say one thing, but do another, the action dominates. Managers must also consider what behaviours they really want. To encourage action, it must be rewarded *and* inaction punished. The first time an action inside the zone of fault tolerance is punished, the wrong signal will be sent.

There are six conditions commonly used to set fault tolerance:

1. When a mistake allows something new to be learned.
2. When a mistake is not part of a pattern.
3. When a mistake is made in pursuit of assigned goals.
4. When a mistake falls within assigned authority.
5. When a mistake is consistent with law and principles.
6. When proper procedures are used.

The first and second conditions arise because there is often more value in the failure of a specific action than in its success. Success does not teach; people replicate successful behaviour until it fails. If an error can teach the company something new, it should be tolerated. But managers must come down hard on repeated (patterned) mistakes to encourage teams to share their experience and to stop the same mistakes from recurring.

The third and fourth conditions arise from the broad delegation of authority that occurs under empowerment. It is easy to have teams drift off the purpose when close supervision is withdrawn and internal dynamics begin playing a role in getting work done. To encourage teams to stick to assigned goals, mistakes made through reaching beyond these goals should be punished. However, as long as the team stays *inside* its goals, mistakes should not be punished, subject to the other conditions on the list.

The fifth condition arises because companies do find themselves running into legal trouble as a result of employees' actions. This last criterion tells employees they are not protected if their behaviour is illegal.

The sixth and last condition is controversial. Teams can cast off their dependence on a manager only to become tied to a procedures manual instead. But procedure can also be important; documentation is key to learning. The firm must know what the team did and a procedures guide can help ensure that value is extracted from errors – in the form of modified procedures.

Trust

Fault tolerance sets the stage for the development of trust. Trust is actually a complex psychological contract that gives employees comfort in taking action. The higher the level of trust that management can generate, the greater the level of empowerment achieved.

Predictability is the weakest form of trust. When it is present, employees can assume that the employer will act in its own interests, although these interests may or may not be shared with the employee. Predictability makes it possible for employees to anticipate what will happen if they undertake certain actions.

There are two methods of building predictability: personal contact and consistency. Personal contact is important because written orders and telephone calls provide little context for action. Employees cannot glean context from the content of orders alone, they also need body language and facial cues, which come only with personal contact. Consistency is also important to predictability. It is as managers handle similar situations in similar fashion that employees come to view behaviour as a guide for future action.

Reliability is a somewhat stronger form of trust. When it is present, employees can assume that the employer will follow through on promises, even if they are not always in the employer's interest. Reliability raises the relationship between employee and employer to a longer-term status and permits more of a two-way exchange of views: sometimes the employer contributes, sometimes the employee.

There are three methods of building reliability: keeping promises, using candour, and offering support. Keeping promises means more than consistent behaviour. For example, a manager may reward employees who come in early by letting them go home early –

behaviour that builds predictability; or the manager may start flexi-time – a promise that those who come in early may *always* go home early. It is keeping the promise that builds reliability. Using candour is also important in building reliability. Candour ensures that the 'promises' to be kept are clearly understood, even at the cost of personal discomfort. Finally, offering support builds reliability as managers talk to subordinates, even if the news is bad.

Mutuality is the strongest form of trust. When it is present employee and employer share expectations of each other and so feel comfortable in taking action with limited communication.

There are two methods of building mutuality: taking time to care and providing as much security as possible given the conditions in which the company must operate. In taking time to care, a manager remembers critical aims/objectives of employees or personal aspects of work relationships. Employment security may be hard to provide, but it generates the maximum degree of mutuality. Consider the position of the partner in a professional service firm: the partner is, to a significant degree, the partnership to which they belong.

Those who establish teams must also understand their own role in the context of empowerment. Managers need to help team members cope with stress. Empowerment is designed for ambiguous environments, but many employees are not – previously they held assigned tasks. Managers must learn how to give and receive constructive criticism and to listen carefully without asserting their remaining authority too strongly.

A company should always aim for the highest level of trust possible to ensure maximum scope for independent action and should never presume to have more trust than it has earned. Without securing at least predictability, employees are unlikely to take actions that have not been directly approved. If mutuality is secured, full empowerment can be almost automatic.

REFERENCE

1. Friesen, G.B., and Mills, D.Q., *Elements of Managerial Style*, unpublished survey research. Further information is available from the authors.

RESOURCES

BOOKS

Friesen, G.B. and Mills, D.Q., *Elements of Managerial Style*, unpublished survey research. Further information is available from the authors.

Mills, D. Quinn, *The Rebirth of the Corporation*, Wiley and Sons, New York, 1991.

Mills, D. Quinn, *Empowerment*, 1994.

Zuboff, Shoshana, *In the Age of the Smart Machine*, Basic Books, New York, 1988.

Winning the talent wars

BRUCE TULGAN

How do you get the best people to pay their dues and climb the ladder in the old-fashioned way? You don't – not in the new economy, says Bruce Tulgan. Organizations will have to move away from the static long-term staffing model and towards a more fluid model. This will require fundamental changes in a whole range of management practices.*

WE are living through the most profound changes in the economy since the Industrial Revolution. Technology, globalization and the accelerating pace of change have yielded chaotic markets, fierce competition and unpredictable staffing requirements.

Starting in the late 1980s, business leaders and managers began responding to these factors by seeking much greater organizational flexibility. Re-engineering increased speed and efficiency with improved systems and technology. Companies in every industry have redesigned almost everything about the way work gets done. Work systems, which in some cases have been in place for decades, have been dismantled and refashioned to improve flexibility, efficiency, and effectiveness.

All of these changes in the economy have been freeing work from the confines of the old-fashioned 'job' with its rigid features: employees going every day to the same organization in the same building during the same hours to do the same tasks and responsibilities in the same position in the same chain of command, paying their dues and climbing the ladder. Now, the rule of thumb is that

*This article is based on Bruce Tulgan's forthcoming book, *Winning the Talent Wars*.

you get the work done, whenever you can, wherever you can, however you can, whatever the work may be on any given day.

As a result, business organizations have become more nimble than ever before and are now much better able to compete in today's high-tech, fast-paced, knowledge-driven, global economy.

But, in the process, the nature of work has been fundamentally reshaped and the relationship between employers and employees radically altered forever. In the new economy, the old-fashioned model of work is all but gone.

The new 'free agent' career path

Business leaders killed the old model of success – the dues-paying career path defined by long-term employment in one company and corporate loyalty – because the new economy called for a whole new relationship between employers and employees. However, very few of those leaders predicted that, in response, the workers with the most marketable skills, the people consistently in greatest demand, would discover that they could do better fending for themselves than they ever had by following the old-fashioned career path. But that's exactly what happened – and a whole new career path is emerging.

People, especially the best educated and most skilled, increasingly see themselves as sole proprietors of their skills and abilities – or as 'free agents'. These free agents think of their employers as 'clients', often juggling several at once. They seem to move seamlessly from one new opportunity to the next – soaking up training resources, building relationships with decision makers, and collecting proof of their ability to add value – and cash out their career investments on a regular basis so they can reassess and renegotiate. To the free agent, success is not defined by where they stand in relation to the hierarchy of a particular organization. What matters is their ability to add value and to sell that value on the open market. Every untapped resource is waiting to be mined. Every unmet need is an opportunity to add value. Every person is a potential customer.

Today, free agency is sweeping across the workforce like wildfire. More and more people are coming to realize that to keep doing what they know how to do well and earn money doing it, they don't necessarily need a permanent job, or even a job as such at all. In the new economy, the individual, not the employer, is in the driver's seat. The skills that make you valuable to an employer belong to you and nobody else. When you leave your employer, those skills and experience and ability to add value go with you. Nowadays, security comes not from stability and commitments, but rather from mobility and options. And all of a sudden, fewer and fewer skilled people are clinging to their jobs and crying 'don't downsize me', and the balance of power in the labour market is shifting.

Perpetual staffing crises

In today's environment of fast-moving markets and fierce competition, experience and seniority no longer rule the job market, and a new breed of talent is in high demand: those who are adaptable, independent, techno-literate, information savvy, and entrepreneurial. Every organization in every industry is spending more time, more energy, and more money than ever before recruiting the talent they need. But the supply of skilled workers is simply not growing fast enough, at any level, to meet organizations' growing needs.

If you ask business leaders and managers, as I do every day, most will tell you that the most pressing and seemingly unsolvable problem facing them is employee turnover. And the problem is not just that turnover is increasing, but that turnover is *changing*. It used to be that the best people were the most likely to stay with the firm. But more and more, it is the best people who are the most likely to leave ... because they can. While employers have human resources teams working double time to solve the problem, it just keeps getting worse.

Perhaps the most troubling news is that the staffing crisis is likely to endure for the foreseeable future. More and more work in all segments of the economy requires more and more skill. Largely for that reason, the demand for skilled workers will keep growing faster than the supply.

Skilled employees are in such great demand, and employers are so concerned about retaining them and getting a decent return on their recruiting and training investment, that employees have more negotiating power in the workplace than ever before. In this climate, employers can no longer expect employees to be motivated by prospects of long-term employment steps up an organization's hierarchy, six-month reviews, annual raises, and other rewards and incentives from the workplace of the past.

So what does this mean for business? Employers cannot go back to promising job security in exchange for loyalty because they need to stay lean and flexible in the post-industrial age, even while they are scrambling for access to the best talent.

Best practice No. 1: Staffing

Throughout most of the industrial era and until recently, the dominant staffing model for most employers was based on long-term employment relationships with long-term employees. People were expected to start in entry-level positions appropriate to their skills and credentials and then, over time, move their way up the ladder. The key features of this model were stability and predictability. Staffing strategy was all about planning for openings in an otherwise static organization chart. With slight adjustments, the positions on the chart remained the same – like the positions on a sports team – only the people who filled those positions would change periodically – like the players on a sports team.

But in today's quickly changing marketplace, where employers can never predict what is just around the corner, the old-fashioned, stable, long-term employer–employee relationship just doesn't fit. The key to continued success for companies is the ability to adapt rapidly to new circumstances, whether they are unexpected or suddenly vanishing market opportunities. Depending on the circumstances, staffing may have to expand rapidly, or contract rapidly – or both at the same time. Certain skills may be required all of a sudden; and others, just as suddenly, may be no longer necessary.

In the new economy, staffing needs will be in continual flux. Employers must gear their staffing strategies around coping with this reality:

1. Shrink your core group.
2. Grow your fluid talent pool.
3. Build a proprietary talent database of individual contributors who could be called on as needed on a temporary basis.
4. Develop solid working relationships with a wide range of vendors who can be counted on for outsourcing.
5. Maintain an internal group of contributors who are not permanently assigned to any particular tasks/responsibilities, teams, locations, or schedules, who can be called on and deployed to fill in staffing gaps wherever and whenever they occur.

Best practice No. 2: Training

Organizations in every industry are investing more in employee training and development than ever before. That's because highly skilled and knowledgeable employees are critical to an organization's competitive position in the new economy. Value adding, problem solving and innovation are the winning elements in today's marketplace. Those elements require smart work every bit as much as, if not more than, hard work. So companies absolutely must train their employees all the way from the corner office to the factory floor, and then train them some more.

But the more companies train their employees, the more marketable those employees become and, therefore, the more likely they are to leave the organization for a better offer. This is what I call the 'training investment paradox'. Employers are simply not getting the return they need on their training investment when their employees turn over too soon, especially when these go to work for the competition (then the competition is getting the investment return).

Organizations need to stop training their employees for the long haul; that approach was based on the assumptions of the old-fashioned, long-term career path. It makes much more sense to train people only on an as-needed basis. By investing in just-in-time learning resources, organizations can separate a large part of their return on investment from the duration of individual employees' employment. Furthermore, just-in-time training is in sync with the learning needs of individuals in today's information environment, because it allows learners to select immediately the precise information they require to fill skill and knowledge gaps as they occur.

Best practice No. 3: Performance management

The key to empowerment is effective delegation: giving individual contributors ownership of tangible results. In the workplace of the past, delegation was not so dynamic. Usually, managers would delegate to employees relatively fixed assortments of tasks and responsibilities. These would be known as 'job descriptions'. And people often became very protective of their own areas of work, claiming job descriptions as their turf. But nowadays, everybody has the same job description: get it done, whatever it is on any given day, as fast as you can.

Simply telling employees 'we want you to treat this project like your own little business' is not enough to achieve effective delegation, which is what is required to create real empowerment. You cannot empower people without establishing the terrain on which they have power. That terrain needs to be made up of tangible goals accompanied by concrete deadlines as well as clear guidelines and parameters. To bring out the very best in the very best people, managers must create clarity on an ongoing basis around three key questions:

- Which roles are being played by which people in pursuit of which missions?

- Where does each employee's responsibility begin and end?
- How and for what will each contributor be held accountable?

Best practice No. 4: The role of managers

Supervisory managers in the new workplace must be performance management coaches and business leaders must hold every supervisory manager accountable for effectiveness in that role. According to our research, the most important predictor of success (productivity, morale and duration of employment) of long-term and short-term employees, as well as of teams, is a coaching-style manager who knows how to give what we call 'FAST Feedback' effectively.

The fundamental principle of FAST Feedback is feedback itself. Feedback is different from other forms of communication because *feedback is always a responsive communication.* Feedback is the fundamental principle of FAST Feedback because, by its nature, coaching is an ongoing series of responses to the performance of whoever is being coached. Giving feedback is the core competency of every coach. According to our research, the FASTer the feedback, the better the coach.

Our formula, FAST, is an acronym that stands for frequent, accurate, specific, and timely. These are the elements employees most often ascribe to feedback they receive from managers whom they describe as 'the best manager I've ever had'. These are also the four elements employees most often say they need, but don't get, in the feedback they receive from most managers.

Frequent

Each employee has their own unique frequency. Giving each employee feedback at their unique frequency is the first key behaviour of the best coaching-style managers. Identifying and tuning into each employee's frequency is the corresponding skill.

Accurate

Every instance of feedback affects trust and performance. Giving feedback that is correct, balanced, and appropriate is the second key behaviour. Stopping to reflect, question assumptions, check facts and rehearse is the second corresponding skill.

Specific

Telling people exactly what they do right and exactly what they do wrong is not specific enough. Telling people exactly what you want them to do next is the third key behaviour. Setting concrete goals and deadlines with clear guidelines is the corresponding skill.

Timely

The closer feedback comes in proximity to the performance in question, the more impact the feedback will have. Giving feedback immediately is the fourth key behaviour. Effective time management is the corresponding skill.

Best practice No. 5: Rewards and incentives

The old-fashioned incentives – long-term employment, steps up the organization's hierarchy, six-month reviews, annual raises, and standard benefits – are no longer enough to motivate the best talent. In the just-in-time workplace, you can't expect people to wait around to be rewarded once they've delivered; long-term rewards are out. People want to know what you have to offer them today, tomorrow, and next week in return for their added value. What is more, in order to really drive the best performance in the workplace of the future, it is necessary to pay contributors not just in cold cash, but also in a wide range of currencies they value (financial and non-financial alike), remembering that different people value different currencies.

Managers need to reward desired performance consistently and with speed and creativity. Three factors should guide rewards and incentives in the workplace of the future:

- Control.
- Timing.
- Customization.

Control

If the role of rewards is to drive performance, managers should make performance the only lever for controlling rewards. That means it is critical to make very clear to individual contributors exactly what performance – what results, within what guidelines, parameters and deadlines – the organization needs and will therefore reward. This must be done on an ongoing basis, because the results required of any contributor in any organization are likely to be in continual flux.

Rewards should not be spread around equally in an effort to treat all contributors the same, unless business leaders are trying to turn their organizations into communes. The issue of fairness often comes up when differential pay for high performers is discussed. So let me offer a way to think about fairness: there is nothing that could be less fair than rewarding high performers and low performers the same. Compensating high performers at a higher rate is not only fair, it's the only fair way. Rewards should not be wasted on people who fail to meet stated goals and deadlines. And individual contributors who perform must be made confident that their performance will result in proportionate financial and non-financial compensation. Every single resource an employer can make available to employees should be positioned as an incentive for performance.

Just as managers must become performance coaches, they must also position themselves as purchasing agents: purchasing the added value (concrete results) of individual contributors every day in exchange for compensation. Just as purchasing agents must negotiate with vendors, managers must learn to negotiate with employees. Employees can be expected to drive a hard bargain and so should managers. And just as it does with vendors, the market ultimately will dictate acceptable terms in each case.

Timing

Reward people when they deliver results – no sooner, no later. Speed matters more than ever nowadays, so give people an incentive to perform quickly. That doesn't mean relaxing standards, but rather encouraging contributors to meet high performance standards as fast as they can. When contributors meet their goals within stated guidelines and parameters, managers should cash them out immediately, and prepare to renegotiate. Immediate rewards are the most effective because there can be no doubt about the reason for the rewards, providing a greater sense of control and a higher level of reinforcement. Further, contributors are more likely to remember the precise details and context of the performance and are therefore better able to replicate the desired performance. And finally, contributors do not spend time wondering if their performance has been noted and appreciated and are less likely to lose the momentum generated by instances of success.

Customization

Managers often complain that today's employees are too demanding:

- 'This one wants Thursdays off.'
- 'That one wants her own office.'
- 'This one wants to bring his dog to work.'
- 'That one wants to go to every training class we offer.'
- 'This one wants to have dinner with the senior VP.'

And so on. But managers are wrong to complain. When a manager discovers the wants and needs of an individual contributor, they have found a needle in a haystack. Different people are motivated by very different incentives. Too often, managers never find out exactly which rewards the different people they manage want most, and are therefore willing to work hardest to earn. In some cases, the desired rewards are so idiosyncratic that a manager wouldn't guess in a million years if the employee didn't offer clues. And even when managers get the clues and find out what their employees want, very often managers disregard the desired rewards as unreasonable or unrealistic.

A much better strategy is to use the discovery of desired rewards as an opportunity to motivate individual contributors with uniquely attractive incentives. Use the desired rewards as bargaining chips in the 'purchasing agent' negotiation for added value:

- 'You want Thursdays off? I'm glad to know that. Here's what I need from you.'
- 'You want your own office? OK. Here's what I need from you.'
- 'You want to bring your dog to work? Great. Here's what I need from you.'
- 'You want to have dinner with the senior VP? Here's what I need from you.'

Trade every customized incentive for concrete goals with clear guidelines, parameters and deadlines.

Best practice No. 6: Retention

In today's tight labour market, business leaders agonize about high turnover because so many employees come and go before they deliver a decent return on the organization's recruiting and training investment. That is why retention will be the number one concern of human resource professionals for the foreseeable future.

You don't have to retain people in the long term as exclusive, full-time, on-site employees with uninterrupted service. In fact, if you did, you would find your organization overly constrained by rigid employment relationships. In the new economy, the best way to get the best work out of the best people consistently is 'on again, off again': sometimes full time, sometimes flexitime, sometimes part time; sometimes on site, sometimes off site; sometimes on an exclusive basis and sometimes as a shared resource. It doesn't matter where, when, or how you get the best people to contribute the most work at the highest levels of speed and accuracy, as long as you get them to make those contributions when you need them.

The key to retention is to redefine it so that it means 'access to the talent you need when you need it'. With that redefinition, the way to retain talent is to stay lean and learn to thrive on short-term flexible employment relationships with the best free-agent employees. The best people who serve you well on a consistent basis will be your new lifelong employees. Retain the best people one at a time, one day at a time, on the basis of an ongoing negotiation with each individual on their own unique terms.

If you are willing to negotiate in order to retain, then you can transform the reasons for the best people leaving into the reasons for the best people staying. According to our research, there are five reasons people typically leave their jobs nowadays (apart from a huge differential in pay opportunity).

Relationships

In the majority of cases, people leave their job because they are unhappy with their boss or manager, further reinforcing the importance of the manager/direct report relationship. The best way to deal with this factor is with preventive measures: making sure that supervisory managers play the role of performance coach. When preventive measures fail, the challenge is to move the individual contributor into the supervisory orbit of another manager without losing the employee altogether.

It is important to note, however, that an employee's relationship with their manager/boss is not the only relationship that may cause that employee to leave (or stay). Other relationships with a powerful impact include those with co-workers, subordinates, vendors, and clients or customers. By working to improve problem relationships or moving contributors out of such relationships and into new ones, many unnecessary turnovers can be prevented.

Schedule

This is almost as big a factor as relationships. Sometimes people want to work more, sometimes they want to work less, often they simply want to work the same hours but on flexitime or compressed time. In many, many cases, even a slight adjustment in a person's schedule will be enough to make them leave a job (or stay).

Work

Often people leave because they want to tackle new challenges – new tasks, responsibilities, or projects – that they feel will not be available to them if they remain in the same job or working in the same organization. If they can find those new challenges in the same job or, at least, the same organization, often they will stay.

Skills

In today's world, where it is critical to keep building your skills faster than they become obsolete, individuals – especially the best, most skilled individuals – feel a strong compulsion to be learning all the time. That is why, when people feel they have exhausted the learning opportunities where they are, they will often leave in search of new ones. As long as such employees are learning voraciously on the job, they are unlikely to leave.

The challenge for employers is to maintain an environment of continual voracious learning. That doesn't always mean formal training programmes or financial support for external education. Often it means creating an infrastructure of learning resources and a culture of knowledge work.

Location

Sometimes due to a change in life circumstances (sometimes not), people want or need to work in a different place. That may mean a different city/town/county, state, or country. In that case, an employer may not have the ability to accommodate this need, but many employers do. When an organization is geographically widespread, all it takes is a transfer.

Of course, employee transfers present many issues, not least of which is that the transferring manager will still lose a valued employee. However, if the complicating factors can be worked out, at least the organization as a whole will retain an employee who would otherwise be lost altogether. It should be noted that sometimes the desire to work in a new location simply means a desire to work at home, some or all of the time. Whenever practical, retaining an employee as a telecommuter is preferable to losing them.

Remember that the factors that cause valuable contributors to leave can often be transformed into factors that cause valuable contributors to stay, if an employer is willing to negotiate. Indeed, it is often an employer's willingness to negotiate and, ultimately, accommodate on such matters that can make an otherwise ordinary employment relationship uniquely valuable to an individual contributor. The strong likelihood is that long-term employment relationships in the workplace of the future will be based on how well the work situation fits with each individual contributor's unique life plan (not the reverse).

RESOURCES

BOOK

Tulgan, Bruce, *Winning the Talent Wars*, W.W. Norton, New York, 2001.

WEB

www.rainmakerthinking.com

MANAGING HUMAN RESOURCES

BROADBANDING

BROADBANDING can be seen as an antidote to the demise of regular promotions and salary increments associated with the traditional career ladder. It involves a compression of the traditional hierarchy of pay grades into a fewer, wider bands, which provide a more flexible and less hierarchy-driven reward system.

Broadbanding originated in the US and was heavily influenced by the pioneering efforts of the General Electric Corporation (GE). It became more established outside GE in the late 1980s as a result of the move to flatter management structures. Indeed, many argue that the switch to broadbanding is a necessary step to support a delayered organization, as a failure to tackle pay will otherwise demotivate employees who have fewer opportunities for promotion.

If there appears to be no reward for their efforts, there is a risk that people will feel disinclined to develop, expand, and innovate. Broadbanding is supposed to mitigate this problem. It allows employees to enjoy salary increases without being promoted to a more senior position. So, for example, a pay increase could result from a sideways move or from developing new skills in their existing job. By focusing attention on career development, continuous improvement, and role flexibility, broadbanding encourages a less rigid interpretation of career progression and provides a sense of direction and achievement. It can also be used to highlight the skills and competencies the organization identifies as important to its future.

Multinationals such as Glaxo-Wellcome, IBM, and British Petroleum have already introduced broadbanding pay systems and other employers seem likely to follow suit.

DOWNSIZING

DOWNSIZING is the *bête noire* of management thinking. It reached its height during the recession of the early 1990s. It advocated a wholesale reduction in staffing levels as the key to greater efficiency and improved financial performance. Originally intended as the antidote to the growing bureaucracy within large American organizations, downsizing became a flag of convenience for many organizations looking to boost profits by cutting headcount.

Downsizing was a natural extension of the prevailing ideology of the time. In the 1980s market forces were elevated to the status of elemental forces. Downsizing was pursued with such vigour and disregard for the human cost, that its victims and survivors alike came to regard it as little more than a cynical exercise. In many cases where companies downsized, corporate income rose significantly while conditions for many working families continued to stagnate or decline. At the heart of the downsizing movement was the assumption that the sole purpose of companies was to increase the wealth of shareholders.

Downsizing was in keeping with other changes taking place in the business world in the late 1980s and early 1990s. Probably the most significant is the trend towards *delayering*. Much of the restructuring over recent years has involved cutting out layers of middle management 'fat' to create 'lean' management structures. American economist Robert Topel estimates that in the US alone, more than 12.2 million white-collar workers lost their jobs between 1989 and 1991 and another 3 million since then.

Public anger at seemingly unnecessary corporate blood letting led to downsizing being reinvented in the more politically correct guise of 'rightsizing'. No one was fooled. Much of the damage, anyway, has already been done. Many companies have lost some of their most experienced middle managers, which some commentators believe contain the 'corporate memory'. An optimistic view of the downsizing binge would be that it may have been a painful but necessary step towards the re-evaluation of the fundamental purpose of business in society.

EMPOWERMENT

EMPOWERMENT is one of the most overused (and misused) words to enter the business lexicon in recent years. As the term suggests, it is all about empowering workers – providing them with additional power. Logically, that means the power to make decisions and pursue the best interests of the organization.

In theory, empowerment is all about the removal of constraints preventing an individual from doing their job as effectively as possible. The idea is to cascade power – especially discretionary decision-making power – down through the organization, so that the people performing tasks have greater control over the way they are performed. Worthy as that aspiration may be, often it fails to translate into practice.

The origins of the empowerment movement date back to the 1920s and the work of Mary Parker Follett, the forgotten prophet of modern management theory. Follett criticized hierarchical organizations; she detested the 'command and control' leadership style, favouring instead more 'integrated' democratic forms of management. She thought that front-line employee knowledge should be incorporated into decision making.

The work of Follett has found a modern-day echo in that of another woman, Rosabeth Moss Kanter, who has championed empowerment in recent years.

Change Masters, the book that helped establish Kanter's reputation, also helped establish the concept of empowerment and greater employee participation on the corporate agenda. 'By empowering others, a leader does not decrease his power, instead he may increase it – especially if the whole organization performs better,' she observed.[1]

But early signals of the empowerment revolution came from Japan. In 1979, Konosuke Matsushita of Matsushita Corporation gave a presentation to a group of American and European managers. Describing the commercial battle ahead, he quietly explained:

> *'We are going to win and the industrial West is going to lose. There's nothing you can do about it, because the reasons for your failure are within yourselves. Your firms are built on the Taylor model: even worse, so are your heads. With your bosses doing the thinking while the workers wield the screwdrivers, you're convinced deep down that this is the right way to run a business.'*

His point was that when a Japanese organization of 100,000 employees was in competition with a Western one of the same size, the Japanese firm would win because it utilized and empowered the brainpower of all 100,000 people, whereas the Western company used only the brains of the 20,000 or so people called managers.

The message was clear – but it took several years and a great deal of painful learning before its implications dawned on Western companies. With typical gusto they seized on empowerment as the answer to all corporate woes. But what they didn't realize is that it is a lot easier said than done.

For one thing, simply telling people they are empowered to make decisions does not mean they have the necessary support to do so. Decisions require resources (money, staff, etc.), authority, and information. In many cases, companies that talked about empowerment failed to provide these or to consider the implications for training and rewarding their newly empowered workforces.

But there is another problem. In organizations where operational decisions have previously been made by middle managers and supervisors, it is unrealistic to expect them to give up that power overnight or for employees lower down to be ready to accept it.

In addition, the downsizing bandwagon saw many companies stripping out layers of middle managers – the very people who were supposed to cascade decision making under empowerment. Not surprisingly, many empowerment initiatives were simply stopped in their tracks by middle managers who had no desire to give up their power at a time when they already felt threatened by redundancy.

In other cases, the wholesale removal of middle management meant that the transfer of skills required to make empowerment successful simply didn't happen. In the most extreme cases, this created a decision-making vacuum at the heart of the organization, with no one prepared to pick up difficult issues.

Those organizations that have made empowerment work have discovered that it requires a fundamental re-evaluation of the role of managers within the organization – as facilitator, coach and mentor, rather than decision maker, boss and police officer.

REFERENCE

1. Griffith, Victoria, 'It's a People Thing', *Financial Times*, 24 July 1997.

FOLLETT, MARY PARKER

AMERICAN political scientist Mary Parker Follett (1868–1933) was ahead of her time. She was discussing issues such as teamworking and responsibility (now reborn as empowerment) in the first decades of the twentieth century. Follett was a female, liberal humanist in an era dominated by reactionary males intent on mechanizing the world of business.

Born in Quincy, Massachusetts, Mary Parker Follett attended Thayer Academy and the Society for the Collegiate Instruction of Women in Cambridge, Massachusetts (now part of Harvard University). She also studied at Newnham College, Cambridge in the UK and in Paris, France.

The simple thrust of Follett's thinking was that people were central to any business activity – or, indeed, to any other activity. She said: 'I do not think that we have psychological and ethical and economic problems. We have human problems, with psychological, ethical and economical aspects, and as many others as you like.'

In particular, Follett explored conflict. She pointed out three ways of dealing with confrontation: domination, compromise, or integration. The latter, she concluded, is the only positive way forward. This can be achieved by first 'uncovering' the real conflict and then taking 'the demands of both sides and breaking them up into their constituent parts'. 'Our outlook is narrowed, our activity is restricted, our chances of business success largely diminished when our thinking is constrained within the limits of what has been called an either-or situation. We should never allow ourselves to be bullied by an "either-or". There is often the possibility of something better than either of two given alternatives,' Follett wrote.

Follett advocated giving greater responsibility to people, at a time when the mechanical might of mass production was at its height. She was also an early advocate of management training and that leadership could be taught. Her work was largely neglected in the West, although not in Japan, which even boasts a Follett Society.[1]

REFERENCE

1. Graham, Pauline (ed.), *Mary Parker Follett: Prophet of Management,* Harvard Business School Press, Cambridge, Mass, 1994.

HERZBERG, FREDERICK

IT is astonishing how little time is spent by management researchers actually talking to people in real situations. The strategist Henry Mintzberg is a notable exception to this, as is Frederick Herzberg (born 1923). In the late 1950s, as part of their research, the clinical psychologist Herzberg and his colleagues asked 203 Pittsburgh engineers and accountants about their jobs and what pleased and displeased them.

This approach was hardly original, but Herzberg's conclusions were. He separated the motivational elements of work into two categories – those serving people's animal needs (hygiene factors), and those meeting uniquely human needs (motivation factors).

Hygiene factors – also labelled maintenance factors – were determined as including supervision, interpersonal relations, physical working conditions, salary, company policies and administrative practices, benefits, and job security. 'When these factors deteriorate to a level below that which the employee considers acceptable, then job dissatisfaction ensues,' observed Herzberg. Hygiene alone is insufficient to provide the 'motivation to work'. Indeed, Herzberg argued that the factors that provide satisfaction are quite different from those leading to dissatisfaction.

True motivation, said Herzberg, comes from achievement, personal development, job satisfaction, and recognition. The aim should be to motivate people through the job itself rather than through rewards or pressure.

After the success of his 1956 book *The Motivation to Work*, there was a hiatus until Herzberg returned to the fray with an influential article in the *Harvard Business Review* in 1968. The article, 'One More Time: How Do You Motivate Employees?', has sold over one million copies in reprints making it the *Review*'s most popular article ever. The article introduced the helpful motivational acronym KITA (kick in the ass) and argued: 'If you have someone on a job, use him. If you can't use him get rid of him.' Herzberg said that KITA came in three categories: negative physical, negative psychological and positive. The latter was the preferred method for genuine motivation.

Herzberg's work has had a considerable effect on the rewards and remuneration packages offered by corporations. Increasingly, there is a trend towards 'cafeteria' benefits in which people can choose from a range of options. In effect, they can select the elements they recognize as providing their own motivation to work. Similarly, the current emphasis on self-development, career management and self-managed learning can be seen as having evolved from Herzberg's insights.

INTERIM MANAGEMENT

IT is hard to pinpoint exactly when the first interim manager emerged, but most commentators agree that the practice started in the Netherlands in the mid- to late-1970s.[1] At that time, it was seen as a way to get around the strict Dutch labour laws, which meant that companies taking on full-time managers incurred substantial additional fixed costs. The opportunity to take on executives on a temporary basis was therefore seen an ideal way to add additional executive resource without the negative effects.

Since then, the practice has spread to other countries. Interim management is seen as one solution to corporate crises and other managerial resourcing issues. It entails hiring highly qualified, highly experienced freelance executives and dropping them into a business dilemma, with a specific brief and a limited length of time to implement it.

Such appointments can actually reassure investors. In September 1996, for example, PepsiCo Inc. appointed Karl von der Heyden to be chief financial officer (CFO) and vice-chairman for a year. A former chief of RJR Nabisco, his main role at Pepsi was to help chart strategy in the wake of a string of operational problems that had plagued the company and to find a 'world-class' CFO to succeed him. Wall Street clearly approved of the idea: when the announcement was made Pepsi shares promptly jumped 50 cents to $29.50.

Today, the use of interim managers – also known variously as 'transition managers', 'flexi-executives', 'impact managers', 'portfolio executives', and 'Handymen' (after management guru Charles Handy, who was one of the first to advocate flexible working patterns) – is establishing itself as a key strategic resource for companies.

In her recent book *Strike a New Career Deal*, Carole Pemberton explains the rise of interim management as follows:

> *'An organization seeks help because there are major projects where it does not have sufficient in-house expertise, but where once the change has been introduced, the job can be managed internally. They [the top management team] know that they are getting an individual who has not only done the job before, but will probably have done it for a far larger enterprise.'*

Scenarios where an interim manager might be considered could include any of the following:

- Implementation of systems, particularly new or updated high-tech installations.
- Helping companies to take advantage of expansion or new opportunities.
- An underperforming company, one in dire need of reorganization.
- Preparing a subsidiary for sale.
- The sudden or unexpected departure or illness of a senior executive.

The wider strategic significance of the interim management concept is becoming apparent. It is very much in tune with other employment trends. According to *Fortune* magazine, for example, one in four Americans is now a member of the contingent workforce, people who are hired for specific purposes on a part-time basis.

There is little doubt that interim management is a timely addition to the corporate resourcing armoury. Interim managers are well matched to the changing business environment that companies now face.

REFERENCE

1. In his 1992 book *Interim Management*, 3. Godfrey Golzen puts the actual year *that interim management started* at 1978.

JAQUES, ELLIOTT

THE Canadian-born psychologist Elliott Jaques (born 1917) has ploughed an idiosyncratic furrow throughout his career. His work is based on exhaustive research and has generally been ignored by the mass managerial market.

Jaques is best known for his involvement in an extensive study of industrial democracy in practice at the UK's Glacier Metal Company between 1948 and 1965. Glacier introduced a number of highly progressive changes in working practices. A works council was introduced and no change of company policy was allowed unless all members of the works council agreed. 'Clocking on', the traditional means of recording whether someone had turned up for work, was abolished.

The emphasis was on granting people responsibility and understanding the dynamics of group working. 'I'm completely convinced of the necessity of encouraging everybody to accept the maximum amount of personal responsibility, and allowing them to have a say in every problem in which they can help,' said Jaques.[1] The Glacier research led to Jaques' 1951 book, *The Changing Culture of a Factory*.

Later in *The General Theory of Bureaucracy* (1976), Jaques presented his theory of the value of work. This was ornate, but aimed to clarify something Jaques had observed during his research: 'The manifest picture of bureaucratic organization is a confusing one. There appears to be no rhyme or reason for the structures that are developed, in number of levels, in titling, or even in the meaning to be attached to the manager–subordinate linkage.'

His solution was labelled the *time span of discretion* which contended that levels of management should be based on how long it was before their decisions could be checked, and that people should be paid in accordance with that time. This meant that managers were measured by the long-term impact of their decisions.

REFERENCE

1. 'Here comes the boss', BBC Radio Four, 1 August 1997.

2

KANTER, ROSABETH MOSS

BORN in 1943, Rosabeth Moss Kanter has a perspective that is resolutely humane. For someone who tends to the utopian, however, she is a diligent and persuasive commentator on industrial reality.

Now Class of 1960 Professor of Business Administration at Harvard Business School, Rosabeth Moss Kanter began her career as a sociologist before her transformation into international business guru. Her first book, *Men and Women of the Corporation* (1977), looked at the innermost workings of an organization. It was a premature epitaph for company man and corporate America before downsizing and technology hit home.

Kanter has mapped out the potential for a more people-based corporate world, driven by smaller, or at least less monolithic, organizations. She introduced the concept of the post-entrepreneurial firm, which manages to combine the traditional strengths of a large organization with the flexible speed of a smaller organization.

Key to this is the idea of innovation. This has been a recurrent theme of Kanter's since her first really successful book, *Change Masters*, subtitled 'Innovation and entrepreneurship in the American corporation'. In the book she defines change masters as 'those people and organizations adept at the art of anticipating the need for, and of leading, productive change'. At the opposite end to the change masters are the 'change resisters', intent on reining in innovation.

Change is fundamentally concerned with innovation (or 'newstreams' in Kanter-speak). The key to developing and sustaining innovation is, says Kanter, an 'integrative' rather than a 'segmentalist' approach. (This has distinct echoes of the theories of that other female management theorist, Mary Parker Follett, whose work Kanter admires.) American woes are firmly placed at the door of 'the quiet suffocation of the entrepreneurial spirit in segmentalist companies'.

Kanter was partly responsible for the rise in interest – if not in practice – of empowerment. 'The degree to which the opportunity to use power effectively is granted to or withheld from individuals is one operative difference between those companies which stagnate and those which innovate,' she says.

THE MANAGERIAL GRID

THE Managerial Grid was invented by Dr Robert R. Blake and the late Dr Jane Mouton. First published in 1964, it seeks to identify an individual's management style.

Crude as it is, the Grid helps people who are not conversant with psychology to see themselves and those they work with more clearly, to understand their interactions, and identify the sources of resistance and conflicts. It arose out of

Blake's experience working as a consultant with Esso (Exxon), where he observed the effects of different managers' personalities in a traditional corporate environment.

The Managerial Grid was a way of characterizing managers in terms of their orientation toward employees (people skills) and production (task skills). This became a three-dimensional model with the addition of motivation as a third axis.

With the Managerial Grid, concern for production is represented on a 1 to 9 scale on the *x* axis (horizontal axis). Concern for people is represented on a 1 to 9 scale on the *y* axis (vertical axis). So a score of 1 on the *x* axis and 9 on the *y* axis would be designated by the co-ordinates 1,9, and indicates someone with a low concern for people and a high concern for task completion. The Managerial Grid argues strongly for a 9,9 management style. The team builder approach in most cases, it is argued, will result in superior performance.

Motivation is the third dimension, running from negative (motivated by fear) to positive (motivated by desire). This is indicated by a + or – sign. According to Blake:

> *'The negative motivations are driven by fear, the positive ones by desire. The 9,1 corner, for instance, is down to the lower right – very high on concern for production, little or no concern for people. At that corner, 9,1+ illustrates the desire for control and mastery. At the same corner, 9,1– represents a fear of failure. These two work together. If I need control I rely to the most limited degree possible on you, because you're liable to screw up and the failure will reflect on me.'*

What the third dimension does is clarify the emotional driver underlying the Grid style. So, for example, 1,9+ describes a 'people pleaser' who cares little for production, and operates wholly from a desire to be loved. On the other hand, 9,1– describes a whip cracker who cares little about people, and operates in fear of something going wrong.

More sophisticated analysis using the Grid also takes account of the reaction of subordinates. Blake and Mouton identified additional management styles that combine various Grid positions. The 'paternalist' style combines the whip cracking (1,9) and the people pleasing (9,1), depending on the response of the subordinate. A subordinate who co-operates, for example, is rewarded with a 'people-pleasing' relationship; one that doesn't is subjected to the whip. The 'opportunist' manager, on the other hand, is a chameleon, taking on whatever Grid style seems appropriate for the interaction of the moment, never revealing their own true feelings.

Mouton died in 1987, but Blake, along with various co-authors, has explored the Grid and its uses in a steady stream of work. Probably the most useful for executives who want to explore the usefulness of the Grid idea is his 1991 book *Leadership Dilemmas – Grid Solutions* (written with Anne Adams McCanse).

MASLOW'S HIERARCHY OF NEEDS

ONE of the best-known theories explaining the actions of people is that of behavioural psychologist Abraham Maslow (1908–1970). In his book *Motivation and Personality*, published in 1954, Maslow hypothesized that people are motivated by an ascending scale of needs. When low-level needs are satisfied, individuals are no longer motivated by them. As each level of needs is met, individuals progress to higher-level motivators. Maslow's Hierarchy of Needs has been used ever since to underpin a variety of people management techniques, especially approaches to motivation.

Maslow asserted that people are not merely controlled by mechanical forces (the stimuli and reinforcement forces of behaviourism) or unconscious instinctive impulses as asserted by psychoanalysis, but should be understood in terms of human potential. He believed that people strive to reach the highest levels of their capabilities. Maslow called the people who were at the top 'self-actualizing'.

Maslow created a hierarchical theory of needs. The animal or physical needs were placed at the bottom, and the human needs at the top. This hierarchical theory is often represented as a pyramid, with the base occupied by people who are not focused on values because they are concerned with the more primal needs of physical survival. Each level of the pyramid is dependent on the previous level. For example, a person does not respond to the second need until the demands of the first have been satisfied.

There are five basic levels in Maslow's Hierarchy of Needs:

- **Physiological needs**: these needs are biological: oxygen, food, water, and a relatively constant body temperature. These needs are the strongest because if deprived of them, the person would die.
- **Safety needs**: except in times of emergency or periods of disorganization in the social structure (such as widespread rioting), adults do not experience their security needs. Children, however, often display signs of insecurity reflecting their need to be safe.
- **Love, affection and belongingness needs**: people have needs to escape feelings of loneliness and alienation and give (and receive) love, affection and the sense of belonging.
- **Esteem needs**: people need a stable, firmly based, high level of self respect and respect from others in order to feel satisfied, self confident and valuable. If these needs are not met, the person feels inferior, weak, helpless and worthless.

- **Self actualization needs**: Maslow describes self actualization as an ongoing process. Self actualizing people are devoted, and work at something, some calling or vocation.

This, Maslow said, explained why a musician must make music, an artist must paint, and a poet must write. If these needs are not met, the person feels restless, on edge, tense, and lacking something. Lower needs may also produce a restless feeling, but the cause is easier to identify. If a person is hungry, unsafe, not loved or accepted, or lacking self-esteem, the cause is apparent. But it is not always clear what a person wants when there is a need for self actualization.

Maslow believed that the only reason people would not move through the scale of needs to self actualization is because of the hindrances placed in their way by society, including their employer. Work can be a hindrance or can promote personal growth. Maslow indicated that an improved educational process could take some of the steps listed below to promote personal growth:

- Teach people to be authentic; to be aware of their inner selves and to hear their inner feeling voices.
- Teach people to transcend their own cultural conditioning, and become world citizens.
- Help people discover their vocation in life, their calling, fate, or destiny. This is especially focused on finding the right career and the right mate.
- Teach people that life is precious, that there is joy to be experienced in life, and if people are open to seeing the good and joyous in all kinds of situations, it makes life worth living.

Maslow's work can be regarded as utopian, but it was undoubtedly a powerful argument for more inclusive and humane thinking to be applied in the workplace.

MAYO, ELTON

The Australian Elton Mayo (1880–1949) had an interestingly diverse career, although he remains best known – if known at all – for his contribution to the famous Hawthorne experiments into motivation.

The Hawthorne Studies were carried out at Western Electric's Chicago plant between 1927 and 1932. Their significance lay not so much in their results and discoveries, although these were clearly important, but in the statement they made – that whatever the dictates of mass production and Scientific Management, people and their motivation were critical to the success of any business; and in their legacy – the Human Relations school of thinkers which emerged in the 1940s and 1950s.

Mayo's belief that the humanity needed to be restored to the workplace struck a chord at a time when the dehumanizing side of mass production was beginning to be more fully appreciated. 'So long as commerce specializes in business methods which take no account of human nature and social motives, so long may we expect strikes and sabotage to be the ordinary accompaniment of industry,' Mayo noted. He championed the case for teamworking and for improved communications between management and workforce. The Hawthorne research revealed informal organizations between groups as a potentially powerful force that companies could utilize or ignore.

Mayo's work and that of his fellow Hawthorne researchers redressed the balance in management theorizing. The scientific bias of earlier researchers was put into a new perspective. Mayo's work served as a foundation for all who followed on the humanist side of the divide.

PACKARD, DAVID

DAVID PACKARD (1912–1996) was one half of the partnership that created one of the business and management benchmarks of the last century. In 1937, with a mere $538 and a rented garage in Palo Alto, California, Bill Hewlett and David Packard created one of the most successful corporations in the world. 'We thought we would have a job for ourselves. That's all we thought about in the beginning,' said Packard. 'We hadn't the slightest idea of building a big company.' That garage was the birthplace of Silicon Valley.

Hewlett and Packard's legacy lies in the culture of the company they created and the management style they used to run it, the H-P way.

From the very start, Hewlett-Packard worked to a few fundamental principles. It did not believe in long-term borrowing to secure the expansion of the business. Its recipe for growth was simply that its products needed to be leaders in their markets. It got on with the job.

The company believed that people could be trusted and should always be treated with respect and dignity. 'We both felt fundamentally that people want to do a good job. They just need guidelines on how to do it,' said Packard.

H-P believed that management should be available and involved – 'managing by wandering about' was the motto. Indeed, rather than the administrative suggestions of management, Packard preferred to talk of leadership. If there was conflict, it had to be tackled through communication and consensus rather than confrontation.

While all about were turning into conglomerates, Hewlett and Packard kept their heads down and continued with their methods. When their divisions grew too big – and by that they meant around 1,500 people – they split them up to ensure that they didn't spiral out of control.

They kept it simple. Nice guys built a nice company. Their values worked to save the company when times were hard. During the 1970s recession, Hewlett-Packard staff took a 10 percent pay cut and worked 10 percent fewer hours. Commitment to people clearly fostered commitment to the company.

Packard retired as chairman in 1993. On his death in 1996, the company had 100,000 employees in 120 countries with revenues of $31 billion.

PETERS, TOM

IN 1982, Thomas J. Peters and Robert H. Waterman's *In Search of Excellence* was published. This marked a watershed in business book publishing. Since then, the market has exploded into a multimillion dollar global extravaganza. And, in parallel, the management guru industry has burgeoned.

Tom Peters (born 1942) was born and brought up near Baltimore. He studied engineering at Cornell University and served in Vietnam. He also worked for the drug enforcement agency in Washington. Peters has an MBA and PhD from Stanford, where he encountered a number of influential figures, including Gene Webb and Harold Leavitt. After Stanford he joined the consultancy firm McKinsey & Company. He left the firm (prior to the publication of *In Search of Excellence*) to work independently.

Tom Peters was both a beneficiary and the instigator of the boom in business books and the rise of the guru business. He was, in effect, the first management guru. While his predecessors were doughty, low-profile academics, Peters was high profile and media friendly. A business sprung up around him. First there were the books, then the videos, the consultancy, and the conferences. The medium threatened to engulf the message.

Peters' critics suggest that while he may have raised awareness, he has done so in a superficial way. He has pandered to the masses. Although his messages are often hard hitting, they are overly adorned with empty phrase making – 'yesterday's behemoths are out of step with tomorrow's madcap marketplace' – and with insufficient attention to the details of implementation.

And, over the years, the message has been radically overhauled. Peters' ideas have been refined, popularized, and, in many cases, entirely changed. What he celebrates today is liable to be dismissed in his next book. His critics suggest that Peters vacillates as readily as he pontificates.

In Search of Excellence celebrated big companies. Its selection of 43 'excellent' organizations featured such names as IBM, General Electric, Procter & Gamble, Johnson & Johnson, and Exxon. The book presented, on the surface at least, the bright side of an American crisis. The Japanese were seemingly taking over the industrial world, unemployment was rising, depression was a reality, and the prospects for the future looked bleak. The management world was ready for good news and Peters and Waterman provided it.

For such a trailblazing book, *In Search of Excellence* is, in retrospect at least, surprisingly uncontroversial. Peters and Waterman admitted that what they had to say was not particularly original. But they also had the insight to observe that the ideas they were espousing had been generally left behind, ignored, or overlooked by management theorists.

Peters and Waterman's conclusions were distilled down into eight crucial characteristics. These have largely stood the test of time:

- A bias for action.
- Close to the customer.
- Autonomy and entrepreneurship.
- Productivity through people.
- Hands-on values driven.
- Stick to the knitting.
- Simple form, lean staff.
- Simultaneous loose-tight properties.

Two years after *In Search of Excellence* was published, an American business magazine covered its front page with a single headline: 'Oops!' It then went on to reveal that the companies featured in *In Search of Excellence* were anything but excellent. The article claimed that about a quarter of the 'excellent' companies were struggling. The single and undeniable fact that the excellent companies of 1982 were no longer all excellent two years later has continued to haunt Peters. 'We started to get beaten up. When the magazine ran the *Oops* story it was a bad week,' says Peters. 'I was certain the phone would stop ringing. I wouldn't disagree that I had been on the road too much and in that respect it was a great wake up call.'

Peters' next two books carried on in much the same vein. *A Passion for Excellence* emphasized the need for leadership. Co-written with Nancy Austin, it was hugely successful but added little in the way of ideas. His next book, *Thriving on Chaos*, was an answer to the big question: How could you become excellent?

Thriving on Chaos opened with the bravado proclamation: 'There are no excellent companies.' This is probably the most quoted single line from Peters' work – either used as proof of his inconsistency, as evidence that he learned from his mistakes, or as a damning indictment of his propensity to write in slogans. *Thriving on Chaos* was a lengthy riposte to all those critics who suggested that Peters' theories could not be turned into reality. Each chapter ended with a short list of suggested action points. '*Thriving on Chaos* was the final, engineering-like, tidying up,' says Peters. 'It was organized in a hyper-organized engineering fashion.'

The major change in Peters' thinking occurred at the beginning of the 1990s. In effect, he dismissed the past and heralded in a brave new world of small units, freewheeling project-based structures, hierarchy-free teams in constant communication. Big was no longer beautiful and corporate structure, previously ignored by Peters, was predominant.

Peters did not mean structure in the traditional hierarchical and functional sense. Indeed, his exemplars of the new organizational structure were notable for their apparent lack of structure. And herein lay his point. Companies such as CNN, ABB and The Body Shop thrived through having highly flexible structures able to change to meet the business needs of the moment. Free flowing, impossible to pin down, unchartable, simple yet complex, these were the paradoxical structures of the future. 'Tomorrow's effective *organization* will be conjured up anew each day,' Peters pronounced.

Key to the new corporate structures envisaged by Peters were networks with customers, with suppliers, and, indeed, with anyone else who could help the business deliver. 'Old ideas about size must be scuttled. "New big", which can be very big indeed, is "network big". That is, size measured by market power, say, is a function of the firm's extended family of fleeting and semi-permanent cohorts, not so much a matter of what it owns and directly controls,' he wrote.

Examining his output, Peters is engagingly candid. 'My books could be by different authors. I have no patience with consistency so regard it as a good thing. I consider inconsistency as a compliment,' he says.

To Peters the moment is all important. If what he sees and what he thinks run totally counter to what he has previously argued, it is simply proof that circumstances have changed. (Not for nothing did Peters name his boat *The Cromwell*, inspired by Oliver Cromwell's comment, 'No one rises so high as he who knows not whither he is going.')

Indeed, what distinguishes Peters – and partly explains his success – is that he is not shackled to a particular perspective. While Michael Porter covers competitiveness and Rosabeth Moss Kanter human resources, Peters stalks restlessly from one issue to another. He has also proved remarkably adept at picking up ideas at exactly the right time. He has moved with the flow of ideas, but has always managed to be ahead of the tide.

If there is a consistent strand through his work, Peters believes it is 'a bias for action'. Forget the theorizing, get on with the job. This is a message that leads academics to shake their heads at its simplicity. With managers, however, it appears to strike a chord.

PSYCHOLOGICAL CONTRACT

DURING the stable 1950s and 1960s, the careers enjoyed by corporate executives were built on an implicit understanding and mutual trust. Influenced by their parents' hardships in the 1930s to value job security, and by their parents' military service in the Second World War to be obedient to those above, the term 'organization man' or 'corporate man' was invented for this generation.

2

Implicit to such careers was the understanding that loyalty and solid performance brought job security. This was mutually beneficial. The executive gained a respectable income and a high degree of security. The company gained loyal, hard-working executives. This unspoken pact became known as the psychological contract. The originator of the phrase was the social psychologist Ed Schein of MIT. Schein's interest in the employee–employer relationship developed during the late 1950s. He noted the similarities between the brainwashing of prisoners of war that he had witnessed during the Korean War and the corporate indoctrination carried out by the likes of GE and IBM.

As Schein's link with brainwashing suggests, there was more to the psychological contract than a cozy mutually beneficial deal. It raised a number of issues.

First, the psychological contract was built around loyalty. While loyalty is a positive quality, it can easily become blind. What if the corporate strategy is wrong or the company is engaged in unlawful or immoral acts?

The second issue was perspectives. With careers neatly mapped out, executives were not encouraged to look over their corporate parapets to seek out broader viewpoints. The corporation became a self-contained and self-perpetuating world supported by a complex array of checks, systems, and hierarchies.

Clearly, such an environment was hardly conducive to the fostering of dynamic risk takers. The reality was that the psychological contract placed a premium on loyalty rather than ability, and allowed a great many poor performers to seek out corporate havens. It was also significant that the psychological contract was regarded as the preserve of management. Lower down the hierarchy, people were hired and fired with abandon.

The rash of downsizing in the 1980s and 1990s marked the end of the psychological contract that had existed for decades. Expectations have now changed on both sides. Employers no longer wish to make commitments – even implicit ones – to long-term employment. The emphasis is on flexibility. On the other side, employees are keen to develop their skills and take charge of their own careers. Employability is the height of corporate fashion.

The new reality of corporate life means that the traditional psychological contract between employer and employee is unlikely to return. But in any employment deal, each side carries expectations, aspirations, and an understanding of the expectations and aspirations of the other side. The challenge is for both sides to make the new psychological contract an explicit arrangement.

SCHEIN, EDGAR

SOCIAL psychologist Ed Schein (born 1928) has eschewed a high media profile during a lengthy academic career. Yet his work has

exerted a steadily growing influence on management theory, particularly over the last 20 years. His thinking on corporate cultures and careers has proved highly important.

Schein joined MIT in 1956 and initially worked under the influence of Douglas McGregor. He has remained there ever since.

Schein noted the similarities between the brainwashing of prisoners of war and the corporate indoctrination carried out by the likes of GE at its Crotonville training base and IBM at Sands Point. 'There were enormous similarities between the brainwashing of the POWs and the executives I encountered at MIT,' says Schein. 'I didn't see brainwashing as bad. What were bad were the values of the Communists. If we don't like the values, we don't approve of brainwashing.' From this work came Schein's book, *Coercive Persuasion*.

The ability of strong values to influence groups of people is a strand that has continued throughout Schein's work. As he points out, recent trends, such as the learning organization (championed by his MIT colleague Peter Senge), are derivatives of brainwashing – 'Organizational learning is a new version of coercive persuasion,' he says.

The dynamics of groups and Schein's knowledge of brainwashing led to a developing interest in corporate culture, a term Schein is widely credited with inventing. His work on corporate culture culminated in the 1985 book *Organizational Culture and Leadership*. He describes culture as:

> *'a pattern of basic assumptions – invented, discovered, or developed by a given group as it learns to cope with its problems of external adaptation and internal integration – that has worked well enough to be considered valid and, therefore, to be taught to new members as the correct way to perceive, think, and feel in relation to those problems.'*

These basic assumptions, says Schein, can be categorized along five dimensions:

- **Humanity's relationship to nature:** while some companies regard themselves as masters of their own destiny, others are submissive, willing to accept the domination of their external environment.
- **The nature of reality and truth**: organizations and managers adopt a wide variety of methods to reach what becomes accepted as the organizational 'truth', through debate, dictatorship, or simple acceptance that if something achieves the objective it is right.
- **The nature of people**: organizations differ in their views of human nature. Some follow McGregor's Theory X and work on the principle that people will not do the job if they can avoid it. Others regard people in a more positive light and attempt to enable them to fulfil their potential for the benefit of both sides.

- **The nature of human activity**: the West has traditionally emphasized tasks and their completion rather than the more philosophical side of work. Achievement is all. Schein suggests an alternative approach – 'being-in-becoming' – emphasizing self-fulfilment and development.
- **The nature of human relationships**: organizations make a variety of assumptions about how people interact with each other. Some facilitate social interaction, while others regard it as an unnecessary distraction.

These five categories are not mutually exclusive, but are in a constant state of development and flux. Culture does not stand still.

Key to the creation and development of corporate culture are the values embraced by the organization. Schein acknowledges that a single person can shape these values and, as a result, an entire corporate culture. He identifies three stages in the development of a corporate culture: birth and early growth, organizational mid-life, and organizational maturity.

More recently, Schein's work on culture has identified three cultures of management that he labels 'the key to organizational learning in the twenty-first century'. The three cultures are the operator culture ('an internal culture based on operational success'); the engineering culture (created by 'the designers and technocrats who drive the core technologies of the organization'); and the executive culture, formed by executive management, the CEO, and immediate subordinates.

Success is related to how well the three cultures are aligned. It is a precarious balance, easily disturbed. For example, when executives move from one industry to another, cultures are often pushed out of alignment.

Another focus of Schein's attentions in recent years has been the subject of careers. He originated key phrases such as the psychological contract – the unspoken bond between employee and employer – and career anchors. Schein proposed that when mature we have a single 'career anchor', the underlying career value that we could not surrender. 'Over the last 25 years, because of dual careers and social changes the emphasis of careers has shifted,' he says. 'The career is no longer over arching. It is probably healthy because it makes people more independent. Lifestyle has become the increasingly important career anchor.'

SUCCESSION PLANNING

SUCCESSION planning is all about having able understudies in place to step into key positions when they become vacant. Although it is often associated with senior management roles, it is a key issue running right through an organization.

In recent years, it has become increasingly evident that the transfer of power from one leader to the next can have a major impact not just on morale and business performance, but on a company's share price.

Until very recently, most companies of any size created succession plans for senior posts, and development plans for key individuals in order to ensure that there was a ready supply of individuals prepared for the top jobs in the future. Usually, this involved accelerated or 'fast-track' programmes for so-called high flyers – graduates and other high-potential recruits.

How appropriate the whole concept of succession planning is in leaner corporate structures is unclear, however. The problem with traditional succession planning – and fast tracking in particular – is that it creates an expectation of upward progression, even though in today's leaner management structures there are far fewer rungs on the corporate ladder. It also fails to take account of non-managerial roles – in particular, knowledge workers in creative roles, who may be vital to the future of the business. The question here is how you retain a brilliant research scientist or software designer who has no desire for promotion.

In effect, then, traditional fast tracking and succession planning are likely to be less effective ways of retaining talent in the future. More flexible approaches will be required, customized to suit employees, their families, and the changing skills mix of the organization.

In recent years, there has also been considerable debate about the best way to handle the transfer of power from one CEO to the next. Certain organizations – UK retailer Marks & Spencer among them – have traditionally prided themselves on promoting from within and have a long history of grooming insiders for the top jobs. The best scenario, they believe, is a seamless succession, where the baton is passed from one executive to the next with virtually no interruption to the momentum and style of the business.

Other companies prefer a different succession strategy. Rather than appoint a new CEO in advance, they prefer a Darwinian approach, aiming to create a strong, highly motivated cadre of senior management from which the new CEO will 'emerge' when the time is right. Cometh the hour, cometh the man (or woman).

But the 'succession of the fittest' approach also has some drawbacks. It encourages political intrigue, as senior managers jockey for power to the detriment of the business. A homegrown CEO isn't always the answer, especially when a company is in trouble. Sometimes a new broom is required. There is also a school of thought that says regular injections of new blood are necessary to add diversity to the corporate gene pool. Either way, the solution is to bring in an outsider.

An external appointment at the top, on the other hand, can drive a coach and horses through the succession plan lower down, especially if the incoming leader brings their own team with them or slashes the management development budget. Such a short-sighted approach can leave holes in the succession plan further down the road, dooming it to failure.

Perhaps the thorniest succession issue of all involves a small group of business leaders – Bill Gates and Richard Branson among them – who are genuinely irreplaceable. These people play such a dominant role in the company that they come to be viewed as inseparable from it. The difficulty then becomes what happens to the business when they go?

The current trend appears to be that many organizations are actively reinstating succession planning. How appropriate such plans are to the needs of 'high flyers', to other employees, and to the organizations themselves is questionable.

THEORIES X AND Y (AND Z)

EVEN though he died over 30 years ago, Douglas McGregor (1906–1964) remains one of the most influential and most quoted thinkers in human relations (what was known in the 1940s and 1950s as behavioural science research). His work influenced and inspired the work of thinkers as diverse as Rosabeth Moss Kanter, Warren Bennis, and Robert Waterman. Most notably, McGregor is renowned for his motivational models, Theories X and Y.

These were the centrepiece of McGregor's 1960 classic, *The Human Side of Enterprise*. Theory X was traditional carrot-and-stick thinking built on 'the assumption of the mediocrity of the masses'. This assumed that workers were inherently lazy, needed to be supervised and motivated, and regarded work as a necessary evil to provide money. The premises of Theory X, wrote McGregor, were:

> *'(1) that the average human has an inherent dislike of work and will avoid it if he can, (2) that people, therefore, need to be coerced, controlled, directed, and threatened with punishment to get them to put forward adequate effort toward the organization's ends and (3) that the typical human prefers to be directed, wants to avoid responsibility, has relatively little ambition, and wants security above all'.*

McGregor lamented that Theory X 'materially influences managerial strategy in a wide sector of American industry', and observed, 'if there is a single assumption that pervades conventional organizational theory it is that authority is the central, indispensable means of managerial control'.

The other extreme was described by McGregor as Theory Y, based on the principle that people want and need to work. If this was the case, then organizations had to develop the individual's commitment to its objectives, and then to liberate their abilities on behalf of those objectives. McGregor described the assumptions behind Theory Y:

'(1) that the expenditure of physical and mental effort in work is as natural as in play or rest – the typical human doesn't inherently dislike work; (2) external control and threat of punishment are not the only means for bringing about effort toward a company's ends; (3) commitment to objectives is a function of the rewards associated with their achievement – the most important of such rewards is the satisfaction of ego and can be the direct product of effort directed toward an organization's purposes; (4) the average human being learns, under the right conditions, not only to accept but to seek responsibility; and (5) the capacity to exercise a relatively high degree of imagination, ingenuity, and creativity in the solution of organizational problems is widely, not narrowly, distributed in the population.'

Theories X and Y were not simplistic stereotypes. McGregor was realistic: 'It is no more possible to create an organization today which will be a full, effective application of this theory than it was to build an atomic power plant in 1945. There are many formidable obstacles to overcome.'

The common complaint against McGregor's Theories X and Y is that they are mutually exclusive, two incompatible ends of an endless spectrum. To counter this, before he died in 1964, McGregor was developing Theory Z, a theory synthesizing the organizational and personal imperatives. The concept of Theory Z was later seized on by William Ouchi. In his book of the same name, he analyzed Japanese working methods. Here, he found fertile ground for many of the ideas McGregor was proposing for Theory Z: lifetime employment, concern for employees including their social life, informal control, decisions made by consensus, slow promotion, excellent transmittal of information from top to bottom and bottom to top with the help of middle management, commitment to the firm and high concern for quality.

2

360-DEGREE FEEDBACK

THE annual appraisal was once a bureaucratic chore to be completed as speedily as possible. Every year, at an appointed hour, a manager sat in an office with their boss. The manager's performance over the previous year was discussed and dissected. The manager emerged from the room and headed back to their desk, until the next year. The traditional form of appraisal may linger on in some companies; in a fast-growing number, however, the annual ritual has been reinvented.

Appraisal's *raison d'être* is straightforward: to improve an individual's – and, therefore, an organization's – performance. To do so, the appraisal has to be responsive to individual needs and be available to individuals throughout the organization. As a result, the modern appraisal tends to be flexible, continuous, revolves around feedback, involves many more people than one manager and a boss, and seeks to minimize bureaucracy.

Appraisal is now seen in the broader-ranging context of 'performance management'. This means that it must embrace issues such as personal development and career planning, in addition to simple analysis of how well the individual has performed over the last year. Extending the range of this approach is the increasingly fashionable concept of 360-degree feedback. This involves a manager's peers, subordinates, bosses, and even customers airing their views on the manager's performance, usually by way of a questionnaire.

The attraction of 360-degree feedback is that it gives a more complete picture of an individual's performance. Different groups see the person in a variety of circumstances and can, as a result, give a broader perspective than that of a single boss. This, of course, relies on a high degree of openness and trust – as well as perception.

To ensure that comments are made as honestly as possible, without fear of sanction, anonymity is the almost universal rule. Inevitably, however, the truth can become clouded by prejudice and politics. People can be incredibly sycophantic or completely negative. Perceptions and the objectivity of the data can also be affected by prejudices and other influential factors.

An additional danger is that if managers are to be judged by subordinates, their motivation will be to be liked. Good management isn't necessarily about being liked, so there is the risk of management by popularity.

Perhaps more significant is that, for traditional managers, 360-degree feedback can be a highly disturbing experience. Managers are not renowned for their willingness to contemplate their weaknesses. Counselling and support are often necessary if the experience is to be a positive one.

More mundanely, actually running 360-degree feedback programmes is demanding and time consuming, which means it is common for companies to bring in consultants to run their programmes effectively. It also means that 360-degree feedback largely remains the preserve of a small number of senior managers. The logistics of expanding the concept to others in the organization are usually not persuasive.

– CHAPTER 3 –

Process management

'Reducing the cost of quality is in fact an opportunity to increase profits without raising sales, buying new equipment, or hiring new people.' PHILIP CROSBY

'People all over the world think that it is the factory worker that causes problems. He is not your problem. Ever since there has been anything such as industry, the factory worker has known that quality is what will protect his job. He knows that poor quality in the hands of the customer will lose the market and cost him his job. He knows it and lives with that fear every day. Yet he cannot do a good job. He is not allowed to do it because the management wants figures, more products, and never mind the quality.' W. EDWARDS DEMING

'Quality in a product or service is not what the supplier puts in. It is what the customer gets out and is willing to pay for. A product is not quality because it is hard to make and costs a lot of money, as manufacturers typically believe. This is incompetence. Customers pay only for what is of use to them and gives them value. Nothing else constitutes quality.' PETER DRUCKER

The quality revolution

STUART CRAINER AND DES DEARLOVE

Stuart Crainer and Des Dearlove explore Deming and Juran's contributions to quality control in both Japan and the US.

IN 1924, a physicist called Walter Shewhart (1891–1967) came up with the idea of a production control chart. A year later, he joined Western Electric as an engineer and found that the desire for exactitude found in theory was inevitably disappointed in practice. Shewhart's response was to develop a statistical approach to quality that emphasized the stability of production and supply, and applied the standards of the end user to the producer. Basically, Shewhart argued that minimal variation in production and maximum human co-operation were the most productive routes forward.

During the Second World War, the US War Department, anxious to enhance productivity as much as possible, brought in Western Electric's Bell Telephone Laboratories to promote its quality control methods. The armaments industry was given a crash course in Shewhart-style quality. Its impact was generally seen as positive. Indeed, Lord Cherwell, wartime scientific adviser to Winston Churchill, said that the Shewhart quality philosophy was the single most significant US contribution to the whole Allied war effort.

Such steps forward seemed to suggest that the Allied victors had the industrial world at their feet. Wartime had been a proving ground for modern management and manufacturing. It had emerged triumphantly, able to produce reliable goods quickly in huge quantities.

In the immediate post-war years, however, the pursuit of more became the driving economic force. Shewhart was largely forgotten in the rush to get on with business life. Quality initiatives like those at Western Electric disappeared ... from the US at least.

Meanwhile, the scale and speed of the revival of the countries defeated and devastated by the war were startling. The destruction was enormous, beyond parallel, at individual, national, and corporate levels. In Germany, the huge Siemens corporation was all but destroyed. By 1945, only about 400 of the 24,000 machine tools originally installed were still operative in the company's Berlin plants. After only 14 days of occupation, the Allied powers allowed work to resume and, by the end of 1945, around 14,000 workers were employed at Siemens' Berlin plants cleaning up and making a bizarre collection of products, including bicycle tyres, coal shovels, cooking pots, and coal-fired stoves.

On 2 September 1945, the Japanese surrendered on board the USS *Missouri*. However, the Japanese had begun planning their future before their final defeat. (As had German industrialists. 'Group directorates' were already established in southern and western Germany by Siemens in the final months of the war. These directorates were later able to start the reconstruction work independently of the head office in Berlin.) In the summer of 1945, Japanese ministers met secretly to discuss the future revival of their country. The aim, according to Foreign Minister Shigeru Yoshida, was to ensure that 'we could indeed rebuild Imperial Japan out of this way of defeat ... science will be advanced, business will become strong with the introduction of American capital, and in the end our Imperial country will be able to fulfil its true potential. If that is so, it is not so bad to be defeated in this war'. This combination of pragmatism, optimism, planning, and blind faith was characteristic of the rebuilding of the country.

The Japanese were greatly helped by General MacArthur's commitment to reconstruction. He wanted to rebuild not through re-establishing the old elite, but through elevating the middle ranks to take charge. One of the immediate post-war objectives was to set up a Japanese radio receiver industry so that the occupying powers could communicate directly to the people. The team of engineers charged with helping Japan's radio industry included a number who had worked at Western Electric and were, as a result, aware of the concept of quality control.

The approach of the American team of engineers in post-war Japan was greatly influenced by Shewhart's work. The team included Homer Sarasohn, W.S. Magil, Frank Polkinghorn, and Charles Protzman. Magil used Shewhart's quality control theories at the Nippon Electric Company in 1946 and lectured on the subject while in Japan.

Then Sarasohn and Protzman were supported by MacArthur in their idea of establishing a management training programme to ensure that their approaches reached as many people in industry as possible. During 1949–1950, Sarasohn and Protzman organized a series of eight-week courses on industrial management to which only top executives in the Japanese communications industry were invited. The students included Matsushita Electric's Masaharu Matsushita, Mitsubishi Electric's Takeo Kato, Fujitsu's Hanzou Omi, Sumitomo Electric's Bunzaemon Inoue, and Sony's founders Akio Morita and Masaru Ibuka.

Another post-war initiative was the creation (in August 1946) of Japan's Federation of Economic Organizations (FEO). This sounds like a glorified talking shop; it wasn't. FEO became one of the mainsprings of Japanese economic renewal, with over 750 large corporations and 100 major national trade associations. It was the power behind the revival of Japan Inc. and announced its main purpose as 'to maintain close contact with all sectors of the business community for the purpose of adjusting and harmonizing conflicting views and interests of the various businesses and industries represented in its huge membership. It is the front office of the business community and is in effect a partner of the government.' FEO's first president was Ichiro Ishikawa, a successful industrialist, who was also president of the Japan Union of Scientists and Engineers (JUSE), Japan's most important quality control organization, founded in 1946.

Quality control was, therefore, well on its way to becoming established in Japan very soon after the end of the war. Its impetus was to become irreversible.

The next move forward came when Ishikawa invited a Census Bureau statistician called W. Edwards Deming (1900–1993) to give a lecture to Tokyo's Industry Club in July 1950. Deming had first visited Japan in 1947 to aid in the development of what was to become the 1951 census. His message was different to the usual quality control theory, in that he emphasized the deficiencies of management. If quality was to happen it had to be led by management. The new generation had to seize the day.

As Ishikawa had sent out the invitations, the lecture was well attended, including 21 company presidents (some have suggested there were up to 45 in attendance). 'I did not just talk about quality. I explained to management their responsibilities,' Deming recalled. 'Management of Japan went into action, knowing something about their responsibilities and learning more about their responsibilities.'[1]

Deming eventually delivered a series of lectures. He asked for no fee, but JUSE sold reprints. The money raised through reprint sales was used to create the Deming Application Prize. This award for outstanding total quality programmes was first awarded in 1951 to Koji Kobayashi.

Over the next three decades, Japanese business put Deming's theories – and those of other quality gurus – into impressive practice. The West did not. Then, in 1979, NBC was fishing around for subjects for a documentary. The basic idea was for a programme on the decline of American business. Executive producer Reuven Frank had began with the far from populist working title of 'What to do About America's Falling Productivity?', which had metamorphosed into 'What Ever Happened to Good Old Yankee Ingenuity?' Neither seemed likely to set the world alight. Then it was suggested to Frank that he send someone along to see an elderly NYU academic who lived in Washington DC.

Clare Crawford-Mason was working on the project with Frank and was assigned to pay the mysterious old man a visit. Later she recalled:

> *'I called the man's office and set up an appointment. It wasn't difficult; his schedule was open. I recall postponing the first meeting. I was directed to go to the side of a residential house and come down the basement steps.*

> *I did. I knocked on the cellar door and walked into a two-room, below-ground office, filled with books and papers and overflowing desks and a blackboard covered with mathematical formulas.'*

She found 'the old gentleman ... pleasant, courtly and vehement'. [2]

The man was W. Edwards Deming. To the outside observer, Deming matched the stereotype of the academic eccentric. He eschewed luxury and wrote the date of purchase on his eggs with a felt-tip pen. (Later, when he was wealthy, Deming continued to drive a 1969 Lincoln Continental and to use public transport.) His staff comprised a single assistant – Cecilia 'Ceil' Kilian, who eventually worked with him for 39 years – and he worked six days a week for 12 hours.

Deming told the NBC team that he had played a central part in the renaissance of the Japanese economy in the post-war years. This was news to virtually everyone in the Western world. Deming was unheard of, an obscure statistician. But he was persuasive and impressive. The facts checked out. He was well known and honoured in Japan. An NBC programme evolved from that mysterious first meeting. It was broadcast on 26 June 1980 with its final title: 'If Japan can, why can't we?'

The NBC programme was a seminal moment in the development of Western management theory and practice. It was also a late and long-delayed recognition of W. Edwards Deming. (There was some irony in the fact that, at that point, Deming didn't own a television and had watched it only once to see the 1969 moon landing.) He gave American businesspeople a lecture in the quality basics. 'Inspection does not build quality, the quality is already made before you inspect it. It's far better to make it right in the first place,' he intoned. 'Statistical methods help you to make it right in the first place so that you don't need to test it. You don't get ahead by making product and then separating the good from the bad, because it's wasteful. It wastes time of men, who are paid wages; it wastes time of machines, if there are machines; it wastes materials.'

After the programme, NBC was inundated with phone calls. The executives of the *Fortune* 500 woke up in front of their TV sets. The programme's message was simple but stark. 'It was the first time anyone had said that if America did not improve its productivity our children would be the first generation of Americans who could not expect to live better than their parents,' says Clare Crawford-Mason.[3]

The early 1980s provided wake-up calls aplenty. Bad news stalked every corner. Western industry was, by common consensus, held to be on its knees. The oil crisis of the mid-1970s was the portent of a period of navel examination, self-analysis. Businesspeople contemplated their poor performing companies and their under-productive workforces with bemusement. By the beginning of the 1980s, Western industrialists were willing to hold their hands up and admit, 'We've screwed up.' They would also have quickly moved on to blaming irresponsible unions and greedy sheiks for this sad situation before desperately professing that they had little clue as to what to do next.

The death knell of post-war industrial optimism and unquestioning faith in the mighty corporation was sounding. Only the profoundly deaf carried on regardless – and there were many who chose to ignore the signals.

There was no shortage of obituary notices. A few days after the Deming TV programme, two Harvard Business School academics, Robert Hayes and Bill Abernathy, had their article 'Managing our way to economic decline' published in the July/August 1980 issue of the *Harvard Business Review*. It proved grim and highly influential reading.

Hayes and Abernathy had wrestled with the demons of decline and emerged dismayed. 'Our experience suggests that, to an unprecedented degree, success in most industries today requires an organizational commitment to compete in the marketplace on technological grounds – that is, to compete over the long run by offering superior products,' they wrote. (It is astounding in retrospect that such commercial facts of life needed restating.)

'Yet, guided by what they took to be the newest and best principles of management, American managers have increasingly directed their attention elsewhere. These new principles, despite their sophistication and widespread usefulness, encourage a preference for (1) analytic

detachment rather than the insight that comes from "hands on" experience and (2) short-term cost reduction rather than long-term development of technological competitiveness. It is this new managerial gospel, we feel, that has played a major role in undermining the vigour of American industry.' [4]

Hayes and Abernathy went on to champion customer orientation as a vital ingredient in reversing the apparently irreversible trend. Their message was that management was the problem. Forget about union militancy, forget about foreign competition, look upstairs to the boardroom.

An article buried in the *Harvard Business Review* does not usually excite or ignite debate; this one did. Hayes and Abernathy announced that the Western corporate post-war dream was approaching its final hours. People asked: what next?

Turning Japanese

One answer was to take Deming's advice and look to the East. This was a new experience. The ability – not to mention the arrogance and torpor – to ignore the rise of Japan was truly astonishing. The emergence of Japanese competitors had been generously signalled by the media.

As early as 1964, *Fortune* noted:

'American manufacturers of radios, television sets and other consumer electronic equipment have been repeatedly confounded by the agile competitiveness of Japan's Sony Corp. A small company even by Japanese standards – its sales last year amounted to $77 million – Sony has astutely used its limited capital to concentrate on a few unusually designed products beamed to a great extent at export markets, particularly the US.' [5]

In the very same article, it was noted that the Sony founder Akio Morita had been based in New York rather than Tokyo since 1963. The other founder of the company, Masaru Ibuka, visited the US in 1952; by 1958 Sony's export sales totalled $2.6 billion.[6]

The *Fortune* article went on to cite a 1960s survey that had asked American radio dealers whether they had ever handled Japanese radios. Most dealers said no. The next question asked whether they had ever handled Sony radios. The majority said yes.[7] *Fortune* concluded that Sony's 'well-made products are usually priced a notch or so above competitive US made equipment and well above the normal run of imports from Japan'.[8]

The warnings were ignored. Suddenly, however, the appetite for knowledge was enormous. A succession of books examined the secrets behind the perceived success of Japan.[9]

William Ouchi's 1981 *Theory Z* venerated Japan's employment and managerial practices. Theory Z was the natural development of McGregor's Theories Y and X. Richard Pascale and Anthony Athos also published the bestselling *The Art of Japanese Management*. This played a crucial role in the discovery of Japanese management techniques, as Pascale and Athos considered how a country the same size as Montana could be outstripping the American industrial juggernaut. 'In 1980, Japan's GNP was third highest in the world and, if we extrapolate current trends, it would be number one by the year 2000,' they warned.[10]

Harsh home truths lurked on every page of *The Art of Japanese Management*. 'If anything, the extent of Japanese superiority over the United States in industrial competitiveness is underestimated,' wrote Pascale and Athos, observing that 'a major reason for the superiority of the Japanese is their managerial skill'. In its comparisons of US and Japanese companies, *The Art of Japanese Management* provided rare insights into the truth behind the mythology of Japanese management and the inadequacy of much Western practice.

Among the key components of Japanese management identified by Pascale and Athos was that of vision, something they found to be notably lacking in the West. 'Our problem today is that the tools are there but our "vision" is limited. A great many American managers are influenced by beliefs, assumptions, and perceptions about management that unduly constrain them,' they commented. The book, they said, was 'not an assault on the existing tools of management, but upon the Western vision of management which circumscribes our effectiveness'.[11]

Adding his voice to the argument was Japanese consultant Kenichi Ohmae. Ohmae (born 1943) did much to reveal the truth behind Japanese strategy making to an expectant Western audience. He demonstrated that the Japanese were human after all; at the time, Western managers were beginning to wonder.

Ohmae explored – and largely exploded – simplistic Western myths about Japanese management. Forget company songs and lifetime employment, there was more to Japanese management than that. Most notably, there was the Japanese art of strategic thinking. This, said Ohmae, is 'basically creative and intuitive and rational'. Japanese companies weren't mired in endless analysis or pointless hierarchies. 'Most Japanese companies don't even have a reasonable organization chart,' Ohmae told Peters and Waterman, authors of *In Search of Excellence*. 'Nobody knows how Honda is organized, except that it uses lots of project teams and is quite flexible ... Innovation typically occurs at the interface, requiring multiple disciplines. Thus, the flexible Japanese organization has now, especially, become an asset.'[12]

Ohmae's *The Mind of the Strategist* reached America in 1982. It had been published in Japan in 1975, though at that time there was no interest in the West in how Japan did anything. Ohmae pointed out that unlike large US corporations, Japanese businesses tend not to have large strategic planning staffs. Instead, they often have a single, naturally talented strategist with 'an idiosyncratic mode of thinking in which company, customers, and competition merge in a dynamic interaction out of which a comprehensive set of objectives and plans for action eventually crystallizes'.

Ohmae also noted that the customer was at the heart of the Japanese approach to strategy and key to corporate values. 'In the construction of any business strategy, three main players must be taken into account: the corporation itself, the customer, and the competition. Each of these "strategic three Cs" is a living entity with its own interests and objectives. We shall call them, collectively, the "strategic triangle",' Ohmae wrote.

> *'Seen in the context of the strategic triangle, the job of the strategist is to achieve superior performance, relative to competition, in the key factors for success of the business. At the same time, the strategist must be sure that his strategy properly matches the strengths of the corporation with the needs of a clearly defined market. Positive matching of the needs and objectives of the two parties involved is required for a lasting good relationship; without it, the corporation's long-term viability may be at stake.'*

The central thrust of Ohmae's arguments was that strategy as epitomized by the Japanese approach is irrational and non-linear. (Previously, the Japanese had been feted in the West for the brilliance of their rationality and the far-sighted remorselessness of their thinking.) 'Phenomena and events in the real world do not always fit a linear model,' wrote Ohmae.

> *'Hence the most reliable means of dissecting a situation into its constituent parts and reassembling them in the desired pattern is not a step-by-step methodology such as systems analysis. Rather, it is that ultimate non-linear thinking tool, the human brain. True strategic thinking thus contrasts sharply with the conventional mechanical systems approach based on linear thinking. But it also contrasts with the approach that stakes everything on intuition, reaching conclusions without any real breakdown or analysis.'*

Unfortunately, faith in the linear model remained strong. (Managers had been ignoring Henry Mintzberg's similar exhortations to increase the level of creativity in strategy formulation for years.) Western managers weren't ready for the ultimate non-linear thinking tool, they wanted something to measure, something to do, something to get hold of.

The quality gospel

They found it in the notion of 'quality'. Western managers grabbed hold of quality with the enthusiasm of the truly desperate. 'I think people here expect miracles. American management thinks that they can just copy from Japan. But they don't know what to copy,' Deming said on the famous NBC broadcast. He became the great deliverer, the ageing sage from Sioux City, Iowa, the miracle worker.

Deming's impact was huge. Ignored for the previous five decades – though celebrated in Japan – Deming made up for lost time. In 1991, US News & World Report identified nine people or events that had changed the world. The Apostle Paul was the first; W. Edwards Deming was the most recent.

Deming's message remained remarkably similar to that delivered in Japan in 1950. First, management was responsible for the mess. 'Failure of management to plan for the future and to foresee problems have brought about waste of manpower, of materials, and of machine-time, all of which raise the manufacturer's cost and price that the purchaser must pay. The consumer is not always willing to subsidize this waste. The inevitable result is loss of market,' he wrote.[13] Quality must be led from the top. Exhortations to work harder do not lead to quality.

Second, the customer was king, emperor, CEO and dictator. Or, as Deming phrased it, 'the consumer is the most important part of the production line'. Quality is defined by the customer.

Third, the old Shewhart mantra: understand and reduce variation in every process. The process, not the product, is the thing (by the time the inspector has a product in his hands, it is too late).

Fourth, never stop and apply quality to everything. Change and improvement affect and must involve everyone in the organization (as well as suppliers) and must be continuous and all-encompassing.

Fifth, train people. Deming's faith in the willingness of people to do a good job was undimmed by his seven decades on earth.

Deming's call to arms was most powerfully put in his well-known Fourteen Points:

1. Create constancy of purpose for improvement of product and service.
2. Adopt the new philosophy.
3. Cease dependence on inspection to achieve quality.

4. End the practice of awarding business on the basis of price tag alone. Instead, minimize total cost by working with a single supplier.
5. Improve constantly and forever every process for planning, production and service.
6. Institute training on the job.
7. Adopt and institute leadership.
8. Drive out fear.
9. Break down barriers between staff areas.
10. Eliminate slogans, exhortations and targets for the workforce.
11. Eliminate numerical quotas for the workforce and numerical goals for management.
12. Remove barriers that rob people of pride of workmanship. Eliminate the annual rating or merit system.
13. Institute a vigorous programme of education and self-improvement for everyone.
14. Put everybody in the company to work to accomplish the transformation.

For some, Deming's Fourteen Points became the commandments of the quality movement. In his efforts to move quality off the factory floor and on to the desk of every single executive, Deming recreated it as a philosophy of business and, for some, of life. 'Unfortunately, a system of totality insists, by definition, that it will solve everything,' noted one obituary of Deming.[14]

Deming did not have a monopoly on quality. A procession of other quality gurus emerged from the shadows with varying degrees of credibility. The career of the most notable, Joseph Juran (born 1904), bore a resemblance to Deming's. Trained as an electrical engineer, Juran worked for Western Electric in the 1920s and then for AT&T. In 1953, he made his first visit to Japan at the invitation of the Japanese Federation of Economic Associations and the Japanese Union of Scientists and Engineers. For two months,

Juran observed Japanese practices and trained managers and engineers in what he called 'managing for quality'.

Juran's weighty *Quality Control Handbook* was published in 1951. He was later awarded the Second Class Order of the Sacred Treasure by the Emperor of Japan – the highest honour for a non-Japanese citizen – for 'the development of quality control in Japan and the facilitation of US and Japanese friendship'.

Juran argued that there was a blessed quality trinity of planning, control, and improvement. In keeping with the desire for simplification and checklists, he produced his 'Quality Planning Road Map', which advocated nine steps to quality nirvana:

1. Identify who are the customers.
2. Determine the needs of those customers.
3. Translate those needs into our language.
4. Develop a product that can respond to those needs.
5. Optimize the product features so as to meet our needs as well as customer needs.
6. Develop a process which is able to produce the product.
7. Optimize the process.
8. Prove that the process can produce the product under operating conditions.
9. Transfer the process to Operations.

Such neat prescriptions helped the quality gospel spread throughout the world. Deming and Juran criss-crossed time zones with the enthusiasm of rock stars whose breakthrough album has just topped the *Billboard* chart. The quality concept – though not necessarily the practice – carried all before it. Deming Associations appeared in France, the UK and other countries. Total Quality Management Institutes were launched, though without Deming's blessing as he didn't like the phrase.

Deming, Juran, and the other quality gurus went out of their way to stress that miracles simply did not happen. Their audience continued to believe in miracles. 'Solving problems, big problems and little problems, will not halt the decline of American industry, nor will expansion in use of computers, gadgets, and robotic machinery,' wrote Deming. 'Benefits from massive expansion of new machinery also constitute a vain hope. Massive immediate expansion in the teaching of statistical methods to production workers is not the answer either, nor wholesale flashes of quality control circles. All these activities make their contribution, but they only prolong the life of the patient, they can not halt the decline.'[15]

The key to halting the decline lay in changes in management. Deming's audience, however, preferred to introduce quality circles and to publish quality newsletters.

Some companies did embrace the quality gospel with genuine vigour and commitment. The Nashua Corporation was the first US company to adopt Deming's quality management principles. Other well-known converts included the Ford Motor Company and Florida Power & Light (the first US winner of The Deming Prize and advised by Asaka Tetsuichi). Ford initially turned to Japanese quality guru Ishikawa Kaoru for guidance but found his lectures too complex and, anyway, its management was tired of having Japan's virtues thrust down its throat at every opportunity. It then turned to Deming, acknowledging that he was opinionated and abrasive but reassuringly American.

Others embraced the idea and then failed to reap the expected dividends. Typical of this group was Kodak, which introduced a company-wide quality campaign in the early 1980s. Its 'corporate policy quality statement' committed Kodak 'to be world leader in the quality of its products and services. We will judge this quality by how well we anticipate and satisfy customer needs'.[16] Kodak seemed to do everything prescribed: employees were trained in statistical techniques, annual worldwide quality conferences were held, top managers were actively involved, and so on. None of this got the company very far. In 1991, Kodak announced a $1.6 billion restructuring of the company and contemplated whether stronger medicine would do the trick.

Quality opened Western eyes; but it did not necessarily open their minds.

REFERENCES

1. Deming, W. Edwards, Speech, Tokyo, Japan, November 1985.
2. Crawford-Mason, Clare, 'The discovery of the prophet of quality', *SPC INK* (newsletter published by Statistical Process Controls Inc, Knoxville TN), autumn 1992.
3. Ibid.
4. Hayes, Robert and Abernathy, William, 'Managing our way to economic decline', *Harvard Business Review*, July/August 1980.
5. 'Around the globe', *Fortune*, July 1964.
6. Ibid.
7. Ibid.
8. Ibid.
9. American companies had, to be fair, taken an interest in how the Japanese had managed to rebuild their economy. Shortly before Deming's TV appearance, teams from Ford and Pontiac visited Japan to see how Japanese car makers organized themselves. They found nothing different.
10. Pascale, Richard and Athos, Anthony, *The Art of Japanese Management*, Simon & Schuster, New York, 1981.
11. Ibid.
12. Peters, Tom and Waterman, Robert, *In Search of Excellence*, Harper & Row, New York, 1982.
13. Deming, W. Edwards, *Out of the Crisis*, Mercury, London, 1986.
14. Reed, Christopher, 'A profit in his own country', *The Observer*, 9 January 1994.
15. Deming, W. Edwards, *Out of the Crisis*, Mercury, London, 1986.
16. Kodak Annual Report 1984.

RESOURCES

BOOKS

Deming, W Edwards, *Out of the Crisis*, Mercury, London, 1986.

Pascale, Richard and Athos, Anthony, *The Art of Japanese Management*, Simon & Schuster, New York, 1981.

Peters, Tom and Waterman, Robert, *In Search of Excellence*, Harper & Row, New York, 1982.

Supply chain management

RICHARD LAMMING

Richard Lamming argues that a strategic approach needs to be taken that links supply activities and related management issues with corporate strategy. Firms require not supply chains but networks.

THE perception of what takes place in the transactions between organizations and their suppliers – of materials, component parts, services, information, and utilities – has changed profoundly over the past 25 years. When, in 1997, *Harvard Business Review* published its 75-year review of management thinking, the central theme of 'production' (as it was called in 1922) had become 'adding value', and featured prominently in the mid-1990s was 'supply chain management'. But what is supply chain management, and what does it entail? Is it different from supply management and what are its implications for strategic management?

The nature of supply

The practice of buying and selling is one of the oldest 'professions' in the world. In the remains of cities within Mesopotamia – modern-day Iraq – there are records of transactions that took place 6,000 years ago, bearing a startling resemblance to today's purchase orders and materials schedules. What *has* changed recently is the scope of concern that the purchaser and seller must have in order to ensure that their organization survives. The copper traders in Ur may have paid the merchants from Dilmun (Bahrain) for minerals from Makan (Oman), and considered they were doing business over great distances. Today, the same distance takes a couple of hours by air and traders in the modern equivalent of each of these countries are dealing with collaborators, customers, and competitors in every part of the globe by internet and mobile, wireless telephony.

Thus, managing the provision of the resources necessary to conduct the operations of the organization – latterly called purchasing, procurement, buying and materials management – is now a matter of competing for scarce commodities to differentiate the product or service in the eyes of the consumer. It is a short, simple step to connect such activity with the operations strategy for an organization.

The supply chain: an imperfect metaphor

The term *supply chain management* is a relatively new addition to the management lexicon. While its origins may be traced to the work of Jay Forrester[1] in the 1950s, the term itself appears to have been coined by Western consultants less than 20 years ago to crystallize the concept of managing an organization with regard to the activities, resources, and strategies of other organizations on which it relies. A contemporary of the supply chain was Michael Porter's concept of the value chain.

Supply chain management is perceived mainly as a manufacturing term, although it is also applied to service sector organizations that use materials, such as telecommunications, retail, hotels and healthcare. Providers of intangible services (e.g. financial services, consultancy, utilities), meanwhile, are at the end of a supply chain for products and services procured for their own use, while some, such as water companies, also have a primary supply chain (e.g. water from the sky to the sewer).

The term 'chain' is used variously to refer to the sequence of activities conducted within the organization itself, to the group of suppliers delivering goods and services to the organization, and to both of these, coupled with the organization's customers. The end of the chain is generally agreed to be the consumer. Still, there is often confusion in use of the term. If the channel to the sales market is 'downstream', then materials and component suppliers are logically 'upstream' (the chain becomes a river!) and thus 'above' their customers: yet there is often talk of going 'back *down* the supply chain'.

The chain is clearly an imperfect metaphor: even a cursory attempt at mapping the process of supply, for anything other than the simplest logistical transportation activities, reveals that there is little about it that is linear – it is more of a 'network', or even a 'mess'.

One example of this 'mess' involves Octel Network Services, Electronic Data Systems (EDS), Xerox, and Motorola. One major client of Octel Network Services, a firm in Dallas that operates more than one million electronic voice mailboxes, is EDS. EDS, in turn, has a $3.2 billion contract to run Xerox's computer and telecoms networks, a deal that involves some 1,700 of Xerox's employees transferring to EDS. Xerox itself provides invoicing and billing services for Motorola, which in turn designs and makes parts of Octel's voice messaging systems, and thus the circle is completed. Such supply configurations do not fit into neat, linear models of the supply chain.

This complexity is reflected in research developments in supply chain management, with a shift away from normative concepts of a linear supply chain to more sophisticated, interactive models of networks and partnerships. The seminal work of Forrester led to a field of study now recognized as *industrial dynamics*, in which analysts present supply chains as physical systems that may be modelled, simulated and thus predicted. This work inspired marketing and logistics researchers to propose further normative frameworks and concepts suggesting that the focal firm could look up and downstream in the chain, influencing other organizations by implementing strategies for improving efficiency in supply and for related activities such as technology transfer.

Towards a strategic approach

Subsequent research has focused on two key areas: a strategic approach to supply chain management, and the concept of supply networks and partnerships. Examples of the strategic view are approaches such as postponement strategies, lean supply, agility and value stream mapping. Marketing researchers have also highlighted this strategic approach, especially in discussing the downstream supply chain – from manufacturer to consumer. There is a general tendency in each of these areas to suggest that there is more to supply chain management than simple logistics, coupled with the observation that purchasing has changed from a clerical function to a strategic process. The concepts of supply strategy and focused operations emerge from this strategic approach, which links supply activities and related management issues with corporate strategy.

Strategic supply and focused operations[2]

All firms have to focus their business to some degree, since they have constrained resources and cannot provide a limitless range or volume of products or services to a global market. The concept of focus is much more specific than this and can have a profound importance for the firm. A firm can focus in a number of ways:

- By choosing to serve particular market segments.
- By adopting a particular type of manufacturing process.
- By focusing different production or service units on particular customers, processes, products, or services.
- By divesting non-core areas of the business.
- By concentrating on a specific activity within the supply chain and forming strategic buyer–supplier relationships with other players in the supply chain.

The last two types of focus relate directly to the management of supply. In these cases, focus appears to be a matter of what the firm *will not do* within the supply network and this becomes part of its strategic intent. For example, focus within the supply network played a key part when, in 1991, Hewlett-Packard entered the PC market with great intensity and was one of the top four PC producers by 1997. H-P decided to move away from being a manufacturer to being an *assembler* of products. This shift in focus placed even greater emphasis on the need for excellent supplier relations, particularly with those suppliers on whom it was most dependent. It also freed H-P from unnecessary investment in manufacturing plant to concentrate on investment in assembly technology.

Very often, as in the case of H-P, focus means understanding specific aspects of the supply chain to determine where the firm can really add value and to subcontract – or 'outsource' – whole areas in the supply process. Focus can also mean divesting areas within the supply chain to concentrate on the core business. In the 1980s, GM acquired computer services company EDS and defence group Hughes Electronics. The aim was to reduce the group's dependence on the highly cyclical US car market and exploit potential synergies with other industries. However, not only did these anticipated synergies prove elusive; the acquisitions also diverted GM away from its core business. GM divested both in the 1990s. It subsequently spun off the components divisions that it had owned for almost a century, under the name of Delphi (Ford followed a similar route in 2000, spinning off its divisions as Visteon).

Focus can also mean that the firm becomes a *virtual* organization, employing far fewer people than before but achieving similar business goals. TopsyTail, a small Texan company, sold $100 million worth of its hairstyling equipment between 1991 and 1997, although it had virtually no permanent employees of its own. Subcontractors handled almost all of the organization's activities, from design and manufacturing to marketing. Similar arrangements exist at Italian motorcycle manufacturer Aprilia and Japanese computer games producer Nintendo.

Strategic supply and outsourcing

Whereas focus can include divesting business assets that were once part of the firm's attempts to diversify, outsourcing is more often associated with the configuration in which the firm finds itself within the supply chain. Mass production strategies assumed that a firm should own as many activities as possible within the supply process. For example, at one time Ford made almost everything that went into its cars, including the steel and glass. In 1980, it made about 87 percent of a car itself. Now it only makes between 30 and 40 percent.

Similarly, in the past IBM produced the silicon as well as the software and hard drives for its computers. This approach – the result of a significant degree of vertical integration – has been replaced by outsourcing strategies. As a result, a new group of 'contract manufacturers' has emerged in the PC industry – companies such as SCI Systems, Solectron, Merix, Flextronics, Smartflex and Sanmina – that manufacture products for major PC players, including IBM and Hewlett-Packard.

In the US such outsourcing has led to a remarkable growth in the number of small manufacturing enterprises: companies with fewer than 100 employees comprised some 85 percent of the US's 370,000 manufacturing firms.[3] However, outsourcing strategies can cause major reactions among those who were once seen as core employees, leading to the type of industrial unrest seen in the GM strike of 1996.

Simply divesting part of what was previously an owned asset is only half the story. For such outsourcing to be successful, strategic buyer–supplier relationships need to be in place, within a more appropriate model for managing: not supply *chains* but *networks*.

From chains to networks and partnerships

The limitations of the linear chain metaphor have also been recognized by researchers focusing on industrial networks and, more recently, supply networks. Researchers have also examined the concept of so-called collaborative partnership strategies in relationships. Use of the term 'partnership' in this context presents a problem, since it departs from the traditional legal connotations of joint liability. The management-oriented derivative term *partnership sourcing* has been defined as 'a commitment by customers/ suppliers, regardless of size, to a long-term relationship based on trust and on clear, mutually agreed objectives to strive for world-class capability and competitiveness', which means 'rejecting the "master–servant syndrome" where the supplier is merely told what to supply'.[4] In this context, then, partnership means a collaboration in which neither the customer nor the supplier holds the dominant commercial interest.

Research over 15 years by a group of academics from around the world, known as the Industrial Marketing and Purchasing group, has concluded that it is not possible to manage in supply networks. Instead, it is suggested, organizations may only seek to manage *within* the network. Forming supply strategy, as an accompaniment to operations strategy, begins with managing the relationships between the organization and other organizations with which it deals directly. As a result, influence may be exerted on the activities of organizations elsewhere in network that are involved in delivering the goods and services that form the focus of the supply strategy. This makes sense for the strategist: form a plan for one's own activities and then try to influence others (either directly or indirectly) so that it may be complemented and therefore successful.

The problems experienced by researchers in conceptualizing and defining the supply chain (or network) are reflected in Western managers' attempts to adapt the logistics literature to develop simple models for managing supply chains, based on the premise that the customer may intervene directly in the supplier's business management. The process of forming a strategy for the operational concerns of the organization outside its boundaries of ownership and physical presence cannot rely on a concept of remote control, however: some better theory is required for managers to employ.

Logically, such intervention must be limited by the need for each firm to manage itself, in order to satisfy its shareholders. The supplier must thus *collaborate* with the customer, to contribute to the overall competitiveness of the chain or supply system in which both operate, and *compete* with it within the system to win the right to conduct the work which either firm might carry out, in order to maintain its own prosperity. It follows that the customers and suppliers at each stage in the chain are actually competitors as well as collaborators.

The task of supply management is thus to bring the marketplace into the relationship, as the arbiter in the competition within the shared interests (i.e. the valuable work that either party might conduct). This paradox leads to a set of dynamic partnering arrangements in the chain which, if they work efficiently in market terms, should lead to individual and mutual prosperity for its members.

These observed collaborative–competitive tensions and paradoxes in supply relationships have prompted some studies to conclude that customers cannot seek to manage suppliers in a traditional sense. They suggest instead that such relationships should employ a complex mix of collaboration and competition. The use (and potential abuse) of power in supplier–buyer relationships is therefore proving another fruitful line of enquiry for current researchers.

The exception to this logic appears to be vertical integration, in which customers may indeed seek to manage their suppliers (subsidiary divisions) in pursuit of a higher corporate goal. Practical flaws have appeared in this established strategy, however, manifested in the observed behaviour and commercial performance of supplier divisions in some vertically integrated groups. As noted above, this factor has, in recent years, led to several instances of large-scale divestment of such holdings.

Japanese firms appear to have built an alternative to traditional vertical integration. Within it, the supply chain relationships appear to have been very efficient. The logistical approaches collectively known as *just-in-time* have been complemented in practice by customer-dominated inter-firm relationships that rarely exhibit the collaborative–competitive balance discussed above. Once again, however, it appears that significant change is under way in these relationships: research in Japan in 1999 revealed that the powerful *keiretsu* groupings are changing in structure and strategy (see

Lamming, R.C., 'Japanese supply chain relationships in recession', *Long Range Planning*, December 2000).

The future of supply chain management

So, it isn't a chain, and you can't manage it – but 'supply chain management' is the term that has, nonetheless, become common parlance around the world, for managers, academics and politicians.

The concept of collaborative partnerships has recently been refined by the identification of different types of supply relationship, selected by customers and suppliers for specific purposes. At the conceptual level, these developments will mean that supply strategists must understand principles that are now only at the exploration stage in research, including such theories as chaos, fuzzy logic and double helix structures.

At the practical level – and in the immediate future – methods for managing supply relationships are being refined from traditional customer-driven approaches to more complex challenges. Two such developments are *transparency*, as a replacement for the traditional, one-way open-book negotiation (in which the customer makes unreasonably general demands of the supplier, whose only possible response is to cheat by massaging data); and *relationship assessment* instead of supplier assessment.

Such challenges may be unwelcome for supply managers who prefer the concept of a chain, but it remains to be seen how long this simplistic metaphor will continue to hold sway.

2

REFERENCES

1. Forrester, J.W., *Industrial Dynamics*, MIT Press, 1961.
2. The discussion and examples on focus and outsourcing are derived from Brown, S.E., *Manufacturing the Future – Strategic Resonance and Enlightened Manufacturing*, Financial Times, London, 2000, and Brown, S.E., Lamming, R.C., Bessant, J.R. and Jones, P., *Strategic Operations Management*, Butterworth Heinemann, Oxford, 2000, Chapter 5.
3. *The Economist*, 27 January 1996.
4. Both quotes are from Sir Derek Hornby, then Chairman of the Board of Overseas Trade, in *Partnership Sourcing*, Partnership Sourcing Ltd, London (1991).

RESOURCES

BOOKS

Brown, S.E., *Manufacturing the Future – Strategic Resonance and Enlightened Manufacturing*, Financial Times Prentice Hall, London, 2000.

Brown, S.E., Lamming, R.C., Bessant, J.R. and Jones, P., *Strategic Operations Management*, Butterworth Heinemann, Oxford, 2000.

Christopher, Martin (ed.), *Logistics: the strategic issues*, Chapman and Hall, London, 1992.

Contractor, F.J. and Lorange, P. (eds), *Cooperative Strategies in International Business*, Lexington Books, Lexington, 1988.

Dimancescu, D., Hines, P.A. and Rich, N., *The Lean Enterprise: Designing and Managing Strategic Processes for Customer-Winning Performance*, AMACOM, New York, 1997.

Forrester, Jay, *Industrial Dynamics*, MIT Press, 1961.

Hines, P.A., *Creating World Class Suppliers*, FT/Pitman, London, 1994.

Hines, P.A., Lamming, R.C., Jones, D.T., Cousins, P.D. and Rich, N., *Value Stream Management*, FT/Prentice-Hall, London, 2000.

Jarillo, J.C., *Strategic Networks: Creating the Borderless Organization*, Butterworth Heinemann, Oxford, 1993.

Lamming, Richard, *Beyond Partnership: Strategies for Innovation and Lean Supply*, Prentice Hall, Hemel Hempstead, 1993.

Macbeth, D.K. and Ferguson, Neil, *Partnership Sourcing: an Integrated Supply Chain Approach*, FT/Pitman, London, 1994.

Womack, J.P., Jones, D.T. and Roos, D., *The Machine that Changed the World*, Maxwell Macmillan, London, 1990.

PROCESS MANAGEMENT

BENCHMARKING

BENCHMARKING became a buzzword of the 1980s and 1990s (although it actually relies on techniques developed by the quality movement). It involves the detailed study of productivity, quality and value in different departments and activities in relation to performance elsewhere.

The principle behind benchmarking is very simple. If you want to improve a particular aspect of your organization or the service it provides, find someone else who is good at the activity and use them as a benchmark to raise your own standards. In effect, it's a way of pulling performance up by the bootstraps.

There are three different techniques that can be used in benchmarking:

1. **Best Demonstrated Practice (BDP):** a technique used successfully for the last 15 years, is the comparison of performance by units within one firm. For example, the sales per square foot of a retail outlet in one location can be compared with the same statistic for a store in another, within the same chain. BDP usually throws up large variances, some of which can be explained by lack of comparability, but much of which is due to superior techniques or simply greater efficiency at one site. That site can then be used as a challenge to lever up all other sites' performance.
2. **Relative Cost Position (RCP):** analysis looks at each element of the cost structure (e.g., manufacturing labour) per dollar of sales in firm X compared to the same thing in competitor Y. Good RCP analysis is very hard to do but very valuable, as much for its insight into competitors' strategies as for cost reduction.
3. **Best Related Practice** is like BDP, but takes the comparisons into related (usually not competing) firms, where direct comparisons can often be made by co-operation between firms to collect and compare data.

Companies that take benchmarking seriously, like the Xerox Corporation, have a web of benchmarking partners both within the organization and outside across a wide spectrum of activities. So, for example, a manufacturing company might benchmark its transport and delivery performance against other business units it owns and against a transportation specialist such as one of the courier companies. The same company might also benchmark its accounting systems against a financial services company, and so on.

CHANNEL MANAGEMENT

CHANNEL management recognizes that companies no longer compete just on the quality of their products and services. The channels they create to reach customers differentiate their offerings and play an increasingly important role in their competitive positioning. In recent years, a number of companies have utilized effective channel management to secure competitive advantage and add value to their business performance. The most obvious example is the use of the internet to create a new channel serving a growing segment of customers who prefer to shop online.

Steven Wheeler and Evan Hirsh, two consultants at Booz-Allen and Hamilton and the authors of *Channel Champions*, define the term as follows: 'Channels are how and where you purchase a product (or service) and how and where you use the product.' A channel, then, they note 'is the essence of how customers and the product interact. It is a business' route to its customer and a business' on-going relationship with its customer.'

Channel management, Hirsh and Wheeler argue, is a systematic means of reaching and taking care of your customers wherever they are and however they like to be reached. It is about identifying the most important customers to the business. It is how you consummate the relationship with customers. It is how you communicate with customers. It is how you create and capture value from the product after the initial sale.

They use the simple example of grocery shopping. Some customers will always prefer the traditional channel, visiting their local grocery store or, more likely, supermarket. But others will welcome the introduction of a home shopping service, via telephone, cable service, or the internet. For both groups of customers, the product – i.e., the groceries – is the same; only the channels change. But it is the channel that imbues the relationship with additional value.

Channel management, then, is not a narrow discipline. It is not merely distribution or logistics; although these are obviously important. Instead, it is a way of thinking. Channel management is a way of making new connections with customers to exploit new commercial opportunities. Think channels, say its supporters, and you should be thinking strategy. Effective channel management offers the chance to re-invent not just your business but also the industry you are in. In a nutshell, Amazon.com became the biggest book retailer in the world simply by offering book buyers a new channel – via the internet.

CRISIS MANAGEMENT

CRISES are a fact of corporate life. In recent years, this realization has fuelled the creation of a whole field of specialized advisers and crisis management specialists.

In corporate terms, a crisis is a major, unpredictable event with a potentially negative impact on the company's employees, products, services, financial situation, or reputation. It is a decisive moment. The American Institute for Crisis Management (ICM) defines a crisis as 'a significant business disruption which stimulates extensive news media coverage. The resulting public scrutiny will affect the organization's normal operations and also could have a political, legal, financial and governmental impact on its business.'

Crises are caused by a multitude of events and factors. Some are pure acts of nature – storms destroying a factory – or the result of mechanical malfunctions, such as when metal fatigue causes an aeroplane to crash. More avoidable are crises precipitated by human error or management. Indeed, the ICM calculates that 62 percent of business crises can be traced back to management and 23 percent to employees.

Companies increasingly accept that crises, in whatever form, are inevitable. While there are a variety of theories and opinions on how best to manage a crisis, some fundamentals are common.

First, accurate information is essential. Any attempt to conceal relevant facts and to manipulate the situation ultimately backfires and increases the damage to the company. Perrier's management maintained that its mineral water did not contain any toxic element in spite of persuasive evidence to the contrary. When it finally admitted the failure, the damage to Perrier's public image was already done. Honesty is the best policy – even if there is nothing to report.

Second, the company must react as quickly as possible. In 1989, Exxon CEO Lawrence Rawl waited two weeks before paying a visit to the scene of the *Exxon Valdez* oil spill. This sent a clear message about where mass pollution figured on his priorities. For all the media clamour, actions speak louder than words.

Third, the response must come from the top. Texaco CEO Peter Bijur took control of the company's reaction to a potentially damaging lawsuit. British Midland's Sir Michael Bishop was the company's spokesman after the M1 air crash. The level of response is an indication of the importance that management places on the problem.

The fourth fundamental is a long-term perspective. The long-term goodwill the company enjoys from its customers should be kept in mind when considering the short-term costs of corrective measures. Immediately withdrawing all your products from supermarket shelves if there is a suggestion of contamination sends a clear signal that you are taking the problem seriously and are intent on sorting it out.

Fourth, predicting problems requires a coherent strategy. Companies need to be prepared for a crisis. Bombs do explode; planes do crash; products do go wrong; boats do sink; and people sometimes make disastrous mistakes. Companies need to review and rehearse options in advance. Systems need to be in place. Most large organizations now have crisis management plans covering a variety of eventualities.

DEMING, W. EDWARDS

W. EDWARDS DEMING (1900–1993) has a unique place among management theorists. He had an impact on industrial history in a way of which others only dream.

Deming was born in Iowa and spent his childhood in Wyoming. He trained as an electrical engineer at the University of Wyoming and then received a PhD in mathematical physics from Yale in 1928. He worked as a civil servant in Washington at the Department of Agriculture. While working at the Department he invited the statistician Walter Shewhart to give a lecture. This proved an inspiration. In 1939, Deming became head statistician and mathematician for the US census. During the Second World War he championed the use of statistics to improve the quality of US production and, in 1945, joined the faculty of New York University as a Professor of Statistics.

Deming visited Japan for the first time in 1947 at the invitation of General MacArthur. He was to play a key role in the rebuilding of Japanese industry. In 1950, he gave a series of lectures to Japanese industrialists on 'quality control'. 'I told them that Japanese industry could develop in a short time. I told them they could invade the markets of the world – and have manufacturers screaming for protection in five years. I was, in 1950, the only man in Japan who believed that,' Deming later recalled.

In fact, Deming was probably the *only* man in the world to believe that Japanese industry could be revived so rapidly. But, helped by him, revive it did in a quite miraculous way. During the 1950s, Deming and the other American standard bearer of quality, Joseph Juran, conducted seminars and courses throughout Japan. The message – and the practice – spread.

The Japanese were highly receptive to Deming's message. The country was desperate and willing to try anything. But, much more importantly, Deming's message of teamwork and shared responsibility struck a chord with Japanese culture.

Deming's message was that organizations needed to 'manage for quality'. To do so required a focus on the customer: 'Don't just make it and try to sell it. But redesign it and then again bring the process under control...with ever-increasing quality...The consumer is the most important part of the production line.' At the time such pronouncements would have been greeted with disdain in the West, where production lines ran at full speed with little thought of who would buy the products.

Instead of the quick fix, Deming called for dedication and hard work. His message was never tainted by hype or frivolity. 'Quality is not something you install like a new carpet or a set of bookshelves. You implant it. Quality is something you work at. It is a learning process,' he said. Also difficult for the West to swallow was Deming's argument that responsibility for quality must be taken by senior managers as well as those on the factory floor. Only with senior management commitment could belief in and implementation of quality cascade down through the organization. Quality, in Deming's eyes, was not the preserve of the few but the responsibility of all.

These exhortations were backed by the use of statistical methods of quality control. These enabled business plans to be expanded to include clear quality goals.

While the Japanese transformed their economy and world perceptions of the quality of their products, Western managers flitted from one fad to the next. Deming was completely ignored. Discovery came in 1980 when NBC featured a TV programme on the emergence of Japan as an industrial power. Suddenly, Western managers were seeking out every morsel of information they could find. By 1984, there were over 3,000 quality circles in American companies and many thousands of others appearing throughout the Western world.

Although Deming was in his eighties by the time he was feted in the West, he dedicated the rest of his life to preaching his quality gospel. His message was distilled down to his famed Fourteen Points.

Toyota is the living exemplar of Deming's theories. As working examples go, it remains impressive. Gary Hamel has pointed out that its Western competitors have simply followed what Toyota has done for the last 40 years. If Western car manufacturers had listened to W. Edwards Deming, the roles might have been reversed. If Western industry as a whole had listened, who knows what might have happened.

FORD, HENRY

THE standard view of Henry Ford (1863–1947) is that he was the first exponent of mass production. While this is true, there was a great deal more to the career, personality, and achievements of the car maker.

Ford built his first car in 1896. He quickly became convinced of the

2

commercial potential and started his own company in 1903. In 1908, Ford's Model T was born. Through innovative use of new mass production techniques, between 1908 and 1927 Ford produced 15 million Model Ts.

Henry Ford did not develop mass production because he blindly believed in the most advanced production methods. Ford believed in mass production because it meant he could make cars that people could afford. And this, with staggering success, is what he achieved.

Ford's commitment to lowering prices cannot be doubted. Between 1908 and 1916 he reduced prices by 58 percent, at a time when demand was such that he could easily have raised prices.

Ford's was a triumph of marketing as much as of production methods. He realized that the mass car market existed – it just remained for him to provide the products the market wanted. Model Ts were black, straightforward and affordable. The corollary of this was to prove Ford's nemesis. Having given the market what it wanted, he presumed that more of the same was also what it required. When other manufacturers added extras, Ford kept it simple and dramatically lost ground. The company's reliance on the Model T nearly drove it to self-destruction.

In the same way that Ford didn't believe in Models Ts in different colours with fins and extras, he didn't believe in management. Production, in the Ford Company's huge plant, was based around strict functional divides – demarcations. Ford believed in people getting on with their jobs and not raising their heads above functional parapets. He didn't want engineers talking to salespeople, or people making decisions without his say-so.

The methods used by Ford were grim and unforgiving. 'How come when I want a pair of hands I get a human being as well?' he complained. Ford will never be celebrated for his humanity or people management skills. Among his many innovations was a single human one: Ford introduced the $5 wage for his workers, which, at the time, was around twice the average for the industry. Sceptics suggest that the only reason he did this was so his workers could buy Model Ts of their own.

JURAN, JOSEPH

TRAINED as an electrical engineer, Joseph M. Juran (born 1904) worked for Western Electric in the 1920s and then AT&T. His weighty *Quality Control Handbook* was published in 1951. In 1953, he made his first visit to Japan. For two months Juran observed Japanese practices and trained managers and engineers in what he called 'managing for quality'.

For the next quarter of a century, the Romanian-born Juran continued to give seminars on the subject of quality throughout the world. Western companies continued to assume that the Japanese were low quality imitators. Then, at the beginning of the 1980s, the world woke up to quality. From being peripheral, Juran and his Juran Institute found themselves near the epicentre of an explosion of interest.

Juran's quality philosophy is built around a quality trilogy: quality planning, quality management and quality implementation. 'In broad terms, quality planning consists of developing the products and processes required to meet the customers' needs.' While Juran is critical of W. Edwards Deming as being overly reliant on statistics, his own approach is based on the forbiddingly entitled Company-Wide Quality Management (CWQM) which aims to create a means of disseminating quality to all.

Where Juran is innovative is in his belief that there is more to quality than specification and rigorous testing for defects. The human side of quality is regarded as critical. He was an early exponent of what has come to be known as empowerment; for him, quality has to be the goal of each employee, individually and in teams, through self-supervision.

Juran's message – most accessibly encapsulated in his book *Planning for Quality* – is that quality is nothing new. If quality is so elemental and elementary, why had it become ignored in the West? Juran's unwillingness to gild his straightforward message is attractive to some, but has made the communication of his ideas less successful than he would have liked.

JUST-IN-TIME (JIT) (KANBAN)

JUST-IN-TIME or kanban is an approach to inventory management based on the efficient delivery of components to the production line at the time they are required. A management technique associated with the Japanese economic miracle after the Second World War, it is one of a range of quality approaches introduced by, among others, the Toyota Motor Corporation and the Kawasaki Heavy Industries Group, and is an essential part of the lean production process.

The goal of kanban was zero inventory. It aimed at a system whereby components for final assembly should arrive just when they were needed, reducing inventory carrying costs. Early production management emphasized ordering materials in economic lot sizes, but the JIT model utilized computer technology to emphasize timing rather than the amount of inventory.

Since the 1980s, international competition and lessons from Japanese practice have encouraged the adoption of just-in-time methods and quality management methods throughout the Western world. Technological advances

2

have also had a significant impact on inventory management.

New mechanical and automated equipment has made stock movement more efficient, with better use of warehousing and major improvements in distribution and logistics management. In particular, IT-based stock control systems with bar coding are integrated with other systems to give better control over order assembly, stock availability and monitoring.

By creating a system that pulls in parts as and when they are needed, JIT dramatically reduces the amount of capital tied up in inventory laying idle, thereby increasing efficiency and reducing costs. Under JIT, the company must manage the overall supply chain efficiently and effectively. Reducing levels of stock in manufacturing is seen as both an internal and external matter, involving relationships between workers at different stages in the production process and relationships with external suppliers.

JIT, however, is not an easy concept to apply. In the past, a number of Western companies attempted to introduce it in isolation from other total quality techniques, without understanding the wider implications, and without instigating the necessary changes in production management.

The human aspects of quality management are sometimes overlooked. Quality management systems that emphasize a 'right first time' philosophy also promote the 'empowerment' of employees via team development, quality circles, and training. In particular, plant maintenance improvements to reduce downtime and secure better reliability of machinery are integral to the successful application of JIT. This is coupled with improved 'housekeeping', to maintain clean, tidy, orderly facilities. Typically, this is part of a 'team or cells' discipline with staff making a vital contribution to the overall efficiency of the approach.

In recent years, many firms have implemented ISO 9000 systems to define quality standards, processes, and control systems with documentation of action taken to ensure quality. Introduction of such systems involves close examination of existing production, operational, and support processes (including inventory standards and flows). Standards and systems are improved as a consequence.

If change is piecemeal and management attention wanes, then JIT is unlikely to produce the desired improvements. An integrated perspective is needed, with coherent strategic direction to secure improvements in productivity/ effectiveness at each operational level, so that the whole supply chain has a competitive edge. JiT is only as good as the weakest link in the production chain.

KAIZEN (QUALITY CIRCLES)

AS much a social system as an industrial process, kaizen is at the heart of the quality philosophy, and involves the use of quality circles – small teams of workers who analyze and make suggestions for improving their own work tasks. In his book *Kaizen*, translated into English in the early 1980s, Masaaki Imai describes the continuous improvement concepts that underpin the quality approach.

The American quality pioneer W. Edwards Deming is credited with introducing the continuous improvement philosophy into Japan. Deming's work inspired small, problem-solving teams of workers, supervisors, and experts (later called quality circles), with the aim of improving the efficiency and quality of work. The idea was developed by Japanese companies, notably Toyota, and quality circles were instrumental in the Japanese economic miracle.

While many Western concepts are based on the notion of a step-change improvement, kaizen is precisely the opposite. The word literally means 'gradual progress' or 'incremental change'. Through continuous gradual improvements, kaizen aims to achieve continual evolutionary rather than revolutionary change – hence the term continuous improvement.

Kaizen consciousness is based on a group of shared values rooted in the Japanese culture. These include self-realization, recognition of diverse abilities and mutual trust. These values lead to a strong belief that individual workers are the experts at their jobs and therefore know better than anyone else how to analyze and improve their work. Integral to the system is an understanding that managers will consider and where possible support workers' efforts to improve work processes.

Interestingly, the pendulum may now be swinging back toward the Western style of thinking and the notion of a 'leap forward'. The pace of change means that many of the high-tech companies that have emerged in recent years take a much more revolutionary approach to innovation, favouring 'discontinuous change' over 'incremental improvement'.

Quality circles are not a panacea for quality improvement but, given the right top management commitment, employee motivation, and resourcing, they can support continuous quality improvement at shopfloor level.

LEAN PRODUCTION

LEAN production is a catch-all term to describe a combination of techniques used to help companies attain low cost status (e.g. just-in-time and total quality management).

Although it is a relatively new term, the genesis of lean production goes back much further. Its origins lie in Japan in the years after the Second World War, specifically with the development of the Toyota Motor Company. In the beginning – in 1918 – the company was called the Toyoda Spinning & Weaving Co. In the 1930s, the development of automatic looms persuaded the company that its future lay elsewhere. Kiichiro Toyoda, the founder's son, had studied engineering and visited the US and Europe. He decided that the future lay in car making and changed the company's name to Toyota in 1936. In the aftermath of the Second World War, Toyoda announced his company's intention to 'catch up with America in three years. Otherwise, the automobile industry of Japan will not survive'. Within 12 years, the company began its assault on the American automobile industry.

Toyota's initial foray into the US proved unsuccessful. Its Crown model was designed for the Japanese market and was ill suited to American freeways. A willingness to adapt and sheer tenacity meant that despite its initial disappointment, in the 1960s the company managed to establish itself in the US. By 1975, it had replaced Volkswagen as the US's number one auto importer. Along the way, the company acquired an unrivalled reputation for build quality and reliability. Toyota is now the third biggest car maker in the world (behind GM and Ford). It sells five million vehicles a year (1.3 million in North America, 2 million in Japan and 0.5 million in Europe).

How the company achieved its remarkable aim is the story of lean production. Visitors to the Toyota headquarters building in Japan can still find three portraits. One is of the company's founder; the next is of the company's current president; and the final one is a portrait of the American quality guru, W. Edwards Deming. Deming was the inspiration and the original source of the techniques that gave rise to the lean production concept.

Toyota has become synonymous with lean production. Through the diligent application of Total Quality Management techniques, it progressed to what became labelled lean production, or the Toyota Production System.

Lean production was based on three simple principles. The first was just-in-time production. There is no point in producing cars, or anything else, in blind anticipation of someone buying them. Production has to be closely tied to the market's requirements. Second, responsibility for quality rests with everyone, and any quality defects need to be rectified as soon as they are identified. The third, more elusive, concept was the 'value stream'. Instead of the company being viewed as a series of unrelated products and processes, it should be seen as a continuous and uniform whole, a stream including suppliers as well as customers.

OUTSOURCING

OUTSOURCING involves an organization passing the provision of a service or execution of a task, previously undertaken in-house, to a third party to perform on its behalf.[1]

It arises from the recognition that no company can excel at everything. Activities involving competencies that are not central to what the business does may be best left to those who specialize in them.

What has made outsourcing a hot topic is its application to information technology. Mary Lacity and Leslie Willcocks, two academics at Oxford University, link this to a decision taken by Eastman Kodak in 1989 to turn over the bulk of its IT operations to three outsourcing partners.[2] In so doing, it ignited the fashion for outsourcing and other *Fortune* 500 companies followed suit. In the UK, similar outsourcing deals followed, involving companies such as British Petroleum, British Aerospace and British Home Stores, and central government departments including the Inland Revenue and the Department of Social Security.

Outsourcing, however, is another simple concept that is hard to apply in practice. Striking the right balance between who gets the projected benefits – in particular, how cost savings are divided between the company and the vendor of the outsourced IT services – requires careful consideration (all too often the bulk of the savings go in profits to the vendor or supplier of the outsourced services, as, for example, do the intellectual property rights from developing new technology).

Outsourcing is no longer being applied just to IT. In the past, for instance, many administrative activities were seen as part and parcel of running the business. It simply didn't occur to companies to outsource areas such as payroll, delivery of finished goods, and secretarial services. That has now changed as it has become fashionable for companies to focus on their core activities – those providing competitive advantage.

In recent years, however, companies and commentators have begun to question the benefits of outsourcing. In a 1998 article, David Bryce and Michael Useem, two academics from the University of Pennsylvania's Wharton School, one of America's most influential business schools, examined the outsourcing experience and evaluated its consequences.[3] They concluded that while outsourcing is not the cure to all known corporate ills, it is an extremely useful and value-creating business tool. 'Outsourcing will never be a silver bullet nor a turnaround engine, but the evidence to date indicates that it is one of contemporary management's more promising new tools.'

REFERENCES

1. Reilly, P., and Tamkin, P., 'Outsoucing: A Flexible Option for the Future?', Institute for Employment Studies, 1996.
2. Lacity, Mary and Willcocks, Leslie, 'Best Practice in Information Technology Sourcing', *Oxford Executive Research Briefings*, Templeton College, Oxford University.
3. Bryce, David and Useem, Michael, 'The impact of corporate outsourcing on company value', *European Management Journal*, Vol 16, No 6, December 1998.

RE-ENGINEERING

RE-ENGINEERING (or Business Process Re-engineering, as it is often called) was brought to the fore by James Champy, co-founder of the consultancy company CSC Index, and Michael Hammer, an electrical engineer and former computer science professor at MIT. The roots of the idea lay in the research carried out by MIT from 1984 to 1989 on 'Management in the 1990s'.

Champy and Hammer's book, *Re-engineering the Corporation*, was a bestseller that produced a plethora of re-engineering programmes, the creation of many consulting companies, and a deluge of books promoting alternative approaches to re-engineering. (Thanks to the popularity of re-engineering, CSC also became one of the largest consulting firms in the world.)

The fundamental idea behind re-engineering is that organizations need to identify their key processes and make them as lean and efficient as possible. Peripheral processes (and, therefore, peripheral people) need to be discarded. 'Don't automate; obliterate,' Hammer proclaimed.

In their book, Hammer and Champy set out what they described as a 'manifesto for business revolution'. Far from revolutionary, however, some commentators have observed that re-engineering was simply a logical next step from scientific management (Taylorism), industrial engineering, and business process improvement (total quality management). What re-engineering had going for it, however, was that it fitted the needs of companies looking for a reason to continue the attack on bureaucracy and complacency, and with them the traditional hierarchical decision-making structures.

Champy and Hammer eschewed the phrase 'business process re-engineering', regarding it as too limiting. In their view, the scope and scale of re-engineering went far beyond simply altering and refining processes. True re-engineering was all embracing, a recipe for a corporate revolution.

To start the revolution, it was suggested that companies equip themselves with a blank piece of paper and map out their processes. This was undoubtedly a useful exercise. It encouraged companies to consider exactly what their core activities were, and what processes were in place, and needed to be in place, to deliver these efficiently. It also encouraged them to move beyond strict functional demarcations to freer-flowing corporate forms governed by key processes rather than fiefdoms. Having come up with a neatly engineered map of how their business should operate, companies could then attempt to translate the paper theory into concrete reality.

The concept was simple; actually turning it into reality has proved immensely more difficult than its proponents suggested. The first problem was that the blank piece of paper ignored the years, often decades, of cultural evolution that led to an organization doing something in a certain way. Such preconceptions and often justifiable habits were not easily discarded. Functional fiefdoms may be inefficient, but they are difficult to break down.

The second problem was that re-engineering appeared inhumane. In some cases, people were treated appallingly in the name of re-engineering. As the name suggests, it owed more to visions of the corporation as a machine than a human, or humane, system. The human side of re-engineering has proved its greatest stumbling block. To re-engineering purists, people were objects who handle processes. Depersonalization was the route to efficiency. (Here, the echoes of Taylor's management by dictatorship are most obvious.)

Re-engineering became a synonym for redundancy and downsizing. The gurus and consultants could not be entirely blamed for this. Often, companies that claimed to be re-engineering – and there were plenty – were simply engaging in cost cutting under the convenient guise of the fashionable theory. Downsizing appeared more publicly palatable if it was presented as implementing a leading-edge concept.

The third obstacle was that corporations are not natural nor even willing revolutionaries. Instead of casting the re-engineering net widely, they tended to re-engineer the most readily accessible process and then leave it at that.

Related to this – and the subject of Champy's sequel, *Re-engineering Management* – re-engineering usually failed to impinge on management. Not surprisingly, managers were all too willing to impose the rigours of a process-based view of the business on others, but often unwilling to inflict it on themselves. Champy suggested three key areas: managerial roles, managerial styles, and managerial systems. In retrospect, the mistake of re-engineering was not to tackle re-engineering management first.

SUPPLY CHAIN MANAGEMENT

TRADITIONALLY, the nitty gritty of moving raw materials and products around was regarded as the truly dull side of business. Companies

knew that products had to be transported, stored, and distributed, but it hardly set their pulses racing. Competitiveness had little to do with whether raw materials arrived on Tuesday or Friday.

Today, the logistics of moving things around has become an exact science: supply chain management. This is, at its simplest, logistics with added strategy (and a plethora of acronyms). It has been defined by Bernard La Londe of Ohio State University as: 'The delivery of enhanced customer and economic value through synchronized management of the flow of physical goods and associated information from sourcing through consumption.'

Supply chain management has emerged as being of critical importance to the modern organization for a number of reasons. First, the balance of power has shifted. In the past, manufacturers dictated terms to retailers. Now, it is retailers who call the tune with sophisticated systems designed so they get what they want when they want it. Companies such as Wal-Mart now store terabytes of information on customers. Manufacturers have to deliver to their increasingly demanding specifications.

Second, time is an increasingly important factor in overall corporate competitiveness. Speed is of the essence, whether it be in terms of product development, production, or distribution. Late deliveries close down production lines or lead to disappointed customers all too willing to look elsewhere.

The third factor is the expansion of information technology (IT). This allows companies to manage the flow of goods, materials, thoughts and information in ways never previously imagined. IT enables each element of the supply chain – whether it be the manufacturer, retailer, or end consumer – to know the situation of the others. For example, if a supermarket runs out of a particular product line, technology enables this to be automatically reordered.

The final factor bolstering the standing of supply chain management is globalization. Truly global businesses require global supply chains. The right raw materials have to arrive in the most obscure of corporate outposts at the right time in the right amount. For major multinational companies, global supply chain management is a highly complex challenge, but one critical to their competitiveness.

TIME-BASED COMPETITION

DESPITE the fact that its underlying logic has been accepted for decades, time-based competition became a management fashion in the early 1990s, largely due to the work of the Boston Consulting Group (BCG). Its chief proponents were two BCG consultants, George Stalk and Thomas Hout. Their book, *Competing*

***Against Time,* calls on companies to seek to compress time at every stage in every process. 'Time is the secret weapon of business because advantages in response time lever up all other differences that are basic to overall competitive advantage,' they write. 'Providing the most value for the lowest cost in the least amount of time is the new pattern for corporate success.'**

They point to Honda's triumph in the 1980s in its lengthy battle with Yamaha. Honda produced 60 new motorbikes in a year and once managed 113 new models in 18 months. Its speed of development far outstripped Yamaha's and Honda emerged triumphant.

Time-based competition contends that organizations should be structured in the most time-efficient way. The rationale is that processes and systems that are needlessly time consuming have a direct impact on competitiveness. Being slow costs you money. Unfortunately, traditional hierarchical organizations are not built with speed in mind. One calculation estimated that over 95 percent of the time products spend in an organization is wasted. Lengthy inventories as well as periods on hold during production cost money.

Stalk and Hout suggest that managers should focus on accomplishing three key tasks. First, they need to 'make the value-delivery systems of the company two to three times more flexible and faster than the value-delivery systems of competitors'. Second, management needs to 'determine how its customers value variety and responsiveness, focus on those customers with the greatest sensitivity, and price accordingly'. Finally, managers must 'have a strategy for surprising its competitors with the company's time-based advantage'.

In general, the logic of time-based competition remains hard to dispute. Fast is undoubtedly good, and being faster than competitors is clearly a route to competitiveness. However, as with many other such ideas, there is the suspicion that this is simply restating the first principles of business. Frederick Taylor's Scientific Management was also based on minimizing time to maximize efficiency and, therefore, profitability.

'Time waste differs from material waste in that there can be no salvage,' noted Henry Ford, who had one eye on the clock and the other on costs. In this and many other ways, Ford was ahead of his time.

TOTAL QUALITY MANAGEMENT

THE quality movement is associated with the Japanese economic renaissance after the Second World War. Total quality management (TQM) is an approach based on the use of quality concepts developed in Japan [see also Just-In-Time and Kaizen]. By the late 1970s,

the diligent application of these techniques by Japanese manufacturing companies had enabled them to overtake many Western manufacturers. Ironically, however, the quality movement was originally inspired by American ideas.

Under TQM, the use of sophisticated statistical production control ensures that quality is built into production, removing the need to check quality later. The aim of TQM is to minimize waste and reworking by achieving 'zero defects' in the production process. TQM is not a single magic bullet, but rather an approach that integrates a group of concepts. These include many of those associated with lean production, such as just-in-time. Although process driven, TQM is underpinned by a management philosophy that advocates continuous improvement and a 'right first time' approach to manufacturing.

It was largely due to the application of TQM among a highly disciplined workforce that in the space of just 25 years, Japanese companies were able to catch up with and outperform their rivals in America and Europe. One of the first American companies to heed the warning was the Xerox Corporation. While other parts of corporate America clung to the notion that the Japanese success story was based not on superior process management but cheap labour costs, Xerox took a long, hard look. It quickly realized that there was more to the superior Japanese performance than the US wanted to admit. Xerox was one of the first American companies to embrace the new Japanese management techniques that had inflicted the damage.

The company became an enthusiastic convert to the quality movement and set about introducing the 'right first time' philosophy into everything it did. In 1983, 'Leadership Through Quality', the Xerox total quality process, was unveiled. Important lessons had been learned.

As interest in the quality movement grew, others began to write and consult on how Western companies could adopt the approach. The best known of these Western thinkers were Joseph Juran and Philip Crosby. In time, a number of Japanese quality gurus also became better known in the West, including Genichi Taguchi, Taiichi Ohno and Shiego Shingo.

By the 1980s, TQM had become a byword for efficiency and success throughout the business world. Indeed, such was the impact of TQM that by the end of the decade it was almost possible to divide the world's top manufacturing companies into two categories: those that had introduced TQM; and those that were just about to. Reinforcing the trend was the widespread adoption of quality accreditation. International ISO 9000 standards created a global quality benchmark (although some companies complained that the bureaucracy the documentation procedures created actually undermined the improvements in competitiveness).

TQM is no quick fix. It requires a fundamental shift in thinking and production techniques. Companies that have successfully implemented TQM confirm that it requires a culture change at all levels – and that can take many years to achieve.

– CHAPTER 4 –

Marketing

'Marketing consists of all activities by which a company adapts itself to its environment – creatively and profitably.' ANON

'Marketing is so basic that it cannot be considered a separate function. It is the whole business seen from the point of view of its final result, that is, from the customer's point of view ... Business success is not determined by the producer but by the customer.' PETER DRUCKER

'Good companies will meet needs; great companies will create markets. Market leadership is gained by envisioning new products, services, lifestyles, and ways to raise living standards. There is a vast difference between companies that offer me-too products and those that create new product and service values not even imagined by the marketplace. Ultimately, marketing at its best is about value creation and raising the world's living standards.' PHILIP KOTLER

'Marketing is too important to be left to the marketing department.' DAVID PACKARD

Major emergent issues in global marketing

H. DAVID HENNESSEY

The first decade of the 2000s will be very different for global marketers compared to the 1990s, says David Hennessey. The basic tenets of marketing will stay the same – satisfying consumers needs – but the actual process of marketing will be radically different.

THE internet has reduced the size of the world to two or three clicks from any company to any consumer or buying organization.[1] The web allows consumers and companies to search, compare, and buy almost any product or service from anywhere around the globe. This can be done in point-to-point transactions or in marketplaces with multiple buyers and sellers. Whether components for an aeroplane, polyethylene resin for a milk container, or a rare book, the search, selection and ultimate transaction will be less costly, more accurate and more efficient than previous exchanges. What this means to executives is that they need to understand how to use the internet to reduce costs and increase value for their customers.

For example, six of the world's leading airline companies have united to form a web-based trading exchange to handle their $50 billion (£32 billion) procurement budgets. The exchange – which includes American Airlines, Air France, British Airways, Continental, Delta and United – will reduce transaction costs, inventory, number of suppliers, and therefore total costs. Industry trading exchanges have been established for oil companies, automotive manufacturers, chemical companies, auto component manufacturers, food retailers, personal computer manufacturers and many other industries. Most companies will either be selling and/or buying through an industry trading marketplace.

It is important for companies to develop internet capabilities and establish or join the appropriate trading marketplaces. First and second movers will most likely develop favourable positions in these new market systems that 'latecomers' will find difficult to usurp. Jack Welch, chief executive of GE, told shareholders at the annual meeting on 26 April 2000, 'Any company, old or new that does not see this technology as literally as important as breathing could be on its last breath.'

Price transparency

As the digital world facilitates product and price transparency, companies with regional or global brands will be able to afford the cost of continual innovation to differentiate their products to consumers. As the cost of research and innovation is spread over the global marketplace, it will be a larger total investment than local brands can afford, but it will be less for global products on a per-unit-sold basis.

At first, the price transparency may make it hard for consumers to differentiate products or services. Therefore, E*Trade, Ameritrade, National Discount Brokers, and other online brokers could become commodities. However, consumers will still look for the best value (perceived benefit received minus price, including time). In many cases, consumers will rely on brand image to help decide, but will also be looking for value-added services such as shipment tracking, quality certification, superior logistics, etc. to choose between similar offerings.

While price transparency will tend to encourage price competition or parity, executives must look for ways to use the new technology and the information to provide increased value. For example,

Schwab has attracted higher net worth customers with higher average balances than other brokers through the use of personalized advice and portfolio tracking. These value-added services along with a trusted brand have reduced Schwab's customer acquisition cost and increased its average trading revenue over other online brokers.

John Chambers, CEO of Cisco systems, spends 50 percent of his time with customers, first to understand their evolving needs, and second to set a clear example that customers are number one at Cisco. Chambers openly admits that he did not do this in his former positions at IBM and Wang, and that the companies lost market position. His advice to executives is: when you think you have the winning formula, it's time to hire more people from other industries, because the rules of the game are changing so fast.

Point-to-point transactions

The internet will allow easy point-to-point transactions, which in many industries will eliminate the need for distributors, wholesalers, agents, and retailers. Because of this disintermediation, travel agents, insurance agents, computer retailers and other channel members will be marginalized unless they can add value to the process. For example, 11 European airline companies, including BA, Air France, KLM, SAS and others, have announced the formation of a joint database to reduce distribution and ticketing costs. This could also displace travel agents.

In the personal computer industry, value-added resellers, distributors and computer retailers were previously the channels used by IBM and Compaq. This approach required extensive inventory in the channel, manufacturers had to take back equipment that did not sell, and the extra profit margin required by the channel members had to be incorporated. Dell has developed a competitively priced direct model that delivers individually configured computers with software loaded on the machine before delivery. The Dell approach requires 7–10 days of inventory compared to 60–65 days for Compaq. The difficulty that Compaq and IBM face is their legacy sales and distribution systems. Executives will need to closely examine new business models being offered and in many cases make difficult short-term painful decisions to be competitive in the longer term.

Point-to-point communications between buyers and sellers will allow global marketers to gain a better understanding of the needs of each customer and become more customer focused. Using the latest information, sellers can tailor their offering to specific needs. For example, booksellers can feature recent books on horses in information sent to the equestrian enthusiast and recent global strategy books to the business executive who has bought similar books in the past.

Specialized industry websites allow marketers to advertise directly to their target audience. For example, the Fish Info Service (www.fis-net.com) is used by fishermen, processors and traders to keep up to date with fish stocks and prices, making this the perfect place to speak directly to this audience.

VerticalNet offers over 50 different business-to-business trade communities, which appeal directly to specialized markets such as fibreoptics, water supply, dentistry and semiconductors. Advertising is a major revenue source for VerticalNet.

Through e-mail, many customers can be contacted directly with high-quality, tailored communications. For example, Germany's Mittelstand companies, large private firms in the engineering field, have used the internet to focus communications with selected customers and suppliers and develop a deep partnership, rather than a mass-market approach.

Global markets

The internet, the euro and the interdependence of major world economies are all fostering companies' opportunities to serve the global marketplace. Large and small companies can serve customers around the globe:

- Given that any customer can reach a company in two to three clicks, it will become common to sell books, art, travel, market information, music, shares of stock, hardware, machinery, planes, trains, automobiles and many other items over the internet. Along with reduced trade and geographic barriers for many products, there will be few limits to what products and services can be sold globally in this way.

- The internet eliminates time zone restrictions and speeds up information exchange.
- The internet allows for two-way interaction, so each business can receive components only when required (JIT), eliminating inventory, warehousing and obsolete stock. Of course, low-value physical products will not be shipped around the globe, but many items will benefit from the efficient worldwide delivery and shipping services now available.

Given the large volume of internet sites and trading marketplaces, a key role of global marketers will be to attract and keep customers at their site. This will require agreements and alliances with search engines and non-competitive sites that serve the customer base. Through search engines and links you will be able to get customers to your site, but that site's quality and perceived value will determine how long a customer stays on it or how many times they return.

Providing product information, negotiating prices, and tracking shipments may be better handled by technology than by a traditional salesperson. In some industries where the salesperson's primary role was to facilitate transactions, they will no longer be required. In other industries, the salesperson's role will be to monitor the customer's industry and work face to face with the customer to add value. This will require salespeople with new skills to assimilate industry information and identify new ways to add value for customers. In business-to-business selling, the salesperson will work closely with marketing to identify and create innovative, value-added products and services.

Global account management

Customers with operations around the globe want to receive the same service, product, and pricing wherever they are doing business.

Standardization reduces acquisition costs, improves quality, and supports global products. Companies such as HP, IBM and Lucent, as well as global advertising and accounting agencies, have found it very useful to establish a global account management programme.

Global account management requires an in-depth understanding of the customer's industry, their position in the industry, and their overall strategy. For example, why is the biggest connector customer building a factory in China? Why is the automotive customer converting from hydraulic power steering to electronic power steering? Why are your automobile component manufacturers establishing a trading marketplace? The experience and training of the global account managers, along with multi-person high-level contact at the customer level, will allow managers to answer these questions and better identify ways to meet the future needs of global customers.

Global account management requires a high level of executive commitment and support, to influence national account managers to do things that will be in the best interest of the global account. National account executives and country managers with different metrics may pursue actions beneficial for that country and not the world. Global account management is also supported by a global information system, which provides all the information necessary to serve a global customer in the best way.

The challenge of global marketing

The new world of global marketing will require significant e-commerce skills. At first, these skills involve using the electronic point-to-point capability of the internet to reduce costs and improve customer value. This will require major changes in pricing, product development, advertising and sales. The digital world provides an amazing variety of new ways to serve customers.

Second, global marketers will be faced with the challenge of co-operation. Companies will be working directly with competitors in trading marketplaces to reduce purchase costs. For example, 11 of the world's leading retailers have set up the Worldwide Retail

Exchange, a business-to-business online exchange to buy, sell, or auction goods and services. This group includes Casino and Auchan of France, Safeway and K-Mart of the US, Kingfisher and Marks & Spencer of the UK, and Royal Ahold of the Netherlands. It follows the establishment of the GlobalNetExchange set up by Carrefour of France and Sears of the US and joined by Metro of Germany, Sainsbury of the UK, and Kroger of the US. These new exchanges will require new skills to obtain the best results while still remaining differentiated in the marketplace.

It is expected that governments may question some of these new arrangements, which is why in many cases the exchanges are operated by a separate company. For example, a computer component exchange including HP, Gateway, Compaq, Hitachi, NEC, Advanced Micro Devices and others will be operated by an independent company yet to be named.

The future of global marketing is difficult to predict in the wired world. Barriers to trade will continue to fall, currency risk and currency conversion costs will decline and geographic borders will become less important, all leading to an increase in world trade. The winning companies will be those that have the vision and can switch to the new approach without being burdened by legacy systems and methods. Most major firms will need to restructure and redefine themselves. There will be winners and losers. Hold on tight, it should be a great ride.

REFERENCE

1. Throughout, reference to consumers includes both consumers and organizations.

RESOURCES

BOOK

Peppers, Don and Rogers, Martha, *The One-to-One Field Book*, Capstone, Oxford, 1999.

Capturing lifetime customer value – beyond CRM to customer stretch

SANDRA VANDERMERWE

The successful modern enterprise sees every customer as an investment. And, like any other investment, each of these customers has a lifetime value, as Sandra Vandermerwe explains. How to capture this lifetime value is the key challenge facing the modern enterprise seeking to grow and compete sustainably.

THE idea of the lifetime value of customers rests on a very different logic from conventional theory and practice, which was based on an era of 'things', where money was made by product and service companies according to volumes, market share, and margins. The new logic acknowledges that strategies based on these 'things', no matter how good or innovative they may be, can never be sustainable because they are too easy to copy, leading to a no-win situation on a diminishing returns treadmill.

'Things' diminish in value as competitors move in – as they invariably do – whereas the value of customers increases over time.

Here lies the key to growth and prosperity in the new economy: enterprises must get customers to 'lock on'. This means that customers want the firm or institution as their sole or dominant choice on an ongoing basis. They do so because they get superior value at low delivered cost, not either superior value or low cost, as traditional theory led us to believe. Since customers stay with an enterprise because they have good and sufficient reason, lock-on becomes self-reiterating over time, which contrasts with the transaction model based on specification and price at a moment in time (see Figure 1).

Figure 1 Customer lock-on

In other words, the more a company does business with a particular customer, the better the relationship. The more knowledge and information they share; the more proactive and precise is the offering. And the more business done together, the lower the cost, thanks to technology and the fact that the knowledge collected – *the* key resource in the value-creating process – can be re-used. This creates a reinforcing loop that improves the depth and quality of the relationship, the amount and quality of the information and knowledge shared, lowering the cost and therefore intensifying the lock-on and so on.

The ability to trigger and sustain this customer lock-on loop becomes the only realistic barrier to competitive entry. So, rather than trying to get economies of scale on the supply side from units churned out of product or service factories and then moving these goods down channels to meet market share goals, the new objective is to get a critical mass of individual customers who 'lock-on' to the enterprise, who will provide for and receive from the enterprise as much value as possible, over as long a period as possible. In other words, in the new economy, economies of scale stem from demand and not from supply.

And since it is individuals rather than markets that lock on, success depends on an enterprise's ability to satisfy individual customers in a highly personalized way by continually giving them the results they want and adapting to their needs. When aggregated, these results become 'market spaces', a descriptive term for the 'playing field' or 'customer activity arena'. It is here that the modern enterprise operates and seeks to dominate in order to maximize share of customer spend over time, rather than maximizing market share in static product categories at a moment in time, in a transactional fashion.

Beyond CRM

Customer relationship management (CRM), customer retention, customer loyalty, and one-to-one marketing – all terms sometimes used interchangeably – have paved the way for thinking about the lifetime value of customers as the competitive paradigm for the new economy. They are made easier to accomplish because of new technologies. However, if we examine these notions, we see that most have stemmed from product thinking, with the focus on using tools – ranging from loyalty cards to the internet – to bring customers back again and again for more static, discrete 'things'. All of this inevitably leads to commodity behaviour and zero gain for everyone, including customers.

Customer relationship stretch goes further. The aim is to become more involved with the customer's experience in a defined 'market space', and to stretch relationships to gain increasing amounts of customer spend over time. Take Unilever: instead of using techniques to induce repurchase (the loyalty approach) and sell more and more detergents and home cleaning items, or using data gathered through technology on buying patterns to improve detergents for customers (the customer relationship approach), it has developed myhome.co.uk, providing cleaning services in the *home and fabric cleaning* market space (the customer stretch approach).

Once lock-on has been accomplished, the new enterprise can move into other market spaces, thus extracting even more spend. As soon as Unilever establishes lock-on with a critical mass of customers, it could easily stretch into another market space, for instance decoration or renovation. This route has been taken by Amazon (from books into CDs, games, software, and even toiletries, healthcare and pet supplies) as well as Virgin (from airlines into retailing, rail services, financial services, and web-based car dealerships, among others).

Moving with customers on the move

Capturing lifetime value means following a customer over time, knowing and anticipating that customers change, and so planning and adapting offerings accordingly. Take the UK's Royal Automobile Club (RAC), now part of Lex Services. The group has moved from an almost exclusive focus on its core breakdown service business (the 'thing'), to finding ways to stretch its share of customers' minds and pockets through the various stages of their lives in the market space the RAC calls *journey management.*

This meant capturing customers early on, hence the decision to buy the British School of Motoring (BSM) – the largest in the UK – which was the RAC's first acquisition in its 100 years of existence. The object was specifically to make the driving school the beginning of a lifelong experience with the RAC for the young, growing their accumulating value for the company over their lifetimes. This represented an intriguing twist in logic: in the past, conventional insuring standards had considered the young too high a risk. 'Better to deal with them when they reached 25 or so and were more stable and drove better-quality cars,' was the conventional industry refrain. This contrasted with the new objective to be involved in the lifetime customer experience – sooner rather than later, and for as long as possible. Said Neil Johnson, RAC's CEO: 'We get them younger, train them better and provide them with "mobility life skills", adapting these skills to their lives as the technology changes while they move from the ages of 17 to 70.'

By 1998, the RAC already had tens of thousands of non-members regularly accessing its traffic information on the internet, including its navigation, mapping and telematic systems, which were designed to help people get from A to B in the best possible way.

Although conventionally non-members of the breakdown services club would not have been allowed access to this information, this is an ideal way to get young people to touch the RAC brand electronically before they actually have to buy or drive a vehicle. So begins a relationship that the enterprise can potentially leverage by selling these individuals the various services necessary over their lifetimes in their journey-managing experiences.

Crossing product and industry boundaries

From the customer's point of view, artificial product and industry separations make no sense. They couldn't care less how companies are organized, who reports to whom, or who owns what.

For example, financial services customers start out as wealth aspirers, borrowing at the onset of adulthood, requiring loans for education or to start businesses (see Figure 2). Many banks try to attract students with cheap loans, hoping to hold on to them afterwards, but because such people are seen as a non-money-making proposition, the services given are poor and the strategy tends to backfire. Then customers become wealth builders: they get married, have children, move around the world, and may build professional practices or businesses. At this stage they become wealth creators – savers and investors – seeking to maintain and enhance their lifestyles and grow their wealth. Once retired, people become wealth protectors: they dis-save, spending their money to sustain and protect their lifestyles. And then wealth passes to the next generation – the wealth inheritors – so continuing the cycle.

Companies such as Virgin Banking or Interactive Investors International (iii.com) aim to cover all these periods of a customer's lifetime financial needs, irrespective of what industry or product 'silo' they happen to be in. They assess the needs that occur at each critical life stage and provide whatever is necessary at that point. For example, Virgin's executives claim that over 25 years, a customer with an income of £50,000 and a mortgage of £100,000 could gain

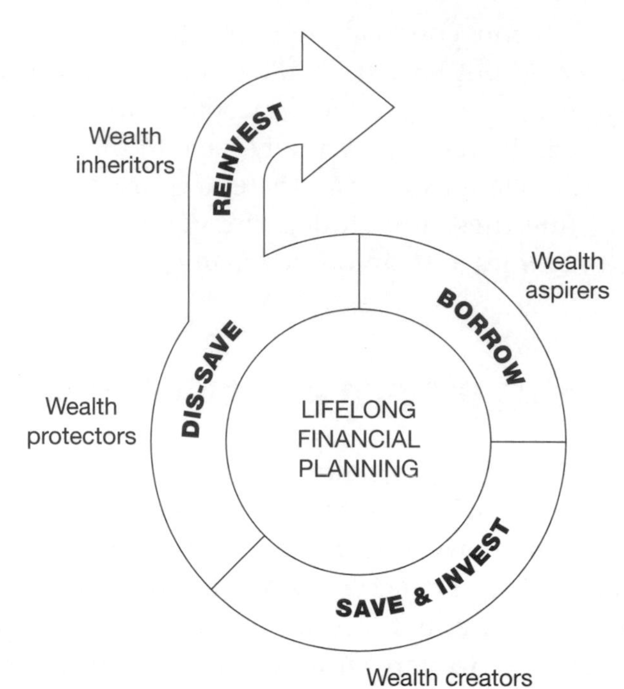

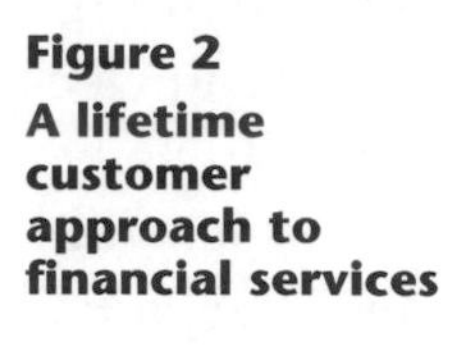
Figure 2
A lifetime customer approach to financial services

as much as £125,000, largely by avoiding the inefficiencies and costs in time, effort, and money of having to deal with different institutions and industries to get the various services they need and obtain the results they want in the *event cash management* market space – cash when, where and how they need it, whether it be insurance, loans, mortgages, or stocks. And thanks to the new e-technologies, companies are able to assemble all the services required for both the predictable and unpredictable events in their customers' lives without having to incur the cost of buying or owning such facilities.

Selling fewer of the core 'things'

In the interest of getting the customer lock-on that leads to lifelong value, the modern enterprise concentrates on the outcome for customers in a defined 'market space'. Often this can mean selling fewer of their core items: water, fuel, airline tickets, paint, insurance. These enterprises thus use a different algorithm, helping customers make better decisions to get results over time, rather than pushing to sell more and more of the 'things'.

For instance, Hempel Paints in Saudi Arabia found that many customers were buying too much paint. They were also choosing a paint that protected the asset (a building, house, or tanker) for five years instead of 10 because it was cheaper, whereas in fact 80 percent of the cost lay in paint application. In addition, customers were storing paint in conditions that shortened its useful life, applying it badly, and repainting at the wrong time, all of which made the cost of the outcome even greater, though the initial deal per unit of paint may have seemed optimal. Hempel decided that in the *asset protection and decoration* market space the opportunity was not in selling customers more paint – where margins were deteriorating in any case – but rather in building and using its existing knowledge and expertise to help customers buy, use, apply and rebuy the correct quantities of paint, at the right time, in the correct way. The alternative was for someone else, probably a new dot-com or consultancy, to perform these activities, thus relegating Hempel to the role of commodity supplier: the *real* threat to corporations today.

Using partners to connect up the customer experience

The modern enterprise's object is to dominate activities (and spend) in its defined market space. This can only be done by providing a totally integrated experience to customers and so locking them on. The company knows that it can't do this alone and that it doesn't have to own or do everything itself to win. So if it doesn't have, or doesn't want to build, certain capabilities necessary to provide an integrated experience, it partners with others to form one customer value-creating delivery system.

Direct Line is an example, getting beyond cheap motor insurance to maximize spend in the *personal mobility* market space. Its repair centre consists of 140 independent shops all integrated under the Direct Line brand. The customer calls Direct Line when they have a problem, the car (and customer) is picked up, fixed, returned, and automatically charged through the customer's bank or card. Claims are made to the insurer by phone. Direct Line 'owns' both the brand and the customer experience. To maintain quality it sets standards – common, consistent and acceptable service levels – ensuring that all players in the customer activity cycle work as one value-creating delivery system. Examples include its 24-hour recovery service; 24-hour collection and delivery to and from the customer's home; contacting the customer within 30 minutes of a call for help; and recovering the stranded vehicle within an hour.

Connecting the various parts of the customer's activities through partnering is facilitated by new technology. Simply and at low cost, the new enterprise can gain from networking and from the knowledge, expertise, and resources of linked partners delivering highly personalized superior offerings.

For example, iii.com links together three data-feed servers and thousands of news sources to provide its customer base of 1.2 million individuals with the latest news, information, and stock performance reports on over 60,000 investment alternatives. And it will put customers in touch with several stockbrokers and allow them to speak to other customers who have had dealings with them before they make their choice. This takes us beyond one-to-one marketing to one-to-many relationship management, which is what obtains the full value of customer spend over time.

Ford connects customers to a series of partners to create the fully integrated experience, while Ford continues to manage and thus 'own' the customer experience. For instance, customers can see what car model all the linked local dealers have in stock instead of having to walk around and ask. The automobile is then delivered to their homes for a test drive. Those interested in used cars can track vehicle ownership, use and service records to make their assessment. Or they can design the new car of their choice, request quotes from a local dealer, and get insurance and financing. Maintenance schedules can be accessed and they can book a service, pay automatically, phone in for help to call centres and, if they want a car for special occasions, get special rental deals from Hertz, also part of Ford. A clearing house of franchised dealers covers emergency breakdowns on a 24-hour basis, and a network of partners enables digital voice-activated phone service for emergency roadside assistance as well as for personalized information such as news, e-mail delivery and stock quotes, together with 100 channels of digital music and other programmes.

Partners may be competitors as firms go multi-brand, recognizing that no single brand can satisfy customers in their various roles, let alone over their lifetime. The new strategy of Ford US is not just for the Ford brand, but also across its family of brands like Aston Martin, Jaguar, Volvo, Lincoln, Mercury and Mazda. Renault goes further in its carevia.com initiative, the first multi-make information and transaction site for used cars by a single manufacturer.

Changing the financial algorithm

The formula for lifetime customer value differs from the conventional model in very significant ways. Most obvious is that what is key is not the profitability of each unit, product, segment, or even country at a moment in time, but the profitability of the customer – over time. The new enterprise knows how to calculate the present value of the future revenue streams obtained from customer lock-on and factor this into resource allocation and investment decisions.

It is also aware that conventional accounting and reporting standards are not only irrelevant but dangerously misleading. Through reliance on such standards, firms were not only organized in product silos, causing disconnects in the customer experience, but were reluctant to do anything that was not regarded as 'profitable', even if it was a vital component of the customer experience. For example, until recently retailing group Marks & Spencer refused to accept credit cards because it thought this too costly. The result was a greater cost to the firm: customers purchased a fraction of what they might have, although brand loyalty and retention rates were probably high.

Early in the 1990s, Baxter Healthcare in North America created and managed a stockless inventory system (which included non-Baxter goods) for hospitals by ordering, delivering, and receiving inventory directly to wards, just-in-time (JIT). The associated service charges to hospitals were more than offset by the superior value they received. Although Baxter lost individual items to competitors when its product was not ideal or too expensive, it did grow its share of a greater customer spend (governments awarded more funding to these hospitals because they were more efficient). But, because the independent service unit was not making a 'profit' in the traditional sense of the word, it was dropped.

Today, Baxter Healthcare uses the lifetime value of the customer in its decision making. And – another key component of the lifetime customer model – it employs different success criteria to mere market share. For example, Baxter Renal UK invested and excelled early on in home care services, making it the expert on personalized services in the home although that unit was not 'profitable'. It began with delivering renal bags, but now the company is able to offer a host of services in the patient's home, such as monitor prescriptions and blood toxin levels to maximize the efficacy of its treatment, and so keep patients on its therapy longer. More recently the company started supplying associated drugs for heart disease or diabetes, as well as the competitive treatment in the home that had previously only been done in hospitals.

All of Baxter's R&D product and service activities are geared to extending the life and wellbeing of the renal patient, not maximizing margins on renal bags. In fact the margins on the bags have dropped, but the lifetime value of the customer has shot up dramatically. And the success indicators used go beyond market share of bags, to include the number of people choosing Baxter's therapy; how long they stay on that therapy; and the amount of high-level services as a percentage of Baxter sales – all of which have increased. In other words, although margins have gone down, Baxter has achieved much more of customer spend, over a much longer period of time.

Similarly, even though Hempel is losing volume sales in its core items, such as paint, this is compensated for by the stretch in its customer relationships, which provides many benefits not yet formalized in traditional accounting. These include:

- Eliminating protracted and expensive negotiations around renewal costs, tendering and bidding – a benefit for both suppliers and customers.
- Amortizing the huge set-up investment costs required in building the customer relationship.
- Low/no acquisition or marginal costs of producing and/or delivering extra value-added products and services.
- Decreased costs of managing customers as systems are joined and familiarity and trust set in.
- Barriers to reaching influencers shrink, giving access to higher levels of decision makers.
- Increased take-up of new innovations, extensions and opportunities for joint ventures.
- Sharing of resources, knowledge, and information, as well as forecasting.
- Selling high-level new services like consulting and project management.
- Cashflow quality goes up – integrated systems save time and money.
- Leveraging from expertise and knowledge gained, which can be taken to other customers and wider markets at great speed.
- Joint risk taking – all parties have a vested interest in the outcome.
- Benefitting from customers' ideas – customers came to Hempel to discuss different paint finishes, but 'the discussion wasn't about the price of the paint any more', said one executive, 'it was about trying different things and opening up new opportunities'.
- Work done by customers, such as the reviews Amazon.com's customers provide on its site.

As firms move from a product to a lifetime customer model, top management will have to accept that all of the investment cannot be recovered in the initial period, as was typically required in the past. Upfront investment in money, time, and energy will have an impact on cashflow in the short term, but enhance it in the long term – and do so exponentially. Also not just revenue inflow but combining cashflow *and* investments (i.e., the P&L and balance sheet), which accounts for 'free cashflow', is what is needed to ensure success in the new economy.[1]

Pricing strategies may also have to change, as they will no longer be based on the 'thing' – the car or renal bag – but on charges made on the outcome per patient, or on the use of a car when and where customers need it. This will require new ways of thinking and accounting.

Customers also have to change the way they look at pricing and prices. They often want to minimize spend up front, which to some extent can be offset by charging customers for use or subscription rather than for owning the 'things'. But it will also mean quantifying the result of buying behaviour that can lead to higher costs later on. As an example, the new 'Measured Response Treatment Plan', pioneered by Imperial College, University of London, means that patients paying insurance can now get treatment that costs more initially, but makes the total treatment much less expensive in the long term because of new ways of diagnosing and monitoring patients.

Getting it – and doing it

The time has come for enterprises to recognize the need to understand and implement a new business model based on customers, rather than on products or services. All firms know what their products or services are worth over time, but few fully appreciate the value of customers over time or how to improve it.

E-technology will facilitate this new business model, but it is not a substitute. Top management's responsibility is to empower people who understand what has to be done – and let them get on and do it. Success will be determined by the ability to lock customers on and capitalize on customer lifetime value in the future – a future yet to be defined, which they themselves can proactively help create.

REFERENCE

1. Free cashflow in this context is discussed by Michael J. Mauboussin and Bob Hiler in 'Cashflow.com', *Frontiers of Finance*, Vol 9 (Credit Suisse First Boston, February 1999).

RESOURCES

2

BOOK

Vandermerwe, Sandra, *Customer Capitalism: Increasing Returns in New Market Spaces*, Nicholas Brealey, London, 1999.

Understanding brand potential

WATTS WACKER

Brands cannot stand still, explains Watts Wacker, they need to develop and grow, while retaining a foundation of authenticity.

BRANDS have always been viewed in a context of consistency. With the world now being defined by a macro environment of 'uncertainty', a brand must, paradoxically, be consistent and inconsistent at the same time. A brand must always be developing, learning, and growing at the same time as much of its bedrock is always seen in a light of consistency. For example, not only is Budweiser the biggest beer brand in the US, Bud Lite is the second largest.

It is also important to reflect on the 'rules of branding' and whether or not they are now obsolete. Two critical 'rules' of branding go back to the roots of modern day marketing (1950):

- The concept of a unique selling proposition.
- That a brand can't be 'number one in pickles and number one in ketchup' at the same time.

Ted Bates gave us the idea of the unique selling proposition. After 50 years of continual sophistication in marketing and continual sophistication in consumers, unique selling propositions may no longer motivate consumers. For example, 'Pringles the potato chip that makes your hands less greasy' is unique, but has no resonance with consumers as far as motivating them to buy the product. Trout and Ries, in their marketing treatise *Positioning Battle for the Mind*, put forth the importance of 'being first'. They also argued that you could not be first in pickles (Heinz) and at the same time be first in ketchup with the same brand name.

Our philosophy is that it is more important to identify your core beliefs and 'fuse' the core beliefs with the consumer's 'take away'. Krispy Kreme's promise – creating magic moments – suggests that it should identify all opportunities that reflect a magic moment as potential and fertile areas for franchise extension. For example, if consumer feedback suggests to Krispy Kreme that there are 100 movies produced in the history of Hollywood that are associated with 'a moment' of great sharing between two people, then those movies should be thought of as potential areas to explore with the Krispy Kreme brand.

The critical thought here is that if you are perceived as 'a wagon master' (as Gateway is), then you should look for every area to which wagon mastering would make sense relative to the emerging needs within individual lives. In the case of Gateway, branding has already shown transference from computer making, to internet service provisioning, to leasing (never having an obsolete computer) over buying.

Great mistakes

It is interesting to note that most great brands have had a major misstep in their past. Ford almost went out of business. British Airways once stood for 'Bloody Awful'. IBM was yet another major brand that demonstrated how easy it is to become vulnerable.

This susceptibility to public display of one's shortcomings has a very humanizing effect on brands. What is critical is not that these shortcomings or failures happen, but what transpires immediately afterward. As Miles Davis once said, 'When you hit a wrong note it's the next note that makes it good or bad.' Great brands that have let down their consumers actually may create even greater opportunities based on how they respond to the specific circumstance. Brands may be well served by 'being wrong and fixing it' instead of striving to be perfect.

... and great concepts

While great brands have a tendency to be viewed as having functional superiority (in a blind taste test Coke is not preferred to Pepsi, but does come out on top when identified as Coke), they see themselves in a larger context than just functionality. Chevrolet did not talk about engineering excellence, it talked about 'seeing the USA'.

It is also important to remember that the people who work on a brand become sensitized to it much more than their customers. Many marketing managers have become bored with their strategies and tactics well before these have reached a level of burnout with their customers. Solarcaine once had some of the world's best advertising ('Mommy, I'm sunburned and feel like a French fry'). Although the spot only ran 20 times in a period of three years, the marketing department was exhausted by having been exposed to it for many thousands of impressions. As a result, Schering-Plough Co. let go of a great concept way too early.

Authenticity

Great brands tend to be referred to by their customers and even their competitors as being genuine and authentic. Whenever authenticity is associated with a brand, the brand tends to have reached a level of involvement in its consuming universe that is of mythological proportions. Anything that causes a 'disconnect' between that authenticity and the actions taken by the brand will result in an immediate and severe consumer response.

For example, Lite beer was built for 35-year-old ex-jocks. As the brand's marketplace began to reach saturation, Miller's response to the desire for continued growth was to 'contemporize' the brand and go after a younger market. Suddenly, the 35-year-old ex-jocks felt like this beer no longer fit them. And the younger group never felt like it was designed for them in the first place.

This problem is to do with the issue of 'cohort brands' versus 'life stage brands'. Cohort brands are those that become attached to a group of people and travel over time with them. (The word cohort comes from the Latin for the Roman legionnaire, who went into the legion and remained with the same group of people.) Life stage brands are used at specific stages of life. For example, mothers use Coppertone on their young children and then slather themselves with the same product. The children themselves grow into the next life stage brand (like Hawaiian Tropic and Tropical Blend), then grow into another life stage and use Bain de Soleil. When they get married and have kids, they come back to using Coppertone.

The importance of understanding life stage versus cohort is also reflected in the ups and downs of Nike. Whether this was to do with the brand itself or athletic shoes in general, at a certain point the target audience for Nike sneakers (teens and young adults) no longer wanted to wear a shoe that was so ubiquitous their parents were wearing the same brand. Levi's underwent similar circumstances when it went from being work clothing to a fashion item.

Another good learning perspective for understanding a brand's potential comes from the experience of Barbie. Great brands reach the level of having iconographic transfer. But nature abhors a vacuum; if you don't define yourself, the *zeitgeist* defines you. Barbie began to be featured in songs and advertisements for other companies (the Nissan GI-Joe/Barbie commercial) in a light that made Mattel feel uncomfortable. More to the point, The Body Shop put ads in its window with Barbie's head on a Rubenesque plastic doll, with copy that said, 'There are three billion women in the world, only six of them are super-models.' Because Barbie was not defining herself in a relevant context, she was being defined by the *zeitgeist* itself.

RESOURCES

BOOK

Wacker, Watts, *The 500 Year Delta*, Capstone, 1997.

WEB

www.firstmatter.com

2

Corporate religion

JESPER KUNDE

Everybody's talking about the new economy, while searching for the answer to the pervasive question: How do you safeguard your company in the new economy and ride the new wave successfully? Jesper Kunde claims that we need a new definition of corporate management, based not on organization but on brand values.

IN the old economy the product played the central role, and companies were organized in order to develop, manufacture, and sell new products. Now everyone is talking about the new economy, assuming that to be the internet. They are wrong. In the shift to disparate modes of thinking, the web has been a unique media, in that it allows companies to interact and communicate with their customers rapidly, globally and individually. But the web only accelerated a development that has been imminent for quite a while: the transition from a product-oriented economy to a value-based economy.

In the new economy it's essential to be unique, because singularity translates into value for your customers. And in the future value will be everything.

We therefore need new definitions of corporate management, definitions which are based on an understanding of brand values.

Brand thinking

Brand thinking is the simplest way of defining and expressing a set of values. I believe the most important management task is being able to put one's company into words, so that everyone inside the company – and outside in the market – shares a common concept of the future.

Don't forget: in the future the company becomes the brand. Moreover, employees and consumers will demand a far more comprehensive understanding of the company behind the brand than they have today.

The first step towards achieving this mutual understanding between a company, its employees, and its customers is a corporate religion (CR). The CR is the 'sticky stuff' between company and market, allowing the company to manage both enterprise and market wholeheartedly.

In psychology, personality is all about perception and is seen from three perspectives:

- What is the world's perception of our company?
- How do we see ourselves?
- How would we like the world to think of us?

The more integrated the three perspectives, the stronger and more consistent we are.

The CR expresses the company's soul and personality – and if these are strong enough, they will penetrate the market in a positive way.

Strong companies break through to the market by creating a singular connected force within the corporation that moves into the market and consistently provide the company with a strong market position. It is of utmost importance to focus on building that powerful link between the internal culture inside the company and the brand position you wish to create in the market.

Everything begins with you

It all begins with the top managers. They need to define who they are and where they want to go. 'Why?' they will say. 'We are already designing strategies and running the company according to solid principles of good management.'

Wrong. In the new economy where value and the ability to communicate it are all important, you need a whole new set of skills to succeed. In the new economy, everything is constantly changing. Companies built to last become companies built to flip – forcing top managements to pay close attention to what goes on in and around their markets, continuously supplying correct interpretations and adaptive actions.

When everything is changing rapidly, it will no longer be the product that is the glue that makes ends meet in your company. Brand values become the most important point of departure in the future. And remember: no amount of harmless, nice-for-all values will do the job.

Only a mission statement that expounds the corporate promise to the market makes it happen. A genuine mission statement describes what the company wants to do better for its customers – and what exactly it is that makes it a unique company in the market.

The mission statement is just the beginning. The next task is to define and phrase the brand values that will link the internal organization with the external position the company wants to conquer.

Precision in formulation adds efficiency to the company. Finding the appropriate words is no easy task and it takes time, but it is worth pursuing. Once the wording is in place and there is consensus, invest heavily in communicating your corporate brand internally and externally.

Believe or leave

In my experience with international concept development, top managers find it very difficult to formulate their company's brand values and generally don't devote resources to this task. They're still chiefly occupied with budgets and organizational structures.

In the new economy, you'd do best to forget about all those budgets and assorted quantities. The great task ahead is figuring out how you transfer your brand values from the old to the new economy. After all, you are never more than the position you own in the heads of your customers.

When everything can change at the drop of a hat, it is important to improve your corporate ability to formulate continuously what your company is about.

In other words, strengthen your capability to revise your company at least once a year. Revision is decisive to success and forms an efficient link between management, employees and customers. Remember: the future calls for incessant fuel injections.

Future top managers need to be on the front line deciphering what is happening for the good of their companies – rephrasing their corporate brands in the process – and communicating the news for all to seize.

Top managers of the future will remain ahead because they know more and consequently demand more of their employees. Corporate religion is about consensus, about uniting many minds in a common purpose. It's crucial for success that everyone has the same attitudes – and goes along the same shared path to create more value. A company which is governed by a corporate religion only has jobs for believers.

RESOURCES

BOOK

Kunde, Jesper, *Corporate Religion*, FT/Prentice Hall, London, 2000.

WEB

www.corporatereligion.com

The brand report card

KEVIN LANE KELLER

Kevin Lane Keller believes that the world's strongest brands share 10 attributes.

WHEN you're submerged in the everyday management of a brand it can be difficult to keep track of all the parts that affect the way that brand is perceived. But it is possible to identify the 10 characteristics that the world's strongest brands share and from that compile a 'brand report card' – a systematic and comprehensive way to evaluate your brand's performance. Applying this report card can help distinguish areas in which the brand is strong, where improvement is needed and provide numerous strategic insights. Equally, compiling similar rankings for your competitors can clarify their strengths and weaknesses as well.

Remember, though, that simply identifying areas of weakness does not mean that they need immediate action. Acting in some areas can be a mistake if it undermines another brand characteristic that may actually create more brand value with consumers.

The top 10 characteristics

1. **The brand excels at delivering the benefits customers truly desire**: customers buy a product not because of a collection of attributes but because those attributes are linked with many other tangible and intangible factors to create an appealing whole. Sometimes, that isn't even something consumers know or say they want.

2. **The brand stays relevant**: brand equity is a function of both product and service quality as well as a number of intangible considerations: 'user imagery' (the type of person who uses the brand); 'usage imagery' (the situations in which the brand is used); the type of personality the brand portrays (sincere, exciting, competent, rugged); the feeling the brand tries to elicit in consumers (purposeful, warm); and the relationship it tries to build with them (committed, casual, seasonal). Strong brands never lose sight of their core values. But they also stay on the leading edge and adjust their intangibles to fit the times.
3. **The pricing strategy is based on consumers' perceptions of value**: it is not easy, though worth the effort, to get the right mix of product quality, design, features and prices. Sadly, many managers are not aware of how price can and should be related to consumer's perceptions. As a result, they either charge too little or too much.
4. **The brand is properly positioned**: well-positioned brands occupy particular niches in consumers' minds. Consumers recognize them as being similar to and different from competitors' brands in predictable ways. The most successful brands create 'points of parity' in areas where competitors are trying to find an advantage as well as 'points of difference' that create advantages over competitors in other areas.
5. **The brand is consistent**: a strong brand strikes the right balance between continuity in marketing and the kinds of change needed to stay relevant. Continuity in this sense means that a brand's image does not get confused or drowned in a chaos of conflicting marketing messages.
6. **The brand portfolio and hierarchy make sense**: most companies create and maintain different brands for different market segments. The corporate brand may act as an umbrella. A second brand name under the umbrella might be targeted at the family market; a third-level brand might be aimed at boys,

for example, or be used for one type of product. Brands at each level of the hierarchy contribute to the overall equity of the portfolio. But each brand should have its boundaries. It can be dangerous to cover too much ground with one brand or to overlap two brands in a portfolio.

7. **The brand makes full use of and co-ordinates a full repertoire of marketing activities to build equity**: a brand is made up of a number of elements that can be trademarked – logos, symbols, slogans, packaging, signage and so on. Strong brands use these elements in varying combinations to enhance or reinforce customer awareness of the brand or its image and also to protect the brand both competitively and legally. There are also specific roles that different marketing activities can contribute to building brand equity. For example, marketing communications can provide detailed product information, show consumers how and why (and by whom, where and when) a product is used, and associate a brand with a person, place or thing to improve or refine its image.
8. **The brand's managers understand what the brand means to consumers**: managers of strong brands appreciate the totality of their brand's image – all the different perceptions, beliefs, attitudes and behaviours consumers associate with the brand, whether the company intended them or not. As a result, managers are confident about making decisions about the brand. If they know what customers like or do not like about the brand and what core associations they have with it, they should be able to take actions that fit with the brand and do not create frictions.
9. **The brand is given proper support and that support is maintained over the long run**: brand equity requires a firm foundation such that consumers have the proper depth and breadth of brand awareness and strong, favourable and unique associations with the brand in their memory. Managers too often want to shortcut and bypass basic

branding considerations – such as achieving the necessary level of brand awareness – in favour of concentrating on 'flashier' aspects of brand building related to image.

10. **The company monitors sources of brand equity**: strong brands generally make good and frequent use of in-depth brand audits and ongoing brand-tracking studies. A brand audit is an exercise designed to assess the health of a brand. Typically it consists of a detailed internal description of exactly how the brand has been marketed (called a 'brand inventory') and a thorough external investigation, through focus groups and other consumer research, of what the brand does and could mean to consumers (called a 'brand exploratory'). Brand tracking monitors the marketing programme to see if it is having the intended brand-building effect on the target market.

Building a strong brand involves maximizing all 10 characteristics, though in some cases when a company focuses on improving one characteristic others may suffer. The trick is to assess how a brand performs on all 10 characteristics and then evaluate any move from all possible perspectives. How will this new advertising campaign affect customers' perception of price? How will this new product line affect our brand hierarchy? Does this shift in positioning gain enough ground to offset any potential damage caused if customers feel we've been inconsistent?

Ultimately, the value of the concept of brand equity to marketers depends on how they use it. It can help them to focus, giving them a way to interpret their past marketing performance and design their future marketing programmes. Everything a company does can help to enhance or detract from brand equity. Marketers who build strong brands have embraced the concept and use it to its fullest to clarify, implement and communicate their marketing strategy.

Rating your brand

You can use the 10 characteristics to rate your own brand (or those of your competitors).

Assess each of the characteristics on a scale of one to 10, where one is extremely poor and 10 is extremely good. Then create a bar chart that reflects the scores. Use this to stimulate discussion among everyone involved in the management of your brands. Remember to try to look at your own and your competitors' brands through consumers' eyes rather than your own.

RESOURCES

BOOK

Keller, Kevin Lane, *Strategic Brand Management,* Prentice Hall, Englewood Cliffs, 1998.

The company is king

TONY CRAM

The customer is king. Think again. Tony Cram takes a look at some unforeseen consequences of Customer Relationship Management.

OPEN a marketing or management journal and you will soon find an article extolling Customer Relationship Management (CRM). CRM books and websites are appearing with increasing frequency. So much so that CRM now appears to be the managerial flavour of the month. But while high powered processing of customer data can be a force for corporate good, all is not plain sailing.

CRM is the latest development in relationship marketing, which evolved from concepts of loyalty marketing in the early 1990s and the focus on customer intimacy of the later 1990s. The idea of understanding and providing for customer needs was highly customer-centric and 'the customer is king' pervaded management thinking and shaped company attitudes.

CRM changes the entire dynamic of this thinking. The new focus is company-centric. Data warehouses with relational databases can connect and analyze millions of transactions to understand the precise value of individual customers. For example, the US-based First Union Bank, knows how much profit a particular customer generates. It can extend this to forecast the potential value of future transactions. This knowledge enables companies to select the customers they want and, directly or indirectly, discard the customers they do not want. High-profile media coverage in April 2000 greeted the decision by the UK bank, Barclays, to close 171 branches whose customers collectively could not generate sufficient profit to make the branches viable. With CRM, the company is king.

It's one on one

CRM is defined as a data-driven approach to identify, profile and select the most profitable customers for focused attention to create the perception of ongoing personal relationships. The leading advocates of CRM are Don Peppers and Martha Rogers who propound a four point plan for managing customer relationships:[1]

1. Identification of customers.
2. Differentiation of customers within the customer base.
3. Interaction with the most valuable customers.
4. Customization of products and services to strengthen the relationship.

They categorize customers three ways. The first of these are the 'Most Valuable Customers' or MVCs and to these they add the 'Most Growable Customers' who represent new or existing customers calculated to offer the highest growth potential. The third group, labelled the 'Below Zeros', cost more to service than the profit they provide. CRM is about discriminating between profitable and unprofitable customers.

The benefit to the company is significant. Information on profitable customers enables managers to channel all efforts into their retention. For example, a mobile phone company uses caller identification on its help line to recognize and give priority to customers with high average monthly line usage. Best customers get a quicker resolution to queries and this enhances customer retention – in fact CRM can calibrate the percentage improvement.

Understanding the characteristics of the most profitable customers can also focus marketing efforts on attracting more customers with the same features and, therefore, a probability of similar profit performance in the future. For example, a business to business services supplier identified senior management stability as a significant characteristic of its most profitable customers. As a result, its business expansion strategy includes targeting prospect companies who exhibit the same continuity of top managers.

With pressure on sales resources, there is great interest in selecting the right prospective customers for long-term profitability. In looking across a variety of industries, global national and regional, I have identified a range of qualities which predict future profitability in potential customers (see Figure 1 for a 15-point checklist).

In effect the core benefit to the company is that it can direct resources productively, avoiding loss-making customers and no hope prospects. Sanwa Bank estimates that its customer service operation increased productivity by 14 percent in 1999 by focusing its resources on its 'A' customers.

From the customer's perspective, the most valuable customers should sense real benefits. At last their true worth is recognized with better products, more closely tailored to their requirements. Service levels should be higher. Over time British Airways becomes familiar with frequent First Class passengers' preferences for food, wine and reading matter and meets them. In the United States, Ford provides differentiated service for repeat purchasers of high profit vehicles, including priority response on the 1–800 service line and favourable treatment on repairs outside warranty periods.[2] In the UK, the Marriott Hanbury Manor Hotel has an added service for its profitable long stay guests – it provides personal business cards bearing the hotel phone and fax numbers.

For valuable customers, response to changing needs is also rapid. Mobile telephone companies are restlessly agile in seeking trends in youth segments and adding the next 'must-have' feature. The new benefit to the profitable customers is a predictive facility. Their suppliers are working hard to identify up-coming trends so that new solutions are in place before the customer discovers the problem. For example, credit card companies like Visa and MasterCard monitor the Icelandic market – the country with the highest credit card penetration and usage. They need to understand the experiences of Reykjavik card holders who no longer carry cash and apply those lessons to other markets.

The downside

Other customers see the flip side. Increasingly the cost of being an average value customer is paid in time. Software help line telephone calls will take longer to be answered because better customers are jumping the phone queue. Airline passengers wait in line while the more valuable travellers overtake them on the priority fast track. Tesco, the UK supermarket, knows that its most profitable customers have a pattern of shopping on Thursday evenings and hence you would expect it to reserve the most proficient check-out operators for that evening.

Another aspect is the diminution of choice. When the most valuable customers are offered first pick, then the average customer may not see the entire selection. There is a scarcity of second-hand Hondas, so when dealerships occasionally have available low mileage models previously driven by Honda management, they offer a 24-hour preview to their best car buyers and service customers. Catalogue retailers send out new season collections to their top shoppers, who experience close to 100 percent availability. Average customers, mailed 10 days to two weeks later, will be disappointed when some popular lines are out of stock.

Marginal and unprofitable customers face real drawbacks. For example, 'unlucky' holidaymakers with a history of losing a camera on every trip are discovering that no insurer will provide cover. Jobless single mothers without assets or prospects are finding it increasingly difficult to obtain banking services. As companies perfect their customer profitability model, some customers emerge as a cost to their supplier, not a contribution. The Wisconsin-based door maker, Weyerhaeuser, has reportedly shed 5,000 customers whose cost of supply was greater than their revenue. The era of cross-subsidization by other customers is coming to a close.

Customer shedding risks

There are real dangers to companies in moving down this track. Despite the profit attractions, there are risks. The media may champion unfortunates who are denied service and pillory the companies involved. The approach must be carefully considered.

For companies there is a five point process to assess the major risks:

1. **Identify loss makers**: overheads of service, support, cost of delivery, inventory costs of variety, and so on, are matched as accurately as possible to individual customers to determine individual customer profitability. Trend data on the customer, and typical performance of customers in the same category, forecasts whether the customer will become profitable in time. For example, banks find students become profitable two years after graduation. Customers who fall into the category of unprofitable today/unprofitable tomorrow are bad payers, those always seeking refunds or returning product, customers who use service support enormously and needlessly, customers who take up disproportionate amounts of time.

   A separate category is customers who abuse staff. The customers themselves may be profitable, but their cost in terms of impact they have on staff morale is sufficiently negative to warrant the customer's sacking. In his book, *Nuts*, Southwest Airlines chief, Herb Kelleher, tells of how he effectively fired the consistent complainer 'Mrs Crabapple'.

2. **Behaviour change**: can you change behaviours or move customers on to an automated system rather than discard them? There may be ways of influencing customers to alter their usage of products or services to make them profitable. Customers made aware of the impact of their specification changes may willingly improve. Training packages on newly installed automation equipment can diminish subsequent call-outs for Rockwell Automation service engineers and make customers more profitable. Financial incentives can

shape customer behaviours effectively. Limit the number of free calls to help lines. Single orders are notoriously expensive to handle, so Books-on-Line www.bol.com, encourages multi-buys with a delivery of £2.95 for up to 10 books purchased at the same time.

Alternatively, where the expensive element in customer service is staff time, you may be able to automate some services. For example, the UK retailer Argos provides in-store terminals which allow shoppers to check product availability themselves. This transforms the profitability of indecisive purchasers of low value items.

3. **Financial modelling**: when those customers who cannot be profitable have been identified as candidates for 'sacking', an important stage takes place. This constructs a financial model of the business without the costs and revenue of these customers. Savings are calculated for the future business without their consumption of service. For example, a brewery was able to close a depot, downsize the workforce and reduce the delivery fleet size, by eliminating low transaction customers located in remote areas. It is critical to evaluate the extent to which low value customers contribute to unavoidable overheads.
4. **Discarding customers**: how can you sack non-profitable customers without a negative impact on company reputation? There are seven techniques to deploy and it is critical that customer facing employees are briefed and trained in executing these approaches. Role play may assist.
   a. Direct comparison: seek a business review and provide comparative data which explains how certain of their needs are better met by other suppliers and recommend specific alternatives.
   b. Withdraw service: provide ample notice of cessation of service and recommend an alternative supply source.

c. Resolution to problems: use the opportunity presented when complaints arise, to explain how an alternative supplier may meet the customers needs better.
d. Wholesalers: redirect low value customers to a wholesaler. Wholesalers traditionally operate on lower cost structures than manufacturers' operations and may be able to take over tranches of customers.
e. Establish service priorities: explain your service priority system, and help less valuable customers to select another supplier who is willing to respond more speedily.
f. Promotion silence: reduce communication. Do not prompt renewals.
g. Discriminatory pricing: significant price increases imposed on loss-making customers can cause them to seek alternative sources. Builders will often quote high for work they would rather not take on.

5. **Learning the lessons**: after the customer list has been cleansed, important conclusions can be drawn. This covers the identification of patterns in desirable and undesirable customers which are then used in selecting new customers. It also addresses how expectations of new customers should be shaped at the outset to ensure profitability. For example, new warranty conditions may be imposed on new customers initially.

None of this can detract from the fact that CRM is a valuable tool. It cannot be un-invented. Your competitors will be applying its strengths to their customer portfolio. Be aware then, that they may be shedding unprofitable customers in your direction. Acquire new business with care. Use the knowledge from CRM to confer benefits on your most valuable customers. Moderate the impact of this on your mainstream customers. Finally, identify customers you no longer wish to serve and smooth their transition to suppliers better able to serve them.

Figure 1
Prospecting for profitable customers – 15 questions to ask

- Is the prospective customer well prepared, have they conducted their own needs analysis? Are they experienced purchasers?
- Is this organization seeking a supplier with complementary skills?
- Are they seeking full supplier qualification, references, accreditation?
- Do they require a high level of personalization and are not buying off the shelf?
- Are they service literate, asking for details of service and support?
- Do they place a high value on time?
- Are they brand aware and conscious of the image benefits you provide?
- Do they have a stable management team?
- Do you share a common culture, with similar values?
- Is a team of buyers involved who share agreed aims?
- Are they eager for multi-level involvement?
- Are they interested in experimenting, testing and learning with you?
- Have they been referred to you by an existing customer?
- Are they returning to you after a period of buying from a competitor?
- Can they demonstrate a pattern of long-term relationships with other suppliers?

Figure 2
How to sack loss-making customers – five point plan

1. Identify loss-making customers.
2. Seek to change behaviour or automate services.
3. Use financial modelling to simulate the impact of sacking.
4. Manage the de-marketing process to avoid negative publicity.
5. Apply the lessons to selecting new prospects and shape their behaviour.

REFERENCES

1. Peppers, Don, and Rodgers, Matha, *The One-to-One Field Book*, Capstone, Oxford, 1999.
2. *McKinsey Quarterly*, No. 4, 1999.

RESOURCES

BOOK

Cram, Tony, *The Power of Relationship Marketing*, FT Pitman, London, 1994.

WEB

www.ashridge.ac.uk

Ten commandments for a brand with a future

THOMAS GAD

Thomas Gad outlines the 10 most important rules for creating brands that will be successful and profitable, as well as building value for the long term.

1. A brand with a future is created in a person's mind (not by the product or service itself)

The traditional view of branding is product and service oriented. It's very much focused on the unique benefit of the product. But the world is changing and is full of examples of extremely virtual phenomena, which do not meet the criteria of the classical product or service. The emergent brands do not have the substance that we are used to attaching to a classic brand. A product or service without a recognized brand is pure utility and availability for the buyer, and can as such be replaced. A brand set in someone's mind is much more unique and, most importantly, individual.

2. A brand with a future must stand for something, be different (not necessarily pleasing to everybody)

'It's better to be something to someone, than nothing to everyone,' the saying goes, and that's very much a truth in branding. The traditional brand does not want to turn anybody down; usually it's a brand for a mass market product defined to attract a mass audience. The problem with that is, of course, that the brand becomes emotionally very shallow. Meeting the new individual audience, the recipe for success is to stand for something special, to have a philosophy and to be different not only in features but in attitude. Such a brand will create brand fans, or even brand groupies, that by sheer loyalty will not only stand by your brand for themselves, they will also enthusiastically introduce it to others. In addition, standing for something different in attitudes and values is often easier than maintaining staying power in product or service differences.

3. A brand with a future is involving like a dear friend

Friendship is one of the easiest ways to understand the subtleties of a brand. If you close your eyes and think about a friend and then try to describe what that friendship is all about, you are very much in the same situation as describing what a very good brand is for you. The words will fail, because the experience is beyond words. To create a brand like that you not only have to stand for something special, you also have to be involving. And to be involving as a brand, you can copy how you would be involving as a friend. Personal attention, recognition, giving nice little surprises, and doing exciting things with your friend would most probably improve your friendship, and the same goes for branding. You might additionally find a common cause in which to engage passionately, and you'll then have the most perfect recipe for success as a brand builder.

4. A brand with a future is always regarded as the company's most valuable asset

The brand is not just a marketing tool, it is quite often the critical 'substance' of your company, yet it is not formally seen as such.

Most of us recognize this, but we seem to ignore it. The reason is that the official system we live in has not been able to adjust to the change. Other, much less important assets have historically received much greater attention, things like property, machinery and technology, assets that are annually audited. So-called human capital is an asset not yet officially valued, but much discussed, and still the value of all these assets usually depends more on the strength of the brand as an asset than on anything else. We have all witnessed how a weak brand, losing trust in its markets, makes the rest of a 'solid' company worth very little.

Of course, this will change over time. Auditors won't forever accept auditing just a small and less important part of a company, and the legal system will not accept having the dominant part of a company value outside of the system, so to speak. The new generation of managers already acknowledge the change, and their focus on their company's brand, or brands, is totally different from that held by the old generation of managers.

5. A brand with a future is used by management to drive the company

There is no tool better than the brand for uniting the forces and the stakeholders inside and around your company. Leading a company today seems like a mission impossible: so many conflicting interests, so much ambition, in so many different directions. Managing is all about focusing mental energies. Any leakage of energy, any unproductive connections, will cause a loss of voltage, affecting the power of the brand on the market. And conversely, a powerful brand in the marketplace will charge up not only the people working inside the company but also the owners and public opinion.

This is a true chicken and egg situation, but what is good is that it's very much within your control as a manager. You can start the process from the inside, you don't have to wait for something else to happen first. Start with setting up a Brand Code and use it as a universal instrument of change.

6. A brand with a future is crystal clear about its role in the marketplace

There was a time when you could be a little bit of everything. It was a nice time, because you didn't have to say no to anything; if you weren't sure what to do, or decide, you just said 'yes' or 'maybe'! If you look at the structure of the traditional enterprise you still see the remains of that. But most of the world's leading companies have focused their businesses, driven by internationalization and tougher competition.

You now have to do very much the same thing with your brand. You not only have to focus on which business you are in, but also what role in that business you want to play. Are you a production brand, with unique know-how in methods or technology? Then you might take the consequences of that and build an ingredient brand, not locking yourself into distributing to one customer or channel only, but co-branding with everybody filling the criteria of your Brand Code. Or maybe you are a relation brand that has a very special knowledge of your customers and a unique distribution platform. Then you might take the consequences of this and build your brand into a meeting place, a portal, in which you should have the freedom to choose any production brand, or any source of production. This new focus on the role of your brand in your business is driven by the transparency of the market, which in turn is induced by the internet.

7. A brand with a future encourages creativity, not least among its customers

Interactivity and creativity form the name of the new game. A future brand has to be experienced as interactive and 'owned' and somehow created by its customers and company employees. Its products and services can always be improved, and continual improvement is the cornerstone of quality, but what is new is really putting the customer to work on this.

The forerunners in this include the software industry, which invented the most ingenious creativity and customer activity instrument of them all – the 'beta test'. Having beta testers not only helps the software producer to make a better, bug-free product, it produces prestige, ambassadors, and 'insiders', and above all it turns critics into supporters, all by using the tool of creativity. Human beings can't resist a creative challenge – if you ask someone to solve a problem that you have, you have the start of a possible friendship. Another software example is Linus Torvalds and Linux, a gigantic creative joint venture where all participators feel like owners, which they are in a way, since no one really owns this software – it's freeware.

Inspire yourself by these examples, and turn your brand into a real concern for a lot of people.

8. A brand with a future enjoys alliances with other brands (rather than maintaining exclusivity at all costs)

The traditional brands were very anxious not to involve themselves with other brands. And possibly rightly so, if you consider that few of them were really brands in the way we now view the term. They were more or less just trademarks or very shallow brands. But strong brands, standing for something special, distinctive, based on deeper values, brands like that have nothing to fear from connecting themselves to other brands, if there is a match in Brand Codes. Ingredient branding, co-branding, and co-branding activities are the latest way to explore the mindspace landscape of values that might be held in common for many brands. Sharing this common ground can make everybody a winner.

It doesn't really matter which is the strongest of the brands involved to begin with. A strong brand might strengthen its brand by co-branding with a less strong one that stands for interesting or refreshing values. And a small brand with a distinctive and exciting brand code can definitely be a winner if it joins a big and well-known one, again provided that the Brand Codes are not critically conflicting.

Every brand has everything to gain by exposing itself and connecting with the right things, in the right environment and the right kind of people. Your Brand Code will be able to help you check out what's right for your brand.

9. A brand with a future is best protected by itself (rather than by trademark laws)

Traditionally, trademark legal protection has been very important for protecting the brand. But in recent years, with internationalization and the transparency of the web, it has become very difficult to control all the legal aspects of a brand. Many established brand owners have had many problems with websites taken in their name and so on.

That legal trademark protection may become less important in the future. In a transparent web-driven culture, consumers will look more for inner values in the brand. The new consumer will know who is behind a certain brand, where something is manufactured, how responsible the company is, and so on. Any fraud or deviation will be more easily discovered, but also reported to other consumers on the web. The deeper relationship with the customer, the total information that the customer will have, makes it meaningless to create bad copies or imitations. A copy or imitation always builds on the lack of knowledge that it is fraud. Of course, a perfect fraud will still be confusing until it's discovered and reported on the web. A fraud against a brand that maintains a base of loyal customers may indeed further strengthen the bond between the customers and the brand under attack.

A distinct philosophy brand with a good Brand Code and a community of brand friends will be more important for protecting the brand than any legal protection of the trademark.

10. A brand with a future is a vehicle for the transfer of both value and values

The tenth and last of the commandments wraps up the nine before – and the book as a whole for that matter – and it connects with the first commandment, giving branding a more general, economic, and philosophical base to stand on.

The purpose of the brand is to be a vehicle for transferring both value and values. From one product generation to the next. From one product to its derivatives, also called line extension. From one kind of a product to another kind, also called brand extension. Between company and product, and vice versa. Between the company, product, and its customers, and between buying occasions. And between the company and staff, owners and public opinion.

Why is this so important? First, the brand is not only an economic but also a philosophical mechanism. It's not just about money, it's about culture and humanity as well. And in the future development of the brand, the philosophical aspect will be essential to produce economic results. In the years to come we may well see a change in business attitude and thinking: from the value chain to a chain of values.

RESOURCES

BOOK

Gad, Thomas, *4D-Branding*, FT Prentice Hall, London, 2001.

WEB

www.differ.com

MARKETING

AFFILIATE MARKETING

AFFILIATE marketing was one of the first marketing models rolled out on the internet. Amazon.com, for example, is one of its most well-known adherents. What internet user hasn't come across the omnipresent Amazon banner while surfing some special interest site?

It works like this. Let's say an e-tailer sets up a site selling Persian Rugs – magicarpetz.com. Magicarpetz then contacts other sites, an interior design portal possibly, or a home furnishings e-store, where prospective rug purchasers may be loitering, and persuades the other company to carry a magicarpetz advertising banner on its site.

The site affiliate in return receives a reward for allowing magicarpetz to place the banner. This reward could be linked to the number of surfers clicking through the banner advert. Or it might be linked to the number of leads produced. Alternatively, it may be linked to actual sales made in the form of a paid commission.

The beauty of the model is that magicarpetz can build an extensive advertising network in prime positions for no upfront costs. In turn the affiliate gets money for nothing other than giving over an unused space on its site to a magicarpetz banner.

Affiliate marketing is not an entirely failsafe marketing technique. There are several potential pitfalls. If a fictional e-tailer, magicarpetz, signed up too many affiliates without checking the quality of their websites it could easily damage its brand image. There are few surfers who have not winced at a homepage piled to the rafters with affiliate links. And then there are the disputes over site traffic. What if the affiliates claim they sent X number of people to magicarpetz, where as magicarpetz reckon its more like Y. Then again it could be such a roaring success that the rugs fly out of the warehouse – but too much time is then spent managing the affiliate program that can't be automated and customer service may suffer as a result.

This is why a number of companies have sprung up offering to manage, to a lesser or greater extent, the affiliate marketing process. The affiliate networks, that include companies such as BeFree, LinkShare and Click Trade, take a lot of the hassle out of setting up an affiliate program. They can plug a would-be affiliate marketer straight into their own ready made network of affiliates numbering anywhere between 50,000 and 250,000. It's not a free service, however. Affiliate network companies make their money, in the main, by charging commission on affiliate earnings – usually around the 30 percent mark.

FOUR Ps OF MARKETING

IN 1960, E. Jerome McCarthy introduced a new concept to the world of business theory. McCarthy took the marketing mix (defined by marketing's eminence grise, Philip Kotler, as 'the set of marketing tools that the firm uses to pursue its marketing objectives in the target market') and identified its critical ingredients as product, price, place and promotion. This became known as the Four Ps of marketing. It is a formula that has stood the test of time, and is still recited by students and known by virtually everyone in business.

At the time of their inception, the Four Ps encapsulated the essence of traditional marketing. A company that successfully focused its attention on all of the Four Ps could develop a soundly based marketing strategy. A company that failed to do so – or that allowed its focus to shift – was unlikely to excel at marketing.

Examining the four categories, first there is the *product* (or the service) being offered. Kotler provided a definition of a product as 'a bundle of physical, services, and symbolic particulars expected to yield satisfaction or benefits to the buyer'. (This has since been distilled down to 'a product is something that is viewed as capable of satisfying a want'.)

Next comes the issue of *pricing*. In recent years this has become ever more complex, with an array of pricing strategies covering everything from premium pricing to seasonal or even daily pricing.

The other two elements, place and promotion, are more wide ranging. *Place* embraces how and where the company makes the product accessible to potential customers. This includes, therefore, distribution and logistics – and, increasingly, cyberspace.

Finally comes *promotion*. This hides a multitude of activities, all of which have enjoyed an explosion of growth over the last 20 or so years. These include communication, personal selling, advertising, direct marketing, sales promotion and public relations.

The Four Ps were a useful summary of the dominant parts of the marketing mix in the 1960s when mass industrial marketing was the order of the day. However, the nature of business has changed. No longer is the emphasis on volumes, but on customer delight. No longer does a company blindly start with the product and then attempt to find a market; the customer is the starting point.

The nature of marketing has also fundamentally changed. The divisions between the Four Ps are increasingly blurred, sometimes non-existent. For example, the Four Ps are of limited value if you are marketing and selling your products over the internet. However, despite great technological leaps forward, product, price, place and promotion are still important. The trouble is that defining their exact meaning, role, and potential is more and more difficult.

KOTLER, PHILIP

WHILE championing the role of marketing over 30 years, Philip Kotler (born 1931) has coined phrases such as 'mega marketing',

'demarketing', and 'social marketing'. His numerous books include the definitive textbook on the subject, *Marketing Management* (now in its eighth edition).

Kotler has a penchant for useful definitions.

> *'When I am asked to define marketing in the briefest possible way I say marketing is meeting needs profitably. A lot of us meet needs – but businesses are set up to do it profitably. Marketing is the homework that you do to hit the mark that satisfies those needs exactly. When you do that job, there isn't much selling work to do because the word gets out from delighted customers that this is a wonderful solution to our problems.'*[1]

Kotler also provides a useful definition of a product as 'anything that can be offered to a market for attention, acquisition, use, or consumption that might satisfy a want or need'. He says that a product has five levels: the core benefit ('marketers must see themselves as benefit providers'); the generic product; the expected product (the normal expectations the customer has of the product); the augmented product (the additional services or benefits added to the product); and, finally, the potential product ('all of the augmentations and transformations that this product might ultimately undergo in the future').

The central shift that Kotler has described is from 'transaction-oriented' marketing to 'relationship marketing'. 'Good customers are an asset which, when well managed and served, will return a handsome lifetime income stream to the company. In the intensely competitive marketplace, the company's first order of business is to retain customer loyalty through continually satisfying their needs in a superior way,' says Kotler.

Kotler regards marketing as the essence of business and more. 'Good companies will meet needs; great companies will create markets', he writes.

> *'Market leadership is gained by envisioning new products, services, lifestyles, and ways to raise living standards. There is a vast difference between companies that offer me-too products and those that create new product and service values not even imagined by the marketplace. Ultimately, marketing at its best is about value creation and raising the world's living standards.'*

REFERENCE

1. Mazur, Laura, 'Silent satisfaction', source unknown.

LEVITT, TED

THE July–August 1960 issue of the *Harvard Business Review* launched the career of American academic Ted Levitt (born 1925). It included his article entitled 'Marketing myopia', which, totally unexpectedly, brought marketing back on to the corporate agenda. 'Marketing myopia' has sold over 500,000 reprints and has entered a select group of articles that have genuinely changed perceptions.[1]

In 'Marketing myopia', Levitt argued that the central preoccupation of corporations should be with satisfying customers, rather than simply producing goods. Companies should be marketing led rather than production led and the lead must come from the chief executive and senior management: 'management must think of itself not as producing products but as providing customer-creating value satisfactions.' (In his ability to coin new management jargon, as well as his thinking, Levitt was ahead of his time.)

At the time of Levitt's article, the fact that companies were production led was not open to question. Henry Ford's success in mass production had fuelled the belief that low-cost production was the key to business success.

Levitt observed that production-led thinking inevitably led to narrow perspectives. He argued that companies must broaden their view of the nature of their business. Otherwise, their customers will soon be forgotten. 'The railroads are in trouble today not because the need was filled by others ... but because it was not filled by the railroads themselves,' wrote Levitt. 'They let others take customers away from them because they assumed themselves to be in the railroad business rather than in the transportation business. The reason they defined their industry wrong was because they were railroad-oriented instead of transportation-oriented; they were product-oriented instead of customer oriented.' The railroad business was constrained, in Levitt's view, by a lack of willingness to expand its horizons.

In 'Marketing myopia', Levitt also made a telling distinction between the tasks of selling and marketing. 'Selling concerns itself with the tricks and techniques of getting people to exchange their cash for your product. It is not concerned with the values that the exchange is all about. And it does not, as marketing invariably does, view the entire business process as consisting of a tightly integrated effort to discover, create, arouse, and satisfy customer needs,' he wrote.

Levitt's other main insight was on the emergence of globalization. In the same way as he had done with 'Marketing myopia', he signalled the emergence of a major movement and then withdrew to watch it ignite. 'The world is becoming a common marketplace in which people – no matter where they live – desire the same products and lifestyles. Global companies must forget the idiosyncratic differences between countries and cultures and instead concentrate on satisfying universal drives,' he said.

REFERENCE

1. Other career-enhancing HBR articles include Robert Hayes and William Abernathy's 'Managing our way to economic decline'; Frederick Herzberg's 'One more time how do you motivate employees?'; Hamel and Prahalad's 'The core competence of the corporation'.

PERMISSION MARKETING

IT was Seth Godin, the former president of Yoyodyne Entertainment

and VP of Direct Marketing at Yahoo!, who first came up with the term Permission Marketing.

The idea was to improve on what Godin termed 'interruption marketing'. Initially the marketer needs to interrupt the viewer's activity in order to grab their attention. So, for example, on the internet an interstitial will be a break in the flow of the viewer's experience. Wouldn't it be better, thought Godin, if at least after the first interruption the marketer obtained the 'permission' of the consumer to market *with* them rather than *at* them.

The premise is that consumers will willingly give up valuable personal information and grant permission for marketers to send them product information so long as they are given sufficient incentive. This then is the challenge for the permission marketer, finding the right incentive to persuade the consumer to grant permission.

Godin rolled out several variations of permission marketing campaign during his stint at Yoyodyne. E-mail and web promotions were built around competitions, gameshows and sweepstakes. For example the company ran a 'Get Rich Quick' campaign where a prize of $100,000 was enough to tempt 250,000 players to the client's site. Following on from this initial contact sponsors were able to build relationships with the customers through e-mail messages that led to the next level of the game. This information was given in return for permission to pitch products.

Godin offers four simple guidelines for permission marketers to remember:

1. People are selfish – they care about themselves not the permission marketer.
2. Never rent or sell permission to a third party.
3. Permission can be revoked – it's not given for ever.
4. Permission is not static – unlike buying an address.

Permission marketers have to be careful not to abuse their permission. They also have to manage the relationship if permission is revoked, and also if the permission has lapsed. It's a fine line between e-mailing product information under permission, and spamming.

RELATIONSHIP MARKETING

RELATIONSHIP marketing refers to the benefits that ongoing relationships with key customers can bring to an organization. The idea behind it goes back to the earliest trading times, but the term entered the vocabulary of management during the 1980s. At that time, management writers observed it at work within the high-tech business community of California's Silicon Valley.

In 1985, marketing guru Regis McKenna wrote the first book devoted to the marketing of high-technology companies, *The Regis Touch*. 'Many of the small highly innovative Silicon Valley companies didn't market new products to the larger computer companies on an individual basis in the traditional way,' he observed. Instead, they sought to establish strategic relationships that allowed the smaller company to work almost as part of the customer's organization.

In a very fast-moving industry, the closeness of these relationships was critical to the ability of smaller firms to develop solutions that met the needs of their customers. It became apparent that their success often depended on personal relationships that had developed into close friendships. Rather than attend to the marketing of products or projects through traditional means, these smaller companies worked extra hard at maintaining ongoing relationships.

Relationship Marketing, McKenna's third book, focused on the interactive relationships vital to market acceptance in the 'age of the customer', and drew wider attention to the concept of relationship marketing.

The logic of relationship marketing is simple: rather than communicate intermittently with key customers, it makes more sense to develop a relationship of mutual trust so that the dialogue is continuous. Everyone in business has been told that success is all about attracting and retaining customers. But once companies have attracted customers, they often overlook the second half of the equation.

Failing to concentrate on retaining as well as attracting customers costs businesses huge amounts of money every year. It has been estimated that the average company loses between 10 and 30 percent of its customers annually. Organizations are now beginning to wake up to these lost opportunities and calculate the financial implications. Research in the US found that a 5 percent decrease in the number of defecting customers led to profit increases of between 25 and 85 percent.

The route to customer retention is relationship marketing, nurturing relationships with customers that create loyalty. Relationship-building programmes now cover a multitude of activities, from customer magazines to vouchers and gifts. In essence, they aim to persuade a person to use a preferred vendor in order to take advantage of the benefits on offer, whether it is a trip to Acapulco or a price-reduction voucher for a calorie-controlled canned drink. Sceptics will say there is nothing new in this. Indeed, businesses have been giving long-standing customers discounts and inducements since time immemorial. What is now different is the highly organized way in which companies are attempting to build relationships and customer loyalty.

The idea is that if you are continually aware of what your customers or partners require and keep them informed of developments within your own organization, the customer– supplier link becomes almost a seamless web. In relationship marketing, the details of the products and services become subservient to the trust that has been established. After all, why would a customer go elsewhere if you are always monitoring and adjusting what you are doing to meet their needs now and in the future? The advantage of such an arrangement is that problems can be averted before they become a crisis. The only reason for losing the customer is if the relationship breaks down.

Technology is likely to have a marked effect on relationship marketing which has evolved into CRM. On the one hand, the emergence of the internet as a global marketplace means that customers are likely to become increasingly promiscuous, able to flirt with suppliers all over the world. At the same time, technology also allows relationship marketing programmes to become ever more sophisticated. When it comes to creating loyal customers, the database is king. Databases mean that companies can target audiences more effectively.

– CHAPTER 5 –

Finance

'There are but two ways of paying debt: increase of industry in raising income, increase of thrift in laying out.' THOMAS CARLYLE

'Nothing so cements and holds together all the parts of a society as faith or credit, which can never be kept up unless men are under some force or necessity of honestly paying what they owe to one another.' MARCUS TULLIUS CICERO

'Annual income twenty pounds, annual expenditure nineteen six, result happiness. Annual income twenty pounds, annual expenditure twenty pounds nought and six, result misery.'

CHARLES DICKENS

'Business is many things, the least of which is the balance sheet. It is a fluid, ever changing, living thing, sometimes building to great peaks, sometimes falling to crumbled lumps. The soul of a business is a curious alchemy of needs, desires, greed and gratifications mixed together with selflessness, sacrifices and personal contributions far beyond material rewards.' HAROLD GENEEN

The value of being in control

LUIGI ZINGALES

Despite many differences throughout the world in the way companies are sold and acquired, there is one common element – investors care about control, which suggests it is valuable. But why? Luigi Zingales outlines why people will pay a lot to control a company.

THIS question of valuing control, though perhaps a little naive, is not without merit. By their very nature, all common shares have equal rights. A majority shareholder is not entitled to receive a penny more per share than all other shareholders. So why should any investor pay a premium to acquire control?

The only possible answer is that, although all shares are created equal, some are more equal than others.

What makes controlling shareholders more equal is that they have the right to shape corporate policy. The crucial question, then, becomes how this right translates into higher benefits for the controlling party that are not shared by other shareholders (the so-called 'private benefits of control').

If private benefits of control exist, then it is easy to explain why control is valuable. But what exactly are they?

The academic literature often identifies them as the 'psychic' value some shareholders attribute simply to being in control. For example, the Michelins probably would value being in control of the famous tyre company founded by their ancestors even if they were not to receive a penny from it.

Although this is certainly a factor in a number of cases, its practical importance is likely to be trivial.

A second, only slightly more convincing, explanation identifies the private benefits of control in the perquisites enjoyed by top executives (and not by their fellow shareholders who pay the tab). There is no lack of examples, as masterfully illustrated in the book *Barbarians at the Gate*. Many executives enjoy golfing and partying with world celebrities at their company's expense and using corporate jets to fly their friends and families around the country. Yet we have to admit that if this is what private benefits are all about we do not need to worry too much about the value of control. In the context of companies worth billions of dollars, the value of these perquisites is simply too small to matter.

Only in the presence of more significant sources of private benefits should the value of control play a prominent role in the theory and practice of finance.

Consider, for example, the value of the information a corporate executive acquires thanks to his or her role in the company. Some of this information pertains directly to the company's business. Some of it reflects potential opportunities in other more or less related areas.

It is fairly easy for a controlling shareholder to choose to exploit these opportunities through another company he or she owns or is associated with, with no advantage for the remaining shareholders. The net present value of these opportunities represents a private benefit of control.

Another source of private benefits is the possibility of internalizing, through other companies controlled by the same party, some of the externalities generated by corporate decisions.

Consider, for example, a shareholder who controls 51 percent of two companies, let's say A and B, operating in the same market. Suppose that there is excess capacity in this market and, thus, some plants need to be closed. In this situation the closure of any plant will reduce overcapacity and so will increase the value of all the other plants.

If the controlling shareholder closes some plants in company B, he or she will experience an increase in value not only of the B shares but also of the A shares. This increase in A shares is a benefit enjoyed by the controlling party and not by B's minority shareholders (unless they own the same quantity of A's shares) and, thus, represents a private benefit of control.

A third source of private benefits is associated with the controlling party's ability to fix transfer prices between a company and its customers and suppliers.

A company controlled by its employees, for example, can pay higher wages and benefits to its workforce. Similarly, a bank controlled by one of its borrowers can make larger and cheaper loans to its parent company.

The ability to manipulate transfer prices can be used even in the absence of business dealings between the controlling company and its subsidiary. Imagine that company A owns 50 percent of company B and 100 percent of company C.

In that case A would find it profitable to transfer B's assets to C at a below market price. For any dollar that B's assets are underestimated, company A loses 50 cents through its B holdings but gains one dollar through its C holdings. A net gain of 50 cents!

I am sure that at this point the reader is wondering whether most (if not all) of the sources of private benefits that I described are *de facto* illegal and, as such, more in the realm of interest of criminal investigators than financial economists.

In fact, there is no doubt that in their most extreme forms these strategies *are* illegal and extremely rare. Nevertheless, there are several reasons why we should expect more moderate versions of these strategies to be more pervasive.

First, in some countries some of these strategies are not illegal at all. Second, even when a law does exist it might be impossible to enforce. For example, educated economists can legitimately disagree on what is the 'fair' transfer price of a certain asset or product. As a result, small deviations from the 'fair' transfer price might be difficult or impossible to prove in court. If these small deviations are applied to a large volume trade, however, they can easily generate sizeable private benefits.

Finally, even if these distortions can be proved in court, it is possible that nobody has the incentive to do so. For example, it might be prohibitively expensive for small shareholders to sue management.

In other words, if private benefits of control were easily quantifiable, then those benefits would not be private (accruing only to the control group) any longer because outside shareholders would claim them in court.

Nevertheless, there are two indirect methods to try to assess empirically the magnitude of these private benefits of control.

The first method is very simple.[1] Whenever a control block changes hands, they measure the difference between the price per share paid by the acquirer and the price quoted in the market the day *after* the announcement of the sale.

The market price represents an unbiased estimate of the value of a share for minority shareholders. Any amount paid in excess of it by the acquirer of the control block represents a minimum estimate of the buyer's willingness to pay for the private benefits of control he or she expects to enjoy.

Using a sample of control block transfers in the US, they find that the value of control is approximately 4 percent of the total market value of a company.

This method also makes clear why the takeover premium cannot be used by itself as a measure of the private benefits of control. When a takeover is announced, the market price incorporates two pieces of information: 1. that the company is likely to be run by a different management team; 2. that somebody is willing to pay a premium for control.

The takeover premium is a combination of these two elements and, in general, it is impossible to separate them. Only when there are two classes of common stock with differential voting rights can we try to disentangle these two components.

This leads to the second method of estimating the value of private benefits of control.

By using the price difference between two classes of stock, with similar or identical dividend rights but different voting rights, one can easily obtain an estimate of the value of a vote. If control is valuable, then corporate votes, which allocate control, should be valuable as well. How valuable?

It depends on how decisive some votes are in allocating control and how valuable control is. If one can find a reasonable proxy for the strategic value of votes in winning control – for example in forming a winning coalition block – then one can infer the value of control from the relationship between the market price of the votes and their strategic role.

I have inferred the value of control from the relationship between the value of corporate votes and a synthetic measure of the distribution of voting power called the Shapley value.[2]

Interestingly, when I applied this method to a sample of US companies I obtained the same value as Barclay and Holderness (4 percent). By contrast, when I applied it to a sample of Italian companies I estimated the value of control at 30 percent of the market value of equity.

In spite of the magnitude of this estimate, all the evidence I collected indicates that if anything it underestimates the true value of control in Italy. But why should the value of control be so much higher in Italy than in the US? And what should we expect it to be in other countries?

Since the value of control is simply the present value of the private benefits enjoyed by the controlling party, the answer is easy.

The magnitude of the private benefits of control, and thus the value of control, depends on the degree of protection offered to minority investors in each country. Without proper disclosure, large investors can more easily hide their abuses and hence find it easier to take advantage of their controlling position.

Similarly, lax law enforcement makes it more difficult to detect and punish these abuses, making them more attractive.

That small investors are better protected in the US than in Continental Europe is not only consistent with casual empiricism but has been documented in a systematic way by La Porta *et al.*[3]

But even in the US, privately held companies carry large control premiums (minority discounts). Interestingly, the reason appraisers adduce for this premium is the lack of protection of minority shareholders in privately held business.

So it is not the good nature of Americans that restrains them from abusing their control position, but rather the rigid oversight by the Securities and Exchange Commission. It is not unusual, for example, for the SEC to investigate large personal expenses that a controlling shareholder bills to his or her company.

Interestingly, once we admit the existence of sizeable private benefits of control, a lot of the standard finance results break down.

For example, the value of a company cannot any longer be estimated simply by multiplying the market price of a share by the number of shares. If one shareholder controls a majority of votes, the market price will simply reflect the value of minority shares and will grossly underestimate the value of a company.

By contrast, when two large shareholders are fighting to reach a majority, the market price of a stock will be mainly influenced by the control value and will overestimate the total value of a company.

More importantly, the efficient working of the financial market may be jeopardized. Large controlling shareholders will be more interested in maximizing the value of their private benefits than the total market value of their company.

Consequently, investors, anticipating this behaviour, will shy away from buying the stocks. This, in turn, will lead to an underdevelopment of security markets. The paucity of observations notwithstanding, there would appear to be a strong negative correlation between the magnitude of the voting premium and the size of the stock market relative to the gross domestic product. This is an important lesson developing countries should not ignore.

REFERENCES

[1] Barclay, M.J. and Holderness, C.G., 1989, 'Private benefits of control of public corporations', *Journal of Financial Economics* 25: 371–395.

[2] Zingales, L., 1994, 'The value of the voting right: a study of the Milan Stock Exchange'. *Financial Studies* 7: 125–148; Zingales, L., 1995, 'What determines the value of corporate votes?', *Quarterly Journal of Economics,* 1047–1073.

[3] La Porta, R., de Silanes Shleifer, F. Lopez and Vishny R., 1996, *Law and Finance,* Working Paper 5661.

RESOURCES

BOOKS

Snaith, Bill and Walker, Jane, *Managing Tomorrow Today: Dynamic financial management,* FT Prentice Hall, London, 2001.

Mastering Finance, FT Prentice Hall, London, 1999.

The revolution in risk management

ANTHONY M. SANTOMERO

Anthony M. Santomero explains why corporations need to manage risk and outlines risk management policy.*

CORPORATE managers are interested both in expected profitability and the risk, or the variability, of reported earnings. This concern is rationalized, or explained, by the existence of costs that vary across the range of possible profit figures associated with any given expected performance. Therefore, the firm is led to treat the variability of earnings as a decision variable that it selects, subject to the usual constraints on management.

How it proceeds to manage the risk position of its activity – how are risks being managed? – is the area of concern here.

The question is easy enough. The answer is more difficult.

The area of risk management can be divided into three sub-fields. While there are overlaps, the questions, answers and open issues vary by area of discussion. It is, therefore, useful to address each of the following questions in turn:

- How should risks be managed?
- What have non-financial firms done by way of risk management?
- How have financial firms addressed the issue?

*This article was written while Dr Santomero was Richard K. Mellon Professor of Finance at the Wharton School.

The three areas can be seen as two separate problems: theory and application. However, in as much as financial firm risk management has developed somewhat separately, it is useful to treat the application of risk management techniques in the financial sector as a separate issue.

This first question is the easiest to answer but hard to implement. To the extent that a firm's manager is making the decision to further advance his or her own best interests the problem becomes the usual one of portfolio choice.

Projects and/or activities are selected using the standard risk-return trade-off that finance has long promulgated. Projects are selected according to their expected profitability, their variance and the covariance of their returns with other projects within the firm.

On the other hand, if the manager's concern over risk is due to its effect on overall firm value, then managers must recognize the effect of volatility on market value. This will lead them to alter their decisions and encourage risk management and control.

In either case, implementing such a risk-management procedure requires a strategy that includes both risk identification and risk reduction. The former involves an analysis of the drivers of firm performance and the reasons for the volatility in earnings and/or market value. The latter is accomplished through the use of standard procedures of risk reduction, such as standard diversification procedures, as well as the establishment of rules that limit potential extreme downside results.

From theory to practice, we move from the neat realm of concept into the difficult area of actual implementation. Here, little information exists on the practices currently employed by nonfinancial firms. General management practices to dampen the variability of cash flow and/or profitability are not documented in any systematic way.

Nonetheless, it is generally accepted that risk management can be conducted in two distinct ways. Either a firm can engage in activities that together result in less volatility than they would exhibit individually or it can engage in financial transactions that will have a similar effect.

The first approach is to embark upon a diversification strategy in the portfolio of businesses operated by the firm; in short, engage in diversification by conglomerate merger. However, conglomerate activity, while once a popular strategy recommended and pursued in the industrial sector, has fallen out of favour. Most firms have learned that they do not necessarily have value-added expertise in more than one area and have found it hard to prosper across industry lines.

As a result, firms concerned about the volatility of earnings have turned to the financial markets. This is because these markets have developed more direct approaches to risk management that transcend the need to invest directly in activities that reduce volatility.

Financial risk management, using financial products such as swaps, options and futures, can accomplish these same ends and has experienced explosive growth. Together, these derivative products have proved to be an important means of risk trading.

In many respects the story associated with risk management for industrial firms is transferable to their financial counterparts. However, the issue is somewhat more complicated for financial firms.

These firms deal in financial markets, as principals and agents, and have a long history of both hedging capability and taking positive risk positions. In fact, it could be argued that their franchise involves taking the financial risk from the non-financial sector.

However, taking financial risk does not imply keeping it. As corporate entities, these organizations, like their non-financial counterparts, must deal with the same issues that motivate the rest of the private sector.

While it could be argued that the existence of regulatory oversight and its implicit guarantee makes these firms less risk averse, the existence of regulators that charter and sustain the institutions' franchise makes risk a real issue of concern.

Management, therefore, must find the correct place for risk management in a sector that has both a reason for taking financial risk and reasons for concern over doing so.

For this purpose, it is useful to distinguish two ways of delivering financial services. These can be provided either as an agent or as a principal. In the former, risk is borne by the two sides of the transaction, with little remaining with the financial institution that facilitated it. In the latter, risk is absorbed by the financial institution itself because it places its balance sheet between the two sides of the transaction.

The choice between these two techniques seems to depend upon the institution's value added or unique expertise in managing the associated risk. For some risks, the institution frequently finds itself in the position of absorbing risk associated with its asset services rather than transferring it while for others the opposite is true.

Empirically, the latter group, where financial transactions transfer risk to the buyer of assets, is growing more rapidly. As information and transaction costs have declined, the fraction of financial assets held by risk-transferring institutions such as mutual funds, pension funds and various unit trusts has increased relative to those held in risk-absorbing institutions such as commercial banks and other depositories. This is due to the decline in the returns offered to these institutions to bear such risks.

Nonetheless, balance sheet risk management is still an important issue in the financial sector. For those institutions that do accept certain types of financial risk, because of their chosen business strategy, risk control and management procedures are essential.

Conceptually, these should involve the same steps and obtain the same results as indicated above. The drivers of uncertainty must be identified and risk reduction strategies outlined. The distinction here is that the risks are somewhat different than those facing the non-financial sector.

The fact that risk matters is, perhaps, not news to senior managers. However, the news is that there is a better understanding of why risk matters and how it should be managed.

Whether a firm is in the manufacturing sector or financial services, it has risks that need to be managed. In today's business environment no organization is immune from risk and none can be without a risk-management and control process.

With the advent of financial change and asset innovation, we have begun to develop a deep understanding of how to fashion an appropriate risk management system. In fact, the implementation of broad risk management systems has become big business – indeed a growth area of management interest and management consulting.

What does such a system involve?

As noted above, it begins with a careful identification of the causes of volatility – the factors that lead to variation in performance.

Next, the risks that have been so identified must be actively managed. Recent research has shown how this is accomplished by the establishment of standardized procedures that measure, monitor and limit the risk-taking activity of a firm so as to reduce the volatility of performance. Such systems usually include four parts:

- Standards and reports, which identify, measure and monitor the factors that cause volatility.
- Limits and controls on each of the factors and on each member of the organization that adds risk to the firm's performance profile.
- Guidelines and management recommendations concerning appropriate current exposure to these same risks.
- Accountability and compensation programmes that lead mid-level managers to take the process seriously.

Shareholders care about risk, the stock market cares and, as has been said, so should senior management. The challenge for these same managers is to embed a risk control system within their organization so as to reduce the volatility of profitability and engender a risk control mentality throughout the organization.

RESOURCES

BOOKS

Walsh, Ciaran, *Key Management Ratios*, FT Pitman, London, 1996.

Holliwell, John, *The Financial Risk Manual*, FT Prentice Hall, London, 2000.

Real options analysis

SYD HOWELL

Syd Howell explores a new technique that is having a fundamental impact on finance and investment.

REAL Options Analysis is a new and fast-growing technique that is changing the way we think about finance, economics, business strategy, and even biology. Nobel Laureate Merton Miller has said that Real Options Analysis 'should dramatically change both the way finance is taught in business schools, and the way the theory of investment is taught in economics departments'. Companies like Shell, Anaconda, and Hewlett-Packard are among its early users.

The kind of decisions that can be affected by Real Options Analysis include:

- Whether we should invest in a research and development project.
- How much we should pay to acquire technical know-how, patents, or licences.
- At what price we should be willing to buy or sell a brand.
- Whether to build new operating capacity, and if so how much.
- Make or buy.
- Whether to expand existing operations by hiring new staff, or by paying overtime, or by hiring temporary staff through agencies.
- At what price to accept a deal that will tie up our operating capacity and/or fix our input or output prices (e.g. long-term deals for electricity supply or generation).

- How to compare long-term financing deals with different conditions.
- When to 'mothball' a plant and when to bring it out of mothballs.
- When to scrap a plant.
- (For government policy) How to design policies and incentives in order to regulate markets and encourage economic growth.

How is real options analysis different?

Real Options Analysis has made some of the traditional tools of analysis, such as DCF (discounted cashflow) and NPV (net present value), partially obsolete. These methods still exist within Real Options Analysis, and in special cases we can use DCF or decision tree methods in traditional ways. But we now know that in many situations the traditional methods lead to wrong answers. In Real Options Analysis it is now usual to call traditional NPV analysis 'naive' NPV.

What is a Real Option?

In logical terms, a real option exists when the future state of the market is impossible to forecast exactly, but at one or more times in the future we will have the right to check out the state of the market, and then take whatever action will be best for us, given the state of the market at that future time.

The heart of real options analysis is about putting a value on this sort of economic opportunity. It involves new ways of thinking about the meaning and value of flexibility.

Some examples of real options:

- We own the rights to a TV cartoon character that was popular 10 years ago, but has now lost popularity. We can invest money to exploit the character at any time (e.g. making spin-off products), but we will naturally only invest if and when public taste changes in the character's favour. (An example of a decision about this real option: at what price should we be willing to sell the rights?)

- We own an electricity generating plant in the US that has a high fuel cost per megawatt hour. We could produce electricity at any time, but we naturally only choose to produce when the price of electricity rises above our variable costs, and this only happens in the summer, during the peak demand for air conditioning. (Examples of decisions about this real option: how much would it be worth investing to upgrade our plant to greater fuel efficiency? What should we sell the plant for? At what fixed flat price should we accept a forward commitment to produce whenever requested?)
- Our R&D department is proposing to develop a new technology to give hair a metallic colouring. If this technology works we could invest in plants to produce the hair colouring on a global scale, but we need not invest in the plants unless and until metallic hair catches on. Right now a strong fashion for ethnic and 'earth mother' styles would make metallic hair hard to sell, and even if metallic hair does ever catch on, the craze is unlikely to last for ever. (Example of a decision about this real option: what is it worth spending to create the technology?)
- We own a fleet of oil tankers, which we charter to oil companies. This year the business is hugely profitable, owing to a sudden demand for oil, but we and other operators have spare tankers in mothballs that we can reactivate by spending money on refurbishment. (Examples of decisions about this real option: how high do charter rates have to rise before we start reactivating our old tankers? Should we accept a longer-term charter contract, at a rate lower than today's spot rate? Even at today's spot rate, our smallest tankers are unprofitable to operate, and it costs us money to

keep them in mothballs – should we scrap our smallest tankers, thus saving the annual cost of mothballing, and gaining the value of the steel?)

- We own a copper mine that is unprofitable at today's ore price (selling price is below variable cost), yet we are still producing because the market may eventually turn up, and because if we stop producing we will have to spend money on drainage, in order to keep the mine safe for possible reopening, after which it will be more costly to reopen the mine. (Example of decisions about this real option: how low does the ore price have to fall before we decide to stop producing? How low does the ore price have to fall before we stop draining the mine and abandon it entirely? What is this loss-making mine worth?)

Option terminology

Terms in capitals in the definitions below have their own separate entry in this section.

Call option: the right to buy something at a known price in the future, however much the market changes between now and then – e.g. (1) the right to invest $100 million to build a factory to produce a new hair colour, whatever the demand for the hair colour, or (2) the right to spend $2,000 to generate a megawatt-hour of electricity, whatever the selling price of electricity.

Put option: the right to sell something at a known price in the future, however much the market changes between now and then – e.g. the right to sell an existing factory for scrap for $20,000, whatever profit or loss the factory may be making.

Exercise price: the known price at which we can exercise any option to buy or sell – e.g. the investment cost of a factory (CALL), or the scrap value of a factory (PUT), or the variable cost of producing one more unit of output (CALL).

Volatility: the tendency of the market value of the underlying asset (on which we hold a real option) to vary away from its present value. The bigger the volatility, the more variation in price over time, and the more attractive it is to hold any option. The reason is that a higher volatility means both a larger upside potential and a larger downside potential. If we hold (say) a call option we can benefit from the larger upside, but we lose nothing from the larger downside, because our option can never be worth less than zero when it expires, however low the value of the underlying asset may fall.

Derivative asset: typically a right of some sort, such as an option, whose value is 'derived' from the value of a so-called UNDERLYING ASSET over which the right exists – e.g. the value of the rights to a new technology for hair colour is 'derived' from the current profitability and economic value of a factory to produce the colour. The UNDERLYING ASSET is the profitability of the factory (if built) and the DERIVATIVE ASSET value is the value of the right (option) to build such a factory, a right that may exist for some time into the future.

European option: option giving the right to invest (or sell out) only on one fixed future date.

American option: option giving us the right to invest (or sell out) at any time we choose, usually up to some fixed final date.

Perpetual option: option that remains open for ever (usually only available for land use decisions or for exchanges between currencies).

Expiry date: the date on which an option to invest (CALL) or to sell (PUT) expires – e.g. the date when a patent or licence expires, or when a pop star or athlete becomes a 'has been' and is no longer useful for endorsements, or when competitors catch up with our technology.

Underlying asset: the asset that a real option gives us the right to buy (CALL OPTION) or to sell (PUT OPTION) – e.g. a factory or a customer base.

Random factor: the variable driving the value of an option. In simple cases, the random factor is the value of the UNDERLYING ASSET on which the option exists – e.g. if our option consists of the patent rights to produce a new hair colour, the underlying asset that this gives us a right to buy is a factory to produce the hair colour; the RANDOM FACTOR is the expected profitability of such an investment. In more complex cases, a random factor may not be an asset price – e.g. it could be an interest rate or an exchange rate.

Random walk: the basic assumption of all real options analysis is that the value of the UNDERLYING ASSET is unforecastable, in the sense that it follows a random walk. This means that at any instant an upward movement is as likely as a downward movement (for technical reasons this is actually true of the logarithm of the asset's value). For a random walk, the best possible forecast of all possible future values is today's value. A random walk is the behaviour expected of values in a perfectly competitive market, so the random walk is a pessimistic or 'bedrock' assumption on which to base our investment strategy if we face very harsh competition.

More complex types of real options

The simplest kind of real option involves a choice between only two alternatives, e.g. to invest/not invest in a new plant; similarly, if we already have the plant, we usually have the choice to produce/not produce during each unit of time.

Some more complex real options offer a choice between the 'best of' more than two alternatives, e.g. we may have a real 'call' option to invest in any of three new plant designs, or not invest at all; or if an existing plant is unsuccessful we have a multiple real 'put' option to scrap it, sell it as a going concern, sell piecemeal, or manage for cash.

A simple real option involves only one 'unforecastable' variable or random factor, e.g. the charter rate for oil tankers, the market price for a call centre operation, the level of demand for an internet service, the popularity of a TV character.

In more complex cases more than one random factor can matter, e.g. for a property developer, the level of rents for the buildings and the interest rate on the project finance are both important and unforecastable factors. If rents fall really low the developer has the option to declare insolvency, and default on the project financing loan, leaving the lender to pick up any further losses; also if interest rates fall really low, the developer can try to refinance the project loan elsewhere. These two possible actions for the borrower are 'options' that the borrower enjoys against the lender: how should they affect the price of the loan, and the market value of the developer's business?

There can also be compound options, where the final value of one option consists of the right to acquire the next option. In this way we can build chains of options. This can justify making (for example) an unprofitable investment in R&D or in test marketing, if this leads to a chain of options for future development, only the last of which will have strong upside potential (if all goes well). Hence Real Options Analysis can offer a quantified rule for going ahead with costly or unprofitable trial businesses (e.g. early experiments in e-business), a type of decision that used to be thought of as intangible or strategic.

How do real options compare with financial options?

Real options arose from work on financial options, when analysts realized that many business decisions have the same logical structure as a financial option.

There are now developments that are unique to real options, but the terminology and methods of real options and financial options remain close to each other, and new developments in financial options continue to affect real options. For example:

- A factory usually has a 'real option' to vary its output, using any fraction of its capacity from zero to 100 percent. This real option corresponds to a type of financial option called a 'bull spread'.
- A football club has a 'real option' to recruit school-age junior players and to try to train them into potential stars, but

there is a risk that this will be 'too' successful, so that the players become superstars and the club has to pay the full market price for their services. This feature of the real option to develop new players resembles an 'up and out' option in finance, and similar problems arise in managing other skilled professionals, such as in law or accounting.

The key difference between a financial option and a real option is that a financial option is a bet about the future share price of a company, and this bet is made between two people who are outside the company. The company itself need not know that the bet exists, and the bet does not change the share price of the company, or the activities of the company itself.

In contrast, a real option is a decision the firm itself faces, about how to create, or use, or dispose of 'real' economic resources, e.g. supplies, energy, the time of staff and managers, wear and tear on equipment. Any decision on these real resources will potentially change the value of the firm itself.

For example, suppose our firm buys buy a five-year licence to assemble a new digital camera, and suppose that the factory would cost $100 million to build. If we buy the licence we are buying an option, and in effect we are betting that some time before our licence expires the market for the camera will be so strong that we can safely invest the $100m cost of building the factory, in the expectation that the net present value of the factory's cashflows (variable revenues less variable costs) will be large enough to repay the investment. Making this investment or not (depending on what happens during the five years) could easily change the value of our firm.

How can real option values affect business decisions?

There are two main ways in which Real Options Analysis can affect a business decision:

- It can show at what price we should acquire or dispose of an economic investment opportunity that resembles a real option. For example, how much should we pay to buy existing intellectual property rights, such as patents, licences or brands; or how much should we be willing to spend in order to create such rights from zero? How should we trade off a fixed payment against a flexible opportunity or threat?
- It can show at what price we should exercise a real option and take up the economic opportunity that the real option represents. For example, how profitable should a market be before we take up our opportunity to invest in it (call), or how unprofitable should a market be before we scrap or sell out (put)?

The answers Real Options Analysis gives to these questions can look very different from traditional NPV analysis.

For example, consider again the problem of whether to invest in R&D to create a new hair colour technology. If research is cheap, Real Options Analysis shows that it can be optimal to develop the new technology even if the market for that technology is currently unprofitable, and therefore on a random walk basis is forecast to remain so on average (50 percent chance of getting better and 50 percent chance of getting worse).

Conversely, if research costs are high enough, it can be optimal not to invest to create a new technology, even if the market for that technology already exists, is highly profitable, and is expected to remain so.

What drives the valuation of a real option?

For acquiring or selling a real option

The key fact about a real option is that it always has some value. For example, if we have the rights to metallic hair colour, these rights can never be worth less than zero (since it costs us nothing to hold the rights without using them, even if metallic hair is totally unpopular at present). But there is always some chance that metallic hair will become popular before our right to make it becomes valueless (since the future is unforecastable) and this small chance gives the rights some value, even at times when metallic hair is out of fashion.

Features that make a real option more valuable typically include greater volatility (i.e. faster market change, such as in e-commerce) and a longer time before the option expires. There is also a technical effect of the risk-free interest rate. For a call, a lower exercise price makes the option more valuable – e.g. if the underlying asset is a market revenue, and the required investment (exercise price) is the cost of a factory, the cheaper the factory required to access the same revenue, the more attractive is the right to build the factory.

For exercising a real option

The heart of the decision on when to exercise a real option (e.g. when we should exercise our right to invest in a factory to produce metallic hair colouring) is straightforward: we calculate the value of the right to invest 'now or later' (i.e. the value of the unexercised option) and we compare this with the value of the actual investment, if made now. It becomes optimal to invest when the net present value of the actual investment 'if made now' is at least the value of the real option (which is the right to invest 'now or later').

How do we calculate the value of a real option?

For a non-technical reader, the answer is 'you really don't want to know'. Some advanced mathematics is needed, including partial differential equations and stochastic calculus, plus rather strange ideas, such as the calculation of a decision tree by using so-called risk-adjusted probabilities instead of the actual objective probabilities. The methods often use a lot of computer time. Some problems need finite difference methods, like those used in physics and engineering, but other problems require the less familiar technique of binomial trees using risk-adjusted probabilities.

Numerate graduates who have worked with partial differential equations for heat flow or fluid diffusion will be well prepared for all this, but they may have problems on first adapting to the slightly different problems and techniques used in finance. Even specialists sometimes make slips in modelling a real options problem, or interpreting a solution. There are no standard calculation packages to help in structuring or evaluating the more interesting real option problems, for which analytical solutions generally do not exist.

RESOURCES

BOOKS

Dixit, A.K. and Pindyck, R.S. *Investment Under Uncertainty*, Princeton, 1994.

Wilmott, Paul, Howison, Sam and Dewynne, Jeff, *The Mathematics of Financial Derivatives,* Cambridge, 1995.

Trigeorgis, L. and Mason, S.P., *Real Options*, MIT Press, 1996.

EVA's charms as a performance measure

TODD T. MILBOURN

Todd T. Milbourn explains the attractions – and limitations – of economic value added.

THERE is an ever-increasing pressure on companies to maximize shareholder value. However, this raises a very important question in the minds of senior executives of how to measure an organization's progress in meeting its corporate goals.

In particular, the question has to do with defining measures of corporate financial performance that correlate highly with shareholder wealth. This issue is also concerned with motivating managers to do what is best for shareholders. The central idea in most organizations is to tie managerial compensation to measures of financial performance that are linked closely to changes in shareholder wealth. In theory, this should motivate managers to take actions that maximize shareholder value.

More precisely, a good performance measure must be responsive to a manager's actions and decisions. In this sense, stock prices (or, for that matter, stock returns) are often ineffective in assessing past performance as they reflect the expectations of all future decisions.

In fact, stock prices are not necessarily that responsive to the actions of even the most senior executive in a company. As one goes further down the organization, the problem becomes even more severe as lower-level employees have even less impact on the stock price.

Economic Value Added (EVA), like other performance measures, attempts to resolve the tension that exists between the need for a performance measure that is both highly correlated with shareholder wealth *and* responsive to the actions of a company's managers.

The number of companies that have currently adopted EVA (or one of its many close cousins, such as McKinsey's Economic Profit) is startling. Stern Stewart Management Services (the founder of EVA) claims that many companies globally have been in discussions with it about adopting EVA as a performance measure.

Why are so many organizations embarking on the EVA trail? This chapter attempts to provide an answer to this question and others, including: why EVA is such a hot topic today. How is it defined and calculated? What are EVA's limitations and what is its future?

If an enterprise's objective is to maximize the value of the shareholders' claim to the assets, then, simply put, a company must do two things: invest only in new projects that are expected to create value, and retain only projects that create value on an ongoing basis.

Finance theory offers managers a guide to choosing capital investments through the net present value (NPV) rule. That is, invest in projects that have positive NPVs and you will create value.

However, when managers seek such a well-defined rule for evaluating their *ongoing* investments, they are often met with frustration. In fact, most organizations are forced to rely on financial measures such as total sales, total earnings or even rates of return on their net assets as a means of differentiating between the 'peaches' and the 'lemons' in their businesses.

However, assessing performance based on these types of measures can often distort the investment behaviour of management away from that of their shareholders' wishes.

Among the many potential conflicts between a company's shareholders and its management, those relating to the misuse of assets are often the most critical. In fact, it is often argued that businesses are overcapitalized relative to the optimal investment level. This is typically caused by the flawed compensation schemes that are prevalent in companies. These schemes often force managers to focus on earnings and market share.

The most fundamental question, then, is why do companies still fail to choose the right projects even when the NPV tool is readily available?

One reason for the misalignment between compensation and capital allocation systems is that NPV cannot be readily used for compensation. NPV is a summary measure based on *projected* cash flows and not *realized* performance.

What is needed for compensation are measures that can be computed periodically. Hence, it is easy to understand why companies reach for flow measures such as earnings and cash flow for determining compensation. Unfortunately, they can also distort managerial behaviour away from what is good for shareholders. A measure such as EVA can help, since it theoretically produces the same recommendations as NPV, as will be shown below.

Investment distortions typically arise because a manager is not 'charged' for the capital he or she uses or even rewarded for the shareholder value actually created. This is the fundamental contribution of EVA. It rewards managers for the earnings they generate but is also conditional on the amount of capital employed to reap these earnings.

If managerial compensation is tied to EVA, then the manager's inclination to consume capital is tempered by the fact that he or she must pay a capital charge evaluated at the weighted average cost of capital on the net capital he or she uses.

One can generalize the example above and draw the following conclusions: earnings-based compensation schemes can cause over-investment of capital, whereas return on net assets (RONA)-based compensation can cause under-investment of capital. Therefore, EVA has evolved as the focal point in many organizations as a means of marrying their project selection and managerial compensation schemes.

Why does EVA offer the correct incentives? The answer is simply because EVA is fundamentally related to shareholder value. At a company level, the present value of EVA equals a business's 'market value added' (MVA), which is defined as the difference between the market value of the organization and the (adjusted) book value of its assets. Moreover, at a project level, the present value of the future EVA equals the NPV derived from the usual free cash flow forecasts.

If EVA and free cash flow analyses give identical NPV estimates, why is it that EVA is useful for compensation and NPV is not? The reason is that one needs flow measures of performance for periodic compensation since compensation is designed to provide a flow of rewards. EVA is a flow measure, whereas NPV is a stock measure.

Moreover, of the available flow measures, EVA is the only one that explicitly takes into account the cost of the capital and the amount of capital invested in the company. In this respect, EVA is superior to another flow measure, cash flow.

The goal of a good financial performance measure is to ask how well a company has performed in terms of generating operating profits in a given period, given the amount of capital that was tied up to generate those profits. EVA is novel in that it provides an answer to this question.

The idea is that the business's financiers could have liquidated their investment in the company and put the liberated capital to some other use. Thus, the financiers' opportunity cost of capital must be subtracted from operating profits to gauge the organization's financial performance.

In this spirit, EVA views NOPAT (net operating profits after tax) as a representation of operating profit and subtracts a capital charge that views the economic book value of assets in place as a measure of the capital provided to the company by its financiers.

Estimating this capital base is the most cumbersome (yet necessary) aspect of calculating EVA. How do we arrive at this number? A company's balance sheet contains one measure of the value of its assets in place. Consider the accounting-based balance sheet in the top panel of Figure 1.

Unfortunately, due to a plethora of accounting distortions, the total asset value on this balance sheet is not an accurate representation of either the liquidation value or the replacement cost value of the business's assets. It is therefore of limited use for asset valuation purposes and must be adjusted.

Stern Stewart is careful to adjust this accounting balance sheet before arriving at an estimate of the value of a company's assets in place. In fact, there are over 250 accounting adjustments that Stern Stewart considers in moving to EVA.

In practice, however, most organizations find that no more than 15 adjustments are truly significant. They include netting the non-interest-bearing current liabilities (NIBCLs) against the current assets, adding back to equity the gross goodwill, restructuring and other write-offs, capitalized value of R&D (and possibly advertising), LIFO reserve and so on. (These accounting adjustments are referred to as 'equity equivalents' and their effects on capital and NOPAT are summarized in the bottom panel of Figure 1.)

The debt balance is also increased by the capitalized value of operating lease payments. The goal of these adjustments is to produce a balance sheet that reflects the economic values of the organization's assets more accurately than the accounting balance sheet. After these adjustments are made, a typical company's 'economic book value' balance sheet would look as it does in the second panel of Figure 1.

EVA is a powerful concept, as it is soundly couched in financial theory. However, before all businesses rush to adopt it, it should be noted that EVA is not the Holy Grail, since it has its limitations.

A frequently asked question is; what does EVA add to conventional valuation analysis? The answer is nothing. EVA-based financial analysis will not (and should not) change the conclusions reached on the basis of cashflow-based valuation analysis.

However, this equivalence is to EVA's credit. In fact, one limitation of EVA is that it is often touted as a new valuation tool, which is simply incorrect. EVA should be viewed primarily as a behavioural tool that is effective in altering the distortions that are prevalent in many companies.

The most severe limitation of EVA is what it (as well as most other financial measures) fails to capture on an *ex post* basis.

Total company value can be derived as the sum of two fundamental components. The most basic component is represented by

Figure 1 Estimating the capital base

Accounting-Based Balance Sheet	
ASSETS	**LIABILITIES AND EQUITY**
Current assets	Non-interest bearing current liabilities (NIBCLs)
Net goodwill	Interest-bearing current liabilities
Fixed assets (net of depreciation)	Long-term interest bearing debt
	Equity (net of write-offs)
TOTAL ASSETS	**TOTAL LIABILITIES AND EQUITY**

Economic (Adjusted Book Value) Balance Sheet	
ASSETS	**LIABILITIES AND EQUITY**
Current assets (with inventory at FIFO) – NIBCLs	Interest-bearing current liabilities
Gross goodwill	Long-term interest-bearing debt
Fixed assets (net of depreciation)	Equity (net of write-offs)
TOTAL ECONOMIC VALUE OF THE ASSETS	**TOTAL LIABILITIES AND EQUITY**

Equity Equivalents	
Add to Capital	**Add to NOPAT**
Equity equivalents	Increases in equity equivalents
Deferred tax reserve	Increase in deferred tax reserve
LIFO reserve	Increase in LIFO reserve
Cumulative goodwill amortization	Goodwill amortization
Unrecorded goodwill	
Capitalized intangibles	Increases in intangibles
Cumulative unusual gain (loss)	Unusual gain (loss)
Other reserves (e.g., bad debt, warranty, etc.)	Increase in other reserves

physical assets in place. If we assume that this is an economic value, then we can equate this part to EVA's estimated capital component. In addition to this component, however, is the present value of the business's growth opportunities. This latter component's value is certainly less tangible, and can be quite large for many businesses. One can view this part of company value as being driven by what the market expects to happen in the future.

Unfortunately, EVA is unable to capture changes in this value. In fact, attempts to capture this value bring us back to simply looking at changes in an organization's stock price. However, the limitations of stock price in judging corporate performance is what motivated our investigation of EVA in the first place.

To be careful not to end on a dismaying note, be aware that measuring and assessing managerial and corporate performance is a very difficult task. While EVA is able to give us a better measure, it is not the remedy for corporate mismanagement. However, to the extent that it has increased managerial awareness of the capital costs in running a business, it has certainly emerged as a very useful concept in corporate finance.

Corporate restructuring

DEAN LEBARON AND ROMESH VAITILINGAM

One of the most high-profile features of the business and investment worlds is corporate restructuring – the mergers and acquisitions (M&A), leveraged buyouts, divestitures, spin-offs, and the like that are contested in the 'market for corporate control'. Virtually without exception, stock prices of participating companies rise in response to announcements of corporate restructuring. But Dean LeBaron and Romesh Vaitilingam ask whether such events are really good for investors beyond the very short term.

THE late 1990s saw yet another wave of M&A activity. Indeed, the number and value of mega-mergers in 1998 set new records, a 50 percent increase on activity in 1997, itself a record year. This reawakened the populist cry that such mergers do not create new wealth, they merely represent the trading of existing assets – rearranging the deckchairs on the Titanic. What is more, it is argued, the threat of takeover means that managements take too short term a view, bolstering stock prices where possible, investing inadequately for the future and, where a company has been taken over in a leveraged buyout, perhaps burdening it with excessive debt.

On the other side of the debate, the primary argument in favour of M&A is that they are good for industrial efficiency: without the threat of their companies being taken over and, in all likelihood, the loss of their jobs, managers would act more in their own interests than those of the owners. In particular, this might imply an inefficient use of company resources, overinvestment, lower productivity and a general lack of concern about delivering shareholder value.

Feeble supervision of corporations often leads to mismanagement, it is argued, and while increased shareholder activism is one option, takeovers are a more radical solution for remedying poor performance and safeguarding against economic mediocrity.

Certainly, a takeover bid is frequently beneficial to the shareholders of the target company in terms of immediate rises in the stock price (although acquisitions often have a negative effect on the profitability and stock price of the acquirer). And managements that resist takeover may be doing it for their own interests rather than those of their investors. Senior executives may use such bizarre devices as 'shark repellents' and 'poison pills', which make it extremely costly for shareholders to replace the incumbent board of directors.

Guru of corporate restructuring: Bruce Wasserstein

In the mid-1980s, there was an avalanche of takeovers of underperforming companies, the targets of institutions and arbitrageurs who suspected that, with the help of plentiful leverage, they could increase corporate values by 'mobilizing assets'. Often that term meant disposal of non-performing assets. In this earlier age of corporate restructuring, Bruce Wasserstein was an *enfant terrible*. M&A deals were being done at premiums of 30–40 percent above market prices and Wasserstein would be in the middle, designing strategies to make them happen.

This was also the heyday of shark repellents and poison pills. Often, the other side would be lawyers and PR people trying to set defences against shareholders who had corporate control in mind, artfully removing shareholder rights whenever they might be exercised to change corporate control. But the SEC (Securities and Exchange Commission) formed an advisory committee to evaluate many of these activities and concluded that the market mechanisms must be left unimpeded.

Wasserstein's youthful energy tapped intensity suited to the pulsing business of deals. Always very well prepared, he worked with arbitrageurs, lawyers, accountants and regulators to move business combinations forward over institutions dedicated to thwart combinations, which, with hindsight, seemed to favour one group of investors over another. He went on to found his own successful investment banking firm, his personality skills leading him on the correct path.

In his 1998 book *Big Deal*, Wasserstein surveys 'the battle for control of America's leading corporations', including his own role in the past two decades or so. He describes five waves of mergers beginning in the mid-1800s:

- The first involved the building of the railroad empires.
- The second, in the 1920s, saw merger mania fuelled by a frothy stock market and rapid industrial growth.
- The third happened during the go-go years of the 1960s and featured the rise of the conglomerate.
- The fourth occurred with the hostile takeovers of the 1980s, driven by names such as Icahn, Boesky and Milken.
- A fifth wave happening today.

Wasserstein attributes the explosion of M&A activity at the turn of the twenty-first century to the need for companies to reposition themselves in today's ever-changing competitive environment:

> *'The patterns of industrial development through mergers, like those of economic activity, are crude and imperfect. However, there do seem to be elemental forces, Five Pistons, which drive the merger process:*
>
> *'Regulatory and political change: many of the most active M&A sectors over the past few years – media and telecommunications, financial services, utilities, health care – have been stimulated by deregulation or other political turmoil. Before deregulation, a number of industries owed their very existence to regulatory boundaries.*
>
> *'Technological change: technology creates new markets, introduces new competitors and is intertwined with regulatory change. Changes in technology make old regulatory boundaries obsolete and sometimes silly.*
>
> *'Financial change: financial fluctuations have a similar catalytic effect. A booming stock market encourages stock deals. A low market with low interest rates can have an especially strong effect after a period*

of high inflation in which the cost of hard assets has increased more rapidly than stock prices. In this environment, it may be cheaper to buy hard assets indirectly by purchasing companies on the stock market. Falling interest rates and available capital lubricate the process.

'Leadership: of course, corporate combinations do not occur in a mechanistic fashion. A human element is involved – the man on horseback who leads a company to seminal change.

'The size-simplicity vortex: scale matters, and bigger seems to mean better to most managers. Maybe it's critical mass, or technology and globalization, or integration, or sheer vanity and ego, but there is a natural imperative towards scale. However, just as some companies keep getting bigger, others shed their skin and become smaller. The imperative towards focus and simplicity is as strong as that for size. The two competing elements create a vortex of change.'

Counterpoint

Why so many mega-mergers? The evidence seems to be very clear, at least on the academic side, that mergers ultimately do not pay off for buyers or sellers. Economically, they equalize themselves out in the normal process of bidding so that the gains do not accrue to one side or the other. Similarly, there is a tendency now to have smaller business units, which, because of the new computer tools, are as functional and more motivational than larger business units.

In the 1980s, the deals were adversarial and there were not enough goodies to go around. Now, they are not adversarial: they are friendly and there are plenty of goodies to go around. The reasons seem to lie first in a compliant US antitrust division – which is strange under a Democratic administration – but even more in the payoffs that go to the agents involved. Executives get their stock options written up and then reissued after they are able to exercise their old options in advance, in order to keep the managements around under the new corporate structure.

In addition, merger accounting allows for a great deal of flexibility of accounting for goodwill and burying old mistakes. A fresh slate is often good and a merger provides that opportunity. And, of course, there are the agents, brokers, lawyers, accountants, and so on who form part of the transaction costs of a merger and act as an incentive to keep it going. It is the agency function that makes it go, plus the high price. That is the current characteristic of mergers, and it does not necessarily bode well for efficient business in the future.

Is the creation of new behemoths really what should be going on? Computer technology is empowering individuals to do marvellous things. Projects are taking the place of process. No longer do we have permanent constabularies of process administrators keeping the wheels of business moving. Instead, we have projects, where the 'administration' may include customers, employees, suppliers and temporary consultants to complete a project and then split apart. Business management of the future is very similar to movie production: bringing people together to engage in a creative function as and when necessary. People can be members of several creative teams at the same time. But in each one, we have to have one who has the 'fire in the belly' to make it happen.

Yet companies do want to merge and become larger, perhaps propelled by the results of management consultant studies that say that is the thing to do. But everything we know is about the empowerment of smaller and smaller groups, the behaviour of smaller units of organizations – which pulls against exactly these structures towards higher and higher, larger and larger units of consolidation. Companies in the US, at least, have learned that instant gratification comes from mergers, while operations come from smaller and smaller units. So we are shifting to having to feed our own financial greed with more and more artifices.

M&A activity seems to be at its highest at the top of bull markets when borrowing is easy. It is probably no accident that the merger waves that Wasserstein describes have tended to occur at moments of the greatest optimism and the highest valuation of financial markets. A hundred years ago there was talk of a new era. Similarly, in the 1920s and the 1960s, and again in the 1990s, the higher the stock market, the more intense the optimism, the greater the tendency towards consolidation. These are cyclical features of markets.

Where next?

Among investment styles and techniques, one is hardly ever mentioned, but it is one that is being used prominently today: event investing. Markets today are looking for events like earnings surprise anticipated – the so-called whisper number; stock promotions – the stocks that are mentioned on news broadcasts; merger news – which allows companies to rewrite history in their accounting statements and write up options for the management; and deals – those between companies for strategic alliances and deals on sales.

Events and anticipation of events are what drives markets in very short-term environments, and that is what is happening today. Yes, we have momentum investing, but much more directly we have event investing, fuelled by communications on the internet, chats, and even the old-fashioned way of your friendly broker calling you with a tip. But our communications have become much faster, more sophisticated and widespread, more popular – so event investing is what is ruling the day.

While mergers dominate as the millennium dawns, demergers may offer the best business and investment prospects for the future. For example, Andrew Campbell and his colleagues at the Ashridge Strategic Management Centre in London calculate that there is one trillion dollars worth of shareholder value locked up waiting to be released by the breakup of multibusiness corporations in the US and the UK. They claim that breaking up these firms into far more focused businesses will create enormous improvements in company performance and, along with it, vastly increased shareholder wealth. And they describe potential investment strategies to gain from it:

- **Speculate ahead of a breakup:** work out which companies may break up and invest in them before other investors have driven the price up and before an official breakup announcement is made.
- **Avoid breakup candidates:** a converse strategy involves avoiding potential breakup candidates altogether and instead investing in those companies that are already

focused – these will outperform companies with value-destroying corporate centres.

- **Invest in a broad portfolio of breakups:** breakups release value, so invest in a broad range of breakups immediately after each breakup is announced.
- **Invest selectively in particular breakups:** identify those companies that will increase in value most once broken off. These tend to be those that are likely to be subsequently acquired by another focused company.

RESOURCES

BOOKS

LeBaron, Dean and Vaitilingam, Romesh, *The Ultimate Investor: the people and ideas that make modern investment*, Capstone, Oxford, 1999.

LeBaron, Dean and Vaitilingam, Romesh (with Pitchford, Marilyn), *The Ultimate Book of Investment Quotations*, Capstone, Oxford, 1999.

Sadtler, David, Campbell, Andrew and Koch, Richard, *Breakup: When Large Companies are Worth More Dead than Alive*, Capstone, Oxford, 1997.

Wasserstein, Bruce, *Big Deal: The Battle for Control of America's Leading Corporations*, Warner Books, 1998.

WEB

www.deanlebaron.com – Dean LeBaron's website.

www.sternstewart.com – website offering access to the *Journal of Applied Corporate Finance*, edited by Don Chew, a good source of recent research and writing on corporate restructuring.

The many roles of financial markets

NARAYANY NAIK

Narayany Naik describes how the economic functions of markets go beyond allocation of capital to include risk management and monitoring company performance among other things.

THE growth of financial markets has been one of the outstanding developments of the past two decades. In that time the composition of financial markets has changed; the share of banks in total recorded financial assets has tended to fall, whereas that of securities markets and even more that of financial derivatives – futures, options and swaps – has greatly increased.

These developments have been most advanced in the US and UK, but the removal of previous restrictions of one kind or another is leading to a similar expansion of financial market transactions in other countries, notably France, Germany and Japan.

The role of banks in the economic system has long been understood, whereas that of securities markets has sometimes been the object of criticism on the grounds that they are driven by 'speculation' – regarded as unproductive – and consume too many real resources. It is essential, however, to recognize the varied economic roles that financial markets, in the widest sense, play.

That financial markets, in the form of both banking and securities markets, are necessary for the effective allocation of real capital hardly needs saying. But the economic functions of financial markets go beyond this and include: the provision of choice in the timing of consumption; the management of risk; the clarification of the role of management; and the provision of information.

Financial markets and instruments enable individuals to choose more effectively between current and future consumption. Borrowing enables them to consume more while 'lending', in the widest sense, enables them to exchange consumption today for more consumption tomorrow.

Market interest rates establish the economic price of this exchange. It should be noted, however, that for individuals as a whole the provision of a higher level of consumption 'tomorrow', with given technology, can only come from the additional output generated by physical investment. So the provision of choice of timing in consumption patterns is linked to the role of capital markets in providing producers with resources in excess of those generated out of their own income. In the process both borrowers and lenders are made better off.

Financial markets also allow efficient risk sharing among investors. There are of two types of risks: those that can be diversified away and those that cannot.

Diversifiable risk can be eliminated by holding assets the returns on which are not perfectly correlated with each other. Financial markets, therefore, enable investors to eliminate diversifiable risk.

Non-diversifiable risk, by definition, cannot be eliminated merely by holding a spread of assets. Individuals need to choose which non-diversifiable risks they are willing to bear and which they want to lay off. But the presence of forward, futures and options markets allows the transfer of non-diversifiable risk from more risk averse to less risk averse individuals and from those who cannot manage risk to those who can.

Financial markets offer a wide array of financial instruments with very different risk-return relationships, making it easier for individuals and organizations to choose a degree of risk according to their risk tolerance levels.

For example, investors who are extremely risk averse may choose to invest a large fraction of their wealth in risk free securities (such as government bonds), more risk tolerant investors may elect to invest in risky stocks while investors with intermediate risk preferences may choose a combination of bonds and stocks.

In some cases risk matching may take place in financial markets. For example, the user of copper loses if copper prices rise whereas the producer of copper gains – and conversely. A forward purchase of copper by the former at an agreed price and a forward sale by the latter can enable them both to 'hedge' their price risk.

It is important to note, however, that if there is not an equal and opposite supply of 'hedging', the gap has to be filled by 'speculators'. So, paradoxically, it is the existence of speculation that makes possible a wider range of risk reduction. Moreover, if speculators are more skilled at judging the 'right', or in the language of economics the 'equilibrium', price than other traders, the effect of their transaction in moving prices towards this level enhances the role of markets in the resource allocation process.

Financial markets also enable the separation of ownership from day-to-day managerial control – a practical necessity for running large organizations.

Many corporations have hundreds of thousands of shareholders with very different tastes, wealth, risk tolerances and personal investment opportunities. Yet, as the American economist Irving Fisher showed in 1930, they can all agree on one thing – managers should continue to invest in real assets until the marginal return on the investment equals the rate of return on investments of a similar degree of risk available in capital markets.

As shareholders are unanimous about the investment criteria, they can safely delegate the operations of an enterprise to a professional manager. Managers do not need to know anything about the preferences of their shareholders, nor do they need to consult their own tastes. Managers need to follow only one objective, namely to invest in projects that yield a higher return compared with that offered by equivalent investments in capital markets (the 'opportunity cost' of capital).

Put differently, the managers' objective becomes that of investing in projects that in present value terms cost less than the benefits they bring in, that is, investing in positive net present value projects. This objective maximizes the market value of each stockholder's stake in the company and therefore turns out to be in the best interest of all shareholders.

The maximization of net present value in competitive markets also implies the maximization of return over cost in terms of the use of real resources and therefore achieves a social optimum in the widest sense (apart from the creation of possible 'externalities' such as pollution on the one hand and the provision of knowledge on the other).

Stock markets aggregate the diverse opinions of market participants and convey how much the equity of a company is worth under its current management.

Suppose the shares of company A are trading at a given price and suppose that company B can use the assets of company A more efficiently under its own management. Then company B may acquire company A and carry this out. If there were no stock market to value performance it would be very difficult for company B to notice that the assets of company A were not being put to the best use. Even if company B had noticed this, it might not be possible for it to acquire company A and thereby transfer the assets.

Thus, by providing information concerning performance the presence of a well-functioning stock market leads to the more efficient utilization of assets and enables poor management to be disciplined through a market for corporate control.

When an organization announces a plan of future action, whether it be starting a new project or taking over another company, the stock price may respond in a positive or a negative way. The management of the organization can observe this reaction and learn what market participants collectively think of its proposed plan.

If the stock price reaction is negative, the management may wish to re-examine its own calculations and reconsider its decision. Thus the stock market helps management by providing a second opinion about its policy. Moreover, as stock prices reflect the value of the assets under current management, they provide a measure of how well the management is doing its job and therefore help the process of evaluating the performance of management.

There is considerable evidence to suggest that financial markets act as efficient aggregators of information and help the efficient allocation of resources via information conveyed through market prices.

Consider the case of a farmer who has a certain amount of land that can be used to grow wheat or corn or oatmeal. He is reasonably certain about how much it will cost him to grow any of these crops and how much output his land will yield. However, there exists considerable uncertainty about the price his crop will fetch after harvesting. This price uncertainty depends not only on the weather but also on the demand and supply conditions that might prevail after harvesting.

However, the farmer can look at the futures prices of wheat, corn and oatmeal and, knowing his cost structure, decide which is the most profitable crop for him. He can also use the futures markets to assure himself a guaranteed price for the crop and then go ahead with planting. In this way financial markets provide signals as to the socially most desired and economically most efficient use of the farmer's land.

Commercial banks clearly play important economic roles as well. In addition to bringing borrowers and lenders together, banks also act as monitors of companies.

If finance is provided entirely through the diverse ownership of stockholders, no single investor has an incentive to incur the cost of monitoring management and ensure that it is acting in the best interest of stockholders. This monitoring only needs to be done by one party; duplication might not result in better monitoring and would waste resources.

Stockholders cannot profitably combine to hire somebody to monitor because of a free rider problem; each would want others to bear the costs of monitoring. When a bank lends to a corporation, it has an incentive to be the single monitor. Further, by holding a large portfolio of loans to different companies, the bank can guarantee that it is undertaking the monitoring and thus overcome the free rider problem.

To summarize, the operations of well-functioning financial markets (banking, stock markets and derivatives markets) bring borrowers and lenders together, improve risk sharing, lead to the optimal allocation of resources, provide information to market participants, allow the separation of ownership from management and help monitor management. Together they improve the quality of investment decisions and the welfare of all market participants.

RESOURCES

BOOK

Young, Patrick and Theys, Thomas, *Capital Market Revolution*, FT Prentice Hall, London, 2000.

The key role of the middle men

HAROLD ROSE

Harold Rose outlines the role of financial intermediaries such as banks, insurance companies and mutual funds.

UNTIL two US economists, John Gurley and Edward Shaw, published *Money in a Theory of Finance* in 1960, banks, insurance companies and other types of financial institution were studied in terms that implied that they had almost nothing in common.

Although important differences between financial institutions are of course still recognized, they are now regarded by academics, at any rate, as all being species of the genus of financial intermediary. The roles financial institutions play are seen as reflecting the advantages of financial intermediation; and the changes in their role, most notably in the case of banks, are to a great extent regarded as reflecting a rise or fall in these advantages.

Financial intermediaries are so called because they transfer funds from those agents in the economy with free cash flows or financial surpluses – an excess of current saving over physical investment – to those with financial deficits. Usually this means on balance a shift of funds from the personal to the business sector.

Banks, insurance companies, pension funds and so on all have this intermediation function in common, although financial flows also involve flows between intermediaries themselves and between businesses in general (in the form of trade credit). Some financial institutions, such as mutual funds, are not intermediaries as defined above.

Three major questions arise: why does intermediation, rather than 'direct' financing, occur; what are the results of financial intermediation; and what changes in the economics of intermediation help to explain the changing weight of different types of institution in the economy?

Intermediaries may originate or develop either on the liabilities or assets side of their business. The conventional history of banks, for example, places their origin mainly in their role as deposit liability takers and similarly with the liabilities of insurance companies. However, leasing companies, say. Have developed on the assets side.

Whatever the case, the development of all financial intermediaries is tied up with two main factors: the insurance principle; and the saving of various kinds of cost.

The insurance principle is involved in the creation of diversified loan or other portfolios, which reduces the risks of financial institutions and their creditors and, by minimizing the influence of random events, also makes it possible for their creditors, such as bank depositors, to judge their performance more accurately.

Moreover, it is the insurance principle, in the form of a low correlation between withdrawals by individual depositors or policy-holders, that makes it possible for a bank to offer demand deposits and a life insurance company to offer surrender facilities. All financial institutions, in one form or another, can be described as selling the law of large numbers.

As for transaction and information cost savings, financial intermediaries may have an advantage over 'direct' financing because they may possess economies of scale, standardization or specialization.

Second, financial intermediaries save costs through what may be called the mathematics of the 'dating' agency. If there are, say, four prospective lenders and four would-be borrowers, there are 16 possible pairings; but if they all transact through a single intermediary acting as an allocating agent only eight links are needed.

Third, financial intermediation avoids the costs that would otherwise result from the duplication of monitoring of borrowers and the management of financial distress and default situations. Without banks, or some equivalent agent appointed collectively, we would individually have to monitor loans to a number of borrowers and individually have to bear the duplicated costs of default management.

Other types of financial institution, such as insurance companies, also relieve us of transaction costs in this way. This is why some economists have stressed the role of financial intermediaries, particularly banks, as being 'delegated monitors'.

Financial intermediaries also solve what would otherwise be the free rider problem, in which we might individually assume that we could leave it to others to bear the costs of monitoring and default management.

Finally, in addition to reducing search and monitoring costs, financial intermediaries reduce information costs not only by specializing in the interpretation of information about borrower quality, for example, but also by receiving information that borrowers, or life insurance policy-holders, would not wish to see published.

Moreover, banks obtain a unique form of information about borrower behaviour by virtue of their knowledge of bank account transactions. These factors help to explain why the US evidence is that the share prices of companies tend to rise on the announcement of a large increase in bank borrowing facilities.

By reducing risk and costs, financial intermediation results in a higher level of saving and investment, but possibly at the cost of a higher degree of financial interdependence and the transmission of shocks within the financial system, so that regulation has become a common feature of financial intermediation.

Financial intermediation has also had the greatly beneficial effect of asset-liability transformation, whereby, for example, a bank is able to make its deposit liabilities more liquid, less risky and individually smaller than its loans. In the development of intermediation a variety of financial instruments has been created, producing more efficient and lower-cost payments services than would otherwise be the case, and enabling us to make a wider range of choices about risk and the time path of consumption.

It is generally accepted that financial intermediation brings economic benefits, but some economists (and politicians) have gone farther and have argued that so-called bank-dominated economic systems are more effective in promoting economic growth than systems in which stock markets form a significant part in the capital-raising process.

A contrast has therefore been drawn between France, Germany and Japan on the one hand and the US and UK on the other. It has been contended in particular that, in systems in which long-term relationships exist between banks and borrowers, the latter are able to take a longer view of investment, whereas stock markets are said to be afflicted by a 'short-termism' that forces firms in the US and UK to follow suit.

This article is not the place to examine such contentions. Suffice it to say, first, that in the view of several economists who have examined the financial system of Germany in particular, the contrast drawn between the role of banks in that country and the UK is not valid; second, that the charge of stock market short-termism remains unproven; and third, that, largely because of international competition, most countries are in the process of dismantling various forms of restriction, a process which is leading their financial systems to become more like that of the UK in particular.

In primitive economies local moneylenders have been the chief form of financial 'institution'. The process of subsequent economic development has everywhere been associated with that of intermediation, with intermediaries' assets rising faster than physical assets: in this phase banks clearly predominate.

In the UK it looked as if the ratio of intermediary liabilities to gross domestic product was levelling out, with the share of bank deposits continuing its long decline before the liberalization of banks and building societies in the 1980s interrupted this phase.

Against a longer perspective the share of bank deposits in intermediary liabilities has been found to decline in many mature economies. Certainly, over the past 20 years or so improvements in security market practices, bringing lower transaction costs and new risk-reducing instruments of various kinds, together with a tougher company law, fuller accounting disclosure and the growth of credit rating agencies, have combined to reduce the relative advantages of banks as corporate credit monitors, at least of quoted company borrowers.

Interest margins on loans to the latter have fallen in the UK and US, where corporate borrowers have turned to securities markets, including Eurobonds and, in the US and elsewhere, commercial paper markets.

Banks have turned increasingly to personal lending; but other types of financial institution and a growing number of large retail stores have used their customer information and modern card technology to invade this field. Card technology in general has reduced the demand for working balances; and this, together with electronic banking, has diminished the need for bank branches. Rising real incomes and, in some countries, tax advantages have favoured the growth of non-bank financial intermediaries such as insurance companies and pension funds.

The result is that, measured in terms of the ratio of bank deposits to total intermediary liabilities, the relative weight of banks has fallen in both the UK and the US.

But the question of whether commercial banks, as distinct from banking in the traditional sense, have lost ground in terms of their share of income or value added in the growing financial services industry is more questionable. And banks retain an information advantage in lending to small firms, which could well represent a growing share of some economies. Banks have also been able to replace lending to large firms by more profitable personal lending.

What is clear is that there has been a widespread tendency for the boundaries between different types of financial institution to become blurred. Deregulation and the abandonment of traditional and cartellized dividing lines have been taking place in many countries of differing political complexions, suggesting that the causes are rooted in common economic forces, of which the most evident have been the pressures of competition brought about by the internationalization of finance and the development of electronic information and payments technology.

So today we see banks offering insurance and retail investment products and insurance companies, and retail stores and, especially in the US, mutual funds offering banking and other financial services.

Whether retail banks choose to undertake investment banking on any scale has become a question of perceived profitability rather than one of any deep structural principle. Some of the most profitable banks are those that have chosen not to become heavily involved in investment banking; and securities firms and other financial institutions lack the means as well as the incentive to become retail banks, which still dominate the payments system and whose branch network, although shrinking, remains a formidable barrier to entry.

But even retail banks combine traditional corporate lending with transactions in various kinds of marketable instruments for their corporate customers. The so-called demographic time bomb will clearly lead to the replacement or supplementation of state pensions by forms of funded market schemes, probably offered by a range of institutions, so further enhancing the role of securities markets.

Modern electronic technology, by reducing transaction and distance costs, is commonly expected to have an extensive influence over a growing range and geographic nature of transactions. The conclusion usually drawn is that the boundaries between financial intermediaries and between these and non-financial firms will become even more blurred. This may well prove to be the case, but the balance of advantage between relatively specialized firms and conglomerates does not depend on technology alone; and outside the world of finance, at any rate, the pendulum seems to be swinging back towards specialization.

RESOURCES

BOOK

Rose, Harold, *Finance – Villian or Scapegoat?*, Institute of Economic Affairs, London, 1994.

ESSENTIALS

FINANCE

ACTIVITY-BASED COSTING

ACTIVITY-BASED COSTING (ABC) aims to provide a dynamic and realistic means of calculating the true cost of doing business. It precisely allocates direct and indirect costs to particular products or customer segments. ABC emerged from Harvard and, in particular, the work of Robert Kaplan (perhaps best known for his work on developing the Balanced Scorecard, a strategic management and measurement system).

ABC is, in some ways, a financial version of re-engineering. The company identifies core processes and analyzes the costs at each stage within the process. This enables it to know how much an activity, such as R&D, costs the business and how much R&D expenditure should be built into the costs of a particular product or service. Properly applied, ABC allows companies to better understand and streamline their cost structures. The drawback is that it requires careful examination of what is actually going on in the business.

According to consulting firm Booz-Allen & Hamilton, companies typically spend 20–25 percent of sales with third-party suppliers for goods and services not directly related to the end product or services of the business. These costs sometimes exceed those spent directly on the end product.

So why don't companies manage their indirect costs better? The simple answer is that you can only save money if you actually know how much you spend in the first place, and where you spend it. That's where Activity Based Costing comes in. If it is to be produced, a product or service – 'cost object' in the language of ABC – requires the input of certain 'activities'. Activities include the traditional business functions (marketing, R&D, production, etc.) as well as indirect costs such as maintenance, storage, and administration. Taken together, these activities are the processes that form the business. There are a number of factors influencing the costs of a particular activity, such as whether it is premium quality. In ABC-speak these are 'cost drivers'.

In addition there are 'activity drivers' – measures of the demand placed on certain activities by particular cost objects. One product may, for example, require greater marketing expenditure than another. Clearly, activities require resources: people and machines. 'Resource drivers' are measures of the demands placed on resources by activities.

ABC does nothing, in itself, to reduce costs. But the better understood the relationship between resources, activities, and processes, the more likely it is that the most cost-effective resources will be channelled to the right activities at the right time in the process. This is the underlying logic of ABC.

DISCOUNTED CASH FLOW

DISCOUNTED CASH FLOW (DCF) refers to a method of valuing a company used by private company investors and venture capitalists to determine the size of their investments in projects.

Discounted cash flow analysis takes all benefits (cash flow, tax credits, net sale proceeds, paper losses) into account, not just cash flow. The aim is to assess a projected stream of economic benefits and calculate the maximum equity contribution that an investor should be willing to make. It also enables an analyst to compare an equity amount with a stream of benefits and calculate an overall rate of return. The investor's minimum rate of return is called the discount rate, the rate at which the investor will discount benefits promised in the future. The discount rate converts benefits promised in the future into an equivalent value today, called present value.

Despite its complexity, discounted cash flow analysis is based on a simple idea – that cash today is worth more than cash promised in the future. It assumes that any investment should yield a return over and above current cash value. It makes no sense, for example, to invest $100 today for the promise of only the same amount in the future. If you invest $100 today, you should receive more than that amount back at a later date.

There are a number of factors involved. The first is the risk incurred. An investor in a property development, for example, is looking for cash flow and appreciation, but neither is guaranteed. The investor bears significant market risk, and risk demands some compensation. Part of the return on investment is compensation for taking risk. (The greater the risk, the higher the rate of return demanded by investors.)

Second, inflation reduces the value of money. An investor needs some return just to preserve the value of the capital. If inflation is proceeding at 4 percent a year, an investor needs a 4 percent after-tax return just to get back what they have invested. The other justification of return on investment, then, is compensation for inflation.

Third is the opportunity cost of the investment. When an investor places money in an investment, they give up the right to use it for anything else – alternative investments or consumption. Economists call this 'opportunity cost'. So, the third part of return on investment is compensation for opportunity cost.

An investor's perception of these three factors – risk, inflation, and opportunity cost – determines their desired rate of return, the minimum return required for a particular investment.

For the purposes of venture capitalists, discounted cash flow assumes that the future value of a company can be estimated by forecasting future performance and measuring the surplus cash flow generated by the company. The surplus cash flows and cash flow shortfalls are then related back to a present value using a discounting factor and added together to arrive at an overall valuation. The discount factor used is adjusted for the financial risk of investing in the company. The mechanics of the method focus investors on the internal operations of the company and its future.

Like any other valuation method, discounted cash flow has its shortcomings. It ignores outside factors that affect company value, such as price-earnings ratios. It also ignores asset values and other internal factors that can reduce or increase company value. Since the method is based on forecasts, a good understanding of the business, its market, and its past operations is essential.

SHAREHOLDER VALUE

SHAREHOLDER value arrived with the sort of trumpeting that usually accompanies a big idea. Yet it really didn't say anything new. Shareholder value simply contends that a company should aim to maximize its value to shareholders. Indeed, this should be its *raison d'être.* The concept gave rise to value-based management, which suggested that generating profits was not enough, and that share price performance in particular should be viewed as a key indicator of corporate competence.

This exposes two very different views about the role of companies. It suggests that shareholders are the only ones that count. This overlooks the responsibility to employees and the wider community.

But to large organizations, this perspective can be attractive for a number of reasons. First, it articulates the reasons for a company's existence with commendable clarity. There is none of the vagueness of making *reasonable* profits and pleasing all the company's stakeholders. It sounds both laudable and achievable – and shareholders are duty bound to like the idea. Second (with some adjustments), it fits with the entire idea of the stakeholder corporation. Shareholders are stakeholders and their numbers are increasingly likely to include other stakeholders, such as employees. Clearly, adding value to the investments of shareholders can have widespread benefits inside and outside an organization.

Advocates of shareholder value claim that it encourages a longer-term view of corporate performance. Instead of desperately seeking to boost quarterly results, executives can channel their energies into creating long-term value growth for shareholders. Institutional investors like the long view and this element was vital in the development of the concept.

Critics voice doubts about whether long-term perspectives are indeed encouraged. After all, they argue, downsizing was popular among shareholders who, perversely, often saw the value of their investments go up when a company announced it was downsizing.

While such arguments are difficult to prove either way, what can be said is that value-based management seeks to bridge the gap between the aims of executives and employees and those of shareholders. In the past, companies tended to measure success solely in terms of profits. If profits increased year on year, executives felt they were doing a good job. If, at the same time, the share price underperformed, they offered reassurance to institutional investors, but little else. In contrast, value-based management is as interested in cash and capital invested than in calculations about profitability. 'Cash is a fact, profit is an opinion,' argues one of the creators of the concept, Alfred Rappaport of Northwestern University's Kellogg School of Management.

While sceptics suggest that shareholder value is simply yet another consulting invention, its popularity among companies like Lloyds-TSB Group and top US conglomerates suggests it is a robust tool to, at least, monitor performance. And, for global businesses, perhaps the greatest advantage of shareholder value is that it provides universally consistent corporate results rather than ones produced to the dictates of local accounting rules.

PART THREE

Management in Action

– CHAPTER 1 –

Leadership

'Our prevailing leadership myths are still captured by the image of the captain of the cavalry leading the charge to rescue the settlers from the attacking Indians. So long as such myths prevail, they reinforce a focus on short-term events and charismatic heroes rather than on systemic forces and collective learning.' PETER SENGE

'Leadership can be felt throughout an organization. It gives pace and energy to the work and empowers the workforce. Empowerment is the collective effect of leadership.' WARREN BENNIS

'The moment you step from independence to interdependence, you step into a leadership role.' STEPHEN COVEY

'The tail trails the head. If the head moves fast, the tail will keep up the same pace. If the head is sluggish, the tail will droop.' KONOSUKE MATSUSHITA

Reinventing leadership

DES DEARLOVE

Leadership is one of the great intangibles of the business world. It is a skill most people would love to possess, but one that defies close definition. Ask people which leaders they admire and you are as likely to be told Gandhi as Jack Welch, Tony Blair as Richard Branson. Yet, most agree that leadership is a vital ingredient in business success and that great leaders make for great organizations. Des Dearlove explores what leadership means in the twenty-first century.

'BROADLY speaking there are two approaches to leadership. You can theorize about it or you can get on and do it. Theorizing about it is great fun, hugely indulgent and largely useless. Doing it – or doing it better – is demanding, frequently frustrating and of immense value,' says Francis Macleod, former chief executive of the Leadership Trust. 'Those who want to change an organization must be able to change people and in that process there is only one starting point that makes sense. Learning to lead oneself better is the only way to lead others better.'

When considering leadership in the business context, most roots lead to the military world. For managers long used to the concept of divide and rule, the temptation to view the business world as a battlefield is, even now, highly appealing. Indeed, the success of Sun Tzu's *The Art of War* as a management text points to the continuing popularity of this idea.

Leadership re-emerged on the management agenda in the 1980s after a period of relative neglect. A great many books were produced purporting to offer essential guidance on how to become a leader. These tended to portray the business leader as a general, inspiring the corporate troops to one more effort.

Useful inspirations do exist in the military world for today's corporate leaders. One of the most persuasive, and underestimated, is Field Marshall William Slim. Slim believed that the leadership lessons he had learned in the army could readily be applied to the business world. In his book *Defeat Into Victory*, he described his thoughts on raising morale:

> *'Morale is a state of mind. It is that intangible force which will move a whole group of men to give their last ounce to achieve something, without counting the cost to themselves; that makes them feel they are part of something greater than themselves. If they are to feel that, their morale must, if it is to endure – and the essence of morale is that it should endure – have certain foundations. These foundations are spiritual, intellectual, and material, and that is the order of their importance. Spiritual first, because only spiritual foundations can stand real strain. Next intellectual, because men are swayed by reason as well as feeling. Material last – important, but last – because the highest kinds of morale are often met when material conditions are lowest.'*

The doyen of the military-inspired approach is the UK leadership writer and practitioner John Adair, who was himself in the army (as well as spending time on an Arctic trawler and various other adventures). Adair identified a list of the basic functions of leadership: planning, initiating, controlling, supporting, informing and evaluating. Central to his thinking is the belief that leadership is a skill that can be learned like any other. This is one of the fundamentals of the military approach to leadership: leaders are formed in the crucible of action rather than through chance genetics.

In the management world, there is a tendency to fluctuate between these two extremes. On the one hand, managers are sent on leadership development courses to nurture, and discover, leadership skills. On the other hand, there is still a substantial belief that leaders have innate skills that cannot be learned.

Modern leadership writers tend to suggest that leadership as a skill or characteristic is distributed generously among the population.

'Successful leadership is not dependent on the possession of a single universal pattern of inborn traits and abilities. It seems likely that leadership potential (considering the tremendous variety of situations for which leadership is required) is broadly rather than narrowly distributed in the population,' wrote Douglas McGregor in *The Human Side of Enterprise*. The American Warren Bennis, inspired by McGregor, has studied leadership throughout his career. Bennis also concludes that each of us contains the capacity for leadership and has leadership experience. He does not suggest that actually translating this into becoming an effective leader is straightforward, but that it can be done, given time and application.

While such arguments are impressively optimistic about human potential, they are disappointed by reality. The dearth of great leaders is increasingly apparent. This suggests either that innate skills are not being effectively developed, or that the business world simply does not encourage managers to fulfil their potential as leaders.

The new leader

The increasing emphasis in recent years has, however, focused on leaders as real people managing in a consensus-seeking manner. Instead of seeing leadership as synonymous with dictatorship, this view is of leadership as a more subtle and humane art. It also breaks down the barrier between leadership and management.

Traditionally, in theory at least, the two have been separated. 'Men are ripe for intelligent, understanding, personal leadership, they would rather be led than managed,' observed Field Marshal Slim. Increasingly, however, management and leadership are being seen as inextricably linked. It is one thing for a leader to propound a grand vision, but this is redundant unless the vision is managed so it becomes real achievement.

While traditional views of leadership tend eventually to concentrate on vision and charisma, the message now seems to be that charisma is no longer enough to carry leaders through. Indeed, leaders with strong personalities are just as likely to bite the corporate dust. The new model leaders include people like Percy Barnevik at ASEA Brown Boveri, Michael Dell, Cisco's John Chambers, Virgin's Richard Branson and Jack Welch at GE.

The magic marking out such executives has been analyzed by INSEAD leadership expert Manfred Kets de Vries. 'They go beyond narrow definitions. They have an ability to excite people in their organizations,' he says. 'They also work extremely hard – leading by example is not dead – and are highly resistant to stress. Also, leaders like Branson or Barnevik are very aware of what their failings are. They make sure that they find good people who can fill these areas.'

Leonard Sayles, author of *Leadership: Managing in Real Organizations* and *The Working Leader*, is representative of a great deal of the new thinking. Sayles suggests that leadership affects managers at all levels, not simply those in the higher echelons of management. 'It is leadership based on work issues, not just people issues, and is very different from the method and style of managing that has evolved from our traditional management principles.'

Sayles argues that the leader's role lies in 'facilitating co-ordination and integration in order to get work done'. He is dismissive of the perennial concept of the great corporate leader. Instead, his emphasis is on the leader as the integrator of corporate systems. The leader is a kind of fulcrum, 'adapting, modifying, adjusting and rearranging the complex task and function interfaces that keep slipping out of alignment'. Rather than being centred around vision and inspiration, Sayles regards the leader's key role as integrating the outputs of their work unit with those of the rest of the organization. To him, 'managers who are not leaders can only be failures'.

Interestingly, and unhelpfully for the practising manager, leadership attracts such aphorisms rather than hard and fast definitions. Indeed, there are a plethora of definitions on what constitutes a leader and the characteristics of leadership. In practice, none has come to be universally, or even widely, accepted.

The very individualism associated with leadership is now a bone of contention. The people we tend to think of as leaders – from Napoleon to Winston Churchill – are not exactly renowned for their teamworking skills. But, these are exactly the skills that management theorists insist are all-important for the twenty-first century.

'In some cases, the needs of a situation bring to the fore individuals with unique qualities or values, however, most leaders have to fit their skills, experience and vision to a particular time and place,' says psychologist Robert Sharrock of YSC. 'Today's leaders have to be pragmatic and flexible to survive. Increasingly, this means being people rather than task-oriented. The "great man" theory about leadership rarely applies – if teams are what make businesses run, then we have to look beyond individual leaders to groups of people with a variety of leadership skills.'

The pendulum has swung so far that there is growing interest in the study of followers. Once the humble foot soldier was ignored, as commentators sought out the commanding officer; now the foot soldiers are encouraged to voice their opinions and shape how the organization works. 'Followers are becoming more powerful. It is now common for the performance of bosses to be scrutinized and appraised by their corporate followers. This, of course, means that leaders have to actively seek the support of their followers in a way they would never have previously contemplated,' says Sharrock.

Phil Hodgson of Ashridge Management College has analyzed the behaviour of a number of business leaders. His finding is that the old models of leadership are no longer appropriate. 'Generally, the managers interviewed had outgrown the notion of the individualistic leader. Instead, they regarded leadership as a question of drawing people and disparate parts of the organization together in a way that made individuals and the organization more effective.' He concludes that the new leader must add value as a coach, mentor, and problem solver; allow people to accept credit for success and responsibility for failure; and must continually evaluate and enhance their own leadership role. 'They don't follow rigid or orthodox role models, but prefer to nurture their own unique leadership style,' he says. 'And, they don't do people's jobs for them or put their faith in developing a personality cult.' The new recipe for leadership centres on five key areas: learning, energy, simplicity, focus, and inner sense.

In an age of empowerment, the ability to delegate effectively is critically important. 'Empowerment and leadership are not mutually exclusive,' says INSEAD's de Vries. 'The trouble is that many executives feel it is good to have control. They become addicted to power – and that is what kills companies.'

Knowing when to let go has become an integral part of the skills of the modern leader. There are many examples of leaders who stay on in organizations and in governments far beyond their practical usefulness. De Vries contends that leaders, like products, have a lifecycle. He identifies three stages in this – entry and experimentation, consolidation, and decline – and estimates that lifecycles for leaders are shortening.[1]

The growing interest and belief in the human side of leadership are, in themselves, nothing new. James McGregor Burns coined the phrases 'transactional' and 'transformational' leadership. Transactional leadership involves leaders who are very efficient at giving people something in return for their support or work. Followers are valued, appreciated and rewarded. Transformational leadership is concerned with leaders who create visions and are able to carry people along with them towards the vision.

The ability to create and sustain a credible vision remains critical. Harvard's John Kotter identified three central processes in leadership: establishing direction; aligning people; motivating and inspiring. The way in which these core elements are put into practice is continually being refined. But at its heart lies an appreciation of the fact that the leader cannot act alone. Peter Drucker has observed that leaders habitually talk of 'we' rather than 'I'. The great leaders appear to be natural teamworkers, a fact overlooked by heroic models of leadership. In *The Tao of Leadership*, John Heider produces another aphorism, but one that cuts to the heart of modern leadership: 'enlightened leadership is service, not selfishness.'[2]

Emotional intelligence

Perhaps the greatest change in our notion of and understanding of leadership in recent years has come through the concept of Emotional Intelligence (EQ). This is based on the belief that the ability of managers to understand and manage their own emotions and those of the people with whom they work is the key to better business performance. Like so many important management breakthroughs, however, its origins lie outside of business.

Rising rates of aggression and depression in US schools led Daniel Goleman to compile the research summarized in his 1995 book *Emotional Intelligence*. He concluded that human competencies like self-awareness, self-discipline, persistence and empathy are of greater consequence than IQ in much of life. Goleman asserted that we ignore the emotional competencies at our peril, and that children can – and should – be taught these abilities at school.

This groundbreaking book did much to raise awareness of the concept of Emotional Intelligence in the business community. The new interest is reflected in the growing number of business books and articles on the subject. Goleman himself is now a rising star in the management guru constellation. *Emotional Intelligence* was on *The New York Times* bestseller list for 18 months and has been translated into nearly 30 languages. The term is now finding its way into management development programmes and on to business school curricula.

Goleman, a psychologist by training, built on the ideas of the Harvard-based psychologist Howard Gardner – credited with the development of the multiple intelligence theory – and the Yale psychologist Peter Salovey. In his book, he adopts Salovey's definition of emotional intelligence. According to Salovey, EQ can be observed in five key areas: knowing one's emotions; managing emotions; motivating oneself; recognizing emotions in others; and handling relationships.

Goleman has gone on to explore the issue of personal and professional effectiveness. In a business world too often obsessed by cold analysis and intellect, he argues, the emotional climate is more important to the success of an organization than was previously recognized. His 1998 book, *Working With Emotional Intelligence*, argues that workplace competencies based on emotional intelligence play a far greater role in star performance than do intellect or technical skill, and that both individuals and companies will benefit from cultivating these capabilities.

In particular, he claims that the emotional dimension is critical in determining the effectiveness of leaders, arguing that in demanding jobs where above average IQ is a given, superior emotional capability gives leaders an edge. At senior levels, emotional intelligence rather than rational intelligence marks out the true leader.

According to Goleman, studies of outstanding performers in organizations show that about two-thirds of the abilities that set star performers apart in the leadership stakes are based on emotional intelligence; only one-third of the skills that matter relate to raw intelligence (as measured by IQ) and technical expertise.

'Our emotions are hardwired into our being,' he explains. 'The very architecture of the brain gives feelings priority over thought.' In reality, it is impossible to entirely separate thought from emotion. 'We can be effective only when the two systems – our emotional brain and our thinking brain – work together. That working relationship, which encompasses most of what we do in life, is the essence of emotional intelligence.'

Goleman has taken his analysis further, applying it to the elusive role of leadership. He argues that part of the problem is that pontification and hypotheses, rather than hard data, have generally been the currency of leadership theorists. This, it must be said, is generally true. The average book on leadership is more likely to feature Churchillian quotations than rigorous analysis of the behaviour of leaders. Goleman redresses the balance with his research covering over 3,000 executives. From this, he identifies six separate leadership styles: 'Coercive leaders demand immediate compliance. Authoritative leaders mobilize people towards a vision. Affiliative leaders create emotional bonds and harmony. Democratic leaders build consensus through participation. Pacesetting leaders expect excellence and self-direction. And coaching leaders develop people for the future.'

These types are useful – and commonsensical. Where Goleman departs from the usual theories is in his belief that leaders need to apply different leadership styles in different situations. Today's coercive leader may need to switch to coaching mode in the next meeting. 'Leaders who have mastered four or more – especially the authoritative, democratic, affiliative, and coaching strategies – have the best climate and business performance,' Goleman writes.

This, once again, makes sense. Leaders require a mix of pragmatism and mental agility to survive the mire of organizational politics, not to mention the demands of the markets. This fits neatly with changes in the business world. Companies are re-evaluating the leadership characteristics they require for the future. Some companies talk about an inward journey. Emotional Intelligence is part of that redefinition.

'We're talking about "relationship savvy",' notes Gill Stringer, executive development manager at telecoms giant BT. 'That's how you inspire people. We're looking to develop interpersonal sensitivity and a mindset that is about collaboration, and understanding what others have to contribute, and seeing partnerships as an opportunity to learn.'

BT went through a major year-long rethink of the leadership profile required to support the company's global ambitions. The new leadership profile was presented to the main board in 1999. Stringer notes:

> *'Our strategy for global expansion includes a high degree of partnering and joint ventures. As boundaries get fuzzier and fuzzier, leadership becomes more and more vital. It's always been a big issue, but the requirements have changed. We don't want people who will sit at the top of their organizational pyramid and say I manage what I control, and I control what I manage. The emphasis is on relationship management.' 'The critical issue is interpersonal sensitivity. This ties in with Emotional Intelligence. These issues are converging now for us not because they are nice to do, but because they are being driven by business objectives. We are moving to a more holistic approach.'*

The good news is that, according to Goleman, Emotional Intelligence can be learned. There are five dimensions to this, he says. These are:

- **Self-awareness**: we seldom pay attention to what we feel. A stream of moods runs in parallel to our thoughts. This, and previous emotional experiences provide a context for our decision making.

- **Managing emotions**: all effective leaders learn to manage their emotions, especially the big three: anger, anxiety, sadness. This is a decisive life skill.
- **Motivating others**: the root meaning of motive is the same as the root of emotion: to move.
- **Showing empathy**: the flip side of self-awareness is the ability to read emotions in others.
- **Staying connected**: emotions are contagious. There is an unseen transaction that passes between us in every interaction that makes us feel either a little better or a little worse. Goleman calls this a 'secret economy'. It holds the key to motivating the people with whom we work.

This is all very well, but there is, as yet, little evidence to suggest that leaders actually have a driving urge to get in touch with their emotions. Emotional leadership will have to wait until corporate executives have got traditional gung-ho bravura out of their bloodstreams.

REFERENCES

1. de Vries, Manfred Kets, 'CEOs also have the blues', *European Management Journal*, September 1994.
2. Heider, John, *Tao of Leadership*, Wildwood House, Aldershot, 1986.

3

RESOURCES

BOOKS

Adair, John, *Understanding Motivation*, Talbot Adair, Guildford, 1990.

De Pree, Max, *Leadership is an Art*, Doubleday, New York, 1989.

McGregor, Douglas, *The Human Side of Enterprise*, McGraw Hill, New York, 1960.

Oates, David, *Leadership: The Art of Delegation*, Century Business, London, 1993.

Sayles, Leonard, *The Working Leader*, The Free Press, New York, 1993.

The new leadership

WARREN BENNIS

The leaders of the future will have to cast off the heavy burden of command and control, hierarchically based leadership. Warren Bennis hails the arrival of new leadership.

THE post-bureaucratic organization requires a new kind of alliance between leaders and the led. Today's organizations are evolving into federations, networks, clusters, cross-functional teams, temporary systems, *ad hoc* task forces, lattices, modules, matrices – almost anything but pyramids with their obsolete top-down leadership. The new leader will encourage healthy dissent and values those followers courageous enough to say no. It will go to the leader who exults in cultural differences and knows that diversity is the best hope for long-term survival and success.

This does not mark the end of leadership. Rather the need for a new, far more subtle and indirect form of influence for leaders to be effective. The new reality is that intellectual capital, brain power, know-how, human imagination has supplanted capital as the critical success factor, and leaders will have to learn an entirely new set of skills that are not understood, not taught in our business schools, and, for all of those reasons, rarely practised. Four competencies will determine the success of new leadership.

1. The new leader understands and practises the power of appreciation

They are connoisseurs of talent, more curators than creators. We all pay lip service to acknowledgement and appreciation. To generalize, most organizations are woefully neglectful of bestowing either. And it is one of the most powerful motivators, especially for knowledge workers.

The leader is rarely the best or the brightest in the new organizations. The new leader has a smell for talent, an imaginative rolodex, unafraid of hiring people better than they are and are often more a curator than a creator. In my research into great groups, I found that in most cases the leader was rarely the cleverest or the sharpest. Peter Schneider, president of Disney's colosally successful Feature Animation studio, leads a group of 1,200 animators. He can't draw to save his life. Bob Taylor, former head of the Palo Alto Research Center, where the first commercial PC was invented, wasn't a computer scientist. J. Robert Oppenheimer, head of the befabled Manhattan project, which produced the first nuclear device, while a brilliant physicist, never matched the accomplishments of the future Nobel laureates working for him at Los Alamos. Max DePree put it best when he said that good leaders 'abandon their ego to the talents of others'.

2. The new leader keeps reminding people of what's important

Organizations drift into entropy and the bureaucratization of imagination when they forget what's important. Simple to say, but that one sentence is one of the few pieces of advice I suggest to leaders: remind your people of what's important.

A powerful enough vision can transform what would otherwise be routine and drudgery into collectively focused energy – even sacrifice. Witness again the Manhattan Project. The scientists there were willing to put their careers on hold and to undertake what was, in essence, a massive engineering feat because they believed the free world depended on their doing so. Reminiscing about Los Alamos, Richard Feynman, the irreverent and future Nobel laureate, told a story that illustrates how reminding people of 'what's important' can give meaning and value to work. The US Army had recruited talented engineers from all over the United States for special duty on the project. They were assigned to work on the primitive computers of the period (1943–1945), doing energy calculations and other tedious jobs. But the Army, obsessed with security, refused to tell them anything specific about the project. They didn't know that they were building a weapon that could end the war or even what their calculations meant. They were simply expected to do the work, which they did slowly and not very well. Feynman, who supervised the technicians, prevailed on his superiors to tell the recruits what they were doing and why. Permission was granted to lift the veil of secrecy, and Oppenheimer gave them a special lecture on the nature of the project and their own contribution.

'Complete transformation,' Feynman recalled. 'They began to invent ways of doing it better. They improved the scheme. They worked at night. They didn't need supervising in the night; they didn't need anything. They understood everything; they invented several of the programs we used.' Ever the scientist, Feynman calculated that the work was done 'nearly 10 times as fast' after it had meaning.

Meaning. Charles Handy has it right in his book *The Hungry Spirit*. We are all hungry spirits craving purpose and meaning at work, to contribute something beyond ourselves and leaders can never forget to stop reminding people of what's important.

3. The new leader generates and sustains trust

We're all aware that the terms of the new social contract of work have changed. No one can depend on life-long loyalty or commitment to any organization. Since 1985, 25 percent of the American workforce has been laid off at least once. That's about half a million on average each year. In 1998, when the unemployment rate was the lowest in 30 years, roughly 110,000 workers were downsized. At a time when the new social contract makes the ties between organizations and their knowledge workers tenuous, trust becomes the emotional glue that can bond people to an organization. Trust is a small word with powerful connotations and is a hugely complex factor. The ingredients are a combination of competencies, constancy, caring, fairness, candour and authenticity. Most of all the latter. And that is achieved by the new leaders when they can balance successfully the tripod of forces working on and in most of is: ambition, competence and integrity. Authenticity, as Groucho joked, cannot be faked. To be redundant, it's real. The current cliché is 'walk your talk'. But it's far more than that.

4. The new leader and the led are intimate allies

The power of Spielberg's *Schindler's List* lies in the transformation of Schindler from a sleazy, down at the heels small time conman who moves to Poland in order to harness cheap Jewish labour to make munitions which he can then sell to the Germans at low cost. His transformation is the singular compelling narrative of the film. And it comes over a period of time where Schindler interacts with his Jewish workers, most of all the accountant, Levin, but also frequent and achingly painful moments where he confronts the evil of the war, of the holocaust, of the suffering, of the injustice. In the penultimate scene, when the war is over and the Nazis have evacuated the factory, but before the American troops arrive, the prisoners give him a ring, made for him, from the precious metals used by the workers. As he tries to put the ring on, he begins crying, 'Why, why are you doing this? With this metal, we could have saved three, maybe four, maybe five more Jews.' And he drives off in tears.

It is hard to remain objective about this scene but, though this was a unique, singular event, it portrays what new leadership is all about: that great leaders are made by great groups and by organizations that create the social architecture of respect and dignity. And through some kind of weird alchemy, some ineffable symbiosis, great leadership brings that about. Without each other, the leader and the led are culturally impoverished. Only a poet could sum up the majesty of this alchemy:

'We are all angels with only one wing.
We can only fly while embracing each other.'

These new leaders will not have the loudest voice, but the most attentive ear. Instead of pyramids, these post-bureaucratic organizations will be structures built of energy and idea, led by people who find their joy in the task at hand, while embracing each other – and not worrying about leaving monuments behind.

RESOURCES

BOOKS

Bennis, Warren, *Managing the Dream*, Perseus Books, 2000.
Laurie, Donald L., *The Real Work of Leaders*, Perseus Books, 2000.

Leadership for the third millennium

ANDREW KAKABADSE

Andrew Kakabadse argues that in the future our concept of leadership will have to change to include the idea of group leadership.

LEADERSHIP, next to religion, has been one of the most examined and debated topics in history. From military leaders such as Alexander the Great to social movement leaders such as Ghandi, the debate has raged as to the characteristics of great leaders.

Yet the composition of leadership still remains devoid of universally acceptable clear criteria and parameters. Some view leadership as the personal relationship between the individual and the group; others as the process of striving towards common goals and values; still others as aspects of behaviour, whether desired and in control of the individual or, alternatively, reactive and driven by forces in the environment.

But leadership thinking cannot concentrate solely on the individual. The impact of the individual, or the team of which the individual is a member, needs to be linked to a broader concept of enterprise value, be that shareholder or stakeholder value. In highly competitive markets the impact of leadership on the organization and perceived worth of the enterprise are concepts that have become inextricably interwoven.

Of the varying views of the elements of sound leadership, it is clear that the managing of opposites is a prime skill. How can one be ethical and political at the same time? How can one be sensitive to others and yet drive through change with discipline and determination? How can one attend to details and yet grasp and pursue half-formed possibilities?

These contrasts promote the first clue as to the requirements of high-performance leadership, namely the balancing of the transformational and transactional elements of leadership. In today's world, balancing the uneasy fit between leading and managing, transforming and transacting, is of absolute necessity.

Leaders who 'transform' fundamentally alter the parameters of the *status quo* through providing a vision for the future and then investing the time and effort in having others share that vision. Through sharing their vision, they clarify the present, explain how the past has influenced the present and promote a view of the future. In order to be effective, transformative leaders need to listen as well as be consistent, persistent and focused in order both to empower others and maintain momentum.

A leader who exhibits such transformative power deeply penetrates the soul and psyche of others and thereby raises in others a level of awareness that rejuvenates people to strive for ever greater ends.

However, leaders are equally required to perform in a transactional manner, simply in order to keep the organization operational. Transactional leadership requires the application of managerial skills in order effectively to address the operational, day-to-day aspects of working life. Managing the detail of budgets, periodically reviewing and following through on projects and initiatives, keeping meetings to time, ensuring that agendas are adhered to and conducting appraisals are examples of transactional management.

How, then, do leaders determine whether to adopt a more transformational or transactional perspective? It is their reading of context, and matching that with their inclinations and aspirations, that determines which element of leadership to pursue. The contextual logic of 'what am I supposed to do' coupled with the individual's views of the world, his or her desire to maintain the steady state or change equilibrium and balance in the world, drives their switching between the transformational and transactional.

As context, or 'making the difference', requires different approaches in different situations, a fundamental issue has been how to approach the analysis of context.

No one person is likely to display the capacity fully to appreciate the different requirements of different contexts. As a number of inputs and viewpoints are required in order to make for a powerful impact in any particular context, leadership needs to be examined from the perspective of role and team contribution rather than personal characteristics.

From the perspective of role, we can categorize executive work as on the one hand 'prescribed', namely, structured and leaving the individual little room to exercise judgement, and on the other as discretionary, whereby considerable judgement is necessary in order for the individual to function effectively in his or her role.

By this distinction, a prescribed role is more of a structured, middle-management transactional job whereas a discretionary role epitomizes the transformational nature of leadership.

The degree of discretion may be planned for in the role and/or driven by the incumbent's capability to influence and determine the boundaries, responsibilities and accountabilities of his or her role. Different bosses set different boundaries and responsibility levels according to contextual pressures, their trust in their subordinates, and each individual boss's wishes and desires. On this basis, any one organization may possess a considerable number of discretionary roles.

Figure 1

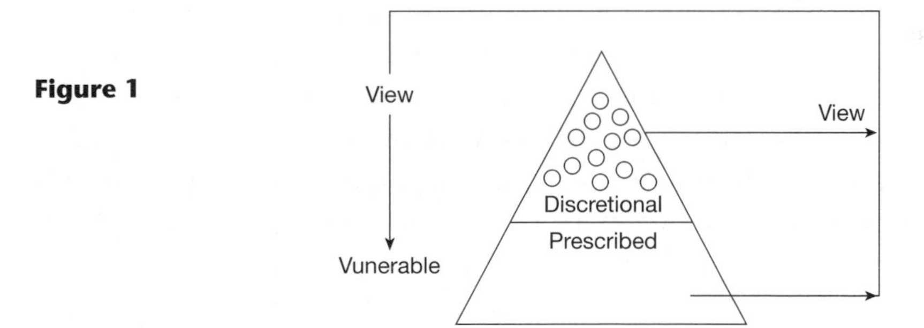

The number of discretionary roles that exist in an organization theoretically determines the number of visions and ways of operating that can shape, positively or negatively, its future. Also, the number of discretionary roles that exist varies from one organization to the next. Further, not all discretionary leader roles need be congregated at the top. Those executives who hold senior management positions – chairmen, CEOs, directors, managing directors and general managers – are likely to occupy discretionary leader roles, the leadership responsibility difference between them being one of degree. However, lower down the organization, younger, key-client account managers may well occupy discretionary leader roles, shaping the future of the company, not because of their involvement in strategic debate but because of their influence on key accounts.

Discretionary leaders from lower down the organization influence strategic direction more by the mistakes they make (for example, losing clients) or by their leaving and taking key-client accounts with them when they exit the organization, than their active participation in direction setting.

Historically, the prime emphasis of leadership concentrated on providing the single individual direction for others to pursue. With the onset of cadre-based organizations, the emphasis changed from one person clearly highlighting the pathways forward to a group-based view of leadership whereby understanding and being responsive to context became the predominant concern.

Being adaptive to context introduced greater complexity to leadership practice, for greater acknowledgement has had to be given to the needs and demands of multiple stakeholders. On this basis, the difference between team-based and cadre-based leadership is one of degree, as much determined by the number of stakeholders that need to be taken into account in the strategic debate.

Whether the leadership philosophy adopted is one of a more transformational or transactional nature depends on an organization's progress through its economic lifecycle. As knowledge-based organizations mature, adopting transactional management is more likely to satisfy shareholder expectations, for the prime challenge, with age, is to introduce scale economies as the prime corporate differentiator.

Yet, irrespective of whether powerful leadership or good management are required, the contextual-based interpretation of leadership assumes constant attention to enhancing leadership capacity, since nothing stays still. Responsiveness to context requires a mindset of continuous development whereby the individual is always ready to adjust and change skills and approach as the needs of stakeholders evolve or even dramatically alter.

The notion of predetermined capabilities of leadership, especially those of providing followers with clear direction, holds little place in today's world, where a follower in one context can be an influential stakeholder or shareholder/owner in another.

RESOURCES

BOOK

Kakabadse, Andrew, *Essence of Leadership*, International Thomson Publishing, 1998.

Leadership role models

RANDALL P. WHITE AND PHIL HODGSON

Leaders can no longer turn to convenient role models in search of inspiration, suggest Randall P. White and Phil Hodgson. Yesterday's role models – whether corporate, military or political – provide lessons valuable for yesterday's leadership. Leaders for the future require future-minded role models.

THE nearest and most appropriate role models for future leaders come from unusual and universal sources, rather than the idiosyncrasies of a few pathfinders.

But, first, what can the new fundamentals of leadership be distilled down to? What does the future leader actually do and hope to achieve?

> *We believe that the leader's role is to identify productive areas of uncertainty and confusion and to lead the organization into those areas in order to gain competitive (or other kinds of) advantage.*

We have identified two groups of people that offer some of the attitudes, approaches and perspectives white water leaders now require. We spent time seeking out the people who seem best equipped to cope in an uncertain world and make uncertainty work. We also identified the specific attitudes and skills used by successful corporate leaders. Our conclusions are far removed from the usual military and sporting role models beloved by leaders the world over.

To our surprise, two groups emerged as particularly adept at handling uncertainty: children and experienced travellers. But, why and, perhaps more importantly, how?

The child as role model

In a world where uncertainty reigns, we all have to escape the safety net of interpreted experience. We must move beyond. We must attain a beginner's mind and come to terms with the 'foreignness' of people and situations. We have to unleash *childlikeness* on the challenges we now face.

The leader as child? The child as leader? It flies in the face of all traditional concepts of leadership roles and role models. Leaders, by convention, are supermen and superwomen, larger than life, strong, indomitable and all-knowing.

But think about how much uncertainty children face just in the process of growing up. Discovering the world around them, their strengths and weaknesses, and infinitely more.

The skills and perspectives of supermen and superwomen are ill-matched against uncertainty. Childlikeness makes business sense. Work can equal play without the bottom line being forgotten. Microsoft, for example, has proved particularly adept at harnessing the learning capabilities and energy we find in children. It may now be a huge corporation but it retains the atmosphere and the behaviours of a precocious upstart. It outwitted the field through its naive smartness and seems determined to hang on to it. Typically, its corporate headquarters at Redmond, near Seattle, is nicknamed 'the campus'. Consciously or unconsciously, Microsoft seeks to utilize the freewheeling, flexible, stay-up-all-night, ideas-driven atmosphere of a college campus. The dividing lines between work and play are blurred to the point of not existing. With 16,000 employees the average age is an astonishing 31 and its programmers are even younger – most are under 25 years old. A Microsoft employee observed in an article that the company 'offers us the life we had in school, except we get paid to do our work. And, unlike schools, we get to do the really cool stuff.[1] Microsoft is school without the homework, the uniform, or the externally imposed discipline.

Of course, there is a downside. Microsoft is poor at meeting its own self-imposed deadlines – Windows 95 was more than nine months late. And we are yet to discover what happens when the programmers get older. Will they suddenly become solid corporate citizens who come down hard on the freeflowing ideas factory, or will they be too burned out to care?

Many other companies have tried to create Microsoft's campus mentality with employees involved in a creative free for all. Most have moved away from the concept by the time they grow to a significant size – believing that a traditional approach is then more appropriate. The child is unleashed and then shepherded away to a quiet corner for a lesson in how to behave in a big corporation.

Interestingly, movie makers are attracted to the idea of letting a child-like mind loose in the grown-up world of business or anywhere else bedevilled by orthodoxy. Peter Sellers' *Being There* featured Sellers as an innocent gardener whose homespun wisdom won him political acclaim. Tom Hanks in *Big* was a corporate executive with a childlike passion for toys. The message was humorous, but underneath there is a more important point. We realize that children can see things as they really are. They can strip away the jargon, the complexity we have loaded onto something, and get to its heart. They ask awkward questions and are not saddled with preconceptions. They live with uncertainty all the time, but are able to cope, grow, develop and learn.

Childlikeness is not childishness – though occasionally a tantrum may be preferable to ignoring a problem. Discussing their working relationship together, David Bowie says of producer and guru figure, Brian Eno: 'Brian has always worked intuitively ... creating a situation of childlikeness in the studio, which sounds glib, but it's not, it's really important, a sense of play. Brian creates an area where you aren't afraid.[2]

There is an element of this childlikeness in many successful artists and sports stars. At his peak, John McEnroe retained all of his childlike qualities. He was constantly willing to try something new, to change the tempo and his entire game was built around the speed, flexibility and intuitive judgement of his touch with the racquet on the ball. McEnroe's downside was that his childlikeness sometimes became childishness.

Practically, what lessons can children teach us? Children can handle, cope with and grow from uncertainty for a number of reasons:

- Creativity.
- Absorbing stimuli.
- Accepting no right way.
- Learning.
- Adaptability.

Creativity

Children are naturally and instinctively creative. Contrast this with organizations which naturally and instinctively distrust creativity. In the traditional company, creative elements are cordoned off. It is risky to do the new and different. The nerds and geeks inhabit a world of their own, set apart from the mainstream. Difficult to manage, organizations choose not to manage them. The stereotype suggests that though they may have bright ideas, they have no grasp of commercial reality. Compartmentalized, they can be controlled and the pernicious effects of their off-beat creativity won't infiltrate the rest of the organization.

Look at what's happened with IT departments. We all know about the ridiculously huge power of technology. Corporations know about it. Executives know about it – some even use it. Yet, evidence suggests that though corporations bankroll investment in IT, it has generally failed to reap significant benefits in corporate effectiveness and performance. The geeks and nerds remain outside the corporate noose of control or understanding.

Managers often have only a limited understanding of what IT can do for their organization. They have a broad sympathy with investing in high technology, but have a restricted view of its practical power and business advantage. For example, a survey by Henley Management College of more than 200 chief executives, directors and other senior managers found that many top managers just did not understand the strategic importance of IT.[3]

It is likely that, if asked, a great many managers would identify the benefits of IT in simple cost terms. IT reduces an organization's staff count, therefore it saves money. (The same goes for re-engineering.) As Harvard's Shoshana Zuboff points out in her book, *In the Age of the Smart Machine*, companies have regarded IT as a means of reducing staff numbers through the automation of their jobs.[4] The trouble is that the jobs which have been automated out of existence are often those which involve direct contact with customers. Zuboff argues that instead of automating tasks, IT's job should be to 'informate' people – an ungainly, but apposite, word combining inform and educate. By regarding IT as a numbers and cost-cutting mechanism organizations are failing to optimize its full potential, which goes far beyond cost reduction.

IT has proved next to impossible to manage. Why? One of the reasons must be that many of those in IT functions are stereotypical techno-lovers. Technophobe executives find it hard to deal with them or communicate with them, and managing them is regarded as close to impossible. The IT experts largely remain marginalized and their creativity often has little impact, or far less impact than it needs to if the organization is to reap the full benefits of IT.

Once upon a time, organizations could – and did – sideline their creatives and get on with the real business of running the company. Not now. Now, creativity has to be part of everyone's job. Cordoning off a vital source of creativity – and potential competitive advantage – is no longer an alternative. Instead, creativity has to be instilled into the lifeblood of the organization. Without creative people, the organization will grind to a halt.

Absorbing stimuli

Children move easily from one activity to another. One minute they are happily contemplating a jigsaw, the next they are painting. They take in different stimuli effortlessly. They move on quickly without letting go of what they have just learned.

As we have seen, executives also jump from one job to another, phone call to video conference, sales call to board meeting. The trouble is that while they are adept at taking in stimuli, they are poor at learning from it so it can be used at a later date. They go through a wide range of experiences and emotions every day of the week and then go home to start afresh on the next day. They are continually letting go of what they have just learned and experienced.

Accepting no right way

Children do not know there is a right way to do anything. This is a positive advantage – for children, and for corporations (though not necessarily for parents). They seek out different methods, however unusual or different. They are not handicapped by the way things have always been done, the way something should be done or the way used by a particular individual.

Children not only think differently. Allied to this, is their innocence – they think the best of people; executives perpetually fear the worst. 'Most people can do something better than the current role they are in,' said one of the executives we interviewed, but such views are often not widely held or translated into practice.

Think what you would do if you were charged with introducing a new brand of car into the country. Your budget is large (but minuscule compared to Ford's or GM's) and your target is to capture a mere 1 percent of the car market. The downside is you are competing against the automotive giants.

Probably you would spend heavily on advertising and set-up dealerships. You would highlight some differentiation in your product and target a particular area. Start with the US West Coast, say California, and then move on.

If we accept there is no single right way, we have to try out new ways. In a corporate context, seeking out new approaches can take on apparently bizarre forms. British writer David Whyte has established a novel niche market. His book, *The Heart Aroused: Poetry and the Preservation of the Soul in Corporate America*, is a surprise bestseller.[5] Whyte is employed by multinationals such as AT&T, Boeing and Arthur Andersen to enhance creativity, and simply to awaken executives to other sources of ideas and value. He reads poetry to them. Some fall asleep, some are inspired. Indeed, Whyte is such an inspiration that one high ranking AT&T executive left the company, having been awakened to the meaninglessness of his job.

Learning

There is a famous observation that it is the mouse that teaches the kitten how to catch mice, and not the mother cat.[6] As the mice become tougher to catch, so the kitten learns how to catch tougher mice. The point is that children, or kittens, progressively learn by playing and play by learning. The lessons for corporations is that when learning is play it is highly effective – look at Microsoft. When learning is work it is ineffective – look at all the executives 'forced' to go on training courses. The learning which sticks has a joy of discovery, playfulness. Many executives have been to brainstorming seminars where an atmosphere of deliberate playfulness often stimulates high levels of executive learning for an hour or so. Corporations of the future are going to need to find ways to extend that hour to cover the entire working day.

Adaptability

Children are good at dealing with the unknown and unexpected. If something unusual occurs they attempt to make sense of it, to understand. Somewhere along the line we have lost this precious curiosity.

'When you're a kid and you're learning it's okay because a lot of things are confusing and you persevere with it,' says Bill Gates.[7] Children persist at learning in a way which is difficult to achieve in an organization full of truculent and ambitious adults ready to make you seem a fool if you've failed or come up with a crazy idea. After all, getting it wrong may cost you your job.

Leaders as travellers

True leaders are also like experienced travellers.

Travellers are romantic figures. We are attracted to the idea of the quest, struggling against the odds, overcoming the might of nature. *In Search of Excellence* was a great title because it suggested a quest – in fact, a more proper description of the book would be, 'Here is our current view of excellence.'

We like the idea of the quest so much that we send managers on outdoor training exercises. We want to turn them into explorers and adventurers, often without thinking why.

Of course, the managers of our times are travellers, skipping from one airport to another, time zone to time zone. They travel, but are they true travellers? Too often, they are mere passengers. And, in the new reality who wants passengers?

As you become more adventurous it is notable that excitement and uncertainty increases. Check where you think your preference for uncertainty puts you on our scale in Figure 1.

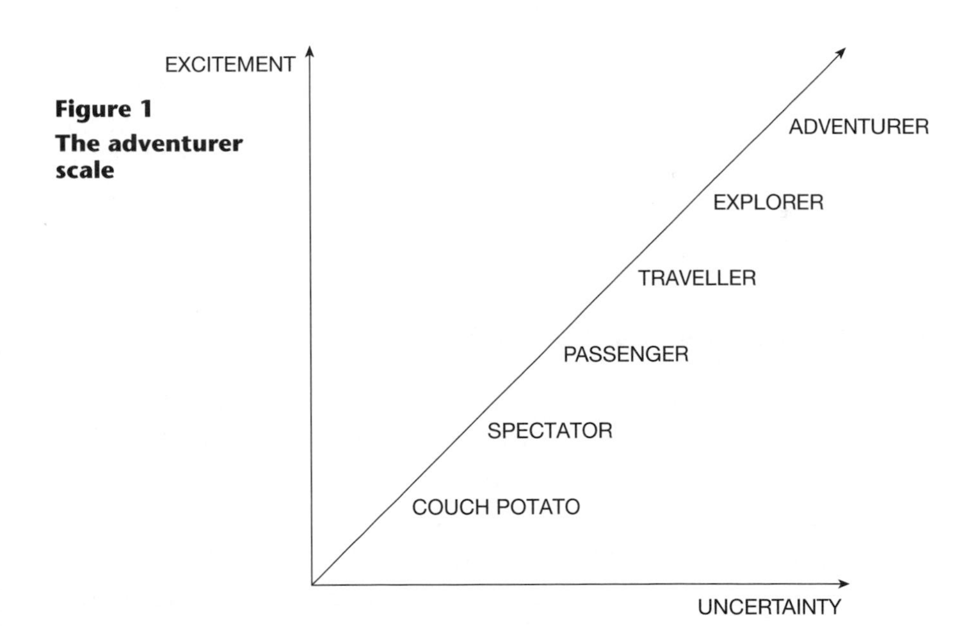

Figure 1
The adventurer scale

The *couch potato* settles for the unexciting security of remaining stationery on the couch with a pizza and the channel changer. Next up the scale comes the *spectator* – some excitement, but a great deal of certainty and no direct involvement in the action; the *passenger* is part of the journey although not contributing to choices made about direction and speed. Moving up the scale towards maximum excitement and maximum uncertainty the *traveller* becomes the *explorer* who can become the *adventurer*. It is noticeable that as excitement and uncertainty increase so, for the most part, does involvement.

But, what is it that experienced travellers do which we are seeking to emulate?

Focus on the quest

They combine focus on their particular quest with a pragmatic realization that there are a multitude of ways of getting there. They take the obscure byways and are entertained and educated by diversions, without losing sight of why they are there in the first place.

Experienced travellers combine focus on given objectives with a flexibility to explore the unexpected byways. Competitive advantage comes from going off the beaten track and moving to an area of uncertainty.

Pragmatically interpreting your corporate and personal quest has important implications for corporate missions. Instead of being fixed and unvarying 'solutions', leaders regard missions as continually evolving.

Take risks to learn and achieve

Travellers take risks to learn to achieve in order to reach their destination, especially one to which they have never travelled before. The best travellers are open to experience – their own and that of others – and can adapt to unforeseen circumstances.

Planes, trains and automobiles are often delayed and sometimes take you where you don't want to go. Experienced travellers shrug their shoulders and change their behaviour and expectations to meet the new demands of the situation. Remember the movie, *Planes, Trains and Automobiles* with John Candy and Steve Martin? The perennially unsuccessful and apparently clueless John Candy character was a far better traveller than the suave and sophisticated character played by Steve Martin.

Understand and play the system

They are like fish in water. Some people move through the system effortlessly – others get gridlocked and struggle with the constraints and distractions. Travellers take it for granted that they can, and do, move through the organization easily and swiftly. Achieving agreement from people, getting clearance for projects, are minor hindrances rather than weighty obstacles to reaching their goals.

This is often an unconscious skill. Travellers do it so well they often don't realize what they are doing. It is akin to a hurdler reaching his or her peak – automatically they take the right number of strides between hurdles. They don't need to think or alter their stride pattern. It is natural and effective.

By talking to people, approaching allies in the right way at the right time, knowing how the system works, travellers are able to work around a great deal of delaying bureaucracy and corporate politics to concentrate on action. They seem at ease in the corporate waters and, additionally, are acutely aware in which environment – which waters – they operate most effectively.

Respect cultural differences and perspectives

Travellers respect, and are sensitive to these differences. Travellers realize that if we were all the same – clones of each other – the world would be a boring uncreative place. But difference also produces difficulty because we do not all think, act and react the same way to the same stimuli. Difference, then, needs to be encouraged and understood.

Thrive on discovery

They are prepared to go where others haven't gone before. Travellers seek out challenges. 'Some people have asked me why I am doing this. It's the excitement that goes with change. I can already feel the juices of adventure building up,' said Bill Cockburn on his appointment as chief executive of the UK retailing chain W.H. Smith.[8] After 34 years with the UK's Post Office, Cockburn still relished the chance to explore new territory.

Or listen to Nobel laureate Seamus Heaney on writing poetry: 'Unless a poem surprises you a little bit, some little gate is opened by the words within themselves, then the poem could be perfectly okay, but it won't hold you forever. There has to be a little surprise, a big surprise is even better, but a little surprise will do. It is to do with the unforeseen being recognized as completely true.'[9] Are you seeking out the big surprises?

Use a combination of hard factual data and inner sense

They use maps, compass, timetables, but also have an inner sense of where to go, what to do and how to behave. When all other sources of information fail, travellers trust their instinct to know what to do.

Enrich their perspectives through their experiences

They learn through each and every experience. No matter how many times an experienced traveller has travelled a particular route, they are always on the look out for the new or unexpected.

Feel comfortable travelling alone or in groups

Experienced travellers support each other, offer ideas and suggestions, but have the confidence to travel alone if needs be. They make good companions, but are not afraid of their own company.

Maximize opportunities

With a few hours to kill after missing a connecting flight they do something, rather than hanging around cursing their misfortune. They regard lost time as a gift rather than a waste. They make the most of learning opportunities at every turn, no matter where they are and what they are doing.

Constantly on the move

Travellers are restless. C.K. Prahalad makes a telling comparison between CNN and CBS. CNN has very little bureaucracy, makes most of its big decisions on the run, and spends less in 24 hours than CBS spends in one hour for apparently equivalent news coverage. The people at CNN are powerful because they keep moving, they don't use fixed authority, they appear to invent it each time afresh. It is very tiring, and people do get burned out, but it is also tremendously competitive to other TV news systems.

The conclusion? Managers should always be seeking an upgrade to experienced traveller class.

Leveraging organizational learning

Children and experienced travellers share a number of things in common. Both are adaptable and flexible. Most importantly, however, they are constantly learning. For them, everything is an opportunity for learning whether it is a new country, a different paintbrush or meeting new people.

If we are to move towards uncertainty, leveraging learning is a corporate and personal imperative no matter what your business, no matter what your aspirations, no matter what your status or skills. Learning is the driving force behind future leaders and the organizations of the future. And learning is the gateway to the other skills of leadership.

'The rate at which organizations learn may become the only sustainable source of competitive advantage,' says Ray Stata of Analogue Devices.[10] The company with a culture geared to and driven by learning may (remember there are no certainties) have a headstart in the hyper-competitive future. The importance of learning more about *how*, *why* and *when* organizations can no longer be understated or put to one side.

In a 1988 article, Arie de Geus, a former planning director at Shell, showed that one-third of *Fortune* 500 industrial companies listed in 1970 had disappeared by 1983. The average corporate survival rate for large companies in the early 1980s was only about half as long as the life of a human being. A look at *Fortune*, or virtually any other listing, provides speedy evidence of the turbulence at work. Last year's loss makers included Time Warner, Tyson Foods, Comcast Corporation, Worldcom and Salomon. It is an international phenomenon. Typically, 43 companies ranked in the UK's top 500 listing left the list in 1995, probably never to reappear.

However, de Geus identified a few organizations that had survived for 75 years or more. De Geus suggested that the key to their longevity was their ability to conduct 'experiments in the margin'. They were always looking for new business opportunities which continually challenged the organization to grow and learn.[11] Corning Glass has been similarly dynamic – it has continually taken in and nurtured start-ups so that they can later be spun-off as separate companies.[12] This ability to grow (although not necessarily in size) and learn has become the backbone of any organization wishing to survive and prosper in changing and turbulent markets.

We would hazard a confident guess that what links the declining fortunes of this disparate groups boils down to a breakdown of learning. They were either too busy learning about yesterday to begin learning about tomorrow, or regarded learning as something you do at school, not in a modern corporation.

Sceptics will argue that the interest in improving learning is similar to the interest in improving quality which was very attractive five years earlier. Sadly, there is mounting evidence that more than half of all quality initiatives fail within two years.[13] Will the learning organization prove similarly disappointing?

Part of the problem is that the faddish popularity of the term 'learning organization' gives the impression that you can install a learning organization as easily as you can install a new piece of equipment. As a latest fad, the learning organization disappoints because it doesn't come in turnkey form. The learning organization is not an end state – a product. In reality the learning organization is not a product; but a process. In fact, the learning organization encapsulates a whole series of complex and messy processes into a single easy sounding phrase.

This messiness means that useful definitions of the learning organization are elusive. In *The Learning Company*, Mike Pedler, John Burgoyne and Tom Boydell say it is: 'an organization that facilitates the learning of all its members and continuously transforms itself.'[14]

Continual experimentation and adaptation to a changing set of circumstances is not a new idea. As we have seen, the decline and failure of many household names and famous industries across the world demonstrates that because you were once very good doesn't mean you will always be good. The rapid rise, and fall, of companies has shown that one good idea will get you going, but a succession of good ideas is needed to keep you in business. This applies to organizations and to each and every individual within them. Learning is the only sustainable source of such inspiration.

Not only that. Learning dynamically bridges the divide between the organization and the individual. The various definitions struggle to reconcile the learning of individuals and the concept of organizational learning.

There is a perennial danger of allowing the concept to overtake the reality. Academic definitions cannot be instantly applied in the real world. As a result, managers need to promote learning so that it gradually emerges as a key part of an organization's culture. Being convinced of the merits of the learning organization is not usually a matter of dramatic conversion.

Ironically, it is fear of failure – or actual failure – which often kick-starts enthusiasm for learning. Alternatively, it may be a change of chief executive, an obvious challenge in the marketplace, or a new opportunity posed by technology. UK software company Logica hit difficulties at the beginning of the 1990s. A new chairman was brought in who set about fundamental changes, rooting out people 'who couldn't learn to think in different ways'.[15]

Learning to think in different ways works – whether it is inspired by a corporate jester, a poet or a new CEO. Most people appear to like learning and find difference attractive and stimulating. It makes them feel better, and it encourages them to come to work, and to work better at work. The difficulty in sustaining this style of organization is found when it has been imposed from above rather as a passing fad or fashion. In this case then, like fashion, the learning organization will last until the next fad comes along.

While learning can now be shown to be a significant component of getting ahead, continuous learning appears to be an even more significant part of staying ahead. But that is often a complex process. The mechanics of creation are complex. But, creating the learning organization is not a dereliction of corporate duty. The onus is not simply passed down to the employee. Instead, it is an expansion of responsibility and of trust that includes everyone in the organization. Managing these two elements, critically, requires leadership and highly sophisticated leaders.

REFERENCES

1. Quoted in Arthur, C, 'All geek to me', *Independent on Sunday*, 15 October 1995.
2. de Lisle, Tim, 'Immaculate conceptions', *Independent on Sunday*, 10 September 1995.
3. *The Future Work Forum*, Henley Management College, 1992.
4. Zuboff, Shoshana, *In the Age of the Smart Machine*, Basic Books, New York, 1988.
5. Whyte, David, *The Heart Aroused: Poetry and the Preservation of the Soul in Corporate America*, Doubleday, New York, 1994.
6. Observed by the early cybernetician W. Ross Ashby and more recently developed by Christopher Bartlett.
7. Quoted in White, L., 'Net prophet', *Sunday Times*, 12 November 1995.
8. Olins, R., 'Can postman deliver at WH Smith?, *Sunday Times*, 5 November 1995.
9. Quoted in Greig, G., 'At the height of his powers', *Sunday Times*, 8 October 1995.
10. *Sloan Management Review*, Spring 1989.
11. de Geus, Arie, 'Planning as learning', *Harvard Business Review*, March–April 1988.

12. For a good description of Corning and its innovative product development process see 'Corning Glass: the battle to talk with light' in Magaziner, I. and Patinkin, M., *The Silent War*, Random House, New York, 1989 (pp. 264–299).
13. Williams, Colin and Binney, George, *Making Quality Work*, Economist Intelligence Unit, London, 1992.
14. Pedler, M., Burgoyne, J. and Boydell, T., *The Learning Company, A Strategy for Sustainable Development*, McGraw-Hill, Maidenhead,1991.
15. Taylor, P., 'Disciplined Logica returns to favour', *Financial Times*, 13 September 1995.

RESOURCES

BOOK

White, Randall P., Hodgson, Phil and Crainer, Stuart, *The Future Of Leadership*, FT/Pitman, London, 1996.

Mutiny on the leadership

TOM BROWN

The study of leadership has become an industry – and a heavy industry at that. Creative takes on leadership are rare. Tom Brown provides his individualistic interpretation of twenty-first century leadership.

OFFICER OF THE COURT: This court is now in session.

JUDGE: High Prosecutor, please proceed.

HIGH PROSECUTOR: You are Tom Brown, are you not? And you are a midshipman aboard the HMS *Leadership*?

BROWN: Nothing more.

HIGH PROSECUTOR: And you understand that you are charged with mutiny, by advocating the removal of the captain of industry aboard the very ship on which you served. Indeed, you attempted to get all the other members of the crew to abandon not only your captain, but all captains of industry serving on all corporate ships. Is that not so?

BROWN: It is.

HIGH PROSECUTOR: Then you do not deny that you disapprove of the current code of conduct for organizational leaders, that – in fact – you seek to rebel against this code which has enriched so many a stockholder for, lo, at least 10 years or more. You do not deny this, do you, sir?

BROWN: I do not.

HIGH PROSECUTOR: Mr Brown, do you realize that if this jury and this court find you guilty of mutiny, you will be haunted for the rest of your life, that you will be tagged appropriately as a renegade, a rebellious rabble rouser who acknowledged immense corporate profits and yet tried to besmirch the men and women who made all that money possible?

BROWN: I do.

HIGH PROSECUTOR: Then, sir, I ask you before all who sit in this courtroom: how do you plead?

BROWN: Not ... guilty ... With the deepest level of respect for this court – not guilty!

HIGH PROSECUTOR: I would ask the Officer of the Court to silence the outcries among the spectators – or remove these people. This is a court of judgment, and management mutiny is a high crime!

OFFICER OF THE COURT: Members of the audience will restrain themselves, or they will be removed!

HIGH PROSECUTOR: Mr Brown, how can you admit to all that you have conceded so far and plead 'not guilty'? This does not follow. This makes no sense.

BROWN: Sir, again, with respect, to mutiny is, in my view, to go against the good of all, not the privileged few. It is true that the so-called leaders of the current generation of corporate executives have created profits that are, well, without comparison in any time in history. But at what cost? Today's leaders captain slow-sinking ships.

HIGH PROSECUTOR: Costs, may I remind you, are almost universally down in the corporate world: no self-respecting captain of industry would dare manage today without the lowest costs, the fewest heads, the tightest turnaround times ... and ... and ..., in sum, captains today focus exclusively on creating a corporate cost structure that maximizes returns on that most precious corporate resource, capital!

BROWN: Precisely. Yet, for some time, I have sensed on my own vessel and others a growing sense of fatigue among the crew and even among frequent passengers, the most loyal and best customers. It's as if things are getting done, but no one cares about doing them – and, thus, no one appreciates the half-hearted, half-done efforts for which they are paying so dearly. Mediocrity, not excellence, has become today's gold standard.

HIGH PROSECUTOR: A mere management midshipman should not fret over such trivial factors in such a robust business climate. You know as well as any that a bulging bottom line served your ship and many others very well. And, may I remind you, that the pensions and investment portfolios of you, your shipmates, and your passengers have all grown in direct proportion to this rising tide of wealth.

BROWN: This is true – but only for some. Most people, even in developed countries, live pay cheque-to-pay cheque, on minimal wages. And as our world has become closer knit because of the broadcast media and the internet, more of those who don't have big pensions and huge savings are seething with expanding discontent, so much so that ...

HIGH PROSECUTOR: Oh, then it's socialism that you want! No captains of industry at all! No profits for those who have the capital and the will to risk it by investing in the great business ships of our time. Your view is an old one, and it is intellectually bankrupt, I might add.

BROWN: I never said that, sir! You presume much too much! I argue for expanded free enterprise in all parts of the world!

HIGH PROSECUTOR: Oh, is that your line? What, then, might I presume? What, then, is your view?

BROWN: The HMS *Leadership* is but one commercial vessel; there are many, as we all know. The names of these ships are branding themselves, or so it seems, in every port on every continent. This can mean only one thing: as a planet, as a world, we are coming together in ways that have never happened before. We are all, as a human population, inter-linked in geo-commercial, geopolitical, and geocentric ways. Nationalism is a point of pride, but it is becoming increasingly less a point of reality ...

JUDGE: Members of the audience will restrain themselves, or they will be removed! Silence! Now! Don't make me use this gavel again!

BROWN: I do not say such things to cut into personal sensitivities; I am instead merely pointing out that, as in all times before us, these times are changing and in quite observable ways.

HIGH PROSECUTOR: Mr Brown, you are charged with mutiny against the captain of the HMS *Leadership* and, by extension, all captains of all commercial ships. Please confine your remarks to defending yourself against that charge.

BROWN: But I am. I am! When we have leaders – in business as well as in government – who operate for the egregious benefit of a limited few, such self-enriching policies and practices are increasingly observable to everyone, everywhere. And crude profit making and power hoarding may be tolerated for awhile, but these actions will sooner or later strangle the very people who make profit and power possible. Our interconnected world makes the actions of any captain increasingly visible. It will also make mass discontent increasingly visible.

HIGH PROSECUTOR: Mr Brown, I am not amused and I am not enlightened by your philosophizing. Just look what the corporate world is reaping these days! Are you losing it? Are you mad? We live in very, very good times!

BROWN: I do not deny that much profit is being reaped, as you put it. But man reaps not only from what he sows, but from what he doesn't sow.

HIGH PROSECUTOR: I'm afraid you have lost me.

BROWN: When leaders promote profits and forget spirit, when they reduce headcount and dismiss community, when they export jobs and import hostility, when they boost productivity yet ignore civility ...

HIGH PROSECUTOR: Your point?

BROWN: Today's leaders have forgotten that enterprises like the HMS *Leadership* were built on a new idea that caught the imagination of workers who rallied an innovation into reality. And, because the new idea helped or pleased a wide arc of people, society backed the fledgling enterprise individually, as consumers, and collectively, as investors. When today's leaders operate only to extract all that they can reap, while turning their back on investing in new ideas and the people who can bring those ideas to life, then ...

3

HIGH PROSECUTOR: Then?

BROWN: Then anger rises in proportion to the sliding sense of morale. And ... society will sooner or later revolt against the limits of that selfishness.

HIGH PROSECUTOR: Please excuse my smile; could you perhaps be a bit more blunt?

BROWN: While I am now on trial for what you allege is 'mutiny', I dare say that there are many people in many organizations who have lost faith in their captains, who are sighing much more than they are working, and who are giving far less to their jobs and to their ships of business or ships of state than they otherwise would. And I would say that this collective sighing gives way, from time to time, to forms of rage that are ugly and counter-productive whether they turn violent or not.

HIGH PROSECUTOR: Officer of the Court, this courtroom must be quiet!

BROWN: Ladies and gentlemen, all of you in this courtroom, please! When the HMS *Leadership* crossed into the twenty-first century, we passed a milestone in time; our clocks have changed but not our attitudes. We are, all of us, shirking our historical mandate if we do not pull together to discover the ideas that will steer us toward the future. What should the twenty-first century city look like? How should the twenty-first century university operate? Who is needed to create the twenty-first century corporation? Leaders who are focused only on reaping all that they can from the present diminish us as a society.

HIGH PROSECUTOR: That's enough of that, Mr Brown. It's obvious that no leader today measures up to your impossible standards.

BROWN: That's not true! They may not make the headlines, but those who are discovering new ways to live and work are leaders. Those who understand that rallying associates, not bullying them, are leaders. Those who have the courage to scrape together the resources they need to nudge their new idea into reality are leaders. Those who stand fast and don't cave into the pressure of the *status quo* are leaders. And those who struggle to improve the common good, to make a genuine contribution to society, are leaders.

HIGH PROSECUTOR: May it please the court, Mr Brown, in my judgment, has just changed his plea to guilty. There is no ship in the corporate fleet with such a captain at the helm ... there is no captain today who measures up to Mr Brown's standards. To the extent he stands by his own words, he is guilty of mutiny. He is guilty ... I cannot say this more strongly: he's guilty!

JUDGE: Do you now wish to plead guilty?

BROWN: If mutiny is synonymous with discovery, enthusiasm, resourcefulness, resolve, and contribution, then guilty I am. Yet I stand firm in asserting that a model of leadership based on commanding, controlling, allocating, exploiting, and profiteering is not one which will survive – or should! – in the twenty-first century. We must fight such forms of leadership. There is a better way. And anyone in this courtroom can become this new kind of leader if he or she will only move each day in new directions.

HIGH PROSECUTOR: Officer of the Court, I cannot hear over all this noise. Officer of the Court! Ladies and gentlemen of the jury, there is nothing more to say. What is your verdict?

RESOURCES

BOOK

Brown, Tom, *Fiscal Fairy Tales*, Berrett-Koehler, San Francisco, 1999.

WEB

www.mgeneral.com

BENNIS, WARREN

WARREN BENNIS (born 1925) has had a lengthy career that has involved him in education, writing, consulting and administration. Along the way he has made a contribution to an array of subjects and produced a steady stream of books, including the bestselling *Leaders* and most recently *Organizing Genius (Secret of Creative Collaboration)*. He is now based at the University of Southern California where he is founder of the University's Leadership Institute in Los Angeles.

From being an early student of group dynamics in the 1950s, Bennis became a futurologist in the 1960s. His work – particularly *The Temporary Society* (1968) – explored new organizational forms. Bennis envisaged organizations as *adhocracies* – roughly the direct opposite of bureaucracies – freed from the shackles of hierarchy and meaningless paperwork.

Despite his varied career and life, Bennis remains inextricably linked with leadership. With the torrent of publications and executive programmes on the subject, it is easy to forget that leadership had been largely forgotten as a topic worthy of serious academic interest until it was revived by Bennis and others in the 1980s.

Bennis' work stands as a humane counter to much of the military-based, hero worship that dogs the subject. He argues that leadership is not a rare skill; leaders are made rather than born; leaders are usually ordinary – or apparently ordinary – people, rather than charismatic; leadership is not solely the preserve of those at the top of the organization – it is relevant at all levels; and, finally, leadership is not about control, direction and manipulation.

Bennis' best-known leadership research involved 90 of America's leaders. From these, four common abilities were identified. The first was management of attention. This, said Bennis, is a question of vision. Successful leaders have a vision that other people believe in and treat as their own.

The second skill shared by Bennis' selection of leaders is management of meaning – communications. A vision is of limited practical use if it is encased in 400 pages of wordy text or mumbled from behind a paper-packed desk. Bennis believes that effective communication relies on use of analogy, metaphor, and vivid illustration as well as emotion, trust, optimism and hope.

The third aspect of leadership identified by Bennis is trust, which he describes as 'the emotional glue that binds followers and leaders together'. Leaders have to be seen to be consistent.

The final common bond between the 90 leaders studied by Bennis is 'deployment of self'. The leaders do not glibly present charisma or time management as the essence of their success. Instead, the emphasis is on persistence and self-knowledge, taking risks, commitment and challenge but, above all, learning. 'The learning person looks forward to failure or mistakes,' says Bennis. 'The worst problem in leadership is basically early success. There's no opportunity to learn from adversity and problems.'

Most recently, Bennis has switched his attention to the dynamics of group working. The relationship between groups and their leaders is clearly of fundamental interest to Bennis. 'Greatness starts with superb people. Great groups don't exist without great leaders, but they give the lie to the persistent notion that successful institutions are the lengthened shadow of a great woman or man.'

Indeed, the heroic view of the leader as the indomitable individual is now outdated and inappropriate. Says Bennis, 'He or she is a pragmatic dreamer, a person with an original but attainable vision. Ironically, the leader is able to realize his or her dream only if the others are free to do exceptional work.'

There is a rich strand of idealism that runs through Bennis' work. He is a humanist with high hopes for humanity. To accusations of romanticism, he puts up a resolute and spirited defence: 'I think that every person has to make a genuine contribution in their lives and the institution of work is one of the main vehicles to achieving this. I'm more and more convinced that individual leaders can create a human community that will, in the long run, lead to the best organizations.'

– CHAPTER 2 –

Learning and knowledge

'Knowledge is the small part of ignorance that we arrange and classify.' AMBROSE BIERCE

'The essence of knowledge is, having it, to apply it; not having it, to confess your ignorance.' CONFUCIUS

'To attain knowledge, add things every day.
To attain wisdom, remove things every day.'

LAO-TZU

'Learning is what most adults will do for a living in the twenty-first century.' S.J. PERELMAN

'The illiterate of the twenty-first century will not be those who cannot read and write, but those who cannot learn, unlearn and relearn.' ALVIN TOFFLER

Developing global leaders

GEORGINA PETERS

Developing tomorrow's global leaders is a problem, writes Georgina Peters, in a world where there is a growing shortage of talented senior executives. Managers need to be given truly international experience and targeted development to provide them with the necessary skills.

BIG name CEOs dominate the media. Hardly a day goes by without some laudatory article on Jack Welch, a celebration of the entrepreneurial rise of Michael Dell, or a peon to the intelligence of Bill Gates. Two simple conclusions can be drawn from the media's fixation with a handful of outstanding business leaders. First, great companies usually have talented leaders. Second, there is a global shortage of such people.

This is hardly startling, but wrestling with the implications is set to keep the minds of HR professionals busy for years to come. Developing tomorrow's global leaders is a constant and sizeable challenge, but one of increasing importance in a world where people and their knowledge can be the difference between winning and losing.

That there is a talent shortage appears widely accepted. It is not only journalists who struggle to unearth new shining stars in the corporate firmament. Research and demographics suggest that the shortage of senior executives is likely to increase in the coming years. Demographic predictions suggest that the number of 35- to 44-year-olds in the US will fall by 15 percent between 2000 and 2015, while the number of 45- to 54-year-olds will rise.

Randall White of the Executive Development Group in Greensboro, North Carolina, takes a philosophical view of the talent shortage, pointing to development as the key issue. 'This is a periodic crisis,' he says. 'Depending on how you define it, we have been in this situation for a number of years. I believe it is a continuous state. If you think about it, there could never be enough talent available. How and when talent is developed is perhaps a more important question.'

The implications of the talent gap are many. One of the clearest is that the onus is on companies to recruit, retain, and develop global leaders for the future. Answers are elusive. Before they begin to tackle this issue, companies are faced with demanding questions. First, they have to understand the skills required of global leaders. These are many and varied. Complex global markets require more sophisticated management skills, including international sensitivity, cultural fluency, technological literacy, and, most critically, leadership.

Renaissance men and women are rare. 'Leadership in a modern organization is highly complex, and it is increasingly difficult – sometimes impossible – to find all the necessary traits in a single person,' says Jonas Ridderstråle of the Stockholm School of Economics and co-author of *Funky Business*. 'In the future, we will see leadership groups rather than individual leaders.' Whatever the scenario, appreciating the competencies required of global leaders is essential to their development.

Role models of global leaders are also few in number. ABB's Percy Barnevik is often mentioned, and Scandinavians generally have a good record in developing truly global executives. In contrast, the corporate leaders most often cited by the media tend to be American. While the American management model remains dominant, it is, with a few exceptions, a model that owes more to colonization than globalization.

The solution suggested by Jonas Ridderstråle is to provide executives with truly international experience. (This is notably lacking from the resumés of Messrs Welch, Gates and Dell.) 'Global leaders require a global cultural perspective. Without a global mindset, there are no global managers,' says Ridderstråle. 'Sending people out on international assignments early on in their career is crucial. Part of developing global leaders is a question of changing attitudes in subsidiaries so that they are given more responsibility. This requires leaders who understand what goes on – culturally and commercially – at that level. Global experience breeds global role models.'

Narayan Pant of the National University of Singapore suggests that companies need to create 'systems where individuals are given the opportunity to evolve leadership'. 'Some Korean organizations post young managers to new countries often alone and with no specific task. They are encouraged to join classes if they like, but essentially do no more than get to understand and negotiate successfully their new environments,' says Dr Pant. 'Experiments such as this are expensive, but they create opportunities to discern the evolution of something extraordinary in individuals – something organizations might not know existed had they not given it a chance.'

The ease with which people can be identified as high fliers and sent to distant corners can be dangerous, warns Terry Bates, managing director of GHN Coaching. 'In the past, people went through induction programmes and the like. They were sent on international assignments knowing the organization well and with its support. Now it is often less systematic. This can be dangerous as people need support.'

And, when it comes to support, HR managers are in the firing line. John Quelch, dean of London Business School, provides a pithy summation of the role of HR managers in developing global leaders: 'Good HR management in a multinational company comes down to getting the right people in the right jobs in the right places at the right times and at the right costs. These international managers must then be meshed into a cohesive network in which they quickly identify and leverage good ideas worldwide.'

The importance of collaboration

The need to continuously develop global leaders and to have a strong input into that process means that companies increasingly work in collaboration with executive education providers. Businesses suggest that executive education is fast becoming their number one path toward two main goals: developing global leaders, and implementing organizational change. The two often go together: leadership can drive change; change requires leadership. 'The new leader,' Warren Bennis, distinguished professor of leadership at the University of Southern California, observes, 'is one who commits people to action, who converts followers into leaders, and who can convert leaders into agents of change.'

Developing global leaders is, therefore, not an internal matter but an opportunity for collaboration with outside providers and organizations. Terry Bates points to the increasing demand for coaching as evidence of the relationship required. A coaching relationship will typically last more than six months. 'Programmes come to an end while coaching continues,' he says. 'Companies offer a great deal of support, but an outside coach is someone executives can really open up to. Increasingly there is dissatisfaction with standardized programmes.'

Development issues

Recruit lovers of uncertainty

For those intent on growing their own, the process begins with selection and recruitment. 'Companies need to search for people who deal well with uncertainty, ambiguity, and change,' advises Randall White. 'They should be wary of people who believe in one right answer to problems. Instead, they must seek out people who are able to adjust their thinking to fit a variety of situations. They must find people with cultural sensitivity – people able to eat peas with chopsticks, as someone once put it. Global leaders do things differently in a variety of locations, situations and culture and make it work.'

Understand individuals

What does career success means to the individual? Not everyone aspires to be chief executive – or even a boss. 'Personal motivation is now an important factor and has to be taken into account. People want to own their own careers,' says Terry Bates.

Stretch people

'There is one linking feature among those who become CEOs,' says David Norburn of London's Imperial College. 'Between the ages of 25 and 35 they have been stretched beyond the norm through things like job rotations, international assignments, functional rotation. They have been treated as mini-CEOs. This requires commitment from senior managers and a degree of selflessness and protectiveness not usually seen.'

Plan succession

'Organizations will need to grow their own talent if they are to definitively address the leadership dilemma,' says William C. Byham, president and CEO of Development Dimensions International, a Bridgeville, Pennsylvania, firm that specializes in HR issues.

> *'At the same time, they are courting failure if they think they can simply dust off traditional success planning initiatives or refill standard talent pools. These are anemic alternatives, at best. A far better strategy is developing an acceleration pool made up of leadership candidates from a range of different leadership levels. Given sufficient resources and attention, an acceleration pool provides the leverage to both respond to the immediate talent gap and grow outstanding talent for the future.'*

Love context

'Leadership is highly context specific,' says Narayan Pant. 'People in organizations need to think deliberately and perpetually about the strange nature of the linkages that connect everything they do. Leadership requires not only the exercise of direction in organizations; it requires the understanding of the contexts in which the action must be exercised.'

RESOURCES

BOOK

Vilere, Albert and Fulmer, Robert, *Leadership by Design*, Harvard Business School Press, 1998.

Leveraging intellect

JAMES BRIAN QUINN, PHILIP ANDERSON AND SYDNEY FINKELSTEIN

How do you get the most out of people? This single question increasingly lies at the heart of a company's competitiveness and future opportunities.

PROPERLY stimulated, knowledge and intellect grow exponentially. All learning and experience curves have this characteristic. As knowledge is captured or internalized, the available knowledge base itself becomes higher. Hence a constant percentage accretion to the base becomes exponential total growth.

The strategy consequences are profound. Once a firm obtains a knowledge-based competitive edge it becomes ever harder for competitors to catch up. Because the firm is a leader it can attract better talent than competitors – the best want to work with the best. These people can then perceive and solve more complex and interesting customer problems, make more profits as a result and attract even more talented people to work on the next round of complexity. Driving and capturing individuals' exponential learning has been the key to strategic success for most intellectual enterprises, from Bell Labs and Intel to Microsoft, McKinsey and the Mayo Clinic.

Knowledge is one the few assets that grows most – also usually exponentially – when shared. Communication theory states that a network's potential benefits grow exponentially as the nodes it can successfully interconnect expand numerically. As one shares knowledge with other units, not only do those units gain information (linear growth), but they share it with others and feed back questions, amplifications and modifications that add further value to the original sender, creating exponential total growth. Proper leveraging through external knowledge bases – especially those of specialized firms, customers and suppliers – can create even steeper exponentials.

There are, however, some inherent risks and saturation potentials in this process. The choices about what knowledge is to be protected – and how – are critical elements in intellectual strategy.

Professional intellect

There are important differences between professional and creative intellect. Professionals are an important source of intellect for most organizations but little has been written about managing professionals. What characterizes the management of such professionals?

While no precise delineation applies in all cases, most of a typical professional's activity is directed at perfection, not creativity. The true professional commands a complete body of knowledge – a discipline – and updates that knowledge constantly. In most cases the customer wants the knowledge delivered reliably with the most advanced skills available. Although there is an occasional call for creativity, the preponderance of work in actuarial units, dentistry, hospitals, accounting units, universities, law firms, aircraft operations or equipment maintenance requires the repeated use of highly developed skills on relatively similar, although complex, problems. People rarely want their surgeons, accountants, airline pilots, maintenance personnel or nuclear plant operators to be very creative except in emergencies. While managers must clearly prepare their professionals for these special emergency circumstances, the bulk of attention needs to be on delivering consistent, high-quality intellectual output. What are the critical factors?

- Hyper-selection. The leverage of intellect is so great that a few top-flight professionals can create a successful organization or make a lesser one billow. Marvin Bower created McKinsey; Robert Noyce and Gordon Moore spawned Intel; William Gates and Robert Allen built Microsoft; Herb Boyer and Robert Swanson made Genentech.

- Intense training, mentoring and peer pressure literally force professionals to the top of their knowledge ziggurat. The best students go to the most demanding universities. The top graduate schools further reselect and drive these students with greater challenges. The best of the students go back to even more intense boot camps in medical internships, law associate programmes or other demanding situations. The result is that the best professionals drive themselves up a steep learning curve.
- Constantly increasing challenges. Intellect grows most when challenged. Hence, heavy internal competition and constant performance appraisal are common in well-run professional shops.
- Managing an elite. Each profession tends to regard itself as an elite. Members look to their profession and to their peers to determine codes for behaviour and acceptable performance standards. Unless consciously fractured, these discipline-based cocoons quickly become inward-looking bureaucracies, resistant to change and detached from customers.

Conventional wisdom has long held that there are few scale economies in professional activities. A pilot can only handle one aircraft; a great chef can only cook so many different dishes at once; a top researcher can only conduct so many unique experiments; a doctor can only diagnose one patient's illness at a time; and so on. Adding professionals simply multiplies costs at the same rate as outputs.

In fact, for years, growing an intellectual organization actually seemed to involve diseconomies of scale. Most often, increasing size brought even greater growth in the bureaucracies' co-ordinating, monitoring or supporting the professionals.

But new technologies and management approaches now enable firms to capture, develop and leverage intellectual resources. The keys are: organizations and technology systems designed around intellectual flows rather than command and control concept; and performance measurement and incentive systems that reward managers for developing intellectual assets and customer value – and not just for producing current profits and using physical assets more efficiently. Companies as diverse as Arthur Andersen, Sony, AT&T, Merck, Scandia, State Street Bank and Microsoft have found ways to do this.

Core intellectual competencies

The crux of leveraging intellect is to focus on what creates uniquely high value for customers.

Through core competency with outsourcing strategies, managers can serve customers substantially better, simultaneously decreasing risk and size while increasing flexibility. Many entrepreneurial ventures such as Apple Computers, Sony, Silicon Graphics, Nike or Norvellus have started in a heavily concentrated and heavily outsourced fashion, leveraging their fiscal capital by factors of three or more – and their intellectual capital by 10s or 100s – as compared with integrated companies.

In today's hypercompetitive climate such core competency with outsourcing strategies let companies be simultaneously the lowest cost, broadest line, most flexible and most highly differentiated producer in their market. No other strategy supports efficiency (through focus), innovative flexibility (through multiple sourcing) and stability (through market diversity) to the same extent.

Organizing around intellect

The exploitation of intellectually based strategies calls for new organizational concepts. In the past, in order to enhance efficiencies, most companies formed their organizations around product clusters, process investments, geographical needs or specialized management functions. However, rapidly changing customer demands and increasingly independent professionals require entirely new structures.

The main function of organizations in today's hypercompetitive environment is to develop and deploy – i.e. attract, harness, leverage and disseminate – intellect effectively. Each of the truly new organizational forms does this is its own way and should be used only for those particular purposes it handles best. But we expect much greater use of four other basic organizational forms that leverage professional intellect uniquely well. These are the *infinitely flat, inverted starburst,* and *spider's web* forms. The key variables in choosing the new forms are:

1. locus of intellect – where the deep knowledge of a firm's particular core competencies lies;
2. locus of customization – where intellect is converted to novel solutions;
3. direction of intellectual flow – the primary direction(s) in which value-added knowledge flows;
4. method of leverage – how the organization leverages intellect.

All the forms tend to push responsibility outwards to the point at which the company contacts the customer. All tend to flatten the organization and to remove layers of hierarchy. All seek faster, more responsive action to deal with the customization and personalization that an affluent and complex marketplace demands. All require breaking away from traditional thinking about lines of command, one-person–one-boss structures, the centre as a directing force and management of physical assets as keys to success. But each differs substantially in its purposes and management. And each requires very different nurturing, balancing and support systems to achieve its performance goals.

Infinitely flat organizations

In infinitely flat organizations – so called because there is no inherent limit to their span – the primary locus of intellect is at the centre, e.g. the operation's knowledge of a fast-food franchising organization or the data analysis capability at the centre of a brokerage firm. The nodes of customer contact are the locus of customization. Intellect flows primarily one way, from the centre to the nodes. The leverage is arithmetic: the amount of leverage equals the value of the knowledge times the number of nodes using it.

Infinitely flat organizations operate best when the activity at the node can be broken down and measured to the level of its minimum repeatable transaction elements (as, for example, the cooking and operating details in fast-food chains or the basic components of financial transactions in brokerage operations).

Such organizations present certain inherent management problems. Without hierarchy, lower-level personnel wonder how to advance on a career path. Traditional job evaluation ('Hay Point') systems break down and new compensation systems based on individual performance become imperative.

The inverted organization

In the inverted form both corporate intellect and customization are at the nodes of contacting customers, not at the centre. Hospitals or medical clinics, therapeutic care-giving units or consulting–engineering firms provide typical examples. The nodes do not need direct linkage between them. When critical know-how diffuses, it usually does so informally from node to node or formally from node to centre – the opposite of the infinitely flat organization.

In inverted organizations the line hierarchy becomes a support structure. The function of line managers becomes bottleneck breaking, culture development, consulting on request, expediting resource movements and providing service economies of scale. Generally, what was line management now performs essentially staff activities.

The inverted organization poses certain unique challenges. The apparent loss of formal authority can be very traumatic for former line managers.

The starburst

Another highly leveragable form, the starburst, serves well when there is very specialized and valuable intellect at both the nodes and the centre. Starbursts are common in creative organizations that constantly peel off more permanent, but separate, units from their core competencies.

In operation, the centre retains a deep understanding of some common knowledge base but, unlike holding companies, starbursts are built around some central core of intellectual competency. They are not merely banks that collect and disseminate funds. The nodes – essentially separate permanent business units rather than individuals or temporary clusters – have continuing relationships with given marketplaces and are the locus of important specialized market or production knowledge.

The flow of intellect is typically from the centre towards the outer nodes. The organization rarely transfers knowledge from one node laterally to another but feeds back to the core specialized information that other nodes may find useful.

The classic problem of this organizational form is that management often loses faith in their freestanding spin-offs. After some time they try to consolidate functions in the name of efficiency or economies of scale. Starbursts also encounter problems if their divisions move into heavy investment industries or into capital-intensive mass production activities where one unit's needs can overwhelm the capacity of the core. In most starburst environments the nodes are so different that even sophisticated computer systems cannot provide or co-ordinate all the information needed to run these firms from the centre. Rather than try, managers must either live with quasi-market control or spin off the subsidiary entirely. Starbursts tend to work extremely well for growth by innovating smaller-scale, discrete product or service lines positioned in diverse marketplaces.

The spider's web

The spider's web form is a true network. In the spider's web there is often no intervening hierarchy or order-giving centre among the nodes. In fact it may be hard to define where the centre is. The locus of intellect is highly dispersed, residing largely at the contact nodes (as in the inverted organization).

The purest example of a spider's web is the internet, which is managed by no one. Common operating examples include most open markets, securities exchanges, library consortia, diagnostic teams, research or political action groups.

The organization's intellect is essentially latent and underutilized until a project forces it to materialize through connections people make with one another.

While it is usually effective for problem finding and analysis, a spider's web presents important challenges when used for decision making. Dawdling is common, as nodes refine their specialist solutions instead of solving the complete problem together. Assigning credit for intellectual contributions is difficult and cross-competition among nodes can inhibit the sharing necessary in such networks.

Because a spider's web is so dependent on individual goals and behaviour there is no best way to manage one except to stimulate a sense on interdependency and identify with the problem at hand. Shared interest of participants, shared value systems and mutual personal gains for members are, of course, the essential starting points for any network relationship.

While managing professional intellect is clearly the key to value creation and profitability for most companies, few have arrived at systematic structures for developing, focusing, leveraging and measuring their intellectual capabilities. But there are ways successful enterprises can design their strategies, organizations, training and measurement systems to maximize the value of their most critical asset – intellect. Technology has created new opportunities and rules for organization design. Customers quickly discover and reward those organizations that understand these new rules.

The strategic potential of a firm's knowledge portfolio

DAVID BIRCHALL AND GEORGE TOVSTIGA

Knowledge, not capital assets, is increasingly becoming the source of wealth in today's global economy, as David Birchall and George Tovstiga explain. Not only is this true for the obviously knowledge-intensive high-technology sectors, traditional manufacturing and utilities industries are also recognizing that using knowledge about customers to provide improved services can build a formidable competitive edge in fast-moving markets.

ASTONISHINGLY, despite the wide consensus on the importance of knowledge to today's organizations, many firms still do not have at their disposal even the most rudimentary tools or methodologies for assessing the breadth and depth of their capabilities-embedded knowledge portfolio.

Knowledge maps that capture, identify, and lay open the firm's knowledge in its various forms are a first step towards managing knowledge in the firm. Knowledge manifests itself primarily in the firm's competencies and capabilities, and it is the tacit knowledge content of competencies and capabilities – rather than the explicit form of knowledge – that underlies the firm's real basis of competitive advantage.

A truly key or core capability – one that provides a clear basis for competitive differentiation – will substantially consist of knowledge in a highly tacit form. Unlike explicit knowledge, which is captured in manuals, procedures, working papers, minutes of meetings, process flow charts, and the like, this tacit knowledge rests in the minds of employees and teams. This feature of a capability carries a number of important implications for competitive differentiation. One of these has to do with the ease with which a capability can be replicated, transferred, or lost to a competitor.

Our premise is that a high degree of tacitness is an effective barrier to diffusion of knowledge. From the external perspective, this represents a protective mechanism; for internal operations, it represents a challenge to be overcome.

A firm's portfolio of knowledge-driven capabilities is a dynamic entity. Clearly, it must be managed in the context of the firm's

Figure 1 Schematic overview of methodology

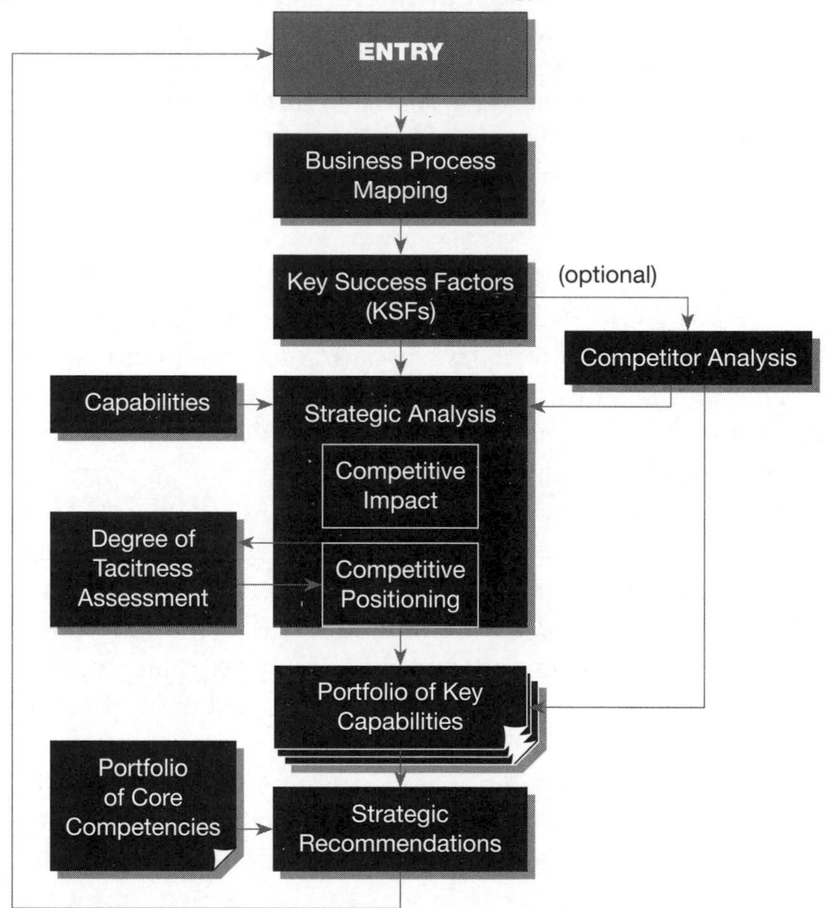

rapidly changing environment. Any analysis of this type must therefore focus on the current as well as the future competitiveness of the firm. The methodology (Figure 1) begins with mapping any one of the firm's business processes from a value-creation perspective.

Business process mapping

The first stage of the methodology focuses on breaking down the firm's business activities in terms of its business process chain. A business process is understood to be any activity or group of activities that takes an input, adds value to it, and provides an output to an internal or external customer.

It is a useful exercise at this stage to think about how individual subprocesses contribute to the value generated by the overall business process chain. Clearly, some of the subprocesses will contribute more to the fulfilment of customers' needs (value generated) than others will. It is these important subprocesses on which we want to focus. An example is shown in Figure 2.

Figure 2 Business process value chain[1]

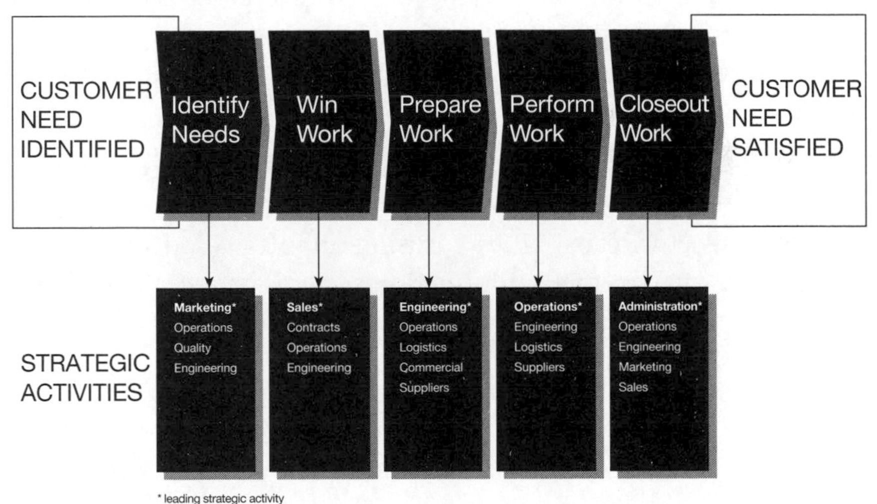

Source: Kaplan and Norton, *The Balanced Scorecard*, Harvard Business School Press, 1996, p. 263.

Key success factors (KSFs)

These strategic variables can be thought of as being common to the firm's industry. They are just as relevant to its competitors and strategic partners. That is, key success factors are characteristic of the marketplace within which the firm is competing, such as an ability to carry out competitive manufacturing and commercial process reviews, and to attract employees with the critical expertise and skills. It is helpful to think about current and future developments in the industry's timeframe and scope, stakeholder profiles, and the general macro environment when selecting key success factors.

Identification of capabilities

The challenge in implementing a competitive strategy lies in identifying and developing those capabilities that constitute the critical building blocks of the firm's core competencies. These, in turn, will have an impact on the most important key success factors of the firm's industry. The capabilities are drawn from the large and diverse array of fundamentally knowledge-based discrete activities, skills and disciplines embedded in the organization.

Capabilities may be broadly broken down into different categories, such as:

- Market-interface capabilities, including selling, advertising, consulting, technical service.
- Infrastructure capabilities, focusing on internal operations such as management information systems or internal training.
- Technological capabilities, directly providing support to the firm's product or service portfolio.

Figure 3 Assessment of degree of the firm's control over capability

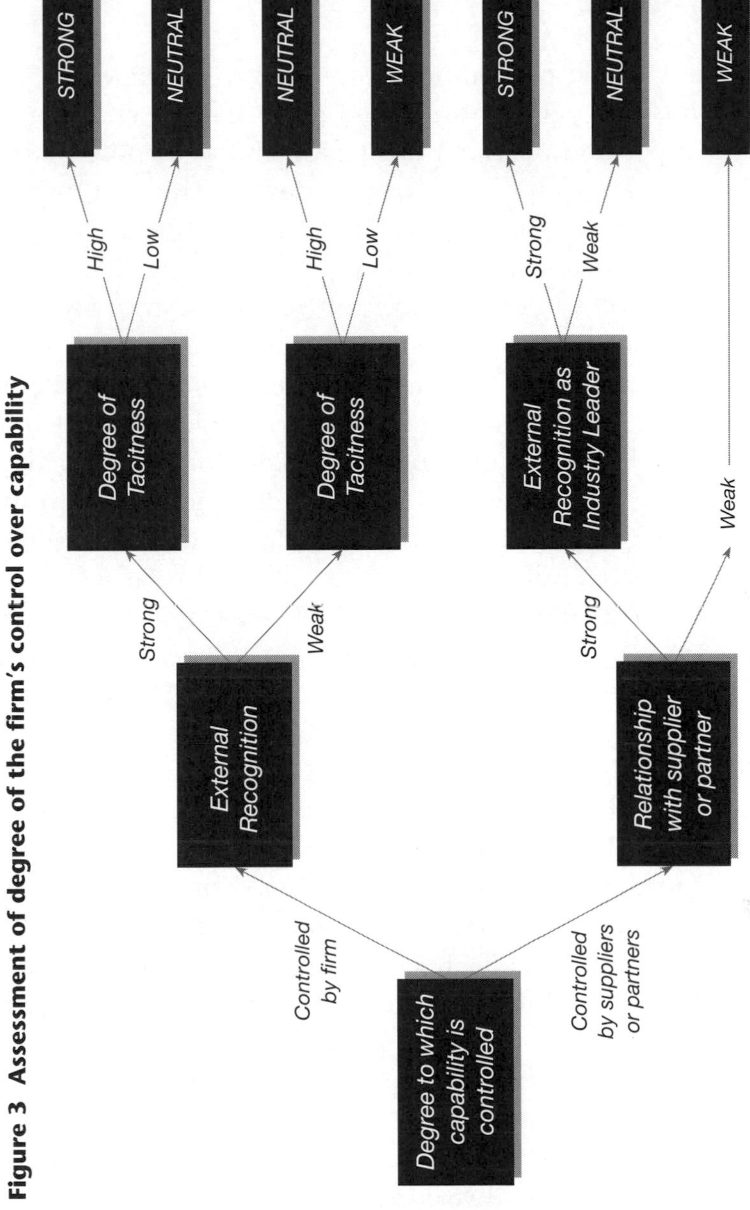

Competitive impact and positioning of capabilities

Capabilities – based on competitive impact – can be classified as *emerging* (has not yet demonstrated potential for changing the basis of competition), *pacing* (has demonstrated its potential), *key* (already has major impact on value-added stream: cost, performance, quality), or *base* (necessary, but confers only a minor impact on value-added streams).

Similarly, a firm's degree of control (relative competitive position) over its capabilities relates to its ability to exploit its current portfolio of capabilities. The firm's degree of control can be *high*, *neutral* or *weak*. For example, a capability may be controlled by a supplier if it is embedded in a bought-in component; or it may be controlled by a partner, as in the case of distribution by an intermediary. A decision tree approach to classifying the degree of control is presented in Figure 3.

The results of the knowledge-by-knowledge classification can be used to construct the firm's capability portfolio, as illustrated in Figure 4. Capability C^1_{int} is a strategically important capability for the firm and one over which it has considerable control. C^2_{int}, on the other hand, is a capability that has become commoditized and therefore is readily replicated by other firms. K_{ext}, in contrast, is an external knowledge domain that is emerging and is likely to have an impact on the products or services offered by the firm. It is an area where mastery is expected to become important and therefore greater control is desirable. The potential offered for integration with existing capabilities for recombinations addressing new market needs is shown in Figure 4, where C^3_{new} represents a capability over which the firm has secured a high degree of control.

Tacit knowledge in capabilities is invariably embodied in 'soft', accumulated experiential knowledge such as would be found in troubleshooting, 'process tweaking' and relational networks. Tacit knowledge embodied in capabilities can exist to varying degrees, ranging from the barely perceptible, subconscious awareness (highly tacit) to just barely codifiable (low degree of tacitness).

Figure 4 Capabilities portfolio

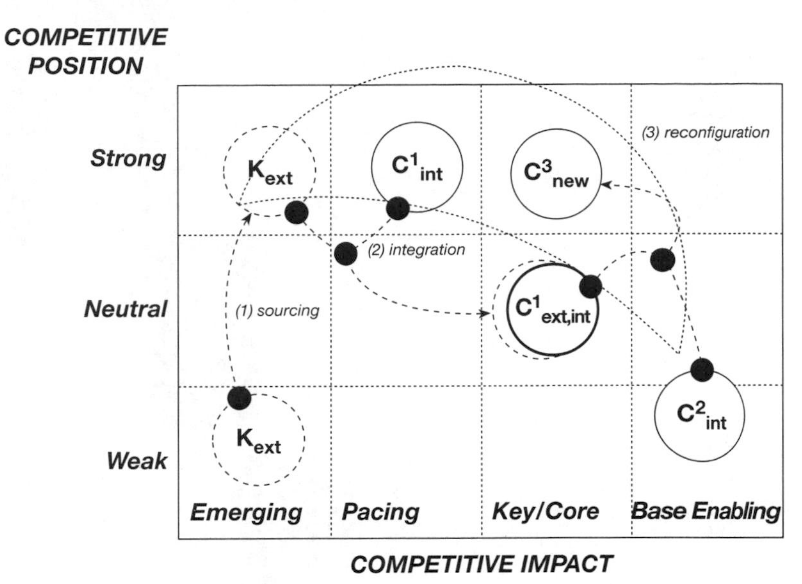

An ordering scheme for determining the degree of tacitness is shown in Figure 5. The greater the degree of tacitness, the greater the difficulty even in identification and then in classification of the capability.

Strategic analysis

The objective of this stage of the methodology is to formulate strategic recommendations on the basis of the capabilities portfolio. Management action could focus on:

1. **Scanning:** recognizing that capabilities can originate from a very diverse set of sources. It further involves developing and nurturing environmental scanning capabilities to detect strong or weak signals, indicating both threats and opportunities.
2. **Protecting:** protecting against any eventuality, whether external (competitive factors) or internal (mismanagement of knowledge resources), that threatens the integrity of the capability portfolio – in either an active or a passive way.

Figure 5 Ordering scheme for assessing degree of tacitness of capability – embodied knowledge

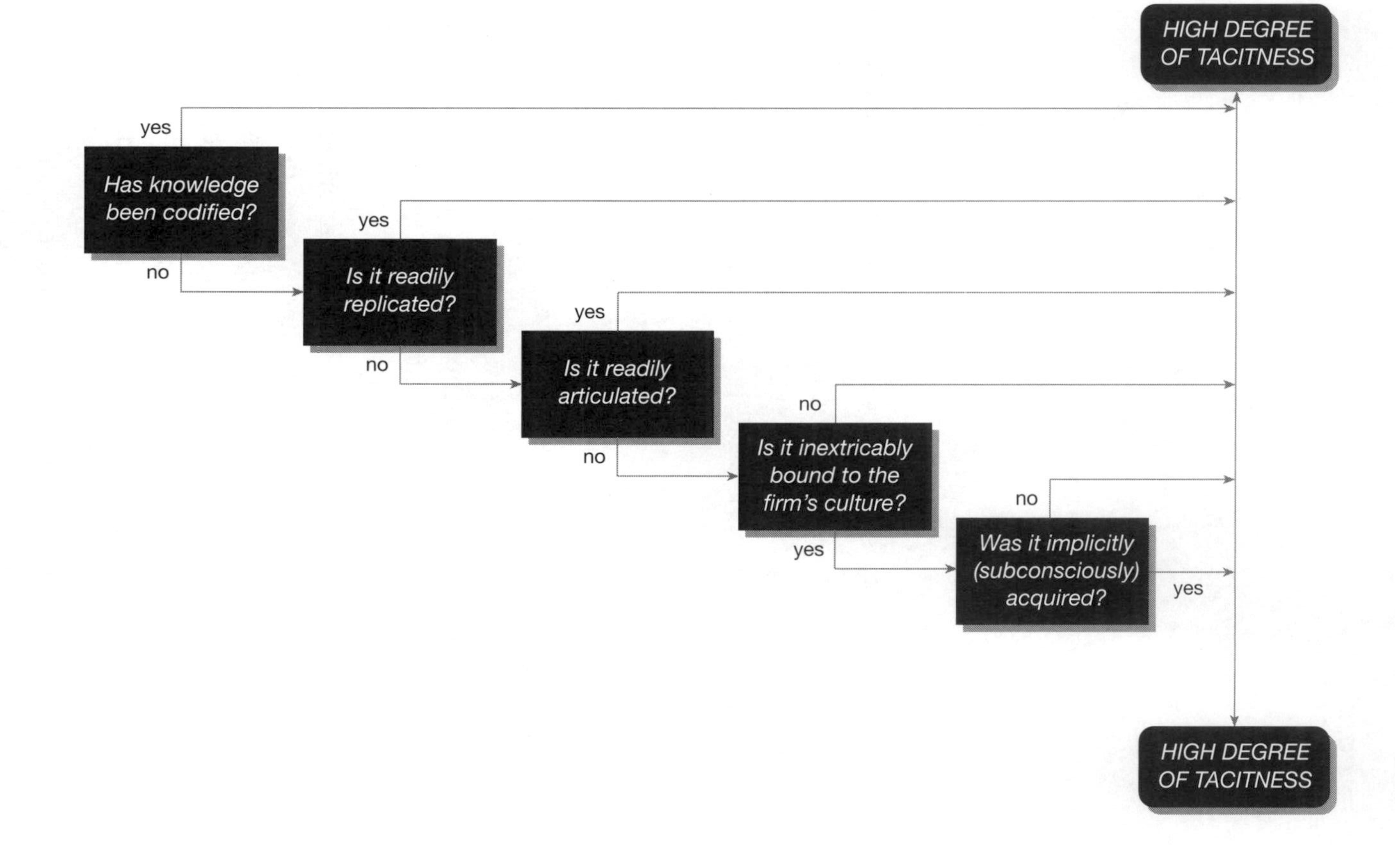

3. **Enriching:** nurturing the business environment most conducive for growth of current capabilities, via in-house capability building, formation of strategic alliances, or acquisitions.
4. **Optimizing:** continually seeking to improve and refine existing capability assets toward better addressing current needs, thereby increasing the degree of control over strategically critical knowledge capabilities.
5. **Disposing of:** disposing of all or parts of a current knowledge capability/asset that is contributing little to the firm's longer-term direction.

This process can be quite involving and complex. Critical assumptions are made throughout; these need to be scrutinized and challenged at each of the stages. It is well worth the effort to review the outcome of the strategic assessment at the end of the process using the following guidelines:

1. Does the final outcome (strategic positioning matrix) make sense? Is the resulting portfolio of capabilities plausible?
2. What are the critical assumptions on which the analysis is based? How valid are they; how sensitive to variation are they? How would the outcome change if you were to modify these assumptions?
3. How, if at all, might the outcome be expected to be different if another group, representing different functional backgrounds in the firm, had carried out the same exercise?

Ideally, of course, this is undertaken as a multidisciplinary exercise – and, depending on the time framework of your industry, on an ongoing basis.

RESOURCES

BOOKS

Chiesa, V. and Barbeschi, M. 'Technology Strategy in Competence-based Competition', in G. Hamel and A. Heene (eds), *Competence-Based Competition,* John Wiley, 1994.

Teece, D. and Pisano G., 'The Dynamic Capabilities of Firms: an Introduction', in Dosi, Teece and Chytry (eds), *Technology, Organization and Competitiveness*, Oxford, 1998.

ESSENTIALS

LEARNING AND KNOWLEDGE

ACTION LEARNING

INVENTED by British management thinker Reg Revans, action learning is a deceptively simple idea. So simple, in fact, that its power was overlooked for years. The basic idea is that managers learn best when they work on real issues in a group, rather than in the traditional classroom. According to Revans: 'Action learning harnesses the power of groups to accomplish meaningful tasks while learning.'

Revans is a former Olympic athlete who worked at the Cavendish Laboratories and for the National Coal Board. He developed his approach in the 1940s, but it was his 1971 book *Developing Effective Managers* that sparked international interest in the concept.

Although largely ignored in Britain, Revans is highly regarded in countries as far apart as Belgium and South Africa. Fans of action learning include Jack Welch, General Electric's celebrated CEO, whose Workout programme is a form of action learning, and Herb Kelleher, head of Southwest Airlines, another American company that has been a trailblazer for the concept.

To explain action learning, Revans created a simple equation: L = P + Q. Learning (L), he says, occurs through a combination of programmed knowledge (P) and the ability to ask insightful questions (Q). In essence, action learning is based around releasing and reinterpreting the accumulated experiences of the people in a group. Working in a group of equals (rather than a committee headed by the chief executive or a teacher), managers work on key issues in real time. The emphasis is on being supportive and challenging, on asking questions rather than making statements.

While programmed knowledge is one-dimensional and rigid, the ability to ask questions opens up other dimensions and is free flowing. The process is a continuous one of confirmation and expansion. The structure linking the two elements of knowledge and questions is the small team or set, defined by Revans as a 'small group of comrades in adversity, striving to learn with and from each other as they confess failures and expand on victories'.

Asking questions and listening to answers is an increasingly important managerial skill. Action learning encourages both. The potential benefits of action learning, however, cannot disguise the challenge it presents. Action learning is no quick fix. It requires a fundamental change in thinking.

All action learning shares a number of features. It:

- Uses a genuine current problem or issue as a learning vehicle (not a past case study).
- Takes a group approach (peers working together provide support and different perspectives).
- Accepts that there are no experts (naive questions illuminate the issues).
- Requires commitment from the sponsoring organization and management.
- Focuses on asking questions rather than providing solutions.

ARGYRIS, CHRIS

CHRIS ARGYRIS (born 1923) is a formidable thinker – even by the lofty standards of his employer, Harvard Business School. Argyris was brought up in the New York suburbs and spent some time in Greece with his grandparents. Prior to joining Harvard he was Professor of Administrative Science at Yale. His qualifications embrace psychology, economics and organizational behaviour.

Argyris's early work concentrated on the then highly innovative field of behavioural science. Indeed, his 1957 book *Personality and Organization* has become one of the subject's classic texts. Argyris argued that organizations depend fundamentally on people, and that personal development is and can be related to work. The problem in many organizations, he believed, is that the organization itself stands in the way of people fulfilling their potential.

Central to Argyris's work has been the entire concept of learning. He has examined learning processes, both in individual and corporate terms, in huge depth. His most influential work was carried out with Donald Schön (most importantly in their 1974 book, *Theory in Practice*, and their 1978 book, *Organizational Learning*).

Argyris and Schön originated two basic organizational models. In Model 1 managers concentrate on establishing individual goals. They keep to themselves and don't voice concerns or disagreements. Model 1 managers are prepared to inflict change on others, but resist any attempt to change their own thinking and working practices. Model 1 organizations are characterized by what Argyris and Schön labelled 'single-loop learning' ('when the detection and correction of organizational error permits the organization to carry on its present policies and achieve its current objectives').

In contrast, Model 2 organizations emphasized 'double-loop learning', which Argyris and Schön described as 'when organizational error is detected and corrected in ways that involve the modification of underlying norms, policies, and objectives'. In Model 2 organizations, managers act on information. They debate issues and respond to, and are prepared to, change. A virtuous circle emerges of learning and understanding. 'Most organizations do quite well in single-loop learning but have great difficulties in double-loop learning,' they concluded.

Corporate fashions have moved Argyris's way. With the return of learning to the corporate agenda in the early 1990s, his work became slightly more fashionable.

INTELLECTUAL CAPITAL

CAPITAL used to be viewed in purely physical terms – factories, machinery, and money. Now, the quest is on for greater understanding of the most intangible, elusive, mobile and important assets of all: intellectual capital.

Intellectual capital can be crudely described as the collective brain power of an organization. The switch from physical assets to intellectual assets – brawn to brain – as the source of wealth creation has been underway in the developed economies for some time. In his book *Intellectual Capital: The New Wealth of Organizations*, Thomas A. Stewart (a leading commentator on the subject) claims that the changes taking place are as significant as the Industrial Revolution.

'Knowledge has become the most important factor in economic life. It is the chief ingredient of what we buy and sell, the raw material with which we work. Intellectual capital – not natural resources, machinery, or even financial capital – has become the one indispensable asset of corporations,' he says.

Intellectual capital is irrevocably bound up with the notion of the knowledge worker and knowledge management. Their root, as with so many other ideas, lies in the work of Peter Drucker. His 1969 book, *The Age of Discontinuity*, introduced the term knowledge worker, to describe the highly trained, intelligent managerial professional who realizes his or her own worth and contribution to the organization. The knowledge worker was the antidote to the previous model, corporate man and woman.

Drucker recognized this new breed, but key to his contribution was the realization that knowledge is both power *and* ownership. Intellectual capital is power. If knowledge, rather than labour, is the new measure of economic society then the fabric of capitalist society must change.

The information age places a premium on intellectual work. There is growing realization that recruiting, retaining and nurturing talented people is crucial to competitiveness. Intellectual capital is the height of corporate fashion.

But converting knowledge into intellectual capital is a new and elusive form of corporate alchemy. 'Intelligence becomes an asset when some useful order is created out of free-floating brainpower,' notes Stewart. 'Organizational intellect becomes intellectual capital only when it can be deployed to do something that could not be done if it remained scattered around like so many coins in a gutter.'

Intellectual capital is useful knowledge that is packaged for others. In this way, a mailing list, a database, or a process can be turned into intellectual capital if someone inside the organization decides to describe, share and exploit what's unique and powerful about the way the company operates.

Intellectual capital is often divided into three categories:

1. Human capital.
2. Customer capital.
3. Structural capital.

Human capital is implicit knowledge; what's inside employees' heads. Customer capital involves recognizing the value of relationships that exist between the company and its customers. But structural capital is knowledge that is retained within the organization and can be passed on to new employees. According to Stewart: 'Structural capital is knowledge that doesn't go home at night.' It includes all sorts of elements including processes, systems and policies that represent the accumulation of the organization's experience over its lifetime.

According to Stewart the knowledge economy also augurs the end of management as we know it. Today's knowledge workers carry the tools of their trade with them between their ears. It is they and not their managers who are the experts and must decide how to best deploy their know-how. As a result, what they do has more in common with work carried out by people in the professions and must be assessed not by the tasks performed but by the results achieved.

From this, he says, it follows that the professional model of organizational design should supersede the bureaucratic. So where does this leave managers? The answer, Stewart suggests, is that the only legitimate role for managers is around the task of leadership – although they don't yet have a proper understanding of what's involved.

He says: 'If "values" and "vision" and "empowerment" and "teamwork' and "facilitating" and "coaching" sometimes sound like so much mush-mouthed mish-mash – which they sometimes are – that's a reflection of the fact that managers are groping towards a language and a means for managing knowledge, knowledge work, and knowledge intensive companies.'

KNOWLEDGE MANAGEMENT

KNOWLEDGE management (KM) is one of the most influential new concepts in business today. A logical follow-on from intellectual capital, knowledge management is based on the idea that companies should make better use of their existing knowledge – everything from licences and patents, to internal processes and information about

customers. The concept has been steadily gaining ground since the early 1990s.

In a now famous statement, Lew Platt, former Hewlett-Packard CEO, is attributed with saying, 'if H-P knew what it knows, we'd be three times as profitable.' This sums up the challenge facing firms that want to create value from the knowledge that exists, in fragmented forms, inside their organizations. The logic is that in an accelerated business world, a company's knowledge base is really its only sustainable competitive advantage.

In their efforts to corral know-how and expertise, some companies have even created the new post of chief knowledge officer (CKO). Those attempting to capture and exploit their hitherto hidden know-how include Unilever, BP, Xerox, General Electric and Motorola. Behind their efforts is the idea that they are sitting on a treasure trove of knowledge that could improve their business operations if only it were captured and made available to everyone in the organization.

'To make knowledge work productive is the great management task of this century, just as to make manual work productive was the great management task of the last century,' Peter Drucker has observed. Managing something as ethereal as know-how, however, is problematic.

Research suggests that many knowledge management initiatives have failed to make a significant contribution to corporate effectiveness. In part, the problem seems to lie with the corporate mindset, and more specifically with overzealous IT departments. Technology has its uses, of course, but it is diverting attention from the human dimension of knowledge creation.

In particular, there seems to be some confusion about what constitutes knowledge and what is merely data. Many knowledge management initiatives have involved the creation of large-scale repositories of information in databases or intranet sites. To some extent, this misses the point, by simply collecting data without the understanding of its significance or usefulness.

Knowledge is not simply an agglomeration of information; it is the ability of the individual or the company to act meaningfully on the basis of that information. Information is not knowledge until it has been processed by the human mind. Technology may be the conduit, but the rubber hits the tarmac at the point where the human brain and the technology meet.

Modern technology makes transmitting information easy, but companies have to create the right environment and incentives to persuade individuals to share what they know. The trouble is that 'knowledge', as the old adage tells us, 'is power'. One of the greatest barriers to effective knowledge management lies in the basic insecurity and fear that prevail in many companies.

The real issue for companies is: How do you persuade individuals to hand over their know-how when it is the source of their power – and the only guarantee of their continuing employment? Until companies address this, knowledge management will remain a pipe dream for most.

THE LEARNING ORGANIZATION

THE work of Peter Senge at MIT's Sloan School of Business has been influential in convincing companies that the ability to learn is a key success factor. Senge has undoubtedly done much to develop and popularize the concept of the learning organization. However, the term was first used by Harvard Business School's Chris Argyris to mean a firm that learns as it goes along, adjusting its way of doing business very responsively.

Closely involved in and greatly influenced by the human relations school of the late 1950s, Argyris has examined learning processes, both in individual and corporate terms, in depth. 'Most people define learning too narrowly as mere *problem solving*, so they focus on identifying and correcting errors in the external environment. Solving problems is important, but if learning is to persist managers and employees must also look inward. They need to reflect critically on their own behaviour,' he says.[1] Problems with learning, as Argyris has revealed, are not restricted to a particular social or professional group. Indeed, it is the very people we expect to be good at learning – teachers, consultants and other 'professionals' – who often prove the most inadequate at actually doing so.

The entire concept of learning was brought back on to the agenda with the publication and success of Peter Senge's 1990 book, *The Fifth Discipline*. This brought the learning organization concept to a mass audience. It was the result of extensive research by Senge and his team at the Centre for Organizational Learning at MIT's Sloan School of Management. Senge argued that learning from the past is vital for success in the future:

> *'In the simplest sense, a learning organization is a group of people who are continually enhancing their capability to create their future. The traditional meaning of the word* learning *is much deeper than just* taking information in. *It is about changing individuals so that they produce results they care about, accomplish things that are important to them.'*

The organizations that thrive, Senge claimed, would be those that discovered how to tap their people's commitment and capacity to learn at every level in the company. This involved encouraging managers and other employees to experiment with new ideas and feed the results back to the wider organization. The book looked at how firms and other organizations can develop adaptive capabilities in a world of increasing complexity and rapid change. Senge argues that vision, purpose, alignment, and systems thinking are essential for organizations. He gave managers tools and conceptual archetypes to help them understand the structures and dynamics underlying their organizations' problems. 'As the world becomes more interconnected and business becomes more complex and dynamic, work must become more *learningful*,' he wrote.

For the traditional company, the shift to becoming a learning organization poses huge challenges. In the learning organization, managers are researchers and designers rather than controllers and overseers. Senge argues that managers should encourage employees to be open to new ideas, communicate frankly with each other, understand thoroughly how their companies operate, form a collective vision, and work together to achieve their goal.

'The world we live in presents unprecedented challenges for which our institutions are ill prepared,' says Senge.[2] Whatever the official line, it is the underlying culture of the organization that sets the tone. Senior managers can talk about learning organizations until they are blue in the face, for all the good it will do if those behaviours are not supported by the culture.

In particular, managers are unlikely voluntarily to shoulder additional responsibilities if the message from the organization's culture is that the most likely outcome of putting their heads above the parapet is having them shot off. One of the clearest indications of an organization's decision-making culture is how tolerant it is of mistakes. To a large extent, this will determine how willing managers are to take risks. It is also an important factor in whether the organization has the ability to learn. Soichiro Honda, the founder of Honda Motor Corporation, once said: 'many people dream of success. To me success can only be achieved through repeated failure and introspection. In fact, success represents the 1 percent of your work which results only from the 99 percent that is called failure.'

Despite current thinking, which suggests that experimentation is vital for companies to remain vigorous, in many corporate cultures there is very low tolerance of mistakes, and individuals' career prospects can be severely damaged if a creative decision goes wrong. Creating learning organizations has proved difficult in practice, not least because companies are set in their ways.

REFERENCES

1. Argyris, Chris, 'Teaching smart people how to learn', *Harvard Business Review*, May–June 1991.
2. Senge, Peter, 'A growing wave of interest and openness', Applewood internet site, 1997.

LEWIN, KURT

KURT LEWIN (1890–1947) was a German-born psychologist who fled from the Nazis to America. Prior to his death, he worked at MIT founding a research centre for group dynamics.

In 1946, Lewin was called into a troubled area of Connecticut to help create better relations between the Black and Jewish communities. Here it was found that bringing together groups of people was a very powerful means of exposing areas of conflict. The groups were given the name T-Groups (the T stood for training).

The theory underlying T-Groups and the Lewin model of change was that behaviour patterns need to be 'unfrozen' before they can be changed and then 'refrozen'. T-Groups were a means of making this happen.

Keen to take the idea forward, Lewin began making plans to establish a 'cultural island' where T-Groups could be examined more closely. A suitable location was identified shortly before Lewin's premature death, which robbed the human relations movement of its central figure. The National Training Laboratories for Group Dynamics were established in Bethel Maine and proved highly influential to an entire generation of human relations specialists, including Warren Bennis, Douglas McGregor, Robert Blake, Chris Argyris and Ed Schein.

THOUGHT LEADERSHIP

THE term 'thought leadership' was coined in the early 1990s by the then editor of the *Harvard Business Review*, Joel Kurtzman. In an economy increasingly driven by ideas and concepts, Kurtzman observed, the ability to plant an intellectual flagpole in new territory was a potent source of competitive advantage. In key sectors, especially the consulting industry and business school sector, thought leadership conferred first-mover advantage to the originator.

Kurtzman subsequently wrote a book called *Thought Leaders* in which he interviewed the leading business thinkers. The term is now generic, and denotes what has become a battleground among the leading consulting firms and the growing ranks of management gurus. The power of thought leadership is that it is a more effective way to brand and market intellectual horsepower than traditional advertising.

The term may be new, but as a strategy the origins of thought leadership go back much further. The traditional leader in this field is McKinsey & Company. McKinsey does not advertise. Instead, it relies on its intellectual prowess to carry the brand. It has long been the intellectual benchmark for consulting firms and, largely, continues to be so. 'The Firm', as it is affectionately known by

McKinsey insiders, bolsters its brand through the *McKinsey Quarterly*, a serious, heavyweight publication that has been around for 35 years and that sometimes makes the *Harvard Business Review* appear frivolous by comparison. Intellectual vigour exudes from every page, which is exactly what McKinsey wants readers to think and experience.

McKinsey flexes its intellectual muscles in a number of other ways. In 1990, it set up the McKinsey Global Institute, the objectives of which are characteristically bold. It aims, according to the firm, '[to] help business leaders understand the evolution of the global economy, improve the performance and competitiveness of their corporations, and provide a fact base for sound public policy-making at the national and international level'. In addition, since the McKinsey-authored *In Search of Excellence* rolled off the presses in 1982, the firm's consultants have been churning out books with admirable dedication.

More recently, the creation of consulting businesses by the Big Five accountancy and auditing firms has increased competition in this area. The need to differentiate themselves from each other has raised the stakes in the thought leadership arena. The top consulting firms now invest millions of dollars in thought leadership as a brand-building strategy.

The battle for thought leadership lacks the glamour of image advertising, but it is incredibly intense. *McKinsey Quarterly* imitators have been launched by rival consulting firms. Booz-Allen & Hamilton, for example, publishes its own heavyweight journal, *Strategy & Business*. Consulting firms have also been busy turning out business books that they hope will position them as thought leaders on the important emerging ideas.

Inevitably, however, the success of the thought leadership strategy depends on the quality and take-up of the ideas that are generated. The whole concept feeds on its ability to generate more and better business concepts. It is a sign that consulting firms have started to believe their own propaganda.

– CHAPTER 3 –

Technology and innovation

'It has become appallingly obvious that our technology has exceeded our humanity.'

ALBERT EINSTEIN

'Business is about communications, sharing data and instantaneous decision making. If you have on your desk a device that enables you to communicate and share data with your colleagues around the world, you will have a strategic advantage.'

ANDREW S. GROVE

'Technocrats are deadly when they're in charge.'

HENRY MINTZBERG

'Technology is dominated by two types of people: those who understand what they do not manage, and those who manage what they do not understand.'

PUTT'S LAW

Managing innovation

JOHN STOREY

John Storey reports the results of a three-year research project exploring how managers understand and prioritize innovation and the ways they interpret the factors promoting or inhibiting innovation in their organizations.

THE importance of innovation is widely proclaimed. The message has been pressed in varying degrees for over a century, but it has perhaps rarely been argued so insistently as now, in the context of the 'knowledge economy'. Yet in comparison with the rhetoric, actual performance on this front appears deficient – especially in the UK, where the DTI's (Department of Trade and Industry) innovation/R&D index reveals poor participation by firms. Organizations are more than happy to use the concept of innovation in their advertising and corporate PR, but, apart from a few notable exceptions, sustained behaviour in practice seems below par.

This gap between proclamation and practice requires some explanation. The 'problem' of innovation is itself of long standing. The barriers to innovation have been investigated at many levels and from diverse perspectives. For example, issues of financing and short-termism have been highlighted at the macro level, while others have focused on organizational structures and cultures.

Innovation involves much more than invention. The Department of Trade and Industry in the UK has defined it as 'the successful exploitation of new ideas'. Such an activity requires a whole series of management processes: environmental scanning, an understanding of threats and opportunities, an assessment of internal capabilities, the acquisition and mobilization of resources and capabilities, and the deployment and management of those resources and capabilities in pursuit of the chosen end. In sum, innovation is, in essence, a *management process*.

The subject of innovation is currently high on the agenda of policy makers and managers. The theme has, however, a long and enduring legacy, and the body of literature and research on the subject is extensive. Despite the wealth of concern and activity, the impact of innovation research on actual managerial behaviour appears to be limited.

Innovation ultimately derives from managerial perceptions of the need for change, the perception of the opportunity to change, and the perceptions about the way to change. Perceptions, beliefs, and assumptions are thus vital aspects to be understood.

In a major three-year research project, a team from the UK's Open University Business School set out to examine the issue of innovation by viewing it through the eyes of some of the most critical participants in the process – i.e., managers, the people who establish priorities, devise strategies, allocate resources, control rewards, and manage performance. The team interviewed nearly 350 managers in over 20 organizations in order to explore how they understand and prioritize innovation and the way they interpret the factors that promote or inhibit innovation in their organizations. A large range of sectors was covered, including pharmaceuticals, computers, banking and finance, television, telecommunications, and call centres, as well as voluntary sector organizations such as Oxfam.

The research found that in most organizations, there is no general consensus among managers about the place or importance of innovation. Even among top team members, there is typically significant variation in judgement about the wisdom of pursuing an innovative, fast follower, or some other strategy.

While an organization may house very creative and inventive individuals, it can be poor at translating novel ideas into products and services with a market impact. The managers in our research produced a wealth of explanations for this phenomenon, including lack of resources (time and money); short-termism; people confined to (and indeed sometimes preferring) their narrow 'boxes'; and fear of failure, as it was safer to follow the routine than take risks. These were the surface explanations, but we were able to reveal problems at a deeper level.

Variations in perceived meaning

The impact of corporate campaigns urging the significance of innovation may be blunted when the interpretation of the message varies so widely. We have indicated some of the broad, generalizable accounts many managers offer when reflecting on innovation. But the *differences* in views are also very important. Managers offered competing understandings of the very nature and meaning of innovation. A map of the different understandings of innovation processes is shown in Figure 1.

Figure 1 The innovation matrix

Product	Process	
Pharmaceuticals	Engineering	**Radical**
Banking and finance	Voluntary organizations	**Incremental**

The figure portrays, in broad-brush fashion, typical emphases of managers from these particular sectors. These patterns were not a matter of surprise and the managers involved were broadly reflecting the dominant cultural understandings in such companies.

What was more interesting was the degree of variation in perceptions and understandings *within* the companies. These differences between managers in the same team meant that attempts to exploit new ideas had to run the gauntlet of competing expectations, strategies and rationales – not to mention entrenched routines and inertia. Many of the key differences hinged on the extent to which innovation was regarded as a result of individual initiative (sometimes referred to as the 'hero innovator') or was seen as the outcome of social co-operation.

Another dimension was the degree of emphasis given to looking inward to the organization's internal resources and capabilities, or external to collaborators in other organizations. By cross cutting these two dimensions we can classify some of the key differences, as shown in Figure 2.

Figure 2 Competing theories of innovation

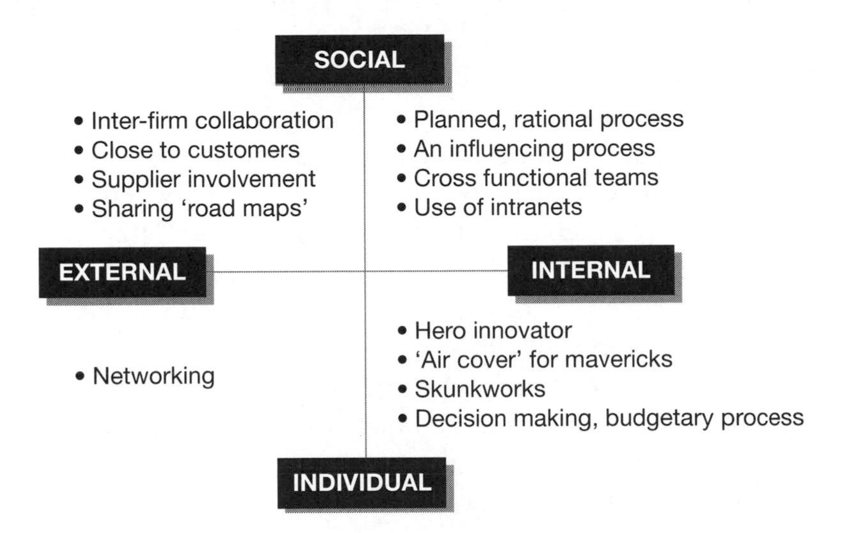

Starting with the top right hand quadrant, we have the idea of innovation as a *planned, rational process*. Managing it entailed a series of stages, with each culminating in a phase or stage review. These review points enabled formal managerial assessment and a decision opportunity to proceed with further investment or project curtailment. Typical phases were idea conception, specification of product, plan the project, prototyping, and so on through to final review. This type of understanding of the process of innovation and its management is allied to the idea of product lifecycles.

Such understandings of innovation were more typical in the contexts of telecommunication equipment manufacturers and pharmaceuticals, where large investments were periodically required in new products or new versions of established products. But even in these settings, we found managers who were critical of this approach.

For example, one telecoms manager observed: 'I think the stage review approach is a serious constraint. It's a good system for killing off creative ideas.' Directors would often use the review procedure as a way to protect their turf and thus, they argued, it was inherently conservative and tended toward low tolerance of risk.

Also in the top right hand quadrant, but operating under a different conception of the nature of the process, is the view that innovation is essentially an *influencing process*. These managers argued that there is a need to build a degree of enthusiasm among colleagues in order to enable a new idea to be accepted. The term 'influence' is rather too mild for some of the instances of change that were being discussed. Innovation for some managers was seen as a *fight for resources*. It involved competition between projects and even between change and the *status quo*. This kind of approach was prevalent in sectors where product innovation was accepted as the norm – for example in pharmaceuticals and computers, but also in some engineering companies.

In yet other circumstances, the perception was even more forthright than this. Innovation in organizations that were perceived as conservative and resistant to change was analyzed by those who wished to change them as requiring *'disruptive interventions'*. This is the politics of change. For example, one of the inner band of innovators at the BBC observed: 'I think you do need to be a bit like Trotsky. There has to be a permanent revolution. I mean, funnily enough the revolutionaries of yesterday inevitably have turned into the conservatives of today.'

Alternative perspectives in this quadrant were that innovation occurred through informal groups and *cross-functional teams* sparking ideas off each other and, by extension, that innovation could be facilitated if virtual teams could be established through the use of intranet technology.

Finally, an important set of perceptions located in this quadrant were those regarding innovation as a *corporate capability* or competence – the capability of the organization to reinvent itself. These managers argued that sustainable innovativeness can only be ensured if the capacity to produce serial innovations is embedded in the wider system. Such conceptualizations are, of course, in tune with current academic theory on knowledge management, the resource-based view of the firm, and the concept of core competence.

Located in the lower right hand quadrant are those perceptions that, while continuing to emphasize an internal focus, switch emphasis toward the role of individuals in delivering innovation. Tom Peters has celebrated the idea of 'skunkworks' – officially tolerated experimentation by individuals. This idea was widespread in Hewlett-Packard. A cultural symbol was the tale of one of the founders using bolt cutters to remove the lock from a supply cupboard so that any engineer could access components and tools in order to experiment – even if this meant playing around at home building toys for the children.

A related popular managerial conception was the idea of the individual *hero innovator*. Indeed, in one of the banks, the majority of managers interviewed made reference to one specific individual and told stories about that person to illustrate innovation. This suggested the general absence of a systematic process for innovation and elevated the notion of an exceptional individual in challenging the system. Closely related to this was the idea that this individual, and the people working under their aegis, would require special protection from powerful board directors. A number of informants used the metaphor of these innovators requiring 'air cover' for their activities. They were seen as vulnerable should that air cover be removed.

Also in this quadrant can be placed those accounts that perceived of innovation as part of the normal *budgetary and decision-making* process. Here a key individual, the managing director, would subject a range of alternative proposals to critical scrutiny and decide what resources should be allocated or withheld.

One such managing director emphasized the need 'to avoid individuals being "let loose" to pursue their "pet intellectual challenges"'. He continued:

> *'My management philosophy is that authority should go with accountability, that generally an organization benefits more from people having a real ownership of a particular part of the business and being given the tools to control that ownership and then deliver on it and be accountable. I am a strong believer in always having that choice made by people who have commercial accountability for a bottom line. I think you can waste an awful lot of time, effort and money, pursuing ideas for the sake of the intellectual challenge and enjoyment. In an organization like ours a lot of money can be consumed that way.'*

Another belief about innovation that belongs in this quadrant was that it occurred through *creative individuals* (by implication the priority is to find them and keep them). One manager in the BBC argued:

> *'Innovation comes first and foremost from the ideas of individuals and from the way in which the ideas are captured. So the ownership of ideas and the development of ideas is absolutely critical, and this is what's interesting about the negotiations that have gone on between production (the creative supplier side) and broadcast (the purchaser). It is now accepted that the ownership of, and exploitation of, the ideas has been recognized as belonging to production.'*

Here we can see that perceptions of innovation are closely aligned with arguments about the strategic future of firms. Thus, this manager continued: 'There was a time when the BBC made this split when people predicted that the BBC would become a commissioning organization like Channel 4. What I think we've won is the battle which says the creative *content* is king and that actually the BBC is dead without it.'

Those managerial perceptions emphasizing an individual focus allied to an external perspective are located in the bottom left hand quadrant. Most important here were those views that stressed the need for certain *individuals to network widely* through company visits, attendance at conferences, and trade exhibitions.

The fourth quadrant locates those managerial perceptions emphasizing an external-facing posture and a view of innovation as a social phenomenon, Thus, many managers stressed the importance of *inter-firm collaboration*. A key part of the collaboration was with customers. When asked what was innovative currently, one manager in a telecoms company replied, 'The front line is undoubtedly customer intimacy. It's about sitting with them as we develop new products and services.'

This was echoed in other companies, although the meaning of being customer focused was open to different interpretations. Some meant only designing new products and modifications to existing products where there was evidence of clear customer demand. This was an attempt to reduce or even avoid risk. Others were more adventurous and were trying to anticipate future demands – sometimes, as in telecoms, those of the customers of their immediate customers.

In a specialist electronics firm, some managers gave priority to collaboration with component suppliers. This was being done in a number of ways, including sharing future plans or 'road maps' with their suppliers so that products and components could be planned and phased-in appropriately.

Applying perceptions of innovation

Where management teams acknowledge and make transparent these competing beliefs, perceptions, and expectations concerning innovation, they can put the findings to practical use. Managers can compare their expectations and make more explicit strategic choices. To take one example, surfacing perceptions about the priority of technological innovation versus product innovation can enable more informed choices about investment of effort and other resources. Figure 3, which draws on ideas from Danny McCaughan, chief scientist at Nortel Satellite Solutions, shows a matrix with various intersecting lines of technology and product advance.

Figure 3 Product/technology innovation

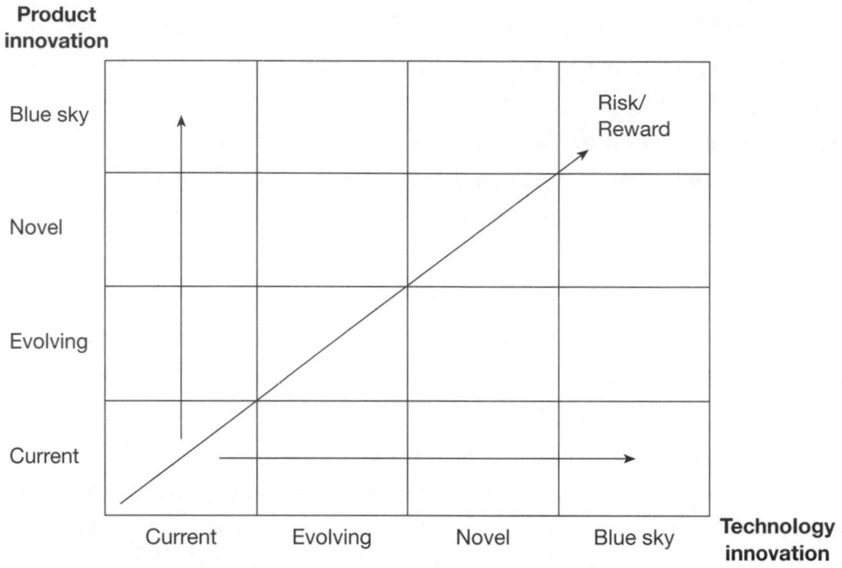

Source: Adapted from McCaughan, D., 'Research and development choices: do it or die,' in the Royal Academy of Engineering, *The Changing Environment*, London, 1998, pp. 30–7.

A decision to focus innovative effort on the vertical (product) axis entails the least technological risk while promoting rapid product evolution and time-to-market competitive advantages. Conversely, a decision to focus on horizontal (technology) innovation may allow feature-additions to existing products. Attempts to innovate simultaneously on technology and product carry the highest risk – and the potential for the greatest gain.

The distinction between technology and product is, of course, sometimes blurred, but the fact that there is a distinction is well recognized in R&D circles. For example, a manufacturer of paint-spraying robot arms for the motor industry might choose to refine an existing product by adding features using current technology. Alternatively, there might be a temptation to invest in novel technology, for example a shift from electro-mechanical devices to an entirely different underlying technology such as electro-activated polymers mimicking human muscle tissue. Another example is the case of the Rolls-Royce RB211 aeroengine, which was both a novel product and a novel technology (initially using carbon fibre-based fan blades). The new technology failed, but the product was rescued and became a great success using more conventional technology.

The product/technology innovation matrix can also be used as the basis for fruitful debates about core competencies and product portfolios. High-tech companies and those at the forefront in sectors such as telecommunications and engineering are comfortable with the concept of allocating varying proportions of R&D funds to different types of activity. This can, for example, entail a larger proportion being spent on the development of existing products and technologies, a slightly lower proportion on technologies with a one-year to three-year horizon, and maybe 10 percent 'ring fenced' for blue sky research. Such instinctive behaviour, however, is quite alien to companies in many other sectors. Realizing such possibilities can in itself be liberating. The model facilitates clearer, more transparent, and better thought-through choices.

Implications and applications

These perceptions of what innovation means and how it happens are very important in influencing behaviour. There are numerous implications that can be drawn from our research; some of the more important are summarized below.

- If the individual creative hero is perceived to be the solution, then organizations may allow considerable freedom to particular individuals. Conversely, the rational, planned perspective results in an orderly, linear approach to research and development. A third belief system produces an attempt to create a culture of experimentation and 'play'.
- Crucially, the largest proportion of managers are to be found in organizations without a track record of significant and sustained innovation. If and when managers in these settings do become attracted to the idea of innovation (or are instructed to embrace it), they tend to champion one or other of the models to which they happen to have been

exposed. Thus, within mainstream organizations with a new top-down edict to 'be innovative', one finds managers variously urging or assuming that this implies the establishment of an R&D unit or a liberal culture. The middle band is thus caught between competing models of innovation that require explication and examination.

- Perceptions and beliefs about innovation have an impact on the allocation of resources. They influence the organization of innovative activity, including, for example, the extent to which innovation is allocated to a select few or is regarded as a diffused responsibility. There are also implications for the way R&D is organized; indeed, for whether there will actually be any R&D and if so on what scale. Competing perceptions affect whether information and forward plans are kept secret or are shared across organizational boundaries and thus they influence the degree of collaboration with suppliers, customers and competitors.
- Clarifying understanding about the nature of innovation in a particular setting (e.g., in a particular organization) can help in the strategy formulation process. Managers can debate their current, compared with their desired, exposure to new markets, new customers, and new technologies and the varied risks and competency requirements associated with these.
- Innovation ultimately results from managerial perceptions of the need for change, the opportunity to change, and the way to change. Perceptions, beliefs, and assumptions are thus important aspects to be understood.

The overall conclusion is that organizations can benefit if perceptions and beliefs about innovation are clarified, made explicit, debated and challenged.

RESOURCES

BOOKS

Clegg, Brian and Birch, Paul, *Imagination Engineering*, FT Prentice Hall, London, 2000.

Cohan, Peter, *Technology Leaders*, Jossey-Bass, San Francisco, 1997.

Innovation as perpetual adaptation

PETER COHAN

Peter Cohan considers the new strategic concept of perpetual adaptation – what it is, why it is important, how it works, and the success of companies that have adopted it.

HIGH-TECH companies have invented a new concept of strategy. They can't afford the time or the capital to build insurmountable barriers around their core capabilities. Instead, they follow a strategy of perpetual adaptation that yields eye-popping financial results and the ability to stay on top of their industries despite tectonic shifts in technology, customer purchase behaviour, and competitor strategies.

What is perpetual adaptation?

Much of the strategic literature over the last 10 years has urged companies to create their futures on a foundation of core capabilities. Leading high-tech companies either ignored the advice or never paid attention to it in the first place. Technology leaders have seen too many companies turn into also-rans by hanging on too long to the capabilities that created their initial success.

Consider the case of Wang Computer. In the early 1980s, Wang grew by selling proprietary wordprocessing systems. By the mid-1980s, personal computers, wordprocessing software, and laser printers had blown Wang out of the water. For a lot less money, workers could produce their own documents.

Wang relied heavily on its closed minicomputer systems and waited too long to get into PCs. Its revenues plummeted from a high of $3 billion to $1 billion, its workforce was slashed from 33,000 to 6,000, and it ultimately filed for Chapter 11 bankruptcy in 1992. In the meantime, companies that made open system components – like Intel, Compaq, Microsoft, and H-P – experienced enormous growth.

The CEOs of companies that have created the strategy of perpetual adaptation have seen at first hand the dangers of these core capabilities-based strategies. For example, John Chambers of Cisco Systems was personally responsible for laying off thousands when he worked for Wang. Bill Gates experienced the implosion of IBM, a process that he had no small hand in causing. (Now Gates' success has drawn the ire of competitors and the US antitrust authorities, leading to a situation where Microsoft, pending appeal, has been ordered to be split.)

A strategy of perpetual adaptation is a reaction to the failures of core capabilities-based strategy. Core capabilities-based strategy causes companies to spend too much time focusing inward on trying to define what they're good at and then imposing these capabilities on the market. It also leads to major disconnects between what customers need and what companies choose to deliver. In short, core capabilities-based strategy leads to corporate extinction.

Perpetual adaptation overcomes the profound weaknesses of core capabilities-based strategy, enabling companies to keep growing and changing. Perpetual adapters make fundamental choices in the way their organizations work along five critical dimensions:

- **Relationship with customers**: how the organization chooses to interact with customers and their level of importance in setting and implementing strategy.
- **Executive grasp of technology** and **business**: how well corporate executives grasp both the technology that drives competition in their markets and the strategic, operational, and financial details that lead to business success.

- **Mission and vision**: how managers choose to define and communicate the fundamental purpose of the organization to employees and other communities.
- **Empowerment and information**: the way the organization distributes power and responsibility, as well as the information needed to make decisions and evaluate performance.
- **Climate**: individual responsibility, personal commitment, and reward and recognition systems.

As Table 1 indicates, these key elements are very different for perpetual adapters.

Table 1 ***Traditional and perpetual adaptation strategies***

Element of Choice	Traditional	Perpetual Adaptation
Relationship with customers	Customers are a source of revenue.	Customers are the magnetic north pole of the company: a source of new product and business ideas and a focus of changing organizational boundaries.
Executive grasp of technology and business	Mastery of strategic planning techniques, delegation of technology to CIO and/or CTO.	Combine deep technology insights with business savvy.
Mission and vision	Maximize shareholder value.	Inspire smart people to create new industry.
Empowerment and information	Underlings vie for CEO's power. Information flows upward through executive information systems. Systems measure aftershocks of change.	Employees are empowered to solve customer problems fast. Information lowers transaction costs for customers and suppliers. Systems anticipate change.
Climate	Standards (stretch goals), structure (linear, analytical planning), and support (emphasis on teamwork).	Responsibility (hire entrepreneurs), recognition (sharing rewards), and commitment (emotionally engaged people).

Why is 'perpetual adaptation' important?

Perpetual adaptation is important for two reasons. First, it leads to superior financial performance and shareholder returns. Second, it is a more highly evolved way of running a business that will permeate industry over the next decade as managers realize its power.

Perpetual adaptation is an approach to strategy invented by America's 20 most profitable high-tech companies. These Perpetual Adapters are presented in my book, *The Technology Leaders*. These 20 companies were selected from over 1,300 US companies based on three criteria:

- They compete in technology-intensive industries as measured by research and development expense to sales.
- They lead their industries in five-year average return on equity and profits per employee.
- They enjoy a reputation among customers and industry experts as producers of innovative, high-quality products.

As Figure 1 indicates, these 20 companies were two and a half times more profitable, grew revenues almost six times faster, and increased shareholder value at over four times the rate of the average US company. This outstanding performance alone might be enough to make the average CEO take notice of their success and seek to emulate the business practices that contributed to these results.

However, it is the uniquely harsh competitive environment under which these companies evolved that makes their success all the more impressive and important for managers to understand. What is so much more difficult about competing in these technology-intensive industries?

- New competitors can jump into their markets with better technology than incumbents have invented. Graduates of engineering programmes know the latest technology and venture capitalists are eager to invest.
- Customers have many choices and they pit suppliers against each other to get the most value for the lowest price.

Figure 1 Perpetual adapters versus average company performance

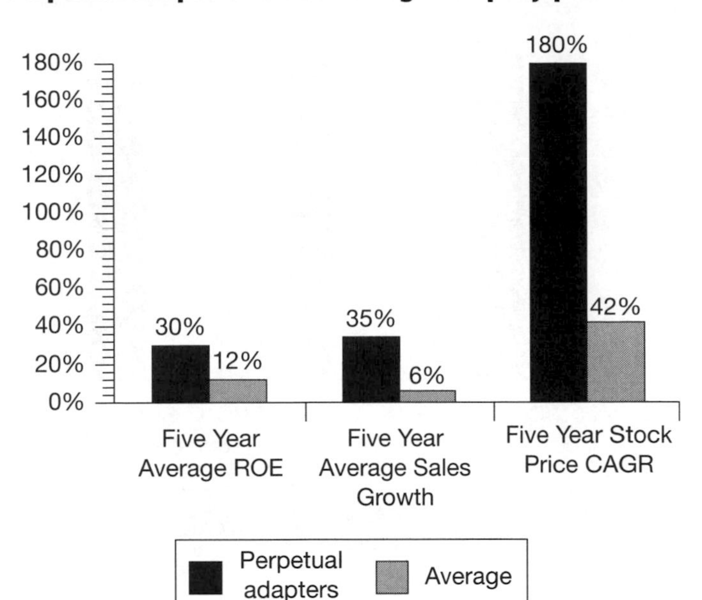

- Even the best-capitalized companies with cadres of top engineers and scientists can be caught flat-footed by a discontinuous technological change that undermines every capability they have built. Responding to these tsunami involves a gut-wrenching process of internal change.
- There is no tolerance for mediocrity. A company either controls the industry-standard technology or it quickly fades away (see Figure 2).

If your company is not competing directly with these perpetual adapters now, consider the following example. Suppose that you are CEO of an insurance company that sells individual annuities through a commissioned salesforce. The competitive environment looks attractive:

- The industry is $200 billion and growing at 10 percent a year as baby boomers prepare for their retirement.
- Regulation makes it difficult for new competitors to jump into your market.

Figure 2 Intel, Microsoft, and Cisco Systems' share of key markets

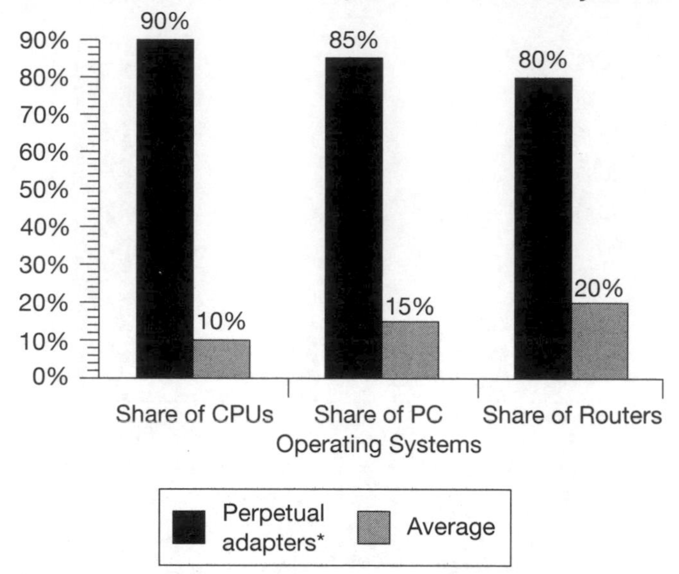

*Intel (CPUs), Microsoft (PC Operating Systems), and Cisco Systems (Routers)

- Price competition is non-existent because customers have no way of comparing prices or the value of different products.

Now, assume that Bill Gates, one of our perpetual adapters, decides that in order to keep up earnings growth, he needs to find a big growing market to attack – annuities. Microsoft simply adds a program to the Microsoft Network (MSN), its online service with millions of subscribers. This MSN program, called Annuity Buyer:

- Explains clearly what an annuity is and gives an overview of how people can compare their prices and value.
- Provides accurate, detailed comparisons of the pricing and value of all annuities available on the market.
- Prices annuities at least 10 percent below the market rate and underwrites them through a Microsoft-owned insurance subsidiary.

- Enables MSN subscribers to purchase these annuities directly over the internet.

Since you don't think of Microsoft as being one of your competitors, you don't even notice its presence in your business until your revenue growth and market share begin to plummet. In the meantime, Microsoft is growing its annuity business at 30 percent a year and approaching $1 billion in revenues. Annuity Buyer offers compelling advantages to customers, including demystifying the purchase process, eliminating contact with the insurance sales professional, lower prices, better value, and no paperwork. And since Microsoft doesn't have a salesforce to support, it can offer lower prices and still enjoy much higher profit margins – giving it ample cash to fund market development.

So perpetual adapters generate far superior financial performance and they represent an evolutionary advance in business strategy that will work its way through most industries over the next 10 years.

How does perpetual adaptation work?

Characteristics of perpetual adapters are that they:

- Redesign everything about their company to avoid losing their customers' business.
- Are led by executives with a strong grasp of technology and tremendous business savvy.
- Create a mission and vision that truly inspire the best people, making it easier to attract them and to create an environment where they achieve outstanding results.
- Push decisions to the individuals who can make rapid, yet informed decisions for the customer.
- Hire entrepreneurs, share rewards, and engage people emotionally.

Let's take a look at examples of each of these.

Customers as magnetic north pole

Cisco Systems, the leading maker of networking equipment, has managed to maintain its leadership by being the first to make fundamental changes in its organization in response to changing customer needs. As Figure 3 indicates, Cisco Systems dramatically outperforms its peers both in terms of profitability and growth.

At its inception, Cisco had tremendous respect for what its customers needed. Cisco was founded by two Stanford University computer administrators who wanted to solve a basic problem facing the university. The problem was that academic departments needed to send data among themselves, but each had a unique computer system with a different method for handling communications. Cisco's solution was both technically workable and politically acceptable. Rather than requiring all departments to standardize on a common communications protocol, a technically feasible but politically difficult approach, it developed a device called a router that could act as a

Figure 3 Profitable growth index for networking companies (1991 to 1996)

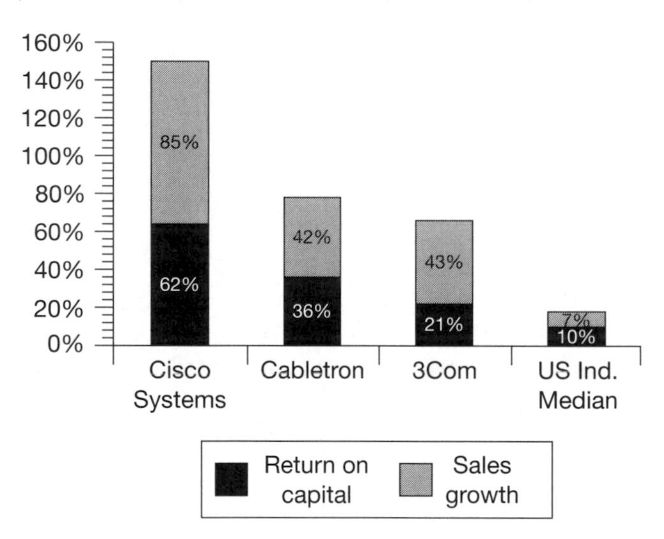

Profitable Growth Index is the sum of the five year average return on capital and the five year average sales growth. US industry median return on capital is 10 percent and sales growth is 7 percent.

central translator for all inter-departmental data communications. This pragmatic, customer-oriented attitude was called 'customer advocacy' by Sandra Lerner, one of Cisco's co-founders.

As Table 2 indicates, customer advocacy remains a permanent part of Cisco's culture. As customer needs changed, so did Cisco. Particularly at the early stages of the company's growth, these changes were made after tremendous internal debate. Nevertheless, despite battles between founders and 'professional management', Cisco's central principle of customer advocacy enabled the company to adapt to the changing demands of its customers. The changes were truly gut-wrenching: bringing in an outside management team, the departure of the founders, making acquisitions to obtain technology instead of developing it in-house and changing the organization structure.

Table 2 ***How Cisco responds to changing customer needs***

Change in Customer Needs	Cisco Response
Customers complained that Cisco was unable to process orders, manufacture product, and offer customer service.	Brought in John Morgridge who created a functionally oriented organization that operated effectively. Founders departed.
A major customer notified Cisco's CEO that it was about to buy switch technology from another competitor.	Morgridge and John Chambers go to the board and obtain approval to make their first acquisition – Crescendo, the Switch vendor from which the major customer was about to place a $10 million order.
Customers begin to complain about Cisco's lack of responsiveness to different product market needs.	Cisco changes from a functional organization to a product-oriented business unit structure and promotes John Chambers to CEO.
Customers in different segments express the desire for end-to-end solutions.	Cisco changes from a product-oriented to a market segment-oriented business unit structure.

Executives with technology and business skills

Bill Gates is the quintessential example of an executive who combines deep understanding of technology with great business skills. Microsoft employees and observers from outside paint similar pictures of Gates. They describe him as a visionary with a maniacal drive to succeed, accumulate great power and make money by taking advantage of his technical knowledge and understanding of industry dynamics. For example:

- According to Jim Conner, program manager of Microsoft's office products unit, Gates is unique in that he combines an exceptionally brilliant intellect with a total focus on creating wealth.[1]
- According to Dave Maritz, former test manager of Windows and MS-DOS, Gates is a maniac. He knows more about the products than any of his employees. Microsoft people go into meetings and come out sweating, because if there is any flaw, Gates will land on it immediately and pick it to bits.[2]
- According to a *New Yorker* article by John Seabrook, IBM seriously underestimated Gates. The company dismissed him as a technically adept but naïve kid. By the time IBM had finished negotiating with Gates, however, they realized that he had decimated them with his thirst for power and profits and his innate knowledge of contract language.[3]

Inspirational mission and vision

It is common to see corporate mission statements that emphasize the importance of maximizing shareholder value. Ironically, perpetual adapters actually create the most shareholder value, without mentioning it in their mission statements.

For example, Microsoft's mission is a personal computer on every desk and in every home, all running Microsoft products. Employees find this mission statement truly inspirational, because it makes them feel like their work will actually make a difference in the lives of millions of people. And this feeling of making a difference helps Microsoft attract the best people and work them hard to bring products to market. And it also creates over 6,000 Microsoft millionaires who got that way through company stock.

Cisco Systems is similar to Microsoft in this regard. Cisco's mission is creating the future of internet working. People who work there are genuinely enthusiastic about their work. They compare working at Cisco to riding on a spaceship. Engineers like to see their products succeed in the marketplace instead of languishing as the object of an internal power struggle between divisions as they do in other companies. And Cisco's stock has appreciated over 11,000 percent since its initial public offering in 1990.

Empowerment and information

Perpetual adapters recognize that their survival depends on the democratic distribution of power and information. They have seen too many business empires collapse because one person had all the information and made all the decisions. Perpetual adapters design their organizations so that decisions fall into three categories:

- Choices that could be made by customers and suppliers by giving them direct access to the information they need.
- Choices that could be made by employees with direct customer contact.
- Choices that require management involvement.

And the objective of the perpetual adapters was to put most decisions as close to the customer or supplier as possible. This approach has many benefits. First, it assures that everybody in the company is focused on solving customer problems quickly and effectively. Second, it ensures that people feel good about their work because they are transformed from passers of information up and down the chain of command to CEOs of their own domains. Third, it makes it much less likely that management will be surprised by a subtle but important change in the marketplace.

Cisco Systems is a case in point. Through an extranet, customers purchase over $3 billion in networking equipment without human intervention. When Cisco acquires a company, it connects the telephone and data lines before the transaction closes to ensure that the employees of the acquired company have immediate access to Cisco people and information. The objective is to make acquisitions seamless to customers. And, perhaps most importantly, Cisco links all employee bonuses and investments in process improvement to corporate performance on independently administered customer satisfaction surveys. Such performance measurement links everyone to the goal of improving customer satisfaction.

Hire entrepreneurs, share rewards, and engage people emotionally

Perpetual adapters convince entrepreneurs to join a larger company of which they are no longer the CEO. The argument is actually quite compelling. While they give up being king of a small hill, they get access to capital, people, and technology that they could not have afforded before. This allows them to do more of what they really want to do – building new businesses – without being distracted by such chores as dealing with Wall Street analysts or approving corporate financial statements. And of course, they get liquidity for their shares in the form of very valuable stock in the acquiring company.

For example, in 1996, Cisco Systems bought a company called Granite Systems. Its CEO had been a founder of Sun Microsystems. He invented the workstation that powered Sun to its greatest market successes. He left Sun with $50 million in stock and started Granite Systems with 40 engineers to develop a business around gigabit ethernet, a very fast networking technology. A while after he started the company, Cisco traded his 60 percent share of Granite Systems for over $100 million worth of Cisco stock. Did he retire?

No. He works seven days a week, 16 hours a day as a Cisco vice president. When asked why, he responds that when a new high-tech market is emerging, he feels a compulsion to be the first one in the industry to get the best product on the market. Cisco Systems is simply the best work environment that he has encountered for achieving this. A decision that might have taken six months to make at Sun could be made in a week at Cisco. It is this ability to attract such entrepreneurs and create an environment in which they can be productive that contributes mightily to the success of the perpetual adapters.

Microsoft uses entrepreneurial incentives as the core of its success cycle:

- Microsoft grants stock options to attract the most talented and creative people in the industry. It pays a base salary below the industry average, thereby helping to preserve its net margins. Employees can exercise 25 percent of their stock options after working at Microsoft for 18 months and another 12.5 percent every six months thereafter. They can also put up to 10 percent of their salaries into stock purchases at 85 percent of market value.
- These talented and creative people, recognizing that their ability to achieve wealth through Microsoft stock appreciation is contingent on producing superior products, work 14-hour days and on weekends to meet aggressive project deadlines. If a deadline appears to be slipping, outside contractors are hired to help avert the slippage, thus adding resources without increasing fixed costs.
- Microsoft introduces superior products to the market, thereby contributing to its sales growth, 25 percent of which goes to the bottom line.
- Its stock price rises substantially, allowing the employees with stock options (many of whom have been exhausted by their efforts) to resign with a substantial financial cushion.
- Microsoft's reputation for producing great products and making its employees wealthy is reinforced, thus attracting a new group of young, talented programmers to the company.

The unstoppable perpetual adapter

Perpetual adapters will take over the business world in the next 10 years. Because they are so much better at adapting to changing technologies, customer needs and competitor strategies, the perpetually adaptive organization will be unstoppable.

The fundamental issue for managers is not whether, but when they will transform themselves into perpetual adapters – before they lose their market leadership, or when they are acquired by a perpetual adapter who has taken it away.

REFERENCES

1. Cusumano, M. and Selby, R., *Microsoft Secrets: How the World's Most Powerful Software Company Creates Technology, Shapes Markets, and Manages People*, New York, The Free Press, 1995.
2. Ibid.
3. Seabrook, J., 'E-Mail from Bill', *New Yorker*, 10 January 1994, p. 59.

RESOURCES

BOOKS

Cohan, Peter, *The Technology Leaders: How America's Most Profitable High-Tech Companies Innovate Their Way to Success*, Jossey-Bass, San Francisco, 1997.

Cohan, Peter, *Net Profit*, Jossey-Bass, San Francisco, 1999.

Harnessing technology, thinking and action

EDDIE OBENG

The move from touchspace to cyberspace requires new skills but, most of all, new thinking for a New World. Eddie Obeng bids farewell to the Old World.

THE digital revolution which began about a hundred years ago with the invention of Morse's Code for the telegraph has finally come of age. The wireless revolution which enabled instant transfer anywhere through cyberspace followed shortly after. The information revolution which allowed mankind to lengthen the lifetime of thoughts and ideas beyond transient noise began centuries ago with their capture on to first stone, then papyrus and then paper. The organization of skills and know-how which allowed the cottage industries to thrive were invented during the renaissance. The financial instruments and tools for global trade – insurance, limited liability, business ownership, shares, stocks, futures – were revolutionary when they were invented in coffee shops and physical markets several generations ago.

So what is so new? If these trends and breakthroughs date back a hundred or hundreds of years how can there be a new economy? The newness refers not to the introduction of the concepts but instead to their impact on the structure of the economy and the business environment. Change has always been persistent. However, because of the scale of the global economy, at inception, even these innovations were discrete, influencing each other but still easily identifiable as step changes. In the past few decades, however, they have begun to impact on one another, rather like neutrons in an atomic reaction, accelerating in their impact as more of the globe was influenced by them until the point of a non-reversible, explosive chain reaction. This we have experienced as an increase in the pace of change. Alone, the explosive growth in the pace of change does not create a new economic structure or business paradigm. The new occurs because the cause–effect relationships which have existed cease to be completely valid. In this case the New World starts at the point for individuals, organizations or economies when the pace of understanding, learning and responses to the pressures of the pace of change lag behind the change itself.

To understand the scale of cyberspace, imagine trying to read everything on your computer and watch all the videos at your local library while trying to listen to all the mobile phone conversations in the country. It is enormous and, more importantly, it works to completely different rules to touchspace.

For example, in touchspace, density is a key concept – the more people you have in your office the bigger it needs to be. In cyberspace, the concept does not work the same way. When you zip a file, where does it all go? This means that the whole organization can access information on an intranet without the scaling implications of trying to physically fit them all in the same space.

In touchspace, finance concepts like raw material and depreciation are important. In touchspace, produced goods consume raw materials. In cyberspace, when you make a copy of a file you do not consume raw materials; furthermore, the original does not wear out with copying and have to be replaced. Again the implications of this relate to sharing electronic information, and help to explain why we are being deluged by e-mail.

Perhaps the most important and least well understood concept of cyberspace is exponential, self-growing information capital. In touchspace, trading is the exchange of goods or services for money, resulting in the seller having the money and the buyer having the goods. In cyberspace, trading means the seller making a copy of the original information (at close to no cost), passing it to the buyer, who exchanges money. In the process the sophisticated seller captures the maximum amount of information about the buyer – demographics, name, address, reason for purchase, etc. At the end of the transaction the buyer has the information; however, the seller has all their original information plus the money, plus all the information they have captured (tax free!). After a second sale the seller has their original information, two sets of money, two sets of information about the buyers and as a result a relational set of information built from the correlation (information capital all tax free!). The mountain of information grows exponentially, available to be used or sold at any time. Information economics is what makes the logic of 'clicks and mortar' mergers, like AOL–Time Warner, exciting.

The 'e' of e-commerce, e-enablement, etc. is simply a reference to the dominance of cyberspace concepts over touchspace concepts and a focus on electronic access, processing and storage. To e-enable your business is to create interfaces and processes which use cyberspace directly to manage and collect electronic information capital and knowledge effectively.

The contribution of the 'e' factor simply compounds the obsolescence of the models and frameworks developed for the Old World. For example, the discussions by traditional experts on the valuation of dot-com businesses fails to differentiate those building information capital of value, such as Amazon.com,[1] from those who are not, such as boo.com.[2]

Figure 1 Success in the Old World

So what's the secret of success in the Old World?

- Think about the best way to make lots of money
  - More of the same – market growth/share
  - Stick to the knitting – focus
  - One / few dominant products
- Think about who you employ
  - Experienced people, who work hard, plan a career with you.
- Think about how you organize them
  - keep them with other experts in their area and away from everyone else
  - keep them apart from everyone else
- Think what happens when you succeed
  - Growth – more of the same

Figure 2 Successs in the New World

So what's the secret of success in the New World?

- Think about the best way to make lots of money
- Think about who you employ
- Think about how you organize them
- Think what happens when you succeed

What are the implications?

The changes to the business environment are structural and redefine the competitive position of every organization. Sometimes I suggest an analogy. 'Imagine the Old World as operating your business in a swimming pool. You could try to make progress by walking through the water; however, it is quite difficult to walk through water so you can make some progress, drive through some change, but it is slow. So, of course not being dumb, you think, swimming pool – I should swim. So you start to swim. Then someone in the organization recognizes that an efficiency improvement can be made by providing snorkels to avoid you having to turn your head to breathe as you swim – and then another improvement a pair of goggles so that you can keep your eyes open under water to see where you are going. And then the ultimate productivity accessory, a large pair of black flippers. Soon anyone who joins the organization is issued with a set of corporate goggles, snorkel and flippers, and in no time at all they fall in at the back of a streamlined hierarchical pack, a triangle of dynamism and efficiency led from the top, cutting through the water in smooth synchrony. And then the New World happens – it is the equivalent of someone sneakily draining the water out of the pool. As the last few inches of water drain out of the pool what happens ...?'

Any business enterprise wishing to survive the structural change described above must make a transition. There are four positions which can be taken.

1. The organization can continue to provide its Old World offer using the same processes and systems.
2. It can look to provide New World offers, which require innovation and learning but can deliver them using the same structures, processes and systems familiar in the old world (e.g. Microsoft).
3. It can concentrate on an Old World offer which is well understood but focus on the processes and systems to deliver the offer (e.g. Amazon).
4. It can concentrate on providing a new offer in a new way (Cisco, Exodus.com).

In the three options which require change, there is a distinct advantage for any organization which can start as a greenfield without the associated overheads and costs, and difficulty of transition. Transition involves gaining commitment and support from people who were successful in the Old World organization to create a new culture – a culture where their skills may not be as relevant and their status and kudos have to be earned all over again. Cultural change is notoriously difficult to deliver successfully, especially since the New World can demand such wholesale change.

How do we respond?

The clear sense of relief of many Old World organizations at the recent fall in technology and new economy stock prices is a sign that as the last few inches drained out of the pool, some swimmers lie on the bottom, arms flailing saying, 'The water will come back you know. I've seen it all before.' Ignoring the New World, though fashionable, is not wise. Organizations have a number of other responses to the challenges posed by the New World. One common strategy is to increase in size through mergers and acquisitions with businesses in the same industry[3] to gain a global reach and market dominance. However, scale tends to reduce speed and flexibility. If you were unable to compete in speed at half the size, it is unlikely that the larger organization will be more successful. Instead, the strategy is to gain market dominance in an industry. The issue though is that as the technologies available in the new economy increase, most industry boundaries are becoming blurred with competition arising from other industries or from new entrants.

Furthermore, in implementing the new strategy it is common to use Old World concepts and approaches. This further reduces the chances of success.[4] The net result is a reduction in organizational effectiveness.

Evolving organizational effectiveness

The combination of the rapid information velocity around the world and the exponential increase in access and usage of cyberspace technologies creates several key issues.

First, customer ignorance ceases to be a source of profit – usually mistaken for commoditization, the problem is that in the old world the slower information velocity limited the choices available to customers. This had the net result that if the suppliers in the market knew each other's prices and could pitch close prices (even without price fixing), the customer came to believe that the average price on offer was probably realistic. At the higher velocity the customer can discover and compare globally, and as a result the 'ignorance premium' disappears.

For comparison, the frameworks the organization must grasp before e-enablement will be effective in the New World are shown in Figure 4.

The traditional model championed by Michael Porter based on focus, differentiation and cost leadership becomes significantly less valid in the New World. Cost leadership comes to mean global cost leadership in a world where the ignorance premium no longer exists. Since there can only be one global cost leader, the framework becomes

Figure 3 Old World

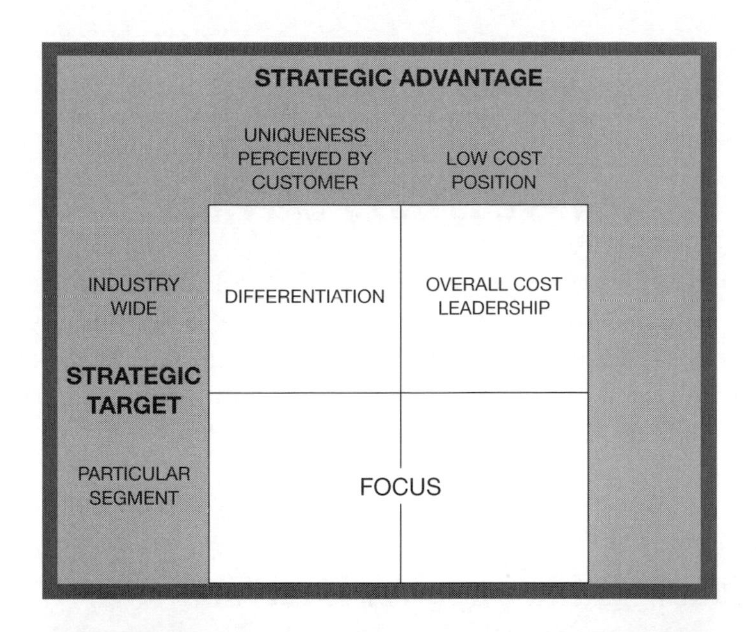

Figure 4 New World

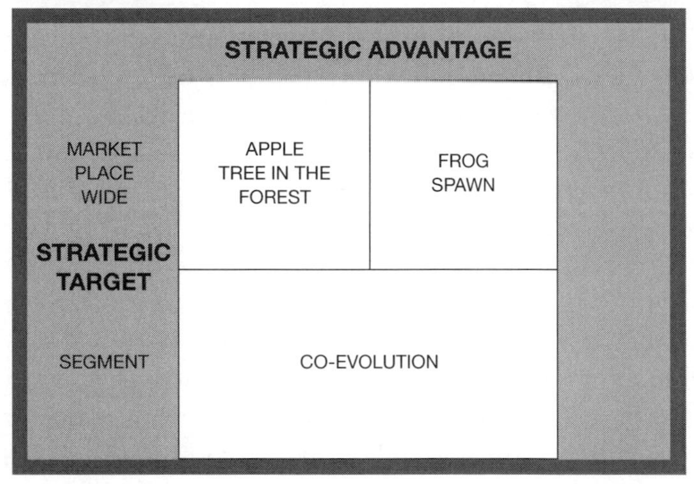

3

pointless to apply. Furthermore, in the New World, as a result of technology divergences,[5] there are more and more ways of satisfying every need. Thus a focus strategy becomes too dependent on the activities of emerging competitors.

The model for the New World has three different positions. Because information velocity has effectively eliminated customer ignorance as a source of profit, differentiation as perceived by the customer ceases to be a tenable solution. Instead really different solutions are required.

Evolving the customer interface

The third option is co-evolution. Co-evolution strategies – growing in tandem with your customers/clients – is particularly dependent on e-enablement for information capture and management. The ability to e-enable this interface is key to such a strategy. The advantage of co-evolution is that it provides stability in a rapidly changing marketplace.

Evolving the supplier interface

With the supplier interface, the goal is to encourage suppliers to offer you their best and latest ahead of the competition, or to reduce their costs of servicing your needs dramatically. For example, Dell provides customer-specific websites where the client organization can buy direct, saving both customer and seller costs.

A second implication of the effect of information velocity and access is that the flow of information in the business-sphere surrounding the organization is probably far greater than the flows into the organization. Most organizations have structured functions – market research, customer service, procurement – which have a specific role of capturing information. However, these functions are usually tasked with gathering specific information focused on the current business model. This data capture is often via traditional media. The net result is that the organization becomes out of touch with its key stakeholder groups. It becomes critical to ensure that all members of the organization directly capture data electronically.

Third, the organization becomes dysfunctional. Apparently the speed of flow of information to a top team of 25 executives is about 1Mb/s.[6] Unfortunately this rate is far below the rate at which information can circulate locally or globally within the organization, creating a structural bottleneck. There are some options.

The first option to do nothing is available so that organizations can fail and be a source of ridicule to spare the rest of us. Getting less better information becomes a clear goal. It becomes important to recognize that information is the result of a combination of a question and an answer.

Increasingly, the organization needs to focus on the questions related to its processes and to recognize that in a fast-changing world where yesterday is a poor barometer for tomorrow, knowing what could happen next and how it might come about is critical.

The shift from a focus on the individual to recognizing the importance of individuals, teams and networks shifts the performance feedback from direct appraisal by your line boss to stakeholder appraisal as a norm. The stakeholders include all the people to whom the individual is accountable. This added complexity provides the vital performance information. However, it can only be practically delivered using an e-enabled solution, such as a groupware based database for capturing all the inputs. Touchspace solutions are cumbersome and are unable to deal with a project by project or process outcome based timing as opposed to an annual cycle.

Evolving key processes: strategy

Traditionally, strategy has been seen as achieving a 'fit' with the environment. Taken from the military model this approach is based on an assumption that the environment remains the same during implementation.

The decision-making process accompanying this approach can be summarized as Analyse, Analyse, Analyse, Create options, Analyse, Select one option, Implement. Unfortunately this is no longer true.

Strategic processes need to be flexible and continuous in an economy of constantly changing competitors, alliances and customer requirements. The selected strategic approach becomes more aligned to a vision (with a sell-by date), with a modular focus based on strategic action which provides advantage in a range of environments, i.e. robust. The decision process here is summarized as: 'Analyse briefly, Decide and implement rapidly with an effective feedback process.' Rapid implementation and feedback are the solution to the difficulty of being able to create a cast iron decision.

E-enablement of the strategic process is the key method for ensuring that the strategy remains valid during implementation.

Evolving key processes: budgeting and planning

Traditionally the budgeting and planning cycle was a primary control mechanism. The time-scale of a year was short in comparison with payback times of five to ten years. The process was aligned with departmental or functional spending, with the result that it was difficult to reassemble figures to match the revenues anticipated. As a result, the process usually takes several months. In a world where yesterday and today are similar, the ability to forecast effectively declines slowly with time.

The New World poses a different challenge – the time it takes to complete a traditional budgeting exercise can be longer than the best forecast horizon available. For example, Jamcracker, an internet application service provider, runs its planning and budgeting on a 'one week forward–one week backward' cycle. Cisco's real time financial information systems are a good example of e-enablement for maintaining control over finances.

In order to operate in the New World, it is necessary not only to alter the frameworks and processes of the organization, but also to support the implementation with significant e-enablement.

REFERENCES

1. *The Economist,* September 1999.
2. *The Economist,* May 2000.
3. *Financial Times* survey, November 1999.
4. Obeng, Eddie, *New Rules for the New World,* Capstone, Oxford, 1997.
5. Obeng, Eddie, *Making Re-engineering Happen,* FT/Pitman, London, 1995.
6. Kevin Baughan, Nortel Networks.

Design to be different

KJELL NORDSTRÖM AND JONAS RIDDERSTRÅLE

In the quest for differentiation, companies are increasingly embracing design as a competitive weapon. Espousing the virtues of design is one thing; inculcating design into a corporate culture quite another.

We live in a surplus society. This is the age of more – more fun, more fear, more freedom, more responsibilities, more products, more services, more competition, more opportunities. We have entered an age of abundance. In November 1998 there were 878 bank websites in Europe – by the summer of 1999, the number had more than doubled. Last year saw the launch of close to 2,000 new business books; 30,000 new CDs; and 20,000 grocery products in the United States alone. The average consumer is now exposed to some 247 advertisements every day.

The competition for our attention is intensive and intensifying. Yet, *more* quite often simply means more of the same. Products have become increasingly homogenous. In 1996, the annual survey of the car industry, produced by J.D. Power, concluded: 'There are no bad cars any longer, because they are all good.' In our age of techno-economic parity, there are few raw materials, technologies and insights that are available to people in the West that are not also available to people in Bangalore, Warsaw, Santiago and Manila. From a strict price/performance view, it no longer really matters what microwave, stereo or vacuum cleaner you buy. Sameness rules.

With markets becoming increasingly global and efficient, most organizations have access to the same input goods. Success depends on our ability to combine and recombine things into something that is desirable. In the corporate equivalent of a blind tasting, the companies which emerge victorious will be those which have, as Stanford's Paul Roemer puts it, the most potent, alluring and attractive recipes. Increasing competitive pressure means that companies incapable of serving the flavour of the future may well be facing their Last Supper.

Different ways to differentiate

In the morass of sameness, differentiation is vital. Successful companies add unique value to a specific group of customers. They are different, offer different things in different ways to different people. Companies seek to be different because it is the route to the corporate Holy Grail of a temporary monopoly.

Once, difference was based on location – being closest to the mine, forest or whatever. However, the development of international markets for raw materials eventually pre-empted these advantages. By the beginning of the twentieth century, difference was based on technological innovation. In certain industries, such as the software industry where increasing returns and lock-ins are powerful forces, this still largely holds true. But for most companies the reality is, and has for a long time been, that products are rapidly imitated and patents sold or acquired in global markets.

When technological innovations became open to all comers, companies pursued differentiation elsewhere. We entered the organizational age. Progressively, throughout the latter half of the twentieth century, organizational innovations gave rise to new temporary monopolies. Through their adoption of an array of organizational innovations, companies differentiated themselves – albeit briefly. Just-in-time, re-engineering, ISO 9000, kanban, outsourcing, downsizing, lean production, and many more were seized upon. In the quest for difference, companies pursued management fads and fashions with increasing zeal. They refocused, leveraged their competencies in all imaginable directions, re-engineered and restructured, in the belief that this was the recipe for future success. These initiatives are laudable and useful, but have now become standard; necessary but not sufficient for securing success. They are available through the international market for expert advice and can potentially become the property of any organization.

The result is that, for most firms, competitiveness can no longer be solely based on a superior location, technological innovation or a new way of structuring the organization. Any advantages these factors might provide are likely to be extremely short-lived. Traditional competitive strategies will get you nowhere. Momentarily you may be one step ahead, but the others will soon catch up.

Figure 1
The historical evolution of sources of competitive advantages

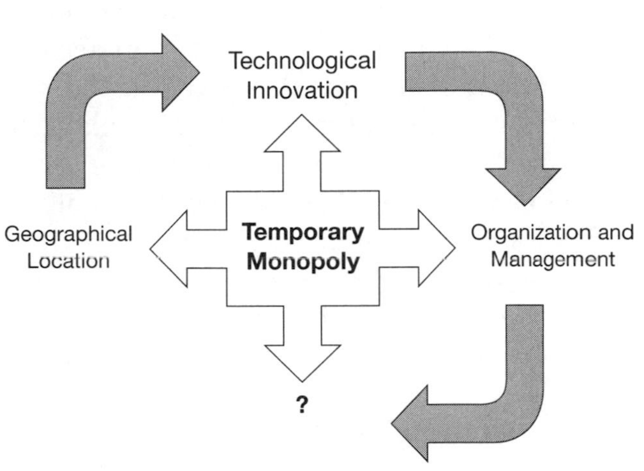

Entering the emotional economy

If being good is no longer enough, there has to be a better way, a more original route to differentiation. There is. Look at the Finnish company Nokia which has come from almost nowhere to become the leading maker of mobile phones in the world. Nokia does not possess groundbreaking technology which its competitors cannot get hold of. Nor has its CEO, Jorma Ollila, stumbled upon a management book yet to be translated from Finnish. It is true that Nokia has world-class, top of the line technology, and that it pioneers new organizational solutions. It is also the case that Nokia seeks out the best IT solutions that money can buy and works with the best suppliers in the world, rather than the closest. All this is necessary. There is no choice. But, it is not sufficient because Ericsson, Philips, Motorola, Sony, Siemens and many more companies are doing the same things.

Nokia, and other such firms, succeed because they have realized that the new economics are emotional rather than rational. True competitiveness must be built around something we all know exists but which is seldom discussed in the business world: emotions and imagination.

The new quest for differentiation requires that companies develop sensational strategies which embrace the emotions, and capture the attention of consumers. Strategies never used to target emotions; they now must. Instead of running faster, companies must play a different game. 'People take technology for granted these days. What they want are warm, friendly products – something to seduce them,' says the designer Phillipe Starck.

As Mr Starck's comments suggest, attracting the emotional customer and colleague is not a question of superior price or performance. Again, this is necessary but not sufficient. Ethics and aesthetics, feelings and fantasy, have little to do with logic, but everything to do with affection, intuition and desire. Sushi is nothing more and nothing less than cold, dead, fish, but that is not the way you persuade people to buy it.

Design is the synthesis of these elements. Design is about truth, love and beauty and, increasingly, about whether a business has a sensational strategy or the same strategy as everyone else. 'Design is not done with rules, but with intuition. Intuition never lies,' says the leading British designer, Jasper Morrison. To some this is frivolous indulgence, a world away from the realities of the bottom line. To them, design is mere decoration rather than pure meaning. 'People have an enormous need for art and poetry that industry does not yet understand,' argues Alberto Alessi, CEO of the eponymous company. The public's appetite for art and poetry enables Alessi to charge some $80 for a toilet brush.

The companies which accept Alessi's viewpoint are cutting a swathe through the competition. Furniture retailer, IKEA, proclaims its vision of 'good design, good function and good quality'. The new American airline JetBlue announces that its priorities are 'simplicity, friendly people, technology, design and entertainment'. 'Customers really respond to products that involve new thinking and connects with their souls,' says Ron Jonson, former vice president of Target, the low cost retailer with close to 1,000 stores, which works with renowned designers such as Michael Graves and Phillipe Starck. Nokia built art and poetry into its 8810 mobile phone which resembles a Zippo lighter. Add some art and poetry to a computer and you get Apple's iMac. Apple claims that around one-third of the people who have bought an iMac did not previously own a computer. Apple's Steve Jobs was asked what distinguishes the company's new Mac OS X operating system. He replied: 'We made the buttons on the screen look so good you'll want to lick them.' He did not utter a single word about megahertz and gigabytes. Such companies understand that although economies of scale and skill still matter, the new game is one of economies of soul.

Design is an increasingly rich source of differentiation. 'We won't make things cheaper than the far-eastern nations, but we can make things better through design and innovation,' says British designer Sir Terance Conran. Robert Hayes of Harvard Business School echoes similar ideas by claiming that: 'Fifteen years ago companies competed on price. Now it's quality. Tomorrow it's design.' A good price/performance relationship is necessary but no longer sufficient. Getting that stuff right buys you a ticket to sit close to the ring, but it will not win the fight.

There is some reassurance for those who insist on old certainties. Even traditional industrial firms admit that emotion and imagination are the way forward. Just listen to one of the head designers at Ford: 'In the past we tended to focus inwardly, looking for functional efficiency. Now the mindshift is to more outwardly focused, emotional satisfaction for the consumer.'

And, inevitably, some companies have been exploiting emotional economics and the power of design for many years. Look, for example, at Sony. 'At Sony we assume that all our competitors' products will have the same technology, price, performance and features. Design is the only thing that differentiates one product from another in the marketplace,' says Norio Ogha, Sony CEO.

Infinite innovation

If design is to be a crucial determinant of competitive advantage, the rules of the game need to be changed. Historically, the competitive game focused on finite dimensions. The new game is infinite. There is no limit to how beautiful, attractive or gorgeous a product can be. The permutations are endless.

Finite dimensions have the attraction of being objectively measurable and clear. As a result, it is easy for consumers to evaluate the performance of different competitors. Finite strategies combined with the internet mean that comparison shopping becomes a picnic for the well-informed customer. By focusing on these finite aspects of the offering, companies enable the customer to become even more of a demanding dictator.

Design, on the other hand, is subjective. It evokes opinions. We love and loathe different things. People differ. So designs must differ. Not everyone likes the pristine expanses of marble and giant-sized revolving doors of London's St Martin's Lane Hotel (designed by Starck). Some may even be appalled. Not all people like the design of Helmut Lang's clothes or Alessi's kettles.

Design strikes at the emotions. It seduces. In an excess economy, it is better to be something for someone rather than nothing to everyone. Differentiation cannot lie in eliciting the same response from everyone. In an emotional economy, it is better to thoroughly annoy 90 percent of the people while capturing the attention and interest of the other 10 percent, than to be merely acceptable to all of them. In the age of affection, mediocrity, average and almost, won't do. People want amazing things, spectacular things.

In a broader sense, design is even more important. In essence, according to Chris Bangle, head of design at BMW, design is meaning. So, if a company is not design driven it is by definition meaningless.

Table 1 ***The transition from rational to emotional competition***

Dimension	From	To
Strategy	Competitive	Sensational
Goal	Being one step ahead	Playing a different game
Implementation	Finite dimensions	Infinite dimensions
View of customer	Objective – rational	Subjective – emotional
Provider of meaning	Everything to everyone	Something to someone

Embracing emotions everywhere

The fear and the attraction of design lie in its infinite possibilities. Design is a fact of life – though not always appreciated – and all embracing. Design concerns all aspects of the organization, from branding to how we deal with customers and colleagues – the office architecture, the stores, packaging, sales people, etc. Design touches all aspects of business life. Companies must, as a result, optimize the emotional experiences they create and offer.

Look at the evolution of retail stores. Until recently, we designed, built, manned, organized and decorated, stores to sell things in them. In an economy where sales almost always equalled physical presence this was reasonable and sound. Now, with the advent of the mobile internet, people will soon be able to bring their own cash register in the phone to the store, have a look at the product and then search the web to find the best deal.

Companies must, in response, add aesthetics and entertainment to the retailing experience – fusing function with fun. All customer offerings contain an aesthetical element. We should, perhaps, think of them as pieces of art. The corollary of this is that we should look to museums and galleries for our inspirations. Rubbermaid has sent groups to the British Museum – they reportedly emerged with inspirations for new kitchen products. Visit MoMa in New York and learn something about the shop of the future. 'The store entrance should be almost stage-like, creating a sensation similar to when you descend into an amazing restaurant. At the same time, it had to have the luxury of a sleek modern residence, so you feel completely enveloped and relaxed,' says Tom Ford on the new Gucci store. Bill Sofield, the architect behind the project, adds 'Because so much of Gucci's image is built around architecture, be it advertising or the clothes, it allowed us to create a new design vocabulary with the stores that speaks to a global consumer.'

Many balk at such notions. They regard design as superficial, driven by the vicissitudes of fashion.

On one level this is, indeed, the case. Business is increasingly fashion driven. The CEO of one of Europe's largest stainless steel companies recently asked us: 'So you think we should enter the fashion business?' The reality is, we told him, you already are in that industry – you just don't know it yet. In fact all companies are – regardless of whether they make stainless steel, sneakers or suits. Today, there is fashion in everything – the beautiful train, the trendy wrench and the stylish lawnmower. Recently, one of us visited a computer games manufacturer in Silicon Valley where games are developed and launched in winter and summer collections. The only fashion victims are those who fail to keep pace.

The reality is that fashion is simply another word for constant improvement. We suspect that few executives would have a problem with constant improvement.

How to make design work for you

So, how do we unleash the potential for emotional competitiveness and corporate imagination? At many companies, the preferred approach for handling increased organizational complexity has been to add yet another box to the organizational chart. Setting up a department for emotions and imagination will not work. By making design a big thing for a select few, the others stop caring. Instead, the critical components and true sources of competitive advantage must be turned into a small thing for all people in the organization. Emotions and imagination cannot be neatly compartmentalized. They are a philosophy, an attitude, a frame of mind, and must concern everyone and everything, go on everywhere and non-stop.

If design touches everything, making design work for an organization involves re-evaluating everything the organization does.

1. Build an organizational tribe

Design is personal and demands a much more personalized company. Oscar Wilde was right when he noted that: 'Consistency is the last refuge of the unimaginative.' A design-driven company that competes on feelings and fantasy must thrive on variation, difference, and diversity. Yet, most of us live and work in organizations built by and for 6.5 percent of the population – middle-aged white males. Tom Peters, a long-term advocate of the importance of design, recently noted that women make some 65 percent of all car-buying decisions in the US. Yet, a mere 7 percent of all car sales people are women, men design virtually all cars, and men dominate the managerial echelons of car companies. This is not only a question of equality, it is a question of quality of decisions and customer offerings.

Variation can lapse into chaos if it is not grounded in solid and articulated values. Design-driven companies require strong cultures. Indeed, these firms resemble organizational tribes. (Or, as someone once said of Nike: 'It is like a cult – but it's a nice cult.') In a tribe people get energy from one another. The Zulus have a word for it: '*ubuntu*' (short for *unmunta ngumuntu nagabuntu*). This can be translated as a person is a person because of other persons. Or as Jung put it: 'I need we to be fully I.'

There is a lot of mystification surrounding the subject of values. In reality, the simplest way to get people to share your values is to recruit people who already do. Herb Kelleher of Southwest Airlines professes to hire attitudes rather than aptitudes. The logic is that you can make positive people into good pilots, but turning great pilots with attitude problems into charming servers of customers is close to impossible. Consequently, smart companies recruit people with the right attitude, then train them in the necessary skills – rather than the reverse. Lenin was right. Find the revolutionaries. Do not try to change people.

2. Extend the tribe biographically

The world of yesterday was geographically structured, and so were its tribes. The new tribes – whether they are Hell's Angels, computer nerds, or Amnesty International – are biographically structured. They are global tribes of people who feel they have something in common, no matter where they were born.

Since design is subjective, success is about targeting such global biographical tribes – core customers. It doesn't matter what kind of tribe, where it's based or how large it is. What does matter is that the targeted tribe has a common bond – values and attitudes – with your organizational tribe.

'We're all listening to the same music, watching the same movies, drinking the same vodka at exactly the same time and now we have stores that will convey the same unified message around the world,' says Gucci's Tom Ford. And Gucci is not alone. Violent drug barons create tribes. Miguel Caballero is the Armani of the armoured apparel world. His company sells customized and fashionable bullet-proof vests. It has targeted a specific tribe. Its home base is Columbia where demand is great.

Pilgrims create tribes. Futurist Watts Wacker tells the story of how every year, 75,000 Chevrolet Suburban vans are sold in Saudi Arabia. The explanation for this sales phenomenon is that the pilgrims who visit Mecca are only allowed to enter the city in a vehicle with specific measurements. The only car that fits the specifications happens to be the Chevrolet Suburban.

The female population remains – astonishingly and, somewhat, depressingly – the most obvious and largely unexploited tribe. Prior to 1994 when Nokia launched the 2110 – the first mobile phone with rounded-off corners and a large display – all mobile phones came in one colour. The 2110 came in a variety of colours and was targeted at women. It was a huge success.

The Norwegian furniture manufacturer Stokke has built an international reputation for its innovative designs. Among its most successful products is the Tripp Trapp, a wooden chair for babies and children. Designed by Peter Opsvik, the height and the depth of the Tripp Trapp are adjustable so that the chair can grow with the child. The Tripp Trapp does not look like a conventional children's chair.

One of the reasons Stokke has succeeded with the Tripp Trapp and its other unusual looking designs is a keen awareness of its tribes. The target audience for the Tripp Trapp is essentially new parents who want the best for their children. So, Stokke gives Tripp Trapps to children's nurseries and kindergartens where parents can see the chairs being used and abused. At times, Stokke has had to take on an educational role. In France, Tripp Trapps failed and then failed again. The problem was that the French had got out of the habit of eating *en famille*. They had no need for a children's chair. Stokke responded in a number of ways. First, it targeted French people who had worked outside the country and returned. It reasoned that they were more likely to have picked up the international habit of eating together. Second, the company sought out publicity opportunities based on the chair's unusual design. It also emphasized the 'newness' of the product, as the French have a predilection for anything new.

Stokke's other products – ergonomically designed furniture – attract a different tribe. These can basically be categorized as 'free agents', freelance professionals. The company sometimes refers to them as 'people who buy Apple Macs'. The trouble with this tribe is that it is disparate with a wide range of ages, occupations and needs. Stokke's approach is to let the tribe come to them. Having decided that face-to-face interaction was important, it established Stokke Centres in major cities. These Centres host regular parties for specific groups such as physiotherapists and musicians to introduce them to the company's products. From being a small, local company with 40 employees in the mid-1980s, Stokke has expanded to become an international organization with 500 people.

3. Identify and involve individuals

Within a tribe there must be room for personalization and individual differences. 'A product that matters needs to say something about the person who owns it,' argues Barry Shepard, co-founder of the design consultancy SHR which helped develop the Volkswagen Beetle. Customers, confused by the array of products and services on offer, are looking to companies for help in expressing their individuality. They want products that in certain respects are as unique as their own fingerprints. Companies must, as a result, deal with micro markets of single individuals and extreme diversity.

Companies must customize – then customize still further. 3M's Post-it notes now come in 18 colours, 27 sizes, 56 shapes and 20 fragrances. All in all, more than half a million combinations are available. Truck maker, Scania, created modularized trucks which allow customers to build their personal truck – cafeteria style. Barbie now comes complete with 15,000 combinations. The management thinkers were right: mass customization is child's play. Change the outfit, the eyes, the colour, the hairdo, the clothes, the name – but don't even think about the legs. All for $40.

In a fragmenting world, niches are becoming ever smaller. Increasing individualization combined with changes in technologies and values mean that micro markets have overtaken mass markets. The next step is one-to-one design, one-to-one manufacturing; one-to-one marketing; one-to-one everything; one customer–one solution. We are entering a one-to-one society. In an age of abundance where sameness rules, people cry out for limited edition products that make them stand out.

The relationship between the producer and the consumer is blurring. Recent developments in Computer Aided Design (CAD) and Computer Aided Manufacturing (CAM) open up many new opportunities. Companies can move from standardized to personalized; from mass production to flexible production and, now, mass customization. With fewer tools we can produce more and better quality models. 'We used to wish we had the technology to do things ... Now technology is giving us things we don't even know how to use,' says Ian Schrager, owner of Schrager Hotels.

4. Replace the rational with the emotional

Regardless of tribal belonging or individual preferences, there are basically four ways in which you can communicate with people: either you appeal to their reason, affection, intuition or their desire. Every time we communicate with someone we use a mix of these elements. The critical question for companies is whether they are using a potent mix. In an age of abundance and information overload, where attention is a scarce resource, are they really getting through?

Most managers are expert in communicating through reason. Reasoning is what the typical manager is rewarded for and trained in. The problem is that success depends less and less on our reasoning skills. The only way to create real profit is to attract the emotional rather than rational consumer. If you try reasoning you will have to deal with the purely economic rationality of the demanding customer. This inevitably results in zero profits as you will compete globally with an infinite number of other similar firms.

Noel Tichy of the University of Michigan says: 'The best way to get people to venture into unknown terrain is to make it desirable by taking them there in their imagination.' The emphasis needs increasingly to be on affection, intuition and desire.

A good case in point is Harley-Davidson. The company and the customer offering are not for everyone. You have to share certain traits with the other members of the Harley tribe. The company is not just selling a motorcycle; it is selling American nostalgia. The arguments for buying a Harley have little to do with rational reasoning – price, performance, etc. – and everything to do with affection, intuition and desire (see Figure 2). CEO Richard Teerling says: 'There's a high degree of emotion that drives our success. We symbolize the feelings of freedom and independence that people really want in this stressful world.'

By inviting its consumer tribe to join the organizational tribe, Harley-Davidson has dramatically extended its community. It uses

Figure 2 A new logic for providing meaning

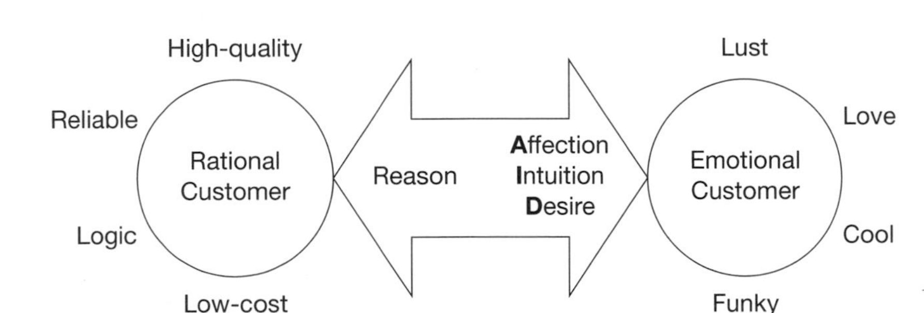

parties to initiate new members. Storytelling around the campfire keeps messages moving throughout the tribe. Closing ceremonies and continuous reinforcement are also part of the deal. What Harley-Davidson and other companies have realized is that a tribe targeting another tribe does not merely have to produce value – the customers also want values.

Value and values are inextricably linked. Raymond Loewe, the father of industrial design who provided mankind with such quintessential things as the Lucky Strike cigarette pack and the Greyhound bus, once said: 'The most beautiful curve is a raising sales graph.' Beauty remains in the eye of the beholder. Companies must amaze, daze, and seduce their customers. They must design to be different – or die.

RESOURCES

BOOKS

Nordström, Kjell and Ridderstråle, Jonas, *Funky Business*, FT.com, London, 2000.
Starck, Phillipe, *Starck*, Taschen, 1999.

WEB

www.funkybusiness.com

DISINTERMEDIATION

DISINTERMEDIATION is all about cutting out middle men. Using the internet as a sales channel is a great way of cutting down the supply chain. The traditional model is that of a manufacturer selling to a wholesaler who in turn sells to the retailer, before finally, passing on the goods to the customer. Each link in the chain between the manufacturer and customer (intermediaries or middlemen) adds to the final cost price of the goods to the consumer.

The ubiquitous internet has the potential to smash the traditional supply chain model. Manufacturers can sell directly to the customer, cutting out the intermediary and passing on the cost saving to the purchaser. This process is called disintermediation and is exemplified by Dell Direct, the online computer company.

Yet, despite the opportunity to cut out the middleman the internet affords, reports of the intermediaries' demise have been greatly exaggerated. Consumers are still distrustful of buying direct from manufacturers. Increasingly sophisticated consumers require price comparison and competing product information before making a purchasing decision. A whole host of websites have sprung up to offer these kinds of services, services like mySimon.com, which use intelligent agents to determine the best possible price, for example. The new middlemen still require revenue to survive, whether through advertising or commissions, and this is likely to impact on the purchase price of the product in an indirect way.

DYNAMIC PRICING

AT first, e-commerce on the has the potential to internet was a reflection of its non-virtual counterpart. Business models were simply cut and pasted from the world of bricks and mortar on to the internet. Now, however, companies are beginning to push the envelope and use the qualities of the internet to be truly innovative.

One such innovation is dynamic pricing. Why should every customer pay the same price for a product or service? The reason fixed pricing was the model of choice, certainly for the last century or so, is that the necessary information to make dynamic pricing decisions was not available. Neither were the complex mechanisms required to deliver it.

Internet technology is bringing dynamic pricing closer all the time. Research by MIT Media Lab under Professor Patti Maes and other technology companies is likely to bring us a world where most prices on the internet are flexible to a degree. But if you're worried about your ability to haggle online, don't. Dynamic pricing will be carried out by bots – intelligent automated software. Despatch your shopping bot and it will haggle for you obtaining prices from other websites' pricing bots. Meanwhile, you'll be able to enjoy a cup of coffee and plan what to do with the money you save.

E-COMMERCE

GENERALLY associated with doing business over the internet, 'e-commerce is any commercial activity that takes place by means of connected computers'. But despite the current hype surrounding the new web technology, e-commerce is no magic bullet. With a few exceptions, most companies are still struggling to create profitable business models based on the internet.

Jeffrey Rayport of Harvard Business School provides a framework for understanding the development of different e-business models. First, there was 'the content business' – 'People who supplied content to online services … got credit for helping keep users online'.[1] Next along was the advertising model, driven by measuring the volume of traffic. More volume meant more sets of eyeballs viewing the content and a better selling proposition to advertisers. The trouble with this model was that a few sites dominated – search engines including Yahoo! and the like, and stars such as Amazon.com and CDnow.

The third business model was selling things over the internet. The enticing logic of this was that companies could be virtual, with dramatically lower overheads than their conventional competitors. The most celebrated example of this is Amazon.com.

This evolves naturally into the fourth e-commerce model: 'never making a profit selling real products for real money'. This in essence means establishing a base of customers and then converting their loyalty into money somewhere down the line. One example of this is Free-PC – this company gives customers a PC in return for information and a long-term relationship.

For all the talk about e-commerce, surprisingly little has been written about how to manage the move from a traditional business to internet-based business. For some, it will happen. It will not be by luck, but by effective management. There are lessons to be learned from the implementation of IT in the 1980s. The companies that used IT to best effect then were those that approached it with a clear idea of what they wanted to achieve.

As Adrian Slywotzky[2] has pointed out, the question that enlightened organizations asked in the 1980s was: 'What business are we in?' In the early 1990s, that changed as companies such as Dell began asking: 'What is the best business model?' The question is now changing yet again. Today, it is: 'How digital is your company?' The key question in the future will be: 'What can e-commerce do for the customer?'

In reality, it is all about applying the new technology to the right part of the business. It is no good simply creating e-channels for the sake of it. Digital technology is most effective when it is linked to a specific strategic goal.

So, for example, when Intel invested $300 million in CAD/CAM technology in 1986, it did so to achieve a clear objective. CAD/CAM was the digital answer to a purely competitive question: How could Intel create a two-year lead over its competitors? Becoming more digital in the design and production of microchips was key to improving competitive advantage.

Other companies are making investments today that will create competitive advantage in the future. The hard part is figuring out where the new technology can make the most difference. The same rigour should be applied to e-channels – B2C and B2B.

According to Booz-Allen & Hamilton consultants Steven Wheeler and Evan Hirsh,[3] e-channels can be leveraged by companies at three different levels:

- As an information platform.
- As a transaction platform.
- As a tool to build and manage the customer relationship.

The impact on the business increases as you move up the levels. Currently, most companies primarily use e-channels as an information platform, although, increasingly, they are experimenting with innovative ways to use them as transaction platforms and to build more sophisticated customer relationships. The most effective e-channels involve an evolution from low-value to high-value platforms.

- **Level 1: Informational platform:** e-channels are already used widely as informational platforms to provide customers with instant information on product specifications and features. They also allow the customer to customize features and options – even colours – to make a personalized purchase decision. For example, Dell and Gateway both have websites that allow the customer to build a PC to their own specification, from a list of off-the-shelf components. The site automatically adjusts the price. In future, smart interfaces – which reconfigure to meet individual customer requirements – and higher internet speeds will make this increasingly powerful.
- **Level 2: Transaction platform:** at the second level, e-channels provide additional information and a mechanism for making transactions. Already, such systems are used to provide quotations, place orders,

check availability and to access additional services – such as applying for finance or insurance. The stumbling block here remains the security of payment. However, this is unlikely to present a serious problem for the future development of e-channels.

- **Level 3: A platform for managing customer relationships:** it is here that e-channels have the most potential impact. By creating an ongoing dialogue with customers, theoretically they offer a way to market to segments of one. To date, however, the practice is a long way behind the theory. Some companies are experimenting at this level through interactive entertainment, special offers targeted at customer segments, and even tie-ins with other products. So, for example, internet service providers and magazines use information push technology to deliver regular updates and advance information via e-mail. Over time, this will become more widespread.

The key attribute of the e-channel is its ability to push as well as pull information. But push too much information at the customer and they will become irritated and pull the plug.

The internet is an exciting new frontier. It opens up new business. The internet is a fascinating new vista. But it would be foolhardy to assume it is an easy option; far from it.

REFERENCES

1. Rayport, Jeffrey F., 'The truth about Internet business models', *Strategy & Business*, Third Quarter 1999.
2. Slywotzky, Adrian, 'How digital is your company?', *Fast Company*, February 1999.
3. Hirsh, Evan and Wheeler, Steven, *Channel Champions: The rise & fall of product-based differentiation*, Jossey Bass, 1999.

INCUBATOR

INCUBATORS are not a new phenomenon although the rise of commercial (for-profit) incubators is linked with the new economy. They are partly a response to the lack of finance and know-how available to young internet entrepreneurs.

One of the key differences between incubators and other kinds of financing for start-ups is the extent of back up provided. Office space, technological know-how, legal and financial advice, web design; all these services are offered by the average internet incubator.

In return incubators take a slice of the equity. And this may be a large slice of the pie, as incubators are effectively another mouth at the trough. Most incubators will have access to VC funding through an associated or partner company. But the VCs will usually want their share as well.

Entrepreneurs with a really compelling idea who lack the infrastructure to convert that idea into a successful company, often find an incubator invaluable.

Well-known incubators include Idealab in the US and Brainspark in the UK. Management consultancies have also got in on the act – McKinsey & Company has its own accelerators and Bain & Co. has its Bainlabs, for example. In another interesting development, some business schools, such as the Haas School of Business at Berkeley in the US and Cranfield School of Management in the UK have developed incubators for their MBA students.

INTELLECTUAL PROPERTY

INTELLECTUAL property has become a critical issue in e-commerce, particularly in the area of domain names and proprietary technology. Lawsuits over the infringement of intellectual property rights are becoming increasingly commonplace, especially in the US.

Legal disputes about intellectual property issues on the internet tend to fall into one of three categories: copyright, trademark and patent. The following definitions are a guide to the meaning of these terms.

Copyright is the exclusive right given to the author of a work – words, music, video, sound, picture, architecture and so on – to reproduce, distribute, display, license or perform their work. So for example *The New York Times* sued Amazon for reproducing a list from the newspaper on the Amazon website. Amazon agreed to change the presentation and the dispute was settled out of court.

A *trademark* is a distinctive word, picture or symbol used to distinguish and identify the origin of a product. Trademark disputes are likely to become increasingly common as domain names are registered and trademarked.

A *patent* means the inventor of a piece of intellectual property is able to prevent others using the patented design for a limited period. This covers hardware and software. The problem with patents is that minor differences in design can negate the protection afforded by the patent. Examples of this kind usually involve media technologies like streaming media, or in the case of Amazon, its patented 1-Click express ordering system.

TOFFLER, ALVIN

AMERICAN futurologist Alvin Toffler (born 1928) is, along with John Naisbitt, the world's best-known purveyor of trends, scenarios and predictions. His work has often been prophetic and is always interesting.

Toffler's first high-impact work was *Future Shock* (1970). '*Future Shock* suggested that businesses were going to restructure themselves repeatedly,' says Toffler. 'That they would have to

3

reduce hierarchy and [adopt] what we termed ad-hocracy. This sounded sensational to many readers.'[1] It also sounded laughable to many others. In 1970 corporate America was at the height of its powers. The oil crisis of the 1970s was yet to happen; corporate giants appeared to have achieved immortality; economists mapped what would happen decades into the future with apparent confidence. At a time of security and arrogance, Toffler preached insecurity and humility.

Toffler differed from mainstream thought in a number of other ways. First, he was not taken in by the burgeoning overconfidence of the time. His starting point was that things needed to change dramatically. Second, he had a keen awareness of the technological potential. The future he envisaged was driven by technology and knowledge. These two themes are constant throughout his work.

While others looked at the impact of technology or of increased amounts of information, Toffler sought out a panoramic view. In his book *Third Wave* (1980), he wrote: 'Humanity faces a quantum leap forward. It faces the deepest social upheaval and creative restructuring of all time. Without clearly recognizing it, we are engaged in building a remarkable new civilization from the ground up. This is the meaning of the Third Wave.'

Toffler ushered in the new technological era and bade farewell to the Second Wave of industrialization. 'The death of industrialism and the rise of a new civilization' meant mass customization rather than mass production. 'The essence of Second Wave manufacture was the long "run" of millions of identical standardized products. By contrast, the essence of Third Wave manufacture is the short run of partially or completely customized products,' he wrote. This notion of mass customization has since been picked up by a wide variety of thinkers and, in some areas, is already in existence.

From a technological perspective, Toffler has been amazingly accurate in his predictions. In 1980, for example, he had to explain what a wordprocessor is. Just a few years later it was reality for many in the industrialized world (or de-industrialized world, according to his perspective).

The company of the future, he predicts, will be a 'multipurpose institution', driven to redefine itself through five forces:

- **Changes in the physical environment:** companies are having to undertake greater responsibility for the effect of their operations on the environment.
- **Changes in the 'line-up of social forces':** the actions of companies now have greater impact on those of other organizations such as schools, universities, civil groups, and political lobbies.
- **Changes in the role of information:** 'as information

becomes central to production, as "information managers" proliferate in industry, the corporation, by necessity, impacts on the informational environment exactly as it impacts on the physical and social environment,' he writes.

- **Changes in government organization:** the profusion of government bodies means that the business and political worlds interact to a far greater degree than ever before.
- **Changes in morality:** the ethics and values of organizations are becoming more closely linked to those of society. 'Behavior once accepted as normal is suddenly reinterpreted as corrupt, immoral or scandalous,' says Toffler. 'The corporation is increasingly seen as a producer of moral effects.'

The organization of the future, Toffler envisages, will be concerned with ecological, moral, political, racial, sexual and social problems, as well as traditional commercial ones.

His perspective became even broader with the 1990 book *Powershift*. In this, he accurately predicted the growth of regionalism and the profusion of local media. The bomb underneath the Western world continues to tick.

> *'The emerging third-wave civilization is going to collide head on with the old first and second civilizations. One of the things we ought to learn from history is that when waves of change collide they create countercurrents. When the first and the second wave collided we had civil wars, upheavals, political revolutions, forced migrations. The master conflict of the twenty-first century will not be between cultures but between the three supercivilizations – between agrarianism, industrialism and post-industrialism.'*[2]

REFERENCES

1. Gibson, Rowan (ed.), *Rethinking the Future*, Nicholas Brealey, London, 1997.
2. Schwartz, Peter, 'Shock wave (anti) warrior', *Wired*, 1993.

3

– CHAPTER 4 –

Power and influence

'Adversarial power relationships work only if you never have to see or work with the bastards again.' PETER DRUCKER

'In the main it will be found that a power over a man's support [compensation] is a power over his will.' ALEXANDER HAMILTON

'Whoever is the cause of another becoming powerful, is ruined himself; for that power is produced by him either through craft or force; and both of these are suspected by the one who has been raised to power.' NICOLO MACHIAVELLI

'Powerlessness is a state of mind. If you think you're powerless, you are.' TOM PETERS

'What you cannot enforce, do not command.' SOCRATES

Career skills for the new economy

BRUCE TULGAN

If you are going to succeed in the new economy, says Bruce Tulgan, you need to understand that you are the sole proprietor of YOU, Inc., and you need to be able to manage yourself.

NO matter where you work, no matter what you do, you are in business for yourself. You are the sole proprietor of your skills and abilities. That means you need to create your success on a daily basis by pursuing four key strategies: learn strategically and voraciously, build relationships with individuals who can help you, add value no matter where you work or what you do, and always keep yourself in balance.

Learn strategically and voraciously

Right now there is more information produced in a day on almost any subject than any person could possibly master in a lifetime. And the knowledge we do have becomes obsolete more rapidly than ever before. Meanwhile, the economy is becoming more and more information and knowledge based, so in order to succeed, a person must wield up-to-date marketable skills and knowledge.

There are two parts of an effective learning strategy in the new economy. First, build a wide repertoire of *transferable skills*, that is, skills that are not likely to become obsolete any time soon, and will make you more valuable no matter where you go or what you do.

For example, knowing a particular software package is not necessarily transferable because software becomes obsolete quickly and different organizations and different jobs require knowledge of different software. However, the ability to get up to speed easily on most new software packages (to learn them quickly and start using them effectively) *is* a transferable skill. Other examples of transferable skills include the ability to negotiate, fluency in foreign languages and good people skills.

Second, *be a knowledge worker* no matter what you do. That means you need to leverage skill, knowledge, and wisdom in every project you undertake, every task you accomplish, and every responsibility you assume. Even if you are digging a ditch, you can leverage skill, knowledge, and wisdom. What is the best way to grip the shovel? What is the most effective technique for striking the ground? What is the most effective technique for lifting the dirt? What kind of shovel should you use? What kind of gloves? What is the best physical posture? What is the best pace?

Skill is the mastery of technique (gripping the shovel, striking the ground, lifting the dirt). Knowledge is the mastery of information (the best kind of shovel, gloves, posture and pace). Wisdom is the most complicated because it comes from the understanding of many, many perspectives (there is more than one 'best' way to hold the shovel, strike the ground, lift the dirt; more than one 'best' shovel, gloves, posture and pace). The wise person understands that the best way for one person may not be the best way for another; that the best way for one situation may not be the best way for another. As long as you use skill, knowledge, and wisdom in your work, you are doing knowledge work.

Build relationships with individuals who can help you

The only reliable anchors you will have in today's fluid world are other people. So build firm loyalties with people you know and trust. But you also need to build mutually advantageous relationships with individuals you don't already know and trust. How do you do that? Always approach relationships in terms of what you have to offer, rather than what you need or want.

Add value, no matter where you work or what you do

Prepare to be an entrepreneur no matter what you do. You have to sell your way into every challenge. Ultimately, the only thing you have to sell is your added value. So what is your 'added value'?

There are five different ways to add value:

- Get a whole bunch of work done (accomplish tasks in a timely, competent manner or deliver an existing product or service).
- Identify a problem that nobody else has identified.
- Solve a problem that nobody else has solved.
- Improve an existing service or product.
- Invent a new service or product.

By the way, don't underestimate the first point – it is by far the most readily available (and often most appreciated) opportunity to add value. Wherever you go, sell your added value.

Always keep your balance

If you are in business for yourself (and you are) you are the employee and the manager; the main office and the factory; the producer, salesperson and distributor. You are YOU, Inc. And you had better take good care of yourself.

There are three elements of you and you need to take care of all three.

- **Your mind:** the key to a healthy mind is variety of input. Also, do not take yourself too seriously (relax). Do take a serious interest in other people, things, events, and issues. And recognize feelings of anxiety so you can learn how to use anxiety without allowing it to paralyze you.
- **Your body:** the key to a healthy body is a solid routine. Also, put healthy food and drink into your body (especially drink a lot of water) and try to limit how much garbage you force your body to process (especially smoke). Get plenty of rest. And get some exercise (stretching and walking are easy and very beneficial) every day (morning is best).
- **Your spirit:** as hard as I look, I can only find one key to a healthy spirit: just believing in something, anything, and spending some time every day with your true beliefs.

Remember this, the ultimate secret to a healthy mind, body and spirit: when you slip up and drag yourself down for a day, or week, or month, or more, you have to forgive yourself, be patient and get right back to healthy habits. What else is there to do?

The art of managing yourself

If you are going to succeed in the new economy, you have to be able to manage yourself. The key to this can be found in the answers to four very simple questions:

- Who are you?
- What do you want to achieve?
- How do you want to conduct yourself?
- Where do you fit in each situation?

Who are you?

Get in touch with your uniqueness

What makes you different from everybody else? If you've always wondered where you fit in, not quite fitting in with the crowd may turn out to be your special niche. Identify something in your background or experience that sets you apart. Is there something that qualifies you to better understand, connect with, or maximize a particular market? Is there something about your unique perspective that lends itself to hard work, problem solving, creativity, or innovation? Exactly what is it that makes you special? You have to get in touch with your uniqueness in order to leverage it in your working life and career.

Examine your priorities

What matters the most to you? Say it's your family. Then what happens when you have a conflict between working all weekend and attending your child's birthday party? No-brainer. Unless, of course, missing work this weekend would cause you to actually lose your job and cause you to no longer be able to support your family. Again, no-brainer.

But what if you are not being honest with yourself? Maybe what's really at stake is that if you don't work this weekend, some of the people at work won't like you as much. Which is more important to you, being popular at work or being there for your children? Again, no-brainer.

Maybe you can figure out a way to do both: what if you could get up at 3am Saturday and Sunday, work like a dog, and then go to the birthday party too? You won't get any sleep. What is more important to you, getting sleep this weekend or meeting your obligations at work and being with the kid? Again, no-brainer. What if you could fake it, make it look like you were at work ... or just stop by the kid's party, you know, make an appearance? What is more important to you, being genuine and really meeting your obligations, or 'looking good' to others and getting away with doing less? Again, no-brainer.

If your priorities are clear and you stay in touch with them, it makes a lot of seemingly tough decisions a whole lot easier.

The next time somebody asks you to do something that you really don't want to do and you feel compelled to do it, ask yourself this question: 'Am I considering this because it is what really matters to me, even though it may be difficult or inconvenient or not fun or get in the way of other things I need to do – or is it because I want to be popular with this person?' Or, the next time you find yourself procrastinating about something that you really need to get done, ask yourself: 'Are all the things I keep doing, instead of the thing I really need to do, more important? Do they matter more to me? Or are they just easier, more fun, or more convenient?'

Grow

If you've ever studied weight training, you know that the way to build muscles is to push them beyond their limits, to the point at which the fibres actually tear, so that they are stronger when they heal. That theory applies to more than just muscles. We only grow when we push ourselves and keep pushing until we feel the pain. Then recover. And then push ourselves some more. Whenever we try to exceed our current level of ability or experience, in any sphere, we move out of our comfort zone into the unknown. We increase the risk of making mistakes and getting hurt.

That's why the key to growth is embracing the unknown, working through mistakes, and tolerating pain. Of course, it would be pointless to venture into the unknown without doing all the research and preparation you can, to risk mistakes without a good backup plan, and to welcome pain that signals injury. But don't turn common sense into an excuse for atrophy. And don't forget that as a living organism you cannot remain static. Atrophy is the only alternative to growth. So push yourself until you feel the pain. Recover. And then push yourself some more.

What do you want to achieve?

Start every endeavour with clear goals

Before you invest your time and energy in anything at all, clarify for yourself exactly what it is you are trying to accomplish. What is the tangible result you should be holding in your hands when you are done?

Hold yourself to strict deadlines

Deadlines are the key to making a plan of action and managing your time effectively. The trick is to use deadlines every step of the way. Break up larger goals and deadlines into smaller pieces, intermediate goals and deadlines.

For example, if you know you need to achieve a particular goal by Wednesday, then you can establish benchmarks along the way: What needs to be done by Tuesday? Monday? Sunday? Saturday? And so on.

Once you have a schedule of intermediate goals and deadlines, the last element in any plan is a list of concrete actions (this is like a to-do list). As you tackle each concrete action and move toward each intermediate goal and deadline, you can monitor your effectiveness along the way. If you find yourself off schedule, you know you need to reassess: are you taking the concrete actions you planned? Are they taking longer than you thought? Or are you running across unexpected obstacles? Do you need to revise the plan? Or do you need to change something about your work habits?

Take action and keep moving forward

Nothing gets done unless somebody does it. In this case, that somebody is you. If you have 100 phone calls to make, you start with the first one and move on to the second and then the third and so on. Each call is a concrete action. But it's important to realize, also, that every phone call involves a whole series of concrete actions, such as identifying the name and number, deciding what you are going to say, dialling the number.

Every concrete action can be broken down into minute components and each minute component is, itself, a concrete action. Sometimes when you get bogged down in the feeling that you are 'not getting anything done', this is a very helpful reality check and it can get you focused and back on track. If you break every task into its minute components and start tackling them one at a time, you will start moving forward.

Use your time wisely

There are 168 hours in a week. How do you use them? There are 1,440 minutes in a day. How do you use them? Most people waste endless minutes and hours without ever realizing they are doing so. How does one waste time? By filling it with activities that don't matter to you. What if you really value just sitting around watching TV? Well then, I would argue that you are not wasting the time you spend watching TV. As long as you know how much time you are devoting to this activity and you are doing so on purpose. And that is the key: are you keeping track of your time and using it with purpose?

Fail, fail, fail, but never give up

If you don't fail, chances are you will never succeed. So court failure. Be greedy with failure. Fail as much as you possibly can. You see, success may be preferable to failure, but statistically failure is far more likely. So turn the odds inside out. Let's say you have a 1 percent chance of success. All that means is that you have to fail 99 times for every 1 time you succeed. So you'd better hurry up and start failing.

There is only so much you can possibly fail. Eventually, you will succeed. Looking at it that way, the odds are in your favour as long as you are not afraid to fail.

Note that most successful people will tell you that failure is a phenomenal learning experience – and it is. But embracing failure is a key to success, ultimately, because if you don't learn to embrace failure and bounce back from it, you'll never master perseverance. When things are going well, it's easy to persevere. Real perseverance is the ability to fail, fail, fail (and even fail some more), but never give up.

How do you want to be?

Be high quality

You are what you write, say, create and do (in no particular order). No matter how grand your intentions or how generous and kind you may be as a person, others will know you by your words, actions, and creations. So, always hold yourself to a high standard:

- Think before you speak (and rehearse).
- Outline before you write (and always do second and third drafts).
- Plan before you take action.
- Double and triple and quadruple check anything and everything you do.

But then go for it – speak, write, create and *do*.

Be full of integrity

If your boss (or customer) of the day wants you to lie, cheat, steal, or harm others, don't do it. Quit if necessary. Blow the whistle if you think it's appropriate. No matter what, don't get involved in unethical dealings. It's not worth any price. Be honest and honest people will gravitate toward you.

But, let's face it, that's the easy part. The hard part is when integrity requires more than sitting on a high horse in judgement of others. Real integrity requires proactive behaviour: breaking your back to deliver, if necessary, when people are counting on you; helping others, even when nobody is there to give you credit; intervening when others are being treated unfairly; and speaking out loud for unpopular causes (if you believe in them).

Be adaptable

People who are too attached to the way things are have a hard time learning new skills, performing new tasks, doing old tasks in new ways, working with new machines, new managers, new co-workers, new customers, new rules, no rules. Usually, the greatest difficulty for such people is the uncertainty: not knowing what will be (or not) just around the corner. Don't be one of these people. Learn to love change. Be flexible enough to go, on any given day, from one boss to another; from one team to another; from one organization to another; from one set of tasks to another.

Where do you fit in each situation?

Be good at evaluating context

No matter who you are, what you want to achieve, or how you want to be, your role in any given situation is determined – in part – by factors that have nothing to do with you, *per se*. These are pre-existing factors, independent factors, factors that would be present even if you were not. These factors determine the context of any situation.

Before you can figure out where you fit, you need to get a handle on the other pieces of the puzzle. Here's what you have to ask yourself, especially when you are new to any situation:

- Where am I (what is this place)?
- What is going on here (what is the mission of the group)?
- Why is everybody here (what is at stake for the group and for each person in the group)?
- When did they all get here (not just today, but in the overall context)?

- Who are all these people (what role does each person play)?
- How are they accustomed to doing things around here (what is standard operating procedure)?

Career skills

As well as being able to manage yourself, other skills are important for the twenty-first century manager.

Critical thinking

Critical thinking is as much a habit as a skill. And it doesn't mean criticizing, disparaging, or finding fault. Rather, it means differentiating between reliable and unreliable information, carefully weighing the strengths of conflicting views, and making reasoned judgements. Critical thinkers do not leap to conclusions: they take the time to consider various possibilities and do not become too attached to one point of view. They do not latch on to one solution: they know that most solutions are temporary and improve over time with new data. Critical thinkers are, at once, open to the views of others and supremely independent in their own judgements.

So the next time you catch yourself jumping to conclusions, stop, and take the time to practise the habits of critical thinking. Suspend your judgement and question your assumptions. Ask yourself, 'What am I assuming here?' More importantly, ask yourself, 'What are all the logical possibilities (who, what, where, when, how, and *why*) that my assumptions exclude?' Then check your facts. Ask yourself, 'What do I really know here? What is my source? Is it a good source? Is there a better source? What facts do I need to gather to make a better decision?'

If you are in the habit of thinking critically, you will handle every situation more professionally, interact more effectively with people, make better decisions, and be able to resolve – at least provisionally – almost any problem. That's what makes critical thinking the ultimate transferable skill. And unlike the hot technical skills, it will never become obsolete.

Human relations

The ability to relate well to people has always been important, but that ability is more important than ever before in the new economy where every individual is in continual motion and other people are your only anchors. Here are eight rules of human relations by which to live and work:

1. **Be a model of trust**: take personal responsibility for everything you say and do, hold yourself accountable, and never make excuses when you make a mistake (just apologize and make every effort to fix it).
2. **Remove your ego**: don't take yourself too seriously, but always take your obligations seriously. Extend personal vulnerability, but never undermine your own credibility.
3. **Listen carefully**: never interrupt when others are speaking and don't let your mind wander. Stay focused on what the other person is saying. When it's your turn, ask open-ended questions first, such as 'What do you mean?' or 'What would be a good example of that?' And make sure to listen carefully to the answers. Then ask specific clarifying questions to make sure you understand, such as 'Do you mean ____?' or 'Are you saying ____?' When you feel confident you understand, don't change the subject, but rather respond directly to what the other person has said.
4. **Empathize**: try to imagine yourself in the other person's position. Ask yourself what thoughts and feelings you might have if you were in that position. Then behave in a way and say the kinds of things that you would appreciate under the same circumstances.
5. **Exhibit respect and kindness**: take courtesy the extra mile. If you think the other person is pressed for time, be brief. If you think something might be wrong, ask if there is

anything you can do to help (but don't be pushy). Never share observations that might be insulting and never hesitate to share a compliment.

6. **Speak up and make yourself understood**: if you don't say what's on your mind, you'll have virtually no chance of connecting with people, getting others to share your interests, influencing their thoughts, or persuading them to do things your way. Of course, sometimes it helps to take a quiet moment and clarify, for yourself, what really is on your mind. If it's something that ought to be shared, take an extra moment to think about the most effective words and actions to get your message across.
7. **Be a motivator**: visualize positive results. Be enthusiastic and share your positive vision. Never speak of a problem unless you have thought of at least one potential solution.
8. **Celebrate the success of others**: always give people credit for their achievements, no matter how small. And go out of your way to catch people doing things right.

Building relationships with decision makers

Everybody knows that building relationships with decision makers is critical to success. That truth has led to the rise of 'networking'. The problem is that there are lots of people out there networking just for the sake of 'networking'. As a result, they are wasting a lot of their own time and wasting the time of busy people.

Don't bother networking with people unless you have a very specific reason, some real business to transact. Wait until you have something very real to talk about – best of all, something very real to offer – before reaching out to build relationships with new people. Then you can approach these relationships with complete confidence.

When you are ready, follow these steps:

1. Clarify exactly what it is you have to offer.
2. Make sure you have the right decision maker with respect to what you want to achieve.

3. Do some research before making contact.
4. Use a mutual connection – but get their permission first.
5. Make your communication interesting and useful.
6. Turn every contact into a multiple contact.
7. Identify and win over 'gatekeepers' – the assistants who screen voice mail, e-mail, paper mail, faxes, overnight packages, and any other communications before their bosses ever see them.
8. Get decision makers to stop and pay attention to you, by making it clear you are offering to add value. Of course, if you sell it, be prepared to deliver.
9. Become Ms or Mr Follow-up. Once you get the ball rolling, don't be the one to let it drop.
10. Keep your contact information up to date and keep others up to date with your own information. People move around a lot these days, so it takes a little more effort to stay in touch.

Managing your boss

Your most valuable career capital consists in your time, labour and creativity. Whenever you are working, you are investing that capital. Maximize your investment. Work closely with good managers: make the most of the learning opportunities they provide; get them to help you formulate ambitious goals and determine realistic deadlines; pay close attention to the feedback they provide; appreciate the recognition, credit and rewards they provide; and never stop earning the responsibility, creative freedom, and flexibility they want to provide for you.

Bad managers, however, are a whole different story. If your manager is getting in your way, you must take control of the situation.

Here's what you need to do to help your manager help you succeed:

1. **Help your manager delegate effectively**: with every assignment, ask up-front for a concrete goal (a clear statement of the tangible results expected of you), a very specific deadline, and all the guidelines and parameters.

2. **Get the feedback you need**: you will probably get six-month and/or twelve-month reviews in most jobs, but those reviews usually feel few and far between. And when they come, they often don't give you the kind of accurate, specific and timely feedback you need to keep moving in the right direction. The best kind of feedback you can get is day-to-day performance coaching from a manager you trust and respect. But if you are not getting that from your manager, you need to give it to yourself. As you accomplish each goal, stop to make a note of the achievement in your calendar or some other contemporaneous record, and then take a moment to evaluate: make sure you take note of what you did well so you can repeat your success. Then look for ways to improve.
3. **Establish specific learning objectives and get your manager's support**: make a list of every task and responsibility for which you are accountable and use this list to brainstorm some specific job-related learning objectives. What skills should you be practising? What knowledge should you be mastering? What wisdom should you be acquiring? Go to your manager with this list and ask what resources might be available to help you undertake some of your learning goals.
4. **When you need something, always ask in the form of a proposal**: don't make requests lightly and they won't be taken lightly. Always include in any proposal you make the following information: what is the benefit of what you are proposing to the organization and/or to the boss? How can it be accomplished with minimum cost and very little chance of something going wrong? What resources will be needed and where do you think they can be obtained? What are the potential problems and what are the measures you propose to avoid those problems? If the problems occur, how will you solve them? Overall what role do you foresee for yourself in this proposal? What is the timeline for the proposal? Regardless of how big or how small your request, make your proposal strong.

5. **Disentangle the micromanager**: always set a day and time for a 'next meeting' with your manager. Whenever the manager tries to get tangled up in your work, remind them of the assignment you are working on (the tangible result and your deadline). Show them your plan (from No.1 above). And if necessary, remind them of the meeting you already have scheduled to review progress on the assignment. It may take time for you to establish an appropriate distance between you and your manager, but if you are patient, this approach will usually give you some space.
6. **Never accept the behaviour of a manager who is intimidating, mean, or abusive**: remember that this is their psychological problem, not yours. Document all abuse and all the solutions you attempt to end it by keeping a notepad with dates and times and names and concrete examples. Seek support among your colleagues (and family and friends), while trying to avoid your abusive boss. After you have compiled a decent record of the abuse, report the behaviour to senior management.

You can adapt the same guidelines to help you in managing other people.

RESOURCES

BOOK

Tulgan, Bruce, *Managing Generation X*, Capstone, Oxford, 1997.

WEB

www.rainmakerthinking.com

Fathers and sons at work

SHERE HITE

Offices inside large corporations are now a blank page, says Shere Hite. We can write on them any kind of social order we want. But many men are finding it difficult to establish a balance between following their traditional roles and being a 'new man' in the twenty-first century.

CORPORATIONS did not use to pose a challenge to the traditional social order. However, with the arrival of large numbers of women in the workplace, especially in management positions, the office no longer resembles that order. In the past, when women were expected to stay at home, men at work were sometimes seen as hunters going out into the corporate jungle to bring home bread for their families. Now Jane is out hunting with Tarzan.

For several decades, corporations did not challenge men's traditional identity. Except for secretaries, it was mostly men who inhabited the corporate landscape, so nothing was out of sync: 'male competition' could follow biblical models (for example, Cain and Abel), i.e., son versus father (or son obeying father), brother versus brother, or brother working with brother, male groups pro or con other male groups. Traditionally, corporations have been kingdoms in which 'sons' and 'fathers' by turn competed with each other or worked together, i.e., younger and older men jousted or fought together for power, glory and money.

In the Freudian view (claiming biological infallibility, therefore to be eternally and universally true), men are by nature in combat (competition), the son fights his father for power, i.e., Oedipus kills his father to 'gain his mother'. But while Freud might claim it is in human nature for sons to try to overtake and dominate their fathers, one does not find this scenario portrayed in classics elsewhere. In Shakespeare's *Romeo and Juliet* the son of Capulet is not angry with his father for making his life difficult, nor does he try to wrest power from his father. Arthur Miller does not portray the son of Willy Loman in *Death of a Salesman* as trying to dominate his father; the son simply wants to leave home and get away from the whole family. On the other hand, many men in corporations do feel that 'the fun of it all' is competing with the other guys; young men sometimes do dethrone older men, taking their crowns.

The 'human-nature-is-unchangeable' view would imply that men can't change, that sons will always by nature challenge fathers. Is this true, or are other interpretations or explanations possible?

Boys and their fathers

Hite Research has turned up two quite different reasons for male attitudes to each other inside corporations, whether fighting or bonding. Both imply that flexibility is a big part of human nature, and that change is not only possible but probable – that what we call 'human nature' is very much shaped and created by society. First, men's loyalty to other men (and desire to be accepted by them, work with them) is – ironically – increased by the lack of closeness that most boys felt growing up with their fathers. In the great majority of cases, the relationship between father and son is not close, although there are exceptions. Boys learn their understanding of relationships with men from this early relationship, no matter how distant it may have been. (If it was distant, they learn that relationships between men are distant.) They tend to repeat this model with their own sons, leading to a competitive mindset.

Boys in my research [for *The Hite Reports on Male Sexuality and the Family*] state over and over, in the most poignant and moving statements, that they did not know their fathers very well, that their fathers rarely talked to them about their feelings, personal thoughts, or relationships. In fact, most boys said that they had

3

never had a real conversation with their father about a personal topic. Most expressed a longing to have had some deeper experience of communication and acceptance.

Boys often become fascinated by the power of this emotionally silent and mysterious monolith, the 'older man': 'I didn't know my father, really, I didn't know what went on in his head. He went to work, he came home, he got angry at odd moments and everybody seemed to have to help rearrange things so his anger would go away and he, the god, would be pacified. I used to ask my mother what was I supposed to be like – him?'

> *'I always identified with the son in* Death of a Salesman. *I didn't want to be that salesman either. So I tried to go along outwardly with the behaviours they all expected of men, damn it, say as little as possible to avoid conflict (or discovery that I was not all I was supposed to be, cracked up to be, I wasn't a "typical man"). Funny thing, one day my one-year-old son said to his mother (when they thought I wasn't around): "Why doesn't Daddy say anything?" I had managed to look just like my dad looked to me.*
>
> *'I felt a sharp pain inside me, almost a stabbing blow, as if someone had put a knife in me. I went and sat down on the sofa and hid my face in my arm, I was crying. It also hurt me when my wife, after my son said that, just murmured something like, "Oh, your father's just like that. He's in his own world, he can't help it," as if she were alienated too. There was just no place to turn. It was then I knew I had to change. I had to make a different life for myself and everyone around me.'*

Like the Michelangelo fresco of Adam reaching for God's hand in The Creation, in which their fingers never quite touch, men often feel that tantalizing sense of 'almost ... almost'. They can almost touch their fathers and yet there is a distance that is unbridgeable. They are left with a feeling that he is unattainable, the other, and that this is how it must be.

This incomplete relationship affects many men for ever. They attempt to reach 'the father', try to make him recognize and see them, the son, at work. This is the same fight that women can have with men in love relationships, essentially trying to get men to open up, be more communicative, relate fully, 'see' them. A cycle persists of the younger man, or a woman, not being able to 'get through' to the grown up, perfectly closed man, consequently feeling less and less loved, coming up against his silence and distance.

The distress of puberty

My research shows, secondly, that what we call male nature is in good part socially created at puberty. Harsh puberty initiation rites make boys learn to bond with and/or fear men in groups; they learn to try (at least outwardly) to conform to the behaviour of the men in groups around them for ever after.

These boyhood events not noticed (or taken seriously) by Freud or others came out strikingly in my research, showing that boys at puberty learn a bitter lesson: they speak repeatedly of their extended pain and emotional turmoil during a period of one to two years around ages 10–12. What they describe is that, while early in life, they felt (most of them) very close to their mother, liked to be with her, felt comfortable at home with her, around ages 10–12 extreme pressure was put on them (usually by older boys at school) to 'shape up', 'be a man', 'don't stay home with your mother', 'don't let your mother tell you what to do'. If they don't heed these messages, they will lose status within the group and possibly even be beaten up or kicked out.

Most boys were emotionally distressed during this period: they didn't want to betray their mother by taking on new, disdainful attitudes, but eventually they came to realize that they had no choice but to join the male group and become 'one of them'. To many, this felt like diving off a high board into a deep pool, not knowing how to swim. This trauma of leaving the mother and all she stands for – joining the 'boys' brigade' – is created by society, although it need not be. Yet it is usually attributed to hormones and not questioned: while debate in the UK has decried the bullying of boys by other boys in school, for example, no laws prohibit this kind of psychological bullying.

Later as adults, many men apply the same logic at work, concluding that they must conform to the group of men in an office or a corporation (or on a construction site) or they will not fit in – and certainly not get ahead. For example, many men – having internalized these lessons about staying with the boys and avoiding the girls to ensure acceptance as part of the men's group – feel nervous about the new presence of career women, and about breaking rules of conformity to male groups around them. Although joining the 'world of the fathers' is a frightening experience for many boys and men (and women) – they describe feeling alone and insecure, suddenly in a new, colder and more competitive world, a world they say over and over that their father did not explain to them – conquering it can become the biggest adventure they undertake in life. Later, however, according to my research, on becoming such a 'fearsome male monolith-power person' themselves, men sometimes feel very unsatisfied and disillusioned.

A new way forward

Many younger men today want to find a new way forward. Often men, as much as women, want to change the atmosphere inside the workscape, but it is difficult for men to behave differently at work than 'traditional male-bonding behaviour'. As boys have learned, the approval of other men ('the older boys at school') is very hard to come by, and once you've got it you'd better not lose it (especially not by behaving with disloyalty, i.e., hanging out with women) or you'll be ousted from the group. Not 'playing the game with the guys' could cost them their job.

Corporate executives today could feel unconsciously uncomfortable being 'disloyal' to the men's group at work, by working closely with women on an equal level or promoting women above men. If men can break the spell of this fear they learned so early in life – a fear that to many has become unrecognizable, 'forgotten' – then the meritocracy that was promised can finally become a reality.

In other words, siding with 'a girl' against a group of men, promoting a woman into a completely male office, can be considered an act of treason, so many men today feel torn between their ethical sense of what is right and their desire not to 'rock the boat'. Once the realization is clear that the situation inside corporate boardrooms resembles the pubertal boys' bully system at school, and that it doesn't have to – that it is counterproductive to today's workscape – things can feel freer and change quickly.

Various factors have come together to set men thinking, embarking on a momentous interior transformation that has as yet to go public. Most no longer want the extreme 'revolution' of the 1960s, but they also don't want the 'return to traditional manhood' of the 1980s; they want a new third way, something they are inventing.

This change in perspective has been in the making for some time. Related to history not hormones, an entire century of social experimentation underlies many men's deep desire for change. They may have lived through 25 years of rethinking, and some were raised by mothers and fathers who had also done major rethinking.

Although twentieth century media spoke more often of the changes that women have made, men have changed dramatically too. During the second half of the century, men revolted *en masse* against the family: first the playboy revolution (symbolized by James Bond films, showing the ever-single, glamorously non-monogamous Agent 007), followed by 1960s flower power, civil rights, and black pride, as well as the birth control pill and 'sexual revolution'. With all these movements, men stressed they wanted more individual self-determination, less conformity (though in some cases they wrongly targeted women as the cause of their feeling 'tied down'). Through the feminist movement of the 1970s, men's thinking about their identity was challenged in a new way.

All of this created a heady mix of ideas in the minds of many men who by the 1980s were ready to call a halt and 'go back to traditional values'. But could they return? The divorce rate passed 50 percent and the number of people living 'single' neared half. The 1990s saw a media focus on extreme versions of sex: sadomasochism, internet pornography and sexual violence as fun ('you're not a real man unless you like it – and participate ...').

Out of all this twentieth century turmoil, what emerged? While media images of men stressed the importance of being 'different', there was simultaneously great pressure on men at work to conform and 'be traditional' – to give off an image of respectable, traditional stability, if one wanted to get ahead.

Many men today find they are coping by living with split personalities: one for work and another for 'outside' or 'private time'. The many books published during the 1980s and 1990s on 'personal growth' – 'self-help' for women and 'business secrets' for men – helped individuals think through issues of self identity and how they see the world; now, after some years, a sea change is taking place.

Quite a few men in my research say they have problems with male authority figures, speaking of feeling torn between wanting to be 'a new man' and wanting to work with the 'male establishment authority figures', the daddies and patriarchs of fable – so exalted in mythology, novels, and elsewhere, their archetypes are all around us. During the 1960s, it was fashionable to declare that 'you can't trust anyone over 35'. Young men believed that old men were all corrupt, had made some kind of trade-off with 'the system', so that they were no longer honest or relevant.

How does a young man make the transition to being an older man in authority without making too many compromises, so that he is still true to himself, stands for something – and likes himself? This can be done, but it is not easy. In today's context, the question of women's status especially challenges men's integrity and sense of fair play. Men at work have very ambivalent feelings about how to treat women in the new situation. Obviously, letting women be equal at work is an idea with justice on its side – but should they go ahead and work easily with women, blend in, make new choices; or should they try to please the older male authority figures who may prefer signals of an old male-bonding variety?

The challenge is for an individual man to understand well enough both sides of his identity, his new thinking and his older training, so that he can elegantly move the entire situation to another stage and make the new world of work valid for everyone concerned – the women there, his boss, and also himself.

According to my research and the statistics around us, most men seem to say that they are quietly undergoing a revolution on their own terms, in their own inner values and beliefs – beliefs about the importance of work, how work should be structured, how private life should be lived, how time should be spent. Many men are rethinking the ultimate values of life, what it means to be alive and part of this world.

Men's new ideas and changes are beginning to make themselves felt at the workplace. We will see more of these changes in the future.

RESOURCES

Book

Hite, Shere, *Sex and Business*, FT Prentice Hall, London, 1999.

Web

www.hite-research.com

CARNEGIE, DALE

DALE CARNEGIE (1888–1955) was the first superstar of the self-help genre. Go forth with a smile on your face and a song in your heart and sell, sell, sell. His successors – whether they be Anthony Robbins or Stephen Covey – should occasionally doff their caps in Carnegie's direction.

First, Carnegie presented the 'fundamental techniques in handling people' – 'don't criticize, condemn or complain; give honest and sincere appreciation; and arouse in the other person an eager want'. To these he added six ways to make people like you – 'become genuinely interested in other people; smile; remember that a person's name is to that person the sweetest and most important sound in any language; be a good listener. Encourage others to talk about themselves; talk in terms of the other person's interests; make the other person feel important – and do it sincerely.'

Born on a Missouri farm, Carnegie began his working life selling bacon, soap, and lard for Armour & Company in south Omaha. He turned his sales territory into the company's national leader, but then went to New York to study at the American Academy of Dramatic Arts. Realizing the limits of his acting potential, Carnegie returned to salesmanship, selling Packard automobiles. It was then that Carnegie persuaded the YMCA schools in New York to allow him to conduct courses in public speaking.

Carnegie's talks became highly successful. So successful, in fact, that he turned them into a string of books: *Public Speaking and Influencing Men in Business*; *How to Stop Worrying and Start Living*; *How to Enjoy Your Life and Your Job*; *How to Develop Self-Confidence and Influence People by Public Speaking*; and his perennial bestseller, *How to Win Friends and Influence People*, which has sold over 15 million copies.

It is easy to sneer at Carnegie's work – it is homespun wisdom adorned with commercial know-how. But it is difficult to sneer at the enduring popularity of his books and his company's training programmes. Long after his death, they continue to strike a chord with managers and aspiring managers, because they deal with the universal challenge of face-to-face communication.

EMPLOYABILITY

THE concept of employability is meant to provide the basis for a new psychological contract between

workers and employers. With companies no longer able to guarantee long-term job security, employability represents a shift to a new deal whereby employers offer shorter job tenure with an undertaking to provide skills development and training that will make staff more employable later on.

Employability grew out of the delayering and downsizing exercises that occurred at the end of the 1980s and early 1990s. As a global recession began to bite, many companies set about restructuring and re-engineering, a process that shocked a workforce accustomed to the concept of 'a job for life'. Downsizing and delayering revoked the unspoken, unwritten contract between corporate man and woman and the company. The bond of trust between employee and employer was irredeemably broken.

In the face of change, HR departments were forced to rethink what the company was able to offer in return for a degree of loyalty. The new message from organizations is: 'we can't offer you a job for life, but we will add to your employablilty.' Typically, this involves a move away from the traditional paternalistic approach to career development towards one where the employee is expected to manage their own career prospects. Today, loyalty can no longer be taken for granted – on either side.

Some commentators argue that the next step down this road is to move to explicit employability contracts. This would involve replacing traditional employment contracts, based on ongoing employment, with renewable fixed-term contracts whereby employees negotiate pay and development opportunities on an individual basis.

But not everyone buys into employability as a concept. One of its most vociferous critics is the influential business commentator Richard Pascale, formerly of Stanford Business School. 'A new social contract based on "employability" is the sound of one hand clapping,' he has observed. 'Its impetus is wishful thinking masquerading as a concept – a lived happily ever after ending to replace the broken psychological contract of the past. The hard truth is, there is no painless remedy. In fact, the death of job security, like any death, means that we have to learn to relate to the pain, not escape from it.'[1]

Employability, says Pascale, is a simplistic attempt to shore up rents in the social fabric. 'There is a fundamental flaw with this convenient new arrangement: philosophically, employability is a slick palliative that sidesteps the need to confront our essential humanness.' There are, he says, three interlocking elements to the problem. First, job loss and employment insecurity are inherently painful experiences that trigger a loss of self-esteem and social identity. Second, corporations and those who work for them cannot resolve these issues by themselves. Third, a new social context is needed to legitimize and deal with the grief associated with the experiences of loss and betrayal in our working lives.

Employability may turn out to be something of a Pandora's box. Having opened the lid on the loyalty issue, most companies have yet fully to come to terms with the wider implications. In the coming years, with skills shortages predicted, they are likely to reap the whirlwind. Having made it abundantly clear that they are prepared to dump employees when times are tough, organizations shouldn't be at all surprised if the most talented employees feel no sense of loyalty to them when times are good.

GAME THEORY

GAME THEORY is based on the premise that no matter what the game, no matter what the circumstances, there is a strategy that will enable you to succeed.

Game Theory was conceived not in the classroom or in the boardroom but in the casino. In the 1930s, when he was a student at Princeton and Harvard, John Von Neumann was an attentive spectator at poker games. Von Neumann was a mathematical genius rather than a gambler and the result was Game Theory, a unique mathematical insight into the possibilities and probabilities of human behaviour.

Game Theory has developed its own Zen-like language of dilemmas and riddles. The most famous of these is the Prisoner's Dilemma. Invented by Princeton University's Albert Tucker in 1950, the Prisoner's Dilemma is an imaginary scenario. Two prisoners are accused of the same crime. During interrogation in different cells they are each told that if one confesses and the other does not, the confessor will be released while the other will serve a long prison sentence. If neither confesses both will be dispatched to prison for a short sentence, and if both confess they will both receive an intermediate sentence.

Working through the possibilities, the prisoners conclude that the best decision is to confess. As both reach the same decision, they receive an intermediate sentence.

The Prisoner's Dilemma has a fundamental flaw: Game Theory is rational; reality is not. Companies that have expressed an interest in Game Theory tend to be from tightly regulated industries, such as power generation, where there is limited competition or cartels (such as OPEC in the oil industry). With a limited number of players, playing by accepted rules, and behaving in a rational way, Game Theory can make sense of what the best competitive moves may be.

Broader interest in Game Theory was reignited in 1994 when the Nobel Prize for economics was awarded to three renowned thinkers: John Nash, John Harsanyi, and Reinhard Selten. In particular, the precociously brilliant Nash is the creator of Nash's Equilibrium – the point when no player can improve their position by changing strategy. Players in a game will change their strategies until they reach equilibrium.

In one classic example, an industry includes two competing companies. Each determines the price of its product. If both were to set high prices, they would maximize their profits. Similarly, if both set their prices at lower levels, they would remain profitable. The trouble comes when they choose different price levels. If one sets a high price and the other a low price, the company with the low price makes far more money. The optimal solution is for both to have high prices. The trouble is if one company has a high price, the other will undercut it and vice versa. Eventually, both companies end up with low prices and lesser profits.

The key lesson from this and other scenarios explored by Game Theory is simply that the interactions of companies and other organizations are interdependent. If a company decides to make an investment it should consider how others – whether they be competitors, customers, or suppliers – will react.

Game Theory is best seen as a way of considering the future, a tool to get people to think. As a rationalist's guide to business paradoxes, it can be a useful business weapon. Instead of seeking out strategies driven by win–lose scenarios, companies begin to explore the merits of other strategies that may be win–win, with mutual benefits for themselves, their customers, their suppliers, and even their competitors.

MACHIAVELLI, NICOLO

POWER is a fact of corporate life. And its patron saint is undoubted: the Florentine diplomat and author Nicolo Machiavelli (1469–1527). Machiavelli's bible on power is *The Prince*. Within it, embedded beneath details of Alexander VI's tribulations, lie a ready supply of aphorisms and insights that are, perhaps sadly, as appropriate to many of today's managers and organizations as they were half a millennium ago.

Machiavelli portrayed a world of cunning and brutal opportunism. 'I believe also that he will be successful who directs his actions according to the spirit of the time, and that he whose actions do not accord with the time will not be successful,' he wrote.

He gave advice on managing change and sustaining motivation, and even had advice for executives acquiring companies in other countries:

> *'But when states are acquired in a country differing in language, customs, or laws, there are difficulties, and good fortune and great energy are needed to hold them, and one of the greatest and most real helps would be that he who has acquired them should go and reside there ... Because if one is on the*

3

spot, disorders are seen as they spring up, and one can quickly remedy them; but if one is not at hand, they are heard of only when they are great, and then one can no longer remedy them.'

Executives throughout the world will be able to identify with this analysis.

Above all, Machiavelli was the champion of leadership through cunning and intrigue, the triumph of force over reason. An admirer of Borgia, he had a dismal view of human nature. Unfortunately, as he sagely pointed out, history has repeatedly proved that a combination of being armed to the teeth and devious is more likely to allow you to achieve your objectives. It is all very well being good, said Machiavelli, but the leader 'should know how to enter into evil when necessity commands'.

THE PETER PRINCIPLE

THERE is precious little to laugh about in the work and thoughts of management thinkers. The few exceptions, therefore, stand out as eccentric beacons of hope.

Laurence J. Peter (1919–1990) was a Canadian academic who targeted the absurdities of the corporation and management hierarchies. He observed incompetence everywhere he looked. The result was the Peter Principle, which said that managers in an organization rise to their level of incompetence, through being promoted until they fail to do well in their current job. 'For each individual, for you, for me, the final promotion is from a level of competence to a level of incompetence,' wrote Peter.

Peter's greatness lay in the fact that his humour is grounded solidly in corporate reality. Anyone who has ever worked for an organization can identify with his observations – 'There are two kinds of failures: those who thought and never did, and those who did and never thought'; 'Fortune knocks once, but misfortune has much more patience'; or 'If you don't know where you are going, you will probably end up somewhere else.'

Peter's book, *The Peter Principle* (co-authored with Raymond Hull), was an antidote to the many hundreds of books celebrating corporate success stories. Around his basic joke, Peter wove a mass of aphorisms and *bon mots*. These included: 'An economist is an expert who will know tomorrow why the things he predicted yesterday didn't happen'; and 'Originality is the fine art of remembering what you hear but forgetting where you heard it.' We all know that farce and failure dog our lives. Peter simply reminded us of this.

TOWNSEND, ROBERT

ROBERT TOWNSEND (1920–1998) did all the right things to become corporate man. He was highly educated – at Princeton and

Columbia – and held a number of important executive positions. But in 1970 he transformed himself into a witty commentator on the excesses of corporate life. His bestseller *Up the Organization* (1970) was subtitled 'How to stop the corporation from stifling people and strangling profits' and was hilariously funny. Its sequel was *Further Up the Organization* (1984); and, most recently, Townsend wrote *The B2 Chronicles* (1997), which recounts the story of a company called QuoVadoTron and includes characters such as Crunch, Dooley and Archibald.

Townsend's genius lay in debunking the modern organization for its excess, stupidity, and absurdity. He was the ultimate sceptic. Those with power, or who think they have power, are dangerous beings. He was, by turn, playful, indignant, critical, and practical. 'A personnel man with his arm around an employee is like a treasurer with his hand in the till,' he noted. His quip on consultants – 'They are the people who borrow your watch to tell you what time it is and then walk off with it' – remains one of the most quoted putdowns of an entire industry.

Townsend had no time for the adornments of executive office and his list of 'no-nos' included reserved parking spaces; special-quality stationery for the boss and his elite; muzak; bells and buzzers; company shrinks; outside directorships and trusteeships for the chief executive; and the company plane. He was, in fact, preaching a brand of empowerment and participation 20 years ahead of its time. Humorous it may have been but, as with all great humour, there was a serious undercurrent.

REFERENCE

1. Pascale, Richard, 'The False Security of Employability', *Fast Company*, April 1996.

3

– CHAPTER 5 –

Managing internationally

'There will be two kinds of CEOs who will exist in the next five years: those who think globally and those who are unemployed.' PETER DRUCKER

'The world is becoming a common marketplace in which people – no matter where they live – desire the same products and lifestyles. Global companies must forget the idiosyncratic differences between countries and cultures and instead concentrate on satisfying universal drives.' THEODORE LEVITT

'Think globally, act locally, think tribally, act universally.' JOHN NAISBITT

'Tough domestic rivalry breeds international success.' MICHAEL PORTER

International joint ventures

PETER LORANGE

If mergers and acquisitions were the strategic mantra of the 1980s, international strategic alliances and joint ventures became the strategic call of the 1990s. These forms of co-operative effort have become an integral part of modern business strategy. Peter Lorange looks at the shifting rationale behind joint ventures.

THE traditional purposes for forming international strategic alliances stemmed from various forms of resource constraints among one, or several, of the co-operating entities. For instance, there might be a problem with finding financial resources to pursue a certain strategic direction; a partner would then be called in to help underwrite the effort. Typically, such alliances might occur when a particular company has an interesting technological opportunity, but lacks the funds to take it further.

A second type of classical international strategic alliance is concerned with access to certain countries. In many parts of the world, it has been difficult for foreign companies to enter the market. It demands resources, willingness to take political risks, and time to develop a meaningful presence in such markets. One solution is to bring in a local partner. Sometimes this partner may not play much of an active role beyond legitimizing the activities of the joint venture in its home country. At other times, however, the true expertise of a local partner might be very helpful. Even though the world is becoming more open to business, with protectionist moves decreasing, this type of international strategic alliance remains prominent.

While the rationale for the above-mentioned type of strategic alliance is clear, it should not be denied that if the initiating actors had free choice, irrespective of resources or other constraints, they would in most cases prefer to go it alone. As such, joint ventures have often been branded as a second-best option. This sense of scepticism tends to be further strengthened when operational problems occur in the alliance. Despite this, there has been growing recognition of the role of international joint ventures as a preferred option, irrespective of resource constraints.

This has been highlighted by the fact that technological and other forces rapidly make all businesses global. Thus, the *speed* of commercializing a new business concept globally is critical. Few corporations can achieve this fast enough on *all* the frontiers on which they may be participating. As a result, it can be an attractive option to share with other progressive corporations in the rapid global development of many activities. We are now seeing increased activity among leading multinationals in teaming up within specific business areas to jointly take them global. The driving force is speed and utilization of a unique common position, not resource constraints *per se*.

We are also increasingly seeing strategic alliances as a way of achieving global economies of scale and/or scope, while at the same time adding flexibility in terms of remaining 'local' in various key markets. The fact that each participant in a joint venture does have a home base and, typically, enjoys certain areas of strength makes it possible for a modern strategic alliance to create an advantage beyond what the wholly owned multinational firm might achieve. This approach, which can create a more credible local perception while also achieving the benefits of global focus, is probably easier to achieve through a network of strategic alliances.

With a shift towards the emergence of positively motivated strategic alliances, where the international joint venture approach *is* the preferred option, it is also more and more common for such alliances to take a longer-term, strategic form. Undoubtedly, it requires a great deal of effort to put together and manage an international joint venture. The investment in time and energy can only be justified if the international joint venture option is covering a central strategic concern.

Formation of international joint ventures

In this discussion I shall draw heavily on a conceptual model for how to form joint ventures developed jointly with Dr Johan Roos.[1] Figure 1 shows this model.

Figure 1 The joint venture formation process

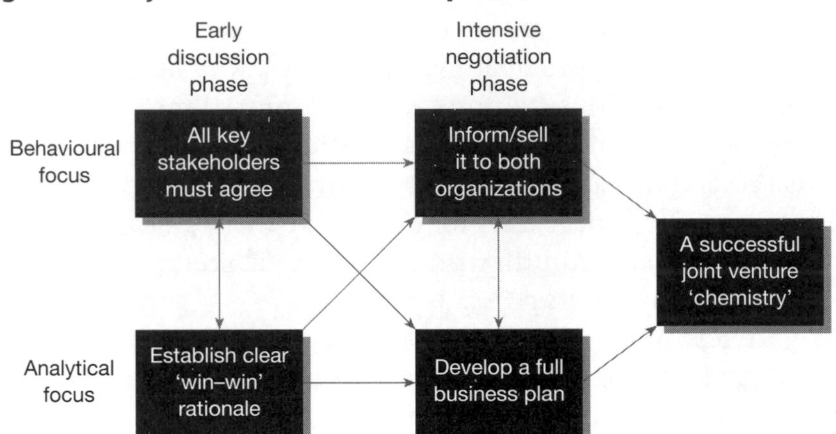

Its main features are as follows: a joint venture is not formulated as a typical discrete or finite decision, but is a result of a 'gradual formation', based on an iterative process among the prospective partners, gradually leading to common understanding and trust. This formation process goes through an initial phase and a main phase. Also, while there are a number of rational and analytical issues to be covered, behavioural and psychological issues related to the various decision makers and stakeholders involved, on both sides, are also prominent. The process is thus partly analytical, partly behavioural.

During the initial phase it is important, from an analytical point of view, to create a clear and easily understood 'win–win *raison d'être'* for the alliance. It is also important that the basic joint venture philosophy and approach is endorsed, explicitly or implicitly, by all key stakeholders in both organizations. During the main negotiation phase that follows, it is necessary to develop a clear analytical plan for *who* does *what* and *when*, together with the resource commitments required. In parallel, however, it is also important to 'sell in' the prospect of a strategic alliance in both participating organizations, so that this new way of working will be welcomed, rather than resisted. A proper formation process is fundamental to making a joint venture work. Even though the joint venture may be based on a brilliant strategy, it is unlikely to yield the expected results unless embedded in an appropriate formation process.

When attempting to create a win–win situation, it is important to keep in mind that realistically this can only be achieved if *all* prospective parties feel reasonably equal. The big multinational corporation must be aware that it may run into nationalistic sentiments when it is dealing with a local entity in developing a strategic alliance. The sensitivity to the perceived dominant attitude of a multinational corporation must be remembered. Similarly, in some cultures the preference for full ownership is very strong. These cultures tend to have a propensity to cultivate a win–lose attitude in their societal activities. It may be particularly difficult to create an appropriate win–win attitude if such a preference is culturally prominent, i.e., when the ultimate motive may be to dominate.

In achieving support from all of the key stakeholders, it is important to remember that it may be hard to find 'who is who' when dealing with international joint ventures. In many companies in different parts of the world the classical hierarchical organization, prominent in many Western companies, simply does not hold. It is often not obvious who are the key stakeholders. For instance, large corporate groups in the Far East can still be run as if they are family owned, even though the formal ownership stake in the various companies of the group may not be too high.

Another cultural characteristic in bringing all key stakeholders on board has to do with the fact that a 'yes' does not mean an agreement. Similarly, a 'no' may not mean no. The way one negotiates is very different from culture to culture. Recent experiences in developing strategic alliances in the former Soviet Union emphasize the difficulties of identifying who the key stakeholders are and being able to determine whether in fact there is commitment to take the joint venture forward or not.

In developing a strategic plan for an international joint venture, achieving a realistic resource focus is often particularly challenging. How can companies ensure that the quality of resources, particularly when it comes to human resources, is adequate on each side? Does each partner have the technological competencies, as well as the commercial competencies, that are assumed? Similarly, it may be difficult to judge the overall financial strength of a prospective partner, given the lack of commonly accepted procedures for reporting accounts. The fact that many international commercial groupings consist of loosely affiliated legal entities makes the issue of developing an understanding of the overall resource realities behind a particular strategic plan even more of a challenge.

Finally, when it comes to the 'selling' of the strategic alliance within both partner organizations, it is important to be sensitive to cross-cultural resistance and national sentiments. Many cultures are fearful of a foreign intrusion. This should be kept in mind when it comes to explaining the rationale for the alliance. Most importantly, the self-respect of both parties must be maintained.

Overall, the formation process for an international joint venture is highly demanding. Research suggests that the more experienced the management teams are on both sides, both in terms of having participated in joint ventures before and, perhaps even more importantly, being truly international in experience and focus, the more realistic international joint venture formations will be.

The evolution of an international joint venture

It has been noted that a joint venture or a strategic alliance never represents a stable situation, but is always evolving from one stage to another. It has also been said by some that a joint venture represents a managerial marathon between the various partners, and that the ultimate winner within such a working relationship is the party that is best able to maintain its drive and commitment to the alliance over time. Why is it that a joint venture typically does not represent a steady state way of working?

This is caused by a number of forces, three of which can be highlighted.

Organizational learning

Learning is likely to take place among the parties to a joint venture, which may allow for more effective ways of co-operation. When an international joint venture is put together, it is frequently based on a concept where each party contributes its part to the business equation and the specific activities to be carried out typically rest with the parents. The joint venture, as an organizational entity, is more or less 'empty'; it is a contract regulating co-operation between the parties.

As time goes on, and the learning accumulates on both sides, it often becomes apparent that executives involved in the strategic alliance should be dedicated to these tasks on a more permanent basis, not only to ensure efficiency, but also so that they can benefit from being together and form an effective team. After all, organizational learning can most effectively take place around a business, rather than around particular, free-coupled functions. One frequently sees activities gradually transferred into a new organizational entity and more and more organizational learning taking place within the joint venture itself. As an additional benefit, this brings an opportunity to develop a more committed organizational culture for the alliance.

Needless to say, there can be particular challenges in developing a designated organization for an international joint venture. It could, for instance, mean moving key executives across borders. It could also mean that the parent organizations may have to give up certain activities, possibly leading to the closure of plants in the home base. Nevertheless, the advantage of business-based organizational learning and the commitment effect that can be achieved from this tends to be very powerful. If one or two of the parents resists such an evolution, insisting instead on the *status quo*, this may lead to a gradual weakening of the joint venture and perhaps even to its ultimate demise.

Responding to competitive threats

A related argument is the growing need to respond more rapidly and forcefully to competitive threats, as well as to be able to take more proactive advantage of related new business opportunities created by the joint venture. When it comes to responding to competitive threats, it goes without saying that this can be a slow and, at times, confused process, with the responsibility for responding split between the two parents. Internal co-ordination problems and debates regarding how to respond are quite frequent within international joint ventures, and an evolution towards a more co-ordinated way of responding is thus key. While this does not necessarily have to be done through a common organization, at least not as a first step, it typically leads to a designation of responsibilities to a few specific executives, perhaps within one of the parent organizations. This 'asymmetry' may then propel further development towards a fully free-standing organization.

The issue of new opportunity seeking is of course also potentially difficult if one or both parents continues to compete actively in other aspects of the business. A parent may be hesitant to see the strengthening of the joint venture organization, fearing that this might lead to the creation of a future competitor. This has to be balanced against the benefits of having a strategic alliance that is able to create positive value from the opportunities as follow-on from the initially established base. Many parent organizations eventually allow the alliance to evolve into a more free-standing organization with the resources and the management capabilities to respond to new business development.

Organizational resistance

There may be resistance among the parent organizations to changes and reconfigurations in the international joint venture. We have already touched on the fact that this also may lead to diminished activities in one or both parent organizations, or lead to change in the relative importance among the parents. It is, therefore, of critical importance that a clear and current concept of the win–win rationale is continually rearticulated among the partners as the alliance evolves. Both parties will be required to reiterate what the win–win equation is at relatively frequent intervals.

There is nothing unnatural about an evolution of the basic rationale behind the joint venture. This can, however, become a problem if the lack of attention to such a reformulation of objectives leads to a creation of dysfunctionality among the parents. A key factor here is being sensitive to national pride and prestige. It is important that the reformulation of the win–win concept is never linked to any sense of 'mistake', or lack of 'performance', or the emergence of winners and losers among any of the parties. Evolution in an international joint venture can only take place based on a feeling of mutual success.

The exit issue

It is clear that an international joint venture can have many risks associated with it. The commercial risks that a joint venture runs may in themselves be quite formidable. In addition, there are the potential risks of the strategic alliance failing due to organizational difficulties. It follows that realistic exit clauses must be built into any strategic alliance.

However, the problem is that these often tend to undermine the very co-operative spirit that is necessary to make an international joint venture work. If discussion and quarrels regarding how to stop the alliance prevail, then it will naturally have a very limited life. Even when it comes to such seemingly straightforward issues as resolving disputes in terms of a vote among the parties where, for instance, a 51 percent majority shareholder votes down the 49 percent minority partner, the joint venture may rapidly be on its way towards becoming ineffective.

What is important is that all parties must act *as if* they are 50–50 parties, despite the fact that the legal side of their alliance agreement may say something different. Only then will the true complementary efforts from the parties emerge, and only then will full positive value creation beyond the capabilities of each partner emerge. If this understanding is not brought to bear, then legally driven actions can handicap the alliance. For executives with their roots in legally driven environments, this can be a problem. Thus, while exit clauses are important, they should not be allowed to hamper the evolution of the alliance.

This leads us to the fundamental issue of how each of the partners might receive their ultimate pay-off from co-operation. In order to address this, it is important to keep in mind that the evolution of the alliance typically leads to the development of a more and more free-standing organization, as we have seen, with indigenous capabilities to tackle its own business. An organization will gradually be created with a commercial value on its own.

At this stage, each of the parents owns an asset that has a commercial value and can be sold. Each has the option to sell out without destroying the value of the joint venture itself. In contrast, selling out *before* such a free-standing organizational entity has taken hold will, in all likelihood, lead to the destruction of the owners' value. Whether one of the partners buys its previous partner or an outside entity is brought in as a new party to the joint venture becomes an issue of negotiation, rather than an issue of how the joint venture's value and operation will continue to take place. Typically, however, one of the existing partners will buy out the other. Such a buyout must be very sensitive to the fact that nationalistic sentiments must not be allowed to create a negative image of what is happening.

The 'black box' issue

It may be desirable for each partner to have some type of safeguard control over its stake in the joint venture. The legal contract does, of course, play an important role here as a way of protecting the parties. It should be kept in mind, however, that an international joint venture's legal contract can be quite difficult to enforce. An appropriate arbitration mechanism must be specified, with a location chosen for where to arbitrate. Similarly, patent protection and technology agreements can contribute in some ways to creating protection for a partner, a 'black box'. Here too, however, the enforcement issue can be a monumental challenge.

A complementary and perhaps more effective black box protection can be created, based on the *latent* power that each partner may be perceived to have *vis-à-vis* the other partners in case the joint venture is broken off. This latent power can, for instance, stem from a technology base that is continually being renewed through innovative R&D, or through maintaining a strong market position – values that any partner appreciates and may be reluctant to cut itself off from.

A technology-based latent power position, developed by a partner through emphasizing its own R&D, can nevertheless only offer protection if it is *signalling* its progress and overall strategic direction to the other party, typically at quite frequent intervals and deliberately. By doing this, the other partner understands that it is part of a flow of new technologies and anticipates future benefits from this. If it breaks off the joint venture, this will naturally mean latent future opportunity losses while no longer being part of the partner's technologically based progress.

Similarly, when it comes to market-driven latent power, demonstrated through investing vigorously in local market development, brand name enhancement, active contact with the distribution chains, etc., it is again important that a partner is able to signal its progress to the other party, so that the latter understands that breaking off the strategic joint venture might lead to a difficult situation in the marketplace. A latent threat of losing the market is, of course, also a strong deterrent against breaking off a joint venture.

Thus, it is an advantage if each of the partners in an international joint venture can take an active stand to develop their complementary black box positions. As such, each party will also perceive that they have teamed up with a true winner, making it easier to justify why this international joint venture should continue. Anticipated future benefits, and the latent threat of seeing such benefits being taken away, are effective ways of protecting one's interest in an international joint venture, complementing a legal-driven approach and patent position.

The future

International joint ventures are already a prominent part of the strategies of many multinationals and leading national companies. More and more can be expected to emerge. Over time, managerial know-how advantage can be expected to accrue for firms that gain practice in being effective participants in such international joint ventures. Success is experience based. The very fact that the company has already previously participated in such co-operative activities will be an asset.

Beyond this, however, it is important to structure a competent way to build up the execution of international joint ventures along the lines suggested. This requires a clearer understanding of the analytical and behavioural sides of creating an effective formation process; more realistic focus on the evolutionary side of a joint venture; clear focus on the aim, enabling the creation of an ultimate exit position to recuperate the value (not, of course, to be confused with premature exit discussions, which can only lead to 'working accidents'); and, finally, the creation of a 'black box' position to help glue the joint venture together in a co-operative way, while still being able to protect one's own interest. All of these elements are essential aspects of successful international joint venture management.

REFERENCE

1. Lorange, P. and Roos, J., *Strategic Alliances, Formation, Implementation and Evolution*, Blackwell Publishers, Oxford, 1992.

RESOURCES

BOOKS

Faulkner, D., *Strategic Alliances*, McGraw-Hill, Maidenhead, 1995.

Lorange, Peter and Roos, Johan, *Strategic Alliances, Formation, Implementation and Evolution*, Blackwell Publishers, Oxford, 1992.

The importance of a global mindset

VIJAY GOVINDARAJAN AND ANIL K. GUPTA

We all make sense of the world in different ways. Vijay Govindarajan and Anil K. Gupta argue the importance of gaining a global mindset.

A 'mindset' is the way we, whether as individuals or organizations, observe and make sense of the world around us. We are selective and biased in what we observe and how we interpret it, usually as the result of our experiences. So the greater the diversity in the experiences of two individuals or organizations, the more likely it is that their mindsets will be different.

These differences matter. It is our perceptions of the environment as well as of ourselves that determine which of a multitude of opportunities and problems we choose to pursue and how we go about doing so.

A firm that wants global presence must develop a global mindset if it is to recognize and capitalize on opportunities for expanding its market. So why does mindset matter? What exactly is a global mindset? And how can a company go about creating a global mindset?

What is a global mindset?

A firm's mindset shapes perceptions in virtually every area: what the nature and size of the opportunity space is; who the customer is; how customer needs are changing; who the firm really competes with; what technologies are central to the industry; and so forth. A firm's mindset has a direct and determining impact on what strategies it pursues and what investments it makes to implement them.

One way to interpret the concept of mindset is to view every mindset as a theory of the world. Looked at in this way, within the concept of an industry, different mindsets represent different and competing theories about the industry. Over time, some theories might prove to be more powerful and their proponents emerge as the victors.

While the concept of mindset applies to both individuals and organizations, it is useful to draw a distinction between the two. When we talk about an individual's mindset we refer to the way that an individual's brain receives and interprets information. But given that organizations do not have brains, what do we mean when we talk about an organization's mindset?

The answer lies in the following set of observations:

- Every organization is a collective of individuals.
- Each individual has a mindset that continuously shapes and is shaped by the mindsets of other people in the collective.
- Depending on the type of decision, different individuals in the collective have differing degrees of influence on the making of a decision.

Building on these observations, we define an organization's mindset as the aggregated mindset of the collective, adjusted for the distribution of power and mutual influence among the people making up that collective. It follows that unless the chief executive is exceptionally powerful or has played a major role in shaping the organization's history and culture (as with Bill Gates at Microsoft), it can be a serious error to regard the chief executive's personal mindset as synonymous with that of the organization.

To understand the meaning of the term 'global mindset', it is useful first to examine its opposite (a more common scenario), the ethnocentric mindset.

Consider the situation at IKEA, a global furniture retailer. Until the late 1980s, Swedish nationals constituted virtually the entire senior management team. Fluency in Swedish was considered essential at senior levels. And when the company entered foreign markets, such as the US, it replicated its historical Swedish concepts such as no home delivery, beds that required sheets conforming to the Swedish rather than US standards, and so forth. In short, IKEA saw the world through a Swedish filter. It was largely blind to alternative views of market reality and believed that given the superiority of its own perspective, such blindness did not matter. It had a closed world view. To its credit, when confronted with disappointing performance in the US, IKEA was a quick learner and realized that an ethnocentric mindset imposes significant constraints on a company's ability to build and exploit global presence.

A global mindset rests on a foundation of openness. An organization with a global mindset operates on the premise that cultures can be different without being better or worse than one another. Such an organization dedicates itself to becoming well informed about different value systems, different norms of behaviour, and different assumptions regarding reality. It accepts diversity and heterogeneity as natural and as sources of opportunities and strengths rather than as necessary evils.

This acceptance of diversity does not, however, imply that the organization with a global mindset becomes a prisoner of diversity and closes itself to the possibility of working across cultures or transferring innovations and superior practices from one culture to another. On the contrary, the openness inherent in a global mindset implies an openness to change over time – in one's own culture as well as those of others. As Percy Barnevik, ABB's architect and first chief executive, observed astutely: 'Global managers have exceptionally open minds. They respect how different countries do things and they have the imagination to appreciate why they do them that way. But they are also incisive; they push the limits of the culture.'

Is your mindset global?

Tables 1 and 2 contain two sets of diagnostic questions that individual managers and organizations can use to assess the extent to which their mindsets are currently global. If you cannot answer 'yes' to every question in Table 1, your mindset is not as global as it could be. And if you cannot answer 'yes' to every question in Table 2, the same goes for your firm.

Table 1 ***Do you have a global mindset?***

- When you interact with others, do you assign them equal status regardless of national origin?
- Do you regard your values to be a hybrid of values acquired from multiple cultures as opposed to one culture?
- Do you consider yourself as open to ideas from other countries and cultures as you are to ideas from your country and culture of origin?
- Does finding yourself in a new cultural setting cause excitement rather than fear and anxiety?
- When visiting or living in another culture, are you sensitive to the cultural differences without becoming a prisoner of those differences?

Table 2 ***Does your organization have a global mindset?***

- Is your company a leader rather than a laggard in discovering and pursuing emerging market opportunities in the world?
- Do you consider every customer, regardless of country, to be as important as a customer in your domestic market?
- Do you draw your employees from the worldwide talent pool?
- Do employees of every nationality have the same opportunity to move up the career ladder to the top?
- In scanning the horizon for potential competitors, do you examine all economic regions of the world?
- In selecting a location for any activity, do you seek to optimize the choice on a global basis?
- Do you view the global arena as not just a 'playground' (that is, a market to exploit) but also a 'school' (that is, a source of ideas and technology)?
- Do you perceive your company as having a universal identity and many homes rather than a national identity?

3

We would not be surprised if the results of these diagnostic tests make many chief executives – even those within large and long-established multinational companies – wince with discomfort. Such a possibility raises the all-important question of whether all, or only some, companies need to have global mindsets.

It is easy to see that those organizations (such as IKEA, Procter & Gamble, and IBM) that already have a global presence and/or global resource commitments would benefit greatly from global mindsets. The same is true of those organizations (such as Wal-Mart, Marriott and UPM-Kymmene) that may not have significant global presence today, but are engaged in becoming global.

However, for organizations that are neither global nor planning to become global, the question of whether a global mindset would be an asset or a liability is difficult to answer. This is because the decision not to become global may itself be the result of a pre-existing, perhaps non-global, mindset. In other words, mindsets often work like self-fulfilling prophecies. The more global an organization's mindset, the more likely such an organization is to value global mindsets and vice versa. Levers for developing a global mindset are explored in Table 3.

From the discussion so far, it follows that in order to exhibit a global mindset an organization's management team must be endowed with two important features: a deep understanding of the world's diversity, and a strong ability to integrate diverse world views.

Ensuring that the management team collectively has a deep understanding of the world's diversity requires that the team consists of people with different national backgrounds and considerable experience in different regions. On the other hand, ensuring that the team is able to integrate diverse world views requires that, notwithstanding their differing backgrounds, each member of the team should have an open mind, some breadth of international experience, and the linguistic skills to engage in direct and rich communication with other team members.

Dow Chemical, ABB and Unilever offer good examples of attempts to create a global mindset. In the early 1990s, of the

Table 3 ***Levers for creating a global mindset***

- Composition of the board of directors – mix of nationalities, international experience, language skills.
- Choice of locations for board meetings.
- Background of the chief executive – international experience, language skills.
- Distribution of the time spent by the chief executive in various regions.
- Composition of the executive committee – mix of nationalities, international experience, language skills.
- Choice of locations for executive committee meetings.
- Background of business unit general managers – mix of nationalities, international experience, language skills.
- Composition of business unit top management teams – mix of nationalities, international experience, language skills.
- Proportion of middle and senior managers who are members of cross-border business teams.
- Proportion of middle and senior managers who have participated in management development programmes consisting of mixed-nationality teams.
- Executive selection procedures that screen for openness to diversity and change.
- Executive career ladders that reward international experience.
- Performance measurement and incentive systems that motivate senior managers to optimize not only local but also global performance.

22 people on Dow Chemical's most senior management committee, 10 were born outside the US and 17 had had significant international experience. In the mid-1990s, ABB's seven-member executive committee consisted of people representing four different nationalities. Further, each of these seven executives had had extensive international experience and was fluent in English.

For many years, Unilever has followed a policy that most people who rise to the top of any business unit should have worked in at least two countries and should speak at least one language besides their native tongue. Unilever is also a good example of a company that commences the globalization process fairly early in a manager's career, through mechanisms such as international placements and a management training centre that brings together 300 to 400 managers from all over the world each year.

The contribution of a global mindset

The economic landscape of the world is changing rapidly and becoming more global at a faster pace. This means that for most medium-sized to large companies, market opportunities, crucial resources, and competitors lurk not just in their home markets, but also increasingly in distant and often poorly understood regions.

How successful a company is at exploiting the emerging opportunities and tackling the emerging challenges depends crucially on how intelligent it is at observing and interpreting the dynamic world in which it operates. A global mindset is one of the main ingredients of such intelligence.

RESOURCES

BOOKS

Jeannet, Jean-Pierre, *Managing with a Global Mindset*, FT Prentice Hall, 1999.

Mastering Global Business, FT Prentice Hall, 1999.

When two worlds collide

FONS TROMPENAARS AND PETER WOOLLIAMS

Fons Trompenaars and Peter Woolliams examine the strategic task facing organizations in generating value through cross border acquisitions, mergers and alliances.

GLOBALIZATION through mergers, acquisitions and strategic alliances is big business – currently worth in excess of $2,000 billion annually. Mergers, acquisitions and strategic alliances are increasingly pursued, not only to implement globalization strategies, but as a consequence of political, monetary and regulatory convergence. Yet, two out of three deals don't achieve anywhere near the initially anticipated benefits.[1]

Organizations are commonly acquired on the basis of their inherent value rather than with the intention of achieving full integration. Increasingly however, motives originate from a range of other expected benefits including synergistic values (e.g. cross-selling, supply chain consolidation and economies of scale) or more direct strategic values (to become market leaders, penetrating a ready made customer base, etc.). The emphasis in the pre-deal and post-deal management is too often focused on seeking to quickly exploit the new opportunities under a mechanistic systems or financial due-diligence mindset.[2] It is assumed that delivering benefits requires the alignment of technical, operational and financial systems and market approaches.

Our research reveals that the real underlying failure to deliver benefits arises from the absence of a holistic structured methodological framework. This means that senior managers do not know what to integrate or what types of decision are important to deliver the anticipated benefits. While any integration programme should be based on operational matters, much more attention and resources need to be given to managing the cultural differences between the new partners/businesses. Relational aspects like cultural differences and lack of trust are responsible for 70 percent of alliance failures. This is even more striking when we realize that building trust is a cultural challenge in itself. Lack of trust is often caused by different views of what constitutes a trustworthy partner. In addition, intercultural alliances involve differences in corporate cultures as well as national cultures. Problems can be due to more or less 'objective' cultural differences, but also to perceptions about each other, including perceptions of corporate culture and national culture.

In response, consideration must be given to leadership styles, management profiles, organization structures, working practices, and a wide range of perceptions in and of the marketplace. In short, culture is pervasive. Even when strategists and senior managers who recognize the importance of culture, frustration continues because they have no means of assessing or quantifying its causes and effects and to take relevant effective action.

Based on our extensive experience working with client companies involved in such mergers and alliances, we have developed a new methodology that we call *Cultural Due Diligence*. This provides an operational framework intended to be facilitated by the HR directorate to make these cultural differences tangible so that their consequences can be made explicit and thereby reconciled to ensure benefit delivery. It is based on the three Rs: Recognition, Respect and Reconciliation.

Recognition

The first task for HR is to help all players recognize that there are cultural differences, their importance and how they impact.

Culture, like an onion, consists of layers that can be peeled off. We can distinguish three layers. First, the *outer* layer is what people primarily associate with culture: the visual reality of behaviour, clothes, food, language, the organizational chart, the handbook for HR-policies, etc. This is the level of explicit culture.

Second, the *middle* layer refers to the norms and values that an organization holds: what is considered right and wrong (norms) or good and bad (values).

Third, there is the deepest *inner* layer: the level of unquestioned, implicit culture. It is the result of human beings organizing to reconcile frequently occurring dilemmas. It consists of basic assumptions, many series of routines and methods developed to deal with the regular problems that one faces. These methods of problem solving have become so basic that, like breathing, we no longer think about how we do it. For an outsider these basic assumptions are very difficult to recognize. Understanding the core of the culture onion is the key to successfully working with other cultures and of successful alliances and cross border collaboration.

Thus, while we instantly recognize the explicit cultural differences, we may not recognize the implicit cultural differences. This explains why the need for cultural due diligence in pre and post merger/acquisition management is usually absent from the agenda. Our research and experience has led us to develop and validate models and diagnostic instruments to reveal and measure these basic assumptions. They are based on the seven dimensions model of cultural differences developed over the last 10 years and are at the core of the new HR cultural due diligence model.

3

Respect

Different cultural orientations and views of the world are not right or wrong – they are just different. It is all too easy to be judgemental – and distrust those who give different meaning to their world from your world. Thus the next step is to *respect* these differences and accept their right to interpret the world in the way they have chosen to cope.

Because of the different views of the world and different meaning given to apparently the same constructs, we find that these differences manifest themselves as dilemmas. We have two seemingly opposing views.

Reconciliation

There is growing conviction that wealth is created in alliances (including mergers and acquisitions) by reconciling values. This is a new contribution to the debate on alliances and mergers in business. Cultural due diligence is the means to bring about reconciliation of these seemingly opposing views.

Our model helps to identify and define behaviours that really make mergers effective. This new approach will inform managers how to guide the social side of alliances of any kind. It has a logic that integrates differences. It is a series of behaviours that enables effective interaction with those of contrasting value systems. It reveals a propensity to share understanding of other's position in the expectation of reciprocity and requires a new way of thinking that is initially difficult for Westerners.

Major dilemmas in need for reconciliation

In a merger or acquisition 'life as taken for granted' within your own organization is abruptly challenged by an alternative logic. The seven dimensional model is a means to elicit, describe and frame the major dilemmas organizations have to resolve when faced with integration of people and systems.

Dilemmas can be characterized by which of the following continua they originate. Consider the dilemmas that arise between:

1. **The universal and the particular**: do people in the organization tend to follow standardized rules or do they prefer a flexible approach to unique situations?

2. **Individualism–communitarianism**: does the organization foster individual performance and creativity or is the focus on the larger group leading to cohesion and consensus?
3. **Neutral–affective**: are emotions controlled or do you display emotions overtly?
4. **Specific–diffuse**: what is the degree of involvement (personal relationships) in business (high=diffuse, low=specific)? Does a specific business project come easily, out of which a more diffuse relationship may develop, or, do you have to get to know your business partner before you can do business?
5. **Achievement–ascription**: is status and power based on your performances or is it more determined by which school you went to or your age, gender and family background?
6. **Sequential–synchronic**: do you organize time in a sequential manner doing one task at a time or in parallel keeping many things live at the same time?
7. **Internal–external control**: are you stimulated by your inner drive and sense of control or are you adaptive to external events which are beyond your control?

When faced with cultural differences, one effective approach is to compare the two profiles to identify where the major differences originate. In practice, the major origin of cultural differences between your organization and the new partner may lie in one or two cultural dimensions. By reconciling the dilemmas deriving from the differences on the dimensions, organizations can begin to reconcile their cultural orientations. Recognition of these differences alone is insufficient. However, it is very important that these are taken into consideration before and during the alliance or merger processes.

Five types of behaviours in alliances or mergers can be distinguished:

1. First, we have the alliance in which one of the partners sticks to its values and proclaims: 'My values first!'
2. The second type of response is to *abandon your orientation and go native*. Here you adopt a when in Rome, do as Romans do

approach. Acting or keeping up such pretences won't go unseen – you will be very much an amateur. Other cultures will mistrust you – and you won't be able to offer your own strengths to the marriage.

3. Third, we find the alliance avoiding and ignoring value dilemmas by operating at arm's length.
4. Fourth there is the type of partnership where a compromise between values is found.
5. Finally, and for mergers/alliances that are more effective and realize and exceed the expected benefits, we find the reconciling alliance in which values are integrated to integrity. Through questionnaires, structured interviews and focus groups, we are accumulating hard evidence that confirms that this new competency correlates highly with effectiveness in environments where one party needs to deal with diversity of values. In short, where parties can reconcile and integrate, the expected benefits of the alliance or merger are delivered and even exceeded.

For convenience we have chosen to define these based on seven dimensions on which the values of diverse cultures vary. These concepts are abstract but all exhibit bifurcation. We can define effective behaviours for each in different cultures.

The new challenge

Other cultures have an integrity, which only some of its members will abandon. People who abandon their culture become weakened and corrupt. We *need others to be themselves if partnership is to work*. This is why we need an approach that will *reconcile differences*, that is, to be ourselves, but yet see and understand how alternative perspectives can help our own.

Once players in alliances and mergers are aware of their own mental models and cultural predispositions, and once they can respect and understand that those of another culture are legitimately different, then it becomes possible to reconcile differences yielding positive business benefits.

Universalism versus particularism

Universalist cultures tend to feel that general rules and obligations are a strong source of moral reference. Universalists tend to follow the rules even when friends are involved and look for 'the one best way' of dealing equally and fairly with all cases. They assume that the standard they hold dear are the 'right' ones and they attempt to change the attitudes of others to match.

Particularist societies are those where 'particular' circumstances are much more important than the rules. Bonds of particular relationships (family, friends) are stronger than any abstract rule and the response may change according to circumstances and the people involved.

In order to test these extreme definitions we have asked 55,000 managers worldwide to consider the following dilemma:

> *You are riding in a car driven by a close friend. He hits a pedestrian. You know he was going at least 35 miles per hour in an area of the city where the maximum allowed speed is 20 miles per hour. There are no witnesses. His lawyer says that if you testify under oath that he was only driving 20 miles per hour it may save him from serious consequences.*
>
> What right has your friend to expect you to protect him?
>
> ☐ My friend has a DEFINITE right as a friend to expect me to testify to the lower figure.
>
> ☐ He has SOME right as a friend to expect me to testify to the lower figure.
>
> ☐ He has NO right as a friend to expect me to testify to the lower figure.

3

Would you help your friend in view of the obligations you feel having for society?

The story above, created by Stouffer and Toby, is another exercise used in our workshops.[3] It takes the form of a dilemma which measures universal and particularist responses.

Figure 1 shows the result of putting these questions to a variety of countries. North Americans, Northern Europeans are almost totally universalistic in their approach to the problem. The proportion falls to under 70 percent for the Latin Americans, Africans and Asians. They would tend rather to lie to the police to protect their friend.

Time and again, universalists respond in such a way that as the seriousness of the accident increases, the obligation to help their friend decreases. They seem to be saying to themselves 'the law was broken and the serious condition of the pedestrian underlines the importance of upholding the law'. This suggests that universalism is rarely used to the exclusion of particularism, rather that it forms the first principle in the process of moral reasoning. Particular consequences remind us of the need for universal laws.

Figure 1 The car and the pedestrian – friend has no/some right and would not help

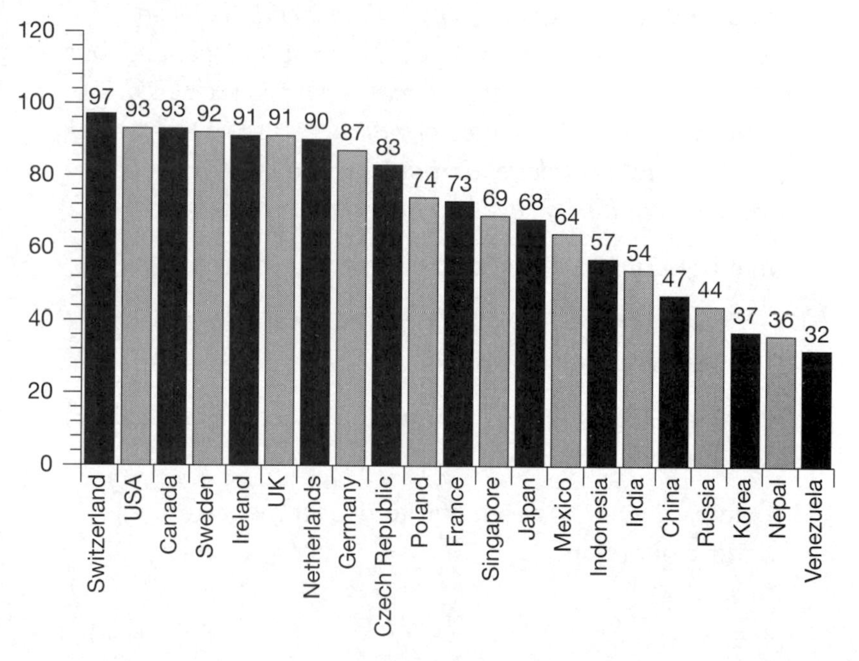

Universalism versus particularism in mergers and acquisition

There are many examples of the universal-particular dilemma impacting international managers. The most dominant one is the global-local dichotomy. Shall we have one standardized approach or shall we try the local more particular approach? There are differing views on whether we are becoming more globally *universal* and alike or whether we are becoming more influenced by *particular* and unfamiliar national cultures.

In retrospect this dilemma has very much jeopardized the success of the KLM-Alitalia alliance. The Protestant Dutch were sticklers for following the contract. The prepayment of some $100 million for the development of Malpensa airport was one of the central conditions. For the Italians it was seen as a sign of the seriousness of the alliance. When the investment was not going to schedule the Dutch began discussing prepayments. A contract is a contract. The Italians had all kinds of reasons why it was not going as planned. Life is hectic and might offer unexpected particular exceptions. 'What's the problem? We'll do it in another way.'

In general, international success in alliances depends upon discovering special veins of excellence within different cultures. Just because people speak English does not mean they think alike. That no two cultures are the same is what brings richness and complexity to multi-nationalism.

A corporation reconciling Axes X and Y must make a conceptual leap. The answer lies in *transnational specialization,* allowing each nation to specialize in what it does best and be a source of authority and leadership within the global corporation for that particular vein of excellence. The reach is truly global but the sources of major influence are national. Leadership in particular functions shifts to whatever nations excel at those tasks. This cycle is in fact helical – see Figure 2.

International alliances need to look for a similar logic: it is the result of connecting particular learning efforts into a universal framework and vice versa. It is the connection between practical

Figure 2 Reconciling universalism and particularism in global alliances

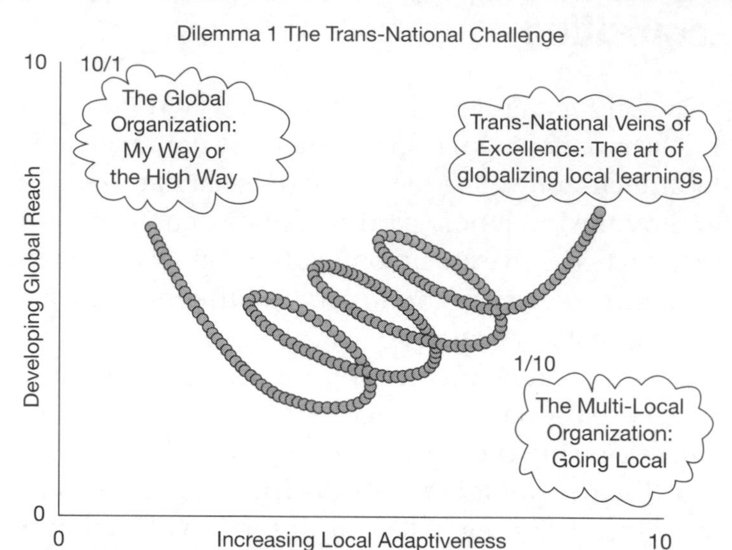

learning in a context of intelligent theories. In this dialectic the best integration processes are developed, disadvantages made into advantages. However, it is not easily achieved and needs the involvement of senior managers.

THE ISUZU AND GM TRUCKS ALLIANCE

MANY cultural dilemmas between the large North American and the relatively small Japanese truck manufacturer have been defined and reconciled on the basis of mutual respect. Both companies have invested in the recognition and reconciliation of the differences. In terms of size, GM was easily able to swallow the little Japanese company. It didn't because it recognized the opportunity to grow together.

After a long series of interviews to see both sides of the picture, we have designed a series of workshops where key participants from both sides reconcile major dilemmas and take advantage of differences.

■ For example, methods were developed to reconcile the more universalistic strength of GM by taking utmost economies of scale out of standardization and the typical Japanese talent of being adaptive to unique situations. We are now trying to jointly define 'learning platforms'. And what to do about the cultural dilemma of a US orientation to codifying knowledge in large handbooks and the capturing of implicit knowledge between Japanese minds that are used to work together for decades. The reconciliation looks simple: let the Japanese write the codified handbooks for the project. They are likely to be shorter and of higher quality.

Individualism versus communitarianism

The conflict between what each of us wants as an individual, and the interests of the group we belong to, is the second of our five dimensions covering how people relate to other people. Do we relate to others by discovering what each one of us individually wants and then trying to negotiate the differences, or do we place ahead of this some shared concept of the public and collective good? The 55,000 managers who have answered the following question show this, although the division here is not quite so sharp as for the universal versus the particular example.

Two people were discussing ways in which one could improve the quality of life:

A. One said: 'It is obvious that if one has as much freedom as possible and the maximum opportunity to develop oneself, the quality of one's life will improve as a result.'

B. The other said: 'If the individual is continuously taking care of his fellow human beings the quality of life will improve for everyone, even if it obstructs individual freedom and individual development.'

With which of the two answers do you agree most?

Figure 3 Individualism versus Collectivism

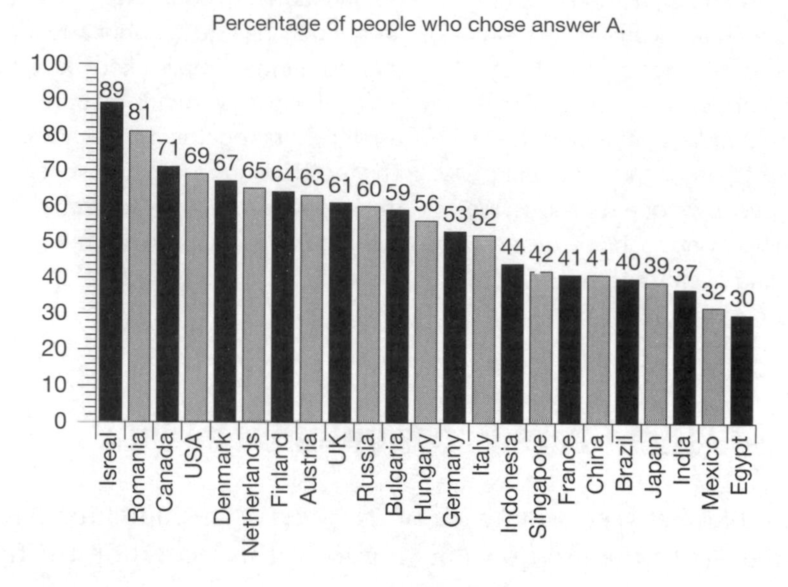

As can be observed there are major differences around the globe. There are some advantages and disadvantages connected to this profile.

We all go through these cycles, but starting from different points and conceiving of them as means or ends. The individualist culture sees the individual as 'the end' and improvements to collective arrangements as the means to achieve it. The communitarian culture sees the group as its end and improvements to individual capacities as a means to that end. Yet if the relationship is truly circular; the decision to label one element as an end and another as a means is arbitrary. By definition circles never end. Every 'end' is also the means to another goal.

The effective international manager is close to the conviction that individualism finds its fulfilment in service to the group, while group goals are of demonstrable value to individuals, only if those individuals are consulted and participate in the process of developing them. The reconciliation is not easy, but possible.

Reconciling individualism and collectivism

An alliance of the R&D activities of a large international oil company operating in the Netherlands with their Japanese counterparts led to an interesting discussion on how to implement a reward structure. The alliance involved predominantly Dutch, British, American, German and Japanese people who needed to work in multicultural teams. Let's see what options are open.

First, an individualized bonus scheme could be implemented which would stimulate the Americans and British to be even more competitive. The communitarian Japanese and Germans would be severely demotivated by this type of reward system. Second, one could go for a team bonus. Great for the Japanese. But would it motivate the Anglo Saxons? No way. So why not take the compromise and have a mixed system of 50 percent variable pay based on team performance and 50 percent on individual bonus. Half of the group might still go for one end while the other half for the other one. The company very successfully sought out reconciliation. For the first time in its history it installed a reward structure where a mixed system of team and individual performance were installed. But individuals could only get a bonus when teams voted them as the best team-players. Additionally, teams were asked to make presentations on how they had nurtured individual excellence. The audience voted on the best team. This system was successfully installed and is known as a version of *co-opetition*. The art of both competing for co-operation and to co-operate to better compete.

Look at Figure 4 which summarizes the reconciliation:

Figure 4

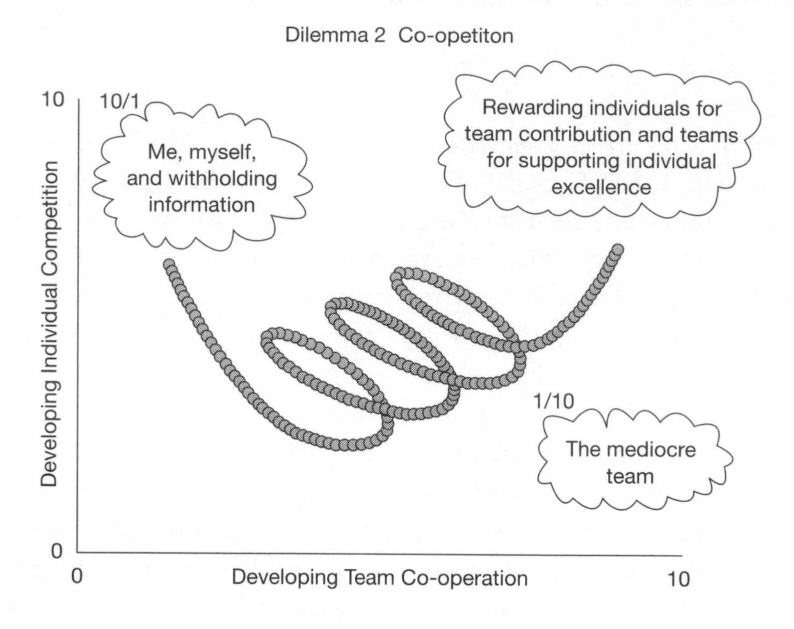

Neutral versus affective

In relationships between people, reason and emotion both play a role. Which of these dominates will depend upon whether we are *affective*, i.e. show our emotions, in which case we probably get an emotional response in return, or whether we are emotionally *neutral* in our approach.

Typically, reason and emotion are of course combined. In expressing ourselves we try to find confirmation of our thoughts and feelings in the response of our audience. When our own approach is highly emotional we are seeking a *direct* emotional response: 'I have the same feelings as you on this subject.' When our own approach is highly neutral we are seeking an *indirect* response. 'Because I agree with your reasoning or proposition, I give you my support.' On both occasions approval is being sought, but different paths are being used to this end. The indirect path gives us emotional support contingent upon the success of an effort of intellect. The direct path allows our feelings about a factual proposition to show through, thereby 'joining' feelings with thoughts in a different way.

The expression of opinions in an open and often passionate way is often compounded by strong personalities of the individuals into fairly fixed opinions and a sometimes adversarial communication style. It is often necessary to restate the importance of basic communications skills such as listening.

Reconciling affective and neutral cultures

Overly affective (expressive) or neutral cultures have problems in relating with each other. The neutral person is easily accused of being ice-cold with no heart; the affective person is seen as out of control and inconsistent. When such cultures meet, the first essential for the international manager is to recognize the differences, and to refrain from making any judgements based on emotions, or the lack of them.

This aspect of culture is quite clearly seen in the amount of emotionality people can stand across cultures. Kodak introduced an advert selling on 'memories' which Americans love, but which was seen by the British as overly sentimental. It was Michael Porter who said that Germans didn't know what marketing was about. In his American conception marketing is about showing the qualities of your products without any inhibition. Germans might see this as bragging. It is not accepted unless you sell second-hand cars. The degrees to which you express positive things in Germany need to be much subtler; a subtlety that might escape Porter.

Specific versus diffuse

One of the seven dimensions concerns the degree of involvement in relationships. Closely related to whether we show emotions in dealing with other people is the degree to which we engage others in *specific* areas of life and single levels of personality, or *diffusely* in multiple areas of our lives and at several levels of personality at the same time. In specific-oriented cultures a manager *segregates out* the task relationship he or she has with a subordinate and isolates this from other dealings. But in some countries every life space and every level of personality tends to permeate all others.

The difference shows itself clearly in the various alliances that can be observed between many of the major airlines. In our work with British Airways and American Airlines, the model helped the parties recognize and respect different ways in which they define the relationship with their passengers. It is typically American to emphasize 'core competencies' and 'shareholder value'. In contrast, British Airways and Cathay Pacific emphasize service with hot breakfasts, champagne and the like.

Thus in this alliance of 'one world' the options are:

1. Go for 'serving the cattle with Coke and pretzels'.
2. Serve not only hot breakfasts but add some massage and shoe polishing and 'go bankrupt on the flight'.
3. Compromise and 'serve the hot pretzel' so it becomes certain that they lose all clients.
4. Reconciliation is the art of trying to specifically define those areas to provide a more personal service and deepen the relationship. Jan Carlzon from SAS called this 'moments of truth'.

The future of the alliance will depend on this very reconciliation: the competence of the employees of the airlines to consistently choose those specific moments to deepen the relationship in the service being provided. A compromise will lead to disaster – and how often have we seen them in alliances of any kind.

Achieved versus ascribed status

All societies give certain members higher status than others, signalling that unusual attention should be focused upon such persons and their activities. While some societies accord status to people on the basis of their achievements, others ascribe it to them by virtue of age, class, gender, education, etc. The first kind of status is called *achieved status* and the second *ascribed status*. While achieved status refers to *doing*, ascribed status refers to *being*.

Achievement-oriented cultures will market their products and services on the basis of their performance. Performance, skill and knowledge justify their authority. These cultures will only make those products into a standard once they have proved they are superior in the market through competition.

Ascription-oriented cultures often ascribe status to products and services. In particular in Asia, status is attributed to those products that 'naturally' evoke admiration from others, i.e. highly qualified technologies or projects deemed to be of national importance. The status is generally independent of task or specific function.

This dilemma is obviously a great challenge when partners have different traditions in how people move up the ladder in the organization. In achievement-oriented cultures your position is best secured by performing continuously. In the worst case you are only as good as your last performance. In ascribed cultures seniority and long-term loyalty are very much more beneficial.

Towards reconciliation in alliances

Despite far greater emphasis on ascription or achievement in certain cultures, the two usually develop together. Those who 'start' with ascribing usually ascribe not just status but future success or achievement and thereby help to bring it about. Those who 'start' with achievement usually start to ascribe importance and priority to the persons and projects which have been successful. Hence all societies ascribe and all achieve after a fashion. It is once again a question of where a cycle starts. The international manager rides the wave of this dilemma.

Sequential versus synchronous cultures

If only because managers need to co-ordinate their business activities, they require some kind of shared expectations about time. Just as different cultures have different assumptions about how people relate to one another, so they approach time differently. This orientation is about the relative importance cultures give to the past, present and future. How we think of time has its own consequences. Especially important is whether our view of time is *sequential*, a series of passing events, or whether it is *synchronic*, with past, present and future all interrelated so that ideas about the future and memories of the past both shape present action.

In alliances between Latin or Asian cultures on the one hand and North-Western cultures on the other, the different time perceptions can have severe implications. Take an alliance between an Italian fashion company which had found a partner in the Netherlands to distribute its designer clothes. The alliance had a very dramatic start. Lots of business was lost because North West European clients expected on-time delivery, very normal for sequential people. The synchronous Italians had a more flexible idea of time and frequently delivered late. Summers in Italy are more extended so why make a problem of delivering a week late? Yes, but that's half of a Dutch or Swedish summer.

Towards reconciliation

The international manager is often caught in the dilemma of the future demands of the larger organization, needing visions, missions and managing change towards it, and the past experiences of local populations. The short termism that plagues Western and, particularly, American companies is often driven by the needs of the stock markets for annual or quarterly results and profits. The risk of a strong future orientation is the failure to learn from past mistakes.

Going back to the sequential–synchronous dilemma above, the solution was very simple. The Dutch manager in charge went to Italy to make friends with the head of logistics. He never had a problem with late deliveries again. Synchronous people can deliver in time. But they like to do it for you, not for your clock.

And just-in-time manufacturing has proven that the best way to speed up a sequence is to synchronize it just in time.

Internal versus external control

The last culturally determined dimension concerns the meaning the actor assigns to his (natural) environment. In cultures in which an organic view of nature dominates, and in which the assumptions are shared that man is subjugated to nature, individuals appear to orient their actions towards others. People become 'other directed' in order to survive, their focus is on the environment rather than themselves, known *external control*.[4]

Conversely, it has been determined that people who have a mechanic view of nature, in addition to the belief that man can dominate nature, usually take themselves as the point of departure for determining the right action. The 'inner-directedness' of this part of the world, is also reflected through the current fashion of customer orientation.

Our research suggests in this instance that there are significant differences between geographical areas. These questions all take the form of alternatives; managers were asked to select the statement they believed most reflected reality. The first of these pairs is as follows:

A. It is worthwhile trying to control important natural forces, like the weather?

B. Nature should take its course and we just have to accept it the way it comes and do the best we can.

Figure 5 shows the percentage of respondents who chose answers like A, i.e. the inner directors.

Figure 5 Internal versus external control

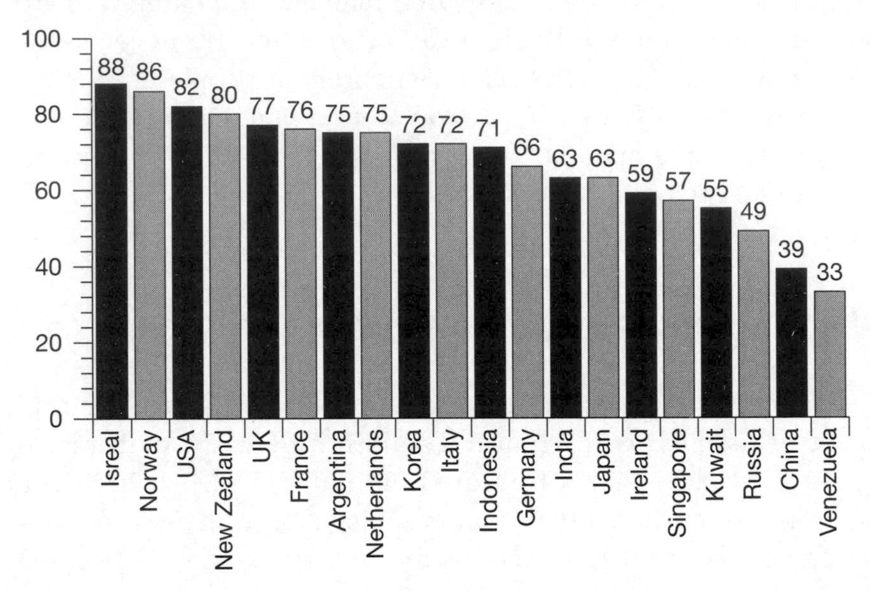

The figures shown above indicate that Western cultures share extremely internally controlled orientations. It is obvious that most Western managers are selected on the competence (false or not) that essentially any environment can be controlled, any market created and any problem overcome by one's own doing. You market what we can produce, better known as technology push. Asians, where you find mostly externally oriented cultures, are supremely equipped to get stimulated by signals from the markets. Correspondingly, Asians operate under the handicap of often not being the ones pushing the latest technological developments.

Reconciling internal and external control

The major issue at stake is to connect the internally controlled culture, leading to the talent of *technology push*, with the externally controlled world of *market pull* in order to achieve a culture of inventiveness. If we take a consumer electronics company like Philips, nobody will deny its great knowledge and inventiveness in its specific technologies and the quality of its marketing. The problem the company faced was that its two major functional areas didn't seem to communicate. The success of an organization is dependent on the integration of both areas. The push of technology needs to help you in deciding what markets you want to be pulled by. And the pull of the market needs to help you in knowing what technologies to push.

The role of the HR professional

Observing the British and Dutch experience in mergers and acquisitions, there is much hope and learning. Consider what Shell and Unilever have proved over the last century or so. If giant alliances between British Steel and Hoogovens and between P&O and Nedlloyd don't reconcile the Dutch directness in communication with the English indirect, diffuse and somewhat fuzzy style of communication, there is little hope.

In our experience HR professionals can play a crucial role in the facilitation of a successful reconciliation of cultures. They need to become 'culture coaches' facilitating the basic processes of post-merger and pre-merger integration.

The challenge facing HR is therefore to:

1. Help employees to know and understand the cultural background of partners from national through to corporate orientations. Many instruments are available for HR practitioners such as individual and group ethnographic interviews as well as validated questionnaires.

2. Help employees to respect those differences by focusing as much on differences as on things shared. It is possible to help people to learn to live 'the logic of the opposite culture' and to share the basic values of the merged company: prerequisites for respect.
3. Seek out the major cultural dilemmas that are affecting business. Again, methodologies are available enabling HR professionals to play a facilitating role in mapping crucial dilemmas.
4. Reconcile differences by integrating seemingly opposing values. These workshops are meant to open up channels and to increase the quality of the communication between the partners of the alliance.

The seven steps to benefit delivery

It is important that this challenge is accepted. The following steps enable HR to implement a cultural due diligence framework to enable players to be effective and add value to the alliance.

1. Link HR activities to the inherent and overt strategy of the alliance/merger

It is a prerequisite that HR professionals are engaged in the integration process as early as possible. Unfortunately, in many situations their expected contribution often is limited to developing an early retirement scheme for those people who become redundant because of the expected economies of scale of the integration.

Bill Clover, former Chief Learning Officer from Amoco, says:

'We were engaged very early in the process of trying to provide consulting and learning solutions which would incorporate relevant cultural aspects in the merger. Unfortunately time worked against us. The speed of the merger, both in the precombination and combination phases, eliminated any serious consideration of programmes related to transition and culture, which did not overtly deal with issues of

performance. Therefore, a key operating principle was that culture was to be dealt with only if "IT" was related to immediate behavioural issues. Anything seen as dealing with issues related to more underlying assumptions, values or dilemmas was perceived as superfluous to the merger process. In all fairness, perhaps we were perceived as inarticulate in building a strong enough case regarding cultural issues. It is my belief that many synergies were lost, and many superb Amoco people lost, in the over anxious rush to meet deadlines. Therefore, in the process while "speed of merger" records were set they were accomplished at the expense of resolution of long-term underlying dilemmas. While people applaud the increase in stock price of the company, it is my belief that this is nothing more than an additive combination of hard assets as opposed to the latent multiplicative value that can come about via the true resolution and reconciliation of underlying cultural dilemmas.'

2. Mix key functions

It is very important that the major functions are mixed and interact from the very beginning. Obviously that implies commitment from the very top of the organizations.

An anonymous source from Chrysler says:

'In HR we are just integrating our activities now. From the beginning I have felt an enormous distance between the German Daimler side and us Americans in Detroit. This reflected in the way we approached training. We have run various workshops: How to deal with the Germans for the Americans and how to deal with the Americans for the Germans. To be honest for me it just reinforced stereotyping.

'Indeed the mixing of the various teams from the beginning is important to map the issues as they occur in the interaction. Too often we have seen that splitting the teams lead to increasing the differences rather than to work early enough on the integration process.'

Martin Gillo, HR director of Advanced Micro Devices says:

'It has been amazingly helpful that we have integrated our teams of Germans and Americans in our alliance to set up our $1.7 billion

3

facility in Dresden. We knew that the integration of German and American cultures were essential to the success of this project. Mapping the cultural differences was an important first step. Having both teams working together was a prerequisite of being able to do this.'

3. Define a code of conduct and shared business principles

Develop a joint definition of what the partners have in common. Top management needs to go beyond the pure technical and economic definitions of the expected advantages of the alliance or merger. A narrow definition of shareholder value hinders the success of a merger or acquisition. The jointly defined code of conduct and business principles that will support the vision and mission of the joint operation is crucial for achieving the integration processes to a successful outcome.

Donald Kalff (Director Strategy KLM), the main architect of the Alliance between Alitalia and KLM, says:

'In our technical discussions we have found so many challenges that we will now need to focus on what we have in common. We will have to make precious time to define our joint code of conduct. That is the best way to build a joint platform on which we can discuss the integration of differences. It is; however, very important that the shared principles are of quality that directs behaviour. Simply alluding to principles like "integrity", "trust" and "respect" are not challenging enough, because nobody will be against them. Values need to engage people in a discussion and form a context in which reconciliation is possible.'

4. Elicit, identify and map the major cultural dilemmas that are affecting business

We have developed and validated diagnostic instruments that enable HR professionals to play a facilitating role in mapping crucial dilemmas. To be able to define the major dilemmas requires clarity of vision and mission. Within this context it is relatively easy to find values that on the surface are in conflict. The main mechanisms we use here to elicit dilemmas are the interactive workshops and cognitive mapping interviews.

5. Reconcile differences by integrating seemingly opposing values

What is needed is an approach where the two opposing views can come to fuse or blend – where the strength of one extreme is extended by considering and accommodating the other. This is *reconciliation*. Working with Charles Hampden-Turner at Cambridge, we have developed a new methodology for reconciling these seemingly opposing values. In summary, it involves re-stating your values or the meaning you put to the issue being considered, reflecting on the other point of view, considering how it informs your view, how it can be used to improve the outcome, recycling and rethinking the process, and using this learning to re-craft a win–win solution. Thus dilemmas are reconciled by following a procedure that involves processing, sequencing, contextualizing and synergizing.

Says Johan Brongers:

'These workshops were meant to open up channels and to increase the quality of the communication between the partners of the alliance. However, they went far beyond those initial purposes. We were able to reconcile major dilemmas that were initially seen as stumbling blocks in working together effectively. This process has become essential to the working together of different cultures. We have been able to make people aware, respect and reconcile differences. This is what celebrating cultural differences are about and the end result is a "better vehicle".'

Tom Pitmon from Applied Materials adds:

'What we believe is essential for the success of embedding this reconciliation methodology, is that it is not taken as a side dish. In order to take advantage of cultural differences it needs to be embedded

3

in the backbone of the HR and management activities, from recruitment through teamwork to interactive CBT media. We have even trained our HRD professionals at Applied as facilitators in the processes in-house.'

6. Giving structured feedback back to the organization

Through taking the above approach, the HR professionals become an important intermediate function to translate workshop results into the strategy implementation of the organization. Managers become increasingly aware that the reconciliation of basic dilemmas they face in the alliance is very close to the development of the strategy of the integration.

7. Transfer merger experiences

The final process is to develop continuous feedback loops into the organization at all levels and functions of the learning that occurs through the reconciliation process.

This needs to become the norm such that the merger of worlds colliding becomes a strategic continuous learning process. Dilemma reconciliations become second nature. It is a bit like being a parent. It becomes normal to jump from one dilemma to another.

Conclusion

If companies and their new partners can achieve reconciliation successfully, they will be well on the way to harmony and shared understanding. The HR community has an increasingly important role in developing the Trans-cultural competence of the individual and the organization through Cultural Due Diligence through which the expected benefits of the strategic, synergistic or intrinsic alliances can be delivered.

REFERENCES

1. *The Economist,* 9 January 1999.
2. KPMG Consulting M&A Report 1999.
3. Stouffer, S.A. and Toby, J., 'Role Conflict and Personality', *American Journal of Sociology,* LUI-5, 1951, pp. 395–406.
4. Rotter, J.B., '*Generalized Expectations for Internal versus External Control of Reinforcement,* Psychological Monograph 609, 1966, pp. 1–28.

RESOURCES

BOOK

Trompenaars, Fons, *Riding the Waves of Culture,* Nicholas Brealey, 1996.

WEB

www.7d-culture.nl

CONTRIBUTORS

Marcus Alexander is a fellow and director of the Ashridge Strategic Management Centre. His research on corporate strategy has been published in books and in articles in the *Financial Times, Harvard Business Review* and other leading publications. He has acted as a consultant to the chief executives of several FTSE 100 companies, and has degrees from Harvard Business School and Oxford University. Previously he worked at the Boston Consulting Group and has also run his own company.

Paul Argenti is Clinical Professor of Management Communications at the Amos Tuck School of Business. Formerly at Harvard Business School and Columbia Business School, he has also taught at the International University of Japan and the Helsinki School of Economics. He is the author of *Corporate Communication* (second edition, 1998) and edited *The Portable MBA Desk Reference.*

Warren Bennis is founding chairman of the Leadership Institute at the University of Southern California where he is also a Professor. He is the author or editor of over 25 books. His latest books are *Organizing Genius: The Secrets of Creative Collaboration* and *Co-Leaders.*

David W. Birchall is director of development at Henley Management College. He is the co-author of *Creating Tomorrow's Organization.*

Tom Brown publishes *MG – The 'New Ideas' Webzine* (www.mgeneral.com) which has readers in more than 82 countries and receives millions of hits per year. In 1997–1998, Tom made history by writing the first interactive online book for leaders, *The Anatomy Of Fire: Sparking A New Spirit Of Enterprise.* He is also the author of the e-book, *S T R E T C H ! – 21 EVENTS THAT WILL ROCK THE NEXT CENTURY*, which projects 'future events' that will make headlines. Formerly director of

Honeywell's Aerospace Management Development Center, Tom is a contributing editor and writes regularly for The Conference Board's *Across The Board*.

David Butcher is Director, General Management Development Programmes at the Cranfield School of Management. David trained originally as a psychologist, and worked for Du Pont and Courtaulds before embarking on a career in management development. He focuses on developing top teams and leadership capability at senior management level, and has worked with organization as diverse as Mars, BP, Ericsson, Morgan Stanley, Williams Formula One and the European Space Agency.

William C. Byham, PhD, is the co-founder, president, and chief executive officer of Development Dimensions International, a Pittsburgh-based human resource organization specializing in leadership development and selection systems. Dr Byham has written 19 books and more than 160 articles, including *Zapp! ® The Lightning of Empowerment*, a seminal book about empowerment.

Peter Cohan is president of Peter S. Cohan & Associates, a management consulting firm. His strategy consulting practice helps companies in technology-intensive industries. His venture capital business is building a growing portfolio of internet venture investments. He is the author of *e-Profit, The Technology Leaders* and *Net Profit*. He previously worked at CSC/Index and Monitor and has an MBA from Wharton.

Stephen Coomber is a business researcher and writer. He is co-author of *Architects of the Business Revolution*.

Stuart Crainer is joint editor of the *Financial Times Handbook of Management*. He is author of numerous books. These include: *The Management Century, Generation Entrepreneur* (with Des Dearlove), *MBA Planet* (with Des Dearlove), *Key Management Ideas*, a biography of the management guru Tom Peters, and *The Ultimate Business Library*. His work appears in magazines and newspapers worldwide. Stuart is one of the founders of the media company Suntop Media. e-mail: stuartcraines@suntopmedia.com

Tony Cram is Director of the Marketing Strategy for Directors and Innovative Business Development programmes at Ashridge Management College and author of *The Power of Relationship Marketing – Keeping Customers for Life* (1994).

Richard D'Aveni is Professor of Strategic Management at the Amos Tuck School of Business at Dartmouth College in Hanover, New Hampshire. He is the author of *Empire Builders: The Struggle for Strategic Supremacy* (The Free Press, forthcoming); *Competing in Highly Dynamic Environments* (The Free Press, 1995) and *Hypercompetition: Managing the Dynamics of Strategic Maneuvering* (The Free Press, 1994).

Des Dearlove is joint editor of the *Financial Times Handbook of Management*. He is a columnist for *The Times*, co-founder of Suntop Media, and author of a number of books. Des's books include *Gravy Training* (with Stuart Crainer), *The Ultimate Book of Business Thinking, Key Management Decisions, MBA Planet* and *The Ultimate Book of Business Brands* (both with Stuart Crainer) and *Architects of the Business Revolution* (with Stephen Coombes). His e-mail is desdearlove@suntopmedia.com

Colin Eden is Director of the Graduate School of Business at the University of Strathclyde in Glasgow, and Professor of Management Science and Strategic Management.

Janis Forman established and now directs the Management Communication Programme for the Anderson School, UCLA. Her books include *The Random House Guide to Business Writing*.

G. Bruce Friesen is an independent organization consultant currently on assignment at the Andersen Consulting Institute for Strategic Change in Cambridge, Massachusetts. He is a 1985 MBA graduate of the Harvard University Graduate School of Business Administration and co-author of *The Empowerment Imperative Workshop: Six Steps to a High Performance Organization* (Human Resource Development Press, Amherst, Massachusetts, 1994).

Thomas Gad invented the 4-D Branding model. He has more than 20 years' experience in advertising, as a copywriter, creative director, and brand strategist. Before starting his own business, Thomas worked for Grey Advertising International with both national Scandinavian and international clients. Thomas founded Futurebrands.com, a Stockholm-based business that has now merged with Conradi Hvid to become Differ.

Vijay Govindarajan is the Earl C. Daum 1924 Professor of International Business and Director of the William F. Achtmeyer Center for Global leadership at the Tuck School of Business at Dartmouth College in Hanover, New Hampshire. An internationally renowned consultant and lecturer, he is currently writing a book entitled *The Quest for Global Dominance* with his co-author Anil Gupta (Harvard Business School Press, 1999).

Anil K. Gupta is Professor of Strategy and International Business at the University of Maryland at College Park, where he was named Distinguished Scholar. He is currently a visiting professor at Stanford University.

H. David Hennessey is Associate Professor of Marketing and International Business at Babson College, Wellesley, Massachusetts, and an Associate of Ashridge Management College. He is co-author of *Global Marketing Strategies*, with J.P. Jeannet (5th ed August 2000, Houghton Mifflin).

Sam Hill is co-founder of Helios Consulting which focuses on growth and marketing issues and has offices in New York and Chicago. Before that, Sam was vice chairman and chief strategy officer of DMB&B, a top 20 global advertising agency; and partner and chief marketing officer at Booz-Allen & Hamilton. He began his career at Kraft General Foods as an engineer. He has an engineering degree from the University of Georgia, an MBA from the University of Chicago. Sam is the co-author of *Radical Marketing* (1999) and *Brand Chemistry* (2000).

Shere Hite is an internationally renowned thinker on human relationships and sexual behaviour. She is Director of the consultancy Hite Research International, which specializes in sexual ethics in the workplace. Shere is the author of *Sex & Business* (Financial Times Prentice Hall, 2000). Her e-mail address is s.hite@hite-research.com

Phil Hodgson is based at Ashridge Management College. He is the author and co-author of numerous books including *What Do High Performance Managers Really Do?*, *The Future of Leadership* and *Relax, It's Only Uncertainty*.

Syd Howell is Senior Lecturer in Management Accounting and Control at the UK's Manchester Business School.

Andrew Kakabadse is Professor of Management Development and Deputy Director of Cranfield School of Management, UK. He is Honorary Professional Fellow at the Curtin University of Technology, Perth, Australia, and Visiting Professor of the Hangzhou University, China. His current areas of interest focus on improving the performance of top executives and top executive teams, excellence in consultancy practice, and the politics of decision making. He has published 20 books including *The Politics of Management*, *Working in Organizations* and *The Wealth Creators*.

John Kay founded the consulting firm London Economics, and was the first director of the Saïd School of Business at Oxford University. One of the UK's leading economists, he writes a column in the *Financial Times* and his most recent books are *Foundations of Corporate Success* and *The Business of Economics*.

Kevin Lane Keller is the E.B. Osborn Professor of Marketing at the Amos Tuck School of Business at Dartmouth College in Hanover, New Hampshire. He is the author of *Strategic Brand Management* (Prentice Hall, 1998). Kevin was previously on the faculty at Stanford Business School where he headed the marketing group.

W. Chan Kim is the Boston Consulting Group Bruce D. Henderson Chair Professor of International Management at INSEAD, France.

Jesper Kunde is the author of *Corporate Religion* (Financial Times Prentice Hall, 2000). Jesper worked for Carlsberg and the electronics company LK before starting the Danish advertising agency Kunde & Co.

Richard Lamming is CIPS Professor of Purchasing & Supply Management at the University of Bath School of Management, and Director of the Centre for Research in Strategic Purchasing & Supply (CRiSPS).

Dean LeBaron, founder of Batterymarch Financial Management, is chairman of Wordworks and of virtual quest.com. Recognized as an investment futurist, he has pioneered indexing and quantitative and emerging market investing.

Peter Lorange is President of IMD, the International Institute for Management Development, based in Lausanne, Switzerland.

Renée Mauborgne is the INSEAD Distinguished fellow and Affiliate Professor of Strategy and Management and president of ITM Research, a strategy research group based in Fontainebleau, France. She has published numerous articles on strategy and managing the multinational in leading magazines and journals.

Todd Milbourn is Assistant Professor of Finance at London Business School. His research interests include corporate finance; executive compensation design; capital budgeting and the economics of asymmetric information.

D. Quinn Mills is the Albert J. Weatherhead Professor of Business Administration of the Harvard University Graduate School of Business Administration. He is the author of numerous books, including *The New Competitors* (1985), *Rebirth of the Corporation* (1991), *Empowerment* (1994), and co-author of *The Empowerment Imperative Workshop* (1994). His e-mail address is Dmills@hbs.edu

Narayany Naik is assistant professor of finance and Citibank Research Fellow at London Business School. He has worked as a project manager with the Taj Group in India and has an MBA from the Indian Institute of Management and a PhD from Duke University.

Kjell A. Nordström is based at the Institute of International Business at the Stockholm School of Economics and is on the board of various companies including Spray Ventures. He is co-author of *Funky Business*.

Eddie Obeng is founder director of Pentacle – The Virtual Business School. Previously he worked with Shell and Ashridge Management College. His numerous books include *Making Re-engineering Happen, Organizational Magic, Cybersense* and *The Project Manager's Secret Handbook*. Eddie is also a regular contributor to *Your Business* on the Money Channel.

Georgina Peters is a business writer. She is a regular contributor to magazines worldwide including *Business Life* and the American Management Association's MWorld.

Jonas Ridderstråle of the Center for Advanced Studies in Leadership at the Stockholm School of Economics is on the board of several internet-related companies. He is co-author of *Funky Business*.

Harold Rose is emeritus professor of finance at London Business School. He was formerly group economic adviser to Barclay's Bank; head of economic intelligence at Prudential Assurance and a director of *The Economist*. His publications include *The Economic Background to Investment*.

Anthony M. Santomero is President of the Federal Reserve Bank of Philadelphia. He was formerly director of the Wharton School's Financial Institutions Center and Richard King Mellon Professor of Finance. He has held visiting appointments at universities throughout the world and is associate editor of leading professional publication including the *Journal of Banking & Finance*.

Richard Scase is visiting professor of Organizational Behaviour at the University of Kent and a corporate keynote speaker. He is the author of *Britain in 2010*.

John Storey is Professor of Human Resource Management and Director of Research at the Open University Business

School. He is editor of the *Human Resource Management Journal* and a fellow of the British Academy of Management. His many books include *Human Resource Management* (editor); *The Realities of Human Resource Management* and *Manager in the Making* (with Paul Edwards and Keith Sisson).

Paul Strebel is Professor of Strategic Change Management and Director of the Breakthrough Program for Senior Executives at IMD. His main area of activity is high speed strategic change, especially the anticipation of industry break-points, the development of strategy and the design and implementation of change processes. Paul is author of *The Change Pact: Building Commitment to Ongoing Change* (Financial Times Pitman) and *Breakpoints: How Managers Exploit Radical Business Change* (Harvard Business School Press), and the editor of *Focused Energy: Managing bottom-up organization* (John Wiley).

Donald N. Sull is Assistant Professor of Business Administration in the Entrepreneurial Management area at the Harvard Business School. He was formerly at London Business School and has an AB from Harvard College and an MBA from Harvard Business School. Before entering academia he was Vice President, Corporate Planning at Uniroyal-Goodrich/Clayton & Dubilier, a consultant with McKinsey & Company, and an adviser to several multinational firms and new ventures.

George Tovstiga is Associate Professor of Technology and Innovation Management at TSM Business School, University of Twente, the Netherlands.

Fons Trompenaars, PhD is founding principal of Trompenaars Hampden-Turner InterCultural Management Consulting and of the Centre for International Business Studies (Amsterdam) and author of *Riding the Waves of Culture.*

Bruce Tulgan is the author of several books including *Winning the Talent Wars*, (W.W. Norton, 2001), *Fast Feedback* (HRD Press, 1999), and *Managing Generation*

X (W.W. Norton, 2000; first published by Merritt, 1995). Bruce is the founder of Rainmaker Thinking, Inc. in New Haven, Connecticut. His e-mail address is www.rainmakerthinking.com

Romesh Vaitilingam is a consultant and financial journalist. He is author of several successful business and financial titles including the bestselling *The Financial Times Guide to Using the Financial Pages* as well as *The Ultimate Investment Library* and *The Ultimate Book of Investment Quotations* (both with Dean LeBaron).

Sandra Vandermerwe holds the Chair in Management at The Management School, Imperial College, University of London. Previously, she spent a decade as Professor of Marketing and International Services at IMD, Switzerland. She is the author of several books, including *Customer Capitalism: Getting Increasing Returns in New Market Spaces* (1999), *The 11th Commandment: Transforming to 'Own' Customers* (1996), and *From Tin Soldiers to Russian Dolls: Creating Added Value through Services* (1993).

Watts Wacker is a lecturer, author, commentator and critic. He is CEO of First Matter and previously was the futurist at SRI International, the Menlo Park think tank, and spent 10 years with the social research organization, Yankelovich Partners. He is the author of *The 500 Year Delta* and *The Visionary's Handbook*.

Jonathan West is Assistant Professor of Technology and Operations Management at the Harvard Business School. He has doctorate and masters degrees from Harvard University and holds a BA from the University of Sydney. He has served as a consultant to corporations and governments worldwide.

Randall P. White is a principle in the Executive Development Group, Greensboro, NC, and an adjunct professor at the Fuqua School of Business, Duke University. He is co-author of *Breaking the Glass Ceiling, The Future of Leadership* and *Relax, It's Only Uncertainty*. Formerly based at the Center for Creative Leadership, he also teaches at Duke University and Cornell University and is on the editorial board of the *Journal of Leaders and Leadership*.

Peter Woolliams, PhD is Professor of International Business at the Anglia Business School, UK and has researched extensively on HR and cross culture.

George Yip is Beckwith Professor of Marketing and Strategy at Cambridge University's Judge Institute, and was previously at Harvard and UCLA business schools. From January 2001, he will be Professor of Strategic and International Management at London Business School. He is the author of *Barriers to Entry, Total Global Strategy* (published in nine languages), *Asian Advantage,* and *Strategies for Central and Eastern Europe,* as well as numerous articles in journals such as *California Management Review, Columbia Journal of World Business, Harvard Business Review*, and *Sloan Management Review.*

Luigi Zingales is associate professor of finance at the Graduate School of Business, University of Chicago. He studied at MIT and Milan's Universitá Bocconi.

INDEX

Bold has been used to indicate the subject headings in the 'Essentials' sections. Page references followed by 'f1', 'f2', 't1' etc. in brackets indicate relevant figures and tables found within the page range shown.